PLAN OF THE BOOK

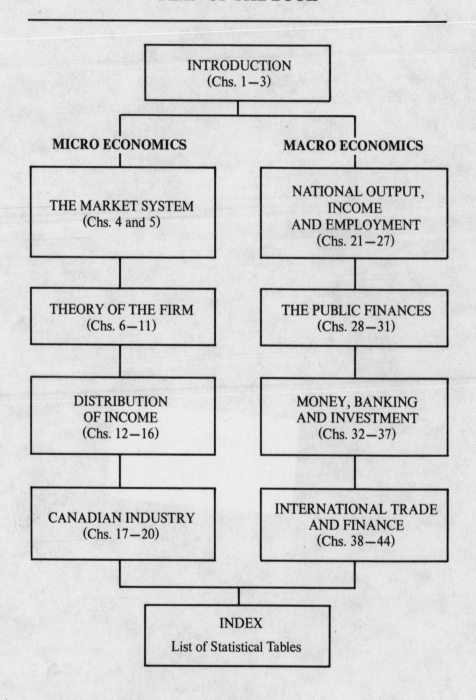

INTRODUCTION
(Chs. 1—3)

MICRO ECONOMICS

THE MARKET SYSTEM
(Chs. 4 and 5)

THEORY OF THE FIRM
(Chs. 6—11)

DISTRIBUTION
OF INCOME
(Chs. 12—16)

CANADIAN INDUSTRY
(Chs. 17—20)

MACRO ECONOMICS

NATIONAL OUTPUT,
INCOME
AND EMPLOYMENT
(Chs. 21—27)

THE PUBLIC FINANCES
(Chs. 28—31)

MONEY, BANKING
AND INVESTMENT
(Chs. 32—37)

INTERNATIONAL TRADE
AND FINANCE
(Chs. 38—44)

INDEX

List of Statistical Tables

Summary of Contents

Table of Contents

PART E: CANADIAN INDUSTRY

PART H: MONEY, BANKING, AND INVESTMENT

Preface

My purpose in this book is to try to provide the senior high school or first-year college or university student with a comprehensive, factual, yet easy-to-read introductory account of the subject matter of *Economics*. This is the social science that describes and attempts to explain the workings of our economic system, particularly the way in which we use our scarce resources to satisfy, as much as possible, our many different wants.

In Chapters 1 to 20, I have discussed the topics normally included under the heading of Microeconomics; in Chapters 21 to 44, those falling under the heading of Macroeconomics. Although the economic concepts examined are of universal application, the setting is Canadian.

In this Second Edition, all the text material has been revised and updated, with new material added where appropriate. The scope of the book has also been enlarged with the inclusion of ten new chapters: 2, 3, 12, 14, 16, 17, 20, 35, 36 and 43. The book's durability and visual appeal have been improved by use of a hard cover, a second colour, numbered key topics, photos, cartoons, etc.

Throughout the book, theoretical concepts have been explained and illustrated with the aid of tables and charts; mathematical treatment has been largely avoided. The examples, statistics, and viewpoints are Canadian and as up-to-date as possible.

Finally, I wish to express my thanks to many different people: to my parents, wife and children; to my colleagues at Ryerson Polytechnical Institute; to all those Economics teachers across Canada who have given me their encouragement and advice; to Statistics Canada and the Bank of Canada for compiling most of the statistics; to the Ontario Ministry of Tourism and Recreation for supplying the photos; and to Trevor Hutchings for drawing the cartoons.

MAURICE ARCHER

Canada is now the world's seventh largest economy

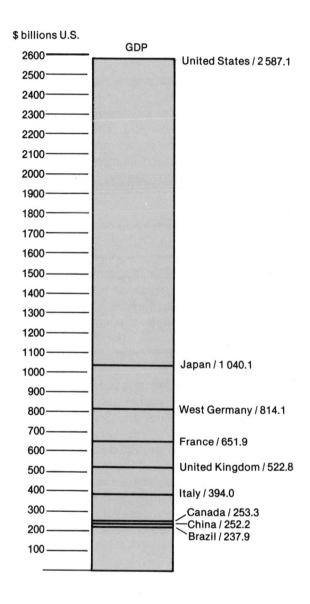

$ billions U.S.

GDP

2600	United States / 2 587.1
2500	
2400	
2300	
2200	
2100	
2000	
1900	
1800	
1700	
1600	
1500	
1400	
1300	
1200	
1100	
1000	Japan / 1 040.1
900	
800	West Germany / 814.1
700	
600	France / 651.9
500	United Kingdom / 522.8
400	Italy / 394.0
300	Canada / 253.3
200	China / 252.2
	Brazil / 237.9
100	

Source of data: World Bank, *World Development Report, 1982*
Note: Figures not available for the USSR, and other East European Countries

1. THE NATURE AND IMPORTANCE OF ECONOMICS

CHAPTER OBJECTIVES

A. To explain the meaning of the term "economics"
B. To emphasize the importance of economic understanding to individuals, business firms, and governments
C. To examine the various types of resources on which our economic prosperity depends
D. To emphasize the need for choice in the use of scarce resources, with the use of a production-possibility curve
E. To explain how in Canada we actually choose what to produce
F. To discuss Canada's economic goals

CHAPTER OUTLINE

1.1   Economics Defined
1.2   Importance of Economics
1.3   Limited Resources
1.4   The Production Possibility Curve
1.5   Economic Choice
1.6   Canada's Economic Goals and Policies

1.1: ECONOMICS DEFINED

Economics is the study of the way in which society uses its scarce resources to satisfy its many different wants. Derived from the Greek words *oikos* (house) and *nemein* (to manage), "economics" means literally "the art of household management."

Two of the most famous definitions of economics are as follows:

Alfred Marshall, "Economics is a study of mankind in the ordinary business of life; it examines that part of individual and social action which is most closely connected with the attainment and with the use of the material requisites of well being," in *Principles of Economics* (Macmillan & Co. Ltd., London, 1930).

Lionel Robbins, "The science which studies human behaviour as a relationship between ends and scarce means which have alternative uses," in *An Essay on the Nature and Significance of Economic Science* (Macmillan & Co. Ltd., London 1935).

Macroeconomics and Microeconomics

Economics is now divided into two main areas: "macro" and "micro"—derived from the Greek words for "large" and "small." *Macroeconomics* is the study of the economic problems that face society as a whole—such as unemployment, inflation, economic growth, and international trade. *Microeconomics* is the study of the economic problems that face the various elements of society: (a) the individual units such as the consumer, the business firm, the government, the wage earner; and (b) the various groups within society such as the household sector, the business sector, and the government sector. Both areas of economics are closely related. Thus, for example, an increase in a country's money supply, as well as affecting the rate of inflation, can greatly affect the fortunes of the individual firm.

Economics: a Social Science

Economics is considered to be a social science because it involves the methodical study of the economic aspect of human behaviour. However, to understand economic behaviour, it also helps to have some knowledge of other social sciences such as psychology, sociology, geography, and politics. The study of many economic problems has also benefited from the rigorous application of mathematical and statistical techniques. In Chapter 3 (Economic Analysis), we examine how economists make use of the scientific method in analyzing economic problems and developing economic theories.

1.2: IMPORTANCE OF ECONOMICS

Today, economics is studied in schools, colleges, and universities throughout Canada. It is also an integral part of the curriculum of most professional associations. There are two basic reasons for this. First, economic reasoning helps one to develop a clear, logical way of thinking that is invaluable in practically any career. In particular, it emphasizes the constant need for choice in using scarce funds and the desirability of weighing rationally the pros and cons of each alternative before making a decision. As Lord Keynes (one of the world's greatest economists) once wrote, economics "is a method rather than a doctrine, an apparatus of the mind, a technique of thinking which helps its possessor to draw correct conclusions."

The second basic reason for studying economics is that it helps us to understand the economic system in which we live, so that, for instance, we can comprehend how economic events such as unemployment occur and how the economic situation of the country and the world at large can affect our personal, business, and government decisions.

From the personal point of view, economics helps us to plan our careers, decide when and where to seek work, make spending, savings, and investment decisions, and understand what is going on around us. The economic efficiency, or productivity, of Canadians (as discussed in more detail in Chapter 20) determines the standard of living that we enjoy. Of course, economic considerations only partly influence our decisions. We are also affected by social, moral and emotional factors—for example, the choice of a more interesting, but lower-paid job; or the decision to marry regardless of income. And even in the purely economic field, many economic events that affect our lives are largely beyond our personal control—for example, inflation, recession, unemployment, and high interest rates. However, we can, through the study of economics, understand why they are occurring and perhaps, through our choice of government, exert some influence on them.

Business firms, in their pursuit of profit, can also benefit from an understanding of the way the economy operates—in setting prices, making production and marketing plans, and making borrowing and investment decisions.

Every country, as one of its goals, tries to improve the economic well-being of its citizens. To do this, government must make a variety of economic policy decisions—for example, with regard to public spending, borrowing and taxation; and to changes in the money supply, in the level of interest rates, in the foreign exchange rate for the currency, and in a host of other economic matters. To do this wisely, requires a thorough understanding of economics, including Canadian and international economic institutions. And most governments are judged at election time on their success in dealing with the bread-and-butter issues of employment, income, and inflation, rather than on empty phrases.

If, in the future, Canadians are to enjoy a rising, rather than falling, standard of living, we must learn how to raise our productivity so as to compete successfully with the newly industrializing parts of the world, particularly S.E. Asia. This issue, perhaps the biggest economic issue for Canada in the 1980s, is discussed in detail in Chapter 20. If we do not resolve it, the extremely high unemployment levels in Canada (discussed in Chapter 23) will continue to haunt us.

Economic History

The economic system that we now take for granted did not develop overnight, nor will it remain unchanged in the years to come. Economic history—the study and analysis of past economic activities—helps us to understand more clearly our present economic system—its strengths and weaknesses, institutions, and directions for the future. We may not subscribe to the theory of economic evolution expressed by Karl Marx in *Das Kapital*—a required economics textbook in many countries of the world. Nevertheless, we can discern logical processes of economic change and development that have been at work over the years and which will continue in the years to come. In the nineteen eighties, as the technological impact of the silicon chip, the microtransistor, and the large-scale integrated circuit, spreads throughout the economy, a new industrial society, dubbed the "Third Wave" by Alvin Toffler, is expected to emerge, that will in one way or another, affect the economic life of us all. And before too long, we are expected to have the "fifth-generation" computers that can listen, see, think, speak and do all manner of industrial and other tasks.

1.3: LIMITED RESOURCES

A shipwrecked sailor, thrown up like Robinson Crusoe on a deserted island, obviously could not produce everything he would like to have with the limited resources available. He would have to determine: (a) what he could produce with these limited resources; and (b) what ranking, or priority, he would attach to his various wants.

First he would have to survey the resources: the land (what it would grow, the minerals and other raw materials it would yield, the fish to be caught along its shores); the labour (his own); and the capital (the tools salvaged from the wreck).

Canada too has a limited amount of resources with which to produce the goods and services that consumers, government, and business would like to have. Traditionally, these resources (referred to by economists as *the factors of production*) have been arbitrarily divided

"Well, Polly, what's it to be today: fish or goat, stockade or boat?"

into three categories—land, labour, and capital—in order to make the analysis of production as simple as possible. Two additional items, entrepreneurship and technology, are now often included among the factors of production. Just as important in our complex, modern society, as the factors of production, are the political and social environments in which our economic activity is carried out—something that we will say more about later in the chapter.

Land

This factor of production consists of natural (as distinct from people-made) resources such as farmland, building land, oil and other mineral deposits, forests, lakes, rivers, and neighbouring oceans, all of which can be used, directly or indirectly, for production and most of which this country possesses in abundance. Canada is, in fact, the second-largest country in the world, covering an area of just under 10 million square kilometres.

Labour

Labour, or human resources, comprises those members of the population who are able to work.

In Canada, this is almost 12 million persons out of a total population of about 25 millions (See Tables S.1 and S.2). The size of the labour force, although important, is only one part of the picture. Equally important are the skills and abilities of its members in performing the complex tasks of modern industrial society. Like Robinson Crusoe, society would be helpless without "technical know-how." Society would also be helpless without a variety of "leaders"—for example, business leaders to plan and organize the production of goods and services; government leaders to steer the economy; scientists, researchers and educators to expand our knowledge; professional leaders to pioneer new standards of service; and labour leaders to safeguard the welfare of the rank-and-file worker.

Capital

This factor of production (sometimes called *real* capital to distinguish it from money capital) is of two basic types: social capital and business capital. *Social capital* (also called the *economic infrastructure* of a country) includes electric-power plants and transmission lines, roads, railways, airports, harbours, and bridges; schools, hospitals, theatres, and

Table S.1
Canada's Population Growth, 1950-1982

Years	Population as of June	Birth rate	Death rate	Natural rate of increase	Immigra- tion rate	Annual growth rate of population
	(000)	(Per thousand of population)				%
1950	13 712	27.1	9.1	18.0	5.4	2.0
1951	14 009	27.2	9.0	18.2	14.0	2.2
1952	14 459	27.9	8.7	19.2	11.5	2.7
1953	14 845	28.1	8.6	19.5	11.5	2.7
1954	15 287	28.5	8.2	20.3	10.2	3.0
1955	15 698	28.2	8.2	20.0	7.1	2.7
1956	16 081	28.0	8.2	19.8	10.4	2.4
1957	16 610	28.2	8.2	20.0	17.0	3.3
1958	17 080	27.5	8.0	19.6	7.4	2.8
1959	17 483	27.4	8.1	19.4	6.2	2.4
1960	17 870	26.8	7.9	19.1	5.9	2.2
1961	18 238	26.1	7.8	18.5	3.5	2.1
1962	18 583	25.3	7.8	17.5	4.1	1.9
1963	18 931	24.6	7.8	16.8	5.0	1.9
1964	19 291	23.5	7.6	15.9	5.9	1.9
1965	19 644	21.3	7.6	13.7	7.5	1.8
1966	20 015	19.5	7.6	11.9	9.8	1.9
1967	20 378	18.3	7.4	10.9	11.0	1.8
1968	20 701	17.7	7.4	10.3	8.9	1.6
1969	21 001	17.7	7.4	10.3	7.7	1.4
1970	21 297	17.5	7.3	10.2	7.0	1.4
1971	21 568	16.8	7.3	9.5	5.7	1.3
1972	21 802	15.9	7.5	8.4	5.6	1.1
1973	22 043	15.6	7.4	8.2	8.4	1.1
1974	22 364	15.5	7.5	8.0	9.8	1.5
1975	22 697	15.8	7.4	8.4	8.3	1.5
1976	22 993	15.6	7.3	8.3	6.5	1.3
1977	23 287	15.6	7.3	8.3	4.9	1.3
1978	23 534	15.2	7.1	8.1	3.7	1:1
1979	23 769	15.4	7.1	8.3	4.7	1.0
1980	24 058	15.4	7.1	8.3	5.9	1.2
1981	24 342	15.2	7.0	8.2	5.3	1.2
1982	24 603	15.1	7.0	8.2	4.8	1.1

Source: Statistics Canada, *Vital Statistics,* and Department of Employment and Immigration

Table S.2
Canada's Labour Force 1966-1982

Annual Average	Population 15 and over	Labour force	Participation rate	Employed	Employment rate
	(000)	(000)	%	(000)	%
1966	13 083	7 493	57.3	7 242	96.6
1967	13 444	7 747	37.6	7 242	96.2
1968	13 805	7 951	57.6	7 593	95.6
1969	14 162	8 194	57.9	7 832	95.6
1970	14 528	8 395	57.8	7 919	94.3
1971	14 872	8 639	58.1	8 104	93.8
1972	15 186	8 897	58.6	8 344	93.8
1973	15 526	9 276	59.7	8 761	94.5
1974	15 924	9 639	60.5	9 125	94.7
1975	16 323	9 974	61.1	9 284	93.1
1976	16 706	10 206	61.1	9 479	92.9
1977	17 057	10 498	61.5	9 648	91.9
1978	17 382	10 882	62.6	9 972	91.6
1979	17 692	11 207	63.3	10 369	92.5
1980	18 005	11 522	64.0	10 655	92.5
1981	18 295	11 830	64.7	10 933	92.4
1982	18 573	11 879	64.0	10 574	89.0
		(Percentage change)			
1967	2.8	3.4	0.1	2.9	-0.4
1968	2.7	2.6	0.0	1.9	-0.6
1969	2.6	3.1	0.1	3.1	0.0
1970	2.6	2.5	0.0	1.1	-1.4
1971	2.4	2.9	0.1	2.3	-0.5
1972	2.1	3.0	0.1	3.0	0.0
1973	2.2	4.3	0.2	5.0	0.7
1974	2.6	3.9	0.1	4.2	0.2
1975	2.5	3.5	0.1	1.7	-1.7
1976	2.3	2.3	0.0	2.1	-0.2
1977	2.1	2.9	0.1	1.8	-1.1
1978	1.9	3.7	0.2	3.4	-0.3
1979	1.8	3.0	0.1	4.0	1.0
1980	1.8	2.8	0.1	2.8	0.0
1981	1.6	2.7	0.1	2.6	0.0
1982	1.5	0.4	0.0	-3.3	-3.7

Source: Statistics Canada, *The Labour Force,* annual, Cat. 71-001

museums; dwelling houses; and government buildings. *Business capital* includes fixed assets such as farm and factory buildings, warehouses, and retail stores and all the accompanying machinery, equipment, and furnishings, including vehicles.

To obtain more of these capital or investment goods, a country has to divert part of its resources away from the production of goods and services that are *consumed*—that is to say, used up immediately, or in a relatively short period of time. Canada also obtains capital goods through investment by foreigners in this country. When we acquire more of these capital goods, we are said to be *investing*.

Entrepreneurship

This term is used to describe the creative risk-taking efforts of enterprising businessmen and women, called *entrepreneurs*, willing and able to assess consumer demand, pioneer the development of new products, establish and manage small and large business enterprises, and produce and market a wide range of goods and services. Because of its vital importance to an economy, entrepreneurship is treated by some economists as a fourth factor of production, separate from labour.

Technology

Economically, a country would be almost powerless without its technology or "technical know-how." This is the expertise, or technical knowledge of how to produce goods and services. A country can have a good labour force and an adequate supply of capital but lack the technology to make the best use of its natural resources—for example, the problems in developing the Canadian oil sands or the Atlantic offshore oil and gas.

Over the years, the world has accumulated a vast amount of technical knowledge which can be passed on to each new generation. If we were to be plunged back into a new Dark Ages, it would take hundreds of years to develop the technical knowledge currently used in industry, medicine, communications, transportation, and so many other fields. That is why, in many eyes, technology ranks as a factor of production *par excellence.*

At one time, improvements in technical knowledge took place very gradually and were considered part of labour and capital. However, the extremely rapid pace of technological change in the twentieth century, much faster than the Industrial Revolution of the nineteenth century, has made economists give this input special attention. Technological change is now frequently cited as one of the most vital factors in a country's economic growth. The importance of technological change to society has been dramatized by Alvin Toffler in his book, *Future Shock*. By dividing the last 50000 years of our existence into lifetimes of approximately 62 years, he suggests that there have been 800 such lifetimes, of which some 650 were spent in caves. Only within the most recent lifetimes have human beings made their most important technological discoveries. Indeed, most of the material goods used by everyone today have been developed only in the present 800th lifetime. Radio, television, telephones, photography, steam engines, propeller-driven ships, electricity, electric-light bulbs, electric motors, internal combustion engines, cars, propeller-driven and jet aircraft, manned space rockets, computers, canned and frozen foods, electric household appliances, electric, atomic and digital clocks, industrial machinery of all kinds, automated manufacturing processes, plastic products, and synthetic fabrics are all examples of goods invented or developed in the last few lifetimes. Moreover, agriculture, not long ago the primary human occupation, has now been replaced in many countries by manufacturing and service industries as the chief source of income and employment.

Political and Social Environments

The contrast between the standard of living of the Western industrial democracies and that of most of the Communist countries of Eastern Europe emphasizes how important the political environment is in influencing economic activity. A government that tries to control almost completely the ownership and use of the means of production also destroys the personal freedom and economic initiative that are essential to rapid economic growth. And as we have seen in, for example, Central America and Lebanon, civil wars, resulting from political differences, can bring economic activity almost to a standstill.

Even within a democracy such as Canada, political decisions constantly interfere with and even overrule economic decisions—so much so that we have been said to have "politicized our economy"—for example, the political decisions in the nineteenth century to build the C.P.R., and later to institute a National Policy of tariff protection for Canadian manufacturers, and in more recent times, the emphasis in government legislation in Canada on income distribution rather than income creation, and the establishment of FIRA and the National Energy Program to promote economic nationalism perhaps at the expense of Canadian income and employment.

The social environment also greatly influences economic activity.

For example, one of the main factors contributing to Japan's economic success is considered to be its disciplined, co-operative labour force and system of life-time employment—both an outcome of the type of society. In Britain, by contrast, management and labour, broadly representing two different social classes, are natural adversaries. In other countries, particularly the Middle East, religion greatly affects business activity.

Scarcity

Land, labour, and capital, both on Crusoe's island and in society at large, are insufficient to produce everything that people want. As a result, economists call them *scarce resources*, even though the absolute quantities may be extremely large. The nature, quantity, and quality of these resources set limits or *constraints*, therefore, on what can be produced.

Alternative Use

Canada's resources, as well as being relatively scarce, are capable of alternative use. Sales reps can be employed to sell any one of a variety of product lines; farmland can be used to grow many different crops; and factories can be designed and equipped to make all kinds of products. We can build more houses if we build fewer schools; more hospitals if we build fewer houses. Or we can spread our resources and build some of each, but not as many as if we used all our resources to build just houses, just schools, or just hospitals.

1.4: THE PRODUCTION POSSIBILITY CURVE

The range of choice open to society is illustrated in economics by means of a *production possibility curve*, or PPC. This curve (also called a *boundary*, or *frontier*) shows, hypothetically, the possible combinations of two different goods that can be produced by society with a given amount of resources.

Let us assume, for simplicity, that society can produce only office desks (capital goods) and hockey sticks (consumer goods). Let us also assume that, by using all its resources, society can produce at the two extremes either 5000 office desks or 16 million hockey sticks. Table 1:1, entitled Alternative Production Possibilities, shows these two extremes, together with some of the various intermediate production combinations.

Table 1:1
Alternative Production Possibilities

	Office desks (thousands)	Hockey sticks (millions)
A	0	16
B	1	15
C	2	13
D	3	10
E	4	6
F	5	0

These various full-employment production possibilities can be plotted on a graph (see Figure 1:1). Along the horizontal axis, we show the number of office desks produced, and along the vertical axis the number of hockey sticks produced. Plotted in the body of the graph is a series of points, A to F, each of which denotes a full-employment production possibility. Thus, point A represents the extreme at which society could produce 16 million hockey sticks but no office desks. Point F represents the other extreme at which society could produce 5000 office desks but no hockey sticks. Points B, C, D, and E represent combinations in between. Thus point D indicates that society, using *all* its resources, could produce 3000 office desks and 10 million hockey sticks. To show that there are any number of possible production combinations, we can draw a smooth curve joining the various points already plotted. We can then read off, at any point along the curve, the number of office desks and hockey sticks that could together be produced.

In practice, many thousands of goods and services can be produced in many thousands of possible production combinations. It is impossible, however, to measure this real-life situation. To do so, we would need a multi-dimensional rather than a simple two-dimensional PPC. Nevertheless, the production possibility curve with just two goods does serve a very useful purpose. It helps drive home an important economic fact: if a society's resources are fully employed, the only way for society to obtain more of one good is by having less of another. To use our previous example, society can have more office desks only by having fewer hockey stocks. Every extra office desk "costs" society so many hockey sticks. For example, from Table 1:1, we can see that if society produces no office desks, it can have 16 million hockey sticks. If it wants 1000 office desks, however, it can have only 15 million hockey sticks. Each desk has "cost" society the opportunity of having 1000 hockey sticks. This is called the *opportunity cost*. It is the cost, in terms of alternative production possibilities, of producing a particular good.

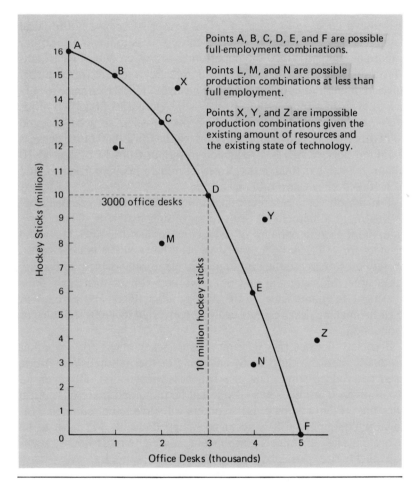

Points A, B, C, D, E, and F are possible full-employment combinations.

Points L, M, and N are possible production combinations at less than full employment.

Points X, Y, and Z are impossible production combinations given the existing amount of resources and the existing state of technology.

Figure 1:1   The Production Possibility Curve

This need for choice is being demonstrated all the time. As one example, the Soviet Union has for many years had a deliberate policy of allocating economic resources predominantly towards the production of military and capital goods at the expense of consumer goods. There are not enough resources to produce sufficient of both. In Canada, as another example, if we want to use more of our resources to fight pollution, we must be prepared to use resources now unemployed or being used for something else.

Why does the PPC have the shape that it does? In other words, why is it drawn concave to its origin? The answer is that the arithmetical data on which it is based have been chosen so as to illustrate another important economic fact: the opportunity cost of producing each additional unit of a good increases as resources are switched from the production of another good. In terms of our hypothetical example, society has to give up only 1 million hockey sticks to get its first 1000 office desks, but it has to give up 2 million hockey sticks to get its second 1000 office desks. The opportunity cost of the third 1000 office desks is 3 million hockey sticks (a reduction in output from 13 million to 10 million). The next 1000 desks "costs" 4 million hockey sticks, and the fifth 1000 desks costs 6 million.

The reason for increasing opportunity cost is that it gradually becomes more and more difficult to substitute materials, labour, and equipment used in one type of production for another type. The wood or steel for office desks cannot very well be used for hockey sticks. Society must increase the output of suitable woods—which, of course, takes time. Management and other workers cannot turn their skills overnight to manufacturing the new product. Plant and equipment used for making desks cannot easily be converted to a different type of production.

If society decides that it wants more hockey sticks (or any other product), then the most easily adaptable of the resources now being used to produce something else will be switched first. However, to obtain even more hockey sticks, it will be more and more difficult to alter the present resource use. Workers will have to be retrained. Unsuitable equipment will have to be scrapped. Plants will have to be relocated. The per-unit cost of obtaining more and more hockey sticks will quickly rise, particularly in the short run.

Production possibility curves can be used to illustrate many different types of economic choice that face society—for example, between consumption goods and capital goods, between capital goods and military goods, and between private goods and public goods.

In practice, society's resources are not always fully employed. This means that the economy operates *within* the PPC rather than on it. Although able to produce up to 5000 office desks or 16 million hockey sticks, society with less than full employment might produce only 4000 office desks or 14 million hockey sticks. So long as it has sufficient unemployed resources, a country can undertake new projects, such as cancer research or a space program, without necessarily forfeiting something else. However, if all resources—land, labour, and capital—are fully employed, then society must do without something else. This is because the economy is operating on its production possibility curve, or boundary.

It should be noted that the production possibility curve is not static. If a country is enjoying rapid economic growth, its PPC will be constantly shifting outwards to the right. Each year, the country becomes able to produce more and more goods and services. However, if the economy is stagnant, the PPC will remain relatively unchanged. And if the country has an increasing population, the average standard of living may actually decline as the same amount of goods and services has to be shared among more people.

1.5: ECONOMIC CHOICE

How does society choose what is to be produced? Who determines what we are to have? What economic goals do our federal and provincial governments pursue? Choice is so fundamental in our economic system that economics is sometimes succinctly defined as the "science of choice".

Consumer Sovereignty

In Canada, the group with the most important say as to what is produced is the consumer sector (See Table S.3). A *consumer* is any private individual with money to spend. Every dollar that one has can be likened to a vote at an election. If one wants more of one good and less of another, one will cast one's dollar "vote" accordingly. In other words, one will purchase only those goods that one wants and in the quantities that one wants. The choice will reflect one's personal needs and desires. Because spending by consumers is still much greater in total than spending by busines firms or by government, we continue to talk about *consumer sovereignty*.

Although Canadian consumers may be said to be "sovereign," that sovereignty is by no means absolute. Advertising, for example, greatly influences how we spend our money. Indeed, it has been suggested that advertising has become so powerful that consumers are often manipulated to buy what business firms want them to buy rather than what they really want themselves.

Table S.3
Spending in Canada, 1950-1982

| Year | Per cent of total | | | GNE at market prices ($ millions) |
	Consumers	Government	Business	
1950	72.7	13.2	15.9	18 491
1951	67.9	16.0	17.6	21 640
1952	65.5	17.9	15.7	24 588
1953	67.4	17.8	16.6	25 833
1954	70.7	18.2	12.4	25 918
1955	70.8	17.4	13.9	28 528
1956	68.4	17.4	18.8	32 058
1957	69.1	17.6	17.5	33 513
1958	71.7	18.0	13.6	34 777
1959	72.0	17.6	14.7	36 846
1960	71.1	17.9	14.4	38 359
1961	69.9	19.9	12.7	39 646
1962	68.3	19.8	13.5	42 927
1963	67.9	19.5	13.7	45 978
1964	67.1	19.1	14.6	50 280
1965	66.1	19.5	16.8	55 364
1966	63.9	20.4	18.0	61 828
1967	64.4	21.2	15.3	66 409
1968	64.7	21.6	14.1	72 586
1969	64.3	21.6	14.7	79 815
1970	62.8	23.1	13.3	85 685
1971	64.0	23.4	13.3	94 450
1972	64.6	23.1	13.1	105 234
1973	63.7	22.1	14.4	123 560
1974	62.4	22.6	15.9	147 528
1975	64.3	24.0	14.7	165 343
1976	64.4	23.4	14.5	191 031
1977	64.8	24.1	13.9	208 868
1978	64.8	23.8	13.9	230 490
1979	63.2	22.7	16.3	261 576
1980	62.9	22.8	15.4	291 869
1981	62.5	23.0	16.6	331 338
1982	62.7	24.8	15.2	348 925

Source: Statistics Canada, *National Income Expenditure Accounts,* Cat. 13-001

Note: Total spending differs slightly from Gross National Expenditure because of imports, exports, and residual error of estimate. Business spending includes non-residential construction, machinery and equipment, and value of physical change in inventories. Government spending includes current expenditure on goods and services and gross fixed capital formation

There is no doubt that advertising is effective in introducing new products to consumers, but it is certainly not so effective in persuading them to continue to buy what they do not like. Business history is littered with products that consumers did not want. Nevertheless, advertising does exert a great influence. Lack of competition in certain industries can also restrict consumer sovereignty; new firms may be prevented from entering the field or existing firms from producing what consumers really want. And, of course, the government (by import duties, sales taxes, government monopolies, and various laws) places restrictions on what consumers may buy.

Consumer sovereignty has meant that the major part of Canada's resources are used to produce food, clothing, cars, housing, furniture, household appliances, and entertainment that are considered necessities by the average Canadian consumer. This method of allocating resources has, of course, led to anomalies—for example, more is spent on tobacco than on theatres, more on entertainment than on education. Nevertheless, it has meant that the wishes of the Canadian public (rather than of the government) are given the top priority in directing the use of the country's scarce economic resources.

Business Spending

Business firms purchase large quantities of materials and parts (or *intermediate goods*) in order to produce the finished products, and supply the services, that consumers, governments and other business firms, want. Such business spending reflects market demand. Thus, the larger the number of cars purchased, the more axles, wheels,.tires, etc. the business firms will have to buy. The business firm's freedom of choice will be restricted to seeking the best value in materials and parts.

Business firms also spend money on *capital goods*, such as plant equipment, for the production of other goods. Their choice in this investment spending reflects their forecast of the production needed to meet expected sales and their view of the most efficient method of production.

Government Spending

Although consumers play the leading role in Canada in deciding what should be produced, our various governments—federal, provincial, and municipal—are also important spenders. Furthermore, they have in recent years shown the fastest rate of increase in spending. Indeed, one of the chief characteristics of the modern Canadian economy is the

"In the free market system, the consumer is always sovereign."

rapidly expanding role of government as a purchaser of goods and services.

Foreign Spending

Much of Canada's output is exported. Foreigners, therefore, greatly influence Canada's pattern of production. The growth of many of Canada's manufacturing industries, to say nothing of its more traditional resource industries, has depended as much on foreign markets, particularly the U.S. one, as on the Canadian one.

Other Government Tools for Allocating Resources

So far we have assumed that spending is the only method of determining how our economic resources are used. But the Canadian federal government, and to a much lesser extent the provincial and municipal governments, have various other tools at their disposal. Those available to the federal government, in addition to spending programs, include taxation, exchange rates, import duties, import quotas, and laws forbidding or encouraging certain business practices. It can use all of these to influence how Canada's resources are used and, equally important the degree of employment of these resources. In other words, it can influence not only Canada's position on the country's production possibility curve, but also whether Canada operates on it or within it — that is, whether Canada operates (see Figure 1:1) at point D (full employment) or at point M (less than full employment).

1.6: CANADA'S ECONOMIC GOALS AND POLICIES

Over the years, various federal governments have emphasized different economic goals for this country. In 1963, the Pearson government, in its terms of reference for the newly established Economic Council of Canada, indicated five basic economic and social goals for Canada: full employment, a high rate of economic growth, reasonable stability of prices, a viable balance of payments, and an equitable distribution of rising incomes. The choice of economic goals, and of the tools to achieve them (for example, tax incentives), by the government is known as *economic policy*.

Naturally, the goals set out by the Federal government in 1963 have been the subject of much discussion. Some years ago, the Economic Council of Canada, in its *Sixth Annual Review*, classified them as mainly *economic performance goals*, the attainment of which permits progress to other more fundamental *achievement goals*. The achievement goals specified by the Council included better education, better housing, the elimination of poverty, improvements in health, the maintenance of national security, increased international aid, rising standards of living and wider consumer choice, and an improved quality of life in a vastly changed and increasingly urban society. The Council also suggested that broader social, cultural, and political goals might also be included among these achievement goals. Since then, other possible achievement goals that have been suggested for Canada are protection of the environment, making cities more fit to live in, the preservation of national unity, and greater national economic independence.

Priorities and Tradeoffs

If a country does not have sufficient resources to achieve all its economic goals at once, it must obviously establish some priorities.In a country with authoritarian rule, these priorities are set by the government, often regardless of the public's wish. In a democracy, the priorities are set partly by the public (through its spending pattern) and partly by the government (through its spending, taxes, and laws). Frequently, a government must "trade-off" the pursuit of one economic or social goal against the pursuit of another. Thus policies designed to achieve a more equitable distribution of income may slow economic growth; and policies designed to combat inflation may increase unemployment.

Political goals may sometimes take priority over economic ones. Thus, the maintenance of law and order in a time of political crisis may cost money that could be used for regional economic development; and greater control over foreign investment in Canada may slow down growth in the economy. Canada, unlike many other countries of the world, needs to devote only a relatively small portion of its economic resources to national defence, because its immediate neighbour, the United States, is both militarily powerful and friendly, and willing to help defend Canada. In other words, Canada is able to devote most of its resources to *non-military goals*. In time of war, of course, many economic goals must be temporarily abandoned in an all-out effort to preserve a country's political identity.

In Canada, governments (like individuals) have found it impossible to pursue all their desired economic and social goals successfully at the same time. Consequently, governments at different times have stressed some goals more than others.

Evaluating Economic Performance

There are two basic ways of assessing a country's economic performance. One simple way is by wandering around the country, observing the people—how well-fed, dressed and housed they are—and the roads, buildings, and other private and public works. Another way is by collecting and monitoring statistical data in a variety of key areas, for example: Gross National Product; employment and unemployment; the rate of inflation (as shown by the Consumer Price Index); productivity; the standard of living (as shown by per capita real income); the balance of international trade and payments; the amount of foreign debt; and the foreign exchange rate for the currency.

The Federal Cabinet

The major economic policy-making body in Canada is the Federal Cabinet in Ottawa, a committee of Ministers headed by the Prime Minister. Particularly influential are the Minister of Finance and the Minister for Economic Development. All the Ministers are advised in their policy-making by Deputy-Ministers and their staff of the permanent Federal Public Service. For more effective performance, the cabinet has various sub-committees of which the Planning and Priorities Committee is the most important as regards economic policy.

Amongst the Ministries, the Department of Finance plays a key role in helping to formulate and implement the government's fiscal policy (changes in taxation and borrowing). Also, in consultation with the Bank of Canada (Canada's central bank), it helps to determine the government's monetary policy (changes in the country's money supply and interest rates) and its exchange-rate policy (the targetted foreign-exchange rate for the Canadian dollar). Another important Ministry is the Department of Regional Industrial Expansion, or DRIE, formed in 1983 from a merger of the Department of Regional Economic Expansion (DREE) and the Department of Industry, Trade, and Commerce (ITC). Also very important economically, as well as diplomatically, is the Department of External Affairs (DEA) which is now responsible for the federal government's export promotion efforts, including the Trade Commissioner service.

From time to time, the federal government also appoints special commissions to conduct investigations of particular economic problems and recommend solutions.

The Provincial Governments

Because Canada is a confederation, with ten provincial governments as well as a federal one, economic policy takes place at two different levels. The federal government has a unique role in monetary and exchange-rate policy but must share the fiscal policy field with its provincial counterparts—who can decide their own rates of income tax and sales tax and their own borrowing requirements. Ideally, the economic policies of the federal and provincial governments should be in harmony—for example, pay-restraint policies. In practice, unfortunately, this is not always so. And such lack of harmony is particularly serious if one or more of the three provincial economic heavyweights (Ontario, Quebec, and British Columbia) disagree with federal government policy.

Economic Council of Canada

Although it is the federal government's responsibility to establish economic policies for Canada, it receives advice not only from its own experts but also from various outside bodies. One of the most important of these is the Economic Council of Canada, established as an independent economic advisory body by the federal government in 1963. Its main functions are: (a) to define realistic five- to ten-year economic and social goals for Canada; (b) to recommend to government and industry the policies most likely to achieve these goals; and (c) to anticipate, as far as possible, Canada's economic and social problems and to advise on preventive or remedial measures. The Council consists of three full-time economists and 25 part-time members drawn from labour, business, finance, agriculture and other primary industries, and the public. It has a large research staff. The Council is required to publish every year "a review of medium- to long-term economic prospects" for Canada. It also publishes studies prepared by members of its staff on different economic problems. Furthermore, it undertakes special economic studies for the federal government.

Summary

1. *Economics* is the study of the way in which society uses its scarce resources to satisfy its many different wants. *Macroeconomics* is the study of the economic problems that face society as a whole.

Microeconomics is the study of the economic problems that face the various elements and sectors of society.

2. Economics is considered to be a social science because it involves the methodical study of the economic aspect of human behaviour.

3. Economics is important because economic reasoning is an invaluable training of the mind and because economic awareness helps improve personal, business, and government economic decisions.

4. *Economic history*—the study and analysis of past economic activities—helps us to understand better our present economic system and future economic trends.

5. Every society has limited economic resources capable of alternative use. Since people have many different wants, they must choose which goods and services to produce. Choice is the essence of economics.

6. A society's limited resources are classified under the broad headings of land, labour, and capital. Entrepreneurship is sometimes considered a fourth factor of production. And technology, a fifth. The political and social environments also affect a country's economic prosperity.

7. The range of choice open to society is illustrated by a production possibility curve, or PPC. Opportunity cost is the cost of producing a unit of one good in terms of the number of units of another good that could have been produced instead.

8. Various groups within society determine what is to be produced. The most important group is consumers—hence the term "consumer sovereignty". The three other main groups are business firms, governments, and foreigners.

9. Canada has many different economic goals. Since they cannot all be achieved at once, priorities must be established. Often, one goal must be traded off against another.

10. There are two basic ways of assessing a country's economic performance: observation and statistical analysis.

11. The Federal Cabinet is Canada's major economic policy-making body. Key economic ministries are the Department of Finance and the Department of Regional Industrial Expansion.

12. The provincial governments also have important economic powers.

13. The Economic Council of Canada is one of Canada's principal economic advisory bodies.

Key Terms

Economics   3
Macroeconomics   4
Microeconomics   4
Economic history   6
Limited resources   6
Factors of production   6
Land   8
Labour   8
Capital   8
Social Capital   8
Infrastructure   8
Business capital   11
Investing   11
Entrepreneur   11

Technology   11
Scarce resources   13
Alternative use   13
PPC   13
Opportunity cost   15
Consumer sovereignty   17
Capital goods   19
Economic goals   21
Economic policy   21
Economic performance
   goals   21
Achievement goals   21
Economic priorities   22
Trade offs   22

Review Questions

1. What is "economics"? Write a brief description, in your own words.
2. Why is economics considered to be a social science?
3. Distinguish between macroeconomics and microeconomics.
4. How can the study of economics benefit you, as an individual person? Give specific examples of the importance of economics to business firms and to governments.
5. What is economic history? Why study it?
6. Compare Alfred Marshall's definition of economics with Lionel Robbins' one.
7. "Economics is a method rather than a doctrine." Explain and discuss.
8. How do modern economists define economics? How do they differ? Why?
9. How can a person be both a Bachelor of Science and a Master of Arts in Economics? Does it make sense? If so, how?
10. Explain and comment on the following popular sayings:
    (a) "There's no such thing as a one-handed economist."
    (b) "Lock six economists in a room and they'll come up with a dozen answers."
    (c) "It's the economists who are running the country these days." Can you add to the list?

11. Economic history can explain the past, but not the present and the future. Discuss.
12. "Most empires have declined for economic rather than military, political, or social reasons." Discuss, with examples.
13. What are the factors of production? To what extent are they scarce?
14. Why is Canada said to be well-endowed with natural resources? What are our major resource deficiencies? What prevents Canada from fully utilizing many of its natural resources?
15. What are the chief characteristics of Canada's population? Size, sex, age, location, growth rate etc. What are its trends?
16. How big is Canada's labour force? How is it growing? Where is it located?
17. Distinguish between real capital and money capital.
18. Distinguish, with examples, betwen social capital and business capital.
19. What is meant by the term "investing"?
20. What is an "entrepreneur"? Why is entrepreneurship considered to be so important? Give some examples.
21. It has been recommended that Canada concentrate on high-technology industries for its future. What does this mean? Give some examples.
22. What difference has technology made to our lives compared with that of our grandparents?
23. How can political and social factors affect a country's standard of living? Give examples.
24. If our resources are so abundant, why do economists call them "scarce"?
25. What is a production possibility curve? What can it illustrate? Give some examples.
26. Why is the PPC drawn concave to the origin?
27. What is meant by "opportunity cost"? Why does it gradually increase?
28. "In Canada we are operating well within our PPC." Explain. Why is this so?
29. "The PPC is not static." Explain. Why not?
30. Canada imports most of its technology. How and why? Discuss.
31. Economics has been defined as the "science of choice". Explain and comment.
32. Explain the meaning and origin of the term "consumer sovereignty." How valid is the concept today?
33. "People buy what the ads tell them to." Discuss.

34. Consumers know what is best for them. Discuss.
35. Business firms buy mainly "intermediate goods" and "capital goods." Explain.
36. Business spending reflects market demand. Explain.
37. Business firms must also anticipate market demand. Why? What happens when their anticipations are wrong? Give examples.
38. How important a say do our governments have in the allocation of our economic resources? How has it changed over the years? Why?
39. How does foreign spending affect us?
40. How can our governments affect the allocation of our resources, other than by their spending programs?
41. Distinguish between economic performance goals and achievement goals. List, in order of priority, the economic goals that you think Canada should pursue.
42. Why do governments have to consider priorities and "tradeoffs"? What economic priorities does your federal government have?
43. Do your provincial and municipal governments have economic goals? What are they?
44. How can we assess a country's economic performance?
45. "Political goals sometimes take priority over economic goals." Explain, with examples.
46. Who decides economic policy for Canada? Which are the key Ministries, from the economic point of view?
47. What is the Economic Council of Canada? What is its role? What other economic advisory bodies exist in Canada?

2. ECONOMIC SYSTEMS

Every society, whatever its political complexion, has the same basic economic problems. These are: what to produce, how to produce, and for whom to produce (or, put in another way, how to share what has been produced). Countries differ, however, in the extent to which government intervenes in their solution. And this forms the basis of our classification of economic systems into three basic kinds: the market system, the command system, and the mixed economic system. Some economists also refer to a "traditional" economic system—in which economic decisions are made mainly on the basis of tradition and custom. However, all economic systems operate partly on tradition (why change something if it works well) and all economic systems, including those of highly traditional Third World countries, constantly undergo considerable economic change (e.g. depressed export prices, expensive oil imports, urbanization, and drought-hit agricultural production).

2.1: THE MARKET SYSTEM

Under this economic system (also known as *free enterprise*, or *laissez-faire*), the basic economic questions are decided in the marketplace. Demand and supply, free from government interference, are the determining forces.

As explained more fully in Chapter 5 (Supply, Demand, and Market Price), if the public wants more of a good, inventories of it will run low and the price of it will tend to rise. This will in turn encourage more production—requiring perhaps the use of additional resources. These may have previously been unemployed or used to produce other less desirable goods and services. If the public wants less of a product, the opposite process will occur.

The characteristics of the market system include the individual's rights: (a) to own property; (b) to earn profit; (c) to compete in business; (d) to decide what and how much to produce, (e) to decide how to produce; (f) as an employer to hire labour and other productive resources; (g) as an employee, to choose one's job and negotiate the terms of employment; and (h) as a consumer, to spend one's money as one sees fit.

Right to Own Property

For most people the right to own property is an important incentive to work hard, to save, and to invest part of one's income. This is because ownership of property can help provide a higher material standard of living and greater financial security, for the future as well as the present. In Canada, a person's property rights are protected by common and statute law, and by the existence of an efficient police force and judiciary. With this assurance, people have gone ahead and built up business firms of all types and sizes and for others the opportunity continues to exist.

Right to Earn Profit

Profit—the excess of revenue over expenses—is the reward that a person receives for assuming the risk of starting and operating a business. Without it, few people would be willing to invest their savings in the ownership of a business—for it is just as easy, if not more so, to make a loss rather than a profit. Unless businesspeople are rewarded for trying to bring new products on to the market and to produce existing ones more efficiently, they will direct their efforts elsewhere. And business investment and operations would have to be undertaken or directed by the government, with questionable results.

Right to Compete in Business

The market system would not operate efficiently if people were not free to start businesses and to close them, as necessary. If government permission were always required, resources would not be shifted into the production of the goods and services that the public wants. In Canada, as we discuss later in the book, competition is by no means perfect—with private oligopolies, government monopolies, production and marketing quotas, etc., all infringing on the businessperson's right to compete.

Right to Decide What and How Much to Produce

In the market system, the businessperson has the responsibility for anticipating consumer demand and deciding what goods to produce and in what quantity. In the command system, by contrast, this is done by planning commissions who seem inevitably, with the complexity of the task and the government bureaucracy involved, to bring about surpluses of some products and shortages of others, all at relatively high cost.

Right to Decide How to Produce

In the market system, the business firm strives constantly to produce and market its goods more efficiently. This is because, by lowering expenses, the firm can increase its profit. Without this freedom and incentive, we would not see the rapid technological change that now characterizes our industry.

Right to Employ Productive Resources

In order to produce the goods and services that the public wants, a business firm must be able to call upon productive resources: labour, land, capital, entrepreneurship, and technology.

In most communist countries, these resources are allocated to factories and farms by the various planning commissions. If a factory manager wishes to increase the labour force or obtain more equipment, he or she must obtain permission from the government. Furthermore, the wage rates or equipment prices to be paid are prescribed by the authorities. In a market system, by contrast, a business firm hires its labour and other productive resources by bidding for them in the marketplace, in competition with other firms. And the firms for whose products the public demand is strongest, will be the ones best able to afford them.

Right to Choose One's Job

In a market system, the individual has the right to choose his or her job. Of course, this right is subject to the type of education, skills, etc. that the person has and the range of jobs available. This freedom means that people are able to move into industries for whose product public demand is increasing and out of those for whose product public demand is falling. The encouragement is, of course, different salaries and promotion opportunities. This freedom also means that people are encouraged to train for jobs for which there is a high demand.

In the market system, the individual has the right to negotiate with the employer the terms of his or her employment. A person is not just allocated a job by a government official and told how much he or she will be paid. A person has the right to decline the salary or wage, and, unlike Oliver Twist, to ask for more. This flexibility enables employees whose services are in greater demand to push up their wage rate and so encourage more people to enter that field—another example of the price mechanism at work, allocating society's resources according to public demand.

Consumer's Freedom of Choice

In the market economy, people are relatively free to spend their money on the goods or services they choose. This means that they can adjust their pattern of spending to suit their personal tastes. A person is not told what to buy, or rationed in the amounts that he or she can have—

"The wonderful thing about our economic system, George, is that everyone has an equal chance."

except by the size of his or her purse. The only government restrictions in Canada on this freedom of choice are the existence of government-operated or regulated monopolies and regulations relating to public health and morals, import restrictions, and varying levels of sales taxes.

Freedom of choice in spending has the important effect, for the economy as a whole, of helping to allocate the use of the country's available productive resources basically in accordance with the public's wishes. Through the working of the price mechanism, an increase in demand for a particular good or service will eventually cause business firms to increase their production of it. And a decrease in demand will cause the opposite effect.

One of the best-known exponents of the market system was the eighteenth-century Scottish economist, Adam Smith. He believed that if people were left alone by government and others to pursue their own private interests, this would result in the maximum benefit for society as a whole. An "invisible hand" would guide people's actions for the common good. Adam Smith's ideas are set out in his celebrated book, *An Inquiry into the Nature and Causes of the Wealth of Nations*, first published in 1776.

The term *private enterprise* is also used to describe this economic system, because most of the means of production and distribution are privately owned.

Advantages of the market system are:

1. The goods and services produced are of the type and quality demanded by the public, not ones ordered by some distant bureaucrat.

2. Entrepreneurs have freedom and incentive to use land, labour, capital, and technology, to produce the required goods and services as efficiently as possible.

3. Employees have freedom to choose and change their job and to negotiate the conditions of their employment.

Disadvantages of the market system are:

1. The public may not choose the goods and services that are best for it—for example, who will pay for schools, hospitals and roads? But governments usually undertake this task—however reluctant the public may be.

2. Business executives may treat labour and other resources in an inhuman or destructive way and may not pass on the benefits of

any efficiency to the public. However, labour unions and collective bargaining now help protect the interests of labour. And, in Canada, the Combines Investigation Act helps reduce unfair business practices.

3. There will tend to be great inequality of income and many people may have very little income to purchase what they need.

2.2: THE COMMAND SYSTEM

Under this system, the government rather than the public decides what is to be produced and how it is to be distributed. Economic plans are made by government planning boards who are also given the authority to carry them out. Such an economic system, operating under government command, is the direct opposite of the market system just discussed.

The characteristics of the command system are:

(a) public (i.e. state) ownership of the means of production (land, buildings, and equipment);

(b) central planning of all economic activity, including what and how much produce, how to produce, and how to distribute;

(c) minor role of the consumer in deciding what is to be produced;

(d) minor role of the price mechanism;

(e) public rather than private investment in farms and factories;

(f) government assignment of jobs; and

(g) outlawing of "profits".

Possible *advantages* of the command system include:

1. A more logical choice of the goods and services to be produced—for example, sports facilities instead of cigarettes.

2. More efficient production methods—for example, no strikes or lockouts, no unemployment, and no labour exploitation.

3. A fairer distribution of the goods and services produced.

Possible *disadvantages* of the command system include:

1. A more illogical choice of the goods and services to be produced—for example, heavy spending on the armed forces instead of producing more consumer goods.

2. A government-directed manufacturing or service firm may be much less efficient than the highly motivated private entrepreneur. There may in fact be considerable "hidden unemployment"—for example, three persons doing the job of one.

3. A much smaller "national cake" to share out. Also, there

may still be economically privileged classes—for example, politicians, government officials, and military leaders—who receive a much larger slice than the others. So the distribution of goods and services, whatever the claims of the ruling political party, may still be inequitable.

2.3: MIXED ECONOMIC SYSTEMS

Very few countries operate today under a purely market system or a purely command one. In most private-enterprise countries, government control has been gradually increasing over the years. Thus, in Canada today the federal government, in addition to being the owner of several large commercial enterprises such as Air Canada and Canadian National Railways, regulates private business activity by a multiplicity of laws. These laws influence in various ways the answers to society's basic economic questions. As another example of government intervention, the federal government, through the Canadian Radio-Television and Telecommunications Commission, regulates and supervises all aspects of the Canadian broadcasting system, both public and private. By setting minimum standards, the federal government also influences the ways in which goods are produced and marketed. By taxes and subsidies, it alters the distribution of income. The provincial and municipal governments also intervene in the working of Canada's economic system by spending, taxing, and borrowing and by a variety of laws covering health, education, labour etc. Also, and very importantly, the government provides various "collectively used" goods such as roads, bridges, schools, hospitals, and services such as police and fire protection and military defence that the private sector would not adequately provide.

In many command or planned-economy countries, on the other hand, government economic control has declined in recent years. This has been particularly so in Hungary. Even in the Soviet Union, although most of the means of production are still owned by the state, the questions of what to produce and how to produce are being entrusted more and more to the managers of individual manufacturing plants and farming co-operatives. In turn, these managers are now attempting to supply what consumers want rather than what the central or regional government decides that they should have. Even the distribution of income, long a strictly controlled function of government, is becoming partly a matter of private decision. Plant managers and other employees, for example, receive bonuses that vary with the amount of profits made; and farm workers sell privately the produce from personally-owned small plots of land. However, central economic control remains the norm.

2.4: ECONOMIC VERSUS POLITICAL SYSTEMS

One must be careful not to confuse economic systems with political ones.

Political systems can be divided, at the most basic level, into two kinds: (a) those which permit the population, at reasonable intervals, to replace the government, if dissatisfied with it, by another group of persons, and (b) those which do not. In the first category would fall Canada, the U.S., Japan, Britain and other democratic countries. In the latter would fall the Soviet Union and other Communist countries, plus all the various military regimes—for example in South America and Africa.

Countries in the first category, including Canada, have a mixed economic system, with the emphasis towards a market rather than a command system. Countries in the second category also have mixed economic systems. But the communist countries have predominantly command economic systems whereas the military regimes have predominantly market economic systems.

To avoid confusion, there are some other terms that we should now define. These are the four "isms"—capitalism, socialism, communism, and fascism—that have both political and economic connotations.

Capitalism is a term used, often in a derogatory fashion, to describe the market, or private enterprise system that Canada enjoys, in which the "capitalists' (the private owners of the means of production) are supposed to be exploiting the workers. Such an interpretation ignores the fact that many large companies are owned by many small shareholders, that governments now closely regulate the activities of business firms, and that labour unions now often seem stronger than employers. Because the Western democracies have a predominantly market system, the term "capitalism" is also used as a derogatory synonym for "democracy".

Socialism is a political system in which: some or all of the means of production are owned by the state; there is a considerable degree of central economic and social planning; and the welfare of society generally is a prime concern of the government. Both democratic and non-democratic countries have professed to be socialist, at one time or another. Thus a distinction is usually made between *democratic social-*

ism, as has been practised, for example, by the Labour Party in Britain and authoritarian socialism as practised by the Soviet Union and other "socialist republics".

Communism is the ideal political system, preached by Lenin and other socialist writers, to which the socialist countries are supposed to be heading—in which each person gives of his or her best and receives according to his or her need. It is also the title assumed by the ruling political party in the one-party socialist states of, for example, Eastern Europe.

Fascism is the political system that originated in Italy and that was practised in that country under Mussolini during the period 1922 to 1943. The political regime in Germany under Hitler, during the period 1933 to 1945, officially called "national socialist", has also been labelled a fascist dictatorship. This is because it also subordinated the rights of the individual citizen to the will of the state and its supreme leader. Under fascism, private ownership of property, including the means of production, was permitted. However, the government reserved the right to intervene at any time in the national interest. In practice, fascism meant aggressively nationalistic policies, central regimentation of the economy, rigid censorship of the press, and the absence of elections and other democratic rights. Economically, fascism meant a mixed economic system, with a strong leaning towards a command system. Today, many of the military regimes throughout the world are labelled "fascist".

2.5: CANADA'S ECONOMIC SYSTEM

The type of economic system now prevailing in Canada can be called *mixed capitalism*, or *limited free enterprise*, because of the increasing economic intervention by government. In this market system, both private and public capital exist side by side and government exercises a considerable amount of control over private business activities.

The basic characteristics of Canada's economic system include (a) the right of individuals to choose their type of work and to bargain with their employer, either individually or collectively, as to the wage and fringe benefits that they will receive; (b) the right of individuals to establish and operate their own private businesses in pursuit of profit; (c) the right of individuals, both employers and employees, to accumulate property—*the institution of private property*; (d) the right of individuals, as consumers, to spend their money as they see fit, and (e) the right of government to intervene in this predominantly private-enterprise economic system, where appropriate, to achieve various economic and social goals.

Weaknesses of Canada's Economic System

The market system that exists in Canada seems to be preferred by most Canadians to a system in which the government tells everyone what job to do, what pay to receive, and what goods and services to produce. However, we have no reason to be complacent. As the system operates in Canada, it has major faults which we are only gradually—if at all—learning to overcome. These faults include: unemployment; inflation; regional economic disparities; poverty; poor labour-management relations; the divergence between private and social costs and benefits; insufficient competition between firms in certain industries operating in Canada; the manufacture abroad of goods for the Canadian market that might be better produced at home; relative low industrial productivity; and the possible misallocation of resources.

1. Unemployment. It is quite shocking (see Chapter 23: Unemployment and its Causes) that such a large percentage of Canada's civilian labour force is unemployed. Even more deplorable is the fact that the unemployment rate is highest among young people. Does the fault lie with a market system that does not create enough jobs? Or are people setting their sights too high and becoming unwilling to accept jobs their parents would have gladly taken? Is the work force becoming too highly educated or mistrained? Or is there insufficient emphasis in Canada on economic growth? Should the government supplement the market system, creating additional jobs through direct spending programs and subsidies to employers? Should people be willing to give up the freedom to choose their own jobs and careers, and to change jobs at will, in return for government-assured employment? Should Canada restrict its imports of manufactured goods to help protect local jobs?

2. Inflation. In our market system, business firms are free to set the prices for their products. Also, wage earners, represented in many cases by labour unions, are free to bargain with employers for wages and fringe benefits. As a result, price and wage levels are constantly being pushed upwards as business firms and labour unions compete to increase their share of the national income. Governments also, reeling under the interest burden of a large public debt, heavy unemployment and other social security payments, and the cost of new energy and job-creation programs, add their spending to already inflationary fires. And by borrowing money to finance deficit spending (i.e., spending more than is received from taxes and other revenue), our federal, provincial, and municipal governments force up interest rates and reduce the capital available for private business investment. People receiving relatively fixed money incomes (pensioners for instance) find that their real income—the goods and services they can buy with their money income—is constantly declining. And the continuation of inflation disrupts social harmony as each labour union and business firm struggles not to be left worse off. Again, we are faced with a variety of questions. Should firms be free to set their prices? Should workers be allowed to bargain collectively for higher wages? Should the federal and provincial governments impose wage and price controls? Should business firms and consumers receive protection from high interest rates?

3. Regional Income Disparities. Why is it, under the market system, that some parts of Canada are much better off than others? Why are Alberta, B.C., and southern Ontario, for example, relatively prosperous economically while most of the Atlantic provinces still find it hard to make ends meet? Why is it that the market system fails to spread economic prosperity evenly throughout the nation?

4. Poverty. How is it possible that poverty exists in an economically rich country like Canada? Why is it that Canada's market system fails to provide everyone with an adequate, if not comfortable standard of living? And what can be done to alleviate the problem?

5. Divergence Between Private and Social Costs and Benefits. By producing goods of the desired quality as cheaply as possible, business firms are helping society to make the best use of its limited resources. However, this has created a problem that many business firms until recently tended to ignore. This problem is the divergence between *private costs* and *social costs*, or, looked at in another way, between *private benefits* and *social benefits*.

Many business firms, seeking the lowest production and marketing costs, choose a course of action that often conflicts with the best interests of society—pollution of the environment is a good example. In the course of business activity, untreated waste products are often dumped into the nearest river, lake, or sea; various chemicals, such as sulphur, are emitted into the atmosphere in the form of smoke and drift down upon our lakes and forests as "acid rain"; large areas of the countryside are denuded by intensive logging of timber or strip mining of minerals; and natural scenery is masked by large billboards and so-called tourist attractions.

Fortunately, more and more firms, partly as a result of growing public indignation, are taking steps to reduce their pollution of the environment. These steps cost money, of course, and must be paid for either by a reduction in profits or by increased prices to the consumer. At the same time, governments are establishing new laws, increasing penalties, and enforcing existing laws more rigorously, to discourage industrial and human pollution.

6. Insufficient Competition. Competition among business firms in Canada to increase their share of the market comprises two basic forms: price competition and non-price competition. In Canada, the amount of price competition varies greatly from industry to industry. In most cases, business firms are extremely reluctant to reduce prices for fear of retaliatory action by competitors. A price war, business firms realize, benefits the public rather than themselves—an example of the divergence between private and social benefit. Advertising (a form of non-price competition) enables many firms to differentiate their products from those of competitors, even though the quality of the product may be the same. This means that consumers may remain loyal to a particular brand of product despite the fact that its price may be higher than that of similar products produced by other firms.

As we see later, the absence of price competition usually means that the public pays more for the goods and services they buy than they otherwise would. In Canada, the federal government, by means of the Combines Investigation Act, tries to discourage firms from restricting competition. On the other hand, through producer-managed marketing boards, liquor control boards, and air transport commissions, etc., it restricts competition in other fields.

7. The Exporting of Jobs. More and more manufacturing firms, often Canadian subsidiaries of U.S. multinational corporations, are reducing or closing down production in Canada, switching all or part of the work to their plants in the U.S., and exporting the finished goods to Canada. Other manufacturing firms, Canadian as well as foreign-owned, although continuing to produce in Canada, are now buying many of their parts and materials from countries such as Japan, South Korea, Malaysia, Taiwan, and Hong Kong, and thereby "exporting jobs" abroad. Other firms, unable to compete with foreign-made goods, have shut down completely, throwing their employees out of work and drastically affecting the economic health of many Canadian communities. At the same time, the federal government continues to reduce tariff and other barriers to foreign manufactured goods. By contrast, other countries such as Brazil, also with many resource-based exports, encourage local production of most of the manufactured goods that they need behind a heavily protected wall of import quotas and exchange controls. Japan, a leading exporter of manufactured goods, makes its local market almost impenetrable to foreign manufactured goods. And the Communist countries, long an advocate of protectionism, accept foreign goods by invitation only. Are Canadians, as some people suggest, becoming once more predominantly a nation of farmers, miners, lumberjacks, and fishermen—the traditional "hewers of wood and drawers of water"? And if so, what should be done about it?

8. Relatively Low Productivity. As we discuss in Chapter 20, Canada's rate of increase in industrial productivity over the last decade has been about the lowest in the Western world. And this is one important reason why manufacturing plants in Canada have been closing down or reducing production.

9. Possible Misallocation of Resources. There is, in theory, an optimum allocation of a society's scarce resources—a perfect "social balance." In practice such a balance is difficult to agree on, let alone achieve. For example, how much of its resources should a society devote to military as compared with civil purposes? What consumer goods and services should it provide? Should it train more doctors and fewer lawyers? More plumbers and fewer civil servants? Should we have less butter and more margarine? Should we pay to have our parks cleaned up rather than pay people to be idle while unemployed?

Canada, with its predominantly private-enterprise economy, has traditionally let the public, with its "dollar votes", have a large say in how our resources are allocated. Thus, spending on liquor and tobacco, for example, far outweighs spending on health. However, in recent years, our federal and provincial governments have been actively altering the way in which we allocate our resources—for example, by financing, with the taxpayers' money, medicare and higher education.

If we compare our society with that of other countries, the different allocation of our resources becomes more apparent. Many people do in fact think that we have achieved a satisfactory social balance in Canada.

Strengths of Canada's Economic System

Although we have just reviewed many apparent weaknesses of Canada's economic system, it is nevertheless true that many people would dearly love to come and live in Canada. Political freedom is one important attraction. But just as important, if not more so, for many people, are the economic benefits.

1. High Average Level of Income. As the result of an impressive output of goods and services, encouraged by our predominantly private-enterprise economic system, Canadians enjoy one of the highest material standards of living in the world. In fact Canada is now considered by the World Bank, which makes international statistical comparisons, to have the fourteenth highest standard in the world. Even though Canada's international ranking has slipped a lot since the end of World

War II, when it was fourth, the actual level is still impressive. Good food, clothing, education, health care, housing, cars, appliances, annual vacations at home and abroad, are the lot of most Canadians. (The decline in ranking has been due partly to the instant wealth, since 1970, of the oil-exporting countries and partly to our own economic neglect).

The standard of living of Canadians now ranks fourteenth in the world

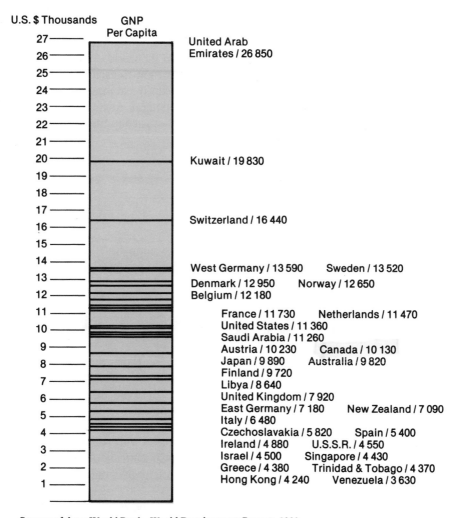

U.S. $ Thousands   GNP Per Capita

United Arab Emirates / 26 850

Kuwait / 19 830

Switzerland / 16 440

West Germany / 13 590   Sweden / 13 520
Denmark / 12 950   Norway / 12 650
Belgium / 12 180
France / 11 730   Netherlands / 11 470
United States / 11 360
Saudi Arabia / 11 260
Austria / 10 230   Canada / 10 130
Japan / 9 890   Australia / 9 820
Finland / 9 720
Libya / 8 640
United Kingdom / 7 920
East Germany / 7 180   New Zealand / 7 090
Italy / 6 480
Czechoslavakia / 5 820   Spain / 5 400
Ireland / 4 880   U.S.S.R. / 4 550
Israel / 4 500   Singapore / 4 430
Greece / 4 380   Trinidad & Tobago / 4 370
Hong Kong / 4 240   Venezuela / 3 630

Source of data: World Bank, *World Development Report, 1982*

2. Limited Economic Bureaucracy. Most Canadians believe that the country has more bureaucrats than it needs, particularly tax collectors. However, it is nothing compared with the economic as well as political and other types of bureaucracy that exist in most command economies such as the Soviet Union. So we should perhaps count our blessings.

3. Personal Economic Freedom. In Canada, people have the freedom to change jobs and the town or part of the country in which they live and work. They also have the right to start a business and work for themselves if they choose. They can also own land, buildings, and other means of production and hire other people to work for them. And they can accumulate capital, to spend later, on whatever they see fit. All these economic freedoms, usually taken for granted in Canada, are non-existent in many other countries of the world.

4. Incentive to Innovate. Because of the right to earn profit and to undertake business, a person has every incentive to innovate whether it be a new product or a new production method. As a result, Canada and other private enterprise economic systems continue to remain in the forefront of technological change.

Summary

1. Every society, whatever its political system, has the same economic problems: what to produce, how to produce and for whom to produce.
2. With the market system (also known as free enterprise or "laissez-faire"), the basic economic questions are decided in the market-place, through the interaction of demand and supply free from government interference.
3. Under the command system, government, rather than the public, decides what is to be produced, how, and for whom.
4. Most countries have a mixed economic system—that is, a market economy with a certain amount of government intervention or a command system with a certain amount of market freedom.
5. Economic systems should not be confused with political systems. However, market systems are more characteristic of political democracies, and command systems of totalitarian, or one-party political regimes.
6. Canada's economic system is a mixed one, with government intervention gradually increasing.

7. Weaknesses of Canada's economic system include: a high level of unemployment; inflation; regional income disparities; poverty for some; poor labour-management relations; the divergence between private and social costs and benefits with environmental pollution and other results; insufficient competition in certain industries; the incentive to produce abroad goods that might better be produced at home; and the possible misallocation of resources—e.g., entertainment rather than health care or, in other countries, "guns rather than butter".

8. Strengths of Canada's economic system include: a high average level of income for Canadians; limited economic bureaucracy; personal economic freedom; and incentive to innovate.

Key Terms

Market system   30
Laissez-faire   30
Private enterprise   34
Command system   35
Mixed economic system   36
Political system   37
Capitalism   37
Canada's economic
   system   38
Unemployment   39
Inflation   39
Regional income
   disparities   40
Poverty   40

Private and social
   costs   40
Competition   41
Exporting of jobs   41
Low productivity   42
Misallocation of
   resources   42
High material standard
   of living   42
Limited economic
   bureaucracy   44
Personal economic
   freedom   44
Incentive to innovate   44

Review Questions

1. What is a "market system"?
2. Who was Adam Smith? And what was his "invisible hand"?
3. What other terms are used to describe the free market system?
4. What are the possible advantages for society of the market system?
5. What are the possible disadvantages? How might it be possible to have the advantages without the disadvantages?
6. What are the characteristics of a command system?

7. What are the possible advantages of a command system?
8. What are the possible disadvantages?
9. Distinguish between capitalism, socialism, and communism.
10. Choose five countries from different regions of the world and indicate which type of economic system they use.
11. Why have some communist countries granted more economic freedom to their people in recent years?
12. Economic systems are closely linked to political systems. Discuss.
13. What economic system exists in Canada? How has it changed in recent years? Give reasons for the change.
14. One major weakness of Canada's economic system is the high rate of unemployment. How high is it? How does it vary by age and location of the persons involved?
15. How might Canada's unemployment problem be resolved?
16. What is "inflation"? What are its disadvantages? Does it have any advantages?
17. Why are some parts of Canada better off than others?
18. Who are Canada's poor? Why are they poor?
19. Explain, with an example, the possible discrepancy between private costs and benefits and social ones.
20. Why do most people favour competition yet resent foreign goods replacing Canadian ones, particularly in Canada?
21. Give some examples of lack of competition in Canada. Who tries to ensure that competition takes place? How?
22. What is meant by the phrase: "exporting jobs"? How does it occur? Why is it taking place?
23. Should foreign goods have unrestricted access to the Canadian market? Explain and discuss the pros and cons. What is the present situation?
24. How is Canada moving, if at all, towards a better "social balance" in the allocation of its economic resources?
25. Why do many people in other countries consider that they would be "better off" living in Canada?

3. ECONOMIC ANALYSIS

CHAPTER OBJECTIVES

A. To explain how economic research is usually conducted
B. To explain how an economic theory is developed and tested
C. To discuss cost-benefit analysis—a practical, everyday application of economic reasoning
D. To indicate that one area of economics is the study of our various economic institutions e.g., the banking system
E. To explain what economists do
F. To offer some tips for clearer thinking about economic problems.

CHAPTER OUTLINE

3.1 Economic Research
3.2 Economic Theories
3.3 Cost-Benefit Analysis
3.4 Institutional Economics
3.5 The Economist
3.6 Economic Pitfalls

Unless we can properly diagnose our economic troubles and prescribe the correct remedies, we will continue to be plagued with high unemployment, inflation, income insecurity, and other economic woes. Economic research and the economic theories that result are our best attempt to understand and explain the workings of our economic system and the ways in which we can adjust it to our needs. Obviously, we have far to go and probably will never arrive.

3.1: ECONOMIC RESEARCH

Over the years, a great deal of research into the working of our economic system has been carried out in Britain, the United States, and other countries, including Canada, and the names of Ricardo, Marshall, Keynes, as well as of many leading contemporary economists such as Samuelson, Galbraith, and Friedman have become known even to the general public. This research has resulted in the formulation of *economic theories* that describe and explain the various cause-effect relationships that exist in our economy—for example, the relationship between national income and employment.

Economic research usually follows a definite scientific pattern: (a) the collection and analysis of relevant data; (b) the formulation of an economic theory or a modification of an existing one; and (c) the testing of the economic theory.

Collection and Analysis of Relevant Data

Sometimes economists or other economic researchers must conduct statistical and other surveys of their own. However, statistical data about a wide variety of economic topics is collected, summarized, and published by Statistics Canada, the federal government's statistical agency. The most important statistical compilation that it undertakes is the census, prepared every ten years. In addition, Statistics Canada publishes an official statistical annual called the *Canada Year Book* and a more concise annual statistical handbook. It also publishes, on a more frequent basis, many other statistical reports, notably the *Daily Bulletin* (with the latest weekly, monthly, and quarterly statistics and details of any new publications), and the monthly *Canadian Statistical Review*. The latter contains key economic indicators, often going back many years, and various graphs and tables. The Bank of Canada also publishes a monthly statistical review, with an emphasis on financial data such as the money supply. Each year, in late April, but sometimes delayed, the Federal Department of Finance publishes its *Economic Review* containing a review of the previous year's economic events and a variety of key economic statistics, including federal, provincial, and municipal government revenues and expenditures, going back for many years. Furthermore, such bodies as the Economic Council of Canada, the Conference Board in Canada, the Private Planning Association, the Fraser Institute, the Canadian Foundation for Economic Education, and various temporary, *ad hoc* commissions provide a steady flow of economic studies of different aspects of the Canadian economy. And then there are the professional economic journals such as *The Canadian Journal of Economics*, published four times a year, by the Canadian Economics Association—an organization of Canadian economists, mainly academics. Newspaper and magazine articles also provide topical economic information and analysis. The economist has to sift this great mass of statistical data and verbal description and abstract what is relevant to the study being undertaken.

3.2: ECONOMIC THEORIES

After a study of the data, the economist suggests the existence of certain relationships—for example, between the money supply and the rate of inflation. This economic hypothesis—a concise statement of the presumed relationship between various economic variables—is called an *economic theory*.

Simplifying Assumptions

Because of the great complexity of most economic problems, arising from the many variables involved, economists are forced, in developing a hypothesis, to make a number of simplifying assumptions—for example, that the supply of a product remains unchanged. In this way, they can concentrate their attention on the relationships that exist among other economic variables. By assuming the money supply and other factors to be constant, for example, they can focus attention on the relationship between government spending and employment.

In addition, since economists must generalize about the economic behaviour of countless consumers and business firms, they must make certain basic assumptions about them—for example, that consumers always act rationally or that business firms always try to maximize profits. In practice, of course, this is not universally or constantly true. Thus, for example, a consumer may buy a poor-quality article for a high price rather than a low price; an investor may be unaware of certain profit opportunities and invest in the wrong company; a businessperson may, for charitable reasons, give away some of his goods rather than sell them for a profit; and a government may, for political reasons, subsidize an economically inefficient plant.

Inductive and Deductive Economic Reasoning

The identification of various economic relationships is achieved by either inductive or deductive reasoning. In *inductive reasoning*, economists infer certain principles from the observation and study of a large number of economic facts. For example, they may infer from a survey of the working habits of a large number of factory workers that the average person works more effectively if given many short work-breaks rather than one or two long ones. In *deductive reasoning*, economists conclude from the study of an established relationship that another relationship logically exists. For example, if they know that a consumer will get less satisfaction from each additional unit that he or she consumes of the same good (the principle of "diminishing marginal utility"), they can deduce that the consumer will not be willing to pay as much for each additional unit as for each previous one. This can have economic significance for a company in deciding its pricing policies. Economic theories are often based on both types of reasoning. Thus, the deduction, based on a knowledge of human nature, that individually-owned and managed business firms usually try to maximize long-run profits can also be inferred empirically from a study of actual business behaviour.

Once the economist has established an hypothesis, or theory, about the relationship between different economic variables, he or she can then predict economic events—for example, that if the government increases its spending when the economy is operating at the full-employment level, this will cause an increase in the general price level. This type of prediction is not, of course, the forecasting of actual events. It is a prediction of what will happen *if* certain events take place and *if* various other economic variables (such as household and business spending) remain unchanged. That is why economists often qualify any statement of an economic relationship with the phrase: "other things being equal".

Most economic theories have been described verbally. However, because most of the variables involved (for example, income, employment, demand, and prices) are quantitative in nature, mathematical symbols have been increasingly employed. Also, as we have already seen, graphs are frequently used to illustrate many of the cause-effect relationships. Sometimes an economic theory is described verbally and then restated in purely mathematical terms. This mathematical treatment has the disadvantage that it renders the theory unintelligible to anyone who does not possess sufficient knowledge of basic algebra. However, it has the advantage that it makes the treatment of the economic problem much more rigorous—definitions, relationships, and assumptions must be explicitly stated; and the limitations of the theory are starkly revealed.

"Other things being equal, you should do well in this course."

Testing the Economic Theory

An economic theory is of doubtful value if it cannot be verified in practice. Consequently, the final step in economic theorizing is to test the predictions that have been made on the basis of the theory. Thus, for example, we could predict, on the basis of exchange-rate theory, that a fall in the foreign exchange value of the Canadian dollar would cause Canada's imports to decrease and its exports to increase. To confirm this prediction we would then need to check exactly what did happen to Canada's international trade when the foreign exchange rate of the Canadian dollar decreased. Of course, we must be careful to watch for any other factors (such as changes in import duties, export subsidies, new trade relations) that might also affect the trade picture.

If the facts confirm the prediction, we can say that the economic theory is valid. Over the years, some economic theories, such as the "sun-spot" theory of business cycles, have become discredited. Others have never got off the ground. However, there are many other economic theories, such as the division-of-labour principle, whose validity continues unscathed despite many years of critical examination.

Empirical testing of economic theories, we should note, has become commonplace only in this century. Indeed, many economic theorists in the past felt that the presentation of an economic theory, based on logical reasoning, was sufficient in itself. Facts were used more as illustrations than controls. This attitude was encouraged by the absence of statistical data about most economic phenomena (the census, for example, was introduced only in the mid-nineteenth century) and by the problem of handling these data even when they were available.

Today, with the regular holding of the census and various other kinds of economic survey, and the preparation and publication of statistical reports, much more data are available. Furthermore, the invention and refinement of electronic computers has made it possible to handle statistical data much more quickly, cheaply, and flexibly than in the past. As a result, the testing of economic theories is now enjoying a boom after several centuries of relative neglect. Over the last forty years in fact, the practice of formulating economic theories in mathematical terms and testing them by statistical techniques has become so widespread that it has come to be recognized as a specialized field of economics, called *econometrics*.

In econometrics, an economic theory is called an *economic model*. A model can consist of a single mathematical equation or a set of simultaneous mathematical equations that set out the assumed relationships between the various economic variables. A model, like the economic theory that it represents, is an abstraction of reality that highlights the relationships to be considered. Because of its relative simplicity, the model enables economists to analyze more easily the possible effects of changes in any key element. From a model of the Canadian economic system, they could estimate, for example, the effects of a change in the country's foreign exchange rate, of a reduction in federal and provincial personal income tax, or of an unusually high rate of immigration.

To visualize the effect of changes in one of the key elements, it is assumed, in simple models, that all the other elements remain constant—in other words, "other things being equal". In practice, of course, they continue to change. Thus, a tax increase may be offset in its revenue effects by a decline in business activity. More advanced economic models, made possible by the advent of more sophisticated electronic computers, have more variables. By systematically changing key elements in a model, economists can draw conclusions about the economic situation—for example, how the levels of income and employment in a country can be affected by changes in the supply of money. The Bank of Canada and several Canadian universities now have sophisticated, computer-programmed models of the Canadian economy that can supply relatively quick answers as to the effects of deliberate changes in one or more of the variables involved.

3.3: COST-BENEFIT ANALYSIS

Since economic resources are: (a) scarce and (b) capable of alternative use, the way in which they are deployed requires careful thought. In our own personal spending, for example, we usually think twice about what we are going to buy, and the larger the amount involved, the greater the deliberation. Thus many people will spend weeks and months shopping for a car or a house. The process of evaluating the costs and benefits of alternative uses of scarce resources is called *cost-benefit analysis*. Its purpose is to improve our choice among these alternatives. Since this type of analysis is used to help solve actual problems, it is also known as *applied economics*.

Cost-benefit analysis involves, first of all, a clear statement of the various alternative possibilities. Thus, an increase in a province's electric power supply, for example, can be obtained by investment in a hydroelectric plant, a thermal plant, an atomic plant, a nuclear plant, or by purchase from an outside producer. Cost-benefit analysis also involves, second, an evaluation of the costs and benefit of each alternative. The costs, in the case of electricity, will depend on relative fuel prices and the capital expenditures involved. Costs, it should be noted, can be very broad in scope, particularly when account is taken of social as well as private costs. Thus, some thermal plants in Canada now use more expensive coal (with a lower sulphur content) than they used to do, in order to reduce environmental pollution. They deliberately incur, in other words, higher private costs to obtain lower social costs. Of course, it is easier for a government-owned enterprise to follow such a policy than for a private business firm, which must justify its actions to its shareholders.

The cost of using resources in one particular way is just one side of the cost/benefit equation. For the use to be worthwhile, the benefits must exceed the costs. Often, of course, it is difficult to measure benefits. In a business firm, expected sales and profits can be given a dollar value. A government goal such as high employment can be expressed as a percentage of the labour force. However, a goal such as greater national unity is impossible to quantify. So also is an individual's goal of pleasure from ownership of a new car or from dining out. Nevertheless, some attempt to measure the benefits is usually undertaken. Often, this measurement is in the form of a comparison with the benefits to be derived from other possible uses of the same money. In devoting money (and thereby resources) to the pursuit of one goal, a government, firm, or individual is, of course, forfeiting the opportunity of doing something else. For example, by spending more on public transportation, a government will have less to spend on, say, public health. In other words, for each course of action, there is an "opportunity cost".

3.4: INSTITUTIONAL ECONOMICS

Another important type of economic analysis is the study of the growth, structure, and operations of Canada's various economic institutions, such as manufacturing, mining, agriculture, banking, other financial intermediaries, and government financial institutions. It also includes the study of the various international economic institutions and systems in which Canada participates. Without this type of analysis and description, our knowledge of the working of Canada's economic system, as well as the international one, would remain incomplete, as well as out of date. Also, the effects of proposed government economic measures, as well as the impact of changes in private spending at home and abroad, would be more difficult to predict than they already are. Furthermore, such study and analysis can point the way to improvements in the country's institutional framework so that the country can operate more efficiently. Thus, for example, a study of Canadian agriculture by a federal task force might suggest more efficient ways of providing government financial aid. Or a study of Canada's capital market might provide a better understanding of the past growth and future prospects of the various Canadian financial intermediaries and thereby help improve the shape of future Bank Acts and other financial legislation. This area of economics is sometimes called *descriptive economics*.

3.5: THE ECONOMIST

An *economist* is a professionally-qualified person who earns his or her living by specializing in the study of economic problems. Both government and industry find it worth while to employ such specialists, full-time and part-time, to undertake analytical research and to provide economic policy advice. In the federal government, for example, economists are required to advise the Minister of Finance on the implications of proposals for tax changes. In an oil company, as another example, the economist must prepare long-range forecasts of the demand for petroleum products and analyze the implications of actions by competitors and by government. Economic policies, public or private, are very much the end-product of the economist. Professional economists working in private industry sometimes describe themselves as *business economists*. Also, not to be overlooked, are the many economists who combine economic teaching and research at our universities with consulting for the private and public sectors.

An economist, if he or she is to be efficient in the job, must understand how the economy operates; be able to recognize and understand the causes of the economic problems that occur; and be able to foresee, in all their ramifications, the likely effects of the measures recommended or undertaken—for example, the effects on the supply of mortgage money of an increase in government borrowing.

Perhaps the most valuable contribution that an economist can make in government, business, or education, is to apply the problem-solving technique of economic analysis to each problem, as it comes along. As we saw previously, this technique involves, first of all, setting out quite explicitly the nature and dimensions of the problem. Second, it involves clear delineation of the various possible courses of action. And third, it involves careful evaluation of the probable benefits and cost of each alternative course. This requires, of course, considerable research. Only then is the economist in a position to make a worth-while policy recommendation.

"What I want you to do, Mario, is to forecast the demand for our product ten years from now."

3.6: ECONOMIC PITFALLS

The study of economic problems can be fascinating. However, clear thinking is essential. For the average student, there are several pitfalls. However, if they are recognized from the start, their ability to hinder is reduced. These pitfalls can be listed under the following headings: preconceptions; self-interest; problems of definition; fallacy of composition; and false analogy.

Economic Preconceptions

Whereas a person begins the study of such subjects as mathematics, physics, or astronomy with little or no background knowledge, the student of economics often has many preconceived ideas or biases about the subject-matter. These are obtained from listening to casual conversation at home and among friends, from reading newspapers, magazines, and books, from listening to radio, and from watching television. Some examples are: "It's always better to buy goods made in Canada."; "Management always tries to exploit the worker"; "We should get rid of foreign capital"; "Workers always try to do the least work for the most money"; "Unions are opposed to technological progress"; "A business always charges the highest price possible for its product"; "The consumer is always being exploited"; "Advertising is an economic waste"; "Saving is a virtue"; "What's good for the company is good for everyone in it."

Economic Self-Interest

In studying economics, a person can easily start looking for economic facts or arguments to fit his or her own particular situation. Thus, the college student quickly appreciates that governments should spend more on education, for the good of the economy; the taxpayer quickly appreciates that high taxes for education and other purposes are destroying private initiative, to the detriment of the economy; the farmer easily believes that farm subsidies should be increased, for the good of the economy; and the federal government realizes that taxes should be increased, perhaps to dampen inflation, again for the good of the economy. To think clearly about economics, a person should, therefore, first recognize where his or her own self-interest lies and consciously try to prevent it from interfering with his or her reasoning.

Problems of Economic Definition

A common source of misunderstanding and disagreement in economics, as well as in other fields, is the fact that different people use the same term to mean different things. Thus a cool weekend can mean one thing to one person and something else to another. In economics, unlike many other disciplines, many of the terms used are also widely used in everyday language. Unfortunately, from the viewpoint of clear economic thinking, the everyday meaning is usually different from the economic one. For example, the verb "to demand" in everyday language means to insist strongly on having something. In economics it means to have not only a desire for a product but also the ability to pay for it. Obviously, then, persons who wish to reason clearly about an economic problem must define carefully what they and others are talking or thinking about. Then, for example, when talking about foreign exchange rates, they would not confuse the "depreciation" of a currency with a "devaluation"; or glibly compare U.S. food prices with Canadian ones, without taking into account the exchange rate differential.

Fallacy of Composition

By fallacy of composition we mean the mistake of assuming that what is true for part of a group must necessarily be true for the group as a whole. Thus, whereas an individual farmer may be better off by increasing his or her production, farmers, as a whole, by increasing their production, may be worse off. This is because the increased supply of goods would probably depress market prices. The same applies to oil-producing and wheat-producing countries.

False Economic Analogy

An analogy is a situation that is similar to, but not identical with, the situation that is being discussed. Thus, in explaining the public finances of a country, a person may use the behaviour of the individual household for purpose of comparison and illustration. In many respects this analogy is useful. However, in some respects—for example, in savings policy—it may be a false analogy. While it may be desirable for an individual household to balance its budget, it may not always, or even usually, be desirable for a government to do likewise. This is because a government must, at different times, increase or decrease consumer demand to keep the economy at high levels of income and employment without runaway inflation. Only by spending more than it receives can a government cause an increase in consumer-demand. And, conversely, only by spending less than it receives, can it cause a reduction in consumer demand.

Summary

1. Research into the working of our economic system has, over the years, resulted in the formulation of economic theories that describe and explain the various cause-effect relationships that exist in the economy.
2. Large amounts of statistical data about the Canadian economy are published by Statistics Canada, the Bank of Canada, and others. These must be sifted and analyzed by the economist or other economic researcher.
3. An economic theory is a concise statement of a presumed relationship between various economic variables. Because so many variables are involved, the economist is forced to make various simplifying assumptions—for example, that consumers always act rationally.
4. The economist in identifying various economic relationships, uses either inductive or deductive reasoning.
5. Once the economist has established an hypothesis, or theory, about the relationship between different economic variables, he or she can predict economic events.
6. Economic theories can be stated verbally and mathematically and illustrated diagrammatically.
7. The final step in economic theorizing is to test the predictions that have been made on the basis of the theory.
8. The process of evaluating the costs and benefits of alternative uses of scarce resources is called *cost-benefit analysis*. This type of analysis is also called *applied economics*.
9. *Institutional economics* is the study of the growth, structure, and operations of various economic institutions. It is also sometimes called *descriptive economics*.
10. An economist is a professionally-qualified person who earns his or her living by specializing in the study of economic problems in government, business, or educational institutions.

Key Terms

Economic research   48
Economic theory   48
Census   48
Economic variables   49
Inductive reasoning   49
Deductive reasoning   50
Economic hypothesis   50
Empirical testing   52
Econometrics   52
Economic model   52

Cost-benefit analysis   53
Institutional economics   54
Economist   55
Business economist   55
Economic preconceptions   57
Economic self-interest   57
Problems of economic
   definition   58
Fallacy of composition   58
False economic analogy   58

Review Questions

1. Who conducts economic research in Canada and why?
2. What is the usual pattern of economic research?
3. What are the main sources of economic data in Canada?
4. Why is it necessary for the economist, in developing an economic theory, to make simplifying assumptions? What basic assumptions are made in economics about consumers and business firms?
5. Distinguish between inductive and deductive reasoning. Give an example of each.
6. What is meant by economic prediction?
7. What are the merits of describing economic theories in mathematical terms?
8. Why was empirical testing of economic theories so long neglected? What is the situation today?
9. Give an example (of your own) to explain the usefulness of cost-benefit analysis.
10. Distinguish between private and social costs and benefits. Show, with examples, how they can easily diverge.
11. Provide three examples of published studies that would fall into the category of institutional economics.
12. What is an economist? What services does he or she provide?
13. Amongst the pitfalls facing the student of economics are economic preconceptions, economic self-interest, and problems of economic definition. Explain each of these with an example.
14. What is meant by fallacy of composition and by false economic analogy? Give an example of each.

Part B:
THE MARKET SYSTEM

Here we examine how the economic force of public demand, modified by government intervention, operates through the price mechanism to direct society's scarce resources into the production of the chosen goods and services.

A Rise in Demand means a higher price and a greater
incentive to produce more.

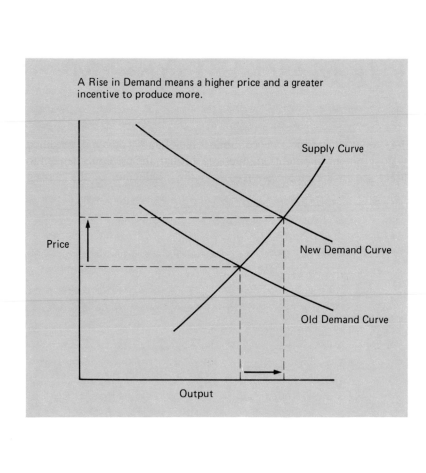

Price

Supply Curve

New Demand Curve

Old Demand Curve

Output

4. THEORY OF DEMAND

CHAPTER OBJECTIVES

A. To indicate how a market demand schedule and a market demand curve are constructed
B. To explain the "law of demand"
C. to explain the concept of marginal utility and how it helps determine a person's equilibrium expenditure
D. To distinguish between a change in demand and a change in the quantity demanded of a good
E. To distinguish between price-elasticity and income-elasticity of demand

CHAPTER OUTLINE

The term *demand* is used in economics to signify the quantity of a good or service that consumers will buy at various prices during a given period of time. Demand, it should be noted, is not necessarily the same as desire since a person must have money to translate desire into demand. Many poor families, for example, would be overjoyed to have more and better food. However, the demand for a certain type of food at any time is the amount that people, with both desire *and* the money, would actually be willing to purchase at various prices. Sometimes, to distinguish demand from desire, the term *effective demand* is used.

Example of a market demand schedule

Price	Fred	Sue	Jim	Liz	Rick	Bill	Tina	Total
$10	1	0	0	1	0	2	0	4
$9	2	0	1	1	0	4	2	10
$8	3	1	3	2	1	7	2	19
$7	4	2	5	2	1	9	3	26
$6	5	4	7	2	2	10	3	33
$5	6	6	9	3	2	12	5	43

* Number of units of the product that would be bought at different prices

Example of a market demand curve (based on the above data)

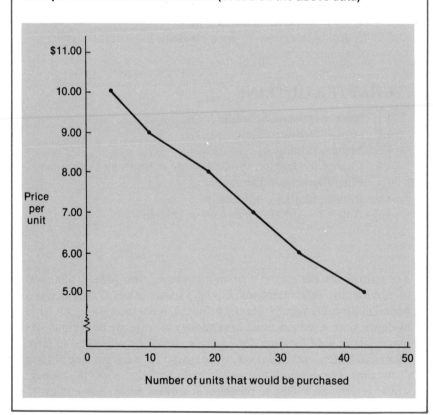

4.1: MARKET DEMAND SCHEDULE

At any one time, all the consumers in a particular area are willing and able to purchase a certain quantity of each good or service at the current market price. This *market demand* is the result of all individual consumers seeking to maximize their total satisfaction (or *utility*) within the constraints imposed by their tastes, the prices of similar goods, and the amount of their incomes.

To describe more fully the demand for a good, it is customary in economics to draw up a *market demand schedule*. This is a numerical statement, usually in column form, of the quantity of a good that would be sold in, say, a week, at each of a series of prices. It is a summation of the individual consumer demand schedules.

For purposes of illustration, we can use a hypothetical example of the demand for lettuce at a supermarket during a given week. At one extreme, $1.00 each, the store would sell hardly any lettuce. Consumers would either go without or substitute something else. At the other extreme, 10 cents each, practically all the lettuce would be sold. At other prices, the number of lettuces sold would vary from almost all to almost none. This is shown in Table 4:1. An imaginary market demand schedule can easily be drawn up. However, without successively charging a variety of prices within a short space of time, it is impossible to ascertain what the demand schedule for a good actually is.

4.2: MARKET DEMAND CURVE

The information contained in a market demand schedule can be illustrated graphically. Thus, in Figure 4:1 the price per lettuce is shown on the vertical axis and the number of lettuces that would be purchased on the horizontal axis. Each point in the body of the chart indicates how many lettuces would be bought at a particular price. Thus, point A indicates that 250 lettuces would be bought at a price of 30 cents each. These points can be joined to form a *market demand curve*. Such a curve, although depicting exactly the same price-quantity relationship as the market demand schedule, is much easier to understand.

Law of Demand

Most demand curves, including the one for lettuce, slope downward to the right. This means that, so long as the other determinants of demand remain unchanged, the lower the price of a good, the more of it will be bought. Conversely, the higher the price, the less will be

Table 4:1
Demand for Lettuce at Store X

Price per Lettuce	Number of Lettuce That Would Be Bought per Week
$1.00	5
0.80	20
0.60	50
0.50	100
0.40	150
0.30	250
0.20	500
0.10	750

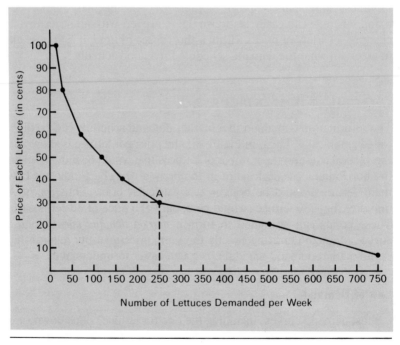

Figure 4:1 Demand Curve for Lettuce at Store X

bought. In other words, there is an inverse relationship between the price of a good and the quantity demanded of it. This inverse relationship is called the *law of demand*.

More of a good is bought at a lower price for two basic reasons. First, there is the *income effect*: persons who had previously bought the good at the higher price can now buy more with the same amount of money. Second, there is the *substitution effect*: consumers will, whenever possible, substitute these goods for other relatively higher-priced goods.

Exceptional Demand Curves

Usually, a demand curve slopes downward from left to right, indicating that more of a good will be bought at a lower price than at a higher price. Occasionally, however, a demand curve slopes upward from left to right, over part of its length, indicating just the opposite. Several possible reasons account for such exceptional demand curves.

1. Fear of future higher prices. If people believe, as in a period of rapid inflation, that prices may rise extremely fast in the future, they may increase their purchases now, even though prices have already gone up. This type of situation occurs, for instance, at the outbreak of war.

2. Ostentatious goods. Some goods occasionally sell better if their price is raised. This is because people tend to assume that a high price signifies high quality. Examples of such goods include jewellery, fashionable clothes, and country club memberships.

4.3: MARGINAL UTILITY

The satisfaction that a person derives from the last unit consumed of a good is called *marginal utility*. It is the difference in total utility obtained from drinking, say, three cups of coffee instead of two. The more a person consumes of a good, the smaller becomes this additional, or marginal utility.

Law of Diminishing Marginal Utility

The relationship between the quantity consumed of a good and the marginal utility that it provides was formulated as an economic theory, or "law" in England and Austria in 1871. The *law of diminishing marginal utility* states that, *as a person increases his or her consumption of a good, the additional satisfaction (or marginal utility) derived from each extra unit of that good will gradually diminish.*

The law of diminishing marginal utility helps us to understand the nature of the demand for a good. Since marginal utility declines as consumption increases, a person will obviously not be willing to pay as much for each successive unit of a good as for the previous ones. Thus, at a particular time, a person might be willing to pay $2.00 for a kilogram of grapes,$1.00 for a second kilo, 80 cents for a third, 50 cents for a fourth, 30 cents for a fifth, 15 cents for a sixth, and 10 cents for a seventh. These figures are shown in Table 4:2 and represent that person's demand for grapes.

Table 4:2
Marginal Utility and Demand

Price of Grapes per kilogram	Quantity Purchased (kilogram)
$2.00	1
1.00	2
0.80	3
0.50	4
0.30	5
0.15	6
0.10	7

The key fact to be noted here is that a person will buy an additional unit of a good only if that person considers its marginal utility to be greater than its price. Thus, if a person considers the marginal utility of the fifth kilogram of grapes to be equivalent only to 20 cents, that person will not pay a market price of 30 cents for it. This is because the marginal utility of the money itself exceeds the marginal utility of the grapes. In other words, a person can be happier by keeping his or her money.

Consumer's Surplus

In the previous example, a person would pay $2.00 for a kilogram of grapes, but less and less for additional kilograms. Now suppose that the market price of grapes is 20 cents per kilo. For the first kilo, our person *would have paid* $2.00, but only paid 20 cents. For the second kilo, the person would have paid $1.00, but again only paid 20 cents. For the third kilo the person would have paid 80 cents, but once more paid only 20 cents. For the fourth kilo, the person was willing to pay 50 cents, but only paid 20 cents. For the fifth kilo, the person would have paid 30 cents, but only paid 20 cents. Altogether, therefore, the person would have paid $4.60 (see Table 4:3), but in fact paid only $1.00. *Consumer's surplus* is the difference between the amount the consumer would have paid for a good and the amount the consumer actually paid. In the example, the difference was $3.60.

Table 4:3
Consumer's Surplus

Kilograms of Grapes Purchased	Total Amount the Customer Would Have Paid	Total Amount the Consumer Actually Paid	Total Consumer's Surplus
1	$2.00	$0.20	$1.80
2	3.00	0.40	2.60
3	3.80	0.60	3.20
4	4.30	0.80	3.50
5	4.60	1.00	3.60

This economic concept emphasizes the fact that consumers often get much more utility from a good than its market price would suggest. The last or marginal unit that they purchase is just worth its price to them, but units that they have purchased before may, in terms of satisfaction, be worth much more. Business firms, in their pricing policies, sometimes try to take advantage of this fact—for example, with regard to new books and movies.

Equilibrium Distribution of Personal Expenditure

A person will distribute his or her money among the various goods and services available so that the marginal utility from the last dollar spent on each item is equal. For, with a given amount of money and current set of tastes, a consumer will have maximized total utility only when he or she no longer has any incentive to switch a dollar from the purchase of one good to that of another. Although we cannot measure marginal utility in absolute terms, we can nevertheless measure it in relative terms. We know whether we can gain more satisfaction by spending more on product A and less on product B, or vice versa.

By concentrating spending on, say, product A, a consumer would find that his or her total utility would increase less with each additional dollar spent. This is because the marginal utility from buying that good is getting smaller all the time. A consumer would be far better off to purchase other goods, B, C, and D, each of which would give him or her a larger marginal utility for each dollar spent.

At first, the marginal utility from purchasing these other goods would be very great. But the more of them the consumer purchases, the smaller it becomes. Conversely, as a person reduces the purchases of product A, he or she will get a larger marginal utility from the last dollar spent on that product. Eventually, a person would reach the equilibrium situation at which the marginal utility from the last dollar spent on each good is equal. Of course, perfect equilibrium can be achieved only if each good is divisible into very small units.

This equilibrium situation is not, of course, one in which a person spends an equal amount on each good. A person's spending pattern also reflects his or her priority of tastes, or scale of preferences. Thus if a person likes product A more than product B, he or she will be able to buy more of A than B before the marginal utilities of the two products are the same.

It is sometimes argued that many people do not bother to weigh carefully the marginal utilities of the various goods and services that they buy. Consumers tend, in other words, to buy impulsively. Obviously, the cheaper the product involved, the less the amount of thought given at the time of purchase. Conversely, however, people tend to deliberate very much when buying a house, car, or other important item. Of course, not every consumer is consistently rational in his or her buying behaviour. Generally speaking, however, the vast majority of consumers do normally try to get the most for their money. If we believe that we will be better off by altering our pattern of spending, we will do so.

Another criticism of marginal utility theory is that a consumer's knowledge of the market is by no means perfect. A person often does not know exactly what he or she is getting for the money spent, nor the range of products available for choice. Nevertheless, within the consumer's field of knowledge, he or she is usually rational enough.

Another criticism is that it is often impossible to switch just one dollar from, say, product A to product B. We cannot, for example, buy one dollar's worth less of an airplane ticket and buy one dollar's worth more of a chair. But the fact that many goods are "indivisible" means only that a consumer's allocation of his money will be more "lumpy" than would otherwise be the case. The average consumer will still try, nevertheless, to maximize his or her total utility.

Paradox of Value

Because the marginal utility of a good falls as more of it is consumed, market price will have to be reduced if more of the good is to be sold. Otherwise, consumers will prefer to spend their money on something else. Consequently, the more abundant a good is, the lower its market price will tend to be. In other words, it is the utility of the *last* unit that is important in determining price, not the utility of *all* the units. This explains why water is so cheap in comparison with diamonds, despite the fact that the world's water supply is more useful than the world's supply of diamonds.

4.4: CHANGE IN DEMAND VERSUS CHANGE IN QUANTITY DEMANDED

It is important not to confuse a change in demand with a change in the quantity demanded as a result of a change in price. A change or shift in demand caused by a change in tastes, income, or other reasons, means a change in the demand schedule and a shift in the accompanying demand curve. Thus, the demand by college students for beefburgers might fall drastically if tuition fees are substantially increased. A new demand schedule, and a new demand curve (see Figure 4:2), would have emerged. A *change in demand* means, in other words, a different quantity of a good being demanded at each of the previous prices.

A *change in quantity demanded* caused by a price change would, on the contrary, leave the demand schedule and demand curve unchanged. For example, people might double their consumption of beefburgers as a result of a reduction in their subsidized price from, say, 50 cents to 40 cents. In this case, there has only been a movement along the demand curve to a new equilibrium position further to the right where more is purchased at a lower price.

Reasons for Changes in Demand

A change in the demand for a good or service may occur for any one of a variety of reasons. Let us briefly consider the most important of them.

1. Change in tastes. People's tastes in food, clothing, shelter, entertainment, and other items gradually change over the years. Education, income, and advertising are all factors influencing a person's tastes. Some tastes, such as for clothing, can change annually as new fashions appear. Others, such as for leisure pursuits, change more gradually.

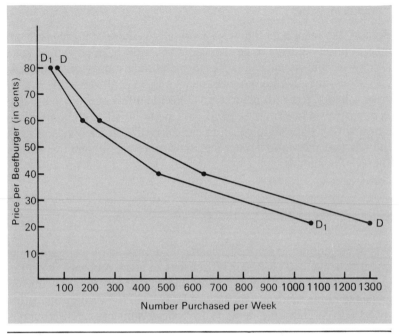

Note: DD is the previous demand curve; D_1D_1 is the new demand curve.

Figure 4:2 Change in the Demand for Beefburgers, as a Result of a Reduction in Student Income

2. Change in income. If a person has a larger money income than before, he or she will buy more of the various goods—assuming, of course, that the increase in income is greater than any increase in the prices of the goods to be purchased. Otherwise, purchases, in terms of quantity, will actually decline. A change in the distribution of a country's income, by increasing some people's income and reducing that of others, will also cause changes in the demand for various goods.

3. Change in relative prices. If the prices of other goods increase or decrease, the demand for a particular good will change because of the income and substitution effects discussed earlier in this book.

4. New goods replacing old. As new goods are invented, the demand for old ones often declines. Thus, the automobile has replaced the horse and buggy; the jet airliner, the transatlantic passenger ship.

5. Change in population. A change in the size of the population and in its age distribution will cause changes in the demand for various goods. For example, the larger the population, the greater the demand for homes; and the younger the population, the greater the demand for schools.

6. Change in expectations. If business managers predict an upturn or a slowdown in consumer demand, their demand for raw materials, parts, and machines will change accordingly. Or if consumers predict shortages, they will want to stock up.

Interrelated Demand

The demand for some goods is related to the demand for others. In some cases, an increase in the demand for one good brings about an *increase* in the demand for another. In other cases, an increase in the demand for one good brings about a *decrease* in the demand for another.

1. Complementary or joint demand. Some goods are used together, like cups and saucers. Consequently, an increase in the demand for cups inevitably means an increase in the demand for saucers.

2. Derived demand. The demand for labour, machinery, parts, and raw materials, depends on the demand for the final goods which they help to produce. A change in demand for such final goods means, there-fore, a corresponding change in demand for the various inputs.

3. Competitive demand. Some goods can be fairly easily substituted for each other—for example, margarine and butter. Consequently, if people increase their demand for one, they usually decrease their de-mand for the other.

4.5: PRICE-ELASTICITY OF DEMAND

The concept of price-elasticity of demand has been devised as a simple means of describing the responsiveness of the quantity demanded of a good or service to a small change in its price. It is defined as the effect of a change in the price of a good on the quantity sold of that good. Numerically, it can be expressed as the percentage change in the quan-tity sold divided by the percentage change in the price (see Table 4:4). For example, if the price of milkshakes were reduced 25 per cent and if the number sold consequently doubled, then the elasticity of demand for milkshakes over that part of the demand curve would be 4. Also since total revenue is equal to prices times quantity sold, we can deter-mine price-elasticity by considering how total revenue has changed fol-lowing an increase or decrease in the price of a product (see Table 4:5).

Table 4:4

Measuring the Elasticity of Demand

Formula for measuring the price-elasticity of demand:

$$ed = \frac{\% \triangle qd}{\% \triangle p}$$

where   ed = price-elasticity of demand

    $\% \triangle qd$ = percentage change in quantity demanded

    $\% \triangle p$ = percentage change in the price of the good

Examples (*n* is the unknown number):

1. What is the elasticity of demand if a business firm increases the price of one of its products by 10% and finds that the quantity sold drops by 16%?

Answer: $ed = \dfrac{16\%}{10\%} = 1.6$

2. If the elasticity of demand for a firm's product is 2, what will happen if the price is reduced by 5%?

Answer: The quantity sold will increase by 10%.

$$2 = \frac{n}{5\%} \therefore n = 2 \times 5\% = 10$$

3. If the elasticity of demand for a firm's product is 0.5, what will happen if the price is reduced by 8%?

Answer: The quantity sold will increase by 4%.

$$0.5 = \frac{n}{8\%} \therefore n = 0.5 \times 8\% = 4\%$$

4. If the elasticity of demand is 1.2, what reduction in price would be necessary to increase the quantity sold by 20%?

Answer: 16.7%

$$1.2 = \frac{20\%}{n} \therefore n = \frac{20\%}{1.2} = 16.7$$

Demand for a good or service can be classified, on the basis of its price-elasticity, into one of three main types: elastic demand, inelastic demand, and demand of unitary-elasticity. Over the length of the demand curve for a particular good or service, all three types of price-elasticity may be present.

Table 4:5

Example of the Relationship between Price-Elasticity of Demand and Total Revenue

1. A business is selling 10 000 units of each of two products, A and B, at a price of $5.00 each, for a total revenue for each product of $50 000. Manager X believes the firm would be better off by raising the price of each of the two products to $6.00.
In fact, the elasticity of demand for each product is different:

$$\text{for A, it is } 2.0$$
$$\text{for B, it is } 0.5$$

What would happen to the total revenue from each product, if Manager X has his way?

Answer (n is the % change in quantity sold):

Product A $\quad 2.0 = \dfrac{n}{20\%} \therefore n = 40\%$

$\qquad$ Total revenue $= \$6.00 \times 6000 = \$36\,000$

Product B $\quad 0.5 = \dfrac{n}{20\%} \therefore n = 10\%$

$\qquad$ Total revenue $= \$6.00 \times 9000 = \$54\,000$

Conclusion: If demand is elastic, total revenue will decrease; if demand is inelastic, total revenue will increase.

Manager X should have been more selective. Give X a second chance. What other factor should we take into account in determining whether the firm will be better or worse off?

Elastic Demand

The demand for a good is said to be *price-elastic* if the elasticity of demand is greater than one. This would be the case if, for example, a reduction in the price of a good caused a more than proportionate increase in the quantity demanded. Thus, in Figure 4:3, a reduction in price from $5.00 to $4.00 per unit has caused an increase in the quantity demanded from 5000 units at point A to 10000 units at point B. Numerically, the elasticity of demand is 100% ÷ 20% = 5. Total revenue, it should be noted, has increased. If the demand for a good were perfectly elastic, the demand curve would be a straight horizontal line and elasticity would be equal to infinity.

The demand for a good or service tends to be price-elastic if one or more of the following circumstances exists:

1. There are close substitutes. Thus, if the price of pears goes up, consumers can buy apples or other fruit instead. Conversely, if the price of pears goes down, consumers can substitute them for other relatively higher-priced fruits. Demand for an individual fruit, it should be noted, may be highly price-elastic, even though demand for fruit as a whole may be relatively price-inelastic.

2. The price of the good absorbs a significant part of the consumer's total expenditure. Thus, a 50 per cent increase in the price of houses may cause a large reduction in the quantity demanded, whereas the same percentage increase in the price of table salt may have little effect.

3. The good is a luxury rather than a necessity. Thus, a rise in the price of sports cars may severely reduce the quantity demanded, whereas a rise in the price of beer (a "necessity" for many consumers) may not cause any reduction in purchases.

Inelastic Demand

The demand for a good or service is said to be *price-inelastic* if the elasticity of demand is less than one. This would be the case if a reduction in the price of a good caused a less than proportionate increase in the quantity demanded. In Figure 4:4, for example, a reduction in price from $5.00 to $4.00 per unit has caused an increase in the quantity demanded from 5000 units at point A to 5500 units at point B. The elasticity of demand over this part of the demand curve is 10% ÷ 20% = 0.5; and total revenue has fallen. If demand were perfectly inelastic, the demand curve would be a straight vertical line and the elasticity would be zero.

Demand for a good or service tends to be price-inelastic if one or more of the following circumstances is present:

1. There is no close substitute. A different painting, movie or book can rarely replace the specific one desired.

2. The money spent on the good is only a small part of a consumer's total expenditure. Thus, consumers will tend to go on buying matches, razor blades, or eleric light bulbs even though their price may have increased substantially.

3. The good is a necessity rather than a luxury. Thus, the demand for salt is quite inelastic.

4. The good is needed to accompany some other higher-value good that consumers wish to have. Thus, consumers must have tapes for their tape recorders and diskettes for their microcomputers.

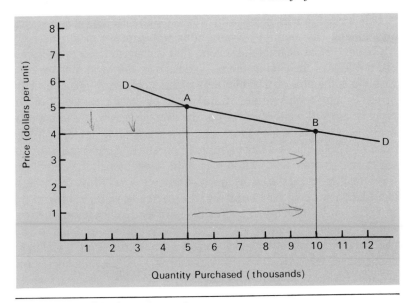

Figure 4:3   Example of Elastic Demand

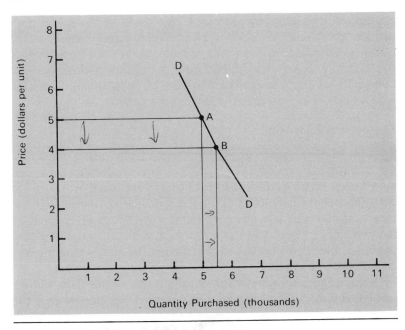

Figure 4:4   Example of Inelastic Demand

5. It is a good to which consumers, after some use, develop a strong attachment—for example, a particular newspaper or magazine.

Gasoline is an example of a good that is characterized by the presence of four of the circumstances listed above. For most modern cars, gasoline is the only acceptable fuel—wood, coal, diesel oil, electricity, or gas cannot be substituted. Cars driven by electricity, diesel oil, or propane are still relatively few. For the average car owner, with a relatively large capital expenditure, the extra cost of an increase in the price of gasoline is of relatively little importance. A car owner will not sell the car in order to do without gasoline, even though the cost of the latter may have increased by many cents per litre. Most car owners consider their car to be a necessity, for driving to work, getting to the stores, to a doctor's office, or for many other reasons. Gasoline, because it is needed to drive the car, is therefore also considered to be a necessity rather than a luxury. Finally, the fourth point, gasoline is needed to accompany the car, since without it the car remains stationary and, for most purposes, useless.

Demand of Unitary Elasticity

The demand for a good is said to be of *unitary elasticity* if the price-elasticity of demand is equal to one. This would be the case if a reduction in the price of a good caused a proportionate increase in the quantity demanded. In Figure 4:5, a reduction in price from $5.00 to $4.75 per unit has caused an increase in the quantity demanded from 5000 units at point A to 5250 units at point B. The elasticity of demand is 5% ÷ 5% = 1. Total revenue remains the same.

Short versus Long Run

Elasticity of demand for a good or service is usually greater, the longer the time period considered. Thus, in the short run, demand for a good may be very inelastic. If the market price were increased by, say 50 per cent, the quantity demanded may fall less than proportionately. In the long run, however, consumers will gradually shift to other products that were not immediately acceptable as substitutes. In the long run, therefore, the percentage fall in demand may be greater than the percentage increase in price.

Demand tends to be relatively price-inelastic in the short run for several reasons: (a) it takes time for the public to become aware of the price change; (b) consumers, out of habit, may be reluctant to switch to or from other products; (c) consumers, anticipating further price changes in a good, may hesitate to change the quantity bought; and (d)

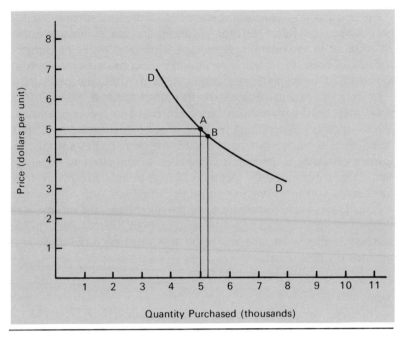

Figure 4:5   Example of Unitary-Elasticity of Demand

because of the durability of some goods, consumers will not replace them immediately.

Cross-Elasticity

Where two goods are in competitive demand, a change in the price of one will not only affect the quantity demanded of that good, but also the quantity demanded of the other. *Cross-elasticity* is the term used to describe the relationship between a change in the price of one good and the corresponding change in the quantity demanded of the other. Income-elasticity of demand, considered next, is considered to be a special case of cross-elasticity.

4.6: INCOME-ELASTICITY OF DEMAND

This is the term used to describe the way in which a person's demand for a good changes as a result of a change in his or her income. Applied to a market as a whole, *income-elasticity of demand* is the change in the quantity consumed of a good following a small change in consumer income.

For most goods, the income-elasticity of demand is considered to be positive; that is, an increase in consumers' money income causes an increase in the quantity demanded. However, where consumers, because of their higher incomes, switch their consumption away from lower-priced to higher-priced goods, such as from cheaper cuts of meat to more expensive ones, the income-elasticity of demand for a good may be negative. Such items are called in economics *inferior goods*—the normal condition for such goods being that demand shifts inversely to a change in a person's income. For food as a whole, the income-elasticity of demand is considered to be quite low, signifying that an increase in money income will lead to only a relatively small increase in consumption. For consumer durables, such as television sets, cars, and kitchen appliances, on the other hand, the income-elasticity of demand is considered to be quite high. This signifies that an increase in money income will result in a relatively large increase in the quantity demanded.

Summary

1. A *market demand schedule* is a numerical statement, usually in column form, of the quantity of a good that would be sold in a certain period of time at each of a series of prices. It is a summation of the individual consumer demand schedules.

2. A *market demand curve*, shown on a two-dimensional graph, illustrates the price-quantity relationship contained in the market demand schedule.

3. An *exceptional demand curve* is one that slopes upwards from left to right. One possible reason for this is ostentation value—people buy more of a good if it is higher priced, equating value with price.

4. Usually, the lower the price of a good, the more of it will be bought; the higher the price, the less of it will be bought. This inverse relationship between market price and the quantity purchased, called the *law of demand*, is illustrated by the downward-sloping demand curve. It is due to the income and substitution effects.

5. *Marginal utility* is the satisfaction that a person derives from the last unit consumed of a good. The *law of diminishing marginal utility* states that as a person increases consumption of a good, its marginal utility will gradually diminish. Consequently, a person will buy more of a good only if its price is lowered. For, if the price remains unchanged, the marginal utility of holding money will exceed the

marginal utility of the good. It is the marginal utility of a good, rather than its total utility, that helps determine how much a person will buy of it—hence the "paradox of value".

6. *Consumer's surplus* is the difference between the amount that a consumer would have paid for a good and the amount actually paid.

7. The *equilibrium distribution* of a person's expenditure is achieved when the marginal utility from the last dollar spent on each good is equal. Perfect equilibrium assumes that the consumer is completely rational; that he or she has a complete knowledge of the market; and that all goods are highly divisible.

8. A *change in demand* caused by a change in tastes, income, or other reasons, means a change in the demand schedule and a shift in the accompanying demand curve. A *change in the quantity demanded* caused by a change in price would, however, leave the demand schedule and demand curve unchanged.

9. The possible reasons for a change in consumer demand for a good include: a change in tastes, perhaps caused by advertising; a change in income; a change in relative prices; new goods replacing old; a change in the size of the population; and a change in consumer expectations.

10. The demand for some goods is related to the demand for others. Thus there is complementary or joint demand; derived demand; and competitive demand.

11. *Price-elasticity of demand* is the effect of a change in the price of a good on the quantity sold of that good. Numerically, it can be expressed as the percentage change in the quantity sold divided by the percentage change in the price.

12. The demand for a good is said to be *price-elastic* if the elasticity of demand is greater than one; *price-inelastic* if the elasticity of demand is less than one; and *unitary-elastic* if the price-elasticity is equal to one. The possible reasons for demand being price-elastic include: the existence of close substitutes; the price of the good absorbing a significant part of a consumer's total expenditures; and the good being a luxury rather than a necessity. Elasticity of demand is usually greater in the long run than in the short run.

13. *Cross-elasticity* is the term used to describe the relationship between a change in the price of one good and the corresponding change in the quantity demanded of the other. *Income-elasticity*, a special case of cross-elasticity, indicates how the demand for a good varies with changes in a person's money income.

Key Terms

Demand 63
Effective demand 63
Market demand 65
Utility 65
Market demand schedule 65
Market demand curve 65
Law of demand 65
Exceptional demand curve 67
Income effect 67
Substitution effect 67
Marginal utility 67
Law of diminishing
  marginal utility 67
Consumer's surplus 68
Equilibrium distribution
  of personal expenditure 69
Paradox of value 71
Change in demand 71
Change in quantity demanded 71

Interrelated demand 73
Complementary or
  joint demand 73
Derived demand 73
Competitive demand 73
Price-elasticity of
  demand 73
Elastic demand 75
Inelastic demand 76
Demand of
  unitary-elasticity 78
Short-run elasticity
  of demand 78
Long-run elasticity
  of demand 78
Income-elasticity
  of demand 79
Inferior goods 80

Review Questions

1. What is a market demand schedule? A market demand curve?
2. What is the law of demand? Explain the income effect and the substitution effect as reasons for downward-sloping demand curves.
3. What is an exceptional demand curve? Why does it occur?
4. Distinguish between a change in demand and a change in the quantity demanded.
5. What are the possible reasons for a change in demand?
6. What are the various types of interrelated demand? Give examples of your own.
7. What is price-elasticity of demand? How is it measured?
8. Distinguish between elastic-demand, inelastic demand, and demand of unitary-elasticity.
9. What causes demand to be price-elastic?
10. What causes demand to be price-inelastic?
11. How does the time period affect the elasticity of demand?
12. What is cross-elasticity of demand?

13. What is income-elasticity of demand? Why is it considered positive for most goods?
14. There is an inverse relationship between the price of a good and the quantity demanded of it. Explain this relationship and the reasons for it.
15. Illustrate the law of diminishing marginal utility with an example of your own. Illustrate also an exception to this law.
16. Explain how business firms take advantage of the existence of "consumer's surplus."
17. How does a person achieve an equilibrium distribution of his or her expenditure? Why is a perfect equilibrium rarely achieved?
18. Suppose that the price of a good is reduced by 5 per cent and the quantity demanded increases by 10 per cent. What is the elasticity of demand?
19. Suppose that the price of a good is raised by 8 per cent and the quantity demanded falls by 5 per cent. What is the elasticity of demand?
20. Suppose that the elasticity of demand for a good is 0.4 and that the government imposes an import duty that raises the price by 12 per cent. What would happen to the quantity purchased?
21. Why is the concept of price-elasticity of demand useful for governments as well as for business firms?
22. List three products for which demand is price-elastic and three for which it is price-inelastic. Explain why the products fall into the two different categories.
23. Give two examples of products for which demand might be (a) perfectly elastic, and (b) perfectly inelastic.
24. Explain, with an example, how price-elasticity of demand affects a firm's total revenue.
25. Give two examples of goods that are characterized by cross-elasticity of demand.
26. Suppose a person's income increases by 12 per cent and the person's demand for entertainment, as a result of overwork, rises by 20 per cent. What is the income-elasticity of demand?
27. Give an example of an "inferior good" and explain how it earned that label.
28. Why is the admission price to a new movie usually so high compared with regular prices? What economic concept does this illustrate?
29. Why are diamonds "a girl's best friend"?
30. How does the existence of substitutes affect the demand for a

product? Give examples.
31. Suppose your parents won $100 000 in a provincial lottery. How do you think it would affect their pattern of spending? For which goods and services would their demand increase and for which would it decrease? Suppose you won the money instead. How would your answers be different? Why?
32. What is the purpose of a demand curve if, in practice, few people ever try to draw them for actual products?
33. The demand for a firm's product may go up, even though demand for the product of the industry as a whole may go down. Explain, with reasons.
34. If poor people demanded more, they would be better off. Comment.
35. What happens in a communist country, if the demand for a product increases?
36. List three products for which the demand has increased in recent years. Explain why.
37. List three products for which demand has decreased in recent years. Give the reasons for this decrease.
38. Look at the stock page of a daily newspaper. How have stock prices changed recently? What causes an increase or decrease in demand for corporation shares?
39. Explain, with a product example, what each of the following demand curves signifies.

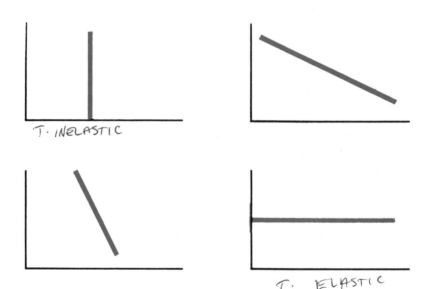

T. INELASTIC

T. ELASTIC

APPENDIX 4-A:
INDIFFERENCE CURVE ANALYSIS

So far in this Chapter we have used the theory of marginal utility to explain the nature of demand. Another approach is that of indifference curve analysis. It starts with two suppositions: (a) that there are many different combinations of the various goods available that will provide a person with maximum total satisfaction; and (b) that consumer behaviour involves a choice between different alternative combinations of goods and services rather than, as in the marginal utility approach, an evaluation of the effects of a little more or a little less of each item.

THE INDIFFERENCE CURVE

Suppose, for instance, that a person can spend his or her money on only two different goods, A and B. We can then plot on a two-dimensional graph (See Figure A.1) the various combinations of these two goods that would make that person equally content. At the extremes, he or she would be just as happy to have 10 units of A and no units of B as to have 8 units of B and no units of A. By joining in the graph all the points which indicate such combinations, we obtain an *indifference curve*. The person is "indifferent" as to his or her position on the curve, since all combinations afford equal total satisfaction. The shape of the curve (convex to the origin) indicates that as a person reduces the consumption of one good, he or she requires larger amounts of the other as compensation. The term, *the marginal rate of substitution*, is used to indicate the amount of product A that must be given up in exchange for an extra unit of product B. Instead of just two goods, one axis of the chart can be used for one good and the other axis for all other goods.

MAP OF INDIFFERENCE CURVES

Instead of just one indifference curve, we can draw for each person a whole series, or "map," of them (see Figure A.2). Each curve represents a different total combined quantity of goods. The larger a person's real income, the higher his or her actual indifference curve. The rational person will try to reach the highest possible indifference curve.

THE BUDGET LINE

The combination of goods that a consumer can actually obtain will depend on his or her money income and the relative prices of the

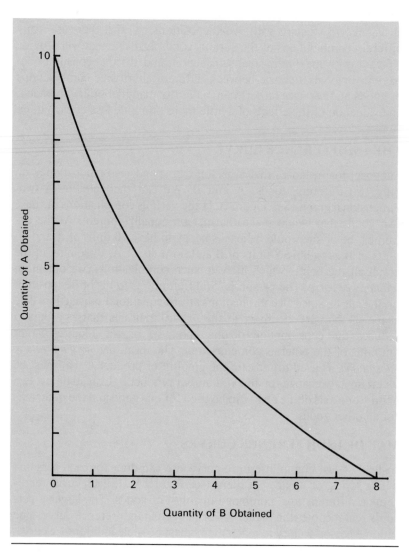

Figure A:1 Indifference Curve

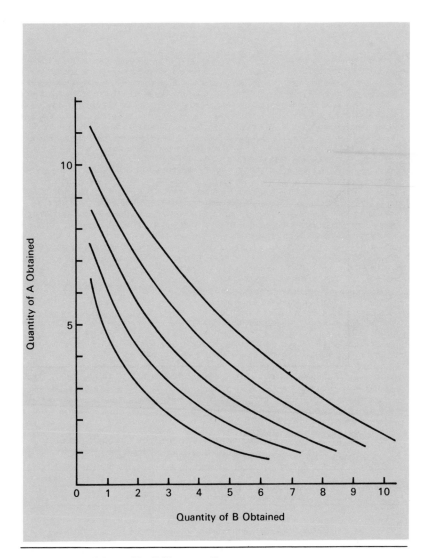

Figure A:2   Map of Indifference Curves

various goods. Let us assume, for example, that a consumer has a monthly income of $500 which is spent entirely on two goods, X and Y, costing $10.00 and $5.00 per unit respectively. The possible combinations of X and Y that can be obtained are depicted in Figure A.3 by the straight line AB. This is known as a *budget line*.

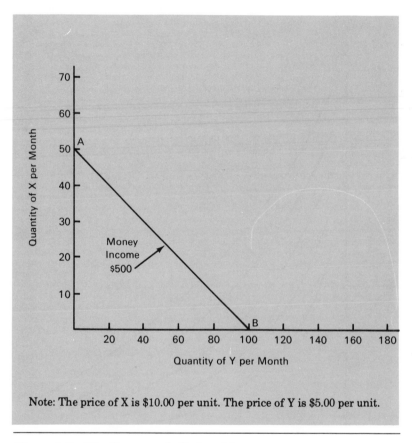

Note: The price of X is $10.00 per unit. The price of Y is $5.00 per unit.

Figure A:3   The Consumer's Budget Line

COMBINING THE BUDGET LINE AND INDIFFERENCE MAP

By combining a consumer's budget line and his or her map of indifference curves (see Figure A.4), we can show theoretically what amount of each good a consumer will purchase, given his or her tastes, income, and the relative prices of the goods shown. This preferred combination of goods is indicated by the point at which the budget line is at a tangent to one of the indifference curves (point P in Figure A.4). At this point, the consumer has attained the highest indifference curve that his or her budget allows and has thereby achieved maximum total satisfaction.

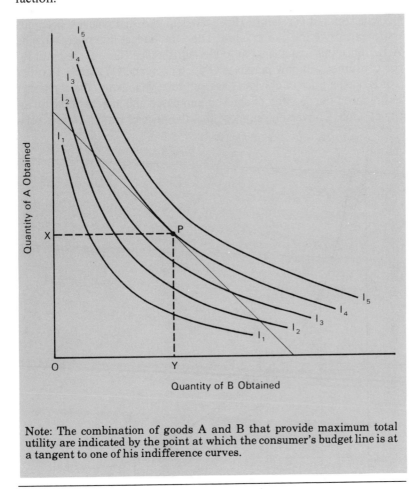

Note: The combination of goods A and B that provide maximum total utility are indicated by the point at which the consumer's budget line is at a tangent to one of his indifference curves.

Figure A:4   How a Consumer Obtains Maximum Total Utility

1 Since the indifference map contains an infinite number of indifference curves, the budget line must be at a tangent to one of them.

CHANGES IN RELATIVE PRICES

We can also make use of the budget line and indifference map to show what happens when the relative prices of goods change.

Let us assume in Figure A.5 that the relative prices of chicken and lamb are indicated by the budget line AB. Since this line is at a tangent to the indifference curve I_1I_1 at the point P, the consumer will purchase OX chicken and OY lamb. However, suppose that chicken becomes more expensive relative to lamb. Then the budget line might now be A_1B_1. Since this is at a tangent to the indifference curve at the point P_1, the consumer will now purchase OX_1 chicken and OY_1 lamb. In other words, as the price of chicken has risen relative to lamb, the consumer has reduced the quantity of chicken purchased and increased the quantity of lamb. Conversely, suppose that the price of lamb increases rela-

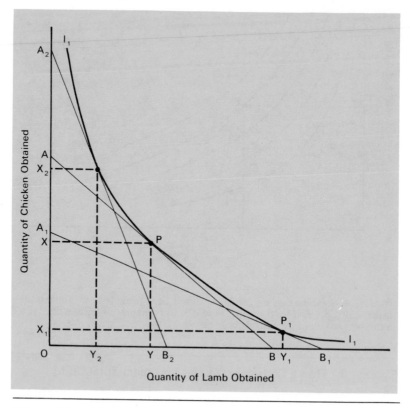

Figure A:5   Effect of a Change in Relative Prices on a
Consumer's Expenditure Pattern

tive to the price of chicken. The budget line, indicating the possible combinations of chicken and lamb with a given income, might now be A_2B_2, and the quantities consumed, OX_2 chicken and OY_2 lamb. The consumer now purchases more chicken and less lamb. In conclusion, we can see that as a good becomes relatively cheaper, a consumer will purchase more; and as a good becomes relatively more expensive, a consumer will purchase less. This pattern of consumer behaviour assumes that all other things remain equal—notably consumer tastes and income.

CHANGE IN CONSUMER INCOME

What happens to a person's pattern of expenditure when his or her income changes? As Figure A.6 indicates, an increase in money income (assuming that absolute prices remain the same) means a movement of the budget line away from the point of origin. A decrease in

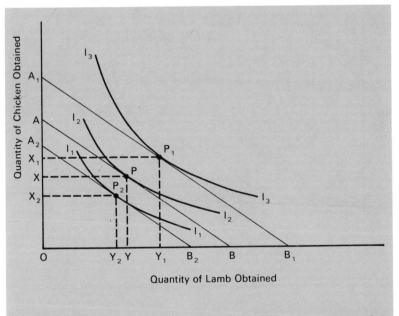

Note: AB is the old budget line; A_1B_1 is the new budget line, representing a higher real income; A_2B_2 is the new budget line, representing a lower real income.

Figure A:6   A Change in Real Income Means a New Budget Line

income means a movement toward the point of origin. This illustrates that, at a higher income, a person can buy more of each good; and at a lower income he or she can buy less. So long as relative prices are unchanged, the pattern of expenditure will remain the same. Only the total amount will have altered. If absolute prices rise, the increase in real income will be less than the increase in money income. Usually, an increase in income causes an increase in consumption. The goods that are bought in greater quantity are called *normal goods*. Sometimes, however, an increase in income may cause a fall in the consumption of a particular good. This occurs when people, because of their larger income, switch to other more expensive goods. The goods that experience a fall in consumption when income rises are called *inferior goods*.

The relationship between a consumer's money income and his or her consumption of a good (over the same period of time) is expressed graphically by what is known as an *Engel curve*. In Figure A.7, the Engel curve indicates that as a consumer's money income (shown on

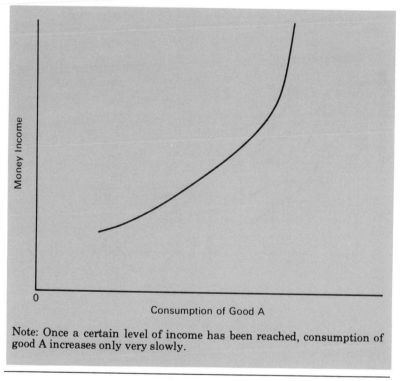

Note: Once a certain level of income has been reached, consumption of good A increases only very slowly.

Figure A:7   Engel Curve for Good A

the vertical axis) increases, his or her consumption of good A rises, but only at a declining rate. This could well hold true for a man's consumption of clothing. Once he has been adequately attired, he may not purchase much more for some time even though his income continues to increase. In the case of other goods—for example, golf balls—consumption may rise even more rapidly than income. Once a certain income level has been reached, the Engel curve would, therefore, tend to flatten out horizontally. This is shown in Figure A.8.

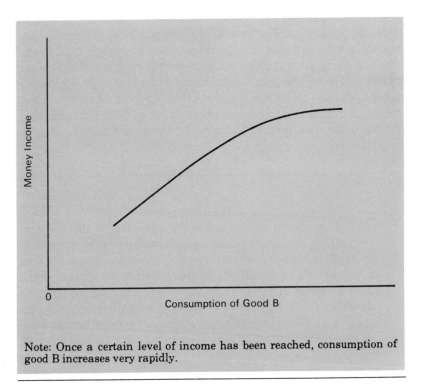

Note: Once a certain level of income has been reached, consumption of good B increases very rapidly.

Figure A:8   Engel Curve for Good B

DETERMINANTS OF CONSUMPTION

In conclusion, we can say that, given a person's tastes, there are two major features that determine his or her consumption of a good: the relative price of the good, and the level of the person's income. If the price of the good, relative to that of other goods, changes, the individual will increase or decrease his or her consumption of that particular good. Similarly, if the individual's real income (the goods and services that can be purchased with the money income) changes, he or she will increase or decrease consumption of all goods. In practice, of course, both factors are at work at the same time, and they usually work in the same direction. Thus, a reduction in the price of lamb will normally cause an increase in its consumption for two reasons: (a) because it is now cheaper relative to other goods; and (b) because the individual now has a larger real income.

Sometimes, however, the price and income effects will work in opposite directions, and very rarely, the income effect may more than offset the price effect. The term *Giffen's paradox* is sometimes used to describe such a situation. This is named after Sir Robert Giffen who observed many years ago that the poor in England tended to consume more bread when the price was high than when it was low. The explanation given was that when bread was cheap, people switched to more attractive, even though more expensive foods, with the result that they ate less bread than before. The opposite occurred when the price of bread was low.

Summary

1. Another approach (the first one was marginal utility theory) used in explaining the nature of demand is indifference curve analysis. An *indifference curve* is a line on a two-dimensional graph showing all the possible combinations of two different goods that would afford a consumer equal total satisfaction. The larger a person's real income, the higher his or her actual indifference curve on such a graph. The combination of goods that a consumer can actually obtain will depend on his or her money income and the relative prices of the various goods.

2. By combining a consumer's budget line and map of indifference curves, we can show theoretically what amount of each good a consumer will purchase, given his or her tastes, income, and the relative prices of the goods shown on the graph. This preferred combination of goods is indicated by the point at which the budget line is at a tangent to one of the indifference curves. We can also make use of the budget line and indifference map to show what happens when the relative prices of goods change.

3. An increase in money income (assuming that absolute prices remain the same) means a movement of the budget line away from the point of origin and hence an increase in consumption. A de-

crease in money income means the opposite. The relationship between a consumer's money income and his or her consumption of a good, over the same period of time, is expressed graphically by an *Engel curve*.

4. Given a person's tastes, there are two major determinants of his or her consumption of a good: the relative price of the good, and the level of that person's income.

Key Terms

Indifference curve 85
Marginal rate of substitution 85
Map of indifference curves 85
Budget line 86
Change in relative prices 90
Change in consumer income 91

Normal goods 92
Inferior goods 92
Engel curve 92
Determinants of
  consumption 93
Giffen's paradox 94

Review Questions

1. What is an indifference curve? Why is it convex in shape? What is a map of indifference curves?
2. The rational person will try to reach the highest possible indifference curve. Explain.
3. What is a budget line? What is its use in indifference curve analysis?
4. What happens to the budget line when relative prices change? How does this affect a person's expenditure?
5. What happens to a person's pattern of expenditure when his or her income changes?
6. Distinguish between normal goods and inferior goods.
7. What is an Engel curve? What does it illustrate?
8. What are the major factors that determine a person's consumption of the various goods and services?
9. What is meant by the term "Giffen's paradox"?

5. SUPPLY, DEMAND, AND MARKET PRICE

CHAPTER OBJECTIVES

A. To explain how a market supply schedule and a market supply curve for a product are constructed
B. To distinguish between between a change in supply and a change in the quantity supplied of a product
C. To explain the concept of price-elasticity of supply
D. To show how changes in market price bring about an equilibrium between the supply and demand for a product
E. To indicate what can happen when government intervenes in the working of the market system by, for example, price control

CHAPTER OUTLINE

We have just looked at demand, which is the quantity of a good or service that consumers will buy at various prices during a certain period of time. Now let us look at *supply*, which can be defined as the quantity of a good or service that producers are willing to sell at various prices during a certain period of time. Afterwards, we can consider how supply and demand interact to determine the market price and amount sold of a good, and how the price mechanism helps to allocate productive resources.

5.1: MARKET SUPPLY

For every good or service, we can, in theory, prepare a market supply schedule showing how much of the item will be offered for sale during a certain period of time at each different market price. Market supply, it should be noted, is not the total stock of a good at any one time, but only the amount that is actually offered for sale at each price.

Market Supply Schedule

A hypothetical market supply schedule for oats (comprising all the individual farmers' supply schedules) is shown in Table 5:1. It shows that the higher the market price, the larger the quantity of oats that farmers would be willing to offer for sale. In any one crop year, once the land is seeded, the supply of oats is largely set. However, in the following season, if a rise in the market price of oats has occurred, land can be switched from other crops. If the price of oats has fallen, compared with the price of other alternative crops, land can be switched out of oats. This supply schedule illustrates what is sometimes called the *law of supply* which can be stated as: *the higher the price of a good, the larger the quantity that will be supplied.* Conversely, of course, the lower the price, the smaller the quantity that will be supplied.

Market Supply Curve

The information contained in a market supply schedule can be shown diagrammatically in the form of a market supply curve. Figure 5:1, for example, is the market supply curve that accompanies the market supply schedule for oats shown in Table 5:1. Price in cents per kilogram is shown on the vertical axis, and the quantity of oats, in thousands of tonnes, supplied by farmers, is shown on the horizontal axis. Usually, as in our example, the supply curve slopes upward from left to right. This indicates that more of a good will be supplied at a higher price than at a lower price; and, conversely, less at a lower price than at a higher price.

In the short run, the supply of most goods is relatively fixed, since it takes time (as with our example of oats) to switch resources from the production of other goods. Consequently, in the short run, the supply curve for most goods will slope quite steeply upward from left to right, signifying that even a large increase in price cannot induce much of an increase in supply. For some goods, such as original works of art, there may be no way of increasing the supply at all. The supply curve, in such instances, would be a vertical line.

Table 5:1
Hypothetical Supply Schedule of Oats

Price (¢/kg)	Quantity Supplied by all Farmers (thousands of tonnes)
70	200
72	210
74	220
76	230
78	240
80	250
82	260
84	270
86	280

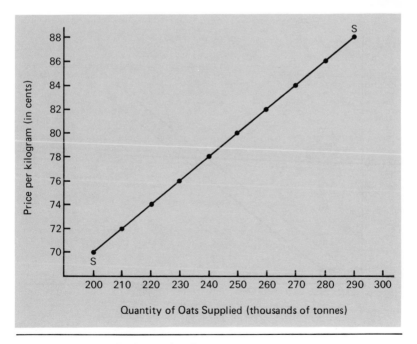

Figure 5:1   Supply Curve for Oats

We saw earlier that there are exceptional demand curves. So also are there exceptional or *regressive supply curves.* Instead of more of a good or service being offered for sale at a higher price, less is offered. Such a situation might occur in a manufacturing plant where the workers, after receiving a substantial increase in their hourly rate of pay, may prefer to work fewer hours. An increase in the price of labour has, in other words, caused a reduction in its supply.

5.2: CHANGE IN SUPPLY VERSUS CHANGE IN QUANTITY SUPPLIED

As with changes in demand, we must be careful to distinguish between a change in supply and a change in the quantity supplied. A *change in supply* means that producers will supply more or less of a good in a certain period of time than they did before at each price. Such a change causes a shift of the supply curve to the right if supply has increased, and a shift to the left if it has decreased. A *change in the quantity supplied* is the terminology used to indicate that supply conditions are unaltered. What has happened is that, as a result of a change in market price, there has been a movement along the existing supply curve.

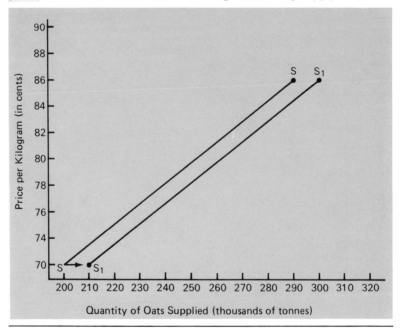

Figure 5:2   Shift in the Supply Curve of Oats, from SS to S_1S_1

In Figure 5:2, for example, we show that the supply curve has changed from SS to S_1S_1. This means that, at the same market price, farmers are now willing to supply more oats than they were before—for example, 210000t at 70 cents per kg rather than 200000t. In Figure 5:3, however, supply has increased from 240000t to 250000t because of an increase in market price from 78 cents to 80 cents per kilogram. In this case, the supply curve, SS, and the supply schedule on which it is based, have remained unchanged.

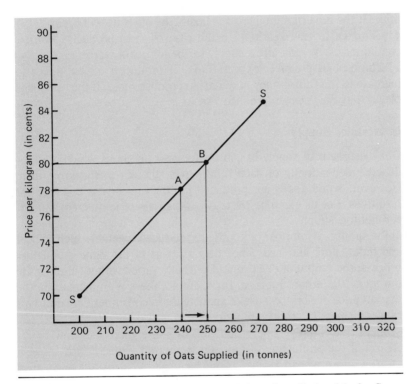

Figure 5:3 Increase in the Quantity of Oats Supplied, with the Same Supply Curve, and an Increase in Market Price

Reasons For Changes in Supply

What causes producers to supply more or less of a good now at each particular price than they did previously? Let us consider the various possible reasons.

1. Changes in technology. If the state of technology improves to permit cheaper production, more can be supplied at each price. The supply curve will have shifted to the right. An example would be the micro-computer.

2. Changes in production and marketing costs. If the per unit costs of production have increased through, for example, a higher wage or raw-material bill, less of the good will be supplied at each price. The supply curve will have shifted to the left. An example would be houses.

3. Changes in taxation. If the government reduces corporation income taxes and sales taxes, producers will tend to supply more at each price. If the government increases taxes, the opposite will occur.

4. Changes in the weather. In the case of farm products, weather conditions can greatly affect supply for better or for worse.

5. Changes in producer expectations. If producers expect prices to increase in the future, they may start to produce more. If the outlook is bleak, they may start to produce less.

Interrelated Supply

Our discussion of supply has so far focused on goods which are produced independently of each other, even though in the same firm. However, some goods are produced jointly, and others compete for resources. Let us examine these two situations of joint supply and of competitive supply.

Joint supply. A number of goods are produced together, such as beef and hides, pork and lard. Since they are part of the same production process, the output of one cannot be greatly varied without altering the output of the other. Suppose, for example, there is an increase in the market price of pork because of an increase in consumer demand. This causes farmers to produce more pork *and* lard.

Competitive Supply. The production of some goods can only be increased if the production of others is decreased. Thus, if farmers wish to grow more wheat because of an increase in its market price, they must grow less of the various other crops. This assumes, of course, that they have no idle land.

5.3: PRICE-ELASTICITY OF SUPPLY

Price-elasticity of supply is the concept used to describe the responsiveness of supply to changes in market price.

Elastic Supply

Supply is considered to be *price-elastic* if an increase in the price of a good or service causes a more than proportionate increase in the quantity supplied of it.

In Figure 5:4, for example, an increase in price from $1.00 to $1.20 results in an increase in supply from 5000 units to 10000 units. In other words, a 20 per cent increase in price has led to a 100 per cent increase in the quantity supplied.

The elasticity of supply is 5, obtained by dividing the percentage increase in quantity supplied (100 per cent) by the percentage increase in price (20 per cent). A formula for measuring the elasticity of supply is given in Table 5:2.

Supply is considered to be price-elastic whenever its elasticity is greater than 1. The higher the number, the greater is the elasticity. Supply is said to be perfectly elastic if producers are willing to supply as much of the good as is required at the existing price. In the case of a perfectly elastic supply, the supply curve is horizontal throughout its length and the elasticity is equal to infinity. The easier it is for firms to increase or decrease production, the more elastic is the supply.

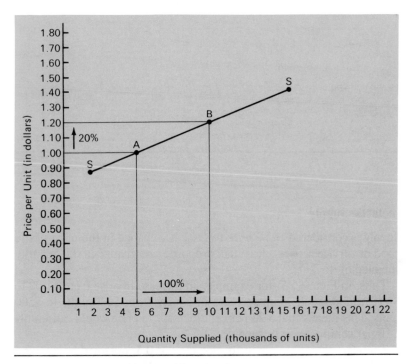

Figure 5:4   Elastic Supply of Product X

Table 5:2

Measuring the Elasticity of Supply

Formula for calculating the price-elasticity of supply:

$$es = \frac{\% \triangle qs}{\% \triangle p}$$

where   es = price-elasticity of supply

% $\triangle$ qs = percentage change in quantity supplied

% $\triangle$ p = percentage change in the price of the good

Examples (*n* is the unknown number):

1. What is the elasticity of supply if a business firm increases its supply of a good by 30%, following an increase in the price of the good by 10%?

   Answer: es $= \dfrac{30}{10} = 3$

2. What will be the effect on the industry supply of a good if price is lowered by 5%?

   (a) if the elasticity of supply is 1.8

   Answer: $1.8 = \dfrac{n}{5} \quad \therefore n = 1.8 \times 5 = 9$

   Supply will decrease by 9%.

   (b) if the elasticity of supply is 0.6

   Answer: $0.6 = \dfrac{n}{5} \quad \therefore n = 0.6 \times 5 = 3$

   Supply will decrease by 3%.

Inelastic Supply

Supply is considered to be *price-inelastic* if a change in the price of the good or service causes a less than proportionate change in the quantity supplied of it.

Thus, in Figure 5:5, for example, an increase in price from $1.00 to $1.20 would result in an increase in supply from 5000 units to 5500 units. This means that a 20 per cent increase in price would cause only a 10 per cent increase in supply.

The elasticity of supply in this example is 0.5, obtained by dividing the percentage increase in quantity supplied (10 per cent) by the percentage increase in price (20 per cent).

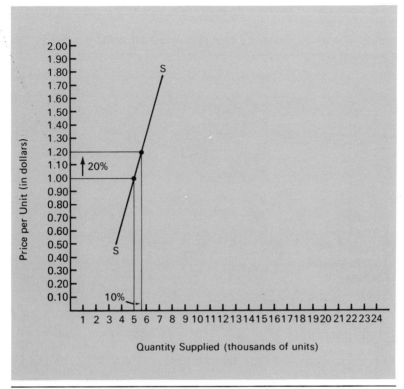

Figure 5:5   Inelastic Supply of Product Y

Supply is considered to be inelastic if its elasticity is less than 1. The smaller the fraction of 1, the more inelastic is the supply. Supply is said to be perfectly inelastic if producers will supply no more of a good or service whatever its market price. A perfectly inelastic supply is represented by a vertical line on the supply chart, and the elasticity is equal to zero.

If it is difficult for a firm to increase or decrease production (often because of considerable fixed investment), supply will tend to be inelastic, particularly in the short run.

Unitary Elasticity

Supply is considered to be of *unitary elasticity* when a percentage change in the price of a good or service is accompanied by an equal percentage change in the quantity supplied of it.

For example, in Figure 5:6, an increase in price from $1.00 to $1.20 causes an increase in supply from 5000 units to 6000 units. The percentage change in the quantity supplied (20 per cent) divided by the percentage change in price (20 per cent) gives an elasticity of 1.

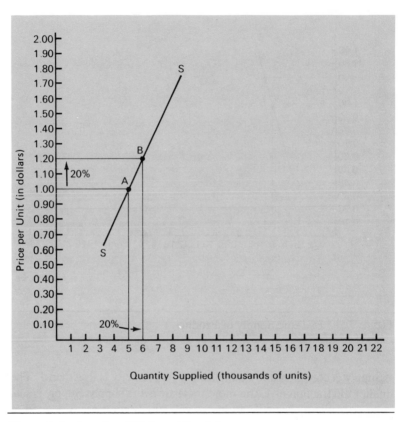

Figure 5:6   Supply of Unitary Elasticity

Short versus Long Run

Because of the fixed nature of business plants and equipment, supply responds much more sluggishly to a change in market price than does demand. In fact, economists have found it useful to distinguish between three different types of equilibria: (a) *momentary*—when output is fixed; (b) *short run*—when output has increased or decreased from existing plants; and (c) *long run*—when output has increased or decreased by firms entering or leaving the industry.

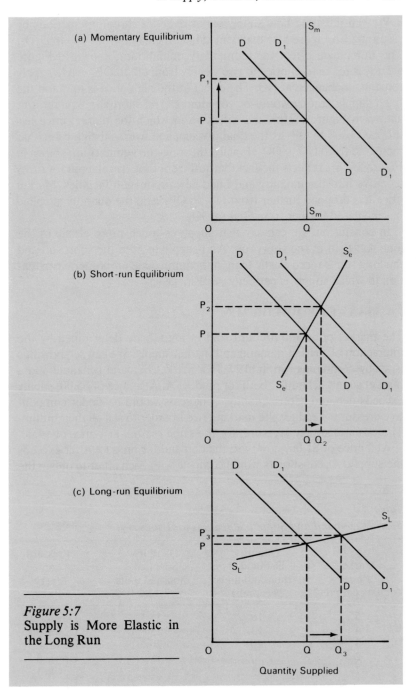

(a) Momentary Equilibrium

(b) Short-run Equilibrium

(c) Long-run Equilibrium

Figure 5:7
Supply is More Elastic in the Long Run

Quantity Supplied

We can illustrate how supply varies over the three time periods by assuming (in Figure 5:7) that demand has increased from DD to D_1D_1. The immediate effect, or momentary equilibrium, shown in Figure 5:7(a), is for market price to rise steeply from OP to OP_1, while supply remains unchanged at OQ. The effect of the high price is to ration the fixed supply among would-be consumers. The short-run equilibrium, shown in Figure 5:7(b), is a situation in which the market price has dropped back to OP_2 as the quantity supplied from existing plants has increased from OQ to OQ_2. Finally, the long-run equilibrium, shown in Figure 5:7(c), reflects the fact that sufficient time has elapsed for firms to move into the industry and build new production facilities. Market price has dropped further from OP_2 to OP_3; and the quantity supplied has increased further from OQ_2 to OQ_3.

In conclusion, we can say that supply is much more elastic in the long run than in the short run. And supply in both the short run and the long run is more elastic than in the immediate or momentary situation in which supply is perfectly price-inelastic.

5.4: MARKET EQUILIBRIUM

The market price and amount sold of a good are determined by the interaction of market demand and market supply. We can see how this is so by combining (in Table 5:3) a market demand schedule and a market supply schedule, both for product A. At a price of $5.00, supply exceeds demand. Consequently, producers would be under competitive pressure to reduce the market price in order to sell all their output. There is also supply pressure, for the same reason, at a price of $4.00.

At a price of $1.00, however, the demand for product A far exceeds the supply. As consumers would compete with each other to obtain the

Table 5:3
Market Demand and Supply Schedules for Product A

Market Price (dollars per unit)	Quantity Demanded (thousand units per week)	Quantity Supplied (thousand units per week)	Pressure on Market Price
5	10	27	Downward
4	13	25	Downward
3	20	20	Neutral
2	30	15	Upward
1	45	5	Upward

limited supply, producers could sell all their output even if they were to charge more. There would consequently be upward pressure on market price. The same thing applies at a price of $2.00. Only at a market price of $3.00 would demand be equal to supply, with therefore no upward or downward pressure on price. This would be a state of *competitive market equilibrium* in which the quantity demanded is equal to the quantity supplied, with no tendency for price to change up or down. In other words, $3.00 is the *equilibrium market price* for product A. The amount sold at this price is 20 000 units per week. This situation can be illustrated by combining the market demand and supply curves that we can plot (see Figure 5:8) from the data contained in Table 5:3. The equilibrium market price and the amount sold are where the two curves intersect.

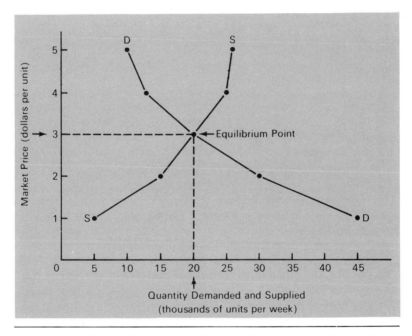

Figure 5:8 Market Demand and Supply Curves for Product A Combined to Show Equilibrium Market Price

Effect of a Change in Demand

What happens to the market price and amount sold of a good if there is a change in the demand for it? Let us assume that the demand for product A has increased because of a change in consumers' tastes. At each price, consumers are now willing and able to purchase more, and a new demand curve D_1D_1 now replaces the old demand curve DD. This new demand curve (see Figure 5:9) now intersects the supply curve SS at point B, so that market price is now $4.00 and the amount sold 25000 units. The effect of the increase in demand has been to increase both the market price and the amount sold of the good.

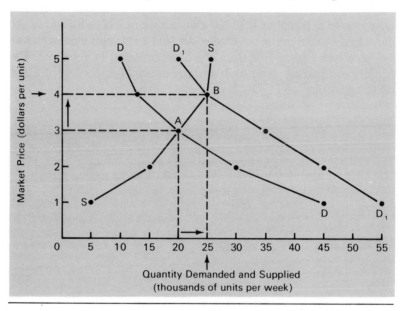

Figure 5:9   An Increase in Demand Causes an Increase in Market Price and Amount Sold

In practice, the effect of an increase or decrease in demand on market price and amount sold will vary according to the elasticity of supply. If supply is inelastic, an increase in demand will cause a relatively large increase in market price and a relatively small increase in the amount sold. If supply is elastic, an increase in demand will cause a relatively small increase in market price and a relatively large increase in the amount sold. This difference is illustrated in Figure 5:10, where S_iS_i is the inelastic supply curve and S_eS_e is the elastic one.

Effect of a Change in Supply

How does a change in supply affect the market price and amount sold

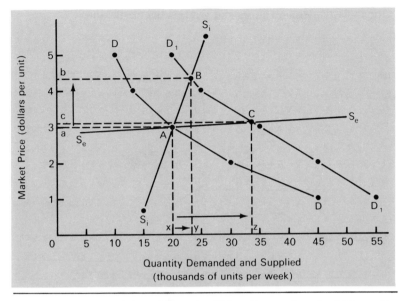

Figure 5:10   Elasticity of Supply Helps Determine the Effect of a Change in Demand

Note: Demand has increased from DD to D_iD_i. With an inelastic supply curve S_iS_i, market price increases from O_a to O_b and the amount sold from Ox to Oy.

With an elastic supply curve S_eS_e, market price increases from Oa to Oc and the amount sold from Ox to Oz.

of a good? Suppose that new technology has lowered the unit cost of production of product A. Producers are now willing and able to supply more at each price. As a result, a new supply curve S_1S_1 replaces the old supply curve SS. The new supply curve (see Figure 5:11) now intersects the demand curve DD at point B, so that market price is now about $2.25 and the amount sold about 27000 units. The increase in supply has caused a *reduction* in the market price and an *increase* in the amount sold.

The actual effect of any increase in supply on market price and amount sold will depend considerably on the nature of demand. If demand is inelastic, an increase in supply will cause a relatively large fall in market price, but only a relatively small increase in the amount sold. If, however, demand is elastic, an increase in supply will cause a relatively small reduction in market price and a relatively large increase in the amount sold. The way in which demand elasticity affects the outcome of an increase in supply is illustrated in Figure 5:12, where D_iD_i

is the inelastic demand curve and D_eD_e is the elastic one.

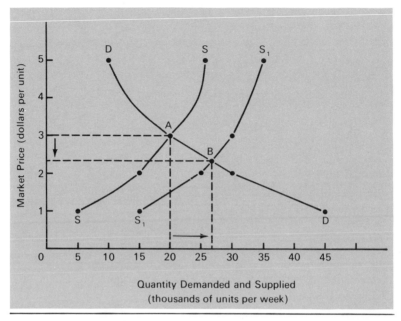

Figure 5:11 An Increase in Supply Causes a Decrease in Market Price and an Increase in Amount Sold

5.5: THE PRICE MECHANISM

Market price, as well as equating the demand for a product with its supply, plays a very important role in our economy in ensuring that business firms produce what the public wants to buy. If, for example, Canadians decide to purchase more tennis racquets, present stocks will be quickly depleted. Retailers will then place more orders with wholesalers and manufacturers. However, if domestic manufacturers and importers are unable to supply enough to meet the increased demand, the price of tennis racquets will rise, for producers will find that they can charge a higher price and still sell all they can supply. However, the higher price, combined with the same expenses, means a larger profit. This larger per unit profit will in turn encourage greater production of tennis racquets; present producers will enlarge their productive capacity and new firms will enter the industry. As a result, we have the situation in which a permanent increase in public demand for tennis racquets has led to an increase in market price which has, in turn,

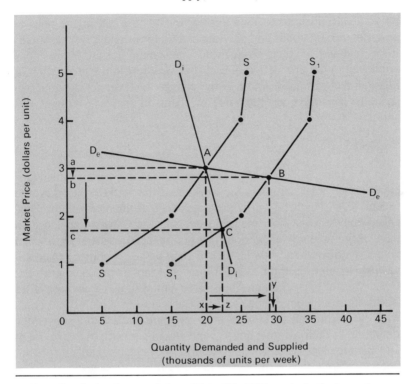

Quantity Demanded and Supplied
(thousands of units per week)

Note: Supply has increased from SS to S_1S_1. With an inelastic demand curve D_iD_i, market price decreases from O_a to O_c and the amount sold increases from O_x to O_z.

With an elastic demand curve D_eD_e, market price decreases from O_a to O_b and the amount sold increases from O_x to O_y.

Figure 5:12 Elasticity of Demand Helps Determine the Effect of a Change in Supply

induced an increase in the quantity supplied by more intensive use of existing productive capacity and by diverting resources from the production of other goods or from any unemployment pool. Conversely, if the public decides permanently to reduce their purchases of tennis racquets, the exact opposite will occur. And if the reduction in demand is sufficiently large, the fall in the market price and in profits will force firms out of the industry.

The action of market price in allocating the use of a country's resources is called the *price mechanism*. A rise in the price of certain goods and services relative to the prices of others, causes resources to be gradually diverted to their production. And a fall in the relative prices of certain goods and services causes fewer and fewer resources to be retained for their production. Thus, many resources are today employed in the production of cars, but very few in the production of horse-drawn carriages. And it is the change in consumer demand, relayed to producers via the price mechanism, 'that has brought this about.

5.6: GOVERNMENT INTERVENTION

Over the years, all levels of government in Canada have gradually increased their intervention in the working of the market system. At the federal level, income-security programs such as unemployment insurance, welfare assistance, medical care, and the Canada Pension Plan have been implemented; various types of financial assistance have been given to industry; and new laws have been passed or contemplated governing income taxation, competition, and labour-management relations. Most of these measures have been aimed at: (a) achieving a fairer distribution of income among persons and regions; (b) protecting people who, often through no fault of their own, are faced with a substantial reduction in their income; and (c) encouraging growth in employment and income. Because of this intervention, the price mechanism does not operate as smoothly as the earlier discussion might suggest.

Price Control

One important type of government invervention in the working of our economic system is price control. It is usually undertaken as part of a comprehensive prices and incomes policy designed to combat inflation. Sometimes, however, it is aimed at a particular product—for example, rental accommodation. What are its economic effects? Suppose, for example, that (a) the present market price of product A is $5.00 per unit; (b) the market demand and supply curves, DD and SS, are as shown in Figure 5:13; and (c) the government forbids any increase in the price for, say, a year. The price control in such a case does not create any immediate problem. The quantity supplied, OQ, at this price and the quantity demanded, OQ, are both equal. There is no surplus or shortage. However, suppose that two months later the demand curve (reflecting an increase in demand) has shifted to D_1D_1 while the supply curve has remained unchanged. Then, at the controlled price of $5.00 per unit, the quantity supplied would still be OQ, whereas the quantity demanded will have increased to OQ_1. In other words, demand at the controlled price exceeds supply with the result that shortages occur.

This gap between demand and supply is shown in Figure 5:13, as the distance AB.

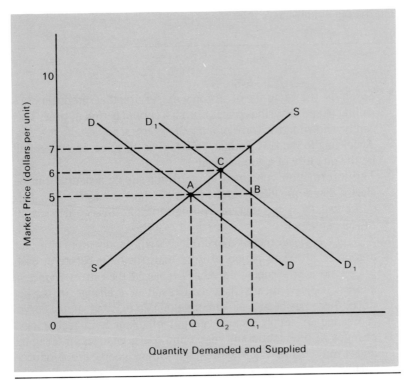

Figure 5:13 The Effects of Price Control on Market Supply and Demand

The economic effect of the price control is therefore to create a shortage of the product. This means that some consumers will go empty-handed or, if the government adopts a rationing scheme, receive a little of the product, but not as much as they would like, (or alternatively, be able to buy it on a lottery basis). The government has been successful in preventing the price of the product rising (a socially desirable goal), but at the expense of thwarting consumers' demand. Only if producers can obtain a market price of $7.00 per unit will they supply enough of the product to satisfy consumer demand. If the government wishes to control the price at $5.00 per unit and see supply increased to OQ_1 it will have to give producers a subsidy of $2.00 per unit. Without price control, the market equilibrium, with the new demand curve D_1D_1 would be a price of $6.00 per unit and a quantity demanded and supplied equivalent to OQ_2. The new demand curve and the old supply curve intersect at point C.

Summary

1. *Supply* is the quantity of a good or service that producers are willing to sell at various prices during a certain period of time. This can be shown in the form of a *market supply schedule*.
2. According to the law of supply, the higher the price, the larger will be the quantity of a good supplied.
3. The information contained in a market supply schedule can be shown diagrammatically in the form of a *market supply curve*. This curve usually slopes upward from left to right, in accordance with the law of supply.
4. A *change in supply* means that producers will supply more or less of a good in a certain period of time than they did before at each price; and a new supply curve has replaced the old. A *change in quantity supplied* means that, as a result of a change in market price, there has been a movement along an existing supply curve.
5. A change in supply occurs because of changes in technology, changes in production and marketing costs, changes in taxation, and even changes in the weather. Some goods are produced jointly; others compete for resources.
6. Supply is considered to be *elastic* if a change in the price of a good or service causes a more than proportionate change in the quantity supplied of it. It is considered to be *inelastic* if a change in price causes a less than proportionate change in the quantity supplied. Supply is considered to be of *unitary-elasticity* if a change in the price of a good causes an equal percentage change in the quantity supplied. Supply is much more elastic in the long run than in the short run.
7. The market price and amount sold of a good are determined by the interaction of market demand and market supply. *Competitive market equilibrium* exists when the quantity demanded is equal to the quantity supplied and there is no tendency for market price to move up or down.
8. If *supply* is *inelastic*, an increase in demand will cause a relatively large increase in market price and a relatively small increase in the amount sold. If *supply* is *elastic*, an increase in demand will cause a

relatively small increase in market price and a relatively large increase in the amount sold.

9. If *demand* is *inelastic*, an increase in supply will cause a relatively large fall in market price, but only a relatively small increase in the amount sold. If *demand* is *elastic*, an increase in supply will cause a relatively small reduction in market price and a relatively large increase in the amount sold.

10. The action of market price in allocating the use of a country's resources is called the *price mechanism*. A rise in the price of certain goods and services relative to the price of others causes resources to be gradually diverted to their production. And a fall in the relative prices of certain goods and services causes fewer resources to be retained for their production.

11. Over the years, all levels of government in Canada have gradually increased their intervention in the working of the market system: one important type of intervention is *price control*. Its main economic effect, apart from holding down prices, is to create a shortage of the product.

Key Terms

Market supply   98
Market supply schedule   98
Law of supply   98
Market supply curve   98
Regressive supply curve   100
Change in supply   100
Change in quantity supplied   100
Joint supply   102
Competitive supply   102
Elasticity of supply   102
Elastic supply   102

Inelastic supply   104
Unitary elasticity
   of supply   105
Competitive market
   equilibrium   109
Equilibrium market
   price   109
Price mechanism   112
Government intervention   114
Price control   114

Review Questions

1. How is supply defined in Economics?
2. What is the law of supply?
3. What is a supply curve? Why does it slope quite steeply in the short run?
4. What is an exceptional, or regressive, supply curve? Give an example of your own.

5. Distinguish between a change in supply and a change in the quantity supplied.
6. What reasons might account for a change in the supply of a good?
7. Distinguish between joint supply and competitive supply.
8. When is the supply of a good considered to be elastic? When is it considered to be inelastic?
9. How does the time period affect the elasticity of a supply of a good?
10. What determines the market price and amount sold of a good?
11. What is competitive market equilibrium?
12. What happens to the market price and amount sold of a good if there is a change in the demand for it? What significance does the elasticity of supply have?
13. How does a change in supply affect the market price and amount sold of a good?
14. What is the price mechanism? How does it help determine the allocation of a country's resources?
15. How does government intervene in the economy?
16. What are the economic effects of price controls?
17. According to the "law of supply," the higher the price, the larger the quantity supplied. Is this always true? Answer, with examples.
18. What happens to the supply curve, if manufacturers decide to produce less of a good even though its price remains unchanged?
19. What can happen to the supply curve of a product if business firms become more optimistic about the future?
20. Suppose that the price of a good rises by 30 per cent and output also increases by 30 per cent. What is the elasticity of supply?
21. Suppose that the price of a good increases by 20 per cent and the output increases by 10 per cent. What is the elasticity of supply?
22. Suppose that the price of a good increases by 8 per cent and that the elasticity of supply is 0.5. How would the supply change? What would be the answer if the elasticity were 2.0?
23. Give an example of a good for which the supply might be (a) perfectly elastic, and (b) perfectly inelastic. Explain.
24. Supply is more elastic in the long run. Explain.
25. Competitive market equilibrium is a notion rather than a fact. Explain.
26. Elasticity of supply helps determine the effect of a change in demand. Explain.
27. "If people weren't so hooked on coffee, we wouldn't have to pay so much for it." Discuss.
28. How have rent controls affected the supply of rental accommoda-

tion in Canada?

29. Show on a graph how the price of gold has changed in recent years. Explain what has happened to demand and supply.
30. How and why has the price of crude petroleum increased so much since 1973?
31. Indicate the typical price range in your district for the following types of home:
    (a) condominium apartment
    (b) townhouse
    (c) semi-detached house
    (d) detached house.

What determines the price of a home? Why are they so expensive?

32. Explain, with a product example, what each of the following curves signifies.

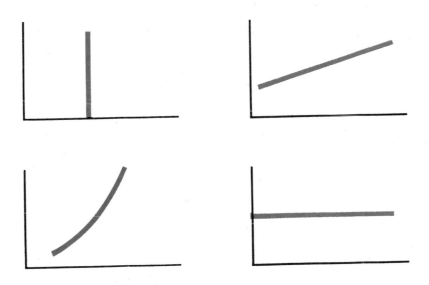

Part C:
THEORY OF THE FIRM

In this third part of the book, we look first at the various costs involved in the production of goods and services and how a firm decides how much to produce. We then consider the different possible market structures in which firms operate in Canada, ranging from the extremes of perfect competition and pure monopoly to the more usual, in-between situations of monopolistic competition and oligopoly.

6. THE COSTS OF PRODUCTION

CHAPTER OBJECTIVES

A. To distinguish between the explicit and implicit costs of production
B. To show how the difference between private costs and social costs can often result in harm to society
C. To distinguish between fixed and variable costs and to examine how they vary as production increases
D. To explain the concepts of average and marginal cost and the relationship between them at different levels of output
E. To discuss the use of cost analysis in business decision-making

CHAPTER OUTLINE

A business firm's main objective is to make a profit. To do this, management must try to increase sales revenue and hold down costs. The larger the difference between the two, the greater is the profit—for revenue minus expenses equals profit.

In business, expenses, as shown in the income, or profit and loss statement, include only items on which money has been spent. However, from the economist's point of view, this is not always logical— because there are certain implicit costs that business firms tend to ignore with the use of conventional accounting procedure.

6.1: EXPLICIT AND IMPLICIT COSTS

The costs of production, as defined in economics, include both explicit costs and implicit costs. *Explicit costs* are expenses such as payment for materials, wages for labour, and rent for a building, that are actually paid out. The items included are the same as those shown under the heading "Expenses" in a business firm's income statement. Also included is depreciation, which is the allocation of the past cost of a capital item such as machinery over the expected years of its use. *Implicit costs* are costs not included among expenses in the income statement, but which are nevertheless incurred.

One important implicit cost can be the amount of owner's time devoted to the business. In many cases, the owners of a business *do* pay themselves a salary and this may even be more than the "going rate" for their services elsewhere. Often, particularly in a new business struggling to get established, or in an old one struggling to survive, this salary may be considerably less than what the owner could earn elsewhere. In some cases, no salary is paid at all. Obviously, to get a truer picture of production costs, a reasonable salary (paid or not) should be included among expenses.

The money that the owners have invested in a business must also not be overlooked. This money could, if employed elsewhere, earn at least the rate of interest currently being paid by the banks. Sometimes the owners will provide part of the capital of the business in the form of a loan. If this is interest-bearing, an interest cost is included among the firm's expenses. However, the equity, or ownership capital, does not receive interest. Therefore, to give a truer picture of the costs of production of a business, we should also include as a cost the return which this equity capital could have earned if invested elsewhere. In economics, this cost is called *normal profit*—the payment required to keep capital in a particular line of business.

6.2: SOCIAL VERSUS PRIVATE COSTS

In the past, the explicit and implicit costs considered by economists have been purely *private*, or *internal costs*. Recently, however, *social* or *external costs* are also being taken into account. These are the costs to society that result from business production. The most important of these are air and water pollution. More and more firms are, of course, taking steps to reduce pollution. If, for example, a business firm builds a taller smokestack or installs special treatment and recycling equipment for liquid wastes, its costs of production are thereby increased. These additional costs are part of its total costs and are therefore included in our analysis of a firm's production behaviour. However, many social or "external" costs, such as draining liquid wastes into a nearby stream or polluting the local air, are ignored.

6.3: FIXED AND VARIABLE COSTS

Some costs of production, such as materials, labour, fuel and power, can be altered relatively quickly. More materials can be purchased or orders cancelled; an extra shift can be worked or some employees laid off. But other costs, such as the wages of plant-maintenance and security staff, the heating costs of an office or factory building, or the implicit annual cost of equity capital tied up, can often be changed only after months or years. In some cases, it may be practically impossible to change them at all, and the plant or store may keep operating until there is no return whatsoever on the capital invested or on the owner's talents employed. Obviously, the longer the time that elapses, the greater the possibility of adjustment.

Short and Long Run

In analyzing a firm's production behaviour, we therefore find it useful to distinguish between the short and the long run. The *short run* is a period of time too short to allow a firm to alter its plant capacity, but long enough to permit it to vary the degree to which this capacity is utilized—for example, by adding or dropping a shift, or by setting up or abolishing a production line. The *long run*, conversely, is a period of time long enough to permit a firm to vary the capacity of the plant as well as the degree of its use. In the short run, the capacity of the plant is fixed; in the long run, it is variable. A short-run adjustment for a firm would be working on Saturday when the normal practice is a five-day week. A long-run adjustment would be building and equipping an addition to the plant. Obviously, the short run is different for each firm; some firms can add to their plant or move to a larger one more quickly than others.

The fixed capacity of a manufacturing plant or a retail store in the short run means that certain of a firm's costs are fixed. For example, so long as the owner's capital is tied up in the land, buildings, and equipment, there is a continuing implicit cost of, say, at least 12 per cent per annum if not more on the equity capital invested. There are also other fixed costs such as interest on borrowed capital; depreciation of capital assets; the wages of management, clerical staff, maintenance and security personnel; rent; insurance premiums; plant and equipment maintenance; and property taxes. These costs would be incurred even if output were nil. *Fixed costs*, therefore, are costs that remain unchanged whatever the level of output.

In business, fixed costs are usually called *overhead*. They can be divided into three parts. The first is *factory overhead*, or *factory burden*, comprising indirect labour costs such as salaries of the plant manager, supervisors, production and inspection clerks, and security staff; indirect material costs such as cleaning supplies; and insurance, rent, and taxes. The second is *administrative overhead*, comprising salaries to general management and "front office" staff such as accounting, personnel, and research. And the third is *sales overhead*, comprising salaries, commissions, and expenses; advertising; and promotion.

Many costs can, of course, be varied in the short run. As output is increased or decreased, payments for materials, labour, power, fuel, and transportation can also be changed. If a firm has not sufficient orders for its goods, it can perhaps lay off some of its workers and reduce the amount of materials purchased. If it is prospering, it can expand its labour force and purchase more materials. It will also use

Table 6:1
A Firm's Fixed, Variable, and Total Costs of Production

Units of Output	Total Fixed Cost (in dollars)	Total Variable Cost (in dollars)	Total Cost (in dollars)
0	100	0	100
1	100	60	160
2	100	110	210
3	100	150	250
4	100	180	280
5	100	220	320
6	100	280	380
7	100	360	460
8	100	470	570
9	100	620	720
10	100	820	920

more fuel, power, and other production inputs. These costs are called *variable costs*, because they vary according to the level of output.

How do costs vary as a firm's output increases? The term *cost function* is used to describe the relationship between costs and the rate of output. Obviously, in the short run, fixed costs are the same whatever the output. The fixed-cost function is shown in Table 6:1 and illustrated in Figure 6:1.

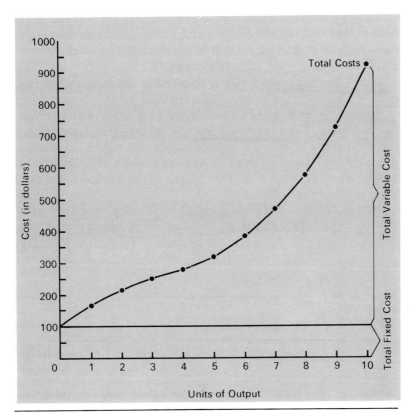

Figure 6:1   Total Cost Comprises Fixed and Variable Costs

But how do variable costs increase? Is it in strict proportion to the increase in output? The answer is no. In fact, up to a certain level of output, the increase in total variable costs will usually be at a decreasing rate. After that, it will be at an increasing rate. The variable-cost function, illustrating this situation, is also shown in Table 6:1 and Figure 6:1, where we can see the relationship between variable costs, fixed costs, and total costs. For simplicity, we have kept the numbers in our example quite small. They can, if desired, be multiplied by hundreds or thousands.

In practice, not all costs fit neatly into one category or the other.

6.4: AVERAGE COST

So far we have looked solely at total production costs in relation to output. However, we will find it useful for our later understanding of price and output determination in different market structures to think also in terms of average, or per unit, costs.

Average variable cost (AVC) is obtained by dividing total variable costs by total output. This cost at first declines, but later begins to rise.

Average fixed cost or (AFC) is obtained by dividing total fixed costs by total output. Since the total fixed cost, or overhead, is the same in the short run whatever the level of output, the AFC will decline as output grows. Thus, in Table 6:2, AFC starts out at $100 but declines as production increases to $10 at 10 units of output. The falling AFC curve is illustrated in Figure 6:2.

Average total cost (ATC) is obtained by dividing total costs (fixed plus variable) by total output, or, alternatively, by adding average fixed cost to average variable cost. In our example, ATC declines from $160

Table 6:2
A Firm's Average Costs of Production

Units of Output	Average Fixed Cost (in dollars)	Average Variable Cost (in dollars)	Average Total Cost (in dollars)
1	100.00	60.00	160.00
2	50.00	55.00	105.00
3	33.33	50.00	83.33
4	25.00	45.00	70.00
5	20.00	44.00	64.00
6	16.67	46.67	63.34
7	14.29	51.43	65.72
8	12.50	58.75	71.25
9	11.11	68.89	80.00
10	10.00	82.00	92.00

at 1 unit of output to $92 at 10 units of output. The ATC curve is also shown in Figure 6:2

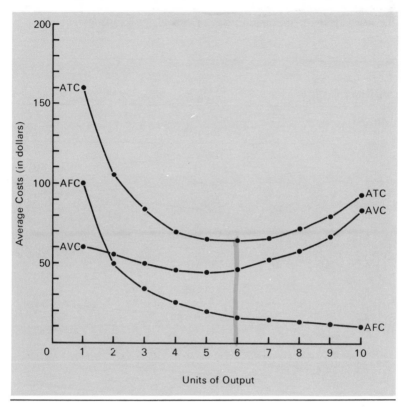

Figure 6:2   The Short-Run Average-Cost Curves

6.5: MARGINAL COST

The term *marginal cost* is used to denote the extra cost of increasing output by one unit. The concept of marginal cost is important because it is the cost that a business manager tends to consider above all when deciding to reduce or increase output. The expected additional revenue from a proposed increase in output must be weighed against the additional marginal cost involved. If the expected marginal revenue is less than the expected marginal cost, the manager will be reluctant to produce more.

In practice, marginal cost at first declines (see Table 6:3) then begins to rise as a firm reaches its optimum production level. Eventually, marginal cost may rise very steeply as overtime rates of pay and other unusual expenses are incurred and as breakdowns become more frequent, with the plant operating at or close to full capacity.

Table 6:3
Marginal Cost

Units of Output	Total Cost (in dollars)	Marginal Cost (in dollars)
0	100	
		60
1	160	
		50
2	210	
		40
3	250	
		30
4	280	
		40
5	320	
		60
6	380	
		80
7	460	
		110
8	570	
		150
9	720	
		200
10	920	

6.6: RELATIONSHIP BETWEEN AVERAGE COST AND MARGINAL COST

If we look at Table 6:4, we can see that when AVC is falling, AVC exceeds MC. And when AVC is rising, MC exceeds AVC. Also, we can see that when ATC is falling, ATC exceeds MC. And when ATC is rising, MC exceeds ATC. This means (see Figure 6:3) that the MC curve intersects the AVC and ATC curves at their lowest points.

The reason for this relationship between average cost and marginal cost is that marginal cost represents the amount by which total variable costs and total costs (fixed and variable) change with an extra unit of output. So long as marginal cost is less than average variable cost and average total cost, the AVC and ATC curves respectively must be sloping downward. Once marginal cost exceeds AVC and ATC, those curves must be sloping upward to represent the fact that the amounts are increasing. Only when marginal cost has stopped declining and has begun to rise would it be equal to AVC and ATC. And this is the point at which the MC curve intersects the AVC and ATC curves.

Firms incur marginal cost as they expand output. If the marginal cost is less than the average cost, the average cost falls. When the marginal cost equals the average cost, the average cost remains the same. When marginal cost exceeds average cost, the average cost rises. Of course, marginal cost only bears this relationship to average variable cost and average total cost. It does not bear it to average fixed cost because fixed cost remains the same whatever the level of output and is unaffected by marginal cost.

Table 6:4
The Relationship between Average Cost and Marginal Cost

Units of Output	Total Cost (in dollars)	Average Variable Cost (in dollars)	Average Total Cost (in dollars)	Marginal Cost (in dollars)
0	100			
1	160	60.00	160.00	60
2	210	55.00	105.00	50
3	250	50.00	83.33	40
4	280	45.00	70.00	30
5	320	44.00	64.00	40
6	380	46.67	63.34	60
7	460	51.43	65.72	80
8	570	58.75	71.25	110
9	720	68.89	80.00	150
10	920	82.00	92.00	200

6.7: SCALE OF PRODUCTION

As a business increases the scale of its production, from say the tens of thousands of units to many hundreds of thousands, its average costs of production per unit of output will decline. This is in addition to the decline in average total costs because of the spreading of fixed overhead among more units of output. Eventually, however, average costs will start to rise.

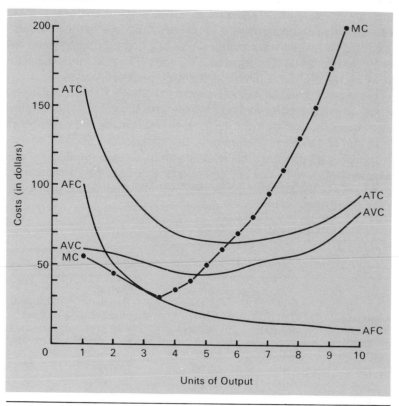

Figure 6:3   The Marginal Cost Curve Intersects the ATC and AVC Curves at their Minimum Points

Economies of Scale

The additional fall in average total costs occurs because of what are called the "economies of scale". These economies, or "savings" arise in several different ways.

1. Greater specialization of labour and equipment. In a mass-production plant—for example, a car manufacturer—the division of labour is extremely great. The work is broken down into small steps and each worker performs a highly specialized task. This specialization often creates boredom and frustration. However, because of greater labour proficiency, it also greatly increases output per worker and so lowers per unit production costs.

Specialization also extends to equipment. With a large quantity of the same good being produced, it is possible to use special-purpose rather than general-purpose machines. Highly specialized machine tools, including industrial robots, although expensive, more than pay for themselves in lower per unit production costs—so long as the production runs are long.

2.More efficient use of common services. There are many common services in a plant, or among branch plants of a single firm, such as production planning and control, research and development, personnel recruitment and training, financing, electronic data processing, advertising, purchasing, and warehousing. Usually, the cost of such services does not increase in proportion to output. Consequently, it is often possible to obtain a reduction in the cost of these services per unit of output as production increases. The larger the output, the wider these costs are spread.

3. Quantity buying. Large-scale production means large purchases of materials and parts. This enables the firm's purchasing managers to obtain quantity price discounts from suppliers and so reduce the cost of materials and parts.

4. Mechanized handling. Long production runs means that workers and machines can be grouped along a production or assembly line. Since the materials and parts always travel the same path, highly mechanized materials-handling methods such as chain-conveyor systems can be used. Mechanized handling lowers per unit costs of handling materials, parts, and finished products.

5. Better use of by-products. In a small firm, by-products are often discarded because the amount is small. With large-scale production, there is an incentive to devise a use for them. With large firms, these by-products, such as wood shavings from sawmills, can be made into a product that can provide a useful source of revenue and so help offset the costs of production.

Diseconomies of Scale

Once production in a plant becomes extremely large, inefficiencies start to arise. These are called the *diseconomies of scale.*

The most important of these diseconomies is the difficulty in managing such a large operation. Up to a certain point, large-scale production can enable a firm to "stretch" its managers further. However, once a firm becomes too large, and there is no proper decentralization of authority, management can become a nightmare, with the whole firm

entangled in red tape. A second diseconomy is the growing number of mechanical breakdowns that seem to arise with very large-scale production. A third one is the likely worsening of labour-management relations and its effect on labour productivity. These diseconomies are one reason why some manufacturers prefer to have several medium-sized plants widely dispersed, rather than just one large-sized plant. The other reason for decentralized operations is the greater competitive effectiveness that comes from being close to one's markets.

Finally, we must remember that, whatever the economies or diseconomies, there must be sufficient demand to justify large-scale production. The *extent of the market* is, in fact, the key to obtaining benefit from large-scale production. If a firm cannot sell all its output, the benefit of any cost reduction obviously disappears.

6.8: COST ANALYSIS AND BUSINESS DECISION-MAKING

In conclusion to this chapter, we should emphasize that business managers are very much concerned with their production costs—because the higher the average cost of each unit produced compared with the factory selling price, the lower a firm's profit margin. Also, in deciding whether to increase output (either by working overtime or by enlarging the plant), managers need to know how average production costs will decline with a larger volume of production. Such information is also essential in making pricing decisions—for cost is one important factor that is considered in setting the price of a product. (Others are management's analysis of consumer demand and the prices of competing products). Also, as explained in the next chapter, an estimate of a firm's total production costs at different levels of output is required if a firm's managers are to make use of break-even analysis in evaluating a new business venture—whether it be a new product, a new machine, or a new branch plant.

By contrast, the concepts of marginal cost and marginal revenue are less generally applied, usually because of the difficulty of actual measurement, except historically, and because of the usual impracticability of varying output in small quantities.

Summary

1. A firm's *total costs* comprise explicit and implicit costs. *Explicit costs* are expenses, such as payments for materials, wages or labour, and rent for a building, that are actually paid out. *Implicit costs* are costs, such as the owner's time, that may not be included

among expenses in the income statement, but which are nevertheless incurred. In the past, the explicit and implicit costs considered by economists have been purely *private* or *"internal"* ones. Nowadays, however, *social* or *"external"* costs are also being taken into account.

2. A firm's total costs, looked at in another way, comprise fixed and variable costs. *Fixed costs* are items such as rent of buildings and management salaries that are fixed, at least in the short run. *Variable costs* are items such as payments for materials that will vary in the short run.

3. In considering price and output determination, we find it useful to calculate *average fixed cost* (total fixed costs divided by total output), *average variable cost* (total variable cost divided by total output), and *average total cost*.

4. The term *marginal cost* is used to denote the extra cost of increasing output by one unit.

5. The *marginal cost curve* intersects the average variable cost curve and the average total cost curve at their lowest points.

6. If there is an increase in the scale of a firm's production, average total costs may fall even faster than usual. This is because of the *economies of scale*—that is, the savings from greater specialization of labour and equipment, more efficient use of common services, quantity buying, mechanized handling, and better use of by-products. However, average total costs eventually rise more and more sharply because of the *diseconomies of scale*—that is, the extra costs of managing a very large operation, even despite attempts at decentralization.

7. The extent of the market is the key to obtaining the benefits of large-scale production.

8. Business managers are vitally concerned, in their decision-making, with production costs. However, the emphasis is usually on total costs (compared with total revenue) rather than marginal costs (compared with marginal revenue).

Key Terms

Review Questions

1. Why do economists include implicit costs among total costs, even though they may not appear in a firm's income statement? What are such implicit costs?
2. What are social or external costs? Why do economists argue that they should be included among a firm's total costs?
3. Distinguish between fixed and variable costs. What is the significance of the time period?
4. How do costs vary as a firm's output increases?
5. What are the various types of average cost? How are they calculated?
6. What is marginal cost? What is its significance?
7. What is the relationship between marginal cost and total cost?
8. What is the relationship between average cost and marginal cost?
9. What are the various economies of scale? What are the eventual diseconomies?
10. The extent of the market is the key to obtaining benefit from large-scale production. Explain.
11. Why, in practice, do business firms neglect to include social costs when making investment and other decisions? Why should they be included?
12. In the long run, there is no such thing as fixed costs. Explain.
13. What are the various categories of business "overhead"? What is the purpose of such a classification?
14. To what extent do business firms use marginal cost analysis in their production decisions?
15. The average cost of production invariably declines as output increases. Comment.
16. Explain why some busines firms are large and others small. Is there an optimum size for each type of production?
17. How does geographical location affect the optimum scale of production?
18. How does government policy affect the optimum scale of production?

19. Many large firms are the result of market power rather than of economies of large-scale production. Discuss.
20. Government transportation subsidies help large-scale Ontario manufacturers at the expense of smaller local firms in other parts of Canada. Discuss.
21. The small size of the Canadian market is no excuse for failure to take advantage of the economies of large-scale production. Discuss, in the light of Canada's export opportunities.
22. Canadian manufacturing costs are too high to permit unrestricted competition by foreign manufacturers in Canada's domestic market. Discuss.
23. Nowadays it makes sense for many Canadian retailers to have most of their goods manufactured abroad. Discuss.
24. Government policies (e.g. minimum wages, unemployment insurance) are making Canadian manufacturing less and less competitive. Discuss.
25. Japan produced its first car only a few years ago. Now it is outselling everyone else. Discuss, with particular reference to relative costs.
26. Canada should have only one car manufacturer. Discuss, with reference to production and marketing costs.

7. REVENUE, COSTS, AND PROFIT

CHAPTER OBJECTIVES

A. To distinguish between total revenue, average revenue, and marginal revenue
B. To indicate how a firm determines its best-profit output
C. To explain the use of the break-even concept in business
D. To explain why a firm may continue to produce even though its total costs may exceed its total revenue
E. To indicate when a firm reaches its shut-down point
F. To define briefly the basic market structures that exist in Canada, as an introduction to the following chapters

CHAPTER OUTLINE

7.1 Sales Revenue
7.2 Best-Profit Output
7.3 Least-Loss Output
7.4 Shut-Down Point
7.5 Different Market Structures

7.1: SALES REVENUE

The money that a firm receives in exchange for its products is called its *sales revenue*. Thus, if a firm sells 5000 units of product X for $10.00 each, its total sales revenue is $50000.

Average Revenue

The total sales revenue, when divided by the number of units of the good sold, gives us the firm's *average revenue*. Thus, if a firm sells 5000 units of its product for a total sales revenue of $50000 its average revenue is $10.00—the same as the price.

Marginal Revenue

If the selling price of the firm's product is $10.00, the sale of one additional unit will increase the firm's total sales revenue by $10.00. If the product is sold only by the thousand, the sale of an extra thousand units will increase sales revenue by $10000. This extra amount of money is called the *marginal revenue*.

In certain types of industry, a firm will always be able to sell more goods at the same price. Consequently, marginal revenue will remain constant—in our example at $10.00

In other situations, more can be sold only at a lower price. If the extra units can be sold to a separate market (for example, a foreign country), the lower price may apply only to the extra units sold. Suppose, however, the firm is selling the extra units to the same market; then the price at which all the firm's output is sold will have to be reduced to increase the number of units sold. The firm's marginal revenue in such a case will be the extra revenue from the sale of the extra unit or units, *minus* the reduction in price on the units already being sold. Thus if a firm can sell an extra 1000 units by reducing its price for all its units to $9.50 each, its marginal revenue would be only $7000. This amount is obtained by subtracting the $2500 no longer received on the other 5000 units from the $9500 received for the extra 1000 units, because of the reduction in price from $10.00 to $9.50 each. If the firm can avoid reducing the $10.00 price for existing sales and sell the extra 1000 units in some other market, even for only $8.00 each, its marginal revenue would be greater—$8000 as compared with $7000.

7.2: BEST-PROFIT OUTPUT

One method of theoretically determining a firm's most desirable output is by comparing marginal revenue and marginal cost. So long as marginal revenue exceeds marginal cost, it will be profitable for a firm to produce and sell more goods. Conversely, if marginal cost exceeds marginal revenue, it would be more profitable for a firm to produce and sell less. A firm would be in an equilibrium situation, with optimum output and sales and with maximum profit, when its marginal revenue equals its marginal cost. This concept is elaborated and illustrated in the following chapters.

Total Revenue and Total Costs

In business, because of the difficulty of measuring marginal revenue and marginal costs, particularly on a current rather than historical basis, management usually concentrates its attention on a comparison of total revenue and total costs. And if a firm's primary goal is to maximize profit (as it often is), it will try to make its total revenue as large as possible and its total costs as small as possible. A firm will therefore usually try to produce and sell that output at which total revenue exceeds total costs by the widest possible margin. In economics, we assume that total costs include "normal profit."

Break-Even Point

Business firms vary greatly in their efficiency and their profits differ accordingly. The more efficient firms make considerably more than "normal profit," while their less efficient rivals may find that their total revenue is only equal to their total costs. Since their total cost includes a normal profit, they are content to stay in the industry rather than look elsewhere. Such firms are operating at a break-even point.

The concept of break-even analysis is widely used in business to decide not only whether to stay in business but also whether to launch a new product, buy new equipment, open a new plant, etc. In the latter case, the first step is to estimate total costs (fixed and variable) at different levels of output. The second step is to estimate the total revenue that these different levels of output would bring. The third step is to compare total revenue and total costs at different levels of output to ascertain the break-even point—the level of output and sales at which total revenue equals total costs. Then, after market research, a management decision can be made on the likelihood of the firm's achieving such a level of sales and the time period required to do so. Of course, a firm would want to do better than just break even. But the break-even point is the minimum goal. If the sales prospects look grim, the investment can be cancelled and little money lost. An example of break-even analysis is illustrated in Table 7:1 and Figure 7:1.

7.3: LEAST-LOSS OUTPUT

A firm may find, perhaps because of increased competition or higher wages, that it is no longer breaking even—in other words, its total revenue is now less than its total costs. Obviously, this may be only a temporary situation and may be remedied by changes within the firm (for example, a more determined marketing effort or a reduction in production costs) or by external factors such as an improvement in the economy or a quota on imports.

Once a firm has invested time and money in equipping a factory and training a labour force, it may continue to operate for some time even though its total costs exceed its total revenue. This is because it has certain fixed costs (such as depreciation of the equipment) that will be incurred whether or not the firm produces.

Thus, even if the less than break-even situation continues more or less permanently, a firm may find it worthwhile to continue to produce so long as its revenue covers its variable costs of production. Ideally,

---

Table 7:1

Example of Break-even Analysis

Situation: XYZ Enterprise Ltd. is contemplating the introduction of a new product. Fixed and variable costs have been estimated for different levels of output. Variable costs are estimated at an average of $5.00 per unit over the expected range of production and includes an allowance for units scrapped. An analysis of demand and of prices charged by competitors for similar products suggests a factory selling price of $10.00 per unit. *Question:* What volume of sales would be required to break even? *Answer:* 10 000 units per month, determined as follows:

Output per month (1000s of units)	Fixed Costs (share of overhead) (in $1000s)	Variable Costs (in $1000s)	Total Costs (in $1000s)	Total Revenue (in $1000s)	Profit or Loss (in $1000s)
1	50	5	55	10	−45
2	50	10	60	20	−40
3	50	15	65	30	−35
4	50	20	70	40	−30
5	50	25	75	50	−25
6	50	30	80	60	−20
7	50	35	85	70	−15
8	50	40	90	80	−10
9	50	45	95	90	− 5
B.E.P. 10	50	50	100	100	0
11	50	55	105	110	+ 5
12	50	60	110	120	+10
13	50	65	115	130	+15
14	50	70	120	140	+20
15	50	75	125	150	+25
16	50	80	130	160	+30
17	50	85	135	170	+35
18	50	90	140	180	+40
19	50	95	145	190	+45
20	50	100	150	200	+50

the revenue should also make some contribution towards covering the firm's fixed costs (ones that would be incurred whether the firm produces or not). It will have to decide at what level of output its losses are minimized. This will be the output at which marginal revenue equals marginal cost, even though total costs at this output exceed total revenue.

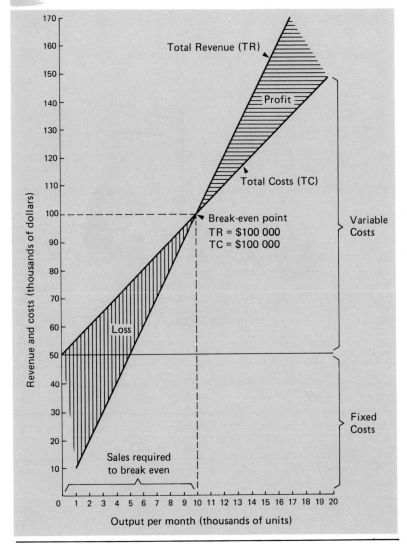

Figure 7:1 The Break-Even Point

"Who's the idiot who set our price below cost?"

7.4: SHUT-DOWN POINT

Only when a firm's total revenue fails to cover its variable costs of production will it be forced to close down—through lack of funds to buy materials and parts and pay wages, utilities, etc. This would be its *shut-down point*. Shut down may be postponed, of course, by borrowing or drawing on financial reserves.

7.5: DIFFERENT MARKET STRUCTURES

We said earlier that consumer demand largely determines what is produced in our economy. Thus, if consumers want more of a good, the increase in their demand will cause inventories to decline and the market price to rise and so induce profit-seeking firms to produce more. Conversely, a reduction in demand will cause stocks to rise, the market price to fall, and so cause firms to produce less. But this use of market price as a mechanism for allocating the use of a country's resources assumes that firms compete effectively with each other in supplying goods. It also assumes that firms may freely enter or leave an industry.

In practice, the degree of competition varies considerably from industry to industry and from place to place. There may be many snack bars in a town, each competing fiercely with others, but only one post office, one liquor store, or one funeral parlour. There may be no doctors in the country, but many in the towns; and even if there are many, they may not wish or be allowed to compete. In some industries, one or a few firms can influence the market price; in other industries, the member firms have no such control. Thus, a provincial electricity commission can set the price for electric power; the chartered banks, the price for the use of their cheques. But the individual rancher has no say as to the market price of beef. In many industries, a firm can make its product appear different from that of competing firms, even though it is basically the same. A firm "differentiates" its product from that of other firms by using a brand name and intensive advertising.

In the face of such diversity, how can we attempt to explain how price and output are actually determined? For many years, economists used only two models for their market analysis: perfect competition and pure monopoly.

Perfect competition was defined as a market in which many firms compete; each produces the same product and each, because of its limited output, cannot influence market price. *Pure monopoly* was defined as a market with only one firm, which can, therefore, set market price. Many economists and other people realized, however, that most business activity fitted into neither category, but fell somewhere in between. Consequently, in the 1920s and 1930s, a new concept, that of *imperfect competition,* was advanced to explain this middle ground. Imperfect competition was divided into two main types: (a) *monopolistic competition*—a market in which many firms sell differentiated products; and (b) *oligopoly*— a market in which just a few firms sell either the same or differentiated products. Economists now therefore make use of four basic models for market analysis, as summarized in Table 7:2.

In the following chapters, we consider how a firm can theoretically determine its best-profit output, least-loss output, and shut-down point in each of these market structures.

Table 7:2
The Four Basic Market Structures

Characteristic	Perfect Competition	Pure Monopoly	Monopolistic Competition	Oligopoly
Number of firms	Many	One	Many	Few
Kind of good	Same	Unique	Differentiated	Same or differentiated
Control over price	None	Considerable	Some	Very much
Condition of entry	Easy	Restricted	Quite easy	Difficult
Non-price competition	None	Advertising Public relations	Advertising Brand names Packaging	Advertising Brand names Packaging
Examples	Agriculture	Local utilities Post Office Telephone	Retail trade Dresses Shoes	Steel Cars Farm implements Household appliances

Summary

1. *Sales revenue* is the money that a firm receives in exchange for its product.

2. *Average revenue* is sales revenue divided by the number of units sold.
3. *Marginal revenue* is the extra revenue received by a firm from the sale of one more unit of the product.
4. Depending on the type of industry, marginal revenue will remain constant or decline.
5. A business firm usually tries to produce that output at which total revenue exceeds total cost by the widest possible margin.
6. The concept of "break-even" point is used to decide not only whether a firm should remain in business but to evaluate new investment opportunities.
7. A firm which has fixed costs may continue to produce, at least temporarily, even though total costs exceed total revenue, so long as it can cover its variable costs and some part of its fixed costs.
8. Shut-down point occurs when a firm's total revenue fails to cover even its variable costs.
9. Economists make use of *three basic market structures* to analyze the economic behaviour of the firm. These are: *perfect competition, imperfect competition* (itself divided into monopolistic competition and oligopoly), and *monopoly.*

Key Terms

Sales revenue   139
Average revenue   139
Marginal revenue   140
Best-profit output   140
Total revenue   145
Total costs   140
Breakeven point   141

Least-loss output   141
Shut-down point   145
Perfect competition   145
Pure monopoly   145
Imperfect competition   146
Monopolistic competition   146
Oligopoly   146

Review Questions

1. Distinguish between total revenue, average revenue and marginal revenue.
2. What is profit? How is it determined? Why should a firm try to maximize its profit?
3. How can a firm determine its optimum or best-profit output?
4. What is a firm's break-even point? Do all firms in an industry operate at this point? Explain.

5. What practical application does break-even analysis have in business?
6. What is meant by a firm's "least-loss output"?
7. What is a firm's shut-down point? How is it determined? What is its significance?
8. Distinguish between perfect competition and monopoly.
9. How does monopolistic competition differ from oligopoly?
10. "Marginal revenue is always the same as the price of the product." Discuss.
11. "Most business firms pay little attention in practice to marginal revenue and marginal cost." Discuss.
12. "Break-even analysis is only as sound as the assumptions on which it is based." Explain and comment.
13. "Today it costs about $500 000 to set up a 24-track recording studio, which must then be booked for about 2500 h every year at $150/h to break even." What is the price, marginal revenue, and total cost? If the studio is booked for 300 h, what would be the rate of return on total capital? State any assumptions that you make.
14. What are the various market structures that economists use to help analyze the economic behaviour of the business firm?

8. PERFECT COMPETITION: MANY FIRMS WITH THE SAME PRODUCT

CHAPTER OBJECTIVES

A. To explain what is meant by "perfect competition" and the purpose of the concept
B. To explain how a firm determines its most profitable level of output, using first the marginal revenue and marginal cost approach and then the total cost and total revenue approach
C. To show how market supply schedules and curves can be constructed for a firm and an industry
D. To explain how each firm and industry arrives at an equilibrium market situation in both the short run and the long run
E. To indicate the effects of increasing costs on market equilibrium

CHAPTER OUTLINE

8.1 Perfect Competition Defined
8.2 Profit Maximization
8.3 Total-Revenue and Total-Cost Approach
8.4 Market Supply Curves
8.5 Firm and Industry Equilibrium

The term "competition" is commonly used in business to describe a market situation in which two or more firms strive in various ways to secure the consumer's dollar. In economics, however, the term *perfect competition* (or *pure competition*) is used in a much narrower sense.

8.1: PERFECT COMPETITION DEFINED

Perfect competition is said to exist in an industry if the following conditions occur:

1. The industry consists of many independent firms. In this way, there is no possibility of collusion among firms to fix prices or restrict output.

2. Every firm produces exactly the same product. This means not only the same physical characteristics, but also such intangibles as product availability and service. Consequently, this excludes industries producing such items as breakfast cereals, toiletries, cosmetics and fast foods, as the member firms "differentiate" their products by advertising and sales promotion.

3. Each firm's output is so small that the firm's output behaviour cannot affect market price. By contrast, if one or just a few firms exist in an industry, they can easily influence industry output or market price.

4. Resources are completely mobile. Workers must be easily able, in the long run, to move from job to job, or from place to place. New firms must be able to enter an industry; old ones, to leave it. Existing production facilities must be capable of being switched from one type of production to another.

5. Firms and consumers must be fully informed. Every firm should be aware of the latest methods of production, the cost of each input, and the state of the market for its products. Workers should know what they can earn in different jobs and in different places. Landowners and financial investors should be fully informed as to possible financial returns on their resources in alternative uses. Consumers should be fully aware of the products available and their relative prices.

Purpose of the Concept

Some industries in Canada—perhaps for example, the production of wheat and other farm products—would, without government intervention, satisfy the first three conditions. These are the closest examples that we have of industries operating under perfect competition. But even in these cases, the existence of government price-support programs and marketing boards means that the third and fourth conditions of perfect competition—no control over market price and no restriction on the movement of resources—are not met.

If no industries operate under perfect competition, as we define it, what is the usefulness of such an economic model? The answer is that the analysis of perfect competition as a market structure reveals how resources would be allocated and market prices set without various market "imperfections," such as product differentiation, resource immobility, poor consumer knowledge, and restrictions on production. It reveals, in other words, what would be the most efficient allocation of resources under perfect conditions. It is particularly useful in helping to understand how output and price are determined in agriculture. It also enables us to see, in the simplest possible setting, how revenue and cost help determine output and even price.

Would perfect competition be the ideal or optimum market situation for a country? Certainly, resource allocation would, under such a market structure, more closely follow the dictates of the consumer as expressed by the price system. Firms would also be under great pressure to use the most efficient methods of production, for high-cost producers would in the long run be forced out of an industry. However, perfect competition would also mean that business firms would be much more vulnerable to competition and that workers at all levels would consequently have much less job security.

8.2: PROFIT MAXIMIZATION

When a firm operates under perfect competition, it can sell all it can produce at the current market price. In other words, demand for its product is perfectly elastic. Whether it produces more or produces less has no effect on market price—because the individual firm's output is too small, compared with that of the industry as a whole, to make any significant impression. Total revenue for such a firm is the number of units produced multiplied by the market price for the industry's product as a whole.

Since the market price is given, all that a firm can do under perfect competition to maximize profit is to alter the amount of its output. The question to answer, therefore, is, "How could such a firm determine its most profitable level of output?"

Marginal Revenue and Marginal Cost

Under perfect competition, marginal revenue is always the same as market price because the price of the good cannot be affected by changes in the individual firm's output. Marginal cost will at first decline. Before long, however, it will rise more and more steeply as the increase in average variable cost more than offsets the decline in average fixed cost, as explained in Chapter 6.

Best-Profit Output

The output at which a firm's profit will be maximized will be that at which marginal revenue equals marginal cost. This best profit level is shown in Table 8:1—at an output of 8 units. At lower levels of production, marginal revenue will be greater than marginal cost. Therefore, the firm can increase its profit by increasing output. Beyond 8 units, marginal cost exceeds marginal revenue. It is more profitable, therefore, to reduce output. The equilibrium position is the output of 8 units where marginal revenue is equal to marginal cost. The best-profit level can also be shown graphically (Figure 8:1).

Table 8:1
Best-Profit Output for a Firm Operating under Perfect Competition

Units of Output	Average Fixed Cost (in dollars)	Average Variable Cost (in dollars)	Average Total Cost (in dollars)	Marginal Cost (in dollars)	Marginal Revenue (price = $90)
0				60	MR > MC
				55	
1	100.00	60.00	160.00	55	
				50	
2	50.00	55.00	105.00	45	
				40	
3	33.33	50.00	83.33	35	
				30	
4	25.00	45.00	70.00	35	
				40	
5	20.00	44.00	64.00	45	
				50	
6	16.67	45.00	61.67	55	
				60	
7	14.29	47.14	61.43	70	
				80	
8	12.50	51.25	63.75	90	MR = MC
				100	
9	11.11	56.67	67.78	115	
				130	
10	10.00	64.00	74.00	145	MR < MC

Note: Average and marginal cost figures are based on total cost data shown in Table 8:3.

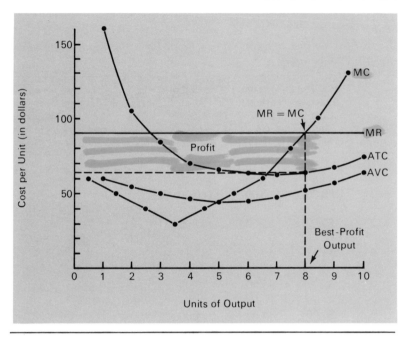

Figure 8:1 Best-Profit Output for a Firm Operating under Perfect Competition

Least-Loss Output

Let us suppose that the market price is reduced. How, by using the marginal revenue and marginal cost method, can we determine the output at which a firm's losses would be minimized? If we look at Table 8:2, we can see that at a market price of $60, the marginal revenue from the first unit of output would only just cover the $60 of marginal cost. However, on each succeeding unit up to 6 units, marginal revenue will exceed marginal cost. At 7 units, marginal revenue will equal marginal cost. And at 8 units and beyond, marginal cost will exceed marginal revenue. Consequently, the firm should produce only 7 units—where MR = MC. At this output, total revenue is $420 (7 × $60); total cost, $430 (7 × $61.43); and total loss, $10. Obviously, in the short run, it is better to produce 7 units for a total loss of $10 than to close down production and incur a loss of $100 (the total fixed cost).

Table 8:2
Least-Loss Output and Shut-down Point for a Firm Operating under Perfect Competition

Units of Output	Average Fixed Cost (in dollars)	Average Variable Cost (in dollars)	Average Total Cost (in dollars)	Marginal Cost (in dollars)	Marginal Revenue (price = $60)	Marginal Revenue (price = $40)
0						
				60	60	40
1	100.00	60.00	160.00			
				50	60	40
2	50.00	55.00	105.00			
				40	60	40
3	33.33	50.00	83.33			
				30	60	40
4	25.00	45.00	70.00			
				40	60	40
5	20.00	44.00	64.00			
				50	60	40
6	16.67	45.00	61.67			
				60	60	40
7	14.29	47.14	61.43			
				80	60	40
8	12.50	51.25	63.75			
				100	60	40
9	11.11	56.67	67.78			
				130	60	40
10	10.00	64.00	74.00			

Shut-Down Point

Suppose that the market price drops even further to $40. If we look at Table 8:2 again, we can see that the average variable cost, whatever the level of output, is always greater than the price per unit. In other words, the price is never sufficient to cover average variable cost, let alone the average fixed cost. It would, therefore, be better for the firm, on purely financial grounds, to halt production. This would be the case at any price less than $44 (the lowest average variable cost). This shut-down situation means that we must slightly modify our previous rule that the optimum output for a firm is where MR = MC. Now we should say that, under perfect competition, a firm will maximize its profit or minimize its loss in the short run by producing that level of output at which price (or marginal revenue) is equal to marginal cost, *so long as the price exceeds the average variable cost.* The shut-down point is, therefore, the point at which P = AVC = MC, as shown in Figure 8:2

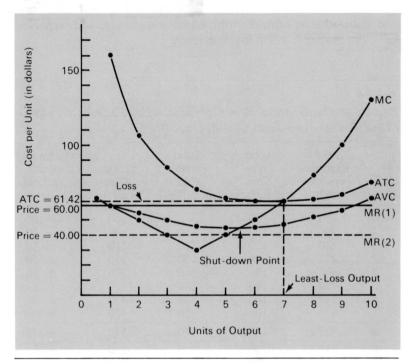

Note: At a price of $60, the least-loss output is 7 units. At this output, total revenue is $420 (7 × $60.00); total cost is $430 (7 × $61.43); and total loss is $10. The price of $60 is greater than the average variable cost ($47.14). The difference of $12.86 goes to help cover the average fixed cost of $14.29. At a price of $40, the firm is financially better off to shut down production. The price cannot even cover the average variable cost. In the chart, the MR line is always below the AVC curve.

Figure 8:2   Shut-Down Point for a Firm Operating under Perfect Competition

8.3: TOTAL-REVENUE AND TOTAL-COST APPROACH

So far in this chapter we have used the marginal-revenue and marginal-cost approach to determine theoretically the output at which a business firm achieves its best profit or least loss, or the point at which it shuts down production. However, the same conclusions can be reached by comparing total revenue and total costs at different levels of output. Thus, in Table 8:3, as an example, we give a hypothetical example of a firm's total revenue and total cost at different levels of output. The total revenue figures are obtained by multiplying the number of units of output by a market price of $90. The total cost figures include normal profit—that is, a rate of return on the owner's time and capital just sufficient to keep the firm in the industry.

Table 8:3
Best-Profit Output for a Firm Operating under Perfect Competition (Total-Revenue and Total-Cost Approach)

Units of Output	Total Revenue (price = $90)	Total Fixed Cost (in dollars)	Total Variable Cost (in dollars)	Total Cost (in dollars)	Economic Profit or Loss (in dollars)
0	0	100	0	100	− 100
1	90	100	60	160	− 70
2	180	100	110	210	− 30
3	270	100	150	250	+ 20
4	360	100	180	280	+ 80
5	450	100	220	320	+130
6	540	100	270	370	+170
7	630	100	330	430	+200
8	720	100	410	510	+210
9	810	100	510	610	+200
10	900	100	640	740	+160

Best-Profit Output

We can readily see that profit, using the total revenue and total cost approach, is maximized at an output of 8 units—where total revenue is $720, total cost $510, and profit $210. At a larger or smaller output, the profit would be less.

8.4: MARKET SUPPLY CURVES

Now that we have seen how a firm, operating under perfect competition, can determine its optimum output at the given market price, we can construct hypothetical market supply schedules and curves for the firm and industry.

The Individual Firm

Given its pattern of production costs, which include normal profit, each individual firm will have a best-profit (or least-loss) output for each different possible market price. An example is given in Table 8:4. These different amounts of a product that a firm would be willing to supply at different prices can be set out in the form of a supply schedule (see Table 8:5). As the price falls, so does the quantity that the firm is willing to supply. Finally, when the price drops below $50, the firm finds it better to produce nothing at all.

Seen from the marginal point of view, a firm will produce up to the point at which marginal revenue equals marginal cost. Since, under perfect competition, marginal revenue is the same as price, an individual firm's marginal cost curve will therefore be its supply curve. There

---

Table 8:4
Best-Profit or Least-Loss Output at Different Market Prices for a Firm Operating under Perfect Competition

| Units of Output | Economic Profit or Loss in Dollars at the Following Different Market Prices | | | | | | | |
	$100	$90	$80	$70	$60	$50	$40	$30
0	− 100	− 100	− 100	− 100	− 100	− 100	− 100	− 100
1	− 60	− 70	− 80	− 90	− 100	− 110	− 120	− 130
2	− 10	− 30	− 50	− 70	− 90	− 110	− 130	− 150
3	+ 50	+ 20	− 10	− 40	− 70	− 100	− 130	− 160
4	+120	+ 80	+ 40	0	− 40	− 80	− 120	− 160
5	+180	+130	+ 80	+ 30	− 20	− 70	− 120	− 170
6	+230	+170	+110	+ 50	− 10	− 70	− 130	− 190
7	+270	+200	+130	+ 60	− 10	− 80	− 150	− 220
8	+290	+210	+130	+ 50	− 30	− 110	− 190	− 270
9	+290	+200	+110	+ 20	− 70	− 160	− 250	− 340
10	+260	+160	+ 60	− 40	− 140	− 240	− 340	− 440

Note: Obtained by subtracting total cost from total revenue at the different market prices. Total cost is obtained from Table 8:3. Total revenue is the number of units of output multiplied by each different price.

is one qualification to be made, however. This observation is only true for that part of the MC curve that is above the AVC curve. For, as we saw earlier, once the marginal revenue is less than the average variable cost, a firm will be better off to shut down rather than to continue producing. The short-run supply curve, based on the MC curve, is shown in Figure 8:3. This curve slopes upward from left to right to show that the firm will supply more of the good at a higher price than it will at a low price.

Table 8:5
The Individual Firm's Supply Schedule

Market Price	Units of Output
100	8.5
90	8
80	7.5
70	7
60	6.5
50	5.5
40	0
30	0
20	0
10	0
0	0

Source: Based on data in Table 8:4.

The Industry

To obtain the industry's short-run supply curve, all we need to do is to combine the supply data for each individual firm. Thus in Table 8:6, we show the amount of a good that would be supplied at different prices by one individual firm and the amount that would be supplied by one hundred individual firms put together.

8.5: FIRM AND INDUSTRY EQUILIBRIUM

We know that under perfect competition an individual firm's output has no influence on market price. But the industry's output as a whole can, of course, affect it. What can happen to market price and output in the short and long run? What is the equilibrium situation?

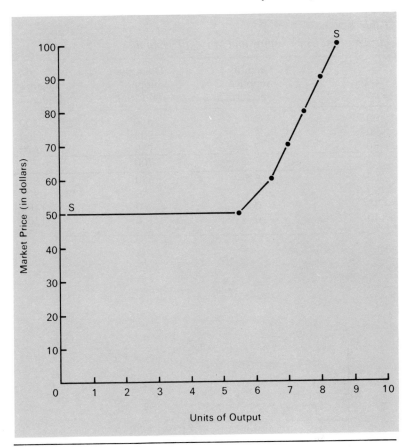

Note: At a market price of less than $50, output will be zero since the price will be less than average variable cost.

Source: Based on data from Table 8:5.

Figure 8:3   The Individual Firm's Supply Curve

Short Run

In the short run, every firm in the industry has fixed production costs. A firm can, it is true, shut down production and thereby eliminate variable costs, but it cannot escape its fixed costs. The equilibrium output and price will therefore be where the industry's supply curve and the market demand curve for that product intersect. This is shown in Table 8:6 and Figure 8:4 at a price of $70 and an output of 700 units.

Table 8:6
Firm and Industry Supply and Market Demand

Market Price	Quantity Supplied One Firm	Quantity Supplied 100 Firms	Quantity Demanded
100	8.5	850	400
90	8	800	500
80	7.5	750	600
70	7	700	700
60	6.5	650	800
50	5.5	550	900
40	0	0	1100
30	0	0	1300

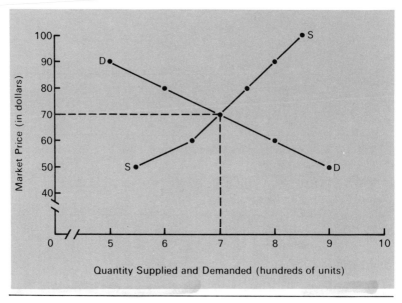

Note: The short-run equilibrium price and output for the industry are $70 and 700 units respectively. The individual firm produces the best-profit (or least-loss) output possible with this market price.

Figure 8:4   Industry Short-Run Equilibrium Output and Price

Long Run

In the long run, a firm can reorganize or re-equip its plan to reduce its costs or switch to the production of something else. Sometimes this will be done by a new owner. In the long run, therefore, no firm has fixed costs. All production costs are variable. If a firm does not find it profitable to produce, it will have had sufficient time to leave the industry. In the long run also, other firms, armed with a lower cost structure, will have had time to enter the industry.

This complete mobility of resources (one of the characteristics of perfect competition) has important implications for our discussion of long-run equilibrium. Combined with the fact that business firms seek to maximize economic profit (or minimize loss), it means that eventually, as a result of all this movement in and out of the industry, every firm that remains will produce up to the point at which its marginal revenue (price) is equal not only to its marginal cost but also to minimum average total cost. If this were not so, firms in the industry would still make a loss and other firms outside could still enter and make a normal profit.

Here we should remind ourselves that, in economics, total cost includes normal profit. The surplus of total revenue over this total cost is called *pure profit*. In the long-run equilibrium situation, there will be no pure profit. The entry of new firms, each competing for a share of the market, will have eliminated it. Conversely, if market demand were to fall, causing a drop in market price, firms which could not make a normal profit would either leave the industry or reduce their output capacity. The long-run equilibrium would once more be the situation in which each individual firm earns only normal profit.

Constant Versus Increasing Costs

We have said previously that the equilibrium market price would be re-established at its former level. This assumes, however, that the entry of new firms into an industry, or the departure of old ones from it, would have no effect on cost structures—in other words, that the industry enjoys constant costs.

If this is the case (and it is quite possible if the industry does not use a large portion of total available resources), the long-run industry supply curve would be perfectly elastic and would appear as a horizontal line. A change in demand would not alter the market price.

In most cases, however, an industry cannot indefinitely increase supply without bidding up the price of its inputs. Consequently, an

162 / Part C: Theory of the Firm

industry usually has an upward-sloping long-run supply curve. This means that a change in demand will cause a change in the equilibrium market price even after firms have entered or left the industry.

Summary

1. Perfect competition exists when: (a) an industry consists of many independent firms; (b) every firm produces exactly the same product; (c) each firm believes that it cannot affect market price because its output is so small; (d) resources are completely mobile; and (e) firms and consumers are fully informed.

2. The main value of analyzing perfect competition as a market structure is that it reveals how resources would be allocated and market prices set without various market "imperfections," such as product differentiation, resource immobility, poor knowledge, and restrictions on production. It is questionable whether perfect competition would be a desirable market structure for a country.

3. Since the market price is given, all a firm can do under perfect competition to maximize pure profit is to alter the amount of its output.

4. A firm can theoretically determine its best profit output, its least-loss output, or its shut-down point by comparing its marginal revenue with its marginal cost. Under perfect competition, a firm will maximize its pure profit (or minimize its loss) in the short run by producing that level of output at which price (marginal revenue) is equal to marginal cost—as long as the market price exceeds the firm's average variable cost of production. Total revenue can also be compared with total costs.

5. Given its pattern of production costs, which include normal profit, each individual firm will have a best-profit (or least-loss) output for each different possible market price. Since a firm will produce up to the point at which marginal revenue (price) equals marginal cost, the individual firm's marginal cost curve will in effect be its supply curve. The supply data for each individual firm can be combined to obtain the industry's short-run supply curve.

6. Although the individual firm's output has no influence on market price, the industry's output can affect it. The industry's output and price are in equilibrium when the industry's supply curve and the market demand curve for the product intersect. In the long run, since movement in and out of an industry is possible, no firm will earn more than normal profit. Each firm will produce up to the

point at which marginal revenue (price) is equal not only to marginal cost but also to minimum average total cost.
7. If market demand increases, pure profit may be earned until the entry of new firms and the enlargement of existing ones eliminate it. The long-run equilibrium would once more be where each individual firm earns only normal profit.

Key Terms

Perfect competition   149
Marginal revenue   151
Marginal cost   151
Best-profit output   152
Least-loss output   153
Shut-down point   154
Total revenue   155

Total costs   156
Short-run supply   159
Equilibrium output   159
Mobility of resources   161
Pure profit   161
Constant costs   161
Increasing costs   161

Review Questions

1. What is the significance of each of the following conditions of perfect competition?
   (a) many independent firms
   (b) exactly the same product
   (c) each firm's output is small
   (d) completely mobile resources
   (e) full information.
2. To what extent does perfect competition exist in Canada?
3. What is the purpose of the concept of perfect competition?
4. Is perfect competition a desirable situation for a country? Justify your answer.
5. Since the market price is given, what can a firm operating under perfect competition do to maximize its profit?
6. How can a firm theoretically determine its most profitable level of output?
7. In economics, a firm's total cost figures include normal profit. Explain.
8. Why would a firm operate at a loss?
9. What is meant by a firm's shut-down point? When does this occur?
10. The output at which a firm's profit is maximized is where the

marginal revenue equals marginal cost. Explain.

11. A firm's shut-down point is where P = AVC = MC. Explain,

12. Since, under perfect competition, marginal revenue is the same as price, an individual firm's marginal cost curve will in effect be its supply curve. Explain.

13. What will be the equilibrium output and price for an industry as a whole?

14. What implications does the assumption of complete mobility of resources have for the long-run equilibrium of an industry?

15. What is the significance, in our discussion of long-run industry equilibrium, of the assumption of constant costs?

9. PURE MONOPOLY: THE SOLE SUPPLIER

CHAPTER OBJECTIVES

A. To explain what is a "pure monopoly"
B. To identify the reasons why monopolies exist
C. To examine the nature of the demand for a monopolist's product
D. To indicate how a monopolist decides how much to produce
E. To explain why a monopolist may engage in price discrimination
F. To discuss how monopoly power can be abused
G. To show what can happen when government regulates a private monopoly

CHAPTER OUTLINE

The economic model of the marketplace that we have just examined (perfect competition) was characterized by one very important fact. The firms in an industry are so many in number and so small in relative size that each by itself is powerless to influence market price. Our present task is to consider the opposite case—a situation in which there is only one firm instead of many and in which the market price, as a consequence, is directly influenced by changes in that firm's output.

The name given to this situation is *pure monopoly*. By first examining the two market extremes—perfect competition and pure monopoly—we shall be in a much better position to understand, in the next two chapters, the type of market structure in which most businesses in Canada actually operate.

9.1: MONOPOLY DEFINED

A *pure monopoly* (also called *complete, absolute,* or *exclusive monopoly*) exists where there is only one firm supplying a product and where there are no close substitutes for this product. By close substitute, we mean a product that a consumer could easily use instead of the one supplied by the single firm. Thus, if one firm produced and supplied all refrigerators, this would be a pure monopoly, for there is no close substitute except perhaps the long-forgotten icebox. The single firm that enjoys this monopoly power is known as a *monopolist*—from the Greek words *mono* for "one" and *polist* for "seller."

In Canada, numerous examples of pure monopolists are to be found, often in key industries. Thus, for instance, there are the provincial and municipal public utility commissions supplying electricity and water, and privately owned firms supplying natural gas, cable television, and telephone services.

Monopoly power, as the previous examples suggest, has its limitations. Even though we may consider that the supplier of electricity has an absolute monopoly, there could come a point (if the price of electricity were raised high enough) when consumers would either do without or turn to something else (such as candles or gas mantles for lighting) that we do not normally regard as a close substitute. Even the post office, which has a legal monopoly on mail delivery, can lose business if its prices are too high or its service too inefficient. Some firms may find it cheaper (if permitted by law) to deliver their own mail, contract the work out to hand-delivery firms, or switch to other forms of data transmission.

9.2: REASONS FOR MONOPOLY

There are several different reasons why monopolies come into existence. These are now discussed in turn.

Ownership of Key Raw Materials

One firm may own or control the supply of an essential raw material used in a manufacturing process. Thus the International Nickel Company of Canada once owned most of the world's known nickel ore reserves. However, new mines in Australia, Central America and Indonesia have changed this picture. More recently the OPEC oil cartel has acted in monopoly fashion.

Government Decree

In return for a substantial fee, or for reasons of public policy, including the raising of additional revenue, governments sometimes grant an exclusive franchise to a private firm or government agency to operate a particular business or to import a certain type of good. It thereby becomes illegal for any other firm to carry on the same business in that area, which often extends over a whole country. Thus the Hudson's Bay Company was given the exclusive right by the British monarch to carry on the fur trade in a substantial portion of Canada. In modern times, the retailing of liquor in most of Canada is governed in this way. Historically such monopolies, like the fur trade, were the monarch's way of rewarding his or her courtiers or a way of raising funds for the monarch's use. Today, the usual justification for the award of monopoly powers is that only one firm can logically provide such a service—for example, a municipal transit system. Competition by several firms would be a wasteful duplication of facilities. Usually, if the firm is not government-owned, the government specifies the area to be served and regulates the rates to be charged. It can no longer be said that monopolies are usually goverment-run to protect the public from being overcharged for a good or service—as many Crown corporations and other government agencies such as Canada Post or Air Canada now charge the public just as much, if not more, than privately owned firms for the goods or services provided. And in the case of wine, beer, and liquor retailing, such monopolies are an important source of provincial revenue.

Sales Franchise

An exclusive franchise may also be conferred by one private firm on another—as with a fast-food sales franchise, which gives the franchisee the exclusive right to use a particular firm's name, logo, techniques etc. in a given geographical area. A popular example is McDonald's.

Patent Rights

A third possible reason for the existence of a monopoly is that a firm may have the patent rights on a particular product or manufacturing process—for example, certain pharmaceutical drugs. Copyrights on books may also be considered to grant a monopoly to the publisher.

Economies of Scale

A fourth and very important reason for the existence of monopolies is the reduction in the average cost of production per unit of output that results from large-scale or "mass" production. These "economies of scale," explained earlier, may be so great that a firm can afford, by price undercutting, to put all its competitors out of business. This battle for "survival of the fittest" leaves only one firm in the industry. Also, the lower average production costs of the survivor may effectively deter any new competitors.

There must, of course, be sufficient demand to justify large-scale production. If a firm cannot sell all of its output, the benefit of any cost reduction disappears.

9.3: DEMAND FOR A MONOPOLIST'S PRODUCT

We saw that, under perfect competition, the demand for an individual firm's output is perfectly elastic. In other words, the individual firm can supply as much of the product as it likes without affecting the market price. Such a firm's marginal revenue is, therefore, the same as the market price. Only changes in the output of the industry as a whole can disturb the equilibrium market price.

For a monopolist, the situation is quite different. The individual firm is in such a case the entire industry. And the demand curve for its products is therefore also the market-demand curve. As such, it is downward-sloping rather than horizontal. This means that the monopolist will be able to sell more of its product only by charging a lower price. Demand is no longer perfectly elastic.

9.4: BEST-PROFIT OUTPUT

How does a monopolist, faced with a downward-sloping demand curve, determine the best-profit output? Less can be charged and more sold, or more can be charged and less sold. But the monopolist cannot have the best of both worlds: price and output cannot *both* be set, because market demand for the product imposes constraints.

Thus, as in Figure 9:1. the monopolist may decide to charge $4.00 for the product, but only 50000 units can be sold. Or the monopolist may decide to sell 100000 units, but must therefore accept a market price of $2.00 each for them. Given the nature of market demand, 100 000 units cannot be sold at $4.00 each.

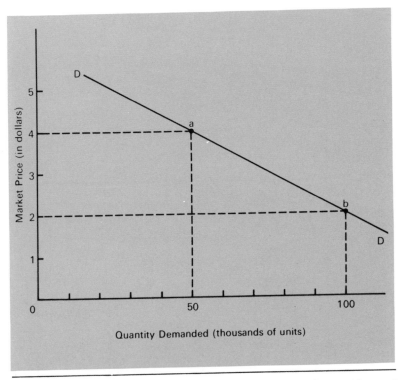

Figure 9:1 The Monopolist Can Set Either Price or Output, but not Both

Elasticity of Demand

Being the sole supplier of a product, the monopolist can, if it so desires, restrict output. However, whether it can gain a monopoly profit (in addition to normal profit) by doing so, will depend partly on the price-elasticity of demand for the product. The more inelastic that demand is, the greater the chance of such a profit—for an inelastic demand means that a reduction in supply will cause a more than proportionate increase in market price and therefore an increase in total revenue. Conversely, an elastic demand means that a reduction in supply will cause a less than proportionate increase in price and therefore a decrease in total revenue.

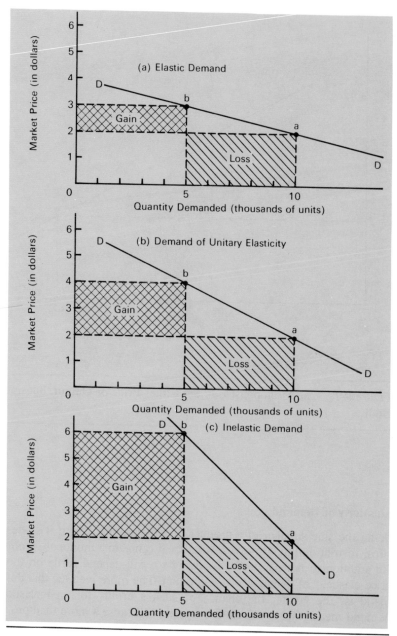

Figure 9:2 How Elasticity of Demand Affects a Monopolist's Total Revenue

Let us suppose, for example, that a monopolist now supplies 10000 units of product A at a market price of $2.00 each. In Figure 9:2 we show three different market demand curves for the same product. Now suppose that the monopolist reduces output by 5000 units. In Figure 9:2(a) where demand is elastic, the price will rise only to $3.00. Total revenue will decline from $20000 ($2 × 10000 units) to $15000 ($3 × 5000 units). In Figure 9:2(b) where demand is of unitary-elasticity, the price will rise to $4.00. As a result, total revenue will remain at $20000 ($4 × 5000 units). In Figure 9:2(c) where demand is inelastic, the reduction in output by 5000 units will cause the price to rise to $6.00.

Demand, we have seen, determines the market price that a monopolist can obtain for its product at different levels of output. Depending on the elasticity of this demand, total revenue may be greater at a higher or lower price. However, before deciding how much to produce, a monopolist must also take into account the costs of production. With enough knowledge of market demand and costs of production, a monopolist could compare total revenue with total cost or marginal revenue with marginal cost to determine its best-profit output.

Total-Revenue and Total-Cost Approach

Using the total-revenue and total-cost approach, the monopolist would, in our example (Table 9:1), gain maximum profit at an output of 6 units, at which total revenue is $540 and total cost is $370.

Table 9:1
Determining the Monopolist's Best-Profit Output
(Total-Revenue and Total-Cost Approach)

Units of Output	Market Price (in dollars)	Total Revenue (in dollars)	Total Cost (in dollars)	Economic Profit or Loss (in dollars)
0		0	100	− 100
1	115	115	160	− 45
2	110	220	210	+ 10
3	105	315	250	+ 65
4	100	400	280	+120
5	95	475	320	+155
6	90	540	370	+170
7	85	595	430	+165
8	80	640	510	+130
9	75	675	610	+ 65
10	70	700	740	− 40

Marginal-Revenue and Marginal-Cost Approach

The monopolist can also determine the best-profit output by comparing marginal revenue with marginal cost. Since the monopolist can only sell more by charging a lower price, it follows that marginal revenue (unlike the situation in pure competition) is *not* the same as market price. The marginal revenue will, in fact, be the price received for the last unit of output *minus* the reduction in revenue on all the other units, which are now sold for less. Therefore, the marginal revenue curve will diverge from the demand curve. The demand curve for the monopolist's output (see Figure 9:3) will also be the average revenue curve.

The monopolist, just like a firm in a competitive market structure, will attempt to maximize profit by producing extra units of output so long as the additional revenue exceeds the additional cost. We can see, therefore, in Table 9:2, that the monopolist's best-profit position (where MR = MC) is 6 units. At any other level of output, there will

Table 9:2
Determining the Monopolist's Best-Profit Output
(Marginal-Revenue and Marginal-Cost Approach)

Units of Output	Market Price	Average Variable Cost (in dollars)	Average Total Cost (in dollars)	Marginal Revenue (in dollars)	Marginal Cost (in dollars)	MR : MC
1	115	60.00	160.00	115	60	MR > MC
2	110	55.00	105.00	105	50	
3	105	50.00	83.33	95	40	
4	100	45.00	70.00	85	30	
5	95	44.00	64.00	75	40	
6	90	45.00	61.67	65	50	
7	85	47.14	61.43	55	60	
8	80	51.25	63.75	45	80	
9	75	56.67	67.78	35	100	
10	70	64.00	74.00	25	130	MR < MC

Note: Because of the indivisibility of units of output, marginal revenue exceeds marginal cost at best-profit output.

Source: Marginal-revenue and marginal-cost data are derived from Table 9:1.

be less profit, or even a loss. This situation can also be shown graphically. Thus, in Figure 9:3, we can see that the nearest complete unit of additional output at which marginal revenue equals marginal cost is 6. If we were to have used fractions of units in Table 9:2, the best-profit output would have been slightly more.

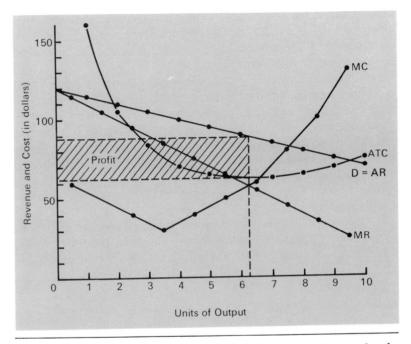

Figure 9:3 Determining the Monopolist's Best-Profit Output by the Marginal-Revenue and Marginal-Cost Approach

9.5: LEAST-LOSS OUTPUT

Although it may enjoy a monopoly position, a firm has no guarantee that it will make a profit. Perhaps consumers are not interested in the product. Or perhaps the item costs too much to produce compared with the price at which it can be sold. There are patents on many new products and processes in Canada for which there is no worthwhile demand. Obviously, in such cases, a firm does not even begin production. It is only worthwhile to enter into production if average revenue is expected permanently to exceed average total cost.

But let us suppose that a monopolist has been supplying a product for some time and is starting to make a loss. The reason for this could be that labour and material costs have increased or that market demand, because of a change in consumer tastes, has declined. What should the monopolist do? In the short run, just like the competitive firm, the monopolist is saddled with the fixed cost of plant and equipment. Thus, it has an incentive in the short run to keep producing so long as the variable cost of production and some part of the fixed cost can be covered. The problem then is to determine the output at which the loss would be minimized.

Let us assume that the monopolist's costs are the same as in our previous example, but that the market price is much lower. Using the total-revenue and total-cost approach, we can see in Table 9:3, that the least-loss output would be 4 units: where total revenue is $220; total cost, $280; and total loss, $60. Obviously, it is financially better for the monopolist to produce 4 units for a total loss of $60 than to produce nothing at all for a loss (the fixed cost) of $100. This situation can also be illustrated in Figure 9:3 by having the ATC curve lie entirely above the demand curve.

In the long run, rather than continue to make a loss, the monopolist would cease production. To continue production, the total revenue must at least be equal to total cost (which includes normal profit).

Table 9:3
Determining the Monopolist's Least-Loss Output
(Total-Revenue and Total-Cost Approach)

Units of Output	Market Price (in dollars)	Total Revenue (in dollars)	Total Cost (in dollars)	Profit or Loss (in dollars)
0	75	0	100	−100
1	70	70	160	− 90
2	65	130	210	− 80
3	60	180	250	− 70
4	55	220	280	− 60
5	50	250	320	− 70
6	45	270	370	−100
7	40	280	430	−150
8	35	280	510	−230
9	30	270	610	−340
10	25	250	740	−490

9.6: PRICE DISCRIMINATION

Usually, a monopolist will charge everyone the same price for the product. However, in certain circumstances, the monopolist may engage in *price discrimination*, charging different prices to different groups of consumers for exactly the same product. Thus, for example, a movie theatre may charge $8.00 for a seat for the first week's showing of a new film and only half that amount later on. The two markets are separated by time. Airline, bus, and railway fares, railway freight rates, and utility charges, may also vary according to time or user. A monopoly firm which practises price discrimination, is called in economics a *discriminating monopolist*.

What are the circumstances that might encourage a monopolist to become a *discriminating monopolist*? First, buyers of the product must consist of separate groups—for example, different income groups. Second, buyers of the product should not be able to transfer it easily from one group to the other; otherwise, members of the group that buy the product at the lower price might sell it to those being charged a higher price and so make it impossible for the monopolist to maintain a price differential. Third, each group of buyers (because of different incomes, different tastes, or different availability of substitutes) should have a different elasticity of demand for the product.

Let us now see, with an example, how a monopolist can benefit from

Table 9:4
A Monopolist's Total Revenue and Total Costs

Units of Output	Market Price (in dollars)	Total Revenue (in dollars)	Total Cost (in dollars)	Pure Profit or Loss (in dollars)
1	115	115	170	−55
2	110	220	240	−20
3	105	315	280	+35
4	100	400	350	+50
5	95	475	415	+60
6	90	540	470	+70
7	85	595	555	+40
8	80	640	630	+10
9	75	675	695	−20
10	70	700	740	−40

price discrimination. Table 9:4 shows how a monopolist's revenue and costs might vary with changes in output. The best-profit output would be 6 units sold at a market price of $90 each. Pure profit at this point would be $70. To sell 10 units instead of 6, the price would have to be reduced to $70. This means that total revenue would increase by $160, while total cost would increase by $270. As a result, pure profit would decline by $110, and the monopolist would be worse off.

Suppose, however, that the monopolist continued to sell 6 units in the first market for $90 each (the best-profit output), but sold 4 additional units in another market. Then, so long as more revenue than the additional cost of producing the 4 units can be obtained, total profit has increased. Since this additional cost is $270, each unit must be sold at more than $67.50. If a price of $75 can be obtained, our discriminating monopolist will have increased the total profit to $100 from the original $70. Whereas total revenue is now $840 (6 units at $90 = $540, plus 4 units at $75 = $300), total cost is only $740.

The monopolist's optimum allocation of output between the two (or more) markets will be where marginal revenue in each market is equal to marginal cost. Until this situation exists, it would be profitable for the monopolist to alter the allocation. Supply will in fact be smaller and the price higher in the market in which demand is more inelastic.

By price discrimination, a monopolist is able to increase profit at the expense of the "consumer's surplus". Thus if, for example, some people are willing to pay $8.00 to see a new movie, the monopolist can charge this price until those people have seen the film. Then $4.00 can be charged to the people who would only be willing to pay this lower amount. By not charging $4.00 from the start, the monopolist has prevented people who would have paid $8.00 from paying only $4.00.

One important example of price discrimination between different markets is the sale of a product in the home (or domestic) market at one price and the sale of the product abroad at a lower one. So long as the foreign price exceeds the variable cost of production, a manufacturer who sells mainly to the home market can profit by this practice. The monopolist has already incurred the fixed costs of production, such as plant and equipment, administration, and research and development, and any extra sales will help pay for them. If the price abroad is less than the home market price, the foreign countries which receive the goods may label such export sales as "dumping" and impose anti-dumping import duties to bring the foreign price up to the Canadian price. Often, to make price discrimination less apparent, a monopolist will try to differentiate the product by name, packaging, or other means.

9.7: POSSIBLE ABUSES OF MONOPOLY POWER

Being the sole supplier of a product, a monopolist has considerable economic power. Just how great this power is will depend on the nature of market demand. If demand is very inelastic (that is to say, a change in price will cause little change in the quantity demanded), the monopolist is in a position to charge a high price for the product. This is the case in Canada with sales of liquor by provincially-owned liquor boards. Unlike a firm operating under conditions of perfect competition, the monopolist is able, by restricting the supply, to obtain pure profit, even in the long run.

Of course, for many products, there is a limit beyond which the monopolist cannot push the price. If the price becomes too high or the supply becomes too small, other products that were not previously considered close substitutes will start to be used instead.

If demand is very elastic (because consumers, rather than pay a high price, would prefer to do without or substitute something else), the monopolist's power is much more limited.

There are other reasons, too, why a monopolist does not have a completely free hand in its pricing and output behaviour. It may, for example, be anxious to avoid adverse publicity. Also, if it abuses its monopoly power by raising prices exorbitantly, it may cause so much public uproar that the government may be tempted to step in. Of course, in Canada, most monopolies providing essential services to the public are already government-owned or regulated. This does, to some extent, help prevent the consumer from being exploited, except by government. Another factor that may help persuade a monopolist to seek less than maximum profit is the possibility of encouraging possible rivals. If, for example, a firm which controls the major sources of a particular mineral ore raises its price too much, mining exploration to find alternative sources of supply will be intensified. In the long run, if the incentive is sufficiently great, most monopolies can be overcome. One classic example was the development of synthetic rubber to replace high-cost natural rubber. Another was the replacement of natural pearls by Japanese cultured pearls.

From society's point of view, the major criticism of monopoly, compared with perfect competition, is that it leads to inefficient allocation of resources. Consumers are prevented from having as much of the monopoly product as they would like. Also, they usually have to pay more for it. This is because average production costs are higher than they would otherwise be and because monopoly profit (in addition to normal profit) is obtained by the monopolist.

Another serious criticism of monopolies is the misplaced political power that can accompany the concentration of economic power.

9.8: REGULATED MONOPOLY

We have seen that a monopolist will charge a higher price and produce less than if subject to competition. Thus, in Figure 9:4 monopoly price and output (determined by the intersection of the MR and MC curves) are OP_1 and OQ_1 respectively. If there were perfect competition, output would increase up to the point at which market price equals marginal cost. In Figure 9:4, this would be where output is OQ_2 and price OP_2. Consequently, to ensure that a monopolist supplies more of the product and to improve the allocation of a country's resources, government could impose a maximum price of OP_2. This would, in effect, make the monopolist's demand curve P_2AD rather than DD. Unfortunately, however, this government-regulated maximum price would cause the monopolist a loss since average cost per unit at OQ_2 output exceeds

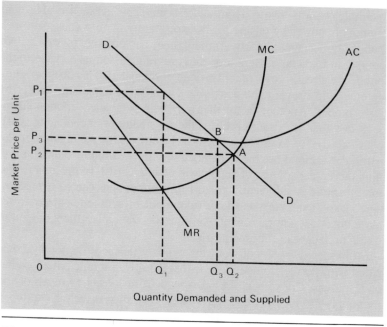

Figure 9:4   Regulated Monopoly and a "Fair Return" Price

market price. To be fair to the monopolist (for example, a public utility) and provide normal profit, the maximum price should cover the average cost. Therefore, the desirable government-regulated price should be OP_3. At this "fair return" price, output will be OQ_3, which is still much more than if the monopolist were left unregulated. As an alternative, the government may insist that the monopolist charge no more than the price OP_2, but make up the difference in the form of a subsidy, as is often done, for example, with government-controlled ferry services.

Summary

1. A *pure monopoly* exists when: (a) there is only one firm supplying a good; and (b) there are no close substitutes for it. The firm is called a *monopolist*.
2. Most of the monopolies in Canada are government-owned or government-regulated.
3. The basic reason for the existence of a monopoly is that no other firms are able to enter the industry. Barriers to entry include: (a) ownership of key raw materials; (b) government decree (c) sales franchise; (d) patent rights; and (e) economies of scale already achieved by the monopolist.
4. With a monopoly, the individual firm is the entire industry. Therefore, the demand curve for the monopolist's product is downward-sloping—rather than horizontal as with perfect competition—indicating that the monopolist can sell more only if the monopolist lowers the price of the good.
5. The monopolist can set *either* market price *or* the amount sold, but not both price *and* output because constraints are imposed by the market demand for the product.
6. Whether a monopolist can gain a *monopoly profit* (in addition to normal profit) by restricting output will depend partly on the price-elasticity of demand for the product. The more inelastic is the demand, the greater the chance of such profit.
7. The monopolist can theoretically determine its best-profit output by comparing total revenue with total cost, or marginal revenue with marginal cost. Unlike perfect competition, where marginal revenue equals market price, the *marginal revenue of the monopolist* is the price received for the last unit of output *minus* the reduction in revenue on all the other units, which are now sold for less.
8. In the short run, a monopolist may continue operating at a loss, so

long as the variable costs of production as well as some part of the fixed cost can be covered. In the long run, to continue production, the total revenue must at least be equal to total cost (which includes normal profit).

9. Sometimes, a monopolist will charge different prices to different groups of consumers for exactly the same product. A *discriminating monopolist* is most likely to exist if: (a) buyers consist of clearly separate groups; (b) the product cannot be easily transferred from one group to another; and (c) each group has a different elasticity of demand for the product. The discriminating monopolist's optimum allocation of output between the various markets will be where marginal revenue in each market is equal to marginal cost. By price discrimination, a monopolist is able to increase profit at the expense of the consumer's surplus.

10. A monopolist is restricted in its ability to abuse its economic position. In addition to the elasticity of market demand, there is government ownership and regulation. The major economic criticism of monopoly is that it leads to inefficient allocation of a country's resources.

11. To ensure greater output by a monopolist and so improve the allocation of a country's resources, government could impose a maximum price for the monopolist's product. This maximum should be set at a level that would enable the monopolist to cover the average cost per unit and so earn normal profit.

Key Terms

Pure monopoly   166
Monopolist   166
Key raw materials   166
Government monopoly   167
Sales franchise   167
Patent rights   167
Economies of scale   168
Best-profit output   168

Elasticity of demand   169
Least-loss output   173
Price discrimination   175
Discriminating monopolist   175
Consumer's surplus   176
Dumping   176
Abuses of monopoly power   177
Regulated monopoly   178

Review Questions

1. What are the characteristics of a pure monopoly?
2. To what extent do monopolies exist in Canada? Give three examples.

3. How do monopolies originate?
4. Describe and explain the nature of the demand curve for a monopolist's product.
5. What control does a monopolist have over the price and amount sold of the product?
6. How does the elasticity of demand for a product help determine the opportunity for monopoly profit?
7. What factors must a monopolist take into account when determining best-profit output?
8. What is the relationship in pure monopoly, between marginal revenue and market price?
9. A monopoly position automatically ensures that a firm makes a profit. Comment.
10. Explain how a monopolist might benefit from price discrimination.
11. What controls exist to prevent the abuse of monopoly power?
12. What are the major criticisms of monopoly power?
13. In regulating a monopoly, government should set a maximum market price for the product that will ensure the same output as under perfect competition. Comment.
14. Why might a government subsidize a monopolist? —TO LOWER PRICE

10. MONOPOLISTIC COMPETITION: MANY FIRMS BUT DIFFERENTIATED PRODUCTS

CHAPTER OBJECTIVES

A. To explain what is meant by product differentiation
B. To define monopolistic competition
C. To analyze the nature of demand for a monopolistic competitor's product, as compared with perfect competition and pure monopoly
D. To explain how output and price are determined in the short run and long run
E. To indicate how non-price competition affects the previous analysis
F. To examine the effects of product differentiation from the consumer's point of view

CHAPTER OUTLINE

So far we have looked at the two extreme forms of market structure—perfect competition and pure monopoly. In practice, most firms are neither perfectly competitive nor purely monopolistic.

10.1: PRODUCT DIFFERENTIATION

Most industries, it is true, consist of many firms in competition with each other. However, although the various firms may produce basically the same good or service (for example, cameras or the services of a travel agent) the product is not exactly the same, which is one of the conditions of perfect competition. Consumers will, for example, prefer one make of camera or one firm of travel agent over another, even though they may cost the same. The reason for this is that most firms, although making basically the same product as their competitors, try to make their own product distinctive—for example, by differences in packaging, by use of brand-name advertising, by better service, and so on. All these efforts are aimed at achieving what is called *product differentiation*.

There is a limit, nevertheless, beyond which a firm cannot go in trying to make its product "unique" and so confer on itself monopoly power. Whatever the amount of product differentiation, consumers will usually switch to another similar product made by a rival firm if the price of the original product is raised too much. Thus, no firm can create for itself conditions of pure monopoly. However, successful product differentiation can make the demand curve for a firm's product more inelastic than it would otherwise be. And in, say, the case of a plastic surgeon or other person with special skills who has devoted customers, the demand curve may be almost vertical—meaning that practically any price may be charged without loss of customers.

To provide a better explanation of how most firms actually behave than do the theories of perfect competition and pure monopoly, a new theory—that of monopolistic competition—was advanced in the 1930s.

10.2: MONOPOLISTIC COMPETITION DEFINED

Monopolistic competition is a market situation in which the following conditions are present.

1. There are many firms, each of which is responsible for only a relatively small part of total supply. This means that each firm can act without much fear of retaliation by other rival firms, in the form either of price-cutting or of non-price competition.

2. Each firm's product, although basically the same, is not identical to that of the other firms in the industry. If some measure of monopolistic power is to be obtained, a firm must be able to differentiate its product from that of its competitors. The firm can achieve this in many ways: for example, by use of a brand, distinctive packaging, effective advertising, good sales techniques, availability of credit, good location of sales outlets, and satisfactory after-sales service.

3. Each firm has only a limited ability to raise the price of its product without losing sales. Through product differentiation, each firm can build its own loyal clientele. But if the price is raised too much, customers will eventually switch to another, cheaper brand.

A *brand* is a general term which includes any name, symbol, design, or combination of these, used to identify some or all of the goods of a particular manufacturer or retailer. The term *brand name* refers to any word or letters contained in the brand and which can be vocalized. *Brand mark* or *trademark* is another name for the symbol used in the brand.

4. New firms can enter the industry. However, entry is more difficult than under perfect competition because the new firm has to compete with firms that have already built brand or store loyalties among the buying public. The new firm will have to spend a great deal on advertising, samples, and other forms of sales promotion to entice consumers away from existing firms. It may also have to invest considerably in research and development to ensure that its product will have a competitive edge over similar products already on the market.

The most important example of monopolistic competition in Canada is the retailing industry. Although there are many firms in each particular line—drug stores, gift shops, flower shops, dry cleaners, restaurants, travel agents, and so on—consumers usually have a definite preference for one store or firm rather than another. This may be because of price differences, but more often because of convenience of location, credit and delivery facilities, or quality of service. And each firm, through advertising, store appearance, and customer service, constantly tries to make itself even more distinct from its competitors.

10.3: DEMAND FOR A MONOPOLISTIC COMPETITOR'S OUTPUT

As we saw in Chapter 8, demand for a firm's output is perfectly elastic when the firm is operating under conditions of perfect competition. A firm can sell as much as it wants without affecting the price. The demand curve is perfectly horizontal. Under pure monopoly, however, the firm *is* the industry and the demand for its products is the aggregate or market demand. So the amount that the monopolist supplies of its product will directly influence the market price. The monopolist can only sell substantially more of its product if it lowers the price significantly. The demand curve for the product is, in other words, downward-sloping from left to right.

By comparison, the demand curve for the product of a firm operating under monopolistic competition is certainly not perfectly elastic. This is because such a firm will have to lower its price to draw customers away from competitors. However, since such a firm is still only one among many suppliers, it does not have to reduce the price drastically (as would a pure monopolist) to encourage consumers to buy more. Conversely, if such a firm were to raise its price, it would soon lose its customers.

In conclusion, we can say that the demand for the product of a firm operating under conditions of monopolistic competition is quite price elastic—not perfectly elastic as under perfect competition but more elastic than under pure monopoly. We can also say that the smaller the number of competing firms and the greater the degree of product differentiation, the closer a firm will be to a pure monopolist's situation. Conversely, the greater the number of competing firms and the smaller the degree of product differentiation, the closer a firm will be to a perfect competitor's situation.

10.4: SHORT-RUN OUTPUT AND PRICE

A firm operating under conditions of monopolistic competition will, the same as any other privately-owned firm, try to maximize its profit or minimize its loss. In the short run, it will attempt to produce that output at which the surplus of total revenue over total cost is greatest. This output, seen from the marginal point of view, is where marginal revenue equals marginal cost. The firm will increase output, therefore, so long as the additional revenue from each extra unit exceeds the additional cost. This marginal revenue, we should remember, is not the same as price. Because the demand curve is downward-sloping, more can be sold only at a lower price. Marginal revenue is, therefore, the price received for the additional unit minus the reduction in price on all the other units. Marginal cost will at first fall but, because of increasing variable costs as the firm approaches full capacity, it will begin to rise steeply. In the short run, a firm operating under conditions of monopolistic competition may make an economic profit, an economic loss, or just break even. These three possible situations are shown in Figure 10:1.

Since, under monopolistic competition, marginal revenue is less than market price, a firm will produce less than it would under perfect

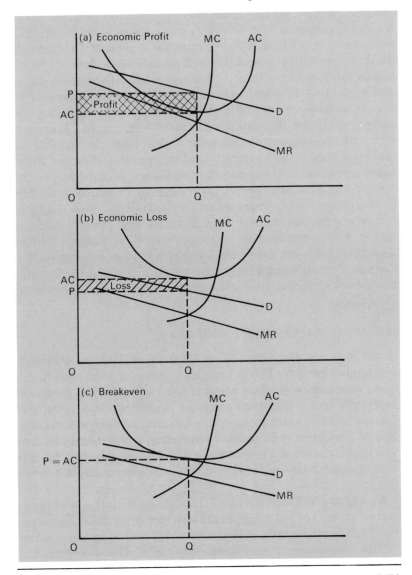

Note: Each firm produces that output (OQ) at which marginal revenue (MR) equals marginal cost (MC). In situation (a), market price (P) exceeds average cost (AC), resulting in a profit for the firm. In situation (b), average cost exceeds market price, resulting in a loss. In situation (c), price equals average cost and the firm merely breaks even.

Figure 10:1 Possible Short-Run Positions of the Monopolistically Competitive Firm

competition. Also, because of the heavy cost of advertising, distinctive design and packaging, after-sales service, and other forms of non-price competition, it will have to charge more for its product. Furthermore, the splintered market means that each manufacturing firm will have a shorter production run than it otherwise would. Therefore, it cannot obtain, and pass on to the public, any benefit from large-scale production. In addition, product differentiation, particularly in retailing, can mean considerable duplication of facilities—one glaring example, at least until recently, was the presence of two, three, or even four gas stations or bank branches at many road intersections. These are important disadvantages of monopolistic competition compared with perfect competition. However, they are partly offset by the benefit to the public of a greater variety of goods and services offered. Also, it is by no means certain that the resources displaced (for example, the gas-station or bank managers and other employees) will find employment elsewhere. There are also strong arguments for the encouragement in Canada of small business firms, not only as a source of employment, but also as a training ground for entrepreneurs and as a bastion of democracy.

10.5: LONG-RUN OUTPUT AND PRICE

In the long run, firms are free to leave or enter a monopolistically competitive industry. This is completely different from the situation under pure monopoly where no other firm can get in. This freedom of movement means that firms which are sustaining a loss—those with average total cost greater than price—will tend to switch to some other type of production or close down completely. It also means that firms which can produce at a profit—those with average total cost the same as or less than price—will tend to enter the industry or stay in if already there.

So long as a firm can keep its ATC no greater than price, it will earn a normal profit. The net effect, in the long run, of all these countervailing forces is that all firms in the industry will tend to earn only normal profit—the situation in which price equals ATC. This situation is illustrated in Figure 10:1 (c). Pure or economic profit will tend to disappear because the entry of new firms into the industry will mean that each firm will now obtain a smaller share of the market and be faced with a larger number of close substitutes for its products. And this in turn means that the demand curve for each firm's product will shift to the left and become more elastic.

However, there are several reasons why, in practice, some firms may for some time continue to make more or less than normal profit. First, some firms will be more successful than others in differentiating their product. To the extent that they are able to build strong customer loyalty to their particular brand or store, these firms may be able to earn an economic profit. This profit, although attractive to would-be competitors, may nevertheless continue to be earned by some firms for the simple reason that nobody can entice their customers away. A second reason for some firms earning economic profit, even in the long run, is that it is often very expensive for a new firm to enter an industry. Also, for various reasons, some firms may not, in the long run, move out of an industry even though they are making a loss. The owner of a small grocery store or restaurant may hang on even though little or no return is received for the capital or time expended. The owner may not be able to find a buyer for the business or may not be willing to risk or be able to afford any other type of life.

10.6: NON-PRICE COMPETITION

Let us now look more closely at competition among firms other than by price. In order to increase its sales, a firm operating under monopolistic competition may do more than just lower its price. It may redesign its product, advertise more, increase its selling effort, or offer better after-sales service. How does this affect our previous analysis? Basically, a change in price means a change in the quantity demanded as a result of a shift along an existing demand curve. A change in the amount of non-price competition is really an attempt to alter the demand curve so that consumers will demand more at each given price. Of course, this additional non-price competition will also alter a firm's cost structure. So, as well as a new pattern of marginal revenue, we would have a new pattern of marginal cost. Equilibrium would, nevertheless, still be at the point at which $MR = MC$. In practice, the ideal combination of price, output, and promotional expenditure will only be found, if at all, on the basis of trial and error.

10.7: PRODUCT DIFFERENTIATION AND THE CONSUMER

Product differentiation, as the key element in non-price competition, helps a firm secure its own loyal band of customers, and there is nothing like having a stable core of demand in a fiercely competitive market. But does product differentiation help the consumer? The answer to this question is highly subjective. Nevertheless, it is possible to claim as a benefit: the variety of product styles and qualities; the attempt by most firms to make their own products more satisfying and attractive to the consumer; the urge felt by a firm to inform consumers about its products; and even the availability of customer credit.

The biggest possible disadvantage to the consumer of product differentiation is that it sometimes helps to perpetuate the existence of many small firms rather than just a few large ones. This can mean, for certain types of product, that the consumer is prevented from obtaining the benefits of large-scale production and merchandising. Thus, many small retail stores may continue to exist even though the public might be better served, from the cost point of view, by fewer, larger units. However, experience indicates that, for many products, the personal service of the small store is still essential.

Some people criticize product differentiation for confusing the consumer with so many similar products. According to this point of view, life would be simpler for a woman, for instance, if she had only one style of dress from which to choose. But for many women, on the other hand, life would be much less interesting. Would we be happier buying only one make and model of car year in and year out, even though the price were less? No one can disagree, however, that changing the appearance of a product just to make the previous ones appear obsolete is economically very wasteful. On the other hand, planned obsolescence helps promote sales and thereby increases national income and employment.

Summary

1. Most firms, even though producing basically the same product as that of their competitors, try to make their own product distinctive. This *product differentiation* is achieved by such means as differences in product design, differences in customer service, differences in packaging, and use of brand-name advertising.

2. To provide a more direct explanation than the theories of perfect competition and pure monopoly of how most firms actually behave, a new theory—that of monopolistic competition—was advanced in the 1930s. *Monopolistic competition* exists when: (a) there are many firms, each of which is responsible for only a relatively small part of total supply; (b) each firm's product, although basically the same, is not identical to that of the other firms in the industry; (c) each firm has only a limited ability to raise the price of its product without losing sales; and (d) new firms can enter the industry. The most important example of monopolistic competition in Canada is the retailing industry.

3. The demand for the product of a firm operating under conditions of monopolistic competition is quite price-elastic—not perfectly elastic as under perfect competition, but more elastic than under pure monopoly.

4. A firm operating under monopolistic competition will attempt to produce that output at which marginal revenue equals marginal cost. However, marginal revenue is not the same as price; it is the price received for the additional unit *minus* the reduction in price on all the other units. This is because the demand curve for the firm's products is downward-sloping; that is, more can be sold only at a lower price.

5. Under monopolistic competition, a firm will produce less than it would under perfect competition. Also, because of the heavy cost of non-price competition, it will have to charge more for its product. However, a greater variety of goods and services will be offered.

6. Because of freedom of movement in and out of an industry operating under monopolistic competition, all firms will, in the long run, tend to earn only normal profit—the situation in which price equals ATC. However, there are several reasons why, in practice, some firms may for some time continue to make more or less than normal profit.

7. A change in the amount of non-price competition is really an attempt to alter the demand curve so that consumers will demand more at each given price. Product differentiation, the key element in non-price competition, provides the consumer with variety of choice, better product design, greater product information, and other customer services. However, by helping to perpetuate the existence of many small firms rather than just a few large ones, product differentiation makes it more difficult for the consumer to obtain the benefits of large-scale production and merchandising. However, for many goods and services, the personal service of the small store is still essential.

Key Terms

Product differentiation   184
Monopolistic competition   184
Brand   185
Brand name   185

Brand mark   185
Trademark   185
Non-price competition   189

Review Questions

1. What is meant by product differentiation? How is it achieved? What is its purpose?
2. Despite product differentiation, no firm can create for itself conditions of pure monopoly. Explain.
3. What are the characteristics of monopolistic competition?
4. Why is retailing considered to be a prime example of monopolistic competition?
5. Explain the nature of the demand for the product of a firm operating under monopolistic competition.
6. What is the optimum output, in the short run, for a firm operating under monopolistic competition? How does this compare with the optimum output under perfect competition?
7. How does freedom of movement in and out of a monopolistically competitive industry theoretically affect long-run profits? What exceptions exist in practice?
8. Explain the nature and purpose of non-price competition.
9. From the viewpoint of the consumer, what are the advantages and disadvantages of product differentiation?

11. OLIGOPOLY: COMPETITION AMONG THE FEW

CHAPTER OBJECTIVES

A. To explain the nature and origin of oligopolies
B. To analyze an oligopolist's marketing and production behaviour
C. To examine the various forms of collusive oligopoly
D. To explain how prices are set in an oligopoly
E. To discuss non-price competition, particularly advertising
F. To examine how oligopolies affect the public
G. To review government competition policy, including the Combines Investigation Act
H. To compare the advantages and disadvantages of competition, from the public's point of view, as a conclusion to our analysis of the different market structures

CHAPTER OUTLINE

In our discussion of monopolistic competition, we stipulated that the number of firms in an industry must be quite large. The implication was that a firm could act with little or no fear of retaliation by its competitors. But what if there are only a few firms in an industry? This situation of competition among the few is called *oligopoly*—from the Greek *oligos*, meaning "few," and *poly*, meaning "sellers."

11.1: OLIGOPOLY DEFINED

An oligopoly is considered to exist if there are only a few firms in an industry and each firm is interdependent in its price and output policy. By a few firms we mean any number from two (sometimes called a *duopoly*) to, say, ten or twenty, depending on the industry. There is, in fact, no generally accepted maximum number. The criterion as to whether a firm is operating under oligopoly or monopolistic competition is whether the firm's price and promotional decisions may cause changes in the other firms' behaviour. If there are so few firms in an industry that, say, a cut in price by one firm causes a retaliatory cut in price by the others, then we are dealing with oligopoly. If there are so many firms that each one can act quite independently, then we are talking of monopolistic competition. The reason for this distinction should by now be obvious: an *oligopolist* (unlike a monopolistic competitor) will have to think twice before cutting price, launching a new promotional campaign, or otherwise disturbing the current market situation. If not careful, the oligopolist may spark a price or other type of competitive war that may leave it worse off than before.

Oligopoly, in its various forms, is a very common form of market structure in Canada. Most of the things we buy, ranging from soap to newspapers, are produced or marketed by a relatively small number of large firms.

It should be emphasized, however, that not all oligopolies are the same. In some industries there are just one or two firms, whereas in others there may be ten, twenty, or more. In some industries, firms produce exactly the same product, whereas in other industries they have a differentiated one. In some industries, member firms enter into "gentlemen's agreements" and other forms of price collusion; in others, they act in strict independence. In some industries, it is relatively easy for new firms to enter; in others, it is not. In some industries, firms are highly interdependent, whereas in others they are much less so.

11.2: REASONS FOR EXISTENCE OF OLIGOPOLY

There are four basic reasons for the existence of oligopolies. First, economies can be obtained from manufacturing or marketing on a large scale. Second, business firms, through advertising and other means, can create artificial barriers to competition. Third, many firms pursue a deliberate policy of acquiring other firms. Fourth, despite the Combines Investigation Act, the federal government encourages some industrial mergers and takeovers.

11.3: PRODUCTION AND MARKETING BEHAVIOUR

When there are only a few firms in an industry, as with oligopoly, the probable behaviour of competing firms becomes of crucial importance. The fewer the firms, the more important this behaviour becomes. A firm must not only try to predict what competitors will do if it pursues a certain course of action, it must also be able to react swiftly to anything that they actually do. If it reacts too slowly, it may already have lost many of its previous customers.

An oligopolist's production and marketing behaviour will also vary according to whether the product is exactly the same as that of rival firms or whether the monopolist is able by various means to differentiate it. That is why it is usual to divide oligopolies into two basic types. The first of these, *pure oligopoly*, is where a few firms produce an identical product, such as steel, cement, or sugar. The second, *differentiated oligopoly*, is where a few firms produce a similar but differentiated product, such as cheese, cars, or television sets.

The most distinctive characteristic of oligopoly, from the viewpoint of economic analysis, is the air of uncertainty that surrounds a firm's possible behaviour. It is impossible for a firm to predict with any degree of certainty how other firms will react if it reduces its price or changes any aspect of its non-price competition. This last fact has given rise to what is called the "Theory of Games," in which as in a poker game, one player (or firm) tries to outwit the others.[1]

11.4: PRICE AND OUTPUT

Because of the many possible combinations of oligopolistic situations (as well as the air of uncertainty as to how other firms will react to, say, a change in price by firm A), no general economic theory of price and output determination under oligopoly has been established. How can we say, for example, that a firm will sell 10000 more units of output if it reduces the price of its product by $1.00, when one or more rival firms may or may not also cut their prices or undertake a retaliatory advertising campaign?

Undoubtedly, an oligopolistic firm will ideally go on producing and selling more up to the point at which marginal revenue equals marginal cost. Just like a firm in any other market structure, it wishes to maximize its profit. And, certainly like any other firm, it will have a definite pattern of production costs. The big question that arises with oligopoly, however, is the nature of the demand for a firm's product. But how can a firm foresee what it can sell at different prices if it does not know how its competitors will react?

Of course, we can build economic models based on a variety of assumptions—for example, that if firm A cuts its price, firms B and C will not. Models of this sort have been in existence since the early nineteenth century. The one that carries most weight today is that advanced by Edward Chamberlin in 1933[2]. This is a model in which there are two firms, each producing the same product. According to Chamberlin's theory, the two firms will reach a tacit agreement to produce between them the output which affords a large measure of monopoly profit. Both firms would recognize that price-cutting, in an attempt to capture each other's share of the market, would be detrimental to both, unless total demand for the industry's product is very price-elastic. Instead, they would both tend to restrict output, even without collusion, and share the market and the monopoly profit between them. Once this understanding has been reached, the price would be reasonably stable as each firm would know that a price cut by one would trigger retaliation by the other. Of course, one firm might undertake such a battle in order to destroy its opponent and, in the long run, capture the whole market for itself.

11.5: CARTELS, UNWRITTEN AGREEMENTS, AND TRUSTS

Two facts—the small number of firms and their mutual interdependence— make it both relatively easy and advantageous for oligopolistic firms to engage in some form of price and output collusion. In this way, they can avoid painful price wars, reduce competitive uncertainty, maintain stable output levels, deter possible new entrants to the industry, and even implement industry-wide price increases.

There are various forms of *collusive oligopoly*. When a formal written agreement is entered into to restrict output and fix prices, the participating firms are described as a *cartel*. Thus, for example, most airlines, including Air Canada and CP Air, are members of IATA (the International Association of Airlines), a cartel that sets air-travel prices. Unwritten arrangements between firms, or even countries, usually with regard only to the price to be charged, are known as *gentlemen's agreements*. Cartels and gentlemen's agreements, since they are voluntary associations of independent manufacturing firms often located in different countries, are by no means always successful in restricting output and keeping up prices. Occasionally, there are disputes among members as well as outside competition. A good example of this has been the Organization of Petroleum Exporting Countries, or OPEC, which after a few years of spectacularly successful price and output regulation, became bitterly divided once the world oil supply began to exceed demand at the current OPEC price.

To ensure better control over firms producing the same product than could a voluntary association, a different form of organization, the *trust*, was devised in the United States in the nineteenth century. This was an amalgamation of a number of different firms, the shareholders of which were given trust certificates in exchange for their shares.

Another method of securing control over a number of previously independent business firms is to establish a *holding company*. This is a firm which is set up purely for the purpose of acquiring the controlling interest in other firms. The firms are acquired either by *merger* (where the owners of the firm being acquired are quite willing to exchange control for shares in the holding company) or by *takeover* (where a controlling interest is obtained by buying up enough shares in the market against the will of the present controlling group of shareholders). The firms acquired in this way usually retain their previous name, but the management is often changed. Together, the holding company and its subsidiaries are known as a *conglomerate* or *group*.

Conglomerates are often highly diversified in their operations because of the desire of the entrepreneurs involved to reduce financial risk or to seize any profit opportunity that becomes available. Conglomerates enable a person with relatively little investment capital to acquire control over business assets worth many times the investor's own. This is because control of other companies can be obtained by ownership of a substantial block of the voting common shares of a company—and not necessarily 51 per cent, if share ownership is widely scattered. The assets of these other companies can, in turn, be used to acquire control of other companies. This practice is known as *leverage* or *pyramiding*.

"And before you could say Dun & Bradstreet, I'd been taken over."

11.6: PRICE LEADERSHIP

Oligopolistic firms, instead of participating in a cartel or unwritten agreement, will often adopt a "follow-my-leader" pricing policy. This is a policy whereby all or most firms in an industry follow the prices set by one large firm—the industry's unofficial price leader. Most firms are forced to follow the leader if it cuts its prices; otherwise, they will suffer a considerable reduction in sales, depending on how strong their customers' loyalty is. Most firms willingly follow the leader in raising prices since they know that the rise will be industry-wide and no firms will be at a competitive disadvantage. They also know that it can mean more profit for all—the actual amount varying according to the price-elasticity of market demand for the industry's product. Furthermore, it eliminates a great deal of the uncertainty from doing business. Often such a follow-my-leader policy becomes a matter of habit.

11.7: RESALE PRICE MAINTENANCE

An oligopolist spends a great deal of time and money in building up the brand image of its products and the distribution network that brings them to the consumer. By ensuring that the product is sold at the recommended retail price, the oligopolist knows that the retailer also obtains a good financial return and can therefore afford to give good customer service. If one store cuts the price of the product, the oligopolist will receive angry complaints from other retailers who sell at the suggested retail price. Also the image of the product in the eyes of the public may suffer. A recent example of this in Canada has been the retailing of art books.

For many years, oligopolists in Canada exerted pressure on retailers to sell only at the manufacturer's recommended retail price. They did this by threatening to discontinue, or actually discontinuing, supplies to the offending retailer. This practice of maintaining retail prices at the manufacturer's desired level is called *resale price maintenance*. It had the result, in practice, of enabling relatively inefficient retailers to survive and preventing more efficient price discounters from growing.

In Canada, resale price maintenance is now illegal. All that manufacturers may now do is to "suggest" the retail price. They may not legally enforce it. However, by owning retail outlets (such as service stations), it has been possible for some oligopolists (e.g., the oil companies) to continue control over the retail price of their products. And there are still occasional reports in the newspapers of attempts by suppliers to force retailers not to charge less than a certain price.

11.8: NON-PRICE COMPETITION

Although oligopolistic firms may be reluctant to engage in price-cutting because of its possibly dangerous consequences, this does not prevent them from competing in other ways. New styles or models of the product, more conveniently located sales outlets, brand name advertising, sponsorship of sporting events, intriguing sales promotional campaigns—all these various forms of non-price competition can together help expand a firm's sales.

If it is successful in its promotional efforts, a firm will have (a) made the demand for its product more price-inelastic (the demand curve falling more steeply from left to right) and (b) caused the demand curve for its products to shift to the right—meaning that consumers will buy more at each possible price than before.

Since these promotional efforts will have increased the firm's share of the market (assuming that total market demand remains the same), rival firms will also intensify their non-price competition. The final result may well be that the market shares enjoyed by each firm remain much the same, but that all firms, because of this extra non-price competition, have incurred higher total costs. Nevertheless, despite this possibility, heavy expenditure on advertising, selling, and other forms of non-price competition, is still a characteristic feature of firms operating under oligopolistic and monopolistic competition. In the case of perfect competition, by contrast, there would be little purpose in such non-price competition, for the product is the same, consumers are fully informed, and a firm can sell all it wishes to produce.

11.9: ADVERTISING

Perhaps the strongest claim that oligopolistic competition is wasteful is directed at the money (and therefore society's resources) spent on advertising. Advertising, formally defined, is the presentation of ideas, goods, or services to customers and prospective customers in a non-personal way by use of such media as newspapers, television, and direct mail. Part of this advertising is purely informative in nature—for example, details about product price and availability. However, another large part consists of subjective claims as to the product's performance and desirability. These claims about the quality of the product are really nothing more than a matter of personal opinion. Occasionally, there may even be misrepresentation, though this is against the law.

It is against the persuasive type of advertising that charges of waste are laid. Instead of spending so much money on this type of advertising, critics argue, why not just reduce the price of the product? Also, critics ask, why should consumers have to submit, when watching a television show or reading a newspaper or magazine, to being brainwashed with advertisements that repeat over and over again the brand name of the product and very little else? Indeed, the advertisements that inform or even amuse are considered to be few and far between. Or why, some people would complain, should the countryside and even city streets be disfigured by a wild variety of billboards and illuminated signs?

Critics also argue that advertising often does not even achieve its goals. If all rival firms advertise their products then the advertising of one firm is largely offset in its impact and persuasive effect by the advertising of the others. If all firms were to spend less on advertising, money would be saved and all firms would still have the same chance of attracting customers. It is also argued that the heavy cost of advertising required to get a brand name established is a deterrent to new firms which contemplate entering an industry.

Another strong criticism of advertising is that it leads to *social imbalance*. By this is meant an unreasonable allocation of a society's resources between private goods, such as cars, dishwashers, and snowmobiles, and social goods, such as hospitals, schools, and roads, and the maintenance of law and order. Because of advertising, it is argued, consumers place a higher priority on, say, entertainment than they do on cleaning up their environment or eliminating disease.

Another criticism is that most of a country's news media depend on advertising as their principal source of revenue. This means, therefore, that large business firms often exert a direct or indirect censorship over program content. This, of course, may be considered a better alternative than government financing of the news media and the possibility of government censorship. But it may not be a better alternative to no censorship at all. Again, it is a matter of opinion.

Another criticism of advertising in recent years is the use by governments in Canada of large sums of the taxpayers' money to advertise the virtues of various government programs. However, the governments argue that the public needs to be better informed and also not just receive the private sector point of view.

What are some of the arguments in favour of advertising? Certainly the need to inform consumers of new products, as well as of new features in existing products, is a necessary task. Even in communist countries, "commercials" abound on state television programs. Thus, advertising keeps the consumer informed about the possible range of choice. Another argument is that advertising encourages consumers to buy and thereby helps bring about production. Without a high level of consumer demand, production in our type of private-enterprise society would tend to stagnate, unemployment rise, and incomes fall. In other words, advertising, both informative and persuasive, is one of the engines of economic prosperity. Also, it is argued, advertising enables a firm to increase its sales and thereby reduce its average costs of production by manufacturing on a larger scale. Consumers will therefore obtain the product at a lower price than would otherwise be the case. However, as we have already indicated, some people question the efficiency of competitive advertising in enlarging demand. Also, critics question whether any reduction in cost would be passed on to consumers, especially if the firm now has fewer competitors. It is also argued that advertising enables the public to enjoy their newspapers and televised hockey games at little or no cost. However, it may also be argued that the public pays for the advertising in the form of higher prices for the products. The alternative, say, for television, would be, as in many other countries, to pay an annual fee to the company (often government-owned) that provides television broadcasting.

11.10: OLIGOPOLY: FRIEND OR FOE?

Is oligopoly, as a market structure, beneficial to society? One point of view is that, since the entry of new firms is restricted in an oligopoly, output is less and price is higher than they would be under perfect competition. In other words, because there is less competition in such an industry, society gets less output and pays more for it than would otherwise be the case. Firms operating under oligopoly, as well as under monopolistic competition and pure monopoly, are guilty, so to speak, of failing to produce up to the point at which marginal cost equals price. The fewer firms there are and the more difficult it is to enter the industry, the further away the industry gets from the purely competitive situation. Also, part of the advertising by such firms is considered by many to be socially wasteful.

In practice, it has been noted that many oligopolistic firms such as car makers, airlines, and radio, television, camera, watch manufacturers and so on have constantly improved the quality of their product and kept price increases relatively small compared with those of other products and the country's rate of inflation. They have also expanded output to take full advantage, wherever possible, of the economies of large-scale production. In many countries for example, Britain, France and Japan governments have in fact openly or discreetly encouraged oligopolies as a means of promoting the orderly growth of industry and the necessary technological research for product development. According to this point of view, a few firms are more beneficial to society than many.

11.11: OLIGOPOLY VERSUS MONOPOLY

From the public's point of view, any agreement to restrict competition means that product prices are kept abnormally high and output restricted. In fact, there are several good reasons for concluding that the effects of a collusive oligopoly are more detrimental to consumers than the effects of even a pure monopoly. First, a pure monopoly is so apparent that its prices are usually regulated by government, as, for example, with Bell Canada. Second, a pure monopolist will not need to undertake the expensive advertising and sales promotion that is essential to oligopolistic firms if they wish to expand or maintain their share of the market or to differentiate their products. Third, it can also be argued, but with less assurance, that a pure monopolist will take better advantage of the economies of large-scale production than a number of oligopolistic firms each with a limited share of the market.

11.12: GOVERNMENT COMPETITION POLICY

At one time, collusion among oligopolistic firms, with regard to product price and market shares, was considered quite respectable among business people and politicians. However, by the 1930s, meetings of cartel members were being held more and more discreetly. Also, the names of the cartels were being changed to more innocent-sounding ones. After World War II, efforts were made by the authorities in many Western European countries to break up cartels. In the United States, trusts had been outlawed as long ago as 1890 by the Sherman Act. Nevertheless, attempts by firms to enlarge their control over the market by buying control of rival firms continue and anti-trust legislation still has to be invoked. However, in some countries (even those concerned with eliminating international cartels) firms in certain industries were encouraged to merge, sometimes with government financial aid. The governments concerned—for example, the British—felt that larger-sized firms might better be able to lower per unit production and marketing costs, undertake expensive research and development, and compete better abroad. Thus, mergers for purposes of "rationalization" were sometimes considered desirable. In Japan, cartels have for many years been officially encouraged as a means of ensuring large-scale production, a high level of research and development, and the more orderly development of industry—promoting thereby a favourable balance of payments, with a high level of exports of manufactured goods providing jobs and income for the country's labour force.

Combines Investigation Act

In Canada, as far back as 1923, the federal Parliament passed a *Combines Investigation Act* authorizing the government to investigate and prosecute firms combining to restrain trade. Under the terms of the Act, a Director of Investigation and Research is responsible for investigating alleged offences and a Restrictive Trade Practices Commission for reviewing the evidence and recommending action by the Registrar General of Canada. An inquiry into alleged offences can be held (a) following an application by six Canadian citizens, (b) on the initiative of the Director, or (c) at the direction of the Registrar General of Canada.

The most important practice outlawed by the Act is the formation of mergers or monopolies. A *merger*, as we have seen, is where one firm gains control of a competitor and thereby reduces competition. A *monopoly* is where a firm gains complete or almost complete control of a certain type of business in a particular area and thereby reduces competition. Such a monopoly is legal only if the monopoly right is conferred by the Patent Act or by any other Act of the federal Parliament.

Pricing practices outlawed by the Act are: (a) *price fixing*—an agreement by business firms, often unwritten, to charge the same price for similar products; (b) *price discrimination*—the practice of selling goods more cheaply to one firm than to another; (c) *predatory pricing*—the practice of charging abnormally low prices in order to reduce or eliminate competition; (d) *price misrepresentation*—the practice by a firm of misrepresenting the price at which it sells its goods; and (e) *resale price maintenance*—the practice by a manufacturer of setting the price at which wholesalers and retailers may sell the product and ensuring that these prices are observed by the actual or threatened cutting off of supplies. All these practices limit competition and prevent the public from being able to buy the goods involved at the lowest price. Such practices interfere, in other words, with the free play of the market forces of supply and demand. The prevention of such practices has, therefore, long been considered to be in the public interest. There are, of course, at the same time, many government-run or government-regulated monopolies in Canada.

Although the Act seems positive enough, particularly with the various amendments made in 1949, 1952 and 1960, its enforcement has always suffered from lack of staff. Various ways have also been devised—for example, consignment selling by oil companies—to avoid prosecution under the Act. In addition, any fines imposed under the

Act have been considered too low to have had any real deterrent effect.

In 1971, because of the inadequacies of the Combines Investigation Act, the federal government proposed new legislation in this area. This followed a three-year study by the Economic Council of Canada on the adequacy of existing competition legislation. However, Bill C256, as it was called, provoked a great deal of criticism, particularly from business and was subsequently withdrawn.

In 1973, the federal government decided to implement changes in competition policy in two stages. The first stage, Bill C-2, was passed by Parliament in October 1975 and came into force on January 1, 1976. Stage I greatly increased the powers of the Restrictive Trade Practices Commission, giving it review power over such trade arrangements as refusal to sell, consignment selling, exclusive dealing, tied sales, market restriction, and trade practices detrimental to small business firms and the public at large. In this respect, the Commission can now hold hearings and issue remedial orders including the prohibition of the offending trade practice. It would not be necessary to use the criminal or civil courts. A second major change was the extension of the coverage of the Combines Investigation Act to all service industries except electric power, rail transportation, telephone service, and bona fide trade union activities. Previously, only industries producing, transporting, storing, distributing, or selling physical goods were included. A third important change was the abolition of the need to prove "complete or virtual elimination" of competition; it is now only necessary to prove a sufficient reduction in competition to cause harm to the public.

In November 1977, new competition legislation (Bill C-13) was introduced by the federal government to replace Bill C-42. However, the Bill was also subsequently withdrawn for revision following many complaints from business.

As we have just seen, any agreement to fix prices or otherwise reduce or eliminate competition is illegal in Canada. However, because most agreements to restrict competition are entered into on an oral rather than written basis, often at social gatherings or sporting events, they are not easy to detect. Nevertheless, there have been several examples of firms which have been successfully prosecuted in Canada for price-fixing and other practices to restrict competition.

11.13: ADVANTAGES AND DISADVANTAGES OF COMPETITION

Let us now conclude our analysis of different market structures and this part of the book by setting out the pros and cons of competition in the market-place.

Advantages

The first advantage of competition, from the viewpoint of the economy as a whole, is the more efficient use of a country's resources. At present, many Canadian manufacturing industries are inefficient because of small plant size, short production runs, and multiplicity of product lines. More competition tends to reduce the number of firms in an industry and enables the remaining firms to achieve economies of scale, such as mechanized materials handling, greater specialization of labour and equipment, and more effective use of their marketing organizations. So long as the displaced labour and equipment can be usefully employed in other production, this rationalization of an industry is beneficial for the economy as per unit production and marketing costs are less. The scope for achieving such economies of scale is even greater if the number of models, styles, or designs offered to consumers is substantially reduced. The continued existence of many small firms, because of government subsidies or resale price maintenance, for instance, may prevent a firm from reaching a size that would permit it to achieve major economies of scale and to spend substantial sums on research and development, which is a vital ingredient of future growth in practically all industries, not just "high-tech" manufacturing. This is why governments in countries such as Japan, Britain, Italy, and Germany have at various times deliberately encouraged the merger of small and medium-sized companies. Such a policy of rationalization not only offers production and marketing benefits at home, but also economies in exporting goods abroad. Thus, the optimum size of firm in certain industries such as steel manufacture, telephone service, and newspapers may in some countries be just one or two firms rather than many. Even without government encouragement, the industry would gradually reduce the number of firms by mergers and takeovers.

At the retailing level, competition has meant the development of supermarkets that can merchandise food more economically than the small corner store. However, we once again encounter the question of social cost. Some people argue that the social cost of the elimination of many small retail stores has outweighed the economic benefits of mass food merchandising.

The second advantage of competition is that it forces business firms to pass part or all of the benefits of improved efficiency on to consumers. These benefits are passed on in the form of lower prices or, at least, prices that do not increase as rapidly as the general price level. Thus, the price of many manufactured goods in Canada has risen relatively slowly because of continuing improvements in plant efficiency and the price of some goods such as ball point pens, electronic calculators, and microcomputers, has even declined.

A third advantage of competition is that it keeps business firms alert. It makes them constantly seek ways to lower production and marketing costs and encourages them to develop new products, all of which ultimately benefit the consumer.

Disadvantages

What are the possible disadvantages of competition? First of all, there is the social and economic disruption caused to a community when a firm is forced to reduce or stop production and lay off its employees. Even though a firm may not be as efficient as a newer firm located elsewhere, this is not necessarily a justification for closing it down completely and depriving its employees of jobs they may have held for many years. This would not be a rational use of a country's human resources, especially when chances of employment elsewhere, particularly for the older worker, may be very poor. Also, the buildings and equipment may not, in fact, be used to produce something else; they may just lie idle. The mobility of human and capital resources is not in practice very great. If it has taken two or three generations to build a firm, should that firm be banished overnight?

A second disadvantage of competition relates to imports. Although imports of goods manufactured abroad—for example, Japanese television sets—can mean lower prices for the Canadian public, it can also mean cutbacks in domestic production of similar items and a reduction in Canadian employment and income. Foreign competition, it is true, can help keep many Canadian producers on their toes, but it can also mean their gradual elimination.

Summary

1. An *oligopoly* is considered to exist if there are only a few firms in an industry, and each firm is interdependent in its price and output policy. *Pure oligopoly* is where a few firms produce an identical product, such as steel, cement, or sugar. *Differentiated oligopoly* is where a few firms produce a similar, but differentiated, product, such as cheese, cars, or television sets. Oligopoly, in its various forms, is the most common form of market structure in Canada.

2. Because of the many different types of oligopolistic situations (as well as the air of uncertainty as to how other firms will react to,

say, a change in price by firm A), no general economic theory of price and output determination under oligopoly has been established.

3. There are various forms of *collusive oligopoly*. When firms in an industry sign a formal, written agreement to restrict output and fix prices, the participating firms are described as a *cartel*. Less formal arrangements between firms, usually with regard only to the price to be charged, are known as *gentlemen's agreements*. Being voluntary, such agreements were not always successful in their aims. Consequently, a different form of organization, the *trust*, was devised. This is an amalgamation of a number of different firms, the shareholders of which are given trust certificates in exchange for their shares. Another method of securing control over a number of previously independent firms is to establish a *holding company* which purchases a controlling interest in other firms. Together, the holding company and its subsidiaries are known as a *conglomerate* or a *group*.

4. Very often, oligopolistic firms, instead of participating in a cartel or gentlemen's agreement, will adopt a "follow-my-leader" price policy whereby all or most firms in an industry follow the prices set by one large firm.

5. For many years, oligopolists in Canada exerted pressure on retailers to sell only at the manufacturer's recommended retail price. They did this by threatening to discontinue, or actually discontinuing, supplies to the offending retailer. This practice of *resale price maintenance* is now illegal in Canada.

6. Oligopolistic firms, although reluctant to engage in price competition, aggressively undertake many forms of non-price competition, notably brand-name advertising. If successful, a firm will shift the demand curve for its products to the right.

7. Perhaps the strongest claim that oligopolistic competition is wasteful is directed at the money (and therefore society's resources) spent on persuasive-type advertising.

8. There are differing views as to whether oligopoly, as a market structure, is beneficial to society.

9. There are several good reasons for concluding that the effects of a collusive oligopoly are more detrimental to consumers than the effects of even a pure monopoly.

10. In Canada, any agreement to fix prices or otherwise reduce or eliminate competition is illegal under the terms of the Combines Investigation Act. However, most agreements, being oral rather than written, are not easy to detect.

Key Terms

Review Questions

1. What is an oligopoly? A duopoly?
2. Distinguish between pure oligopoly and differentiated oligopoly.
3. Give three examples of oligopoly in Canada. Why do oligopolies exist?
4. What is an oligopolist's best-profit output? What is the main difficulty in determining an oligopolist's price and output behaviour?
5. What is the essence of Chamberlin's theory concerning the optimum output of an oligopolist?
6. Why do oligopolists find it both relatively easy and advantageous to engage in some form of price and output collusion? What forms does this collusion take?
7. Distinguish between a cartel and a conglomerate.
8. Why do governments of some countries discourage mergers and takeovers, while governments of other countries encourage them? What is the situation in Canada?
9. What is price leadership? Why does it exist?
10. What is resale price maintenance? What are the arguments for and against it?
11. Why do oligopolistic firms fear price competition, but aggressively engage in non-price competition?
12. Why is the persuasive-type advertising used by oligopolistic firms

considered to be wasteful? What are the arguments in favour of it?

13. From society's point of view, does oligopoly seem to be a desirable market structure?
14. What has the federal government done to promote competition in Canada? How effective have its efforts been?
15. What advantages does competition have for society? What disadvantages?
16. How has competition affected the retailing of food in recent years?
17. How has competition affected the supply of manufactured goods in recent years?
18. How do business firms view competition?
19. Most competition in Canada takes the form of non-price competition. Why is this so?
20. What steps can business firms take to reduce competition?

References

1   See, for example, John Von Neumann and Oskar Morgenstern, *Theory of Games and Economic Behaviour*, Princeton University Press, Princeton, N.J., 1944.
2   Edward Chamberlin, *The Theory of Monopolistic Competition*, Harvard University Press, Cambridge, Mass., 1933.

Part D:
DISTRIBUTION OF INCOME

Here we examine the various basic types of remuneration (wages, rent, interest, or profit) that the factors of production receive in our society and why some factors, including people, receive more and others less.

"Okay, Reg, you win. A $1 million signing bonus, $500,000 a year for five years, and your mom gets to travel with the team."

12. DEMAND FOR THE FACTORS OF PRODUCTION

CHAPTER OBJECTIVES

A. To emphasize how the demand for labour and other factors of production is derived from the demand for a firm's product
B. To explain how the productivity of one factor may decline if more of it is used with the same amount of the other factors
C. To indicate how, in certain industries, an increase in the amount of all the factors may increase productivity
D. To analyze how the demand for a factor is determined under different market structures for the product
E. To explain how a firm decides on the best combination to use of the various factors of production

CHAPTER OUTLINE

12.1 Derived Demand
12.2 Diminishing Marginal Returns
12.3 Economies of Scale
12.4 Factor Demand under Perfect Competition
12.5 Factor Demand under Imperfect Competition
12.6 Elasticities of Factor Demand
12.7 Changes in a Firm's Demand for Factors of Production
12.8 Industry Demand for Factors of Production
12.9 Combining the Factors of Production

The various factors of production (as described in Chapter 1, Unit 1.2) are land, labour, capital, entrepreneurship, and technology.

12.1: DERIVED DEMAND

A business firm is willing to employ the various factors of production for one reason only—namely, to help produce the goods and services that households, business firms, and governments want to buy. If a firm cannot sell its output, it will not want to hire more factors of production or even retain those that it already has. Conversely, the more goods a firm can sell, the bigger its demand for labour and the other factor inputs. That is why the demand for the factors of production is called a *derived demand*.

Because of its derived nature, the demand for one factor compared with another will depend, first, on that factor's *productivity*—that is, the amount of output that results from the services of each unit of that factor; and, second, on the market value of the output which that factor helps to produce. Thus, a leading hockey player is in great demand not only because of his skill as a hockey player (high productivity) but also, just as important, because the public is willing to pay a large sum of money to watch him perform (market value of output).

12.2: DIMINISHING MARGINAL RETURNS

The demand for a factor of production is influenced by the fact that output does not increase in proportion to the amount of the factor used. This fact was formulated as an economic principle, the *law of diminishing marginal returns*, by the English economist, David Ricardo, in the early nineteenth century. The law states that: *when the amount of one factor of production is increased relative to other factors that are fixed in amount, the extra output (or marginal return) from each additional unit of the variable factor may at first increase but will eventually decrease.* In other words, there will at first be *increasing marginal returns* as more of the variable factor is used, but eventually there will be *diminishing marginal returns*. These diminishing marginal returns may even become negative. This is because the extra units of the variable factor may cause so much confusion, and hamper production so greatly, that total output may actually decline.

Let us illustrate the law of diminishing marginal returns with a simple, hypothetical example. Assume, for example, that a farmer owns a tractor, plough, and other farm machinery, plus a hundred acres of land that he uses to grow wheat. In Table 12:1, we show how many bushels of wheat would be produced as the number of workers is increased (assuming all the workers are equally efficient). The farm machinery and the land are the fixed factors, and the number of workers the variable factor. With the farm machinery and one hundred acres of land and no workers, the output of wheat would be nil. With the same amount of land and machinery and one worker, output is 1000 bushels. With two workers, output is 2500 bushels. With three workers, it is 3500 bushels. With four workers, it is 4000. And, finally, with five workers, it is 3800 bushels. What has happened? At first, there were increasing marginal returns—the extra output from employing one extra worker rose from 1000 bushels to 1500 bushels. But then diminishing marginal returns set in. The extra output from employing a third worker is only 1000 bushels; that from the fourth worker only 500 bushels; and the fifth worker, instead of adding to production, causes total output to decline by 200 bushels.

Table 12:1
An Example of Diminishing Returns
Extra Units of Labour Combined with a Fixed Amount of Land

Number of Workers	Total Output (bushels of wheat)	Extra Output from Each Additional Worker
0	0	
1	1,000	1,000
2	2,500	1,500
3	3,500	1,000
4	4,000	500
5	3,800	−200

12.3: ECONOMIES OF SCALE

We have considered what can happen to output if the amount of one factor of production is increased relative to the other factors. But what happens to output if a firm employs more of every factor of production, leaving the relative proportions unchanged?

Bigness, or *mass production,* often enables a firm to reduce production costs per unit of output by, for example, quantity purchasing of materials, highly mechanized materials handling, effective use of special-purpose equipment, and greater specialization of labour. As the marginal cost of production falls, a firm's average variable cost curve (see Figure 12:1) and therefore also its average total cost curve will decline. Eventually, however, bigness of production will result in extra costs rather than economies, and the AVC and ATC curves will start to slope upwards to the right.

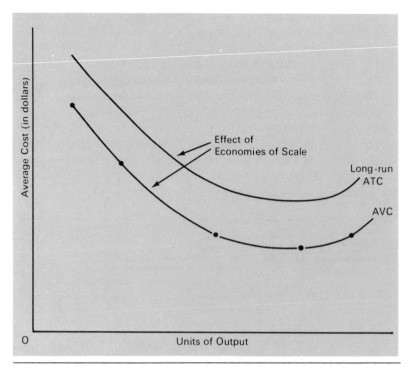

Figure 12:1 Economies of Scale Cause Declining AVC and ATC Curves

By increasing the amount employed of all the factors of production, a firm can obtain greater additional output from each factor than it would if that factor alone were increased. This greater output from the extra units of all the factors of production is described as *increasing returns to scale*. The more productive each factor of production is, because of mass production, the lower the cost of the product. And the lower the price, the bigger the demand for the product, and the bigger the demand for the factors that produce it.

12.4: FACTOR DEMAND UNDER PERFECT COMPETITION

We have noted that the demand for a factor of production is a derived one; that is, it will vary according to (a) the factor's productivity, and (b) the market value of the output which that factor helps to produce. Now, on the one hand, the market price of a product may remain the same whatever the amount produced. This is the case with perfect competition—a market structure in which the market price of the goods produced remains the same whatever the level of a firm's output. On the other hand, the market price of a product may fall as more is produced. This is the case of imperfect competition. Depending on which market structure we assume, the demand for a factor of production will be different. Consequently, even though imperfect competition is the typical market structure in modern society, we shall examine factor demand under the two possible situations.

Let us use a numerical example to explain how the demand for a factor of production is determined under perfect competition. In Table 12:2, we show, first of all, what might happen to output if more and more units of one factor, say factor A, are added to a fixed amount of other factors. In accordance with the law of diminishing marginal returns, we see that the additional output of, say, product X, from each extra unit of factor A becomes less and less as more of the variable

Table 12:2
Marginal Revenue Product Determines a Firm's
Demand for a Factor of Production under Perfect Competition

Units of Variable Factor Input Combined with a Fixed Amount of Other Inputs	Total Output (in units)	Marginal Physical Product (in units)	Marginal Revenue Product (in dollars)
		30	60
1	30		
		28	56
2	58		
		26	52
3	84		
		24	48
4	108		
		21	42
5	129		
		18	36
6	147		
		15	30
7	162		
		11	22
8	173		
		7	14
9	180		
		3	6
10	183		

Note: It is assumed that market price remains the same at $2.00 per unit whatever the output under perfect competition.

factor is employed. Whereas the first unit of the variable factor increased output by 30 units, the tenth unit increased output by only 3 units. This additional output from each extra unit of the variable factor is called the *marginal physical product,* or *MPP.* The difference in total revenue, as a result of the employment of an additional unit of a factor of production, is called the *marginal revenue product,* or *MRP.* The MRP of factor A comprises two things: (a) the marginal physical product of that factor, and (b) the marginal revenue from the sale of product X. Algebraically, this can be stated as: $MRP_A = MPP_A \times MR_X$.

From the viewpoint of factor demand, a firm will employ additional units of a factor of production only so long as MRP exceeds the cost of the extra factor input. This extra cost we can call *marginal resource cost,* or *MRC.* A firm will stop hiring any more of a particular factor of production at the point where the MRP of that factor is equal to its MRC.

In Table 12:2, the firm would take on a tenth unit of the variable factor only if its cost were less than $6.00. If its cost were more, the firm would lose money by employing it—for the MRP is only $6.00. This same reasoning can be applied to every additional unit of the variable factor—only if the MRP is greater than the MRC will the firm hire it. The MRP schedule provides the information required to construct a firm's demand curve for a factor of production. Thus, from Table 12:2, we can see that at a factor price slightly less than $60.00, the firm will employ 1 unit. At a price slightly less than $56.00, it will employ 2 units. At a price slightly less than $48.00, it will employ 3 units, and so on. The demand curve, based on this data, is shown in Figure 12:2.

12.5: FACTOR DEMAND UNDER IMPERFECT COMPETITION

Unlike the situation under perfect competition, the market price for a firm's output under imperfect competition (that is to say, monopolistic competition, oligopoly, or pure monopoly) does not remain the same whatever the volume of sales. The market price will have to be reduced if a firm wishes to expand its sales. Previously, to obtain the MRP under perfect competition, we multiplied the marginal physical product of each additional factor input by one set market price. Under imperfect competition, however, we must multiply the MPP by the market price at that particular level of total output and subtract the reduction in market value of all the other units produced.

In Table 12:3. we retain the production data used previously. However, we illustrate, with different prices at different levels of output,

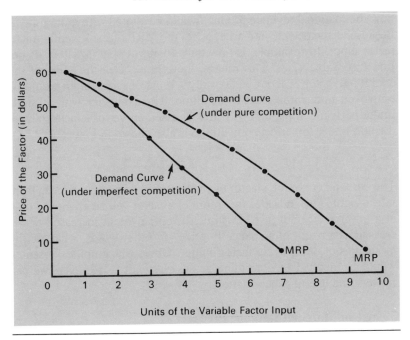

Figure 12:2 A Firm's Demand Curve for a Factor of Production.

Table 12:3
Marginal Revenue Product Determines a Firm's
Demand for a Factor of Production under Imperfect Competition

Units of Variable Factor Input	Total Output (in units)	Market Price per Unit	Total Revenue	Marginal Revenue Product
1	30	$2.00	$ 60.00	$60.00
2	58	1.90	110.20	50.20
3	84	1.80	151.20	41.00
4	108	1.70	183.60	32.40
5	129	1.60	206.40	22.80
6	147	1.50	220.50	14.10
7	162	1.40	226.80	6.30
8	173	1.30	224.90	−1.90
9	180	1.20	216.00	−8.90
10	183	1.10	201.30	−14.70

Note: It is assumed that market price falls as output increases.

how the marginal revenue product would be altered with more output. Because of the decline in market price, the MRP of the seventh unit of factor input, for example, is now only $6.30, instead of $30.00 as before (see Table 12:2). This means, therefore, that if the MRC of the additional factor is about $6.00, only 7 units of factor input would be employed under imperfect competition. This compares with 10 units under perfect competition. A firm's demand curve for a factor of production under imperfect competition is also shown in Figure 12:2.

12.6: ELASTICITIES OF FACTOR DEMAND

The demand curve for a factor of production is downward-sloping from left to right. This indicates that more of a factor will be employed only at a lower price. But just how much is employment increased or decreased as a result of a change in price? In other words, what are the elasticities of demand for factor inputs? Obviously, empirical research would be needed to determine actual elasticities. However, we can make some useful generalizations.

Change in Marginal Revenue Product

We can begin by asking a question. If the price of a machine were to fall, how would this affect the amount employed? We have already seen that a factor will tend to be employed up to the point at which its marginal revenue product, or MRP, is equal to its marginal resource cost, or MRC. Now we have just said that the MRC has been reduced. Therefore, the answer to our question will be determined by what happens to the MRP. Perhaps the MRP will decline only very slowly as more of the factor is employed. This would be more likely in a situation in which a firm can sell more of its output at the existing price than one in which it would have to lower the price to sell more. It would also be more likely in a situation in which management can put the extra machines to most efficient use. If the MRP declines slowly, then the elasticity of demand for the factor of production would tend to be quite elastic. A reduction in its price would bring about a large increase in the amount employed. Conversely, if the MRP were to decline sharply as more of the factor is employed, it would not be long before the MRP had dropped to the same level as the MRC and no more of the factor would be employed. In such a situation, therefore, demand for the factor would be relatively inelastic.

We can also usefully ask another question. How would a rise in the price of labour affect the amount employed? This is the reverse of the previous case. Because of the increase in salaries or wages, the MRC is now greater than the MRP. A firm can consequently save money by employing less labour. If a reduction in the number of employees causes the MRP to rise quickly, the firm will soon be back to a position of equilibrium where, once again, MRP = MRC. In such a case, demand for labour is relatively inelastic. An increase in its price has caused a relatively small change in the amount employed. However, it is possible that the MRP of labour is reduced. It will therefore require a large reduction in the number of persons employed before the MRP of labour once more equals its MRC. In this case, the demand for the factor of production is relatively elastic. Consequently, a rise in the wage rate could eventually result in many workers losing their jobs.

Demand for the Product

The elasticity of demand for the product will be another important determinant of the elasticity of demand for the factors of production. Thus, if a reduction in the price of a product (caused by reduced factor prices) causes a large increase in the quantity demanded of that product, there will also be a large increase in the quantity demanded of the factors of production that are required to make that product. An elastic demand for the product will therefore tend to cause an elastic demand for the factors of production involved in its manufacture. Conversely, an inelastic demand for a product will tend to cause an inelastic demand for the various factor inputs required to produce it.

Substitutability

Another consideration that will affect the elasticity of demand for a factor of production is the degree to which a firm can substitute one factor for another in the production or marketing process. Technologically, at any particular point of time, there is only one method that is the most efficient for producing a good, given the relative costs of the various materials, parts, and factor inputs. But if the MRC of one factor changes relative to another, a different method of production (e.g., automatic tellers, industrial robots, word processors, etc.), involving less of the more expensive factor may now become the most efficient. In some cases, the degree of substitutability is very low; in others, it is very high. The higher it is, the more elastic will be the demand for that factor. Thus, if the price of factor A falls, more will be demanded not only because MRP now exceeds its MRC, but also because that factor can now be profitably substituted, to some extent, for factors B and C. Conversely, if the price of factor A rises, less will be demanded, not only because its MRP is now less than its MRC, but also because more units of factors B and C can be used instead. If factor A cannot be substituted at all for factors B and C, or vice versa, this will help to make the demand for factor A inelastic. Finally, we should note that a change in technology may in fact offset a change in relative factor prices.

Relative Importance of the Factor

If one factor accounts for only a small part of the total cost of production of a good, a change in the price of that factor will not greatly affect the price of that good. If, however, one factor (say, labour) accounts for most of the cost of a good, an increase in wage rates might cause a large increase in the price of the good. And this increase in the price of the product will, depending on the elasticity of demand for it, cause a large reduction in the amount sold. This will, in turn, cause a cutback in production and a fall in the amount of labour and other factors employed. The more important a factor is as a percentage of total cost, the greater therefore is the elasticity of the demand for that factor.

12.7: CHANGES IN A FIRM'S DEMAND FOR FACTORS OF PRODUCTION

We have just considered some of the forces that help determine the shape of the demand curve for a factor of production. Let us now consider what may cause a shift in this demand curve so that a firm instead of employing, say, 1000 workers at an average wage of $400 per week now wants to employ 1500 at the same price.

One reason for a change in factor demand would be a change in consumer demand for the product. If consumers decide that they want more of the product at the same price, there will also be an increase in demand for the factor inputs. Conversely, if consumers want, say, fewer North American-made cars (compared with foreign ones) at existing prices, there will be less demand for labour and other factors employed in the North American car industry.

A second reason for a change in factor demand is a change in the productivity of that factor, which would cause its MRP to become greater or less than its MRC. How would a factor be able to produce more units of output than before? There are several reasons. First, the proportion in which it is combined with other factors may be altered. Thus, if more capital is used, labour becomes more productive. A man with a forklift truck, for example, can move many more goods than a man without. Second, the quality of the factor may improve. Thus, an airline pilot trained recently might be considered to be more productive than a pilot trained twenty years ago; or a memory typewriter be considered more productive than a non-memory one. Third, technical know-how may enable factors to become more productive. Thus, without the discovery of the means of flight, labour, in the form of a pilot, would have been of little use. Improved technology has in fact greatly increased the productivity of all factors of production during the twentieth century.

A third reason for a change in the demand for a factor is a possible change in the price of other factors. Thus, if the price of labour rises, a firm will probably increase its demand for labour-saving machines. These machines, as well as being cheaper than labour (no wages or fringe benefits), may even be more hard-working (twenty-four hours a day, no coffee breaks), more loyal (never quitting and never answering back), and even more reliable (never going on strike, and rarely reporting sick). It is therefore not surprising that machines are rapidly being substituted for labour in so many industries in Canada. Fortunately, from the viewpoint of labour employment, machines cannot do everything that a person can.

12.8: INDUSTRY DEMAND FOR FACTORS OF PRODUCTION

So far, in our discussion, we have looked at factor demand by the individual firm. But if we are to go on in the next two chapters to look at the supply of each factor compared with demand, we must be able to talk in terms of total, or industry demand. To obtain the industry demand curve for a factor of production we might at first be tempted merely to add together the individual firms' factor demand curves. However, there is a serious complication. It is that, under every market structure except pure monopoly, a change in the price of a factor input would cause the whole industry, not just one firm, to alter its output to regain the position where MRP equals the MRC of the factor input. This increase in total output will cause the market price of the product to change, which will, in turn, cause a change in each firm's demand for factor inputs. The only way, in fact, to obtain the industry demand curve for a factor input is to determine, for each eventual market price, what amount of factor input each firm would demand to achieve its best-profit position. These individual firms' demands at each price could then be added together to form the industry demand curve. Obviously, this is a theoretical rather than a practical exercise.

*"Eventually, we hope to do without peo-
ple completely."*

12.9: COMBINING THE FACTORS OF PRODUCTION

In deciding how to produce, every business firm is faced with the problem of how to combine the various factors of production in the most efficient way. The manager of a firm must decide how much of each factor of production to employ in order to produce the desired output. If a manager uses more of a factor than is really needed, he or she is being wasteful.

Least-Cost Combination

We have seen that a firm will employ more units of a variable factor of production as long as the benefit outweighs the cost. We have also seen that because of diminishing marginal returns, together with declining market price under imperfect competition, the marginal revenue product from the variable factor eventually declines. In practice, a firm is able, at least in the long run, to vary all the factors of production, not just one. The first question is, therefore, in what proportions should a firm employ all the various factors of production? Only by using the factors of production in the correct proportions will a firm be able to produce the desired output of a good at least cost. And only by achieving this least-cost combination will it maximize profit.

To achieve this least-cost combination, a firm will not only compare the expected benefit from an additional unit of a factor with that unit's cost, but will also compare the benefit that could be obtained by spending the same amount of money on alternative factors of production. Suppose for example, a firm believes that it can increase the monthly value of its output by $1000 by renting an additional machine for $600. Obviously, it will choose the extra machine. Because there is more benefit to be obtained by using more capital, it will increase the proportion of capital to labour. The least-cost combination of all factors of production will in fact, exist where the last dollar spent on each factor yields the same MPP. This combination may be summarized as follows:

$$\frac{\text{MPP of Factor A}}{\text{Price of Factor A}} = \frac{\text{MPP of Factor B}}{\text{Price of Factor B}}$$

The validity of this *least-cost rule* can easily be seen. If, for example, the MPP of a dollar's worth of factor A were greater than the MPP of a dollar's worth of factor B, then a firm's output could be increased at no extra cost by employing more of A and less of B. This switch in spending would go on until equality is achieved.

At any time, a firm may discover that because of, say, a new wage scale or a change in productivity or price of output, this equilibrium no longer exists. Therefore, the firm would have an incentive to alter the combination of its factors of production, for it may now be more profitable to use more machines and less labour. If there were complete mobility of resources, as under perfect competition, equilibrium would eventually be restored. This would be achieved, on the one hand, by an increase in the MPP of labour as less of it is used relative to capital and other factors; and, on the other hand, by a decrease in the MPP of capital as more of it is used relative to labour and other factors.

Optimum Size

We have seen how, in theory, the various factors of production can be combined in a firm in the best relative amounts—for example 3A to 1B. But just how many units of each factor should be used? 300A and 100B? 330A and 110B? Or some other combination? The answer is that a firm will continue to increase the absolute amount of each factor until the marginal revenue product of that factor is equal to its marginal revenue cost. So long as the additional benefit from employing more of a factor of production outweighs the additional cost, a firm will obviously go on increasing the amount used of that factor. Only when the additional cost threatens to equal or exceed the additional benefit will the firm call a halt. The overall equilibrium situation will be where:

$$\frac{\text{MRP of Factor A}}{\text{MRC of Factor A}} = \frac{\text{MRP of Factor B}}{\text{MRC of Factor B}} = 1$$

To check the validity of this statement, let us assume the following situation:

$$\frac{\text{MRP}_A: 15}{\text{MRC}_A: 10} \quad \text{and} \quad \frac{\text{MRP}_B: 12}{\text{MRC}_B: 16}$$

In other words, the marginal benefit of factor A exceeds its marginal cost, while the marginal cost of factor B exceeds its marginal benefit. Clearly, the firm can increase its profit by increasing the amount of factor A employed and reducing the amount of factor B. Equilibrium will be reached only when the MRP of each factor is equal to its cost.

Some Practical Considerations

To be realistic, we should remind ourselves that the theory of production that we have discussed depicts the optimum situation toward which a firm tends to gravitate. There are in practice many obstacles that can prevent this equilibrium from being achieved. First, a firm's knowledge of what an additional worker or machine will contribute is sometimes based more on hope than on fact. Second, in most firms it is impossible to add or subtract units of factor input at will. Since one factor, labour, is composed of human beings with feelings and family responsibilities, a firm cannot always be governed solely by financing considerations in reducing its labour force. Furthermore, a labour union often reduces the ease with which workers (and even machines) can be added or removed from a plant. Third, different units of the same factor are not equally productive—for example, one worker may do much more than another. Fourth, in the short run, a firm may not be willing to hire extra factors if it cannot be sure that demand for the product will continue at the same level. Despite all these reservations, the theory of production does provide a reasonable explanation of how firms, motivated mainly by profit, tend to decide how much of the various factors of production to employ and in what relative proportions. The theory does not, of course, attempt to explain the actual technology of production.

Summary

1. Industry's demand for the factors of production is said to be a *derived demand* because it depends on the demand for the goods and services that these factors help to produce. The demand for one factor compared with another will depend on (a) that factor's productivity, and (b) on the market value of the output which that factor helps to produce.

2. The *law of diminishing marginal returns* states that when the amount of one factor of production is increased relative to other fixed factors, the extra output or marginal return, from each additional unit of the variable factor may at first increase but will eventually decrease. The existence of diminishing marginal returns will influence the demand for that factor.

3. When a firm employs more of each factor, leaving the relative proportions unchanged, it may obtain *economies of scale* that will lower production costs per unit of output. These arise from such means as quantity purchasing, specialization of labour and equipment, and mechanized materials handling. By increasing the amount of each factor of production, a firm may therefore obtain a more than proportionate increase in output. This is called *increasing returns to scale*. The lower production costs can permit a lower

price, an increase in the quantity demanded of the product, and more demand for the factors of production involved in producing it.

4. Under perfect competition, a firm will continue to hire more of a factor of production so long as the marginal revenue product, or MRP, exceeds the marginal resource cost, or MRC. Equilibrium is where MRP = MRC.

5. Under imperfect competition, the market price of the good produced will have to be reduced if more of it is to be sold. Therefore, the marginal revenue product is the marginal physical product multiplied by the market price at that particular level of output *minus* the reduction in market value of all the other units produced. Equilibrium employment of the factor will also be where MRP = MRC.

6. Demand for a factor of production will be more elastic if the MRP declines only slowly as more of the factor is employed. Conversely, demand will be more inelastic if the MRP declines rapidly as more of the factor is employed. The elasticity of demand for the product also helps determine the elasticity of demand for the factors involved in its production. Other determinants are the degree to which a firm can substitute one factor for another in the production process; and the relative importance of the factor in the total cost of the good.

7. A shift in the demand curve for a factor of production can be caused by a shift in the demand for the final product; a change in the productivity of that factor; or a possible change in the price of other factors.

8. The only way to obtain the industry demand curve for a factor of production is to determine, for each eventual market price, what amount of factor input each firm would demand to achieve its best-profit position.

9. For a given level of output, a firm will achieve its least-cost combination of factor inputs when the last dollar spent on each factor yields the same marginal physical product.

10. To achieve its optimum size, a firm will continue to increase the absolute amount of each factor of production until the marginal revenue product of that factor is equal to its marginal resource cost.

11. There are some obstacles that may, in practice, prevent a firm achieving the equilibrium production situation that economic theory indicates. These obstacles include lack of knowledge as to marginal physical product; the indivisibility of factors of production;

the inclusion of social, as well as economic, criteria in increasing or reducing the use of a factor; variations in output between one unit and another of the same factor; and uncertainty as to the future level of demand for the final product.

Key Terms

Derived demand 214	Marginal physical product 218
Productivity 214	Marginal revenue product 218
Marginal returns 214	Marginal resource cost 218
Law of diminishing	Elasticity of factor demand 220
marginal returns 214	Substitutability 221
Economies of scale 215	Least-cost factor combination 225
Mass production 215	Least-cost rule 225
Factor demand 216	Optimum size 226

Review Questions

1. The demand for the factors of production is said to be a "derived demand." Explain.
2. What is "productivity"? How does it help determine the demand for a factor of production? What other consideration is vital as a determinant of demand for a factor?
3. What is the law of diminishing marginal returns? How does it affect the demand for a factor of production?
4. What is meant by the economies of mass production? How do they arise?
5. What is meant by "increasing returns to scale"? What is their relationship to the economies of mass production? Why are they said to depend on the extent of the market?
6. Distinguish between the marginal physical product of a factor of production and the marginal revenue product.
7. A firm will stop hiring more of a particular factor of production at the point at which the MRP of that factor is equal to its MRC. Explain.
8. How is the MRP of a factor of production affected by imperfect competition?
9. How do changes in the MRP of a factor of production affect the amount employed of that factor?
10. How do changes in the MRC of a factor of production affect the amount employed of that factor?

11. How does the elasticity of demand for a product help determine the elasticity of demand for the factors involved in its production?

12. How does substitutability help determine the elasticity of demand for a factor of production?

13. How is the demand for a factor of production affected by the relative importance of that factor in the production process?

14. A shift in the demand curve for a factor of production can occur for any one of three reasons. What are they?

15. How can we obtain the industry demand curve for a factor of production?

16. How can a business firm theoretically achieve the least-cost combination of factors of production for a given level of output?

17. How can a business firm theoretically determine its optimum size?

18. What practical considerations limit the applicability of the economic theory of production?

19. Will the use of computers in various industries result in greater demand for labour or less (a) in the short run and (b) in the long run? Discuss.

13. WAGES: LABOUR'S SHARE OF INCOME

CHAPTER OBJECTIVES

A. To explain why wage rates differ from one occupation to another
B. To explain how wage rates are determined (a) when employers compete to seek workers and workers compete to obtain jobs; (b) when there is only competition among workers; (c) when there is only competition among employers; and (d) when there is no competition among employers or among workers
C. To discuss the effects on the labour market of government-set minimum wage rates
D. To emphasize how real wages today are much greater than in our ancestors' days
E. To point out how relative wage rates for different occupations can alter as the years go by

CHAPTER OUTLINE

How does a country share among its population the goods and services produced? In our modern society, this question is answered in terms of monetary income. The more money a person receives, the larger the amount and the better the quality of goods and services that he or she can buy.

A person's income is obtained mainly in the form of payment for the use of the productive resources (or factors of production) that such a person has at his or her command. The most obvious of these is the person's own time and efforts as a member of the labour force. However, additional sources of income, discussed in the next chapter, include rent from land and buildings; interest from the loan of money capital; and profit from the operation of a business.

13.1: WAGES DEFINED

The term *wages* is used in economics to embrace all the different types of payment—wages, salaries, commissions, bonuses, royalties, and fringe benefits—made to the various kinds of labour in exchange for their services. The *wage rate* is the price paid to a particular kind of labour for its services over a specific period of time. In practice, the wage rate is usually hourly for factory workers, shop assistants, and many clerical personnel; annually or monthly for professional and managerial staff.

The most important determinants of the standard wage rate for one type of employment compared with another are demand and supply— the number of job vacancies on the one hand and the number of workers seeking employment on the other.

13.2: DIFFERENT DEMAND/SUPPLY SITUATIONS

For convenience, we talk about "labour" as a factor production. In reality, labour is by no means homogeneous. No one worker is exactly the same as another. Consequently, we must recognize that at any one time there is not just one demand/supply situation for labour, but a whole series of them—as many, in fact, as there are different types of labour. The demand/supply situation for company presidents, for example, is different from that for company treasurers; and that of plant engineers different from that for plant supervisors. If, for example, the demand for company presidents falls relative to the supply, their salaries will drop, even though, at the same time, the salaries of executive secretaries may rise because of an increase in demand for them relative to their supply. Because of the existence of these different demand/ supply situations, wage rates differ considerably from one job to another. They also differ for the same job, from one region to another and, even more, from one country to another. This is because physical distance causes separate labour markets even for the same type of worker.

Differences Between Workers

Although human beings are often said to be equal, in practice they differ greatly from each other in a variety of ways: in intelligence, ability to get along with others, willingness to accept responsibility, conscientiousness, ability to communicate, creativity, appearance, ability to withstand mental pressure, ability to organize, physical strength, attitude, skills, and dexterity—the list is almost endless. These differences mean, first, that some persons cannot perform certain jobs at all. For example, a successful bank manager might be a hopeless surgeon, even with the necessary medical training; or a skilled typist might be a hopeless bookkeeper. Second, some workers, although they may be able to perform the same job, may not be as efficient at it as some others.

Another important reason for differences between workers is the varying amounts and types of education, training, and experience that they have received. If it requires many years of academic and practical training to become, for example, a doctor, engineer, chemist, or accountant, it is to be expected that the number of such persons will be relatively small, particularly when compared with the number of unskilled workers.

There are also other differences between persons, such as personal appearance, that may be crucial when it comes to securing a particular job.

When we look at workers as a whole, we can see that they really consist of a number of *non-competing groups*. Plant managers form one group, geologists another, and so on. In the short run, a person's mobility between one group and another is usually very limited, which is why these groups are called "non-competing." Over time, some persons may be able to switch from one group to another—for example, a chemical engineer may become a college professor; or a lawyer, a politician. However, even in the long run, most groups remain largely noncompeting. Few professional musicians will ever become accountants and few accountants will ever become professional musicians, even if comparative wage scales provided a financial incentive. In other words, each group represents a separate demand/supply situation, which accounts for the great differences in wage rates. Only if persons can easily switch from one occupation to another can such wage differences be

eliminated. Thus, only if a large number of persons had the ability, inclination, and opportunity to be successful television performers, for example, would wage rates for such performers drop to the level enjoyed by the vast majority of factory workers. But so long as only a limited number of people can perform certain jobs, disparities in wage rates will continue.

Hazardous or Unpleasant Jobs

All jobs do not exert the same appeal on prospective employees. Many people would not, for example, contemplate becoming police officers or firefighters because of the danger involved. Hardship, excessive travel, responsibility, and nervous tension are all examples of factors that tend to create separate demand/supply situations for particular types of jobs. In particularly demanding jobs, the wage rate resulting from the interaction of demand and supply will contain a premium—an equalizing difference—to offset these aspects. Thus, a police constable will receive more than a clerk; a garbage collector more than a street sweeper. Worker A, earning less at another, more pleasant job, will not attempt to compete with worker B, who is willing to perform a hazardous or unpleasant job for the extra money.

Geographical Immobility

Another reason for separate demand/supply situations, even for the same job, is that many people are reluctant to move from the area in which they have grown up. Such a move can mean that they must leave relatives, friends, and their old home, find a new school for any children, and adjust to a new community and even climate. Obviously the younger a person is and the fewer the family ties, the easier it is to move. Nevertheless, there are still many people in, say, the Maritime or Prairie provinces who would be reluctant to move to better-paying jobs in Calgary, Toronto or Vancouver, even if they were available. Geographical immobility is even greater, of course, between different countries—because of distance, immigration restrictions, cultural differences, etc.

The Multiplication Factor

This seemingly odd title refers to the fact that some employees are able, through the communications media, to multiply their services. Thus a television performer, although making only one personal performance, may be enjoyed at the same time, or even months or years later, by thousands or even millions of persons. Similarly, a successful novelist, although writing each book only once, can provide entertainment, through the printed word, to hundreds of thousands of interested readers. Because services can be multiplied in this way and therefore generate multiplied revenue, the person who provides them can command extremely high fees or salaries—for example, hundreds of thousands of dollars for ice-hockey and baseball stars.

Varying Degrees of Competition

In some employment situations, there is a high degree of competition among employers and employees. In others, there is relatively little. In the following pages, we analyze the various possible situations.

13.3: COMPETITIVE LABOUR MARKET

In this type of labour market, many different firms compete with one another to employ each particular kind of labour. Every firm has its own demand curve for each kind of labour, based on the expected monetary benefit (the marginal revenue) that additional units of that factor will confer. The industry demand curve for each kind of labour is the sum of these individual firms' demand curves, calculated at each particular wage rate.

In this labour market, workers also compete to obtain jobs. For every vacancy advertised, there are many applicants; and there is no union to restrict the number of workers entering a firm. It is possible to visualize the supply of each kind of labour, in these circumstances, as the number of workers willing to offer their services at each of a variety of wage rates. The lower the wage, the fewer the number of applicants—as workers will tend to remain at their present jobs or look for opportunities in other fields. The higher the wage, the larger the number of applicants.

In Table 13:1 we give an example of the demand for, and supply of, a particular kind of labour. We can see that the equilibrium wage rate is $10.00 per hour. This is the rate at which the industry's demand for this kind of labour (1000 workers) is equal to the supply (1000). The corresponding demand and supply curves are shown in Figure 13:1. Since the wage rate for labour is determined by the interaction of industry demand and market supply, no individual firm can exert any influence on this price.

For any individual firm, the price of each kind of labour is fixed and the supply unlimited. All the firm can do is to decide how much of this labour it will employ. It does this by comparing the extra financial benefit to be obtained from employing more workers (the marginal reve-

Table 13:1
Wage Determination in a Perfectly Competitive Labour Market

Wage Rate per Hour (in dollars)	Number of Workers Demanded by All Firms	Number of Workers Offering Their Services
6.00	2200	200
7.00	1800	400
8.00	1500	600
9.00	1200	800
10.00	1000	1000
11.00	800	1200
12.00	600	1400
13.00	450	1600
14.00	300	1800
15.00	150	2000

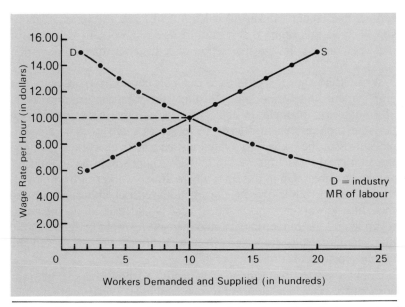

Note: One thousand workers are demanded and supplied at a wage rate of $10.00 per hour.

Figure 13:1 Demand for and Supply of Labour in a Perfectly Competitive Market

nue) with the extra cost of employing them (the marginal cost). In a competitive labour market, the marginal cost is the same as the wage rate. If the marginal revenue exceeds the marginal cost, it will be profitable to hire more workers. If the marginal revenue is less than the marginal cost, it will be more profitable to employ fewer of them. Only when the marginal revenue equals the marginal cost will there be no incentive to alter the number of workers employed.

13.4: MONOPSONY

Another possible type of employment situation is monopsony—that is, a labour market in which there is only one firm recruiting labour, but competition among individuals to supply it. This is the exact opposite, incidentally, of a term we used earlier—monopoly, meaning only one seller.

Because the monopsonist is the only buyer of labour services, the labour supply curve that it faces will be the market supply curve that slopes upward from left to right, indicating that more labour will be supplied only at a higher wage rate. This is in complete contrast to a competitive labour market in which a firm faces a horizontal labour supply curve, indicating that it can hire as many workers as it likes, at the wage rate set by the interaction of industry demand and market supply.

What effect does this difference in supply curves have on wages and employment under monopsony? To explain, we make use once again of a numerical example. In Table 13:2, we can see that the wage rate that the monopsonist must pay increases as more workers are employed. Also, the higher wage rate must be paid to all workers, not just the additional ones employed; otherwise, there would be all kinds of employee unrest. Up to the point where fifteen workers are employed, the marginal revenue exceeds the additional cost of labour. With more than fifteen workers, the marginal cost would exceed the marginal revenue and the monopsonist could increase its profit by reducing the number of persons employed. Only with fifteen workers would the monopsonist be maximizing its profit.

Unlike the firm operating in a competitive labour market, the monopsonist's extra expenditure for each additional worker will be more than the going wage rate. This is because the wage rate, which has risen as more labour is demanded, is higher not just for the additional worker but for all the other workers already employed. Thus, for example, in hiring the fourteenth worker, the marginal cost, on an hourly basis is not $10.00 (the wage rate) but $23.00. This comprises $10.00

Table 13:2
Wage and Employment Determination under Monopsony

Number of Workers Employed	Wage Rate per Hour (in dollars)	Total Cost of Labour (in dollars)	Marginal Cost of Labour (MC) (in dollars)	Marginal Revenue of Labour (MR) (in dollars)	
10	6.00	60.00	——	35.00	MC < MR
11	7.00	77.00	17.00	33.00	
12	8.00	96.00	19.00	31.00	
13	9.00	117.00	21.00	29.00	
14	10.00	140.00	23.00	27.00	↓
15	11.00	165.00	25.00	25.00	MC = MR
16	12.00	192.00	27.00	23.00	↑
17	13.00	221.00	29.00	21.00	
18	14.00	252.00	31.00	19.00	
19	15.00	285.00	33.00	17.00	
20	16.00	320.00	35.00	15.00	MC > MR

for the fourteenth worker plus $13.00 for the previous thirteen workers (an additional $1.00 each). Because of this fact, the wage rate and the amount of labour employed will both be less under monopsony than they would be in a competitive labour market. This can best be demonstrated by use of graphic analysis. In Figure 13:2 we can see that the monopsonist would hire fifteen workers (the point at which the marginal revenue curve intersects the marginal cost curve) compared with about nineteen workers in a competitive labour market. The monopsonist will also pay only about $11.00 per hour, compared with over $15.00 under pure competition.

We should, however, recognize the middle ground between monopsony on the one hand and a competitive labour market on the other. Thus, if only a few firms operate in a labour market, they may very well co-operate, formally or informally, to hold down the wage rate. This situation, in which there are just a few buyers in a labour market, is described as *oligopsony* (as contrasted with oligopoly which means just a few sellers). Where there are many buyers but the type of labour demanded is somewhat dissimilar and some firms prefer candidate A over candidate B or vice versa, the term used is *monopsonistic competition*. This latter market model is very close to the situation that exists in most labour markets.

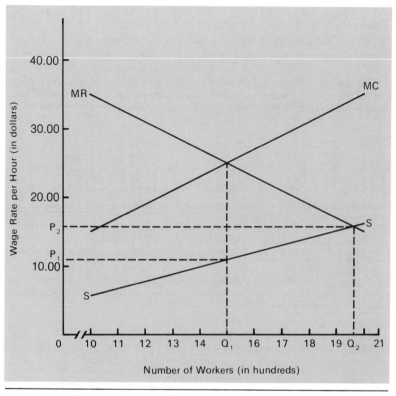

Note: The monopolist hires Q_1 workers (the labour force at which MR = MC) and pays a wage of P_1 dollars. Under pure competition, a firm would hire Q_2 workers and pay a wage rate of P_2 dollars.

Figure 13:2 A Monopsonistic Firm Will Pay a Lower Wage Rate and Hire Fewer Workers than Would a Firm Operating in a Perfectly Competitive Labour Market

13.5: LABOUR UNION MONOPOLY

In practice, not all individuals compete freely with each other in offering their services in the labour market. This lack of competition among workers comes about in the vast majority of cases through the existence of a strong *labour union*—an association of workers practising a similar trade or employed in the same company or industry.

A *craft union* is an association of workers practising the same trade—for example, the United Brotherhood of Carpenters and Joiners of America. An *industrial union* is an association of many different types of workers, but usually all employed in the same firm or industry—for example, the United Automobile, Aerospace, and Agricultural Implement Workers of America.

Restricting the Labour Supply

One way in which a labour union can affect wages and employment is by *restricting the labour supply*. Table 13:3 shows the demand for a particular type of worker at different wage rates. It also shows the supply of workers without a union and the supply of workers with a union. We can see from the Table that without any restriction of supply the wage rate would be $9.00 per hour; and the number of workers employed, 800. With a union, the supply of qualified workers, we assume, has been cut in half. As a result, the demand for and supply of workers are equal at a wage rate of $11.00 per hour—a point at which only 600 workers are employed. The effect of the labour union's action in restricting supply has been, therefore, to raise the wage rate by $2.00 per hour and reduce the number of persons employed by 200. The shift in the supply curve of labour and its effects on wages and employment are illustrated in Figure 13:3.

Table 13:3
A Labour Union May Restrict the Supply of Labour
Causing a Higher Wage Rate and Less Employment

Wage Rate per Hour (in dollars)	Number of Workers Offering Their Services (without union)	Number of Workers Demanded	Number of Workers Offering Their Services (with union)
6.00	200	1100	100
7.00	400	1000	200
8.00	600	900	300
9.00	800	800	400
10.00	1000	700	500
11.00	1200	600	600
12.00	1400	500	700
13.00	1600	400	800
14.00	1800	300	900
15.00	2000	200	1000

Note: It is assumed that the existence of a craft union has reduced the available supply of qualified workers by half.

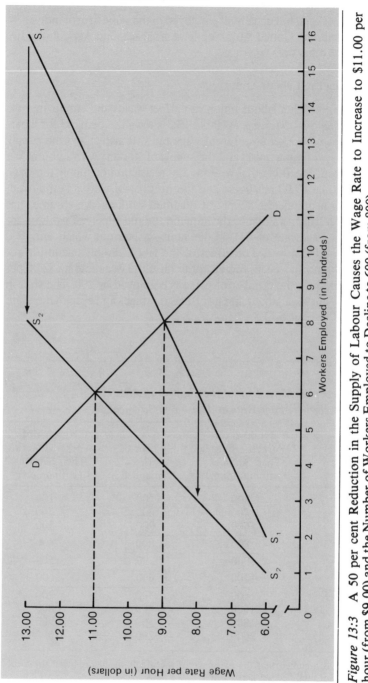

Figure 13:3 A 50 per cent Reduction in the Supply of Labour Causes the Wage Rate to Increase to $11.00 per hour (from $9.00) and the Number of Workers Employed to Decline to 600 (from 800).

Industrial unions, unlike the craft unions and professional associations, do not usually attempt to restrict the supply of labour. Since their membership consists of the unskilled and semi-skilled non-managerial workers in an industry, they are in no position to require long training periods, entrance examinations, and the like. Instead, their main concern is to try to ensure that every non-management worker in an industry is a dues-paying member of the union.

Although industrial unions are not greatly concerned with restricting the supply of workers, they are very much concerned with wage rates and conditions of work. In negotiating a labour contract with management, the union will try to obtain the best possible overall package of wages and fringe benefits. A high wage rate will obviously be the centrepiece of such a package.

A craft union will also be very much concerned with the rate of remuneration of its members. Thus, in a particular area, the craft unions—for example, in construction—will negotiate wage rates for the next one or two years with the employers. Also, professional associations will set a schedule of fees to which members are expected to adhere.

The ability of a craft union to enforce these negotiated wage rates is usually very great. If an employer tries to pay less, a strike will be called. However, the union's power extends only to those firms that have participated in the agreement. In construction, for example, the labour employed by most small builders is non-union. As far as professional associations are concerned, the policing of a fee schedule is often very difficult. That is why, for example, you will sometimes hear a lawyer quoting a fee at so much below "tariff". This tendency to charge less than the recommended fee will continue so long as the supply of lawyers tends to exceed the demand for them.

Increasing the Demand for Labour

A labour union may attempt to increase the wage rate and the number of union members employed by causing an increase in the "quantity" demanded—in other words, a movement along the demand curve for union labour. It may also try to achieve a shift of the demand curve to the right, meaning that more union labour is demanded at each wage rate than before. One way it can achieve these two aims is by trying to discourage employers from using non-union labour. Another way is to advertise products as being "union-made" in the hope that consumers will prefer such products over others. A third way is to include clauses in a labour contract that prevent an employer from substituting labour-saving machinery in the production process. A fourth way is to pressure Parliament for additional tariff or quota protection from foreign competition for the industry's products. At a more general level, a labour union can try to promote the demand for the industry's products by pressuring government to adopt a full-employment policy. It can also try to reduce competition for jobs by restrictions on immigration. Some of these policies—such as opposition to greater mechanization or automation—may eventually prove detrimental to labour's interest, particularly if they make an industry unable to compete with lower-priced imports. Figure 13:4 shows how an increase in the demand for labour may increase the wage rate and the number of workers employed.

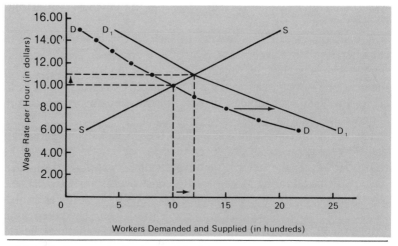

Note: An increase in the demand for labour causes the wage rate to increase to $11.00 per hour (from $10.00) and the number of workers employed to increase to 1200 (from 1000).

Figure 13:4 Effects of an Increase in the Demand for Labour on the Wage Rate and Number of Workers Employed

13.6: BILATERAL MONOPOLY

Sometimes a labour market lacks competition among both employers and employees—firms are not actively competing with each other to recruit employees and workers are not competing with each other in trying to obtain jobs. On the one side, there may be just one large firm or a few large firms acting jointly; on the other, there may be a large and powerful labour union. This situation is called *bilateral monopoly*. It combines a situation of monopsony (one buyer of labour services) with a situation of union monopoly (one seller of labour services).

To illustrate this type of labour market, Figure 13:5 combines the monopsony situation of Figure 13:2 with a labour union's desire for a wage rate of $14.00 per hour (the horizontal part of the supply curve S_1S). It is clear that no wage rate is logically acceptable to both parties. Therefore, the actual wage rate will be somewhere in between; its actual position will be determined by the relative bargaining strengths of management and labour.

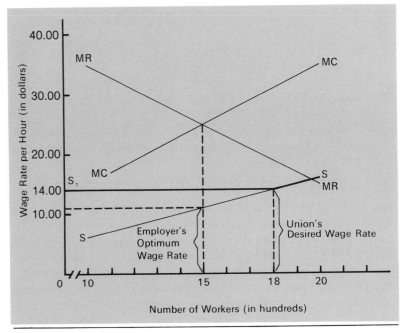

Note: The monopsonist seeks a wage rate of just over $10.00 per hour. But the labour union wants a wage rate of $14.00 per hour. The actual rate will be determined by relative bargaining strengths.

Figure 13:5 With Bilateral Monopoly, the Wage Rate Cannot Be Logically Determined

13.7: MINIMUM WAGE RATES

In many countries, the government sets a minimum wage rate for labour. In Canada, the federal and provincial governments carry out this task. The minimum wage rates are normally set above the level that would be established by the forces of demand and supply. How does this affect the number of workers employed? In Figure 13:6 we can see

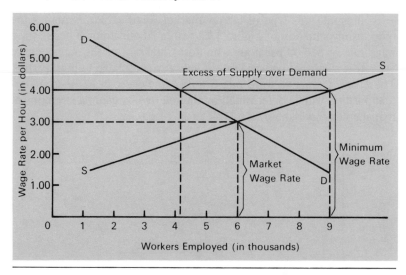

Figure 13:6 Government-Imposed Minimum Wage Rate Raises the Wage But Reduces Employment

that, in the absence of a minimum wage rate, the actual wage rate would be $3.00 per hour; the number of workers employed, 6000.

If the government imposes a minimum wage rate of $4.00 per hour, firms would employ only just over 4000 workers—a reduction of almost one-third of the present labour force. At this minimum wage rate, however, more workers would seek jobs. The labour force seeking work would in fact rise to 9000—a one-third increase over its present size. The effect of the minimum wage rate is therefore to provide a higher wage to those still employed, but to eliminate jobs for many others. The severity of unemployment will depend not only on the level of the minimum wage rate, but also on the elasticities of labour demand and supply.

The same result would occur from a union-negotiated minimum wage rate in a particular firm or industry. It is difficult for a labour union to gain the best of both worlds—higher wages and more employment. If it insists on a higher wage rate, it must usually accept less employment for its members. The only other way for a labour union to have both higher wages *and* more employment is if the marginal revenue of labour increases. This can be achieved by greater labour productivity, by an increase in the demand for the product causing the price to rise, or by both combined.

The possible unemployment of a number of its members will in theory have some moderating effect on a union's wage demands. The important consideration is the elasticity of demand for labour. Will the higher wage rate cause a large or a small reduction in the demand for labour? The more elastic the demand, the greater the reduction in the number of workers employed. This reduction may not take place immediately, but a firm will gradually substitute more and more labour-saving equipment and, in an assembly-type operation, use more and more parts manufactured more cheaply abroad. Even if it does not dismiss workers, it will achieve the same result by slowing the rate of recruitment of new workers. In practice, it appears that many labour unions believe that the sacrifice of some jobs, particularly those of future rather than present workers, is a necessary price for obtaining higher wages, better fringe benefits, and better working conditions for those union members who remain employed.

13.8: THEORY AND PRACTICE

There are in practice industries in which competition among employers to recruit new staff is considerable. There are also industries in which just a few firms—for example, car manufacturers—take a common hiring stand, particularly with regard to wage rates. On the employee side, there are industries in which employees have strong labour unions, and others—particularly industries comprising many small firms—in which competition among applicants for jobs is intense.

Most firms will hire an additional worker if his or her production is worth more than the wage and fringe benefits to be paid. However, it is by no means easy, in practice, to determine what exactly is an extra worker's productivity. Very often, additional hiring is based on a manager's opinion (possibly inaccurate) that an extra man or woman is needed. And since, according to one of Parkinson's Laws, work expands to fill idle hands, it soon becomes impossible to prove that the extra worker's tasks could perhaps have been done at no extra cost by someone else already on the payroll. Also, many employees, such as management trainees, may not be immediately productive.

Because of this lack of precise information about present or future worker productivity, hiring often tends to be done in an irregular fashion. In times of general economic expansion, a firm is fairly liberal in its hiring policy and the payroll is expanded. Conversely, in times of general economic contraction, even some of the supposedly "indispensables" may be fired and the payroll squeezed. The major variable is a company's sales prospects—how much can be sold and at what price. A worker's productivity may be the same, but a firm may believe rightly or wrongly that sales revenue will rise or decline. And revenue is just as important a part of labour's marginal revenue as is labour's marginal physical productivity. Furthermore, hiring to some extent reflect the subjective likes and dislikes of the recruiter. This means that a person may hire someone who is personally compatible, but who is not necessarily the most productive. In such a case, the extra labour cost may exceed the additional benefit received by the company.

In practice, labour is considerably immobile. Many workers are unaware of other suitable job opportunities. Also they are also often extremely reluctant, because of family, pension, and other ties, to change jobs. Furthermore, government intervenes in many labour markets by setting minimum wage rates, paid vacations, and other conditions of employment.

13.9: HIGHER REAL WAGES TODAY

In Canada today, a worker usually earns much more in real terms than did his or her parents and grandparents. Relatively abundant food, good clothing, free public education, medical care, automobiles, paid vacations, travel, household appliances, and even ownership of a home are all part of the good life that the average employed worker now enjoys. However, there is much more pollution of the land, the air, and the water than there was in our ancestors' days. And there still is, of course, much individual poverty that varies with the state of the economy and the level of unemployment.

The increase in real wages that has occurred over the years can be attributed in part to an improvement in the quality of labour. Generally speaking, we are healthier, better educated, better informed, and better trained than our ancestors. We may even claim to possess more entrepreneurial ability. Compared with our ancestors, we should therefore be able to produce more, even if our efforts were combined with only the same amount of land, capital, and technology as they possessed.

These other factors of production, however, have shown the most remarkable improvement over the years. Land, in its economic sense, means mineral resources as well as the soil. Discovery of major deposits of iron ore, nickel, and other minerals as well as vast resources of coal, oil and natural gas have contributed spectacularly to the increase in the Canadian worker's real wages. So also have the vast amounts of hydro-electric power that Canada's rivers and waterfalls have made possible, and the relatively easy transportation facilities provided by the St. Lawrence River and the Great Lakes. Even the soil itself has been transformed by fertilizer, drainage, and irrigation so that it can produce more. Also new crops such as rapeseed (or canola) have been successfully developed in Canada.

"I've just worked it out, Doris. At our rate of saving, I'll only need to work another ninety-three years to pay off our debts."

Another factor that has played an extremely important role in raising the Canadian worker's productivity is capital investment—the use of buildings, machinery and equipment in production. This normally requires the diversion of a part of a country's productive effort from the production of goods for consumption to the production of goods, such as factories and machines, that can produce other goods. In most countries, the desire to raise living standards quickly often means that capital formation is neglected. In a developing country, which has an abnormally large capital need because of its many resources waiting to be exploited, the local capital supply is usually insufficient. Also, in some relatively well-developed countries such as Canada the emphasis on a high standard of living means that a large part of the money to pay for major capital spending programs, both public and private, is often sought abroad. Whatever the source, this capital is indispensable in raising a country's productive capacity. And the large amounts of private industrial capital in Canada, as well as the vast amount of social capital, such as roads, railways, dams, hospitals, bridges, and so on, have meant that despite a larger labour force, the amount of capital per worker has greatly risen. This extra capital per worker, in large part due to investment from abroad, has greatly contributed to the rise in real wages of Canadian workers.

Another important reason for higher real wages in this country is the amazing growth in technology, much of it imported from the United States and elsewhere. Without this technical knowledge, most of our natural resources would still lie untapped as they did for so many hundreds and even thousands of years. Today, minerals, lumber, and other resources are made into usable products with the aid of electrically driven machines that multiply our power and dexterity many times over. Even the land, thanks to the development of more productive hybrid crops, now provides astonishing yields per acre. The "communications explosion" and transportation revolution have also meant that people are better informed and more widely travelled than was conceivable even only fifty years ago.

13.10: WAGE MOVEMENTS BETWEEN DIFFERENT OCCUPATIONS

If we look at economic history once more, we will observe that the difference in wage rates between one occupation and another has also changed over the years. This has been caused, as we should expect, by changes in demand and supply. Let us consider two examples.

At the beginning of this century, domestic servants were easy to obtain and cheap to employ. Nowadays, by contrast, the case is just the opposite. The reason for the increase in their wages relative to other occupations is twofold. First, the demand for domestic help is still quite high, despite the invention of labour-saving household devices: a large professional class, with both husband and wife at work, willing and able to hire domestic help, has emerged in Canada. Second, the supply of such labour has been reduced. This reduction has been caused by competition from alternative forms of employment such as retail stores and manufacturing firms; by the higher standard of education and training of the mass of the population who can therefore qualify for other forms of employment; by the widespread attitude that domestic service is degrading in a democratic society; and by the restrictions placed on the immigration of unskilled labour into Canada.

As another example, steelworkers used to work early in this century for 50 to 60 hours per week for an extremely low hourly wage. Nowadays, their wages compare favourably with accountants, lawyers, and teachers. On the demand side, there has been a growing need for steel in a new and developing country; consequently, more and more capital per worker, together with more sophisticated steel-making technology, has raised labour productivity. On the supply side, a strong labour union—the United Steelworkers of America—has emerged and has effectively insisted on a shorter work week, higher wage rates, and greater fringe benefits. Only now is the prosperity of Canada's steelworkers being adversely affected by cheaper foreign steel.

In our type of society, there is nothing static about relative wage scales. Over the past decade, for example, nurses, teachers, and lawyers have all known wide variations in the demand for their services. If demand for and supply of a particular type of labour alters, the wage rate will alter too. It is not surprising, therefore, that different groups of labour are constantly trying to expand demand for their services on the one hand and to restrict the supply and impose minimum pay rates on the other. The problem is, of course, that there is no objective measure to indicate what a particular kind of worker is worth; it is all a matter of supply and demand and sometimes government regulation.

Summary

1. The terms *wages* is used in economics to embrace all the different types of payment—wages, salaries, commissions, bonuses, royalties, and fringe benefits—that are made to the various kinds of labour in exchange for their services. The *wage rate* is the price

that is paid to a particular kind of labour for its services over a specific period of time. Wage rates vary considerably in Canada between different occupations and between different parts of the country because of different demand/supply situations.

2. Labour consists of a number of groups of individuals with different skills and abilities and with limited mobility from one group to another—hence the term "non-competing groups."
3. Sometimes the wages for a job will contain a premium to compensate for danger or unpleasantness.
4. Unwillingness to move from one part of a country to another, or from one country to another, helps create and perpetuate different demand/supply situations, even for the same job, and therefore different wage rates.
5. Some workers can multiply their services by use of TV, radio, or print.
6. Different degrees of competition, by firms seeking workers on the one hand, and workers seeking jobs on the other, also help create wage disparities. There are four theoretically possible basic situations: (a) the *competitive labour market*—with competition among firms to recruit employees and competition among workers to obtain jobs; (b) *monopsony*—with no competition among firms, but competition among workers; (c) *labour union monopoly*—with competition among firms but no competition among workers; and (d) *bilateral monopoly*—with no competition among firms and no competition among workers. A labour union can influence wages and employment by restricting the supply of labour; by direct negotiation; and by causing an increase in the demand for labour.
7. In many countries, the government sets a minimum wage rate for male and female labour. This can result in a higher wage to those still employed, but eliminate jobs for many others.
8. Today's workers usually earns much more in real terms than did his or her parents and grandparents.
9. Relative wage rates can vary over the years between different occupations.

Key Terms

Review Questions

1. How is the term "wages" used in economics?
2. "Labour is by no means homogenous." Explain.
3. What are "non-competing groups"? How does their existence affect wage rates?
4. Give three examples of jobs which offer a danger, hardship, or isolation premium.
5. How does a person's reluctance to leave his or her home town affect wage rates?
6. What effect does immigration have on wage rates?
7. What are the characteristics of a competitive labour market?
8. What is monopsony? How does the supply curve of labour for a monopsonist differ from that for a firm operating in a competitive labour market?
9. What effect does the difference in the labour supply curve for a monopsonist have on wage and employment determination?
10. What is oligopsony? How does it differ from monopsonistic competition?
11. Distinguish between a craft union and an industrial union.
12. Why do labour unions and professional asociations restrict the supply of particular types of labour? What effect does this restriction have?
13. How can a labour union achieve higher wages and increased employment? What is the usual relationship between these two goals?
14. What is bilateral monopoly? Give two Canadian examples.
15. The amount of labour employed in a particular occupation is not, in practice, determined scientifically. Comment.
16. What are the possible economic and social effects of a government-set minimum wage rate?
17. Why are wages higher in real terms today than they were in the past?
18. Do wage rates for different occupations always bear the same relationship to each other? Answer, with examples.
19. What are the reasons for income inequalities in Canada?

20. How does a country share among its population the goods and services produced? Is this a satisfactory way? What alternatives, if any, exist?

21. Why are doctors, lawyers, and dentists among the highest-paid occupations in Canada? Will this increase the supply?

22. Why are self-employed entertainers and artists, employees, and people who fish, among the lowest paid? Will this decrease the supply?

23. "If I don't make it as a professional hockey player, I'll become a wildlife biologist!" Discuss.

24. Why is geography an important factor in explaining wage differences?

25. Competition in the labour market is against the workers' interests. Discuss.

26. The competitive labour market is the exception rather than the rule in Canada today. Discuss.

27. Profit-sharing, rather than the payment of wages, would reduce management-labour antagonisms and improve the allocation of a country's resources. Comment.

28. Explain and discuss how Canada's immigration policy affects the labour market in this country. What changes, if any, would you like to see? Why?

29. Marginal revenue and cost analysis does not really apply to labour. Discuss.

30. Today's Canadians are smarter than their parents and grandparents. Hence they are paid more. Discuss.

31. Plumbers now earn more but provide less service than their predecessors. Discuss.

32. In France, garbage is collected daily and letters are delivered six days a week. How does this compare with the situation in Canada, where jobs are hard to find? Discuss.

33. "In our type of society, there is nothing static about relative wage scales." How do you predict relative wage scales will change in the future for a variety of occupations? What trends are already apparent?

14. LABOUR UNIONS AND LABOUR LEGISLATION

CHAPTER OBJECTIVES

A. To indicate what exactly is a labour union
B. To explain the origins of labour unions in Canada
C. To examine the various types of labour unions
D. To indicate the political role of labour unions
E. To describe how workers bargain collectively for pay and other conditions of work
F. To explain how, during contract negotiations, conciliation is required by law before a firm may lock out its workers or the employees go on strike
G. To indicate how, during the life of a collective agreement, any grievances must ultimately be settled by arbitration
H. To outline the major types of labour laws in Canada

CHAPTER OUTLINE

14.1: LABOUR UNION DEFINED

A *labour union* or *trade union* is an association of workers, practising a similar trade or employed usually in the same company or industry. As we noted in the previous chapter, there are both craft unions and industrial unions. Whatever the case, the basic purpose of the union is to improve the economic welfare, including pay and job security, of its members through collective, rather than individual, bargaining of wage rates, hours of work, order of layoffs, and so on, with employers. Many labour unions use the term "union" in their official title, but many others use terms such as association, brotherhood, federation, alliance, or guild.

In the various Labour Relations Acts and Codes in Canada, the term "trade union" is used. In fact, the terms "trade union" and "labour union" are often used interchangeably. However, the term "trade union" is more commonly used with reference to a group of workers possessing a certain type of industrial skill or "trade" (in other words, a craft union), whereas the term "labour union" is more commonly used with reference to a group of unskilled and/or multi-skilled workers employed in a particular industry. Throughout this chapter, we use the term labour union.

There are, in addition to the labour unions referred to above, many employee associations that have not been officially recognized, under the term of a Labour Relations Act, as the bargaining agent for employees in a particular firm. Although without legal status, these unofficial or "quasi labour unions" are nevertheless recognized by the employer as the spokesman for its employees—bargaining on their behalf or at least presenting the employees' complaints to the employer.

Not all industries have the same degree of union membership. Thus, there is very little unionization so far among workers in agriculture, trade, finance, insurance, real estate, and service industries generally. However, this picture has been changing in recent years with, for example, nurses, teachers, and bank clerks joining the ranks of organized labour. In some industries—for example, railway transport, transportation equipment, leather, paper and allied industries—the degree of unionization is extremely high.

Certain persons are usually excluded from coverage under the federal and provincial Labour Relations Acts. This means that the employer has no legal obligation to recognize or bargain collectively with any unions representing such persons. In Ontario, for example, persons excluded from coverage under the Labour Relations Act include: domestics employed in a private home; persons employed in agriculture, hunting, or trapping; members of the police force; and full-time firefighters.

Public sector employees are covered by separate collective bargaining legislation.

14.2: HISTORY OF LABOUR UNIONS IN CANADA

Labour unions in Canada date from the early nineteenth century when the immigrant British began to organize associations of carpenters, printers, and shoemakers. However, geographical proximity and and financial and professional help from U.S. unions in establishing and expanding unions in Canada soon caused much closer ties to develop between organized labour in the two North American countries than between Canada and Britain. In the early part of the twentieth century, the Roman Catholic Church played an important role in organizing unions among French-speaking workers in Quebec.

During the nineteenth century, labour unions and their organizers had an extremely difficult time. First of all, they ran into bitter hostility from employers. Second, they could be prosecuted in the criminal courts for conspiring to restrain trade and, in the event of a strike, sued in the civil courts for losses caused to an employer. This situation continued until the beginning of the twentieth century when unions were given statutory protection from such actions.

14.3: TYPES OF LABOUR UNIONS

Until the 1930s, the craft union was the predominant type of labour union in Canada. However, the emergence of large mass-production industries employing vast numbers of unskilled and semi-skilled workers created a vacuum that the craft unions, with their rigorous entrance requirements, were neither able nor prepared to fill. Consequently, a new type of union, the industrial union, with membership open to almost all non-management workers, whatever the job, came into being. The exceptions include security personnel and persons employed in a confidential capacity.

Labour unions, as well as being divided into craft unions and industrial unions, differ in another way—the geographical scope of their membership. On this basis, labour unions can be classified as international, national, or local. *International unions* are unions with members in the United States and Canada that in practice have their head offices in the United States. An example of such a union is the International Chemical Workers' Union.

National unions are unions with totally Canadian membership—for example, the Canadian Union of Public employees.

Local unions are of two types. The *directly chartered local union* is organized by, and receives its charter from, a central labour congress and is not part of an international or national union. The *independent local union* is a local labour organization not formally connected to or affiliated with any other labour organization.

Table S.4
Union Membership in Canada, in thousands of persons, 1921-1982

Year	Union Member-ship	Total Non-Agricultural Paid Workers	Union Member-ship as a Percentage of Non-Agricultural Paid Workers	Union Member-ship as a Percentage of the Civilian Labour Force
1921	313	1 956	16.0	9.4
1926	275	2 299	12.0	7.5
1931	311	2 028	15.3	7.5
1936	323	1 994	16.2	7.2
1941	462	2 566	18.0	10.3
1946	832	2 986	27.9	17.1
1951	1 029	3 625	28.4	19.7
1956	1 352	4 058	33.3	24.5
1961	1 447	4 578	31.6	22.6
1966	1 736	5 658	30.7	24.5
1967	1 921	5 953	32.3	26.1
1968	2 010	6 068	33.1	26.6
1969	2 075	6 380	32.5	26.3
1970	2 173	6 465	33.6	27.2
1971	2 231	6 637	33.6	26.8
1972	2 388	6 893	34.6	27.8
1973	2 591	7 181	36.1	29.2
1974	2 732	7 637	35.8	29.4
1975	2 884	7 817	36.9	29.8
1976	3 042	8 158	37.3	30.6
1977	3 149	8 243	38.2	31.0
1978	3 278	8 413	39.0	31.3
1980	3 397	9 027	37.6	30.5
1981	3 487	9 330	37.4	30.6
1982	3 617	9 264	39.0	31.4

Source: Canada Department of Labour, *Directory of Labour Organizations in Canada*
Note: The method of reporting was changed in 1980. Thus statistics up to and including 1978 are for Dec. 31 of each year. But statistics for 1980 are for Jan. 1 (i.e.— equivalent to Dec.31, 1979). This explains the absence in the above Table of 1979 figures

Table S.5
Largest Unions in Canada, by Membership, 1982

1.	Canadian Union of Public Employees	274 742
2.	National Union of Provincial Government Employees	230 000
3.	United Steelworkers of America	197 000
4.	Public Service Alliance of Canada	157 633
5.	United Food and Commercial Workers	135 000
6.	International Union, United Automobile, Aerospace & Agricultural Implement Workers of America	121 829
7.	International Brotherhood of Teamsters, Chauffeurs, Warehousemen and Helpers of America	93 000
8.	United Brotherhood of Carpenters and Joiners of America	89 010
9.	Social Affairs Federation	84 000
10.	Quebec Teaching Congress	82 122
11.	International Brotherhood of Electrical Workers	70 993
12.	Canadian Paperworkers Union	66 210
13.	Service Employees International Union	65 000
14.	International Association of Machinists and Aerospace Workers	64 384
15.	International Woodworkers of America	63 000
16.	Labourers' International Union of North America	55 447

Source: Labour Data Branch, Labour Canada, *Directory of Labour Organizations in Canada 1982,* Minister of Supply and Services Canada, Ottawa, 1982

14.4: LABOUR UNION ORGANIZATION

The basic unit of labour organization, formed in a particular plant or locality, is known as the "local". In the case of an industrial union, a local may consist of either the employees of several small firms in a given area or the employees of one large firm. In the case of a craft union, the membership usually consists of persons practising a common skill—for example, brick-laying—in a given area.

The internal organization of a typical local will vary considerably from one union to another. An example is shown in Figure 14:1.

The union local will have its own constitution, and will draw up its own by-laws governing the conduct of its officers and members. Power is usually exercised by an executive committee, comprising the president, vice-president, and business agent.

Union Officials

In the smaller locals, all the various executive positions are held on a voluntary part-time basis by working members. These persons are elected by the members of the local, for periods ranging from several months to several years. Only in the larger locals is there a full-time *business agent* whose salary is paid either by the local itself or by the national or international office. The part-time officials are reimbursed for time taken from work for union business. Where there is a business agent, he or she will handle much of the work of the union, helping perhaps in the enrolment of new members and in the representation of the union in grievance matters and in contract negotiations.

Part of the executive committee's work is delegated to the various other sub-committees: the organizing and membership committee (which is responsible for recruiting new members); the bargaining committee that looks after negotiations for a new collective agreement; the grievance committee (which is concerned with the processing of members' grievances with the employer); the recreation committee (which looks after dances, parties, excursions, and so on); and the education committee (which disseminates information about union aims and activities to present and prospective members and others).

In the plant itself, other union officials, the *shop stewards* or *zone representatives*, look after the interests of union members—for example, in handling complaints (e.g. incorrect pay) or in filing grievances. The senior steward for a particular area or division is known as the *chief steward*.

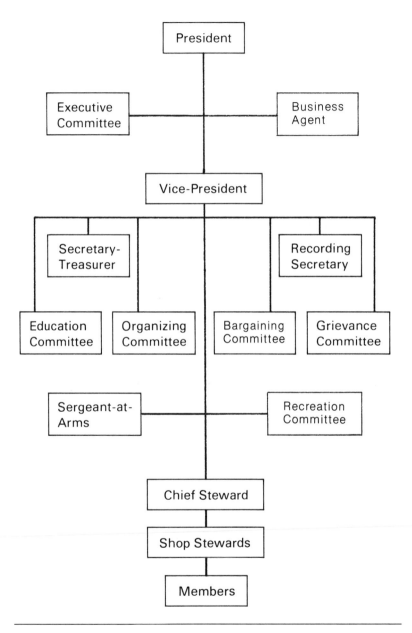

Figure 14:1   Internal Organization of a Typical Union Local

The powers of a union local can vary considerably according to the trade union of which it is a part.

Decentralization

Unlike their counterparts in other parts of the world, most North American labour unions are highly decentralized. In other words, most of the action takes place at the local level rather than at head office. It is the union local, close to the place of employment, where the new members are enlisted; where the employers send the union dues that are deducted from the worker's pay; where the meetings are held to discuss the problems facing the members at work; where social activities are organized; where grievances are discussed; where the strike committees are formed; and where the president and other local officers, as well as shop stewards, are elected.

Of course, the degree of autonomy that a union local enjoys will vary greatly from labour union to labour union. Nevertheless, compared with those in other countries, labour unions in North America are highly decentralized—with the local unions, to say nothing of the independently chartered local unions, enjoying a great deal of autonomy. Only in certain circumstances has the head office of the national or international union the right to interfere in local affairs. This high degree of local autonomy or decentralization is sometimes described as "grass-roots unionism". In some other countries, by contrast, the unions may not even have plant-level local organizations. All union matters are administered from a central office.

Local Collective Bargaining. In line with the decentralized nature of North American labour unions, most of the collective bargaining takes place at the local level. In the case of some large companies, the various locals will use a company-wide bargaining committee to bargain over certain company-wide issues, leaving local issues to be bargained on a local basis. Such a settlement might result in what is commonly called a company-wide "master agreement" with local supplements. In other words, each local union usually negotiates with the company that employs its members. In other countries such as West Germany and Sweden, collective bargaining is conducted at the national level by representatives of all the unions and employers in a particular industry and the agreement reached is binding on union members nation-wide.

14.5: POLITICAL ROLE OF LABOUR UNIONS

Labour unions, through the various provincial and national labour organizations, can exert pressure in municipal, provincial, and federal politics by offering support to political parties willing to help promote union aims. Labour unions also make direct representations to the provincial and federal governments on matter of urgent economic importance such as a high unemployment, high interest rates, or the need for price or profit controls.

Labour Councils

In Canada, the locals of many labour unions are affiliated with a Labour Council established by charter of the Canadian Labour Congress for their particular city or district—for example, The Toronto and District Labour Council (C.L.C.). The delegates from the various locals elect the council's officers, who are responsible for furthering the interests of the labour union movement at the community level—for example, by lobbying municipal governments or by organizing strike aid. These district councils are sometimes called joint boards or conference boards.

In industries organized along craft lines (such as painting and decorating), unions or union locals in a particular area may form a special council to co-ordinate members' activities and resolve jurisdictional problems. Such a council is sometimes called an Allied Trades Federation.

Labour Federations

Most provinces have a Federation of Labour, chartered by the Canadian Labour Congress, which acts as the central organization for the labour union movement in the province. The Federation holds annual conventions where delegates from the affiliated locals vote on policy matters and elect officers. The purpose of the Federation is to represent labour's interest at the provincial level, particularly in the establishment or amendment of labour legislation by the provincial government.

Canadian Labour Congress (CLC)

The major central organization for labour unions in Canada is the Canadian Labour Congress, with headquarters in Ottawa and regional offices in most of the provinces. Most international, national, and local unions, and all labour councils and federations are directly affiliated with the CLC and send delegates to its biennial conventions. The purpose of the CLC is primarily a political one: to act as the common spokesman, particularly in Ottawa, for organized labour throughout Canada. It is also active in helping to settle *jurisdictional disputes* among the affiliated unions. These are disputes in which two or more unions claim the right to be certified as the bargaining agent for the same group of employees—employees who may or may not already be represented by a union.

The primary goal of labour unions in Canada is to secure from employers greater economic benefits for their members. This includes better pay and fringe benefits as well as greater job security and improvement in working conditions, including occupational health and safety. This union philosophy, with its emphasis on economic rather than political goals, is sometimes called "business unionism". However, so far as most Canadian and American union leaders are concerned, North American style democracy and the private enterprise system, despite their faults, have provided their members with one of the highest material standards of living in the world.

14.6: COLLECTIVE BARGAINING

By belonging to a labour union, a worker not only feels psychologically more secure, but also receives the benefits of collective bargaining. Rather than bargain individually with the employer about wages, hours of work, holidays, and so on, the worker bargains as a member of a large group. This group, the union, is often able to employ professional negotiators to help obtain the most favourable terms for its members.

Occasionally, the management of a business firm will voluntarily recognize a labour union as the bargaining agent for the firm's employees. Usually, however, this recognition is that required by law once the union has satisfied the Labour Relations Board's requirements as to minimum employee support. A procedure for certification of the union as bargaining agent for a firm's employees is set out in each provincial Labour Relations Act. At the federal level, the procedure is set out in the Public Service Staff Relations Act and the Canada Labour Code— the former for federal government employees and the latter for other workers coming under federal labour jurisdiction such as airline, railway, and bank employees.

Once a labour union has been certified as the collective-bargaining agent for the workers in a particular plant, the employer is required to enter into negotiations and bargain "in good faith" with the union for a labour contract, setting out the rights and obligations of workers and management. Such a contract is usually for one, two, or three years' duration.

"Steady boys. By the look of the mood in here, they must've gotten wind of that little hike we voted ourselves last night."

14.7: COMPULSORY CONCILIATION

If the employer and labour union are unable to negotiate a collective agreement, they must by law make use of a conciliator (a provincial government employee) who will try, by persuasion, to help them resolve their differences. If these new efforts are unsuccessful, management may try to enforce its point of view by methods such as a *lockout*—that is, closing the plant and "locking out" the employees. The employees, on the other hand, may go on *strike*—that is, withdraw their services and try to prevent management from hiring anyone else to take their place. To prevent striking employees from engaging in acts of personal intimidation or property damage, management may call on the police and private security services and ask one of the courts to issue a court order called an *injunction*, ordering a person or persons to stop doing something. If appropriate, use may also be made of the criminal law. As a last resort, if no agreement is reached, the government may intervene and, in the public interest, impose a settlement.

14.8: ARBITRATION

Every collective agreement must, by law, contain an arbitration clause. This means that if an employee grievance remains unresolved after having been considered at each of the steps of a clearly defined grievance procedure, it must be settled by *arbitration*—that is, by the decision of an outside person (or persons) who reviews the facts and make a decision legally binding on both management and labour. A *grievance* is an alleged violation of one or more terms of the labour contract or of customary practice in the firm.

14.9: LABOUR LEGISLATION

Under common law (the body of law that has developed over the centuries based on precedent, or prior judicial decision), an employer and an employee have a number of well-established obligations towards each other.

Thus management must, for example, provide the employee with a safe place in which to work; must employ reasonably careful and competent fellow workers; must fulfil any contractual agreements with the employee or the labour union that represents him or her; must reimburse the employee for any expenses properly incurred in the course of his or her duties; and must provide the employee with reasonable notice of dismissal, or wages instead.

The employee also has a number of obligations toward the employer. He or she should not be persistently late or absent without permission; should not disobey orders so long as they are reasonable and legal; should not be dishonest, disloyal, or clearly incompetent; should not be grossly immoral or habitually drunk at work or elsewhere; should not be habitually negligent or destructive at his or her job; and should not be chronically disabled, either because of accident or illness. Should the employee fail to fulfil any of these common law obligations, his or her employment may be terminated without notice.

Because of the Constitution Act, 1867, which gave the provincial governments the right to pass laws concerning "property and civil rights," most labour legislation in Canada is of provincial origin. The federal government is, however, empowered to pass labour laws with regard to industries specifically under its jurisdiction. These include: navigation, shipping, interprovincial railways, canals, telegraphs, steamship lines and ferries, airports, air transportation, radio stations, and works declared by Parliament to be for the general advantage of Canada or of two or more provinces. It also has jurisdiction over persons employed under federal government work contracts and on works partly financed by federal government funds. It also has the right to legislate on matters delegated to it by the provincial governments such as unemployment assistance and old age pensions.

Industries Under Federal Jurisdiction

Industries under federal jurisdiction, including firms employed under federal contract, are regulated by the terms of the *Canada Labour Code*. This Code, which came into force in July, 1971, consisted of five parts—each one absorbing a former Act. However, Part 1 (Fair Employment Practices) was subsequently replaced by the Canadian Human Rights Act and Part 2 (Female Employees' Equal Pay) was repealed.

Labour Standards

Part 3 of the Canada Labour Code requires that employers in industries under federal jurisdiction: (a) limit the hours of work of employees to a maximum of 8 hours per day and 40 per week; (b) pay one and one-half times the regular rate of wages for any hours in excess of the standard hours, if such hours are permitted by the Ministry of Labour; (c) pay a specified minimum hourly wage for all employees aged 17 and over, and a specified minimum wage for persons under 17; (d) provide each employee with a minumum of two weeks' vacation with vacation pay (4 per cent of the employee's annual wages) after every completed year of employment or, should the employee leave during a year, pay him or her the vacation pay for the completed portion of his or her year of employment; and (e) provide each employee a holiday with pay on each of the general holidays (New Year's Day, Good Friday, Victoria Day, Canada Day, Labour Day, Thanksgiving Day, Remembrance Day, Christmas Day, and Boxing Day) falling within the period of employment.

Safety of Employees

Part 4 of the Code tries to ensure safe working conditions for all employees in industries and undertakings under federal jurisdiction by: (a) specifying all the elements of a complete industrial safety program and the general obligation of employers and employees to perform their duties in a safe manner; (b) authorizing regulations to deal with problems of occupational safety; (c) authorizing the use of advisory committees and special task forces to assist in developing the industrial safety program, all to be accompanied by continuous consultation among federal and provincial government departments, industry and organized labour; (d) providing for research into causes and prevention of accidents; (e) authorizing an extended program of safety education; and (f) providing for regional safety officers and federally-authorized provincial inspectors to enforce the Code.

Industrial Relations

Part 5 of the Canada Labour Code regulates industrial relations in industries under federal jurisdiction. The Code recognizes the right of employees to organize and bargain collectively through trade unions. However, both employers and employees are required to bargain in good faith, and to include in the labour contract a provision for the arbitration of disputes. The Code prohibits unfair labour practices (such as discrimination and coercion) by both employers and employees, and provides for government conciliation officers or boards to help mediate differences between the two parties in contract negotiations. The administration of Part 5 of the Code is the responsibility of the federal Minister of Labour. Part of his or her authority—for example, the provisions covering the certification of bargaining agents—has been delegated to the Canada Labour Relations Board.

Fair Employment Practices

Under the Canadian Human Rights Act, discrimination is prohibited in any matter, including employment, on grounds of race, national or ethnic origin, colour, religion, age, sex, or marital status. However, exceptions are permitted for bona fide occupational reasons or if a person's employment is terminated at normal retirement age. The Act also prohibits pay differentials between male and female employees based on sex discrimination alone. Merit and/or seniority must be the only criteria for wage differentials. The Act is administered by the Canadian Human Rights Commission and heavy fines may be imposed for violations.

Provincial Labour Legislation

By virtue of their constitutional power, the provincial legislatures have enacted a large number of labour laws, many of which are frequently being revised. The most important of these provincial labour laws are reviewed in the following pages.

Minimum Wage Rates

All the provinces have legislation under which a provincial government board sets minimum wage rates for persons employed in industries in the province. This legislation is intended to ensure that a minimum standard of living is enjoyed by all employees and their families. For a few types of industrial employment, a higher minimum wage may be set under industrial standards laws. Provincially-set minimum wage rates now cover almost all employment except farm labour and domestic service.

Limited Working Hours

The number of hours of work which an employer may demand from an employee are limited by provincial statute in most provinces—for example, 8 hours per day and 40 hours per week. Many employees do, however, work more than this on a voluntary basis in which case they must be paid at one and one-half times the regular hourly rate for this "overtime". In many provinces, hours of work and wage rates in particular industries are regulated under the various Industrial Standards Acts or, in the case of Quebec, under the Quebec Collective Agreement Act. These Acts encourage conferences of employers and employees to discuss and recommend minimum wages and maximum hours of work for employees in their industries.

Annual Vacations with Pay

All the provinces have legislation providing for compulsory paid vacations for employees in most industries. Vacation pay stamps are used in some provinces. Vacation requirements, after a year of service, are normally two weeks' paid vacation.

Minimum Age

Every province has set a minimum age below which a person may not be employed. In Ontario, for example, this limit is fifteen for factory work, eighteen for mining below ground, and fourteen for work in shops, hotels, or restaurants. Persons under sixteen may not, however, work in Ontario during school hours unless they have been granted special permission, or unless they are on school holidays.

Fair Employment Practices

All provinces prohibit any discrimination by employer and labour union against new employees and new members by reason of race, colour, nationality, ethnic origin, or religion. Certain provinces also prohibit discrimination on the grounds of age or sex. The Acts expressly prohibit the publication of advertisements, use of application forms, and the making of inquiries in connection with the hiring of an employee by an employer, which express or imply discrimination on any of the forbidden grounds.

Equal Pay

Provincial legislation throughout Canada tries to ensure equal pay for men and women for the same or similar work.

Apprenticeship

Some provinces require that certain tradespeople—for example, plumbers, carpenters, electricians, and barbers—undergo a period of apprenticeship training and pass a test before being allowed to offer their services as qualified craftspersons.

Notice of Dismissal

In many provinces, an employer is required by law to give written notice of termination of employment in case of individual dismissal. In Ontario, the notice requirement also includes collective dismissal. In Quebec, notice must also be given in case of mass lay-off.

Accident Prevention

Most provinces have a Factory or Industrial Safety Act to help protect the health and safety of workers in factories and other workplaces. Matters covered include sanitation, heating, lighting, ventilation, and the guarding of dangerous machinery. There are also provincial laws regulating the design, construction, installation, and operation of mechanical equipment such as boilers and pressure vessels, elevators and lifts, and electrical installations; the use of gas- and oil-burning equipment and radiation-producing equipment such as laser sources; and the standards of qualification for workers who install, operate, or service such equipment.

Public Holidays

Most provinces, including Ontario, have legislation governing public holidays. In these provinces, an employee must receive the regular pay even though he or she does not work; if he or she does work, special overtime rates must be paid. The number of holidays named varies from seven to nine. The provisions for payment also vary slightly between provinces.

Labour Relations

There is a Labour Relations Act or Labour Code in every province which sets out the rights of employer and employees. Persons not usually covered by the Acts include domestic servants; persons employed in agriculture, horticulture, hunting, or trapping; police officers; firefighters; and teachers.

Some of the most important provisions of the Ontario Labour Relations Act are the following. Every persons is free to join a trade union of his or her own choice and to participate in its lawful activities. Similarly, a person is free to join any employers' organization and to take part in its lawful activities. Another provision of the Act is that the employer and the trade union which has been certified by the provincial Labour Relations Board as the bargaining agent for the employees, must bargain in good faith and make every reasonable effort to make a collective agreement. This collective agreement, or labour contract, lasting usually one, two, or three years, sets out in writing the rights and duties of employer and employee. Other provisions, such as compulsory conciliation and the inclusion of an arbitration clause in each collective agreement, were discussed earlier in this chapter.

Summary

1. A *labour union* (or *trade union*) is an association of workers, practising a similar trade or employed usually in the same company or industry whose main purpose is to improve the economic welfare of its members by collective rather than individual bargaining with employers.
2. Labour unions in Canada were started in the early nineteenth century. Although British immigrants helped start them, subsequent financial and other help from U.S. labour unions has been a stronger influence. Until the twentieth century, labour unions and their organizers could be prosecuted for conspiring to restrain trade.
3. Until the 1930s, the craft union was the predominant type of labour union in Canada. However, large mass-production factories created a need for a new type of union—the industrial union—with membership open to unskilled and semi-skilled workers.
4. Labour unions can also be divided according to geographical scope of membership. An *international union* has members in both Canada and the United States; a *national union* has only Canadian members; and a *local union* has only local membership within Canada.
5. The basic unit of organization of a labour union is the "local".
6. A Labour Council acts as the spokesperson for organized labour in each municipality. A Labour Federation represents labour unions in the province as a whole. The Canadian Labour Congress acts as a national spokesperson for organized labour. A second, but less powerful, central labour organization is the Confederation of National Trade Unions, with membership mainly in Quebec.
7. Employees who are members of a certified labour union bargain collectively (i.e., as one body) with employers as to the terms and conditions of employment, according to a procedure set out in the

relevant federal or provincial labour relations statute.

8. By law, an employer and a labour union must use the services of a conciliator (a person who tries, by persuasion to bring about an agreement) to negotiate a new collective agreement before the employer may "lock out" its employees or the union call a "strike".

9. An *injunction* is a court order that an employer may obtain instructing strikers to do or not to do something—for example, refraining from physical obstruction.

10. Every collective agreement must, by law, contain a clause whereby every grievance must eventually, if otherwise unresolved, be settled by arbitration.

11. Under common law, an employer and employee have a number of well-established obligations towards each other. Under the Constitution Act, 1867, the provincial governments have the major responsibility for labour laws in Canada. However, the federal government has the right to pass labour laws with regard to: (a) industries under federal jurisdiction; and (b) industries under federal contract. Provincial labour legislation relates to such matters as: minimum age for employment; minimum wage rates for male and female employees; maximum hours of work per week; annual paid vacations; public holidays; weekly rest day; equal pay; fair employment practices; apprenticeship training; workmen's compensation; and labour relations.

Key Terms

Labour union   255
International union   257
National union   257
Local union   257
Union local   260
Executive committee   260
Business agent   260
Shop steward   260
Decentralization   262
Labour council   263
Labour federation   263
CLC   263
Jurisdictional dispute   264

Business unionism   264
Collective bargaining   264
Compulsory conciliation   266
Lockout   266
Strike   266
Injunction   266
Arbitration   266
Grievance   266
Labour legislation   266
Labour standards   268
Safety of employees   269
Industrial relations   269
Fair employment practices   270

Review Questions

1. What is a labour union? What is its purpose?
2. How, why, and when did labour unions come into being in Canada?
3. Distinguish between craft unions and industrial unions. Which came first? Why?
4. What are international unions? Why do they exist? Why do Canadian workers belong to them?
5. Explain the typical organization of a labour union local.
6. Distinguish between the role of the business agent and that of the shop steward.
7. What external ties does a union local possess? Why?
8. What is meant by "business unionism"?
9. What is "collective bargaining"? What are its benefits for the employee?
10. How does a labour union become certified as a bargaining agent?
11. Explain the nature and purpose of compulsory conciliation.
12. How can (a) labour unions and (b) employers exert pressure on each other to arrive at a new labour agreement?
13. "Outstanding grievances must be settled by arbitration". Explain.
14. What are the common law obligations of the employer to the employee, and vice versa?
15. How is the responsibility for labour legislation divided in Canada between the federal and provincial governments?
16. What are the major areas covered by provincial labour legislation?

"How come you didn't make a profit last year?"

15. RENT, INTEREST, AND PROFIT

CHAPTER OBJECTIVES

A. To explain the economic meaning of "rent"
B. To distinguish between economic rent and "transfer earnings"
C. To indicate how economic rent occurs and how the concept applies to people and other resources as well as to land
D. To explain why interest rates (the payment for the use of borrowed funds) vary for different type of loans
E. To discuss the concept of profit as a reward for risk-taking by business firms

CHAPTER OUTLINE

15.1 Rent: The Return to Land and Other Resources
15.2 Interest: The Return to Capital
15.3 Profit: The Return to the Entrepreneur

15.1: RENT: THE RETURN TO LAND AND OTHER RESOURCES

In everyday conversation, we use the term "rent" to mean the price of using, for a certain period of time, a house, car, boat or other type of property owned by someone else.

Economic Rent and Transfer Earnings

In economics, rent has a different meaning. In fact, *economic rent*, as it is called, is the payment over and above that required to keep a factor of production, such as land, in its present use.

The most money that a factor of production can earn in alternative employment is called its *transfer earnings*. Thus, land on the outskirts of a town, now worth $10 000/ha for residential housing development, may only be worth $2000/ha as farmland (the best-paid alternative employment). The implicit earnings of, say, $1000 a year at a 10% annual rate of return would therefore comprise $200 of transfer earnings and $800 of economic rent. As another example, an accountant now employed for $40 000 a year may only be able to obtain an alternative position paying $30 000 a year. The present labour income would therefore comprise $30 000 of transfer earnings and $10 000 of economic rent. Economic rent is, in other words, that part of a factor's earnings that is surplus to its transfer earnings.

The more difficult it is for a factor of production to obtain alternative employment, the larger is the rent portion of its income. One of the chief characteristics of land, in the eyes of early economists, was precisely the fact that land, if not used for growing crops, could be used for little else. Consequently, since the transfer earnings were very small, most of the earnings of land comprised economic rent.

Relatively Fixed Supply of a Factor of Production

How does economic rent arise? In other words, why is a factor of production paid more than the maximum amount that it could secure in alternative use? The reason is that the factors of production are in relatively fixed supply: as demand increases for a factor with little change in its supply, the market price of the factor will rise. Thus, the value of land along the main street of a town will steadily increase (discounting the effects of inflation) because of the mounting pressure of demand.

The term *rent* was originally applied exclusively to land because of the very fact that its supply was fixed. It is true, of course, that land can be reclaimed from the sea and even deserts irrigated and made fertile. It is also true that land can be eroded, flooded, and otherwise destroyed. However, the amount of land involved is only a fraction of the total supply. The supply of land in any particular area is consequently almost completely inelastic. Whatever the price people are willing to pay, the supply of land cannot be increased. All that can happen is that the amount of land in the area may change hands. Because of this fixed supply, any increase in the demand for land will automatically cause a rise in its price. Thus, in Figure 15:1, an increase in demand, from D_1D_1 to D_2D_2, causes land rent to rise from OP_1 to OP_2.

Although the total amount of land is fixed, the supply of land for specific purposes is not. Any specific parcel of land can be used for several different purposes. Thus, the supply of building land in a particular suburban area can be increased (at the expense of the amount

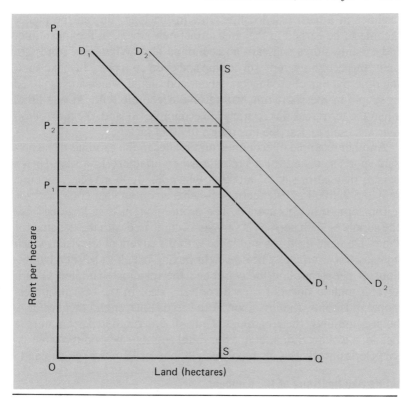

Figure 15:1 The Price (or Rent) of Land Is at the Point at which the Downward-Sloping Demand Curve Intersects the Vertical (Completely Inelastic) Supply Curve

of farmland) if the necessary water, road, sewer, and other services are installed. Often private developers will bear much of this cost. It is quite true to say, therefore, that the higher the price they can obtain per hectare of serviced land, the greater will be the supply. Because land can be used for many different purposes, the supply of land for any one particular purpose can be increased if a higher price is offered. The supply curve of such land, instead of being vertical, would be upward-sloping from left to right. Supply, in other words, would be relatively inelastic instead of completely inelastic. In such a case, the economic rent would be less than where the amount of land available for that particular purpose is absolutely fixed.

In the short run, other factors of production as well as land are relatively fixed in supply. These factors include, for example, shopping facilities in a particular locality. Only in the long run can the higher income to be earned in that area attract new stores. In the meantime, the existing stores will earn an economic rent. When new stores are built, this economic rent will decline and even disappear. Just like land, the other factors of production, labour and capital, which are also fixed in supply in the short run, will receive economic rent. At one time, when the term rent was restricted in economics to land, the term *quasi-rent* was used to describe this return to other factors.

Another example of economic rent relates to the earnings of highly-paid sports stars and other professional entertainers. In a year, such a person may earn, say, $500000 of which $480000 may be economic rent and $20000 transfer earnings—what an entertainer could perhaps get in some other occupation. The economic rent is so large because the supply of such persons is very small compared with the demand for them. Demand itself has multiplied with the advent of television which enables, for example, a heavyweight boxing match to be seen by millions of people around the world and the reigning champion to earn several million dollars for each contest. Also, in the case of professional musicians, the invention of the record-player and the tape deck helped multiply their earnings. Only if every other person were a Beatle, a Rolling Stone, or a Who would pop stars be paid the same as, say, clerical workers—for supply would then have overtaken demand.

Some Applications of the Concept

The concept of economic rent has been used at various times as the basis for recommending:

1. A special land tax. Henry George, a printer in the U.S. in the nineteenth century, advocated in his book, *Progress and Poverty*, that a government's tax needs should be met by a single tax that would be levied on the unearned "surplus" on land.

2. Public confiscation and ownership of land. Whereas capital is accumulated in society only in response to a definite financial incentive, land and other natural resources have always been in existence. Whether a reward is paid for their use of not, so the argument runs, they would still be there. Also, unlike capital goods, land does not periodically have to be replaced. However, most of the present owners of land have purchased it from someone else. Why should they be penalized, the owners would argue, compared with people who have invested their savings in something else? Or compared with people who, instead of saving, used all their income for consumption?

3. The imposition of a capital gains tax —particularly on profits made from speculation in land. Because of a growing population, together with the benefit of the construction, mainly at public expense, of roads, sidewalks, sewers, and water mains, land appreciates in value without any effort on the owner's part. All or most of this increase in value should, it is argued, be taxed away for the benefit of the community as a whole. In fact, many municipal governments do already impose "lot levies" before approving new residential or other construction.

15.2: INTEREST: THE RETURN TO CAPITAL

Capital, in its real sense, consists of factory, commercial and office buildings, equipment, trucks, and other manufactured aids to production and marketing. These items are produced, at the expense of current consumption, because they enable business firms to have a larger output at lower per unit cost than if labour and land alone are used.

Real and Money Rates of Return

The extent to which capital, as a factor of production, increases output is called its *gross productivity*, or *real rate of return*. This amount, when calculated in monetary terms, minus an allowance for depreciation of the capital goods involved, constitutes the net productivity, or *marginal efficiency*, of that capital. Thus, the rate of return on a new piece of equipment, obtained by relating the increase in output (minus depreciation allowance) to the cost of the equipment, may work out at, say, 15 per cent a year.

Capital, in its monetary sense, is the money used by business firms to purchase capital goods and to help cover operating expenses. This money comes in part from lenders and in part from the owners of businesses themselves. The cost of the "borrowed capital" is called the *rate of interest*. So long as a business firm can use the money borrowed to earn a higher rate of return, it is worthwhile to borrow and pay this rate of interest. For the cost of money invested in a business by its owners (the "equity capital"), economists impute a rate of interest equal to its *opportunity cost*—in other words, what it would have cost the firm if the money had been borrowed instead of being supplied by the owners. This implicit cost is just as valid, from the economist's point of view, as the rate of interest paid for the use of other people's money.

Looked at from the lender's point of view, the rate of interest is the reward that the owner of money receives for temporarily giving up its use. Instead of lending it, a personal investor could, after all, have spent it. For abandoning this immediate pleasure, he or she is entitled to some recompense.

Different Rates of Interest

In practice, there are many different rates of interest, not just one. The rate that is charged will depend upon a number of factors, as listed below.

1. Risk involved. Part of the variation between interest rates is explained by the varying degrees of risk involved in obtaining repayment. Thus, if a person has a good *credit rating* (i.e. is considered to be trustworthy by lenders) and can offer stocks, bonds, accounts receivable, or other collateral as security for repayment of a loan, a bank will offer one of their lowest rates of interest. The lowest rate is called the *prime rate*, and is usually reserved for a bank's very best (least-risk) clients.

2. Length of time. Another part of the variation in rates is explained by the differences in length of time for which the money is borrowed. Thus, the rate of interest on short-term loans is usually lower than on long-term ones.

3. Size of loan. Another reason for some variation in interest rates is the size of the loan. Whatever the amount borrowed, the applicant must be interviewed and references checked. Also, instalments of principal and interest must be collected, and any delinquency followed up. Per dollar borrowed, the cost is higher for a small loan than for a large one, and this difference is reflected in the interest rates charged.

4. Geographical differences. Finally, between one part of the country and another, interest rates may vary to reflect local differences in the demand for and supply of funds. However, with branch banking and highly advanced means of communication, local differences are nowadays relatively slight. Even differences in rates of interest between different countries are now smoothed out by international flows of short and long-term funds.

15.3: PROFIT: THE RETURN TO THE ENTREPRENEUR

Business executives consider profit, or net income, to be the surplus of total revenue over total expenses. The more goods and services a firm can sell and the more it can charge for them, the greater will be its total revenue. The more efficiently a firm can produce and market its goods and services, the lower will be its total expenses. It is on this basis of total revenue minus total expenses that business firms calculate and report their profits or earnings.

Implicit Returns to Other Factors of Production

Because firms which have owner-managers do not always pay their managers a normal salary or even any salary at all, but give them a share of profit instead, part of the reported profits is really an implicit return to labour. This is particularly true of unincorporated businesses whose owners, even though running the business, are not permitted by law to pay themselves a salary. All they are allowed to do is take a drawing against future profits. Also, in businesses which own the land they use, the declared profit really contains an implicit rent. And for every business, there is an implicit return on that part of the capital which, instead of being borrowed at interest, is invested by the owners. This implicit return should at least be the same as the going rate of interest on borrowed capital. Business profit therefore contains implicit returns to labour, land, and capital, as well as a residual "economic" profit.

Pure Profit

Most economists consider profit to be an entrepreneur's reward for the acceptance of risk. *Pure* or *economic profit* is in fact the reward that the entrepreneur receives for undertaking the risk of establishing and operating a business. Practically every business-investment decision is accompanied by risk. This is because it is impossible to predict accurately, for example, how consumers will react to a new product; what competing firms will do; when and how governments will intervene; and how domestic and export markets will be affected by changes in the state of the economy. In return for his or her willingness to undertake the risk of losing money, both personal and borrowed funds, and wasting valuable personal time, the entrepreneur demands and merits a special reward. Without it, the entrepreneur would not undertake the risk; and the economy would forgo the income and jobs that could have been created.

Occasionally, a business enjoys some form of monopoly power which enables it to charge more for its products than it would in the presence of competition. Consequently, a *monopoly profit* may arise. Economists recognize that economic profit, although mainly a compensation for risk, may also contain such a monopoly profit.

Some economists, stressing the role of the entrepreneur as a fourth factor of production, consider profit to be the reward for entrepreneurial activity in general, not just risk taking. The more successful an entrepreneur is in combining resources to produce and market what the public wants, the greater will be the profit. Clearly, this concept of profit is very similar to the one already described, for risk and entrepreneurship are inextricably linked.

Whatever the approach used, one thing is clear. Since profit is a residual amount, over and above the explicit and implicit returns paid to labour, land, and capital, it may be positive or negative. The likelihood of making a profit is no greater than the risk of making a loss. Entrepreneurial ability or good management makes the difference.

Pure profit exists only in a dynamic situation, for, in the long run, other firms would move into an industry in pursuit of profit. And as they do, the effects of increased competition would be to reduce the profit earned by everyone. Of course, a certain minimum amount of profit must be earned by a firm, otherwise it would no longer continue to produce. This minimum amount, which is just sufficient to keep capital in a particular line of production, is known as *normal profit.* However, artificial barriers, such as brand advertising and other forms of product differentiation, help established firms to maintain some degree of additional profit by restricting newcomers.

The Purpose of Profit

The purpose of profit may be said to be that of motivating people to assume the risk of establishing and operating a business. Without the lure of profit, people would put their savings to a much safer use. Furthermore, only by producing what consumers want, is it normally possible for a firm to make a profit. Thus, the profit motive is instrumental in allocating a society's factors of production to the uses that society most wants. Of course, this profit motive should not be permitted unrestricted play; otherwise we might once again suffer the economic and social abuses of nineteenth-century *laissez faire*—or unrestricted free enterprise. Thus, as with the Combines Investigation Act, the government intervenes where necessary in the public interest.

The possibility of increased profit is also the most important motivating force for business firms to reduce costs and improve the efficiency of production. In communist countries, by way of contrast, production quotas assigned by regional-planning committees have long been used instead of profit as the motivating force. However, the result has been the output of many poor-quality goods which, although perhaps achieving the production quota, have often been relatively unsaleable. In non-communist countries, the profit motive has provided the incentive for business firms to emphasize not only quality but also the production of goods and services that consumers really want.

The more profit a firm makes, the more it can reinvest or pay out in dividends to its shareholders. In turn, shareholders have more money and a greater claim on the goods and services currently produced.

Profit Controls

Some people treat profit as a dirty word, synonymous with worker exploitation, ignoring its importance as a stimulus to saving, investment, risk-taking, innovation, sheer hard work, and an efficient allocation of a country's resources. As a result, governments have periodically restricted profits either generally by, for example, increased income taxes or price controls or selectively by, for example, rent controls. The economic effect of such restrictions is (a) to discourage investment by individuals and business firms; (b) to encourage them to invest in other more attractive countries; (c) to encourage individuals to increase their current consumption, rather than to save and invest part of their income; and (d) to distort the flow of public savings toward tax-incentive investment vehicles such as RRSPs, RHOSPs, MURBs, Canadian-produced feature films, etc.

In some cases, both past and present, business firms have earned extremely large profits. From the social point of view, excessively large profits, compared with the capital or entrepreneurial energy invested, may be considered undesirable. And most governments today redistribute part of this profit by taxation on the one hand and social security payments, etc. on the other. The question is, of course, just how much taxation and redistribution should there be if the "golden goose" is to survive?

Finally, we should not forget that so long as a competitive situation exists, new firms can enter an industry and thereby help eliminate excessive profits.

Summary

1. At one time, rent was considered by economists to be solely the return to land. Nowadays, in economics, rent is defined more broadly as the payment that any factor of production, not just land, receives over and above that required to keep it in its present use.
2. The most that a factor of production can earn in alternative employment is called its *transfer earnings*. Economic rent is, therefore, that part of a factor's earnings that is surplus to its transfer earnings.
3. Economic rent is caused by an increase in demand for a factor of production compared with a relatively fixed supply of it. The term "rent" was originally applied exclusively to land because of the

very fact that its total supply was fixed.

4. Although the total amount of land is fixed, the supply of land for specific purposes is not. This means that the supply of such land is relatively inelastic rather than completely inelastic, and its rent is correspondingly less.

5. In the short run, labour and capital are also relatively fixed in supply and therefore earn economic rent. Formerly, the term *quasi-rent* was used to describe this return to factors of production other than land.

6. The significance of the economic concept of rent is that society often pays far more than is necessary to keep a factor of production in its present use. The concept has also been used, at different times, and with varying response, as an argument in favour of a special land tax, the public confiscation and ownership of land, and the imposition of a capital gains tax.

7. Capital, in its real sense, consists of plant, equipment, trucks, and various other people-made aids to production. The extent to which capital causes output to increase is called its gross productivity, or real rate of return. Capital, in its monetary sense, is the money that is loaned by various financial institutions and the public to business firms.

8. The cost of borrowing capital is called the *rate of interest*. For money invested in a business by its owners, economists impute a rate of interest equal to its *opportunity cost*—that is to say, what it would have cost if borrowed. In practice, there are many different rates of interest because of differences in risk involved to the lender; length of time of the loan; size of the loan; and geographical location of the borrower. The money paid to a lender, after allowance for the factors just mentioned, constitutes the *pure rate of interest*.

9. The business concept of *profit* (the surplus of total revenue over total expenses) usually makes no allowance for implicit returns to land, labour, and capital. Most economists consider profit (a "residual" amount) to be a businessperson's reward for risk-taking; others consider it a reward for entrepreneurial activity in general, not just risk-taking.

10. In addition to this *pure*, or *economic profit*, there may also be an element of *monopoly profit*, depending upon the amount of competition in an industry.

11. The minimum amount of profit required to keep a firm in an industry is called *normal profit*.

12. The purpose of profit is to motivate people to assume the risk of

establishing and operating a business.
13. The actual amount of profit is determined by sales revenue (price, the attractiveness of a firm's products to consumers, the amount of competition, etc.) minus the costs of production and marketing.

Key Terms

Rent   277
Economic rent   277
Transfer earnings   277
Quasi-rent   280
Interest   281
Gross productivity   281
Real rate of return   281
Marginal efficiency
  of capital   281
Borrowed capital   281
Rate of interest   281

Equity capital   281
Implicit cost   281
Credit rating   282
Prime rate   282
Profit   282
Implicit return   282
Pure profit   283
Monopoly profit   283
Normal profit   284
Profit control   285

Review Questions

1. How is the term "rent" used in economics?
2. What are transfer earnings? What is their relationship to economic rent?
3. What gives rise to economic rent?
4. Why, at one time, was the term "rent" applied almost exclusively to land?
5. To what extent is the supply of land fixed?
6. In the short run, there are other factors of production, as well as land, that are relatively fixed in supply. Explain.
7. What is the meaning of the term "quasi-rent"?
8. What is the significance of the economic concept of rent?
9. Distinguish between real capital and money capital.
10. How can the rate of return be calculated on a new piece of industrial equipment?
11. What is the rate of interest? What significance does it have for business investment? Why does it fluctuate so much?
12. Why are there many different rates of interest, not just one? What is the pure rate of interest?
13. How does the business concept of profit differ from the economic one?

14. Distinguish between normal profit and monopoly profit.
15. What is the purpose of profit, from society's point of view?
16. What factors determine the level of a firm's profits?
17. How are profits controlled? What are the effects of such controls?
18. "Economic rent should be the subject of a special tax." Explain and discuss.
19. All interest rates should be the same and should not fluctuate over time. Discuss.
20. Interest rates are the main determinant of the level of business investment. Discuss.
21. Compare and discuss the following statements: (a) "There is no place for profit in a democratic society;" (b) "Profit may be termed the engine of economic growth".

16. POVERTY AMIDST PLENTY

CHAPTER OBJECTIVES

A. To explain what is meant by the term "poverty"
B. To indicate how many Canadians are considered to be poor
C. To distinguish between the various type of poor people in Canada
D. To identify the reasons for the existence of poverty in Canada
E. To outline the various government programs designed to help keep family income at a reasonable level
F. To explain the concept of a guaranteed annual income
G. To examine income inequality in Canada and the reasons for it

CHAPTER OUTLINE

16.1 Poverty in Canada
16.2 Types of Poor
16.3 Causes of Poverty
16.4 Government Income-Security Programs
16.5 Proposals for a Guaranteed Annual Income
16.6 Income Inequality

16.1: POVERTY IN CANADA

Canada, using a predominantly private-enterprise economic system, has been very successful over the years in raising its real GNP. And despite population growth, it has succeeded in achieving and maintaining (although it has slipped somewhat over the last 30 years) one of the highest standards of living in the world—now about fourteenth.

However, this same economic system has also meant great economic insecurity for the individual. Dependent primarily on the market place, a person can easily find (because of age, illness, accident, loss of a spouse, technological change, or general economic recession) that personal income can become very small or even cease altogether. This decline in income means, of course, a smaller share of the goods and services produced by society.

To ensure that every Canadian enjoys a reasonable minimum standard of living and has some protection against economic vicissitudes, the federal and provincial governments have adopted a variety of income-security programs. Unfortunately, these programs, although involving considerable government expenditure, have not been as successful as was originally hoped. Thus, although Canada is considered to be part of North America's "affluent society," Canadians do not have to look far to find evidence of poverty. As the Special Senate Committee on Poverty pointed out in 1971: "The grim fact is that one Canadian in four lacks sufficient income to maintain a basic standard of living."[1]

Poverty Defined

For many years, the term "poverty" was used to describe a situation in which a person or family was unable to afford a minimum level of physical subsistence. Thus, a poor person was one who was unable to pay for the food, clothing, and shelter needed to keep him or her alive and well.

Nowadays, poverty is more usually defined as a standard of living that is low relative to that enjoyed by most people in society. Thus, although a family in Canada may be reasonably well off when compared with the poor of many other countries, such as India or China, it may nevertheless be poor by Canadian standards. In accordance with this view, the Economic Council of Canada has defined *poverty* as:

> ... insufficient access to certain goods, services, and conditions of life which are available to everyone else and have come to be accepted as basic to a decent, minimum standard of living.[2]

In other words, poverty is a *relative* concept rather than an absolute one.

The Measurement of Poverty

One way of measuring poverty would be to compare the way that different people live and to award points for various factors. Thus a family that is under-fed, under-clothed, and badly housed, even though the parents earn a reasonable income (and spend it on other things), would still be considered poor. Obviously, however, the task of measurement would be immense, costly, and unpopular. Another and much simpler way is to use income as the measuring stick. A person earning $20000 a year under this system would be considered better off than one earning $10000.

A key consideration in defining poverty is the number of persons in a family. Thus a single person receiving $20000 a year is much better off than a family of ten, with the same total income.

Geographical location is another important factor. Thus, a person earning $10000 in, say, Ontario, may be worse off, because of differences in housing and other costs, than someone earning $8000 in Newfoundland. Similarly, someone earning $10000 in Toronto may be worse off than someone earning $7000 in a rural Ontario community.

Obviously, the level of income below which a family can be considered "poor" is a matter of opinion. However, the National Council of Welfare and other organizations commonly use as their poverty lines the "low income cut-offs" employed by Statistics Canada to produce data on Canada's low-income population.

Statistics Canada found, in a survey of family expenditure, that Canadian families spend, on average, 38.5 per cent of their income on food, clothing and shelter. Therefore, because poor families devote an above-average proportion of their limited income on the basic necessities, the low income cut-offs were set at the income level at which 58.5 per cent of income (that is 20 percentage points above the average) is spent on food, clothing and shelter. Consequently, any family or single person whose income is below this level is considered to be "low-income".

The income that is taken into account in the calculation is money income received by all family members aged 15 or over from: wages and salaries before deductions, net income from self-employment, investment income, government transfer payments such as Family Allowances and pensions, and other miscellaneous income.

Statistics Canada has taken into account the size of household by using seven categories of family size, ranging from a single person to seven or more persons. It takes into account place of residence by using five groups of communities: metropolitan areas with half a million or more people (Vancouver, Edmonton, Calgary, Winnipeg, Hamilton, Toronto, Ottawa-Hull, Montreal, and Quebec City); large cities (100000 to 499999); medium-sized cities (30000 to 99999); smaller centres (cities of 15000 to 29999 and small urban areas under 15000); and rural areas (both farm and non-farm).

Taking into consideration size of household and place of residence, Statistics Canada has produced a whole set of low income cut-offs for

Canada rather than just one. These low income cut-offs (See Table S.6) are then adjusted each year according to changes in the cost of living, as indicated by the Consumer Price Index.

Although the Statistics Canada low-income cut-offs are widely used as poverty guidelines, it should be pointed out that Statistics Canada itself states in its publication, *Income Distribution by Size in Canada*, that the cut-offs should not be interpreted as poverty lines as these involve a value judgment as to the minimum level of income below which an individual or family would generally be regarded as poor. As Michael Fraser, director of the Fraser Institute, has pointed out, a number of factors are ignored by the cut-off levels. First, they ignore an individual's personal wealth. Thus, a low income for a person who owns his or her home does not mean the same thing as for a person who is renting. A second factor that is ignored is the availability to many low-income persons, particularly senior citizens, of subsidized services such as free public transportation and reduced rate meals, pharmaceuticals, medical care, entertainment, and even travel. Third, statistics interpreted as poverty lines, ignore the fact that people, in their lifetime, pass through many different income stages. For example, is a person "poor" because he or she is working at a first job after leaving school and is perhaps still living at home or in shared accommodation? Within ten years, that person's income may have doubled, even in real terms. So, as well as taking into account place of residence and family size, Statistics Canada (and those who use low-income data) should perhaps include age as an important variable. Fourth, the composition of Canada's population should also be considered. Because of the passage of the baby boom through the population, Canada has a disproportionately large percentage of people at early and late stages in their earnings life cycle—when personal income is usually expected to be relatively low. And this should not be allowed to distort the average income so as to conclude that an extremely large segment of the Canadian population is poor—for example, the 3.5 millions suggested by the Canadian Council on Social Development.

Other groups that have put forward poverty lines for Canada include the Special Senate Committee on Poverty and the Canadian Council on Social Development. The poverty line suggested by the former is well above that obtained by using Statistics Canada's low income cut-off figures.

Health and Welfare Canada, from a national survey, concluded that single elderly persons required an after-tax income of $8722 in 1981 to cover essential needs, which was higher than what the Statistics Canada figures would suggest as the minimum income required.

Table S.6
Low Income Lines, Estimates for 1983

No. in Family	Population of Area of Residence				
	500 000 and over	100 000 - 499 999	30 000 - 99 000	Less than 30 000	Rural
1	$ 9 538	$ 9 058	$ 8 497	$ 7 856	$ 7 052
2	12 583	11 942	11 142	10 339	9 218
3	16 832	15 952	14 908	13 867	12 344
4	19 397	18 434	17 233	16 030	14 268
5	22 604	21 401	19 959	18 594	16 591
6	24 687	23 325	21 802	20 279	18 114
7 or more	27 172	25 729	24 047	22 363	19 959

Source: Statistics Canada

"*According to the newspaper, we're just below the poverty line..*"

The Poverty Rate

What percentage of Canada's population can be classified as poor? It depends, of course, on which poverty levels of income that we use and whether we consider them to be a true criterion of poverty, even in its relative sense. However, out of a total population of 25 millions, anywhere between one-tenth and one-fifth (that is, from 2.5 to 5 million persons) might be considered poor.

16.2: TYPES OF POOR

Those Canadians whose individual or family income today falls below the poverty line are by no means all the same. They include, in fact, many different types of poor people, each with problems of their own—problems that often require different solutions.

One useful division is between the *urban poor* and the *rural poor*. Another is between the *working poor* and the *welfare poor*. The poor can also be divided according to the principal cause of their poverty—for example, physical disability, old age, lack of a male family head, or unemployment. Furthermore, because of the cultural differences involved, special attention is frequently given to Canada's native peoples—the Indians, Métis, and Inuits—who together form about 2 per cent of Canada's total population.

The Urban Poor and the Rural Poor

How do the urban poor differ from the rural poor? The most important difference is that in the urban areas over half the poor are unattached individuals, whereas in the rural areas the bulk of the poor are families.[3]

In both urban and rural areas, poverty among the aged is high. However, in rural areas, a young family is just as likely to be poor as an old one. The poor in urban areas tend to earn more than the poor in rural areas. Furthermore, the difference in income between the poor and non-poor is much greater in urban areas than it is in rural areas.

The relatively large number of unattached individuals living in poverty in urban areas would seem to reflect the migration of young people from rural areas to the cities in hope of a more exciting time, if not a more worthwhile job. Although average income among the poor may be lower in rural areas, the cost of living (particularly accommodation) is normally much lower than in the urban areas. That is one of the reasons why many young families prefer to be poor in the country rather than in the city.

Among the rural poor are many farm families. Caught in a squeeze between slowly increasing prices of farm products on the one hand and quickly rising costs of production (hired labour, machinery, seed and fertilizer) on the other, the average small farmer in Canada has gradually found himself and his family working for a pittance wage. Only large-scale highly mechanized farming, including intensive factory-like chicken and hog production, seems to be profitable. But it is an option open to only a relative few. Among the rural non-farm poor, there are many Indians and Métis.

The Working Poor and the Welfare Poor

By far the largest group of poor persons in Canada is the *working poor*—people who work for very low rates of pay in such industries as laundries, textile mills, and retail stores, and as farm owners or employees. These are people who are able to find a job and prefer to work, even though they might be better off financially on welfare.

There are also many people in Canada, the *welfare poor*, who, for various reasons, are unable to work and rely on social assistance for all or part of their income. These welfare poor include: persons permanently disabled or ill; female heads of families; persons unemployed, aged, or temporarily disabled; and persons working but not earning sufficient to live on. Contrary to popular belief, studies in Canada and the United States suggest that only about 2 per cent of welfare recipients are people who prefer to receive welfare rather than work for a living.

Native Peoples

Living on 2279 reserves covering more than 6 million acres, the Indian population of Canada now totals about 300000. As one Indian chief explained to the Special Senate Committee on Poverty, not all native people are poor, but those who are can be described as "the poorest of the poor." Most Indians, in fact, have considerably worse housing, sanitation, educational and health services than other poor people in Canada. Indian poverty, according to the Senate Committee, can be mainly attributed to "a basic misunderstanding and/or lack of appreciation of native cultures and the values on which they are based." A second factor, according to the committee, is "a paternalism that is blind to the rights of native peoples as people and to their need to preserve and develop their own identity and self-respect."[4] Others have argued that the average Indian lacks the inherent ability to cope with the demands of modern technological society. However, even when Indians possess the necessary skills or education for employment, they are widely discriminated against both by employers and fellow-employees—often because they are considered, rightly or wrongly, to be unsatisfactory workers.

Canada's Inuit, numbering about 17500, live mainly in the North-west Territories, Arctic Quebec, and Labrador. As the area is developed, notably in the pursuit of oil and natural gas, more and more Inuit are abandoning their previously independent fishing and trapping way of life to work as employees. Some have established their own production and marketing co-operatives, specializing in Arctic foods, parkas, sculptures, and other handicrafts. But, as with the Indians, considerable poverty continues to exist, even measured by local standards.

16.3: CAUSES OF POVERTY

There are many different reasons for poverty in Canada.

1. *The determination of salaries and wages by the market forces of supply and demand results in very high incomes for certain persons (see Table S.7), but very low incomes for others.* A person employed at minimum wage-rates in certain areas can find that his or her income is insufficient to provide a decent standard of living. Only when both husband and wife work can many families in Canada make ends meet. Thus, a person, although employed full-time, can be poor because his or her abilities, education, training, character, age, and other characteristics are insufficient or unsuitable to secure or retain a higher-income job. People in this situation form Canada's "working-poor". In the case of many poor Canadian farmers and small-business owners, their way of life is bound up with their choice of occupation. Before switching occupations, even if jobs were available, such poor would need to be almost penniless.

2. *Many people who could perform a useful job are unable to find work.* The harsh winters in Canada have traditionally meant high seasonal unemployment. But more important in causing unemployment, as we see in Chapter 23, are such factors as the fluctuations of the business cycle, "stop-go" government monetary and fiscal policies, increased foreign competition, new capital-intensive manufacturing techniques, and a very high rate of new entrants to the labour force. Others for whom job openings are available lack the necessary education and skills.

3. *Some people are unable to work because of old age, temporary or permanent illness, or physical disability, and the need (in the case of single-parent families) to stay home to look after young children.*

4. *Prejudice (because of ethnic origin, race, language, or sex) prevents people from obtaining better jobs, or even jobs at all, despite human rights*

Table S.7
Average Income in Different Occupations in Canada, 1980

	Number of Persons	Average Income ($)	Total Income ($ millions)	Occupational Share of Total Income (%)
S/e doctors & surgeons	29 383	62 273	1 829.8	.90
S/e dentists	7 699	55 328	426.0	.21
S/e lawyers	16 345	45 921	750.6	.37
S/e accountants	9 696	39 317	381.2	.19
S/e engineers & architects	3 709	36 477	135.3	.07
Other s/e professionals	37 986	17 851	678.1	.33
Investors	987 516	16 560	16 353.1	8.08
Employees	10 175 814	15 555	158 288.1	78.16
Property owners	106 012	15 370	1 629.4	.80
S/e salesmen	33 588	14 306	480.5	.24
Farmers	276 523	13 265	3 668.1	1.81
Business proprietors	501 773	12 049	6 045.9	2.99
Fishermen	39 138	10 795	422.5	.21
S/e entertainers & artists	17 972	9 188	165.1	.08
Pensioners	934 447	8 323	7 777.7	3.84
Unclassified	1 587 277	2 193	3 481.5	1.72
Total	14 764 878	13 716	202 512.8	100.00
Business Proprietors				
Finance	2 813	36 076	101.5	.05
Real Estate	1 999	25 961	51.9	.03
Other Business	11 694	23 986	280.5	.14
Insurance Agents	1 616	22 254	36.0	.02
Wholesale Trade	10 188	16 542	168.5	.08
Recreation Services	5 780	16 319	94.3	.05
Forestry	7 797	15 764	122.9	.06
Construction	79 434	12 930	1 027.1	.51
Retail Trade	138 027	12 104	1 670.6	.82
Business Services	6 435	11 310	72.8	.04
Utilities	63 111	11 097	700.3	.35
Manufacturing	16 348	10 795	176.5	.09
Other Services	156 531	9 857	1 542.9	.76
Total	501 773	12 049	6 045.9	2.99

Source: Revenue Canada, *Taxation Statistics,* 1982 Edition

Note: Doctors, lawyers, and similar professional classifications shown above include only those earning the major part of their income as professional fees. Professionals whose principal source of income is in the form of salary are classified as employees

legislation.

5. *The children of poor people, through lack of educational and other opportunities, are often unable to break out of the "poverty circle"—a situation in which poor families, because of economic circumstances, are condemned to remain poor.*

6. *Some people are unwilling to accept a job that involves relocation, responsibility, strenuous mental or physical work, or other disagreeable conditions.* That is why, for example, labour sometimes has to be recruited in foreign countries for jobs that Canadians will not accept—such as fruit-picking, tobacco harvesting, and other agricultural work. However, it can also be argued that such jobs would be accepted by Canadians if the wage-rates were higher.

7. *The difficulty that many of Canada's native peoples have in accepting and adjusting to a different culture and the inability or unwillingness of the remainder of society to accept them as equals.*

16.4: GOVERNMENT INCOME-SECURITY PROGRAMS

Today most Canadians recognize that they have a social obligation to help the less fortunate members of society. This recognition is expressed by donations to the various churches and church organizations such as the Salvation Army and to civil organizations such as the United Appeal. Much more important, though, are the contributions that most people make through taxes. This is because a large part of this tax revenue is used to help pay for a variety of government income-security programs all of which are designed to help people maintain a minimum, decent standard of living. Although most people object to paying so much in taxes, they nevertheless usually support the principle of collective social responsibility, a basic Christian ethic, whereby the economically strong help the economically weak.

Government income-security programs include unemployment insurance, the Canada and Quebec pension plans, old-age security, family allowances, youth allowances, workmen's compensation, and social assistance.

Unemployment Insurance

By the terms of the Unemployment Insurance Act, all regular members of the labour force in Canada are compulsorily insured against loss of wages through unemployment. In fact, about 95% of all employees are covered. The main exceptions are the self-employed, some part-time workers, and workers over 65 years of age. Both employers and employees pay contributions, with the employer collecting and remitting both to the government. Contributions are adjusted yearly. The government also makes a contribution. The program is administered by the Canada Employment and Immigration Commission, or CEIC.

Under the Act, a person can draw unemployment benefit for up to a certain number of weeks, so long as he or she has made a minimum number of recent contributions (depending on the economic region) and meets certain conditions of availability, capability, and searching for work. Persons who have made more contributions can claim a wider range of benefits. There is a two-week waiting period, once a claim has been accepted, before any benefit is paid. The benefit rate is 60% of average weekly insurable earnings, with a maximum benefit period. Persons collecting unemployment insurance benefits may work part-time and earn up to 25% of their weekly benefit rate before deductions. Any amount above that is deducted from the benefit cheque. Persons who have been dismissed for misconduct, quit their job voluntarily, or turned down a suitable job offer are disqualified from benefit for up to six weeks beyond the normal two-week waiting period.

The program is being constantly revised so current benefits and eligibility requirements should be checked at the local CEIC office. The current scale of benefits has been criticized by some (for example, the Canadian Federation of Independent Business) as being too generous and helping to destroy the work ethic. Others claim that it is not enough.

Canada Pension Plan

Every province except Quebec (which has its own comparable pension plan) participates in a federally-run pension plan. This plan, the Canada Pension Plan, began in 1966 and covers, on a compulsory basis, practically every employee, whatever his or her occupation, between the ages of 18 and 65 (or 70 if the person continues to work and does not apply for the retirement pension). It is financed by equal contributions from employee and employer.

The plan provides the following benefits: a retirement pension; a disability pension; benefits for the children of disabled employees; a widow's pension; benefits for the children of a deceased employee; benefits for disabled widowers; and a lump sum payment to a deceased employee's estate. A formal application must be made to receive them.

Benefits under the plan are portable. This means that if a person changes his or her job or place of residence, the pension rights remain the same. With a private plan, employees frequently lose all or part of the employer's contribution if they leave their jobs.

To take into account changes in the cost of living, all benefits under the plan are revalued annually so long as the Pension Index (which is, in turn, based on the Consumer Price Index) has increased by more than 1 per cent over that of the previous year. Thus, a person's benefits will not remain at a fixed dollar amount, but will increase each year as prices rise. This feature overcomes, to some extent, the common fear among pensioners that inflation will gradually wipe out the real value of their pensions.

Old Age Security

Under the Old Age Security Act, a person who is sixty-five or more and who has satisfied the Canadian residence requirements is entitled to receive an old-age pension in addition to any retirement pension under the Canada Pension Plan. A person receiving an old-age pension and living in Canada may also receive an additional monthly allowance, called a *guaranteed income supplement*, if he or she has little or no other income. There is also a special *spouse allowance* payable to the spouse of an OAS pensioner.

These three programs (the old age pension, the guaranteed income supplement, and the spouse allowance) all of which provide benefits for the elderly in Canada, are non-contributory. In other words, a person does not have to have paid contributions during past years (as with the Canada Pension Plan) to be eligible. The benefits are paid for from the government's general tax revenue. They are also indexed to the cost of living and adjusted each quarter.

Family Allowances

These are payments made by the federal government each month to supplement family income, for the benefit of each dependent child under 18 years of age. There is no limit on the number of children in a family who are eligible. The allowances are made on a *demogrant* basis—that is, every family, whatever the need, receives them so long as there are children of eligible ages. To help offset the fact that the allowance is paid, whatever the level of family income, such benefit is subject to income tax. Also, it has been proposed that benefits be made payable on a sliding scale, the actual amount of benefit depending on the size of family. The benefits are indexed to the cost of living and adjusted each January. Quebec has its own family allowance program. Alberta and Quebec vary the rate according to the child's age. And Quebec adds a provincial supplement.

Child Tax Credit

A person is entitled, under this Federal program that began in 1979, to receive a certain sum for each child under 18 years of age, additional to the Family Allowance. As net family income exceeds a stated exemption level, the credit is gradually reduced.

Workmen's Compensation

In every province, a Workmen's Compensation Act provides for the establishment of a fund, financed solely by employers, to pay compensation to an employee for industrial injury or disablement. An employee does not have to prove negligence on the part of his or her employer to obtain compensation. On the other hand, compensation may be withheld if the accident arose from the employee's gross misconduct—for example, being drunk on the job. If an employee is disabled, he or she may receive all necessary medical care and hospitalization; cash payments to compensate for loss of wages; a life pension for permanent disability; and rehabilitation services. If an employee dies as the result of an industrial accident or disease, his widow receives a monthly pension; a special lump sum payment; an allowance for funeral expenses; and a monthly allowance for each child below a certain age limit.

Social Assistance

Each province makes social assistance or "welfare" payments to families and individuals who can prove that they are in need. Half the money is provided by the federal government through the Canada Assistance Plan. Special allowances are also paid, after a means test, to blind and otherwise disabled persons. There are also war veterans' allowances for qualified veterans in need; and special federal social assistance to Indians and Inuit.

Under the Canada Assistance Plan, the federal government also shares the cost of various assistance and service programs administered by the provincial governments. These services include: (a) health care, including medical and surgical services, nursing, dental and optical care (including dentures and eye-glasses), drugs, and prosthetic appliances; (b) assistance to mothers with dependent children; (c) the maintenance of needy persons in such residential welfare institutions as home for the aged, nursing homes, homes for unmarried mothers, and child-care institutions; and (d) welfare services such as rehabilitation, casework, counselling and assessment, adoption, and homemaker and day-care services.

16.5: PROPOSALS FOR A GUARANTEED ANNUAL INCOME

Although Canada has a variety of income-security programs designed to help the needy, this whole welfare system, costing many billions of dollars a year, has been the subject of much criticism. One of the strongest condemnations was by the Special Senate Committee on Poverty, which stated:

> The social-welfare structure so laboriously and painstakingly erected in Canada over the past forty years has clearly outlived its usefulness. The social scientists who have studied it, the bureaucrats who have administered it, and the poor who have experienced it are of one mind that in today's swiftly-changing world, the welfare system is a hopeless failure. The matter is not even controversial; everybody's against it. But what is to take its place?[5]

The major criticism that is made of Canada's present welfare system is that it discourages the welfare recipient from trying to improve his or her position through employment. Any money that such a person earns is usually deducted from his or her welfare cheque. This system also encourages the welfare recipient to try to cheat the government by doing jobs on the side. A second important criticism is that the system creates dependence. The poor must ask for help if they are to obtain financial assistance. By doing so, they lose their sense of self-pride. A third important criticism is that it is unfair to the "working poor" who may work long hours at unpleasant jobs to earn the same amount of money, or just slightly more than someone living on welfare.

Obviously, the elimination of poverty in Canada is not just a matter of making payments to those in need. Sound government monetary and fiscal policies to promote economic growth are also needed to create jobs. So also are good trading relationships with foreign countries that provide important markets for our goods. There must also be suitable training and education for new entrants to the labour force and retraining opportunities for persons whose jobs may have disappeared because of technological change. Health care, education, and housing must be expanded and improved. However, government income-security payments can play an important part in eliminating poverty—certainly in helping those Canadians such as the old and disabled who are in no position to help themselves. The question is, therefore, how best to use the limited amount of money that the government is willing to spend on helping the poor?

A proposal that has been gaining some ground in Canada in recent years is that of a guaranteed annual income. This is a program whereby the federal government would pay everyone above a certain age an amount of money sufficient to bring that person's annual income up to a minimum guaranteed level. The usual method recommended for doing this is a "negative income tax". In other words, the government, instead of taking money in income tax from a person's pay packet every week or month, would, in the case of a poor person, *add* money, the actual amount depending on how low the level of earned income actually was.

The advantage of the negative income tax method is that it is selective: allowances are paid only to those who need them as established by a simple declaration of income. Such a system is considered to be more equitable and efficient than demogrant programs such as the old-age pension and family allowances which are paid to everyone with the required demographically measurable characteristic (age or family status) irrespective of financial need. The federal government has, in fact, turned, in its present welfare programs, more and more towards selective-type payments and away from demogrants. Thus, for example, instead of increasing the level of all old-age pensions, it has offered guaranteed income supplements to those old people who actually need the money.

The Special Senate Committee on Poverty, in its report, recommended, with respect to a guaranteed annual income, that:

1. The Government of Canada implement a Guaranteed Annual Income (G.A.I.) program using the Negative Income Tax (N.I.T.) method, on a uniform, national basis.

2. The proposed G.A.I. program be financed and administered by the Government of Canada.

3. The proposed G.A.I. plan be designed to cover all Canadians who need it. Initially, G.A.I. would not cover residents of Canada who are not Canadian citizens and Canadian citizens who are single, unattached individuals under forty years of age.

4. Basic Allowance Rates under the G.A.I. be set initially at 70 per cent of the poverty line for each family size as determined by the methods outlined in the report and raised progressively as quickly as possible.

5. The G.A.I. plan incorporate a work-incentive mechanism to ensure that those who work receive and keep more income than those who do not. It proposed that Basic Allowances initially be reduced at the rate of 70 cents for every dollar of other income.

6. Income-maintenance under the proposed G.A.I. plan be divorced from the provision of social services. The latter would remain the responsibility of the provincial governments.

7. The Canada Assistance Plan (C.A.P.) be retained and updated to serve as a vehicle for federal-provincial co-operation and cost-sharing in the delivery of social services. C.A.P. would also be used to cover, on a "needs" basis, those not covered initially by the G.A.I.

8. All existing federal income-maintenance legislation be progressively repealed. Social-insurance programs such as Unemployment Insurance, and the Canada Pension Plan, would be retained, as would certain contractual programs related to Canada's native peoples. The G.A.I. would immediately replace the Family Allowance, Youth Allowance, and Old Age Security programs, operated by the Federal Government.

9. The G.A.I. program be based on the principle that no one would receive less income under the G.A.I. than he or she now receives from other federal programs such as Old Age Security and income supplements. Other allowances or insurance payments would be treated as "other income" and augmented through the G.A.I. program where they are less than the G.A.I. allowances.

10. Income tax exemption levels be raised so that no Canadian whose income is below the "poverty line" would be subject to income tax.[6]

Under the plan recommended by the Senate Committee, income floors would be set for a single person, for a family of four, and for a family of ten. Others have recommended that the government set two basic floor levels. Thus, people who are able to work might be guaranteed an income set at 70 per cent of the poverty level. Those who are unable to work might be guaranteed 100 per cent.

The federal government, after considering the possibility of a guaranteed income plan, reached the conclusion that it would be too costly for the country, at least at the present time.[7] The government also decided that some joint federal-provincial pilot studies employing the G.A.I. technique should first be carried out. So far, therefore, the government has preferred to revise existing programs rather than launch a national guaranteed annual income plan. However, it has allocated some money for experimental guaranteed income projects.

The pilot projects, first undertaken in Manitoba, seek the answers to a variety of questions. For example: will G.A.I. aid encourage recipients to work and earn more than those on regular welfare? Will it discourage husbands from deserting their families so that dependants will receive welfare? Will it help lower the school drop-out rate of children from welfare families? Will it depress local wages for the unskilled because people cannot afford to work for uneconomic wages? Will it cause rents and prices to rise in low-income communities because more money is available? Above all, will G.A.I. aid be cheaper and simpler to operate than conventional welfare?

16.6: INCOME INEQUALITY

Throughout history, people have been arguing about the way in which a country's wealth should be divided. Why should a peasant slaving away in the master's fields from dawn to dusk earn a pittance while the absentee landlord, with money to burn, lives it up in town? This simple line of reasoning has brought about many political upheavals over the years. The French revolution of 1789 and the Russian revolution of 1917 are two of the most dramatic. But revolutions sparked by economic injustice, alleged or real, are still continuing throughout the world.

Before the widespread use of money, the problem of sharing a country's economic wealth was one of physically allocating the produce of the land. With the use of money, the actual division of wealth came to be decided in terms of purchasing power. Today, as a result, the question "for whom to produce?" is answered in terms of income. The larger a person's income, the greater his or her ability to buy the various goods and services produced.

Personal incomes (as Table S.8 confirms) vary greatly in Canada. Some people earned little or no income at all, while others received extremely large incomes.

The Lorenz Curve

Another way of measuring income inequality is to consider how *total* income is shared. Thus, if each 1 per cent of the population received 1 per cent of the total income, there would be complete income equality between each 1 per cent of the population. This can be shown graphically (Figure 16:1) by what is known as a Lorenz chart—named after M.O. Lorenz, a German statistician of the 1900s. Such a chart measures, on the vertical axis, the percentage of total income received, and, on the horizontal axis, the percentage of persons receiving that income.

If there were complete equality of income distribution, then 10 per cent of total income would be received by 10 per cent of the population; 20 per cent of the total income by 20 per cent of the population; 30 per cent by 30 per cent; and so on. This situation would be depicted in the Lorenz chart by a straight diagonal line called a Lorenz curve,

Table S.8
Income Inequality in Canada, 1980

Income Class (based on total income)	Number of Persons	Percentage of Persons in this Class or a Lower One	Total Income Received by this Class or a Lower One
Loss and Nil	959 008	6.50	.14
1— $1 000	597 610	10.54	.16
1 000— 2 000	525 975	14.11	.39
2 000— 3 000	613 534	18.26	1.14
3 000— 4 000	604 960	22.36	2.19
4 000— 5 000	627 811	26.61	3.58
5 000— 6 000	634 967	30.91	5.30
6 000— 7 000	587 997	34.89	7.18
7 000— 8 000	574 590	36.83	9.31
8 000— 9 000	574 727	42.68	11.72
9 000— 10 000	553 383	46.42	14.31
10 000— 11 000	550 172	50.15	17.16
11 000— 12 000	529 534	53.74	20.16
12 000— 13 000	515 724	57.23	23.34
13 000— 14 000	489 440	60.55	26.59
14 000— 15 000	457 249	63.64	29.86
15 000— 16 000	423 565	66.51	33.10
16 000— 17 000	402 067	69.23	36.37
17 000— 18 000	398 379	71.93	39.81
18 000— 19 000	370 800	74.44	43.19
19 000— 20 000	354 925	76.85	46.60
20 000— 25 000	1 435 101	86.57	62.38
25 000— 30 000	834 288	92.22	73.58
30 000— 40 000	674 784	96.79	84.88
40 000— 50 000	227 638	98.33	89.86
50 000— 100 000	206 311	99.73	96.38
100 000— 200 000	32 597	99.95	98.48
200 000 and over	7 742	100.00	99.86
Total	14 764 878	100.00	100.00

Source: Revenue Canada, *Taxation Statistics,* 1982 Edition

rising from left to right. Usually, however, this line is bent rather than straight. The greater the curvature of the Lorenz curve, the greater the inequality of distribution. The flatter the curve, the more equal the distribution of income.

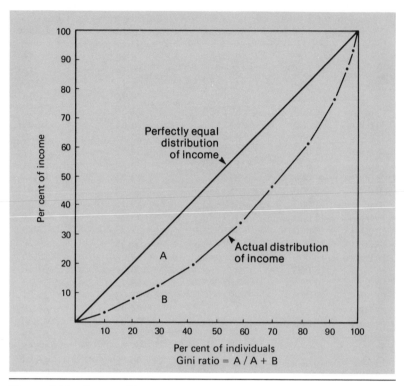

Figure 16:1 Lorenz Curve

Since most married couples pool their incomes, Lorenz curves can also be constructed showing the distribution of income among families and unattached individuals. They can also be plotted to show the distribution of wealth rather than income. However, such data, for Canada, is still hard to obtain.

Reasons for Income Inequality

There are two basic types of income that a person can receive: employment income and investment income. Let us briefly consider why one person may have higher employment or investment income than another.

Employment Income

One reason for inequality of employment income is that human beings are different physically, mentally, and emotionally. This means that some people can do things better than others. It also means that some people, given the right motivation, work harder than others, accept more responsibility, and take more risks. Whatever type of society exists, some people emerge as leaders and others as followers. These differences in physical, mental, and emotional abilities between different people are often inherited traits. However, a good family life, education, training, and a good general environment can help a person to make the most of what he or she has.

Another important reason for inequalities in employment income in Canada is the difference in education, training, and experience of different members of the labour force. Some people are better qualified than others to hold down a higher-paying job. If it requires many years of academic and practical training to become, for example, a doctor, lawyer, engineer, or accountant, it is to be expected that such a person's income will be greater than that of an unskilled worker. Even in socialist countries, persons with highly skilled jobs receive larger incomes than the semi-skilled and unskilled.

Inequalities of employment income are also attributed to differences of social and ethnic background. Native-born white Anglo-Saxon Protestants (or WASPs), so it is said, are assured of economic success. However, compared with many other countries, merit is much more important in Canada as a determinant of economic success than social background. And in most provinces, a human rights code legally forbids discrimination in employment on grounds of race, colour, nationality, ethnic origin, or religion. However, the very existence of such a code implies that discrimination did, and still continues to, exist.

Sex and age are also responsible for differences in rates of pay, despite equal pay legislation. They can also even determine whether a person obtains a job or not.

Finally, looking at Canada as a whole, differences in employment income between equally able and qualified persons can arise because of geographical location.

Investment Income

Investment income consists mainly of income derived from the ownership of savings deposits, stocks, bonds, and real estate. Why might one person have a larger investment income than another? One important reason is that many people are able and willing to save and invest part of their current income. Another is that some people are shrewder investors than others. This means that, over a period of years, people gradually accumulate varying amounts of wealth in its different forms. This accumulated wealth, through both investment return and the realization of *capital gain* (the profit on resale of an asset) provides investment income. Of course, in old age, this investment income, together with pensions, may form the only income. However, for many people, investment income does provide an additional source of income even during their working lifetime. And the larger the amount of wealth, and the shrewder the form and timing of the investment, the greater this income is.

Some people inherit wealth from parents and relatives. This can, depending on the temperament of the recipient, form a large windfall income for a few years or, if invested wisely, a continuing source of investment income. In the past, it was relatively easy to pass wealth from one generation to the next. Nowadays, government-imposed death duties make it more difficult. Nevertheless, through trusts and other means, considerable sums are still passed in Canada from parents to children and grandchildren.

Income Inequality: Good or Bad?

Should everyone receive the same income?

In practically every type of society, one of the most important human motivating forces is the acquisitive instinct. In order to make money, people have taken all manner of risks, worked all kinds of hours, and endured all kinds of hardships. Without this driving force, Canada would not be as developed a land as it is today.

Of course, this motive is not the only one for human activity. But it is, for most people, the most important. Consequently, if the opportunity to earn an above-average income is removed, some other motivating force must be found. In wartime, it is often a sense of patriotism. In peace-time, nationalism, religion, political creed, may all inspire men and women in their work.

However, the experience of most communist, or socialist countries is that where the profit motive does not exist, compulsion must take its place. People must be told where to work, for how long, and at what wages. So long, therefore, as Canadians are unwilling for government to control every aspect of their economic life, they must be assured of the possibility of additional reward for additional effort. The need for above-average earnings does not mean, however, that there should be be no effort to help people whose income, often through no fault of their own, is unusually low.

Summary

1. Canada's economic system, although providing one of the highest standards of living in the world, has meant great economic insecurity for the individual. Consequently, the federal and provincial governments have adopted a variety of income-security programs. However, these programs have not always lived up to expectations. And perhaps one in four Canadians can be classified as poor.
2. Nowadays, poverty is usually defined as a standard of living that is low relative to that enjoyed by most people in the society. It is a *relative* concept rather than an absolute one.
3. There are various ways of measuring poverty. The most usual is to establish a "poverty line" level of income and classify anyone receiving income below this level, as poor.
4. There are many different types of poor people, and each group has problems of its own. One useful division is between the urban poor and the rural poor. Another is between the working poor and the welfare poor. Canada's native peoples are usually the subject of special attention.
5. There are many different reasons for poverty in Canada: income inequality, unemployment, old age, illness, physical disability, prejudice, lack of education, unwillingness to relocate, and in the case of native peoples, difficulty in adjusting to a different type of society.
6. Government income-security programs include unemployment insurance, the Canada and Quebec pension plans, old-age security, family allowances, youth allowances, workmen's compensation, and social assistance.
7. A guaranteed annual income has been proposed as a good replacement for the present system of income-security programs. Under it, the government would pay everyone above a certain age an amount of money sufficient to bring that person's annual income up to a minimum guaranteed level.
8. Incomes vary greatly in Canada. A Lorenz curve is a useful means of depicting this graphically.
9. Reasons for inequality of employment income include differences in physical, mental, and emotional abilities; difference in education, training, and experience; differences in social and ethnic background; sex; age; and geographical location.

10. Reasons for inequality of investment income include differences in willingness to save and invest, differences in shrewdness of investments, and differences in inherited wealth.
11. One of the most important human motivating forces is the average person's acquisitive instinct. If the opportunity to earn an above-average income is removed, some other motivation to work must be found. Compulsion has not proven very effective.

Key Terms

Poverty 290
Poverty line 291
Poverty rate 295
Urban poor 295
Rural poor 295
Working poor 296
Welfare poor 296
Poverty circle 299
Unemployment insurance 299
Canada pension plan 300
Old age security 301

Family allowance 301
Child tax credit 302
Workmen's Compensation 302
Social assistance 302
Guaranteed 303
annual income 303
Negative income tax 304
Income inequality 306
Lorenz curve 306
Employment income 309
Investment income 309

Review Questions

1. What is meant by "poverty"? Compare poverty in Canada with that in one or more economically underdeveloped countries.
2. How is poverty measured in Canada?
3. What are the "low income cut-offs" used by Statistics Canada?
4. What are the main criticisms of using the low income cut-offs as poverty lines?
5. What has been the poverty rate in Canada in recent years? How realistic is it?
6. In what ways do the urban poor differ from the rural poor?
7. Who are the "working poor"?
8. What are the main reasons why many people require welfare assistance in Canada?
9. What are the various causes of poverty in Canada?
10. How do governments in Canada try to reduce income insecurity for the individual?
11. Explain how a guaranteed annual income could be implemented.

What could be its advantages and disadvantages?
12. To what extent do personal incomes vary in Canada?
13. What is a Lorenz curve? What purpose does it serve?
14. Give five reasons for income inequality in Canada.
15. To what extent is income inequality desirable?
16. Without adequate motivation, people would lose interest in their work and the economy would suffer. Discuss.

References

1. Special Senate Committee on Poverty, *Poverty in Canada* (Ottawa: Information Canada, 1971), p. vii.
2. Economic Council of Canada, *Fifth Annual Review* (Ottawa: Queen's Printer, 1969), pp. 104-5.
3. N.H. Lithwick, *Urban Poverty*, Research Monograph No. 1, in *Urban Canada: Problems and Pospects* (Ottawa: Central Mortgage and Housing Corporation, 1971).
4. *Poverty in Canada*, p. 35.
5. *Poverty in Canada*, p. vii.
6. *Poverty in Canada*, pp. xv and xvi
7. Department of National Health and Welfare, *Income Security for Canadians* (Ottawa: Information Canada, 1970), pp. 26-27.

17. CANADIAN MANUFACTURING, MINING, AND ENERGY

CHAPTER OBJECTIVES

A. To examine the nature of Canadian manufacturing and the problems that face it
B. To examine the state of Canada's mining industry
C. To review Canada's energy supplies and discuss the federal government's energy policy

CHAPTER OUTLINE

17.1 Manufacturing
17.2 Mining
17.3 Energy

In the nineteenth century, Canada was a predominantly agricultural country with most families making their living by raising crops and tending livestock. But today the main sources of income and employment for Canadians are industrial ones—manufacturing, mining, power, construction, transportation, communications, wholesale and retail trade, and other services. Government is also an employment and income sector of growing importance.

17.1: MANUFACTURING

Originally, the term "manufacturing" meant making a product by hand. Nowadays, however, manufacturing means the production of goods by people using power-driven machinery. For purposes of analysis, manufacturing industries can be classified as primary or secondary.

Primary manufacturing is the processing of basic raw materials such as metal ores and crude lumber. Industries of this type, which have existed for many years in Canada, now sell their output primarily to markets in Canada, the United States, Western Europe, and Japan. *Secondary manufacturing* is the production of finished goods and parts from processed raw materials. Many industries produce the parts that are used by other industries for assembly into a finished product, such as farm machinery or an automobile. A major part of this secondary manufacturing emerged during and after World War II. It has been aided in its growth, since the late nineteenth century, by tariff protection from lower-priced imports. This has not only encouraged domestic manufacturers to expand, but also foreign, mainly U.S., producers to set up branch plants in Canada for manufacturing or assembly. However, since World War II, tariff protection has been gradually reduced and Canadian manufacturing firms have had to overcome stiffer competition or go under.

Much of the output of Canada's secondary manufacturing industries is sold in the Canadian market. However, export sales, particularly to the United States are growing in importance. The Canada-United States automotive products agreement (discussed in Chapter 43), signed in 1965, has resulted in a tremendous expansion in bilateral trade in vehicles and parts.

Types and Location

The various types of manufacturing being carried on in this country are shown in Table S.9. The most important industries, in term of value added, are foods and beverages, transportation equipment, petroleum and coal products, paper and allied products, and primary metals.

Most of Canada's secondary manufacturing industry is to be found in a few key areas, notably southern Ontario, southern Quebec, and the Vancouver area of the West Coast. Primary manufacturing is much more widespread.

Manufacturing Processes

Many different processes are used to manufacture finished and semi-finished products from raw materials and parts. One classification is as follows:

1. **Extractive**. This is the process of extracting materials and products from land, sea, and air—for example, iron, copper, and nickel from the land, salt from the sea, and oxygen from the air.

2. **Conditioning**. This occurs when a raw material is changed into a

Table S.9
Canadian Manufacturing Shipments, by Industry, in millions of dollars, 1981

Industry	Annual monthly average	% of total
Foods and beverages	2 631.7	16.7
Tobacco products	121.9	0.8
Rubber	379.8	2.4
Leather	102.5	0.6
Textile	410.3	2.6
Knitting mills	81.5	0.5
Clothing	336.5	2.1
Wood	714.9	4.5
Furniture and fixtures	223.0	1.4
Paper and allied industries	1 294.5	8.2
Printing, publishing and allied industries	531.5	3.4
Primary metal	1 193.3	7.6
Metal fabricating[1]	1 035.3	6.6
Machinery	711.9	4.5
Transportation equipment	1 849.7	11.7
Electrical products	737.3	4.7
Non-metallic mineral products	393.2	2.5
Petroleum and coal products	1 633.3	10.4
Chemical and chemical products	1 059.4	6.7
Miscellaneous manufacturing	333.4	2.1
Total shipments	15 776.0	100.0

Source: Statistics Canada, *Inventories, Shipments and Orders in Manufacturing Industries,* Cat. 31-001

Note: (1) Excludes machinery and transportation equipment

more valuable form—for example, wool into cloth, and hides into leather.

3. Analytical. This is the process of breaking down a raw material into a number of different products—for example, petroleum into gasoline, fuel oils, lubricating oils, and paraffin.

4. Synthetic. In this process, various raw materials are combined into a finished product—for example, flour, salt, and yeast into bread.

5. Assembly. Here, a number of component parts and materials are put together (i.e., assembled) to form a finished product—for example, a telephone. Sub-assembly is the same process, except that the product—for example, a loudspeaker—will be used as a component part of the final product, the television set.

Characteristics of Manufacturing

Modern manufacturing is characterized by a high level of mechanization and, to a lesser extent, automation; it makes use of electric power to drive the production machinery and conveyor systems; it employs a high degree of specialization, both of workers (division of labour) and machines; it uses mass-production techniques and standardization whenever advantageous; it requires common timing, or "synchronization," of deliveries, manufacturing, assembly and sub-assembly operations; and it employs highly sophisticated production technology. Because of these facts, production costs per unit of output are much lower than under the earlier handicraft system. In other words, the same number of workers and capital can, in the same amount of time, produce much more than previously.

Let us now look at these characteristics of modern manufacturing a little more closely.

1. Mechanization. When machines are used to perform work previously done by hand (usually with relatively unsophisticated tools), the system of production is said to be *mechanized*. Most manufacturing industry in Canada is now highly mechanized. First, it has been possible to invent machines to perform most routine tasks more efficiently than the average worker, equipped only with hand tools, can. Second, as labour costs have risen and machines have become relatively cheaper, more and more of them have been purchased and relatively fewer workers hired. As a result, each worker now usually operates and controls a larger amount of machinery. The modern manufacturing process has, in other words, become more and more *capital-intensive* and less and less *labour-intensive*. This is also true of the handling and transporting of raw materials, parts, and finished products from one

place to another within the modern manufacturing plant.

2. Automation. It was only a matter of time before machines were invented to control other machines. This process of *automation* has meant that even fewer workers are required relative to a given amount of capital. Their job is primarily one of control, maintenance, and "trouble-shooting" in the event of a mechanical breakdown. Fortunately, from the labour-employment point of view, automation has by no means become as widespread as mechanization. A familiar example of automation is the thermostat in the home, which switches the furnace on and off according to the temperature. Another is the computer-controlled office elevator system. But many manufacturing processes have now been automated.

3. Electric power. We tend to take electric power for granted, but it is only an invention of the last century. Previously, manufacturing had to rely on steam-power (a nineteenth-century invention) and before that on water-power, wind-power, animal-power, and human-power. Without the existence of electricity and electric motors, manufacturing would have been stunted in its growth, and the key modern tool, the electronic computer, would have been impossible.

4. Specialization. The great increase in output per worker that specialization in manufacturing affords has long been pointed out by economists. Thus Adam Smith, the eighteenth-century Scottish economist, used the example of a nail factory to point out the economic benefits of the "division of labour". By specializing in the performance of one or two tasks, rather than trying to make a complete good, a worker can become highly proficient in his or her work. Consequently, a group of workers, each performing his or her own specialized tasks at great speed, can produce much more than if each were to work as an independent craftsperson. This principle of specialization, or *division of labour*, and the benefits it affords, have also been extended to machines and manufacturing plants. However, a prerequisite for specialization is a large enough market to enable all the output to be sold. If the scale of production is small, the scope for specialization is more limited.

5. Mass production. Many goods are now produced in great quantities at one large factory rather than at many small plants or workshops. By concentrating production in this way, a manufacturer is best able to make use of power-driven production machinery and materials-handling equipment. The large volume of output also enables the firm to enjoy the benefits of specialization of labour and machines; to obtain quantity discounts for purchases; and to spread its relatively fixed costs of production and marketing—for example, administrative salaries, factory rent, research and development, advertising, and marketing organization—as widely as possible. Long production runs, in other words, mean lower per unit costs of production and marketing. The only limit to these economies of scale is the volume of output which, in turn, is limited by the extent of the market.

6. Standardization. Each material and part used in the manufacturing process must conform to strict standards of size, shape, strength, and quality. Only in this way can a manufacturer make use of machines tooled to handle certain size materials and parts, and ensure that the product meets the desired performance and safety requirements. Work methods are also standardized, after careful time and motion studies, to ensure that plant employees work in the most efficient way.

7. Synchronization. Modern manufacturing operations are usually quite complex, involving large numbers of workers, a vast array of machines, and a continuous inflow of materials and component parts to be assembled or otherwise made into finished goods. Therefore, precise timing of the various manufacturing and assembly operations is critical. Also, one of the ways in which Japanese automobile manufacturers have been able to cut costs is by keeping inventories of materials and parts to an unprecedented minimum, by exact timing of deliveries from locally situated suppliers. And North American car manufacturers are now switching to "just in time" inventory control. Nowadays, in many manufacturing plants, a delay in a sub-assembly or other manufacturing operation, or in delivery of materials or parts, can easily hold up a whole production line. Because of this need for synchronization, each worker must keep up a certain pace in his or her work or else delay the work of many others.

8. Technology. The technical knowledge employed to produce and market goods has increased at a fantastic rate in the twentieth century. In fact, most of the goods purchased today were not available two or three generations ago. Compared with the nineteenth century, it takes a much shorter time between the invention of a new material, product, machine, or method and its commercial application.

9. CAD/CAM. With the lower price and increased sophistication of modern electronic computers, more and more firms in Canada and elsewhere are turning to computer-assisted design and computer-assisted manufacturing, or CAD/CAM for short. Experience so far shows that the use of computers in designing products and manufacturing processes, as well as in planning and controlling production, can greatly improve productivity—that is, a greater value of output per person employed.

10. Robotics. Already in Canadian auto plants, industrial robots are busy welding and painting cars. These robots operate under the instructions of built-in microcomputers and can be programmed for a variety of repetitive manufacturing tasks. Unlike earlier robots, they are not built to perform only one task. By changing the program (a quite simple task), the plant supervisor can easily switch the modern industrial robot from one task to another, as called for by changes in production plans.

Problems of Canadian Manufacturing

Canada, with its almost 25 million population, is a relatively small market for manufactured goods compared with the United States or the European Economic Community. Long production runs are only possible, therefore, if there is a substantial export market as well as the local Canadian one. This has been achieved in some industries— for example, cars and trucks—by integrating the production plans of Canadian-located plants with sister plants south of the border. In some other industries, exports, particularly to the United States, have also enabled firms to achieve economies of mass production. However, in many industries, dependence on the relatively small home market has stunted growth. Furthermore, the existence of a large number of firms within the same industry, each differentiating their product by advertising and other means, has limited the individual firm's growth even more. Of course, not all goods can be mass produced. That is why we still have so many small business firms in Canada—in manufacturing as well as in service industries.

Another serious concern at the present time, as discussed in Chapter 20, is the slow rate of increase in Canada's industrial productivity compared with other countries.

The large sales that Canadian manufacturers make to the U.S. market, although highly beneficial in terms of income and employment for Canadians, do have some dangers. If the United States adopts a more protectionist attitude, as it has in recent years, U.S. imports of manufactured goods from Canada can be severely affected. Consequently, the greater the dependence on the U.S. market, the more vulnerable Canadian manufacturers (and their employees) become. However, attempts to diversify Canada's exports of manufactured goods geographically have not been very successful. In recent years, for example, the value of Canadian goods exported to the European Economic Community, or EEC, our second biggest market, has gradually declined, whereas the value of our exports to the United States has continued to edge up. This trend is expected to continue as the foreign exchange rate for the Canadian dollar remains relatively stable compared with the U.S. dollar but continues to strengthen against the European and other foreign currencies, making Canadian goods more expensive in non-U.S. markets.

Canadian manufacturers also have to worry about foreign competition, both in their export markets and in the Canadian market itself. Other countries such as South Korea, Taiwan, Malaysia, Singapore, Hong Kong, and Japan, with lower labour costs, fewer strikes, and equal or better technology for the production of many goods, provide formidable competition. Only the transportation costs involved in bringing the goods to North America and government pressure to obtain "voluntary" restrictions of exports from these countries for certain goods have prevented even deeper inroads. Nevertheless, Canadian manufacturers have in recent years stopped production of certain product lines such as television sets. Also, following the old adage of "if you can't beat them, join them," many Canadian manufacturers have been forced to switch their production of parts and certain finished goods from Canada to the Far East, at the expense of Canadian income and employment.

Investment capital is not short in Canada. However, funds have not easily been available for new business ventures where the element of risk is high. The difficulty of obtaining such funds has often inhibited a firm's growth and even led to the sale of all or a controlling percentage of the firm's common shares to U.S. or other foreign investors.

As in many other countries, labour strikes have increasingly disrupted Canadian manufacturing industry. Although conciliation is compulsory under provincial labour legislation, management and labour often find it difficult to reach a negotiated agreement. Prolonged strikes, with all their harmful effects on the public as well as on the parties directly involved, seem to be a necessary prelude to a new labour-management contract. Also, wage settlements in certain industries have been so high that the resultant higher prices for the goods produced have impaired their competitive effectiveness, particularly abroad.

17.2: MINING

The Canadian mining industry has been an important source of income and jobs for Canadians since the earliest days of Confederation. Iron, copper, nickel, zinc, and coal are the "big five" in production value, followed by potash, gold, uranium, cement, and sulphur (see Table S.10). In the early 1980s, Canada's mining industry was generally depressed as a result of a drop in world demand for mineral products associated with the world economic recession.

Table S.10
Canada's Principal Mineral Products, 1981

	$ millions	Per cent of total
A. *Metals*		
1. Iron Ore	1 748.1	12.2
2. Copper	1 529.8	10.6
3. Nickel	1 238.1	8.6
4. Zinc	1 089.6	7.6
5. Gold	922.1	6.4
6. Uranium	794.2	5.5
7. Silver	458.1	3.2
8. Lead	263.6	1.8
9. Molybdenum	218.8	1.5
10. Platinum group	136.2	0.9
11. Iron, remelt	113.1	0.8
12. Cobalt	108.4	0.8
13. Tantalum	23.2	0.2
14. Columbium	18.6	0.1
15. Selenium	8.7	0.1
16. Cadmium	4.1	0.0
Sub-total	*8 683.8*	*60.4*
B. *Non-Metals*		
1. Coal	1 072.5	7.5
2. Potash	990.4	6.9
3. Sulphur, elemental	647.7	4.5
4. Asbestos	548.4	3.8
5. Titanium dioxide	131.7	0.9
6. Salt	131.6	0.9
7. Peat	51.6	0.4
8. Sulphur in smelter gas	47.4	0.3
9. Gypsum	46.9	0.3
10. Sodium sulphate	39.4	0.3
11. Quartz	33.5	0.2
12. Nepheline syenite	16.8	0.1
Sub-total	*3 779.1*	*26.3*
C. *Structural Materials*		
1. Cement	665.9	4.6
2. Sand and gravel	518.2	3.6
3. Stone	312.1	2.2
4. Lime	153.9	1.1
5. Clay products	119.1	0.8
Sub-total	*1 769.2*	*12.3*
D. *Other Minerals*	*135.6*	*0.9*
Grand Total	*14 367.7*	*100.0*

Source: Statistics Canada, Cat. 26-202

Foreign Sales

Much of the capital used to develop Canada's mines has come from abroad; and much of the output is shipped to the United States rather than processed and used in Canada. This has led to a continuing argument that Canada is being stripped of its natural resources to feed the mineral-hungry industries of countries such as the United States and now, to an increasing degree, Japan.

Certainly, Canada would be better off, in terms of income and employment, if it had the manufacturing industry that could profitably utilize these raw materials. But with a market of only about 25 million people at home, and limited ability to compete abroad with other more efficient manufacturing countries, there seems little hope for many years that Canada can make use of all the minerals that are at present mined. And certainly, according to the doctrine of comparative advantage (discussed in Chapter 41) Canada should be prepared to export minerals in exchange for other products.

The argument has also been advanced that these minerals should be left in the ground until Canadian industry needs them. But this would mean abandoning Canada's present mining industry, and all the employment and income that it generates, for the sake of retaining mineral stockpiles that may in the future be replaced in industry by something else, or by minerals found elsewhere. A saner argument would seem to be to encourage as much processing as possible of these minerals in Canada before they are shipped abroad (perhaps by means of an export tax on unprocessed minerals), and gradually to develop efficient Canadian manufacturing industries to use as many of these minerals as possible.

However, if Canada is to obtain access to the large United States market for its manufactured products, it must also be willing to sell at least part of its minerals.

Tax Incentives

A controversy that has surrounded the Canadian mining industry for many years is whether it should receive special tax concessions. Until 1971, mining firms, and also oil and gas firms, were permitted to write off almost all their exploration, development, drilling, and property acquisition costs before paying any income tax. Furthermore, the income from new mines, or from abandoned mines that were reopened, was exempt from income tax for the first three years of operation. Combined with the previous concession, this meant that a mine was free of tax for six or seven years, during which time the firm would often try to extract as much ore as possible, often with little regard for the ecology. Some mines might even be closed at the end of the tax-holiday period.

Mining, oil, and gas firms were also given a special "depletion allowance" to compensate them for the fact that their wealth—the mineral resources—was being used up in the process of earning income. This concession was a deduction of one-third from their taxable incomes each year. Shareholders of mining companies were also permitted a depletion allowance on their dividend income in calculating their personal income tax.

Just like any other firm, a mining company was allowed to depreciate assets, such as machinery, that gradually wear out. However, the rate of depreciation was an attractive 30 per cent per annum, based on a diminishing balance. Mine shafts and haulage ways built after a mine had begun operation could be written off completely in one year. Also, certain provincial taxes could be included as expenses for income tax purposes. There were also other benefits.

In 1971, the federal government, as part of its overall tax reform, made a number of changes in the tax treatment of mining companies. However, it continued the general direction of its previous tax policy. As the Minister of Finance stated: "Substantial tax incentives are maintained to recognize the risks involved in exploration and development, the international competition for capital, and the levels of incentives available in other companies."[1] Amongst the changes, the three-year income tax exemption on new mines was withdrawn after 1973, and replaced by an accelerated write-off of capital equipment and on-site facilities, including townsite facilities. Also, the system of automatic depletion for mining and petroleum corporations was replaced in 1976 by a new system by which only one-third of actual expenditures can be deducted. Shareholders' depletion allowances on dividends from mining and petroleum corporations were abolished in 1971.

These tax concessions have in the past undoubtedly spurred the development of Canada's mineral resources. However, critics such as Eric Kierans charge that this is just the problem; federal taxation and incentive programs place too much emphasis on the development of natural resources at the expense of manufacturing, a sector which creates many more jobs. Furthermore, these tax concessions, the critics say, are made even worse by the fact that they stimulate a boom in mining investment and the funds that flow in from abroad drive up the foreign exchange rate of the Canadian dollar. This makes Canadian manufactured goods more expensive abroad and so retards the growth of this important job-creating sector. Another sore point is the fact that such a large portion of Canada's extractive industries is still foreign-owned. The tax concessions, it is argued, mean that the Canadian government is providing foreigners with money to help buy more of Canada. In the 1980s, this same criticism is being made with regard to the tax concessions provided under the National Energy Program for oil and gas exploration in Canada's "frontier" lands.

Mineral Policy

Amongst the federal government's plans for the future is a national advisory committee on the mineral industry made up of industry representatives. This committee would advise the government on such matters as mining economics, mineral exports, and environmental problems. Another initiative is the development of a mineral resource policy for Canada.

A set of fifteen guidelines for such a policy was outlined by Mr. Jack Austin, the federal Deputy Energy Minister, in March, 1971.[2] These were as follows: (1) maintenance of an adequate domestic mineral supply at reasonable prices so that shortages or uneconomic prices do not impede the development of secondary industry in Canada; (2) standards established within which the public and private sectors, whether Canadian or foreign-owned, are expected to operate with respect to land tenure, pricing and marketing, operating practices, further processing, the degree of domestic ownership and control, employment practices, land conservation and reclamation, and integration of land and resource development; (3) to encourage an increasing degree of domestic mineral processing and mineral-based manufacturing instead of exporting raw or lightly processed products, and to optimize the return from mineral exports in term of price and value in relation to tonnage; (4) the expansion of Canadian ownership and control over mineral resources, while taking appropriate account of a continuing need for foreign capital and achieving maximum benefit from foreign capital invested in the mineral industry; (5) to maintain and improve Canada's competitive position in world mineral markets; (6) to establish an infrastructure by either government or industry to include power, transportation, communication, education, community facilities, and other factors necessary for rational mineral exploitation; (7) to ensure that technical and economic information systems are set up to disseminate data such as geological and mineral maps and reports, statistics, and technical information; (8) to alleviate regional economic disparities through optimum exploitation of mineral potential in "disadvantaged regions"; (9) to forecast problems related to mineral depletion and declining regions in order to cushion the effect of impending mine closings; (10) to conserve mineral resources through optimum recovery of minerals from deposits; (11) to establish pollution-control standards and to minimize costs external to the mineral project itself; (12) maximum reduction possible in foreign "discriminatory actions" such as tariffs and non-tariff barriers that affect Canada's mineral trade; (13) to ensure that mineral exploitation contributes an equitable share of the tax revenue to the nation; (14) an increase in the development and application of domestic skills in mining; and, (15) overall development of Canadian mineral resources in a manner that contributes to, and reflects, general government policies.

Provincial Incentives

In Canada there are provincial as well as federal incentives to mining. Thus, for example, the Ontario government has an incentive plan to aid mineral exploration in designated parts of the province. Under the plan, the government pays one-third of the cost of an approved exploration program up to a stated maximum for each project.

17.3: ENERGY

Canada is blessed with an abundant supply of oil, natural gas, coal, and electric power (see Table S.11). However, much of the crude oil is in presently unaccessible form or geographical location.

Oil and Natural Gas

Canada's present large oil industry began in 1947 with the discovery of the Leduc oilfield in Alberta. Previous discoveries of significance had been made at Petrolia, in south-western Ontario, in the 1850s, and at Turner Valley, near Calgary, Alberta, in 1913. Nowadays, Alberta is by far and away the leading oil-producing province, followed by Saskatchewan and British Columbia. Alberta is also the leading producer of natural gas, followed by British Columbia. Oil and natural gas are shipped by pipeline from Alberta to markets in the United States and central Canada.

The discovery, in the late 1960s, of vast quantities of oil and natural gas in Prudhoe Bay, on Alaska's north shore, meant that a large new U.S. source of supply was found for the United States market. It has also meant a difficult environmental problem for Canadians. Since the oil and gas are brought overland to Alaska's south shore and then shipped by ocean tanker to Seattle, or ports further South, there is grave risk of pollution to Canada's West Coast should a mishap occur in, for example, the foggy waters of Juan de Fuca Strait. Discoveries of

Table S.11
Electric Energy in Canada, 1982

A. *Net Generation*	Million kilowatt hours	Per cent of total
Hydraulic	255 136	68.0
Thermal	120 313	32.0
Total	375 449	100.0
Utilities	339 514	90.4
Industries	35 935	9.6
Total	375 449	100.0
Net exports(1)	31 366	8.4
Total available(2)	344 083	91.6
Total	375 449	100.0
B. *Electric Energy*		
Available by Province		
Newfoundland	8 487	2.5
Prince Edward Island	511	0.1
Nova Scotia	6 664	1.9
New Brunswick	8 490	2.5
Quebec	117 943	34.3
Ontario	106 683	31.0
Manitoba	14 366	4.2
Saskatchewan	10 115	2.9
Alberta	26 404	7.7
British Columbia	43 612	12.7
Yukon & N.W.T.	808	0.2
Canada	344 083	100.0

Source: Statistics Canada, *Electric Power Statistics,* Cat. 57-001

Note: (1) Less imports; (2) total net generation less exports

natural gas on King Christian Island, as well as of oil and natural gas on Canada's Arctic north slope make the problem of transportation—overland to Alberta or by tanker to the Atlantic Ocean—an urgent, and environmentally very hazardous, problem. If a pipeline is built in the Canadian North, this will involve an investment of many billions of dollars—far more than was involved in the construction of the St. Lawrence Seaway project. Because much of this money would have to come from the United States, the undertaking of such a project would inevitably cause an appreciation of the foreign exchange value of the Canadian dollar. This, in turn, would make it harder for Canadian firms to export their goods and services, and so, it is feared, create another economic problem for Canada. However, on the positive side, the sale of Arctic oil and natural gas would be a welcome new source of income for Canada and a welcome replacement for costly imported oil.

On Canada's east coast, oil and gas have been discovered in economic quantities off Nova Scotia and Newfoundland as a result of off-shore drilling. This, it is hoped, will provide the Atlantic provinces with the same economic stimulus received by Alberta in the late 1940s.

The National Energy Program

In 1980, the federal government announced a National Energy Program (or NEP) with the aim of ensuring by 1990 oil supply security for Canada and substantial Canadianization of the petroleum industry. And the NEP, spearheaded by Petrocan, a new Crown corporation, now with immense financial assets, has given considerable impetus to oil and gas exploration throughout the country. For example, gas from the Scotia Shelf is expected to be brought ashore by 1987. Although less accessible, the Hibernia field in the Grand Banks off Newfoundland, which is estimated to contain 1.8 billion barrels of recoverable oil, making it the largest oil pool in Canada, is also being developed. One problem that has slowed development has been the need to secure federal-provincial agreement over the resources. In Nova Scotia's case, such agreement has already been reached, with revenues to be divided about 42 per cent to the industry, 30 per cent to the Nova Scotia government, and 14 per cent to the federal government. Newfoundland is still negotiating.

Under the National Energy Program, to help offset the high cost of off-shore exploration (more than $300000 a day to operate a rig off the East Coast) the federal government gives to the oil companies, on the basis of their degree of Canadian ownership, what are called Petroleum Incentive Program (PIP) grants.

Companies with a 75% Canadian Ownership Ratio (or COR) receive the maximum grants, which cover 80% of their direct exploration spending. Foreign-owned companies are eligible for grants covering 25% of their direct exploration costs. In addition, there are tax write-offs for all companies, whatever the degree of foreign ownership. However, as from 1983, to curb the increasingly high cost of frontier oil exploration, written permission must first be obtained from the federal Energy Minister for wells costing $50 million or more, in order to qualify for the full benefit offered by federal grants.

A factor that has hampered oil and gas development in Western Canada is the 1981 two-tier oil pricing agreement between the Alberta and federal governments. Under this agreement, increases in the price of Western oil from wells discovered prior to the end of 1980 were restricted to a fixed percentage of the world price, with a maximum of 75 per cent of the average imported price in Montreal. Oil discovered subsequently could be sold at the world price. At the present time, this means that about 85% of Canadian oil is sold at the Special Old Oil Price (SOOP) and the other 15% at the New Oil Reference Price, or NORP, equivalent to the world price. Under the agreement, the price of natural gas is also restricted, with a maximum of 65 per cent of the wholesale price of oil in Toronto.

According to the critics, Canadian oil prices were held below world prices to please voters in Central and Eastern Canada. This in turned discouraged investment in the oil industry (for example, the Alsands and Cold Lake oil sands projects) and resulted in Canada moving from a substantial surplus in oil trade with other countries to a substantial deficit. Although Canadians would have paid more for their oil, Canada would now be self-sufficient and the economy much better off— especially as the federal government has had to subsidize the importation of foreign oil to keep Eastern Canadian oil prices below world prices. Politically, the Alberta government has championed the cause of a world price for its oil production whereas the federal government has tried to keep its 1980 election promise to consumers to keep Canadian oil prices below world levels.

In 1983, the Ottawa-Alberta energy pricing agreement was adjusted. Although the two-tier oil pricing structure was maintained, the cut-off date for oil qualifying for world prices was moved back from December 30, 1980 (the date under the 1981 agreement) to March 31, 1974, the year in which the steepest OPEC world oil price increases occurred. The federal government also agreed that all production from in-fill wells (wells drilled after an initial discovery is made), even in fields discovered long before 1974, will also now qualify for the world price. The net effect of the change in the agreement is to permit more Alberta oil (now about 35% of the total) to be sold at the world price, and yet still give consumers a lower than world price for many of the oil products they buy.

One factor bedevilling investment in oil exploration and development in Canada is the world price of oil. Since most of Canada's oil is costly to extract and bring to market, a drop in the world price can easily make a project uneconomic. Thus, to be economically viable, Hibernia oil (from offshore Newfoundland) would, at the present time, have to sell for at least $25 to $27 U.S. per barrel; output from the Alsands project for at least $30 U.S.; and Sable Island (Nova Scotia) natural gas for an oil equivalent of $16 to $18 per barrel. In other words, Canada is a high marginal cost oil and gas producer that requires relatively high and rising world prices to make investment attractive, even with government incentives. If the world price of oil were to drop substantially (for example, from $30 U.S. to $20 U.S.), the development of Canadian resources would become unprofitable at the present time. Already in 1982, the $13.5 billion Alsands project in Northern Alberta was halted because of unwillingness of the last two private-sector participants (Shell Canada and Gulf Canada) to proceed. Also, plans for an Alaska Highway natural gas pipeline were further delayed. To encourage oil development and conservation, the Canadian government (whatever the political party) is expected in the future to move away more quickly from a "made-in-Canada" oil price towards world prices for all oil sold in Canada—whether produced in Canada or purchased from abroad. Even with world prices and government exploration incentives, no frontier oil is expected before 1990. Although progress is being made in the Grand Banks, the other frontier hope (the Beaufort Sea and the Arctic Islands) is still doubtful—because of conflicting reports of actual oil and gas reserves and the problem of transportation to market (tanker or a revived Mackenzie Valley pipeline?). In the West, of the several oil megaprojects that have already bitten the dust, only Imperial Oil's Cold Lake heavy-oil project is likely to be revived, and then on a reduced scale and with special tax and other concessions from the federal and provincial governments.

Coal

After World War II, oil and natural gas began to replace coal as a fuel for heating and transportation, both in Canada and abroad. As a result, Canada's coal industry entered a period of decline. In Nova Scotia, the long-established coal industry was squeezed between falling demand on the one hand and rising costs and shrinking reserves on the other. In the West, however, low-cost, open-pit mines in Alberta and Saskatchewan have been able to supply, at reasonable profit, the increasing fuel needs of thermal-electric power plants. Mines in Alberta and British Columbia have also, in recent years, begun to export metallurgical coal to Japan and make a significant contribution to Canada's balance of payments. However, in the early 1980s a world coal glut and increased Australian competition, made the prospects for Canadian Western coal producers less rosy.

Electricity

By 1980, Canada's electric-power generating capacity totalled about 80000 electrical megawatts, practically all of it built in this century. As most parts of Canada are rich in water-power, hydro-electricity has been the main type of electricity generated. Amongst the various provinces, Quebec is the most richly endowed, with over 40 per cent of Canada's water-power resources and the largest amount of developed capacity. British Columbia is the second most energy-wealthy province. Ontario, although a large producer of hydro-electricity, also makes substantial use of conventional and nuclear thermal-electric power. However, a decline in electricity demand in the early 1980s has slowed the development of the nuclear energy industry. Newfoundland, by contrast, still has a rich, relatively untapped hydro-electric potential. However, exploitation has been hindered by disagreement between Newfoundland and Quebec as to the terms on which electricity may be transmitted across Quebec territory to U.S. export markets. In the Maritimes, plans for a massive Nova Scotia tidal-power development, harnessing the Bay of Fundy, are still awaiting funds.

Summary

1. Industry, rather than agriculture, is now Canada's main source of income and employment.
2. Manufacturing, in its modern sense, means the production of goods by people using power-driven machinery. *Primary manufacturing* is the processing of basic raw materials. *Secondary manufacturing* is the production of finished goods and parts from processed raw materials.
3. Canada's most important manufacturing industries, in term of value added, are food, beverages, primary metals, paper and allied products, and transportation equipment.
4. Manufacturing can be divided into the following processes: extractive, conditioning, analytical, synthetic, and assembly.

5. The most important characteristics of modern manufacturing are: mechanization, automation, use of electric power, specialization of labour and equipment, mass production, standardization, synchronization, and advanced technology, including CAD/CAM and robotics.

6. Problems that face Canadian manufacturing include the relatively small domestic market (just 25 million people); the dangers from excessive dependence on the U.S. market; the existence of a relatively large number of firms in many Canadian industries, which helps to prevent long production runs; foreign competition at home and abroad; appreciation in the foreign exchange rate for the Canadian dollar; difficulties in obtaining additional capital; and uneasy labour-management relations.

7. In Canada's mining production, nickel, copper, iron, zinc, and asbestos are the "big five," followed by lead, potash, gold, silver, and coal.

8. Much of the capital to develop Canada's mines has come from abroad, and much of the output is shipped to the United States rather than processed and used in Canada. Although mineral exports constitute an important source of national income, it would be preferable to have more of these minerals processed in Canada or, even better, to have them used by Canadian manufacturing industry and exported as finished or semi-finished goods.

9. A controversy that has surrounded the Canadian mining industry for many years is whether it should receive special income tax concessions as an incentive to the development of the country's mineral resources.

10. Guidelines for a Canadian mineral resource policy have been set out by the Federal Government.

11. Provincial governments also provide financial incentives for mineral exploration.

12. Canada's present large oil industry began in 1947 with the discovery of the Leduc oilfield in Alberta. This province is now Canada's leading producer of both oil and natural gas. However, large oil and gas fields have recently been discovered in the Canadian Arctic and in the off-shore Atlantic.

13. In 1980, the federal government announced a National Energy Program for Canada with the aim of ensuring national oil self-sufficiency by 1990 and substantial Canadianization of the petroleum industry.

14. After years of decline, Canada's coal industry, now centred in Alberta and British Columbia, has begun to revive, supplying both

thermal-electric power plants in Canada and markets in Japan.
15. At the beginning of this decade, Canada had about 80000 mega-watts of electric-power generating capacity, predominantly hydro-electric. Quebec is Canada's most richly endowed province as regards water-power resources and developed electricity generating capacity.

Key Terms

Manufacturing 315	Mass production 320
Primary manufacturing 316	Standardization 321
Secondary manufacturing 316	Technology 321
Extractive process 316	Synchronization 321
Conditioning process 316	CAD/CAM 321
Analytical process 318	Robotics 321
Synthetic process 318	Mining 323
Assembly process 318	Tax incentives 325
Mechanization 318	Depletion allowance 326
Capital-intensive 318	Depreciation allowance 326
Labour-intensive 318	Mineral policy 327
Automation 320	National energy
Division of labour 320	program 330

Review Questions

1. What is manufacturing? Distinguish, in your answer, between primary and secondary manufacturing.
2. What are the most important types of manufacturing industry in Canada? Which are the country's key manufacturing centres?
3. What are the five basic types of manufacturing processes?
4. Distinguish between mechanization and automation. What are the implications for employment in Canada of the growing use of capital-intensive methods of production?
5. What is the significance of electric power in manufacturing growth?
6. What is the nature of specialization in industry? How does it contribute to industrial productivity?
7. What is mass production? Why is its use restricted to certain kinds of products? Why does it require standardization and synchronization?

8. What is technology? Why is it so important to Canada's economic and social future?
9. Explain the terms CAD/CAM and robotics. What impact are these items expected to have on Canadian manufacturing industry?
10. What are the major problems facing Canadian manufacturing industry today?
11. What are the principal types of ore obtained from Canada's mines? Why is it that such a large proportion of the output is exported? How beneficial is this to Canada?
12. The Canadian mining industry has for a long time received special tax concessions. What is their purpose? How justified are they?
13. What are the key features of the federal government's mineral policy? How suitable a policy does it seem for Canada?
14. Where are Canada's oil and natural gas deposits to be found? What are the principal markets? What transportation problems face the development of newly discovered deposits?
15. What has been the history of Canada's coal industry?
16. How great is Canada's capacity to generate electric power? Where is this capacity located?
17. What is the federal government's energy policy? Discuss.

References

1. The Hon. E.J. Benson, Minister of Finance, *Summary of 1971 Tax Reform Legislation* (Ottawa: The Queen's Printer, 1971), p.45.
2. *The Globe and Mail,* Toronto, March 26, 1971.

18. CANADIAN AGRICULTURE

CHAPTER OBJECTIVES

A. To highlight the two basic economic problems that face most Canadian farmers
B. To discuss government price-support programs
C. To review the role of agricultural marketing boards
D. To examine crop insurance as an income-stabilization device
E. To review the various types of farm credit programs
F. To explain the role that has been played by transportation subsidies
G. To discuss the future role of government in assisting Canadian agriculture

CHAPTER OUTLINE

In Canada, as well as in the U.S., Western Europe, and other countries of the world, agriculture is considered to be part of the social as well as economic fabric of society. In other words, farming communities, spread across the country, as well as being an important source of jobs and income outside the urban, industrial areas, help provide political and social stability. In Canada's case, with the vastness of its territory and the scantiness of its population, a prosperous agricultural industry give incentive to settlement and development. Also, from the economic point of view, Canadian agriculture makes a substantial contribution to the country's GNP and to its balance of international payments.

18.1: BASIC ECONOMIC PROBLEMS

Over the years, Canadian agriculture has suffered from the fact that the Canadian farmers' average income has been both relatively small and dangerously unstable. To help alleviate this situation, the federal and, to a lesser extent, the provincial governments have introduced a variety of programs of financial and other assistance. However, by helping to overcome one problem, government is seen by many critics to have created another. Canadian agriculture, it is alleged, now depends for its continued existence on a government paternalism that stifles any attempt by farmers to solve their own economic problems. Furthermore, the taxpayer at large is required each year to help pay for farm surpluses that cannot be sold and to maintain in use substandard farmland that is not really needed. But this is only one side of the story.

Low Average Income

For many years, the average income of farmers, relative to that of workers in other occupations, has steadily declined. Also, farming is one of the hardest forms of physical work. And, today, with the high degree of farm mechanization, the scientific approach to farming, and the amount of government regulation, a good farmer needs to be a labourer, mechanic, manager, bookkeeper, and veterinarian, all wrapped into one. It is not surprising, therefore, that the sons and daughters of farm families are moving to the cities where incomes are usually higher and the jobs less physically demanding. Of course, not all farmers suffer from low income; as in any occupation, incomes vary greatly. There are, for example, many prosperous wheat farmers in the Prairie provinces, but there are also many poor ones. Throughout Canada, many farmers are struggling along at a subsistence level, trying to make a living from relatively unproductive, marginal land.

The causes of this relative decline in average farm income are not hard to find. Basically, the demand for Canada's agricultural output has failed to increase as fast as the supply. On the demand side, people can only eat a limited amount. The demand for food is, as economists would say, relatively income-elastic. Thus, a doubling of a person's income does not mean a doubling of that person's expenditure on food. Spending on food must compete, in priority, with spending on transportation, housing, home furnishings, entertainment, travel, and many other non-food items. Once people are reasonably well fed, they tend to spend any additional income on these other items. Of course, many people in this country and abroad go short of food, but demand, as we saw earlier, implies the ability to pay as well as the desire to have. Unfortunately, without money, many people cannot obtain all the goods, including food, that they would like to have.

The demand for Canada's agricultural output is also affected by competition from farmers in other countries. Within Canada, for example, fruit and vegetable farmers find that much of their market is taken by imports from Florida and California. And recently farmers have complained, to no avail, to the Anti-Dumping Tribunal about the import of subsidized Italian wines and canned tomatoes. However, trade works both ways. Thus, the demand for Canadian beef has been greatly increased by export sales to the United States. Similarly, the demand for Canadian wheat has been greatly increased by sales to the Soviet Union and China. However, the signing in 1983 of a new five-year U.S.-Soviet grain agreement, means extra competition for Canada. Under the agreement, the annual minimum Soviet grain purchase from the U.S. will be 9 million tons, out of a total Soviet import requirement of 30 million tons or more, in a bad Soviet harvest year. On the whole, Canadian farm exports exceed imports by about $4 billion each year, and provide about one quarter of Canada's trade surplus. Key products are wheat, barley, and other grains; meat products, especially fresh and frozen pork; and fishery products.

On the supply side, Canadian agriculture has been characterized by a dramatic rise in output per acre. New and improved strains of high-yield crops, improved methods of cultivation, new chemical fertilizers and insecticides, and farm machinery of all kinds have been the principal causes. This increase in the supply of farm products has far exceeded the increase in demand. As a result, the prices received by farmers and ranchers for their products have declined over the years relative to the prices received by manufacturing and service industries. A farmer's net income consists of the gross income from the sale of the output minus expenses. But, whereas the price paid for the output has not increased greatly despite inflation, the prices of the inputs have increased tremendously. The wages for hired help are one of these

"The trouble is, the public's just not eating the right foods.."

expenses, but just as important has been the increase in the price of the other inputs such as farm machinery, seed, and fertilizers. Unlike the manufacturer, the farmer is not easily able to pass on these higher costs to the consumer in the form of higher prices. As a result, the profit margin, even for the most efficient farms, has gradually decreased.

Unstable Income

It is bad enough for farmers that their average income is relatively low, but, even worse, that this income is unstable. The most important cause of this instability is changes in supply. Good weather can mean bumper harvests, but it can also mean a drastic fall in market price; bad weather can mean small harvests and high prices. In addition, all kinds of diseases and pests can affect crop and livestock output. Also, a few good years usually encourage an expansion in output; and this overproduction in turn depresses market prices and farm incomes. Canadian producers of eggs, chickens, and hogs are all examples of farmers who have suffered badly in the past from an excess of supply in relation to demand. Only government price supports, which we will discuss later in this chapter, have prevented other farmers from sharing this fate.

Changes in demand are also responsible for unstable farm income. The prices of farm products tend to decline much more when demand falls than do the prices of non-farm products. This is because the supply of farm products is much more inelastic than the supply of other products. A farmer with land, buildings, and equipment is committed to farming. If the price of the farm output falls, the farmer cannot easily switch to the production of something else. Also, in the export market, competition from foreign producers of wheat and other farm products can cause sudden changes in demand.

In the case of Western grain farmers, another problem has been the closing down of West coast ports by grain workers' strikes. Normally, the West Coast grain terminals run at full capacity all year round. Therefore a strike or lockout can severely disrupt Canada's $5 billion grain export trade. The West Coast ports of Vancouver and Prince Rupert handle about 45 per cent of prairie grain exports.

18.2: GOVERNMENT ASSISTANCE

The decline in prosperity of Canadian agriculture relative to other sectors of the economy and the instability that has characterized agricultural prices and incomes over the years, have resulted in a variety of federal and provincial government programs to assist farmers.

Government became involved in agriculture as far back as the early days of Confederation, with grants and sales of land to prospective settlers. However, until the 1930s, government activities were confined mainly to land conservation and rehabilitation. In the 1930s, however, government intervention took an additional dimension—that of income assistance. Thus, in 1935 the federal government passed the Prairie Farm Rehabilitation Act to help farmers in Alberta, Manitoba, and Saskatchewan develop water supplies and otherwise rehabilitate farms which had suffered badly from prolonged drought and soil drifting. It also passed the Canadian Wheat Board Act to provide farmers with stable minimum prices for their wheat. Furthermore, in 1939, the federal government passed the Prairie Farm Assistance Act to provide indemnities to farmers whose crops might be damaged or destroyed by various natural hazards, and who are not covered by a provincial government crop insurance plan.

Early in World War II, the federal government imposed price ceilings on agricultural products so that the public would not face steeply rising food prices. To compensate farmers for their loss in potential income, the government made cash payments to them and subsidized the purchase of feed, seed, fertilizer, limestone, machinery, and other agricultural inputs. After the War, the price controls were gradually removed and most of the subsidies eliminated. However, the continued relative deterioration of the agricultural sector of the economy, the economic and social importance for Canada of a healthy farming industry, and the political value of the farm vote (one-third of federal M.P.s are from rural areas) have led to successive Canadian governments providing more and more assistance. One extremely important form of this government assistance has been price-support programs.

18.3: PRICE SUPPORTS

A *price support* is an undertaking by the government that a farmer will receive a minimum price per unit for all or a specified amount of his or her output. Since the purpose of the price support is to keep up the level of a farmer's income, this minimum price is usually higher than the one that would be set by the normal interaction of market demand and farm supply.

Price-Support Methods

How can a government implement a price-support program? Basically, there are three ways: (a) by buying up surplus output at the floor price; (b) by leaving output unrestricted, but enabling producers to sell all their output by subsidizing the price to consumers; and (c) by paying farmers to restrict output or by penalizing them if they produce more than their allocated quota.

The first of these methods, buying up any surplus, prevents competition among sellers faced with a limited demand which would force the market price down. Thus, in Figure 18:1, the government will have to purchase the amount Q_2Q_3. The total revenue received by producers would be the minimum price, OP_2, times the quantity, OQ_3. This is equal to the rectangle OP_2AQ_3. Of this sum, conumers would pay an amount equal to the rectangle OP_2EQ_2, and the government would pay the remainder, equal to the rectangle Q_2EAQ_3. The federal government uses this approach, for example, to ensure that Canadian dairy

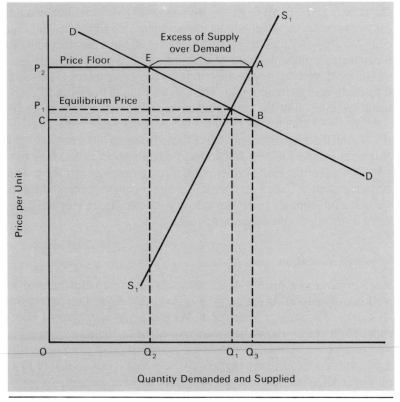

Note: Without a price floor, the equilibrium market price is OP_1, and the quantity demanded and supplied are equal at OQ_1.

With a minimum price of OP_2, the quantity demanded, OQ_2, is much less than the quantity supplied, OQ_3.

Figure 18:1 A Price Floor Causes Supply to Exceed Demand

farmers achieve the Target Returns level—a fair return on their labour and investment based on a cost of production formula.

The second way in which a government can implement a price-support program is by making deficiency payments to farmers. Thus, in Figure 18:1, a government could ensure that producers sell all the output, OQ_3, that they would produce at the floor price, OP_2, by enabling producers to sell it at a price OC. At this price, the amount demanded would be as large as the amount supplied—namely OQ_3. The producers would receive a total price per unit of OP_2, of which the part OC would come from the consumer and the part CP_2 from the government. The total revenue received by producers would be equal to the rectangle OP_2AQ_3. Of this amount, $OCBQ_3$ would come from the public, and CP_2AB from the government. This technique is used, for example, as part of the federal government's support program for dairy farmers—with a subsidy paid on each 100 litres of milk produced for industrial milk and cream production.

The third method of price support is for the government to persuade farmers to restrict their output. Thus, as we can see in Figure 18:2, the quantity supplied at the minimum price, OP_2, would have to be restricted to OQ_2. Such a policy would mean a new supply curve, S_2S_2, to the left of the original supply curve S_1S_1. However, it is not easy in a democratic society to persuade farmers voluntarily to reduce their output. Consequently, cash payments are often given as an incentive. This system is used in Canada and the U.S., with regard to grain production. Canada also imposes levies (or penalty payments) on, for example, dairy farmers who produce above quota.

Resource Allocation

Since government price-support programs interfere with the normal working of market forces and the price mechanism, they affect the allocation of a country's resources. With the first two types of price-support programs (buying up surplus output at the government-set minimum price or making deficiency payments) farmers are encouraged to produce more than they otherwise would. Thus, in Figure 18:1, output is OQ_3, not the amount OQ_1 that it would be with no price-support programs. Also, under these conditions, consumers must pay considerably more.

In economic theory, we tend to assume that if output is reduced, the human and other resources that are consequently freed can gradually be diverted to other uses that are more highly prized by consumers. In practice, there is great immobility of farm resources. Crops, livestock,

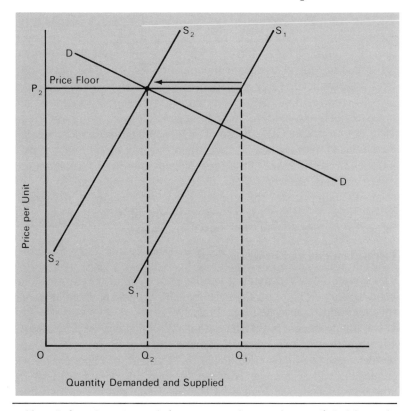

Note: Before the crop restriction program, the quantity supplied, OQ_1, at the minimum price, OP_2, exceeded the quantity demanded.

With crop restriction, a new supply curve, S_2S_2, intersects the demand curve, DD, at the minimum price. Since no surplus or shortage exists at this price, there is a state of market equilibrium. This will continue so long as individual farmers adhere to their production quotas and so long as demand remains unchanged.

Figure 18:2 Crop Restriction Means a Shift in the Supply Curve

and other farm products can be varied, it is true, in response to changing consumer demand. However, there is no way that a country's farms can be converted into manufacturing or service industries, except in a relatively minor way—for example, by "dude" ranches. Consequently, most price-support programs are adopted for political and social reasons to help prevent the economic decay of whole rural areas.

If farms rate low in consumer priority compared with, say, beauty parlours this will be reflected, by means of the price mechanism, in Canada's resource allocation. However, our governments have long acted in accordance with the view that they often know what is better for the national interest than the consuming public; and the preservation of a country's farms and rural way of life, including the geographical spread of our relatively small population, may well be worth more than a theoretically ideal allocation of resources.

With crop restriction, the third type of price-support program, supply is deliberately reduced to keep up market price. Thus, in Figure 18:2, output is only OQ_2 instead of OQ_1. Although keeping productive land unused appears less wasteful than burning or dumping surplus production, it still makes little sense when viewed against the amount of starvation in the world. Also, the consumer is still required to pay a relatively high price for the product. Therefore, the ideal system would appear to be one which encourages maximum effective land use, a fair return to the farmer, and a fair price to the consumer.

Price-Elasticity and Program Costs

The cost to the government of various price-support programs will depend to a large extent on the nature of the demand and supply curves for the product concerned (see Table 18:1).

1. Paying producers to restrict output. With this type of program, the government will spend more if demand and supply are elastic. This is because setting a floor price above the equilibrium market price will create a much wider gap between the amount demanded and the amount supplied (see Figure 18:1). The larger the excess of supply over demand, the more the government will have to pay producers to cut back output to the same amount as the quantity demanded. The more price-inelastic are demand and supply, the smaller the cost of such a program.

2. Buying up surplus output. As with the first method, the cost of the program will be larger, the more price-elastic are demand and supply. Instead of paying producers not to produce, the government purchases the surplus. The wider the gap between market demand and industry supply, the more the government has to buy.

3. Subsidizing the price to consumers. With this method, the cost of the program will be larger if demand is inelastic rather than elastic. This is because the surplus output would have to be sold to consumers at a price considerably less than the floor price. The more inelastic the demand, the more the price would have to be reduced to increase the quantity demanded. This means that the more inelastic the demand, the greater the difference between the floor price guaranteed to the producer and the price paid by the consumer. The difference is the government subsidy. On the supply side, the more elastic the supply, the greater the cost of the program. This is exactly the same as with the

Table 18:1

*How Elasticity of Demand and Supply Affects the Cost
to the Government of a Price-Support Program*

Government Cost of Price-Support Program	Type of Price-Support Program		
	Paying Producers to Restrict Output	Buying up Surplus Output	Subsidizing the Price to Consumers
Cost of program will be larger if *demand* is:	elastic	elastic	inelastic
Cost of program will be larger if *supply* is:	elastic	elastic	elastic
Cost of program will be smaller if *demand* is:	inelastic	inelastic	elastic
Cost of program will be smaller if *supply* is:	inelastic	inelastic	inelastic

two previous methods of price support.

Canadian Government Policy

In 1944, the federal government passed an Agricultural Prices Support Act that empowered a Prices Support Board to set minimum prices for any agricultural product that it saw fit. To prevent the market price falling below this floor, the Board was authorized under the Act to purchase the product at the minimum price. In practice, the Board provided temporary emergency help for a variety of products including apples, beans, and turkeys. Two products, eggs and butter, received continuous price support.

The Agricultural Prices Support Act, designed to help farmers adjust from conditions of war to those of peace, continued in force until 1958. During its period of operation, the Board spent about $100 million in price supports. However, it was replaced in 1958 by a new and more ambitious measure, the Agricultural Stabilization Act. Under this Act, the federal government, by means of an Agricultural Stabilization Board, committed itself to support, at not less than 80 per cent of the previous ten-year average market or base price, the prices of nine commodities: cattle, hogs, and sheep, butter, cheese, and eggs; and Eastern wheat, oats, and barley. The government also gave itself the discretionary right to support the prices of other agricultural products.

Because of the large surpluses of hogs and eggs that developed in the 1950s, the federal government later altered its price-support program for those products. Instead of offering to purchase any amounts of hogs and eggs that could not be sold at the floor price, the government decided to let farmers sell these surpluses in the market place at whatever price they would bring. The Board would then pay farmers the difference between the government-set floor price and the national average market price. It should be noted that these *deficiency payments* are not paid on all of a farmer's output, only on a set amount, or quota, established for each farm. In this way, additional output is discouraged, and the total amount of farm subsidies held down. The deficiency payment method was also later used to support the price of sheep, soybeans, sugar beets, wool, honey, cattle, and tobacco.

18.4: THE CANADIAN WHEAT BOARD

Wheat, oats, and barley produced in Western Canada are products not included within the scope of the Agricultural Stabilization Act because they are the subject of special legislation. Under the Canadian Wheat Board Act of 1935, the federal government established a crown corporation, the Canadian Wheat Board, for the purpose of "the marketing in an orderly manner, in interprovincial and export trade, of grain grown in Canada." For many years the Board concerned itself only with the marketing of wheat. However, in 1949, it extended its control to oats and barley. Today, the Board has extensive control over the marketing of Western wheat and more limited control over the marketing of Western oats and barley.

How is wheat actually marketed? Each farmer is allowed to deliver a certain quota of wheat to the local elevator, the owner of which acts as an agent for the Wheat Board. The wheat is then sold by the board either at home or abroad. The farmer is paid an "initial price" for his or her wheat that is set by the federal government at the start of each crop year, on the basis of the expected selling price. This initial price is, in effect, a guaranteed floor price. In recent years, however, the actual price at which the Wheat Board has sold the wheat has usually exceeded this floor price. The difference is then paid to the farmers. However, they are charged a certain amount per bushel for elevator and freight costs.

Canadian wheat, although considered one of the best hard wheats in the world, has for many years faced a difficult market situation abroad. Internationally, Canada has co-operated with other major wheat producers to ensure the orderly marketing of wheat. Thus it was a member until 1969 of the International Grain Agreement that went into operation in 1949-50; and, since 1969, has been a member of the International Grains Arrangement. However, the selling prices established for different types of wheat under the International Grains Arrangement have been repeatedly undercut as a result of an excess supply of wheat in relation to demand. Only large sales of wheat to the Soviet Union and China have enabled Canadian wheat farmers to earn as much as they have without the need for government subsidy. However, diplomatic recognition of China by other wheat-producing countries such as Australia and the United States has resulted in more competition for Canada in that market. Also, Britain's entry into the Common Market has reduced Canada's wheat exports to that country as Britain now purchases more European wheat. Clearly, if Canadian wheat is to continue to be sold in substantial quantities abroad, the Canadian Wheat Board will have to reduce its export price. This will become even more necessary if importing countries continue the present trend of using softer, less expensive wheat for baking. In the future, therefore, Canadian wheat farmers may well have to rely on the Wheat Board's floor price for a reasonable income.

Until 1970, the Canadian Wheat Board placed no restriction on the amount of land planted to wheat. However, the growing wheat surplus—a stockpile of 25.8 million tonnes in 1970—led the federal government to introduce a program to reduce the amount of land used for growing wheat.

After World War II, oats and barley were once more sold on the open market. However, in 1949, the marketing of these coarse grains was also put under the control of the Canadian Wheat Board. Each farmer is given a quota of grain that can be sold to the Board at an established price. Since this price usually exceeds the price elsewhere, the floor price provides substantial aid to the farmer. Unlike wheat, oats, and barley, Prairie rye and oilseeds are still sold on the open market.

18.5: THE CANADIAN DAIRY COMMISSION

Since the 1930s, the marketing of fluid milk in Canada has been regulated, for public health as well as economic reasons, by provincial governments. Each province has its own milk control board that sets minimum prices at which fluid milk may be sold. In 1967, however, a Canadian Dairy Commission was established by the federal government to complement the activities of the provincial boards. Specifically, the commission's purpose was to regulate the production and marketing, including pricing, of milk and milk products entering into interprovincial and international trade. More broadly, the Commission aimed "to provide efficient producers of milk and cream with the opportunity of obtaining a fair return for their labour and investment and to provide consumers with a continuous and adequate supply of dairy products of high quality." To achieve this aim, the Commission offers to purchase creamery butter, the two top grades of cheddar cheese, and dry skim milk at officially-set floor prices. It also provides subsidies to producers of industrial milk and cream, based on assigned output quotas. Despite these quotas, which determine a dairy producer's eligibility for subsidy, Canadian farmers still produce large surpluses of dairy products. Some of these, such as evaporated milk and skim-milk powder, are sold abroad, usually at a loss. Like other marketing boards, the CDC is criticized by consumer groups for unnecessarily raising the price of dairy products to the Canadian public.

18.6: OTHER MARKETING BOARDS

In an attempt to obtain better prices for their products, Canadian farmers began many years ago to establish marketing cooperatives. Although these organizations enabled farmers to ensure better grading and packing of their products, develop a common brand image, and negotiate sales from a position of collective strength, they suffered from the fact that membership was purely voluntary. As a result, most have now been replaced by farmer-controlled marketing boards, imposed by provincial statute, which have control over the entire production and marketing of a particular product in each particular province. Canada now has over 120 such government-authorized but producer-controlled and managed boards, together accounting for about one-quarter of the total value of all farm product sales. A board may be established under provincial law once a majority of the farmers producing a particular product have voted in favour.

Marketing boards operate in different ways to achieve their basic objectives of raising farmers' income and eliminating wide fluctuations in it. Some boards limit themselves to promoting their product by advertising and other means. Others have also undertaken to improve transportation, assembly, storage, market research, and other marketing functions for their product. Another tool used by some marketing boards is the two-price system under which a board sells its product at a higher price in one market than another, or charges a higher price for one use rather than another. Thus, wheat may be sold at a lower price abroad than at home, or milk sold at a lower price for industrial use than for domestic consumption. Like the early co-operatives, marketing boards try to obtain the full benefits of collective bargaining in negotiating sale orders for their products. Because of compulsory

membership and compliance with the regulations, no farmer within the same province is free to undercut the price offered by the board. Another important tool for maintaining prices at a reasonable level has been the establishment of input quotas by various boards for their member producers. Thus, for example, the Ontario Fine-Cured Tobacco Growers Marketing Board allocates acreage rights to members, and the British Columbia Broiler Growers Marketing Board allocates broiler floorspace rights. Other boards such as the milk marketing boards use sales quotas instead, whereby each producer is permitted to sell only a specified amount of the product.

One of the biggest problems that faced marketing boards for many years was that most of them, except for the Canadian Wheat Board, were provincial in scope. That is, the efforts of one board could be undone by competition from another board in another province. The "chicken and egg war" that broke out between several provinces in 1971 was a case in point. Obviously, national marketing boards were needed, except for products such as tobacco that are produced in only one province. This need was partly met in 1972 with the federal government's Farm Products Marketing Act, which authorized the establishment of a national marketing board for poultry and eggs and permitted producers of other commodities to establish national marketing boards. Canada now has four federal marketing boards—one each for eggs, milk, chickens, and turkeys.

Supply-management marketing boards have been criticized for some years by consumer and industry groups in Canada such as the Grocery Products Manufacturers of Canada who claim that they give farmers too much control over the price of chickens, eggs, milk and turkeys in Canada. And there is serious concern that new marketing boards may be set up in the future for beef, hogs, and potatoes. The major criticisms are that such marketing boards restrict the supply of the product, artificially drive up prices, permit inefficiencies, and disallow economies of scale. It has been suggested that, to prevent abuse, the power to fix prices should be transferred from the marketing boards to a quasi-judicial board similar in nature to the Canadian Transport Commission or the CRTC.

Disposal of Surpluses

If a government adopts a policy of buying up surplus output at the minimum price, it faces the problem of handling, storing, and disposing of this food or other product. Obviously, it cannot sell this surplus output in the domestic market because this would depress the market price to the level at which it would have been without the government price-support program and thus make nonsense of the price floor. It might, however, give some of the surplus away to needy people who would not otherwise have provided part of the demand. This would prevent any interference with the floor price, but the government would have to ensure that none of the food disposed of in this manner finds its way to the normal market.

In practice, most governments try to dispose of surpluses abroad, sometimes in the form of gifts. For example, U.S. dried eggs and bottled orange juice concentrate became something of an institution in Britain during World War II. Canada, too, has made gifts of food at various times in recent years, normally in response to a particular disaster such as earthquake, famine, or disease. Canada has also provided gifts of food that can be sold locally to raise funds for economic development projects.

Instead of giving surpluses away, governments often try to sell them to foreign countries. Canada's wheat sales to China and the Soviet Union are a successful example of this policy. However, a government does not always have a free hand in this matter. If it sells surplus products abroad at a price less than that charged in its own country, it can be accused of "dumping." This means that, in many countries, local producers can successfully appeal to their governments to raise import tariffs on such goods to bring their price up to the level charged at home. This, in turn, may make it unprofitable for foreign importers to buy such surplus products. Sometimes, a government can sell its surplus abroad for more than it paid for it at home, but this is unusual.

Another difficulty in selling surpluses abroad is that the world market may be the main market for a country's product. In these circumstances, a government may buy up surplus output in order to keep up the price in the international market. This is the policy that Brazil, Colombia, and other major coffee producers follow. Disposing of surpluses then becomes a real problem. It was solved in Brazil's case for many years, to the horror and chagrin of coffee drinkers the world over, by dumping coffee into the Atlantic Ocean or by just burning it. In recent years, however, Brazil has switched its price-support program to one that requires coffee producers to restrict output.

Sometimes world producers will agree, in order to avoid disastrous price competition, to limit exports to commonly agreed-on quotas. This was the arrangement, for example, under the International Coffee Agreement, the International Sugar Agreement, and the International Grain Agreement. However, it is difficult to enforce the quotas assigned to member countries, to say nothing of the problem posed by producing countries who are unwilling to participate. It was this prob-

"You boys figure it out. We'd be a lot better off producing less, but selling it for more.."

lem of member and nonmember countries selling below the agreed world floor price that caused Canada to abandon the International Grain Agreement in 1969.

18.7: CROP INSURANCE

One of the problems that has always bedevilled Canadian farmers is the risk of loss from natural hazards such as drought, floods, hailstorms, frost, rust, and insects. Unfortunately, private insurance companies have found from sad experience that crop insurance is too risky a business to be profitable. Consequently, farmers have had to turn to the government for help of this kind. The Prairie Farm Assistance Act, passed by the federal government in 1939, was designed to meet this need. Under the Act, farmers marketing grain through the Canadian Wheat Board are required to pay a levy of 1 per cent of the value of sales. In return, they are paid an indemnity if the crop is damaged or destroyed. In practice, total indemnities have considerably exceeded total levies, the difference being paid by the federal government.

In 1959, the federal government went a step further in crop insurance. In that year, it passed the Crop Insurance Act, which gave provincial governments the necessary authorization to set up crop insurance programs of their own. It also provided for the federal government to pay part of the cost. The provincial crop insurance programs, covering practically all crops, including fruit trees, instead of just a few, are now considered to have made the Prairie Farm Assistance Act redundant.

18.8: AGRICULTURAL AND RURAL DEVELOPMENT

In 1966, the federal government passed an Agricultural and Rural Development Act (ARDA), replacing the Agricultural Rehabilitation and Development Act of 1961. The purpose of the new Act was to help people living in rural areas adjust to a changing social, economic, and technological environment. This was to be achieved by means of federal-provincial shared-cost programs covering land use, soil and water conservation, development of rural income and employment opportunities, and all necessary research. Federal money for the programs was provided under a special Fund for Rural Economic Development Act (FRED), also passed in 1966. Both the Act and the Fund were terminated in 1969 when the Department for Regional Economic Expansion (DREE), now replaced by the Department for Regional and Industrial Expansion (DRIE), was established to promote rural and other types of regional economic development.

18.9: FARM CREDIT

To make a reasonable living from the land, the modern Canadian farmer has to combine large amounts of machinery with a relatively small amount of labour. This machinery is, of course, expensive. Also, the need to reorganize farms into larger, more economical units to operate requires considerable financing. As well, short-term financing is customarily required to bridge the gap between the time at which a crop is planted and the time at which cash is received from its sale.

Although most farmers traditionally save a large part of their net income, outside financing is virtually indispensable to help meet their purchasing needs. A great deal of the money required, particularly short and medium-term financing, is obtained from private individuals, chartered banks, farm supply companies, and credit unions. However, the federal and provincial governments have also provided help in a variety of ways. We shall now briefly describe the most important of these government financing programs.

Farm Credit Corporation

In 1959, the federal government passed the Farm Credit Act. This Act established a federal government agency, the Farm Credit Corporation, to make long-term mortgage loans to farmers. Previously, only a limited amount of long-term financial help had been available from a Canadian Farm Loan Board established in 1929. For some loans, the security is land alone; for others, it is land, livestock, and machinery. The rate of interest charged to farmers is very close to that which the corporation itself pays for its funds. The Farm Credit Corporation is now the most important source of long-term loans for farmers. Other sources of long-term mortgage loans are the loan corporations set up by various provincial governments.

The Canadian Federation of Agriculture, on behalf of Canadian farmers, has complained in the early 1980s that funds available to farmers through the Farm Credit Corporation are insufficient. Another complaint in 1983 centred on the fact that, after government-supplied funds were used up in two months by farmers trying to refinance their operations to stay in business, the Department of Finance restricted FCC borrowing in foreign money markets to only $250 million, as compared with the $600 million desired.

Farm Syndicates Credit Act

By this Act, effective from 1965, the federal government authorized the Farm Credit Corporation to make loans to syndicates of three or more farmers for the purchase of farm machinery, buildings, and installed equipment. These loans are for up to 80 per cent of the value of the machinery, with a maximum total amount.

Animal Disease Eradication

The federal government compensates herd owners when their animals have to be put away because of disease. The compensation is usually their market value.

Farm Improvement Loans Act

This Act, passed in 1944, encourages the chartered banks to make short and medium-term loans to farmers by providing a federal government guarantee for such loans. Bank financing under the Act, with a maximum amount per farmer, has been used predominantly for the purchase of farm machinery and equipment, livestock, and farm improvement.

Prairie Grain Advance Payments Act

Under this Act, the Canadian Wheat Board is authorized by the federal government to make interest-free advance payments to Prairie grain farmers who are prevented from delivering their grain because of insufficient elevator space.

Federal Business Development Bank

This government-owned bank makes mortgage loans to new and existing agricultural enterprises when the funds cannot be obtained on reasonable terms and conditions elsewhere. There is no fixed maximum amount.

Provincial Aid

Most provincial governments have established programs of financial aid to farmers. In Alberta, for example, a farmer may borrow funds from the government, under the Farm Purchase Credit Act, to help buy a farm. In British Columbia, as another example, loans are available to farmers, under the Farmers' Land Clearing Assistance Act, to finance the clearing and breaking of land.

18.10: TRANSPORTATION SUBSIDIES

One of the ways in which the Federal Government helps farmers is by transportation subsidies.

Livestock Feed Assistance Act

Under this Act, the federal government helps pay the cost of transporting feed grains from the Prairie provinces to Eastern Canada and to British Columbia. The purpose of the Act is to ensure that feed-grain prices remain relatively stable without great differences between one part of Canada and another. A special Board administers the freight and storage assistance programs involved.

Crow's Nest Pass Agreement

By this agreement, made between the federal government and Canadian Pacific Railway in 1897, railway freight rates for grain being shipped from the Prairie provinces to Thunder Bay ports were held at the 1898 level. This was in return for substantial federal subsidies to build a 300-mile rail line through the Crow's Nest Pass in the Rockies. Later, in 1925, the fixed rate was legislated—for the Canadian National as well as the C.P.R. and extended to all Prairie delivery points and to West Coast ports. Farmers, so it is estimated, now pay about one-fifth of the actual cost to the railways of shipping the grain. This transportation subsidy to farmers is met by the federal government which, under the National Transportation Act of 1967, reimburses the railway companies for the revenue loss incurred. However, because of the low rates, the C.P.R. has not found it worthwhile to invest in new track and rolling stock and this has hampered Canadian grain exports. Whereas Canada now exports about 31 million tonnes of grain a year, it could, with better transportation, export 40 million tonnes by 1990. In 1982, the federal government announced its intention to abolish the special railway freight rates for grain shipments and pay a subsidy instead to the railways and farmers. In return, the railway companies would undertake to improve their grain handling facilities.

18.11: FUTURE ROLE OF GOVERNMENT

One important conclusion of the Federal Task Force on Agriculture some years ago was that government should reduce its direct involvement in agriculture. To achieve this, the Task Force recommended a number of measures. They included: (a) the control and reduction of farm surpluses to manageable proportions by switching production to

Table S.12
Canadian Farm Cash Receipts, by Source, in millions of dollars, 1982

Source	$ millions	Per cent of total
Crops		
Wheat	3 496.6	18.7
Wheat C.W.B. participation payments	463.7	2.5
Oats	53.6	0.3
Oats C.W.B.participation payments	0.6	0.0
Barley	791.5	4.2
Barley C.W.B.participation payments	111.6	0.6
C.W.B. net cash advance payments	2.8	0.0
Rye	54.1	0.3
Flaxseed	106.0	0.6
Rapeseed	583.6	3.1
Soybeans	192.7	1.0
Corn	399.9	2.1
Sugar Beets	28.2	0.2
Potatoes	251.4	1.3
Fruits	264.5	1.4
Vegetables	439.0	2.4
Floriculture and nursery	307.1	1.6
Tobacco	376.8	2.0
Other crops	285.9	1.5
Deferred grain receipts	-706.5	-3.8
Liquidation of deferred grain receipts	823.5	4.4
Sub-total	8 543.9	45.8
Livestock and Products		
Cattle	3 223.9	17.2
Calves	362.5	1.9
Hogs	1 957.3	10.5
Sheep	3.4	0.0
Lambs	24.1	0.1
Dairy products	2 640.3	14.1
Poultry	773.6	4.1
Eggs	462.7	2.5
Other	178.3	1.0
Sub-total	9 626.21	51.6
Forest and maple products	99.0	0.5
Dairy supplementary payments	274.4	1.5
Deficiency payments	25.0	0.1
Provincial income stabilization program	102.9	0.6
Total cash receipts from program farming operations	18 671.5	100.0

Source: Statistics Canada, *Farm Cash Receipts,* Cat. 21-001
Note: Figures exclude Newfoundland

other agricultural products in greater demand or by taking land out of production; (b) the phasing out of certain agricultural subsidies and price supports; and (c) the improvement of farm management. Financial assistance would be provided temporarily to facilitate crop switching and land retirement; educational and other assistance would be provided to younger farmers switching to other occupations; and financial assistance would be provided to older farmers.

These recommendations undoubtedly sound harsh to people who make their living from the land, particularly when they see that many people living in urban areas receive their income from tariff-protected manufacturing industries or from tax-supported government departments. Nevertheless, the question remains: to what extent should Canadian agriculture stand on its own feet?

From the purely economic point of view, there is the question of the most efficient allocation of Canada's resources. Should the federal and provincial governments try, at considerable public expenses, to keep in use farmland that is only marginally productive? Is money well spent, in social as much as economic terms, in trying to slow the present drift from the land? Is it worth spending large sums of public money to reclaim marshland in certain parts of the country when more than enough good farmland is unused elsewhere?

Also, the public may well ask, just how effective has government aid been in solving the farmers' twin problems of low and unstable income? As regards low income, most government payments, because they are usually geared to assigned production quotas or existing farm sizes, help the rich farmer just as much as the poor one. In other words, financial assistance is not being given to farmers selectively. It is not being directed where the need is most urgent or where the benefits are likely to be greatest. Also, in the case of farm loans, the farmer who often needs the greatest help, very often does not possess the land, buildings, and other collateral to qualify for a loan. Those who do receive farm credit are often the ones who could obtain loans in competition with other business borrowers and who could afford to pay the normal rate of interest. The same criticism may be applied to transportation subsidies that benefit all farmers, not just the poorer ones. However, this brings us to another question. Are the poorer farmers poorer because their farms are inherently inefficient? If this is the case, then financial aid may well be like pouring water (the taxpayers') into a bottomless well.

With regard to income stability, government price-support programs have meant that farmers can now count on a much more stable income than was previously the case. However, because the government is unwilling to sell farm surpluses in the domestic market when the market price is reasonably high, these surpluses, purchased with the taxpayers' money, must be held in storage—eventually to be sold abroad, often at ridiculously low prices, to be given away, or even to be destroyed. Certainly, the government has not attempted to follow the more reasonable policy of buying up farm surpluses in good crop years and reselling them in bad ones. Instead, it has held the floor price at a level higher than would be the case if surpluses were resold at home over a period of years. In other words, it has provided incomes to farmers which are not only stable but also higher. But this may well be in the national interest.

Income Stabilization Policy

At the present time in Canada, income stabilization is being achieved by both marketing boards and price-support programs. However, many people believe that the latter are preferable because they do not involve any attempt to control supply, fix prices, or otherwise interfere with the free market. In 1983, the Ministers of Agriculture for all provinces except Newfoundland set up a task force to develop a national price support program for farmers that would replace the present hodge-podge of schemes.

All Canadian farmers would be eligible to participate in such a scheme except those already protected by supply-management marketing boards. The scheme would be funded equally by the federal and provincial governments on the one hand and by participating farmers on the other. Although requiring a government subsidy, this could be much less than under equivalent programs in the U.S. and the European Economic Community. The price-support levels would be kept below the cost of production to ensure that market forces, not subsidies, control the supply and prices of agricultural products. Others suggest a higher support price based on a cost-of-production formula.

Agricultural Exports

A more controversial issue in the area of government support for agriculture is the federal government's decision to create a Crown corporation, Canagrex, to expand Canada's exports of agricultural products.

Summary

1. Over the years, the Canadian farmer's average income has usually

been both relatively small and highly unstable. Consequently, governments have introduced various programs of financial and other assistance which have in turn led to allegations of excessive government paternalism and an undue tax burden on the nation.

2. The two main reasons for the relative decline in average farm income are (a) the failure of demand for agricultural output to increase as fast as supply; and (b) the increase in the cost of agricultural inputs.

3. The two main causes of unstable farm income are changes in the weather (affecting supply) and changes in demand.

4. Until the 1930s, government assistance to farmers was confined mainly to land conservation and rehabilitation. Thereafter, it also included income assistance.

5. One government measure to keep up farm income has been price supports. This has taken three forms: buying up surplus output at the government-set floor price; subsidizing the price to the consumer; and persuading farmers, with cash incentives, to restrict output.

6. Government price-support programs, since they interfere with the normal working of market forces and the price mechanism, affect the allocation of a country's resources.

7. The cost to the government of the various price-support programs will depend to a large extent on the elasticities of demand and supply of the products involved.

8. Canada now has a Wheat Board, Dairy Commission, and other federal and provincial marketing boards to control the production and marketing of various farm products.

9. Provincial governments, through crop insurance programs, provide a vital service to farmers, not available from the private insurance companies.

10. Another important form of government assistance to agriculture is the provision of a variety of farm credit programs.

11. The provision of government-subsidized railway freight rates, under the Crow's Nest Pass Agreement and other later legislation, was to be reduced or eliminated in the 1980s.

12. Although controversial, government is expected to continue its income-stabilization efforts for farmers.

13. The federal government also intends, through a new Crown corporation, Canagrex, to try to increase Canadian exports of agricultural products.

Key Terms

Price support   342
Deficiency payment   344
Crop restriction   344
Initial price   348
Grain quota   349
Surplus   350

Marketing board   350
Dumping   353
Crop insurance   355
Farm credit   356
Transportation subsidy   358
Canagrex   361

Review Questions

1. Why is average farm income relatively small compared with that of other sectors of the economy?
2. Why has farm income been relatively unstable?
3. What new dimension did government assistance to Canadian farmers take in the 1930s? What was its significance?
4. What are the main types of government price-support programs? What is their purpose?
5. How do price-support programs affect the allocation of a country's resources?
6. How do the elasticities of demand and supply affect the cost to the government of price-support programs?
7. Explain the nature and purpose of the 1944 Agricultural Price Support Act. How did the 1958 Agricultural Stabilization Act change government assistance to farmers?
8. Explain the nature and purpose of the Canadian Wheat Board.
9. How is wheat now marketed in Canada?
10. How is milk marketed in Canada?
11. Why do farm surpluses occur? Why does their disposal seem to be such a problem?
12. Explain the nature, purpose, methods, and limitations of marketing boards in Canada.
13. Why is crop insurance an important form of government assistance to agriculture?
14. What was the purpose of the 1966 Agricultural and Rural Development Act (ARDA)? How was it financed? What agency now performs this work?
15. What are the ways in which government helps provide credit and loans to farmers?
16. What types of transportation subsidy does the Canadian government provide to farmers?

17. What were the recommendations of the Federal Task Force on Agriculture with regard to the future role of government in Canadian agriculture?
18. Why can't farmers manage on their own? Discuss.
19. What is the most efficient type of agricultural price-support program from society's point of view?
20. "Canada should be the breadbasket of the world." Discuss.
21. "Paying farmers not to produce is as sinful as throwing coffee into the sea." Discuss.
22. "Canada should follow the example of the oil-producing countries by forming an international wheat cartel and raising the price of wheat." Discuss.
23. "If marketing boards are permitted in agriculture, they should be permitted in other industries." Comment.
24. "There seem to be many prosperous farmers in Canada." Discuss.
25. "It is against Canada's national interest to let people build houses on good farmland, wherever it may be." Discuss.

19. BUSINESS ORGANIZATION

CHAPTER OBJECTIVES

A. To explain how persons organize their business activities from the ownership point of view
B. To describe the nature, advantages, and disadvantages of the sole proprietorship form of business ownership
C. To explain the partnership form of ownership, including the differences between a general partnership and a limited partnership
D. To analyze the corporate form of business ownership, including a discussion of common and preferred shares, and the nature and role of the multinational corporation
E. To describe the co-operative form of ownership
F. To examine the various forms of government enterprise

CHAPTER OUTLINE

The business firm is the unit of ownership that people use to pool their funds and/or abilities for business purposes. It usually has, as its principal long-term aim, the maximization of profit by producing and marketing the goods and services that society wants. It can be set up as a sole proprietorship, a partnership, a corporation, or a co-operative. Each form of business ownership has its own characteristics, as summarized in Table 19:1. Also, in the last thirty years, there has been a tremendous expansion in the number of multinational corporations, mainly U.S.owned, in Canada. There is also in Canada a great number of business enterprises owned and operated by the federal, provincial, and municipal governments.

Table 19:1

Characteristics of the Various Types of Business Ownership (A = good; B = fair; C = poor)

	Sole Proprietorship	General Partnership	Limited Partnership	Business Corporation (Private)	Business Corporation (Public)
Ease and cost of establishment	A	B	B	C	C
High personal motivation	A	A	A	A	A,B
Quickness and freedom of action	A	B	B	A,B	A,B
Privacy	A	B	B	B	B,C
Possible management disputes	A	B	B	A,B	B
Ease of dissolution	A	B	B	C	C
Availability of capital	C	B	B	B	A
Professional management	C	C	C	B,C	A,B
Easy transferability of ownership	A	C	C	B	A
Continuity of existence	C	B	B	A	A
Personal liability for business debts	C	C	A,C	A	A
Relatively frozen investment	B	B	B	B	A
Legal restrictions	A	B	B	C	C
Income tax	B,C	B,C	B,C	A,B	A,B

19.1: SOLE PROPRIETORSHIP

A sole proprietorship is a business owned by one person. Although the owner may employ other people, the owner alone is responsible for its debts.

Advantages

The most important advantages of this form of business organization are: ease of establishment, high personal motivation, quickness and freedom of action, privacy, and ease of termination.

The legal requirements for starting a small business are minimal. Only certain types of business require a municipal licence or a provincial vendor's permit. And only if the owner wishes to use a name for the business other than his or her own, does the name and other particulars of the business need to be registered with the provincial government.

The proprietor is highly motivated because he or she receives all the profits, has pride of ownership, and meets a personal challenge. Being the boss, the owner is free to make business decisions without the approval of someone else. The owner is able to maintain privacy about the financial affairs of the business and is in a good position to keep secret any special processes, formulas, recipes, or business contacts. Also, the owner can legally terminate the business merely by closing its doors.

Disadvantages

The sole proprietorship form of ownership also has some disadvantages. These include: unlimited personal liability, limited talent, limited capital, lack of continuity, and possibly heavier income taxation than if the business were incorporated.

Unlimited personal liability means that a sole proprietor's personal assets can be seized, if necessary, to pay outstanding business debts. Thus, a person's life savings could be wiped out by a business failure. The sole proprietor usually has no one else on whom to rely to run the business. Good assistants are difficult to find and expensive to retain. The owner will also find it more difficult to borrow money than if there were business partners to whom the lender could also turn. If the sole proprietor becomes ill or dies, the business can easily come to a halt. Depending upon his or her level of business and other personal income, the sole proprietor may pay more income tax than under the corporate form of business organization This is because the personal income tax is at a progressive rather than a flat rate.

19.2: THE PARTNERSHIP

A partnership is a business firm that has two or more owners who pool their talents and/or their funds, but which is not incorporated. It can be either a general or a limited partnership.

In a *general partnership*, all the partners, called general partners, may take part in the management of the business and all have unlimited personal liability for business losses. In a *limited partnership*, there are both limited partners and at least one general partner. The limited partner is liable for business debts only up to the amount of his or her investment. However, in return, that partner (or partners) must not take part in the management of the business. Otherwise, he or she may be considered by the courts to have been a general partner. Usually a written partnership agreement is drawn up to govern the conduct of the partners. An example of such an agreement is shown below. There is no set form prescribed by law.

PARTNERSHIP AGREEMENT

AGREEMENT made this 15th day of December 19--

BETWEEN Lorne Park, of 7 Curlew Drive, Mississauga, Ontario and T.L. Kennedy, of 3572 Ashbury Road, Burlington, Ontario.

IN CONSIDERATION of the sum of One Dollar paid by each party to the other (the receipt whereof is hereby acknowledged) the parties do hereby mutually covenant and agree as follows:

1. That the said parties will, as partners, engage in and conduct the business of a hardware store.
2. That the name of the firm shall be Mississauga Hardware.
3. That the term of the partnership shall commence on the 1st day of January, 19--, and shall continue until one month after one partner has notified the other partner in writing of his intention to withdraw from the partnership.
4. That the place of business shall be Sherwood Mall, Mississauga, Ontario.
5. (a) That the capital of the firm shall be $50000, to be contributed in equal cash amounts of $25000 each on the signing of the Agreement.
   (b) That neither party's contribution to the partnership shall bear him interest.
6. That the partnership capital and all other partnership monies shall be deposited in the Sherwood Mall branch of the Bank of Nova Scotia, from which all withdrawals shall be made only by cheques

signed jointly by both partners.

7. (a) That books of accounts be kept in accordance with standard accounting procedures.

(b) That these books be kept on the premises and open to the inspection of either partner.

8. That each partner shall be entitled to draw 500 dollars per week from the funds of the partnership on account of his profits.

9. (a) That at the end of June of every year, an inventory shall be taken and the assets, liabilities, and gross and net income of the business ascertained.

10. That neither partner shall, without the written consent of the other, draw, accept, sign, or endorse any bill of exchange, promissory note, or cheque, or contract any debt on account of, or in the name of the partnership, except in the normal course of business and up to the amount of $500.

11. That each partner shall devote his whole time and attention to the partnership business, and shall not, during the term of the partnership, engage in any other business.

12. That should one of the partners die, his executors shall be entitled to receive the value of his share of the partnership property at the time of his death, together with 1 per cent interest a month in lieu of profit from that day on until final settlement of the property.

13. That on termination or dissolution of the partnership, other than by the death of a partner, an audit shall immediately be made of the firm's assets and liabilities and the balance be divided equally between the partners.

14. (a) That in the event of a disagreement between the partners as to the conduct of the business, as to its dissolution, or as to any other matter concerning the business, the same shall be referred to arbitration within 10 days of written notice being served by one partner on the other.

(b) That each partner shall appoint one arbitrator, who shall in turn appoint a third arbitrator.

(c) That the matter referred to arbitration shall be decided by simple majority of the arbitrators.

IN WITNESS WHEREOF, the parties hereto set their hands and seals, the day and year first above written.

Witnesses: *David Bell*　　　　　　*Lorne Park*

David Bell　　　　　　　　　　　Lorne Park

Pauline Gloucester　　　*T.L. Kennedy*

Pauline Gloucester　　　　　　T.L. Kennedy

Advantages

The most important advantages of the partnership form of business organization are: more capital, more talent, high personal motivation, and relatively few legal restrictions.

1. More capital. A partnership pools the funds of a number of people, whereas a sole proprietorship has only the one owner's money. Also, an individual with a good business idea, talent, or experience but no money can often establish a business only by joining with someone else who does have capital to invest. It is also normally easier for a partnership to obtain credit from suppliers or borrow money from a bank than it is for a sole proprietor. This is because the creditor or lender can have the security of the business and personal assets of several persons for repayment rather than those of just one person.

2. More talent. Not everyone feels competent to run a business on his or her own. Two or more partners, by combining their energies and talents, can often make a success of a business whereas one person alone might fail. This is particularly true when a business demands a variety of talents such as technical knowledge, financial skill, and sales ability. The partnership also offers the means of retaining valuable employees by making them partners in the business.

3. High personal motivation. As with the sole proprietorship, the owners of a partnership business know that all the profits (less the government's share) will go to them. Consequently, they have every motivation to make it successful. This is in addition to the pride of ownership and personal satisfaction that comes from being self-employed.

4. Few legal restrictions. To set up a partnership, legal fees may be incurred in preparing a written partnership agreement, if the partners do not wish to rely on their own wisdom alone. Also, the partnership must be registered. Once this is done, however, the only legal requirements are a municipal business permit, if necessary, and observance of tax, labour, fire, and other regulations.

Disadvantages

The main disadvantages of the partnership type of business ownership are: possibly higher income tax; unlimited personal liability; possible management disputes; limited capital (compared with a public business corporation); relatively frozen investment; and possible lack of continuity.

1. Possibly higher income tax. Like a sole proprietor, a partner must pay personal income tax on any business income. Because the personal income tax is graduated, the rate of tax constantly increases. However, if the business is set up as a corporation, any income earned by the business would be subject to a flat (not graduated) rate of income tax, with a special deduction if the business is small (i.e. has a maximum annual income of $200000) and Canadian-controlled. Thus a Canadian-controlled private corporation (or CCPC) enjoys, in Ontario, a special 24% corporate income tax rate on active income (as distinct from investment income). Once a small business starts to prosper, the tax advantages of incorporation can be substantial. However, this special tax rate does not apply to a firm that provides medical, legal, or other personal services.

2. Unlimited personal liability. In both a general and a limited partnership, the general partner can be forced to sell his or her personal assets to pay any outstanding business debts. This liability is both joint and several. This means, first, that all the partners are together liable for the debts of the partnership; second, that one partner may be required to pay *all* the debts of the business if the other partners fail to pay their shares. If a person is unwilling to assume this risk, he or she can become a limited partner, with liability only up to the amount of his or her investment.

3. Possible management disputes. Because more than one person manages the business, occasional disputes will inevitably arise. If the disputes are serious, they may cause the partnership to terminate. Unfortunately, it is not easy to foresee whether the personalities of the partners will clash. This can be a real disadvantage to a partnership, particularly if one of the partners has formerly operated alone and is not accustomed to collective decision-making.

4. Limited capital. A partnership has more capital at its disposal than a sole proprietorship, but less than a business corporation, particularly a public one. Most large enterprises today require greater sums than can be obtained from a few investors alone. Unlike a public business corporation, the general partnership cannot solicit funds from the general public by selling shares or bonds. Additional long-term funds can, however, be arranged by mortgaging fixed assets. The need for long-term funds can be substantially reduced by leasing buildings, equipment, and vehicles, rather than buying them. A corporation can raise long-term funds by selling shares of capital stock to the limit authorized in its charter. It can also borrow long-term funds by issuing a bond. The partnership, with its unlimited personal liability for general partners and difficult transfer of ownership (as explained next), cannot usually attract large amounts of capital.

5. Relatively frozen investment. It is not easy for a partner to sell his or her share of the partnership to obtain cash to meet some sudden need. The partner must first obtain the approval of the other partners for the transfer of ownership to a new partner. If approval is not forthcoming, the other partners must usually buy out the retiring partner's share, depending on the partnership agreement. However, this process is slow.

6. Lack of continuity. A partnership legally terminates if one of the partners dies, becomes insolvent, incapacitated, or insane; commits a breach of the partnership agreement; acts against the best interests of the business—for example, by being constantly absent; or, if the partnership is for an indefinite period, gives notice of his or her intention to dissolve the partnership. The need for terminating the business is usually overcome in practice by the inclusion in the partnership agreement of a clause providing for the purchase of that partner's share of the business should any of these events take place. The money to purchase a partner's share is often provided for by a term-insurance policy on the life of each partner with the partnership as the beneficiary. However, a partnership certainly does not have the continuity of a business corporation which continues to exist whatever the fate of its owners.

19.3: THE BUSINESS CORPORATION

A business corporation (or limited company as it used to be called) is a business firm that is a legal person in its own right. As such, the corporation has its own name, its own address, its own capital, and its own life. Because of its separate legal existence, any debts incurred by it can be repaid only out of its assets. There is no recourse to its shareholders. This is completely different from the sole proprietorship and general partnership, in which the owners are legally responsible for all the obligations of the business and must therefore, satisfy any outstanding claims by creditors of the business from their own personal funds.

Private or Public

Business corporations can be either private or public. In a private business corporation, the transfer of shares of ownership requires the approval of the corporation's board of directors; and the shares or bonds must be sold privately. A public business corporation, conversely, is a one that can transfer its shares of ownership freely. This means that it can sell its stocks and bonds to the general public, using advertisng where necessary to do so, so long as it has the approval of the provincial securities commission. The term public corporation is also sometimes used in practice to mean a government-owned or Crown corporation.

Federal or Provincial Incorporation

A business corporation may be established on the authorization of either the federal or the provincial government. Federal incorporation is considered most appropriate when a firm expects to do business in a number of provinces. This is cheaper and more effective than incorporating in each of the various provinces in which business is to be undertaken. Also, it provides the firm with protection against discriminatory provincial legislation. Provincial incorporation is quite adequate, as well as being cheaper, if business is to be transacted in one province alone. All laws of general application such as income, sales, and property taxes, business licences, and compulsory annual statistical returns apply equally to both types of business corporation.

To establish a corporation in Ontario, for instance, there need be only one applicant who must be eighteen or more years of age. Also, the name of the proposed corporation must not be the same or similar to the name of a known corporation, association, partnership, individual, or business, if its use would be likely to deceive, unless consent has been given by the party concerned. The corporation must include the word "Limited," "Incorporated," or "Corporation," or the abbreviation "Ltd.," "Inc.," or "Corp." as the last word of its name.

Capital Stock

The ownership of a corporation is represented by its *capital stock*. This consists of common shares and, in many cases, preferred (or preference) shares. The holders of these shares are known as *shareholders* or *stockholders*. Authorization to issue shares is obtained from the government concerned in the articles of incorporation (or, depending upon the province, the charter or memorandum of association) that establishes the corporation. The shares are issued as and when funds are required. Most corporations now issue their common shares at no-par value. The term *par value* means that a corporation has placed a definite monetary value on the share, usually stated on the *stock certificate* (the written evidence of ownership) at the time of issuance. *No-par value*, or *without par value*, means that no price is stated. Preferred shares have a par value since it is usually the basis on which their fixed dividend is calculated. The actual price or value of any share at any particular moment is what it will fetch in the market. This is known as the market price or *market value* of the share.

	Trans Code	Line No	Stat	Comp Type	Method Incorp
	A 18	**0** 20	**0** 28	**A** 29	**3** 30

	Share	Notice Req'd	Jurisdiction
	S 31	**N** 32	**ONTARIO** 33 47

ARTICLES OF INCORPORATION
STATUTS CONSTITUTIFS

Form 1
Business Corporations Act 1982

Formule numéro 1
Loi de 1982 sur les compagnies

1. The name of the corporation is: Dénomination sociale de la compagnie:

A	B	C		T	O	Y	S		I	N	C	O	R	P	O	R	A	T	E	D									

2. The address of the registered office is: Adresse du siège social:

1284 Ontario Street

(Street & Number or R.R. Number & if Multi-Office Building give Room No.)
(Rue et numéro ou numéro de la R.R. et, s'il s'agit d'un édifice à bureaux, numéro du bureau)

Toronto, Ontario   M 5 H 3 H 1

(Name of Municipality or Post Office)   (Postal Code)
(Nom de la municipalité ou du bureau de poste)   (Code postal)

City of Toronto   in the   Municipality of Metropolitan

(Name of Municipality, Geographical Township)   dans le/la   (County, District, Regional Municipality) Toronto
(Nom de la municipalité, du canton)   (Comté, district, municipalité régionale)

3. Number (or minimum and maximum number) of   Nombre (ou nombres minimal et maximal)
   directors is: One (1)   d'administrateurs: Five (5)

4. The first director(s) is/are   Premier(s) administrateur(s):

First name, initials and surname Prénom, initiales et nom de famille	Residence address, giving street & No. or R.R. No. or municipality and postal code. Adresse personnelle, y compris la rue et le numéro, le numéro de la R.R. ou, le nom de la municipalité et le code postal	Resident Canadian State Yes or No Résident Canadien Oui/Non
Mr. John Smith	456 Anywhere Street Toronto, Ontario M5H 3L1	Yes

The *book value* of a share is the value, as shown in the company books or accounts, at which it was originally issued. The *asset value* is each share's portion of the corporation's assets. It is calculated by dividing the *net worth* of the corporation (total assets minus total liabilities) by the number of shares that have been issued.

Common Shares

Each common share of a corporation's capital stock entitles the owner to certain benefits: to vote at shareholders' meetings; to share in the profits of the corporation; and to share in the assets of the corporation should it be liquidated.

1. Voting rights. Normally, each common share entitles the owner to one vote at the shareholders' meetings. In some companies, two classes of common stock, A and B, are issued, with the class A shares carrying the voting rights. Any person or group owning a majority of the voting common shares, or even sometimes just a substantial percentage, can appoint the board of directors and thereby control the management of the corporation. In raising additional long-term capital by selling more common shares, the directors must therefore always take into account how these new shares may affect voting control.

The term *holding company* is used to describe a firm that exercises control over a number of subsidiary companies by means of ownership of all, a majority, or, in some cases, just a substantial proportion of the voting shares of these companies. The holding company and its subsidiaries are known as a *conglomerate* or *group*.

2. Share of profits. The common shareholders of a corporation have the right to any profits that remain after preferred shareholders have received their fixed rate of dividend. This right does not mean, however, that the profits have to be paid out to them. *Dividends* are in fact that part of a corporation's profits which the board of directors decides to pay to the shareholders. One of the duties of a corporation's board of directors is to decide how much of the profits is to be distributed to shareholders in the form of dividends and how much is to be kept in the business as retained earnings. If the dividend policy is unsatisfactory, the shareholders can change it only by replacing or influencing the board of directors.

One of the most important reasons why directors retain earnings in the business is to provide additional long-term equity capital. From the shareholder's point of view, a conservative dividend policy is not entirely unfavourable. In the first place, the corporation will be in a stronger financial position, and this should be reflected in increased earnings. Secondly, the extra assets usually cause the market price of the shares to rise in anticipation of an increase in dividends. This increase can result, when the shares are sold, in a capital gain for the seller.

In many instances, business corporations which have built up a substantial amount of retained earnings (or *earned surplus*) will declare a *stock dividend*. This is a distribution of additional shares to existing shareholders. Since the net worth of the company is now divided among a larger number of shares, the asset value of each share is reduced. The shareholder will benefit if the decline in market value of his or her shares is not as great as the reduction in asset value. The shareholder may also benefit by having lower-priced, and possibly more marketable shares. The corporation itself has benefited by distributing stock rather than cash, which it can retain for company use.

Another device, somewhat similar to a stock dividend, is a *stock split*. In this case, a company does not issue new stock backed by retained earnings; it merely splits existing shares into several new ones. Of course, each new share has a smaller amount of company assets behind it. For example, a four-for-one-split reduces the assets behind each share to a quarter of the amount behind each old share. A stock split is often made when the market price of the present shares is too high to make them easily marketable—for example, $500 each. Often, when the stock is split, the market price of each new share may be more than the exact proportionate amount of each old share. This is because the new lower-priced shares are more attractive to investors.

When additional capital stock is to be issued, a corporation may give its existing shareholders the opportunity to buy new stock at less than the current market price, before offering the stock for sale to the general public. These privileges, which lapse within a short period of time, are called *rights*, and are usually in proportion to the amount of stock that each shareholder now owns. The number of rights granted to a shareholder are stated on a certificate called a *warrant*. These rights can be traded in the securities market. The term *warrant* is also used to describe a certificate which gives its holder an option to buy a certain number of shares of a company over many months or even years at successively higher prices. Such a warrant is sometimes attached to bonds and preferred shares as a promotional feature. Like a right, a warrant may be traded.

3. Share of assets. Usually the least important benefit to a shareholder is the right to share in the assets of the corporation on its liquidation. Normally a corporation is terminated because it is unprofitable; as a result, little money is usually left for shareholders from the sale of the company's assets, once the various tax collectors, bondholders, and other creditors have been paid—especially when a corporation is forced into bankruptcy by its creditors.

Preferred Shares

The capital stock of a corporation may consist of preferred or preference shares as well as common shares. Where this is the case, the preferred shares, as the name implies, enjoy a favoured or "preferred" position with regard to profits and assets.

1. Voting rights. The right to vote is normally withheld from the holders of preferred shares in exchange for the preferences given. However, the right to vote at the shareholders' meetings may become effective if preferred dividends have not been paid for a certain number of months or years. In this way, the preferred shareholders are given the opportunity to influence management, usually by having a representative on the board of directors.

2. Share of profits. Preferred shareholders are entitled to receive from the profits of the corporation a fixed dividend on their shares before anything is distributed to the common shareholders. This fixed annual rate of dividend is set as a percentage of the par value of the share or as a specific amount per share.

The right to a preference in receiving profits applies, it should be noted, only to distributed profits. A company is not contractually obliged to pay a preferred dividend each year: the profits may be retained as additional long-term capital. However, preferred shares are normally cumulative, unless otherwise specifically stated. Therefore, any dividend withheld in one year must be paid in subsequent years, before any dividend can be paid on the common shares. Where a preferred share does not have this right, it is described as *non-cumulative*.

In paying dividends, some corporations give a preference to one preferred share over another. Where this is done, the different types of preferred shares are ranked Preferred A, Preferred B, and so on.

3. Share of assets. Should the assets of a corporation be sold—for example, on voluntary liquidation—preferred shareholders rank before common shareholders in their claim to a share of the proceeds. They are, however, only entitled to receive the sum stated on the preferred share certificate. The common shareholders are entitled to receive all the remainder.

4. Other features: redeemability, convertibility, participation. Preferred shares, in addition to their other characteristics, may also be *redeemable*, or *callable*. By making the preferred shares redeemable, management gives itself the option of repaying this type of equity capital at a pre-set price whenever it finds it advisable—for example, to replace an issue carrying a higher dividend rate with one carrying a lower rate. The holder of the redeemable preferred share must, however, be given due notice and be paid a prescribed premium.

Another feature sometimes added to a preferred share is that of *convertibility*. A convertible preferred share is one that is convertible at the option of the owner into common stock at a fixed price or at a set ratio—for example, one preferred share for every two common shares. This option is given for a fixed number of years, or for as long as the shares are outstanding. The purpose of making preferred shares convertible into common shares is to add a speculative element to them. A preferred share may also be *participating*. This means that once the preferred shares have received their fixed dividend, and once the common shares have received a stated amount—for example, $1.00 per share in any one year—the preferred shares are entitled to receive a predetermined part of the remaining profits.

Advantages of the Corporate Form of Ownership

The main advantages that the corporate type of business ownership can offer are: limited liability for the owners; possibly lower income tax; continuity of existence of the firm; relatively easy transferability of ownership; professional management for the owner's investment; and more capital.

1. Limited personal liability. Unlike the sole proprietor and the general partner who stand to lose part or all of their personal assets if their business fails, the shareholder of a corporation can only lose the investment that he or she has made in purchasing the shares.

2. Possibly lower income tax. Canadian-controlled private corporations or CCPCs, need pay a rate of only 25 per cent (in provinces with a 10 per cent provincial tax rate) on the first $200000 of active annual business income. In Ontario, the rate is 24 per cent. This compares with the graduated personal income-tax rates that a sole proprietor or partner must pay, rising to as much as 50 per cent on taxable income over $56000. Once a corporation has earned $1000000 of business income, it is no longer eligible for the reduced rate. The general rate of corporation income tax is 46 per cent. However, profits from manufacturing and processing are taxed at a flat rate of 40 per cent.

3. Continuity of existence. Because the corporation is itself a legal person, separate and distinct from its shareholders, its life is unaffected by the death or other personal misfortunes that may befall any of its owners. The corporation's existence can be brought to an end only by the vote of its shareholders to dissolve it.

4. Transferability of ownership. It is very easy to transfer shares of ownership of a public business corporation from one party to another. All that is required is to find a buyer and record that buyer's name in the stock register. And stock exchanges, stock brokers, and trust companies exist to facilitate this task. With the private business corporation, however, the transfer of shares must first be approved by the board of directors.

5. Professional management. In many private business corporations, the major shareholders are usually actively engaged in the management of the business. Therefore there is no gap between owners and managers. However, the structure of the business corporation, in which a board of directors is empowered to set basic business policies and appoint a president to carry them out, permits people to invest their money in a business without themselves becoming involved in its management. This feature is taken full advantage of in the public business corporation whereby many large businesses are now operated with predominantly professional, hired management.

6. More capital. An extremely important advantage of the corporate form of ownership is its suitability for raising large amounts of capital. This is particularly true of the public business corporation which can have an unlimited number of shareholders and can advertise the sale of its stocks and bonds to the public. An investor's liability is limited to the amount invested whatever happens to the corporation; the firm (and the investment) will continue whatever happens to the investor; the investor can easily sell his or her shares of ownership for cash should the need arise; and the investor does not need to spend time in the management of the business.

A private business corporation is, however, relatively handicapped in its ability to raise long-term funds. First, it may not advertise the sale of its shares of capital stock to the general public, or otherwise solicit funds from them. Second, the ownership of the shares is not easily transferred once they have been initially sold—for the approval of the board of directors must be obtained and existing shareholders must usually be given the first right to purchase the shares. Private business corporations, often family-owned businesses, consequently tend to rely heavily on reinvested profits for their capital expansion.

Disadvantages

Compared with the sole proprietorship and partnership, the corporate form of business ownership has the following main disadvantages: the initial cost; more government regulation; less privacy; and possibly less personal incentive.

1. Initial cost. To set up a corporation, it is necessary to pay a fee to the government. This fee will vary in size according to the amount of capital stock authorized. Usually, also, it is prudent to pay for a lawyer's services in handling the incorporation. To set up a provincially incorporated private business corporation, the total initial cost, including legal fees, the corporate seal, and shareholders' registers, can easily range from $500 to $1000.

2. Government regulation. A number of government regulations are directed specifically at business corporations. Corporations must, for example, maintain a set of books specifying shareholders, directors, capital, and so on; keep certain books of accounts; have annual shareholders' meetings; and file annual tax returns with the federal and provincial governments. Corporations must also limit their transactions to those specified in their charter, articles of incorporation, or memorandum of association (depending on the province) or permitted generally by the Act under which they were incorporated. These powers can be amended only by the issue by the government of supplementary articles, or other similar document of authorization.

3. Less privacy. The Business Corporations Act requires that a business corporation furnish its shareholders with an annual income statement and balance sheet. Many firms believe that this information helps their competitors and consider it highly detrimental to have to reveal anything at all. A private business corporation offers greater privacy because its financial statements do not have to be published. The subsidiaries of many foreign firms in Canada are in fact set up as private business corporations to help safeguard their privacy. The same applies to many Canadian firms.

4. Possibly less personal incentive. In most private corporations, particularly the small ones, the managers of the business are also the major shareholders. Their personal desire to perform well is, like that of the sole proprietor or partner, highly motivated by the fact that all the profits earned will be theirs.

In the public business corporation, which is often quite large, the president and the department managers, or vice-presidents, are usually paid employees. Although they may have great personal ambition and dedication to the business, their personal incentive and loyalty are rarely as strong as that of an owner. This is partly overcome in some firms by stock options, profit-sharing plans and annual performance bonuses.

19.4: THE MULTINATIONAL CORPORATION

Many firms sell part of their output abroad, license foreign companies to use their manufacturing processes, or even establish their own overseas manufacturing plants. Many firms also import goods from abroad. Because of their involvement with foreign countries, these firms are sometimes called international. However, in many international firms, manufacturing involvement abroad has become so great that head office management now makes marketing, production, financial, and investment decisions on a global rather than domestic or national basis. Where this is the case, the term *multinational corporation* (*multinational enterprise* or *transnational enterprise*) is used.

Existence in Canada

Multinational companies have existed for many years: the Hudson's Bay Company in Canada was one of the first. Nevertheless, only since World War II and more specifically since the 1950s, has the number and size of these enterprises increased tremendously. Because of American managerial ability, technological know-how, and financial resources, most of these multinational firms are U.S.owned. Because Canada is geographically so close, has abundant resources, has well-developed markets in certain areas, and is politically stable, much U.S. investment has been directed towards this country. Furthermore, an increasingly large proportion of this investment has been direct rather than portfolio. In other words, it has involved mainly the purchase of shares of ownership rather than the straight lending of money. As a result, more and more business firms in this country have become subsidiaries of U.S. multinational corporations. That is why Canada is sometimes said to have a "branch-plant economy." Since 1974, however, the Foreign Investment Review Agency, or FIRA, screens all foreign investment to help ensure that it will provide significant benefit for Canada, particularly in term of employment and income.Canada also has, it should be noted, quite a large number of multinational corporations of its own, with subsidiaries in other countries.

Reasons for Growth

The main reason that a domestic or national corporation becomes multinational is financial: it hopes to increase or maintain sales revenue, reduce or hold down costs, and thereby improve its profitability and financial solvency. Revenue is often threatened when a country imposes tariffs, quotas and other barriers on imports. By establishing manufacturing facilities within the country, a firm can retain its hold on the foreign market, even though its exports are restricted. Also, more positively, the establishment of overseas manufacturing facilities offers new sales prospects, even to firms which have not previously exported to that country. Furthermore, a foreign subsidiary, as well as producing and selling profitably in the local or regional market, may well buy parts and equipment from plants located in the home country that are also owned by the multinational corporation. On the cost side, lower local costs for raw materials and labour are a great attraction to overseas manufacturing. This is so even after allowance for differences in labour productivity. Often special tax concessions and development grants are also available from foreign governments. Thus a Canadian or U.S. multinational may produce parts or finished products in its plants abroad for shipment and sale in the home country—hence the accusation by Canadian or U.S. workers and their unions that such companies are "exporting jobs".

As regards financial solvency, control over foreign sources of raw materials helps ensure that production in the home country will not be held up. The financial stability of an enterprise is also enhanced by having plants in a number of countries. Political upheavals and wars usually affect some countries but not others. By geographical diversification, a business firm is hedging its bets.

Internal Organization

The internal organization of the multinational corporation is quite diverse. Usually, key decisions such as new capital investment and new labour contracts are made at head office in the home country, usually the United States. Other powers are delegated to regional and country offices. The usual organization is a blend of functions (marketing, production, finance) and geographical areas. Research and new product development, an extremely important activity in the typical multinational corporation, is usually controlled and integrated by head office even though parcelled out among research laboratories in various countries.

19.5: THE CO-OPERATIVE

Another type of business organization is the co-operative.

Characteristics

One main characteristic is that each member, whatever his or her investment, is entitled to only one vote at members' meetings. This is the opposite of the business corporation where a shareholder has as many votes as common shares. Also, no voting by proxy is permitted in a co-operative—a person must be present at the annual meeting in order to cast a vote. Second, a fixed rate of interest is paid on capital invested by the members. And, third, profits not retained in the business are paid out to members in the form of patronage returns which vary with the amount of business transacted. If, for example, a member has bought one per cent of the goods sold, that member receives one per cent of the profit paid out.

Incorporation

Co-operatives are permitted to incorporate under the Corporations Act of their province, and many have in fact done so. By incorporating, the co-operative retains its essential co-operative features of democratic control (one member, one vote), fixed interest on capital, and patronage returns, yet also enjoys the benefits of limited personal liability for its members and continuity of existence for itself.

Origin

Co-operatives are believed to have originated in England in the first half of the nineteenth century. Specifically, a retail co-operative was established in Rochdale, Lancashire, in 1844. In Canada, the co-operative movement has been most popular in the Western provinces.

Types

The principal types of co-operative business in Canada are: consumer (or retail) co-operatives which specialize in retailing goods; marketing co-operatives which engage in the marketing of members' fruit, milk, and other farm products, and in the purchasing of seed and fertilizer for them; financial co-operatives (also called credit unions or *caisses populaires*) which borrow from some members and lend to others; insurance co-operatives which supply members with fire, life, hail, and public-liability insurance; and service co-operatives which supply members with such services as housing, rural electrification, medical insurance, transportation, recreational facilities, rental of machinery, and even funerals.

Purpose

The main purpose of the co-operative enterprise, whatever its specialization, is to provide members with goods or services at a lower price than that normally charged. This lower price may be offered immediately when the goods or services are bought, later in the form of a patronage return, or in both ways combined. Marketing co-operatives enable growers to establish common processing, grading, packaging, and advertising facilities, and to use a common brand name for their products.

Advantages

From a member's point of view, the co-operative has several advantages: first, the member can buy goods and services more cheaply or sell goods more profitably; second, the member can always have a say in its management because of the "one member, one-vote" stipulation; and, third, the member can enjoy limited personal liability and know that the business has continuity of existence, so long as the co-operative is incorporated.

Disadvantages

The disadvantages of the co-operative include: first, its limited ability to raise capital; and, second, the possibility that the democratic control may prevent good management.

19.6: GOVERNMENT ENTERPRISES

Governments own and operate many businesses in Canada and, even though there is not the same degree of public ownership as in many countries of Western Europe, the number is steadily increasing. Nevertheless, Canada still remains vastly different from the communist countries where ownership and operation of industry is almost entirely in the hands of the state.

Federal

At the federal level, certain government-owned businesses are run by regular government departments. However, most federally-owned businesses are operated by *Crown corporations*, which are recognized in the eyes of the law as independent legal persons. Unlike ordinary business corporations, all or most of the shares of capital stock are owned by the federal government rather than by private individuals. Also, they are ultimately accountable to Parliament, through a minister, for the conduct of their affairs.

Most government-owned businesses are run by a special type of Crown corporation, known as a *proprietary corporation*. Such Crown corporations are engaged in lending and other financial operations, as well as in the production and marketing of goods and services to the public. They include Air Canada, The Canada Post Corporation, the Canada Development Corporation, the Canadian Broadcasting Corporation, the Canada Mortgage and Housing Corporation, the Canadian National Railways, and Polysar Corporation Limited. Unlike other Crown corporations, they do not usually require parliamentary appropriation of funds to finance their operations.

Another type of Crown corporation is the *agency corporation*. Such a corporation manages trading or service operations of a quasi-commercial nature and the procurement, construction, and disposal activities of the federal government. Examples of this type of crown corporation include Atomic energy of Canada Limited, Canadian Patents and Development Limited, Crown Assets Disposal Corporation, and the National Harbours Board.

A third type of crown corporation, though less of a business, is the *departmental corporation*. These are responsible for government administrative, supervisory, and regulatory services. Such corporations include the Agricultural Stabilization Board, the Economic Council of Canada, the National Research Council, and the Canada Employment and Immigration Commission.

Provincial

At the provincial and municipal level, government-owned and operated public utilities supply electricity and water; provincial boards retail liquor; development corporations provide grants and loans; and housing corporations provide shelter. Also, a number of provincial governments have become partners in manufacturing operations usually to attract industry to slow-growth areas. All these various enterprises are operated by corporations with all or part of the shares of ownership held by the provincial or municipal governments. Sometimes the enterprise is called a "Board" or "Commission," according to whether a Board of Directors or a Commission (of Commissioners) is entrusted with its management. Thus, there are liquor boards and hydroelectric commissions.

Summary

1. The business firm, organized as a sole proprietorship, partnership, corporation, or co-operative, is the unit of ownership that people use to pool their funds and/or abilities for business purposes.

2. A *sole proprietorship* is a business owned by one person who alone is responsible for its debts. The most important advantages of this form of business organization are: ease of establishment, high personal motivation, quickness and freedom of action, privacy, and ease of termination. The disadvantages include unlimited personal liability, limited talent, limited capital, lack of continuity, and possibly heavier income taxation. Unlimited personal liability means that a sole proprietor's personal assets can be seized, if necessary, to pay outstanding business debts.

3. A *partnership* is a business firm that has two or more owners who pool their talents and/or their funds, but which is not incorporated. In a *general partnership*, all the partners, called *general partners*, take part in the management of the business and all have unlimited personal liability for outstanding business debts. In a *limited partnership*, there are both limited partners and at least one general partner. The limited partner is liable for business debts only up to the amount of his or her investment. However, in return, the partner must not take part in the management of the business. The most important advantages of the partnership form of business organization are: more capital, more talent, high personal motivation, and relatively few legal restrictions. The main disadvantages are: possibly higher income tax, unlimited personal liability, possible management disputes, limited capital (compared with a public business corporation), relatively frozen investment, and possible lack of continuity.

4. A *corporation*, or *limited company*, is a business firm which is a legal person in its own right. A *private business corporation* is one which has restrictions placed on its right to sell shares of its capital stock. A *public business corporation* has no such restrictions and can advertise the sale of its shares and bonds to the general public, if approved by the provincial securities commission. A business corporation may be established under the authority of either the federal or the provincial government.

5. The ownership of a corporation is represented by its *capital stock*, comprising common shares and, in many cases, preferred, or preference, shares. Most common shares are issued with *no-par value*. Each common share entitles the owner to vote at shareholders'

meetings on a one-vote-per-share basis, to share in the profits of the corporation, and to share in the assets of the corporation should it be liquidated. The board of directors of the corporation, as one of its basic policy decisions, decides on the dividends to be paid to the common shareholders. Sometimes a *stock dividend* will be declared, or a *stock split* made. A corporation may also make a rights issue to its shareholders. Preferred shares do not usually confer voting rights on their owners. They do, however, confer a right to a fixed dividend, based on the par value of the stock, before any dividends are paid to common shareholders. Preferred shares may be cumulative or non-cumulative. They may also be redeemable, convertible, or participating.

6. The *advantages* of the corporate form of business ownership, from the owners' point of view, are: limited personal liability for the shareholders, possibly lower income tax, continuity of existence, easier transfer of ownership, professional management, and more capital. *Disadvantages* include the high initial cost, government regulation, less privacy, and possibly less personal incentive.

7. In recent years, there has been a tremendous expansion in the number and size of *multinational corporations*. These are international firms that have manufacturing operations in various countries and make marketing, production, financial, investment, and other major business decisions on a global rather than purely domestic basis. For various reasons, more and more business firms in Canada have become subsidiaries of U.S. multinational corporations. Hence the label sometimes applied to Canada of a "branch-plant economy." However, Canada's Foreign Investment Review Agency, or FIRA, now tries to ensure that foreign investment provides "significant benefit" for Canada. Canada also has multinationals of its own.

8. A *co-operative* is a business firm in which each owner or member has only one vote and in which profits are distributed according to the amount of business the member has transacted with the co-operative. Co-operatives are permitted to incorporate under the Corporations Act of their province. In Canada, there are consumer co-operatives, marketing co-operatives, insurance co-operatives, and service co-operatives. The main purpose of the co-operative enterprise is to provide members with goods or services at a lower cost than would otherwise be possible.

9. There are many government-owned and operated businesses in Canada. The federally-owned ones are usually run by Crown corporations. At the provincial and municipal level, boards and com-

missions supply, for example, electricity, public transit, and liquor.

Key Terms

Sole proprietorship 366
Unlimited personal liability 367
Partnership 368
General partnership 368
Limited partnership 368
Partnership agreement 368
Business corporation 372
Capital stock 373
Shareholder 373
Par value 373
No-par value 373
Stock certificate 373
Market value 373
Book value 375
Net worth 375
Common share 375
Holding company 375

Conglomerate 375
Dividends 375
Stock dividend 376
Stock split 376
Rights 376
Warrants 376
Preferred shares 377
Non-cumulative 377
Redeemability 377
Convertibility 378
Participation 378
Corporate income tax 378
Multinational corporation 381
Direct investment 381
Portfolio investment 381
Co-operative 382
Crown corporation 384

Review Questions

1. Explain briefly the nature and purpose of the business firm.
2. What is a sole proprietorship? What are the advantages of this form of business ownership?
3. What is unlimited liability? Why is it considered a disadvantage of the sole proprietorship form of business ownership? What other disadvantages exist?
4. Distinguish between a general partnership and a limited partnership.
5. What are the most important advantages of the partnership form of ownership?
6. What are the most important disadvantages of the partnership form of ownership?
7. What is a business corporation? Distinguish between a private and a public one.
8. Why might federal incorporation be preferred to provincial incorporation? And vice versa?

9. What is the requirement for establishing a corporation in your province?
10. What is capital stock? Distinguish between par value and no-par value shares. Why are shares issued without a par value?
11. Distinguish between the market value, the book value, and the asset value of a share.
12. What are the privileges of a common shareholder?
13. What is a holding company? A conglomerate?
14. Distinguish between a stock dividend and a stock split.
15. Distinguish between a right and a warrant.
16. What are the privileges of a preferred shareholder?
17. Distinguish between cumulative and non-cumulatve preferred shares. What is a redeemable preferred share?
18. A preferred share can be convertible and/or participating. Explain.
19. What are the advantages of the corporate form of business ownership?
20. What are the disadvantages of the corporate form of ownership?
21. What is a multinational corporation? What encourages a domestic or national business corporation to become a multinational one?
22. Explain the nature and purpose of the co-operative form of business ownership.
23. What is a crown corporation?
24. How do provincial and municipal governments organize public utilities and other government-owned business enterprises?
25. Why do most business firms start out as sole proprietorships? Discuss.
26. Why would an entrepreneur operating as a sole proprietor decide to take in partners? Discuss.
27. In a limited partnership, all the partners have limited liability. Discuss.
28. Why might a sole proprietor decide to incorporate his or her business? Explain and discuss.

"Guys, I've called this meeting because there seems to be something wrong with our productivity.."

20. CANADIAN PRODUCTIVITY

CHAPTER OBJECTIVES

A. To explain what is meant by the term "productivity"
B. To emphasize the fact that a country's productivity determines the standard of living of its people
C. To show how Canadian productivity is lagging behind that of other nations
D. To identify the reasons for slow productivity growth in Canada
E. To explain how poor productivity makes Canadian firms more vulnerable to foreign competition
F. To indicate why S.E. Asian goods are usually cheaper and often better-made than many Canadian ones
G. To examine the research and development efforts that are now being undertaken in Canada
H. To review government efforts to assist the growth of Canadian productivity
I. To emphasize the vital role of both management and labour in improving Canadian productivity
J. To discuss the federal government's industrial strategy

CHAPTER OUTLINE

20.9   Government Assistance
20.10   The Role of Management and Labour
20.11   Canada's Industrial Strategy

20.1: PRODUCTIVITY DEFINED

In the 1980s, a critical economic concern for Canada is productivity. The term *productivity* is normally used in the sense of *labour productivity*—meaning the value of the average output per person employed over a given period of time such as an hour, a week, or a year. Logically, however, we can also talk about the productivity of the other main factors of production: land and capital. In fact, land varies greatly in productivity throughout Canada and the world. And capital also varies in its productivity, depending on whether the machines being used in a manufacturing plant are new or old, and on the way in which they are maintained. We can also talk about *total factor productivity*—the output of all the factors of production combined.

20.2: CANADA'S PRODUCTIVITY RECORD

Canadian productivity, defined as real GNP per employed person, has deteriorated significantly since 1973. After increasing at an annual rate of 2.5 per cent between 1966 and 1973, productivity declined 0.1 per cent a year from 1974 to 1981. Other studies show that from 1973 to 1981, productivity in Japan grew at an annual rate of 6.8 per cent, in France 4.6 per cent, in West Germany, 4.5 per cent, and in Canada 1.6 per cent, just less than in the U.S. According to the European Management Forum, an independent organization that evaluates the international competitiveness of 22 industrial nations, Canada ranked thirteenth in ability of companies to produce goods at competitive prices; twenty-second in productivity trends; twentieth in the introduction of labour-saving technology; and nineteenth in employee turnover. According to another source, the OECD, Canada's annual productivity growth over the period 1960-1980 was 2.4 per cent, compared with an average of 3.9 per cent for 16 OECD countries. The only country with a lower productivity growth rate was Britain, with 2.3 per cent.

In recent years, the productivity growth rate has risen quickly in many countries. Unfortunately, Canada has lagged well behind. For example, U.S. Department of Labour figures show that, in the period 1950-1981, manufacturing productivity increased by 110 per cent in

Table S.13
Canadian Labour Productivity in Manufacturing, 1951-1981

Country	average annual percentage			Annual percentage growth rates		
	1951-1973	1967-1973	1974-1981	1979	1980	1981
Canada	4.3	5.0	1.1	1.7	-3.3	0.3
U.S.	2.8	3.1	1.5	0.7	0.2	2.8
Japan	10.0	11.9	6.2	8.9	6.8	3.2
France	5.3	6.0	4.2	4.9	1.6	1.6
Germany	5.8	5.3	4.4	4.9	1.4	2.7
Italy	6.6	7.1	3.6	7.3	5.8	3.4
U.K.	3.4	4.7	2.2	3.3	0.6	5.9

Source: U.S. Department of Labour, Bureau of Labour Statistics, Office of Productivity and Technology, *Output per Hour, Hourly Compensation and Unit Labour Costs in Manufacturing, Eleven Countries, 1950-81, December 1982*

Note: Labour productivity is defined as output per hour worked

the U.S., 194 per cent in Canada, 267 per cent in Sweden, 341 per cent in Denmark, 350 per cent in France, 414 per cent in West Germany, 462 per cent in Netherlands, 470 per cent in Italy, and by 1334 per cent in Japan. Although Canadian productivity increased faster than in the U.S., this position has been reversed in more recent years.

All the statistics show, in other words, that Canada's labour productivity growth is now one of the slowest in the non-communist industrialized world. This conclusion also applies to total factor productivity. This characteristic of our economy—ailing productivity—has even been called the "Canadian disease". And forecasts by the Economic Council of Canada and the Conference Board of Canada for the 1980s, estimate productivity growth, in the event of no major change, at no more than one per cent a year.

20.3: PRODUCTIVITY AND THE STANDARD OF LIVING

A person living in one country may work much harder than a person living in another, yet receive much lower real wages—that is, the goods and services that he or she obtains in exchange for the money wages received. As we become well aware, when travelling abroad, the material standard of living that the average person enjoys varies greatly between different parts of the world.

The basic reason for this disparity in living standards is the difference in productivity. This may be caused by differences in the persons themselves. For example, a farmer in country A may be physically weaker, less knowledgeable, less determined, etc. than a farmer in country B—which would help account for part of the lower productivity in country A. But there are other important considerations. The farmer in country A may have very little farm equipment or other capital goods. Also what he has may be out-dated or in poor state of repair. And this would also help keep his output low relative to the farmer in country B. Furthermore, the land that he works may be rocky, dry, and otherwise infertile, compared with that in country B. Consequently, the farmer in country A may never achieve the standard of living that is enjoyed by the farmer in country B, even though he or she may work harder.

Even though the farmer in country B may now enjoy a high standard of living (due in part to a large amount of capital per worker and abundant natural resources), his standard of living may deteriorate as the years go by. This would be the case if the farmer in country B let his capital goods deteriorate or grow out-of-date; if he neglected his resources; and/or worked less hard and less skillfully. The situation could become even worse if the goods produced by the farmer in country B become so expensive or so poor in quality that consumers, not only in other countries but in country B as well, prefer to buy the goods produced by the farmer in country A.

In summary, as a country's productivity rises, so normally does the standard of living of its people. Conversely, as a country's productivity declines, so does the standard of living. Britain is considered to be a good example of a country whose productivity and standard of living have declined in modern times. Japan, West Germany and other West European countries are examples of countries whose productivity and standard of living have substantially increased. Canada's productivity and standard of living were rising for many years after World War II. However, since the mid-1970s, the rates of increase of both have been slipping compared with those of many other countries. Whereas at the end of World War II, Canadians had the fourth highest standard of living in the world. Now it is about the fourteenth.

The implications of a declining rate of increase in productivity are several. Because the amount of goods and services being produced is increasing relatively slowly, money wages, which are increasing more quickly, will buy less. Also, the government will not be able to afford to provide as many social services for the public. There will be increasing social hostility between the "haves" and the "have-nots"; labour-management relations may worsen; and the country's goods will become less competitive with those of other countries, both at home and abroad, because they now cost more to produce and must therefore be higher priced.

20.4: PRODUCTIVITY AND WAGES IN CANADA

Whereas the growth of labour productivity has been relatively slow in Canada in recent years, real wages per worker have increased faster. In other words, higher wages have not been matched by higher productivity. This widening gap between productivity and wages has not only reduced the international competitiveness of Canadian goods but has also increased inflationary pressures in Canada. This is because the money earned is chasing relatively fewer goods and services. Also, although productivity in Canada is lower than in the U.S., our principal export market, average wages in Canada are higher—a fact which is gradually making it more and more difficult for Canadian manufacturers and other producers to compete in the U.S. market and elsewhere. Only if the exchange rate for the Canadian dollar sinks even further can Canadian export prices remain competitive—but this means that Canada would have to pay more for its imports and for the servicing and repayment of its large foreign debt which is denominated in U.S. dollars and other hard currencies.

20.5: REASONS FOR THE DECLINING RATE OF INCREASE IN PRODUCTIVITY IN CANADA

Many different factors have been blamed for the declining rate of increase in productivity in Canada. The only agreement among economists and others in this matter is that there is not just one cause but many together that are to blame. These various possible causes are listed below, in no particular order.

1. There has been a reduction in the amount of capital employed per worker. However, Canadian industry is much more capital intensive than that of the U.S., yet Canadian productivity is lower. Nevertheless, more investment in new products and new production processes could have been made in Canada.

2. There has been a gradual shifting of workers away from sectors of the economy such as manufacturing that have a high measured productivity (partly because of more capital per worker) to service industries in which productivity, as well as being hard to measure, appears to increase only very slowly.

3. A large number of women and young persons entered the Canadian labour force in the 1970s as a result of changing attitudes and the post-war baby boom which, according to some analysts, means a less experienced work force.

4. The increase in energy prices adversely affected the use of capital.

5. Relations between management and labour in many firms, particularly large ones, have continued to be antagonistic, with resultant strikes, walkouts, and low worker morale, and an attitude by many union leaders that improvement in productivity is not the proper concern of a labour union.

6. Too many people have been educated for the wrong jobs.

7. There is insufficient competition in Canada—due to weak anti-monopoly legislation and the existence of too many government-protected monopolies and oligopolies.

8. The highly graduated rates of personal income tax in Canada discourage a person from working harder and undertaking business risk.

9. The fact that Canada's manufacturing sector (in which productivity gains can be most spectacular) is so small.

10. There has not been enough spent on research and development aimed at improving production.

11. There has been an undue emphasis over the last two decades in Canada on the redistribution of wealth to the detriment of the rate of creation of new wealth.

12. The Canadian market is so small that it prevents long production

runs, with corresponding economies of scale, unless substantial quantities of the product can be exported—and relatively few Canadian firms are good at exporting, even to the U.S. market.

13. A labour union complaint: the failure of the Canadian government to insist on greater Canadian content in imported goods or on other restrictions on imports.

14. Canada's cold climate.

15. Canada's small population being spread over such a wide country, causing high transportation costs.

16. Government safety and pollution requirements that require nonproductive expenditure from the GNP point of view.

17. Foreign ownership of so much Canadian industry.

18. Shipping of so many resources abroad without sufficient processing in Canada.

19. Poor business management.

20. Insufficient tax incentives to industrial investment.

21. Insufficient tax incentives for the export of manufactured goods.

22. Insufficient savings and investment in Canada compared with consumption. We should consume less out of current production and save and invest more, government tax incentives or not.

23. Lack of a coherent industrial strategy by the federal government.

20.6: VULNERABILITY OF CANADIAN FIRMS

Many Canadian firms have already succumbed to foreign competition as a result of their inability to compete at home or abroad on the basis of price, product quality, or both. And many other firms now import component parts and even complete products that were formerly manufactured in Canada. The most vulnerable Canadian firms, now and in the future, are of two basic kinds. The first are those that produce a good that can be manufactured more cheaply in lower-cost countries and can be economically transported to Canada and other world markets. Some examples are textiles, clothing, shoes, home entertainment equipment, business office equipment, cars, motorcycles, bicycles, and base metals. In the last instance, the production of base metals such as manganese, the ore-producing countries now do their own refining instead of just exporting the ore.

The second kind of vulnerable Canadian firms are those that produce a good or service that will be made obsolete by technological change. For example, Canadian copper producers who see their product being replaced in power transmission by aluminum, and in communications by fibre optics; or metal manufacturers who have already seen many of their markets taken over by plastics. The Swiss watch industry fell into both categories of vulnerability when it was devastated in the 1970s by, first, the competition of S.E. Asian low-cost producers and, second, by the invention and manufacture of quartz and digital watches in North America.

In the future, as another example of the changes in store for us, automobiles are expected to become completely non-metallic; and high-performance toughened adhesives, or industrial "superglues", are expected to transform basic manufacturing methods for just about everything from washtubs to machine tools to aircraft. At least one pundit has forecast that in the next few decades, Canada and the U.S. will gradually witness the disappearance of such traditional industries as automobiles, clothing, appliances, steel, and a host of others—and that a massive structural change is already taking place in the North American economy as S.E. Asian manufacturers increase their penetration of the world market. The salvation of Canadians, so it is suggested, is to concentrate on resource-based "high-tech" industries. A report by the Science Council of Canada has suggested that Canada is already falling behind in the race to exploit the new computer technology. For example, Canada is now a major net importer of computers and automated office systems. However, a recent report by the Economic Council of Canada is more optimistic.

A particularly significant trend that is emerging in modern industry is the application of labour-saving computerized technology. Sometimes called CAD/CAM (Computer-Assisted Design/Computer-Assisted Manufacture), this approach has already received much attention in Canada. Nevertheless, Canada is still in the early stages compared with Japan where so-called "manless" plants, with numerous programmable robots, already produce a variety of high-quality products in the auto, steel, electronics, and machine-tool industries. In these new plants, computer equipment and special programming are combined with traditional mechanical automation, in a process called "mechatronics". This trend has been called the "second industrial revolution" and by Alvin Toffler, the "Third Wave" and promises to change the manufacturing process and the industrial workplace as drastically as did steam-power in the nineteenth century, and mass-production techniques in the early twentieth century. A key characteristic of these new manufacturing plants is the use of a central computer linked to satellite computers. Electronic instructions are given to the various robots which then act accordingly. The satellite computers monitor the work being done and make adjustments as and when necessary.

20.7: COMPETITION FROM S.E. ASIA

For many years, goods made in Japan and other S.E. Asian countries were considered to be cheap but shoddy imitations of those made in North America and Western Europe. However, in the last few decades the picture has completely changed. Now, many Western consumers buy the S.E. Asian product for quality as well as price. And this dramatic change has threatened the existence of many traditional Western industries—automobiles, watches, steel, ships, toys, calculators, TV sets, motor cycles, bicycles, pens, clothing, textiles, etc. and, before long, so it is anticipated, computers and pharmaceuticals.

The easy explanation for the inability of many Canadian or U.S. firms to compete effectively with the S.E. Asian product (from Japan, South Korea, Hong Kong, Taiwan, Singapore, Malaysia, and now mainland China) is the lower cost of labour in those countries. This is estimated at about one-third of the North American wage—with Japan now a relatively-high-labour-cost country in the S.E. Asia region. However, the S.E. Asian producers have several other advantages. First, they have adopted and, where necessary, adapted the latest Western industrial technology, as well as developed new technology of their own. Second, they have invested large sums of money in modern plant and equipment so that (a) the amount of capital per worker in many industries is extremely high and (b) the condition and technological efficiency of that capital is excellent. Thus, for example, Japan now has more industrial robots than all the other countries of the world combined. Third, the quality control standards for materials, components, and finished products are usually more demanding than in the West where product testing is often done on a sample basis. Fourth, the quality of labour (dedication, intelligence, trainability, manual dexterity, patience etc.) is high. Fifth, the motivation of the worker and management is generally greater—the "have nots" struggling to improve their lot, unspoilt by the commonplace luxuries of the West. Sixth, their business management is often more efficient—whether it be in the area of labour relations (the Theory Z style of participative management), marketing, finance, or production planning and control. Seventh, there is much closer co-operation between government and business than there is in Canada and the U.S. This involves joint planning and implementing, often with government financial assistance for research and development, of an industrial strategy for the country. All these factors, when taken together, mean that S.E. Asian productivity is often higher than Canadian productivity and provides a sharp competitive edge that has already sliced through many world markets.

20.8: INDUSTRIAL RESEARCH AND DEVELOPMENT

Innovation—the invention of new products or production processes—is one acknowledged key to productivity growth. And innovation usually requires, as a prerequisite, a serious and sustained industrial research and development effort. Unfortunately in Canada, private sector R & D has not been impressive. Most large firms, usually Canadian subsidiaries of U.S. multinationals, have been content to borrow any new technology from their parent companies abroad and pay a licising fee for its use in Canada. And the U.S. parent companies, as we discuss in more detail in Chapter 37 (Foreign Ownership of Canadian Industry), are usually inclined to concentrate their R & D centres in the U.S. However, despite what has just been said, there are a number of large and small Canadian firms that are leaders in innovation (Northern Telecom, Mitel, etc.) and who even sell successfully in the Japanese market—considered to be one of the hardest for a foreign firm to crack.

At the present time, Canada is spending about 1.2 per cent of its GNP on research and development with the federal government hoping to raise that figure to 1.5 per cent. By contrast, the U.S., West Germany, and Japan already each spend about 2 per cent of their GNP on R & D.

20.9: GOVERNMENT ASSISTANCE

Oddly enough, governments in Canada have a better reputation for R & D support than do private business firms, although it is the latter who will go under if they do not keep ahead in the technology race. Nevertheless, even in the public sector, federal expenditures—through tax incentives and grants—have declined (in constant 1971 dollars) since their peak in fiscal year 1973-74. Also, since the early 1970s, federal expenditure on R & D, as a percentage of Canada's GNP, has steadily slipped. However, in the federal budget of April 1983, new government proposals for R & D support in Canada were announced. Specifically, the income tax credit for R & D expenditures by business firms was increased by 10 per cent and more government money was to be made available in R & D grants. The federal government also asked for submissions from the private sector on a government R & D paper. One suggestion, already made, was that the government broaden the application of the R & D tax incentives to include "technological development" rather than the narrower and pure-research oriented "scientific research".

At the federal level, most of the programs of assistance for industrial research and development are now administered by the Department of Regional and Industrial Expansion. Previously, they were under the Department of Science and Technology which is now responsible for advising on science policy for Canada.

In 1983, the federal government proposed the establishment of a National Centre for Productivity and Employment Growth, with financing of $5 million a year. The centre's main function would be to bring together management, labour, and government to work on the problem of improving productivity, to distribute information on methods for improving productivity, and to act in an advisory capacity to help the government formulate productivity policies.

The federal government has also in the early 1980s given a great deal of thought to the development of a technology strategy for Canada. Suggestions include: the establishment of R & D income tax shelters for individuals; the establishment of national technology centres across Canada—for example, a biotechnology centre in Saskatoon, a manufacturing technology centre in Winnipeg, and a food-processing technology centre somewhere in New Brunswick; a stronger Buy Canadian policy; and encouragement of foreign multinationals to do more R & D and manufacturing in Canada.

At the provincial level, Ontario as one example, has set up six technology centres around the province—for example, the Ontario Centre for Microelectronics in Ottawa that plans to help small and medium-sized businesses to develop new electronic products and to use microelectronics to solve manufacturing problems and the Ontario Centre for Automotive Parts Technology in St. Catherines.

20.10: THE ROLE OF MANAGEMENT AND LABOUR

If Canada is to remain competitive both at home and abroad it must raise labour productivity by applying the latest computer-assisted manufacturing technology. However, labour unions in Canada have in the past been reluctant to accept such changes without adequate safeguards for the livelihood of their members.

In Japan, by contrast, workers have been extremely willing and able to accept this new manufacturing technology even though it is labour-saving. This seems to be the result of three factors. First, the system of life-time employment used by most large Japanese companies which assures the worker of a new job if his or her old one disappears. Second, the fact that the average Japanese worker has a relatively high level of technical education and training. And, third, the much more co-operative attitude between management and labour, based on dedication to employer and country.

It should be noted here that labour productivity depends only partly on the persons employed. Thus the slow improvement in productivity in Canada cannot be blamed solely on the Canadian worker's alleged lack of effort, lack of skill, hostility towards management, unwillingness to accept new technology, lack of pride in his or her work, etc., although these must share some of the blame. Just as important is the way in which production is organized and the employees managed (including the way in which the workers are motivated).

An essential prerequisite of the acceptance of rapid technological change in Canada is therefore an improvement in labour-management relations.

In the vast majority of North American companies, management treats the average employee as if he or she is basically lazy, dull, unambitious, selfish and resistant to change. This conventional approach was labelled by Professor Douglas McGregor in 1957, in his book, *The Human Side of Enterprise*, as the Theory X style of management. Other companies adopt a more positive attitude towards their employees, giving them more training and responsibility whenever possible, and treating them more like human beings than mere cogs in a vast production machine. McGregor labelled this approach "Theory Y". Nevertheless, even with the Theory Y approach, the company always comes first, and if sales drop, heads soon start to roll. In Japan, by contrast, a somewhat different system of management seems to exist—one that blends discipline, loyalty, employee participation, quality circles, greater mutual trust, greater openness and exchange between employer and employee, job security and other elements, into a more fruitful whole. This style of management has been called by W.G. Ouchi, in a book about it, "Theory Z".

A *quality circle* is a group of employees who meet together, on a regular basis, with or without a member of supervisory management, to discuss ways in which work methods, manufacturing or assembly operations, and the quality of the product can be improved. Although the idea originated in the U.S., it seems to have been applied more extensively, and with perhaps better results, by the Japanese. However, more and more Canadian companies are making use of quality circles and other ways of improving worker motivation and productivity such as by profit-sharing and employee stock-ownership plans.

At the national level, the federal government, organized labour, and private business are now starting to co-operate again—for example, in a proposed Canadian Labour Market and Productivity Centre.

*"You mean, we should have been follow-
ing Theory Z, not Theory Y?!"*

20.11: CANADA'S INDUSTRIAL STRATEGY

The long-term program that a government adopts toward its country's industrial sector is known as its *industrial strategy*. Thus, for example, in 1879, the Canadian government greatly increased the level of tariffs on imported manufactured goods as a deliberate policy of protecting and thereby promoting local manufacturing industry. Although tariff protection in Canada and other countries has since declined as a result of multilateral trade agreements, other tools are nowadays being used to encourage manufacturing growth. The Federal Business Development Bank, the Canada Development Corporation, and the Department of Regional and Industrial Expansion all provide federal financial assistance to industry. There are also financial incentives and technical assistance to undertake research and development and to promote exports of manufactured and other goods. Industry in general, and small businesses in particular, have benefited in recent years from reductions in corporate income taxation. At the individual industry level, federal government initiatives have led to the auto pact with the United States (which gave a powerful boost to car, truck, and parts production in Canada), the development of Arctic oil and gas fields, and the establishment of a computer industry. At the regional level, provincial governments, usually through development corporations, have also tried to promote industrial growth by loans and equity participation. Also, joint federal-provincial initiatives have led to new enterprises being started in Canada—such as the helicopter manufacturing plants now scheduled for Ontario and Quebec.

As the years go by, changes in demand, production, technology, and overseas sources of supply cause changes in the relative prosperity of different industries. Therefore, unless an industry can adjust, it may soon become stagnant. Already in Canada and other countries there are such pockets of industrial depression. Consequently, a country's industrial strategy, as well as needing to be clear and internally consistent, should be flexible. It is not surprising, therefore, that there has been much talk in Canada in recent years of the need for a new industrial strategy to cope with changing times. Let us now consider some of the factors that such a new strategy must take into account.

1. Employment. Canada has a high rate of unemployment. Should only industries that are labour-intensive be encouraged? Should industrial growth be artificially encouraged in otherwise slow-growth regions of the country?

2. Productivity. Productivity per worker varies greatly from one industry to another. It is greater in the capital-intensive, high-technology industries such as oil and chemicals than in, say, the leather and clothing industries. Should only high-productivity industries be encouraged despite the fact that they are capital-intensive rather than labour-intensive?

3. Growth. The long-term growth prospects for some industries (for example, electronics) are better than for others. Should the emphasis of government assistance be placed only on industries with above-average growth prospects? Should traditional, but ailing, industries such as textiles and footwear be encouraged to survive?

4. Resources. Large quantities of Canada's raw materials are now exported with relatively little processing. Should there be incentives to encourage greater processing in this country, and thus increase income and employment opportunities for Canadians from resources that are gradually being depleted?

5. Imports. Apart from automobiles, much of Canada's exports consists of food and raw materials, while most of its imports are manufactured goods. Should imports of manufactured goods be discouraged by means other than tariffs—a policy followed by, for example, Japan and many Latin American countries?

6. Market size. Countries throughout the world are entering into regional free-trade arrangements. Canada, if it is to maintain or improve the average standard of living of its 25 million people, cannot be self-sufficient. And, despite political misgivings, Canada cannot turn away from the large, rich U.S. market just across the border. The automobile pact, by treating the North American market as one, and by dividing production between Canadian and U.S. plants, has increased prosperity all round by taking better advantage of the economies of mass production. Should Canada try to arrange similar pacts for other products, and even with other countries—for example, with the European Common Market countries?

Industrial and Regional Development Program (IRDP)

In 1983, a new program for Canadian national economic development was announced by the federal government. This program, to be administered by the Department of Regional and Industrial Expansion (DRIE), will provide substantial government financial assistance in the form of grants, loans, and loan-guarantees, to Canadian businesses. It applies to six separate phases of the corporate and product life cycle, as follows: industrial infrastructure; industrial innovation; plant establishment; modernization and expansion; marketing; and industrial renewal. The basic purpose of the program is to make Canadian industry more competitive so as to maximize its sales potential in both the domestic and foreign markets. An Industrial and Regional Development Board, with both business and labour representatives from across Canada, is to advise the government on overall industrial policies and strategies. Also, task forces are to be assembled for key industrial sectors (such as the aeronautics and automotive industries) to advise on specific development programs for those sectors.

How the new program will work out is uncertain. Some critics argue that it is nothing more than a spruced-up package containing almost the same kinds of industrial development assistance already available for years. The only new additions are funding for new product research and development, marketing studies, the application of new manufacturing technology, and tourism projects. On the other hand, there will now be one standardized instrument for basic industrial development rather than a bewildering variety of programs. In fact, the IRDP replaces nearly 80 industrial development programs previously offered by ITC and DREE. Also, the budget has been increased.

One problem with IRDP is the need to reconcile, in the allocation of funds, the aims of developing a more productive industrial base in Canada (the philosophy of ITC) with the aim of assisting the economically disadvantaged regions of Canada (the philosophy of DREE). This is to be attempted by dividing Canada's 260 census districts into four economic groups, ranging from the poorest 5% of its population (tier IV) to the most affluent 50% (tier I). Project funding varies according to tier group—with a firm in a tier IV district receiving a larger percentage of assistance than a firm in a tier I district. Furthermore, funding assistance to establish a new plant is not available to firms in tier I districts.

The program is to be administered in a decentralized way, with most applications for assistance being processed locally by DRIE staff. Also, regional executive directors are to orient the focus of the IRDP to the specific development needs of their province.

Summary

1. *Productivity* is the value of the average output per person employed over a given period of time.
2. According to the statistics, productivity has been increasing more slowly in Canada than in most other industrial countries.
3. If productivity declines, so does a country's standard of living.
4. Wages in Canada have been increasing faster than labour productivity.

"Russ, I want you to fit some 'quality circles' into our organization.."

5. Many reasons (as listed in the Chapter) have been put forward for Canada's slow productivity increase. The only consensus is that it is not just one factor, but many combined, that are the cause.
6. Canadian firms are vulnerable in two ways: to lower-cost imports and to changes in technology.
7. S.E. Asian firms, notably in Japan, not only have the competitive advantage of lower labour costs but also seem able to apply new technology faster in manufacturing production, seem willing to invest the large sums of money required, and enjoy greater management-labour co-operation.
8. Spending on research and development in Canada is considered to be inadequate.
9. Canada's federal and provincial governments are now taking steps to help encourage productivity in Canada.
10. A critical issue in Canada, in any discussion of productivity, is Canada's adversary system of management-labour relations as compared with Japan's "Theory Z" style of management.
11. Federal and provincial governments have assisted Canadian industry in various ways. However, it is argued that Canada badly needs a more definite *industrial strategy*—that is to say, a long-term government program to promote industry. Some of the considerations that such a strategy must take into account are: employment opportunities, productivity, growth prospects, use of natural resources, competition of imports, and market size, including export opportunities.
12. In 1983, the federal government announced a new Industrial and Regional Development Program for Canada.

Key Terms

Productivity 392
Labour productivity 392
Total factor
  productivity 392
Standard of living 394
High-tech industry 398
Labour-saving computerized
  technology 398
CAD/CAM 398

Mechatronics 398
Second industrial
  revolution 398
R & D 401
Innovation 401
Government assistance 401
Theory Z management 403
Industrial strategy 405
IRDP 406

Review Questions

1. What exactly is "productivity"?
2. How successful has Canada been in raising productivity? How does our record compare with that of other industrial countries?
3. The standard of living is higher in Canada than in the Third World countries because Canadians work harder. Discuss.
4. Explain, in terms of productivity, the fact that the standard of living has declined in Britain since World War II but risen in such countries as Switzerland, Denmark, West Germany and Japan.
5. To what extent does productivity explain regional differences of living standards within Canada?
6. What are the economic implications of the fact that wages have been increasing faster in Canada than productivity?
7. Many reasons have been suggested for slow productivity growth in Canada. Which do you consider to be the five most important reasons. Why?
8. "Labour productivity depends only partly on the person employed". Explain and discuss, with reference to Canada and Japan.
9. What types of Canadian firms have gone out of business in recent years because of low-cost foreign competition?
10. What types of Canadian firms have gone out of business in recent years because their products have become obsolete?
11. What has been called the "second industrial revolution"? What was the "first"?
12. What is CAD/CAM? Why is it attracting so much business and government attention in Canada?
13. "The reason that imports from S.E. Asia are cheaper than Canadian-made goods is mainly lower labour costs". Discuss.
14. What is industrial "innovation". Explain, with examples.
15. What are our federal and provincial governments doing to encourage R & D?
16. "Japan's biggest competitive advantage over Canada is the attitude of its labour force". Discuss.
17. How have the federal and provincial governments assisted manufacturing industry in Canada?
18. What is an industrial strategy? What problems could such a strategy help Canadian manufacturers solve?
19. Explain the nature and purpose of the IRDP.

Part F:
NATIONAL OUTPUT, INCOME, AND EMPLOYMENT

Beginning with this part of the book, we turn our attention to macro-economics—the study of the economic problems that face society as a whole. These problems include: producing enough goods and services; creating enough jobs; avoiding excessive inflation; maintaining a satisfactory balance of international payments; and achieving other desirable economic goals.

Canada now produces twice as many services as goods . . .

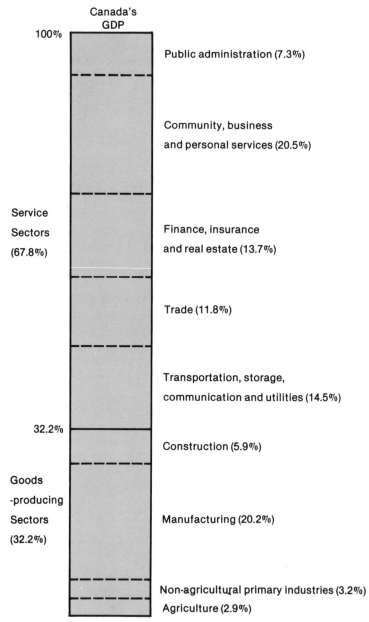

Canada's GDP

100%

Public administration (7.3%)

Community, business and personal services (20.5%)

Service Sectors (67.8%)

Finance, insurance and real estate (13.7%)

Trade (11.8%)

Transportation, storage, communication and utilities (14.5%)

32.2%

Construction (5.9%)

Goods -producing Sectors (32.2%)

Manufacturing (20.2%)

Non-agricultural primary industries (3.2%)

Agriculture (2.9%)

(% share in 1982 of Gross Domestic Product in constant 1971 prices by each industrial sector)

Source of data: Statistics Canada, *Gross Domestic Product by Industry,* monthly, Cat. 61-005

Most people in Canada now work in the service industries . . .

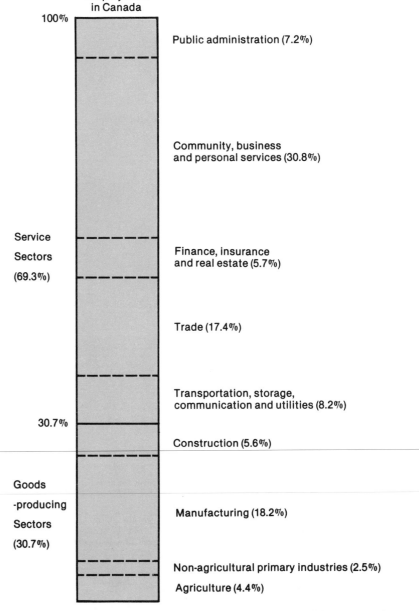

Employment
in Canada

100%

Public administration (7.2%)

Community, business
and personal services (30.8%)

Service
Sectors
(69.3%)

Finance, insurance
and real estate (5.7%)

Trade (17.4%)

Transportation, storage,
communication and utilities (8.2%)

30.7%

Construction (5.6%)

Goods
-producing
Sectors
(30.7%)

Manufacturing (18.2%)

Non-agricultural primary industries (2.5%)

Agriculture (4.4%)

(% share in 1982 of total employment in Canada by each industrial sector)
Source of data: Statistics Canada, *The Labour Force,* monthly, Cat. 71-001

Money paid to the public as wages and salaries, rent, interest, and dividends

The factor market

Business firms

Households

The product market

Money paid by the public to business firms for goods and services supplied

Business firms and households, linked together in the market system, mainly determine the three basic economic problems of our society: what to produce, how to produce, and for whom to produce.

21. THE CIRCULAR FLOW OF INCOME

CHAPTER OBJECTIVES

A. To make use of an economic model to illustrate how the various sectors of the Canadian economy operate in relation to each other
B. To explain the economic relationship between the business firm and household sectors of the economy
C. To explain the nature and use of an input-output table
D. To distinguish between savings and investment
E. To explain how governments affect the circular flow of income
F. To explain how other countries affect the circular flow of income

CHAPTER OUTLINE

21.1 The Circular-Flow Model
21.2 Relationship between Business Firms and Households
21.3 Savings and Investment
21.4 Governments and the Circular Flow of Income
21.5 Other Countries and the Circular Flow of Income

21.1: THE CIRCULAR-FLOW MODEL

What is the basic structure of the Canadian economy? To help us answer this question, we can make use of a circular-flow model. This is an economic model that demonstrates by means of income flows how the various sectors of the economy—business firms, households, and governments—operate in relation to each other. It also shows how the economy is affected by relations with other countries. For Canada, this foreign sector is particularly important because of the large flow of goods, services, and investment capital, to and from other countries. *Business firms* include all sole proprietorships, partnerships, corporations, and co-operatives engaged in business activity. *Households* comprise family units and unattached individuals living on their own. *Governments* include federal, provincial, and municipal governments.

21.2: RELATIONSHIP BETWEEN BUSINESS FIRMS AND HOUSEHOLDS

Our first version of the circular-flow model (Figure 21.1) illustrates how the business and household sectors of the economy are intimately tied together. We ignore, for the moment, the existence of governments and other countries. We can see, first, that business firms pay money to households in exchange for the services of labour and other factors of production. This money, which constitutes the *money income* of Canadian households, is in the form of wages and salaries, rent, interest, and dividends. Households in Canada in turn pay money to business firms in Canada in exchange for goods and services. Thus, the *circular flow of income* is the flow of money from business firms to households and back again, all within the country.

The money that business firms receive back from households is used to pay for more production. Money continues to flow in a circular fashion: first, from business firms (the producers of goods and services) to households (the suppliers of labour and other factors of production on the one hand, and the purchasers of goods and services on the other); and, second, back again to business firms (the sellers of goods and services, as well as the producers). The top half of our circle represents income; the bottom half, expenditure.

Not all the production (and marketing) costs of a business, we should note, are payments for the services of factors of production. The other costs are payments to other business firms for *intermediate goods*—the materials and parts used in the production process. Thus, if the selling price of firm A's product is $100, perhaps $60 will be paid to firm B for materials and parts. Factor payments by firm A will, therefore, be only $40. This $40 is equivalent to the *value added* by firm A to the intermediate goods purchased from firm B. Firm B may in turn pay $40 to firm C for materials—which means that factor payments by firm B, equivalent to its value added, are only $20. Thus, the money received by each firm is used partly to pay for factor services and partly to pay for intermediate goods. And so it goes on, from firm to firm. Eventually, however, all the money is received back by households, either for their labour or for their capital and land. Thus, if we trace a steel

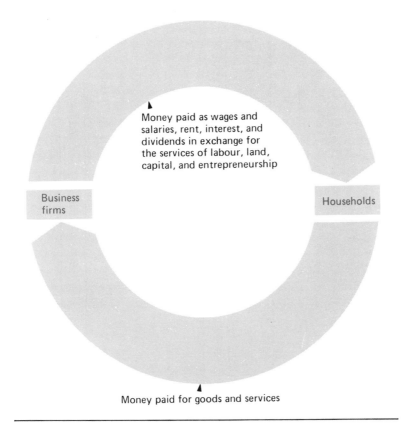

Money paid as wages and
salaries, rent, interest, and
dividends in exchange for
the services of labour, land,
capital, and entrepreneurship

Business
firms

Households

Money paid for goods and services

Figure 21:1   The Circular Flow, Showing the Position of Business
Firms and Households

product back to the original iron-ore, we find that even the price paid
for the ore was in fact shared among various individuals: by the owner
of the mineral rights, by the investors who provided the equity capital
to establish the mine, by the lender who provided loan capital to help
finance the undertaking, and by the workers in the mine—all owners
of factors of production.

Input-Output Analysis

The fact that one industry's output is often part of other industries'
inputs means that many industries are closely related. Consequently, a
fall in the demand for the output of one industry, or a labour strike that
cripples its activities, is soon felt throughout the economy.

Table 21:1
A Simplified Input-Output Table (with Hypothetical Data)

User Producer	Agriculture	Mining	Manufacturing	Construction	Service	Exports	Households	Total output
Agriculture	20	—	80	—	50	100	250	500
Mining	—	—	300	—	—	400	—	700
Manufacturing	100	80	120	60	40	100	200	700
Construction	20	30	50	20	30	—	100	250
Service	10	10	50	20	10	50	150	300
Imports	5	—	25	5	5	—	50	90
Labour (households)	150	50	300	50	200	—	50	800
Total input	305	170	925	155	335	650	800	

All the various inter-industry flows of goods and services within a country can be summarized in the form of an *input-output table*. Such a table shows, for each industry listed in vertical order on the left-hand side, to which industries (listed horizontally, from left to right, across the top of the table) its output is sold. A simplified example is shown in Table 21:1. Input-output tables were first devised by an eighteenth-century French economist, François Quesnay. The principal modern exponent of this type of analysis—useful for forecasting the effects of government economic policies—is Harvard's Professor Wassily Leontief[1]. Many countries, including Canada and some provinces, have computed input-output tables for their own policy-making and analysis. However, because of the expense and the fact that the inter-industry relationships are constantly changing with new technology, these tables are prepared only intermittently.

Conclusion

We have seen, so far, that the producers of goods and services, by making payments to the various factors of production, provide households with monetary income. This monetary income can then be used by households to purchase the goods and services that have been produced. So long as there are no *leakages* (income not passed on) this circular flow of money from business firms to households and back again will remain consistent in volume, and will enable producers to sell all they make. Thus, if households receive $100 billion as income, they will return this sum to business firms as expenditure on final goods and services.

But what happens to the circular flow of money if households do not spend all the income they receive? This leads us to the question of savings and investment.

21.3: SAVINGS AND INVESTMENT

Households may spend all of their income on the purchase of goods and services that they use up, or *consume*, immediately or within a relatively short period of time. They may even spend so much on current consumption that they fail to maintain or replace the country's capital stock of buildings and equipment. This is called *dis-saving*. In practice, most households will not spend all their income on consumption goods and services. They will also save a part. In economics, *saving* is defined as the act of abstaining from present consumption. These savings (S) constitute a leakage in the circular flow of money.

Hoarded money is obviously withdrawn from the circular flow—at least until it is stolen or inherited by someone else. However, it constitutes only a very small part of total savings. In fact, most households either invest their money savings themselves or lend them to those who wish to invest. Thus households may, for example, deposit their savings into an account with a bank or other financial institution. This money can then be loaned by the bank to business firms, other individuals, or governments. Also households may purchase stocks and bonds or make mortgage loans.

In economics, *investment* is defined as (a) the purchase of new machinery, equipment, and buildings, and (b) increases in business inventories of goods and materials. Machinery and equipment are called *capital goods*, or *producers' durable goods*. Buildings include both residential and non-residential structures. Investment, as defined in economics, is not the purchase of existing wealth; it is the replacement of, or addition to, the existing capital stock.

The total, or gross, investment (*I*) that takes place acts as an *injection*—that is, an increase in income that originates outside the circular flow. This injection tends to cause an increase in the size of the circular flow of income. However, if the amount invested is equal to the amount saved (see Figure 21:2), there will be no change in the size of the circular flow of income. Thus, if *I* and *S* are $20 billion each, the injection exactly offsets the leakage, and the circular flow of income remains at $100 billion. This assumes, of course, the absence of governments or other countries, which, as we shall soon see, also create leakages and injections. One very important injection for Canada, also shown in Figure 21:2 is the investment here of foreign capital.

Not all saving, we should note, is done by households. Business firms also save considerable sums. They receive, on the one hand, revenue from goods and services produced and sold. They pay, on the other hand, for materials and parts and for factor services used. The surplus of their revenue over expenditure is the profit or net income of the business. If it is not all spent, a reduction in the circular flow of money will occur—more money is flowing into the business sector than is flowing out.

But what actually happens? First of all, business firms reinvest a large part of their profit. Also, by including depreciation among expenses (although no money is currently paid out) there is additional saving and reinvestment. Thus, a large part of business saving is immediately used to purchase more capital goods or to increase inventories of materials, parts, and finished goods. If the savings are equal to the investment, the leakage is offset by the injection.

Another part of a business firm's net income may be accumulated in cash. However, the amount of cash in excess of a firm's immediate

Reinvested profit and depreciation allowances

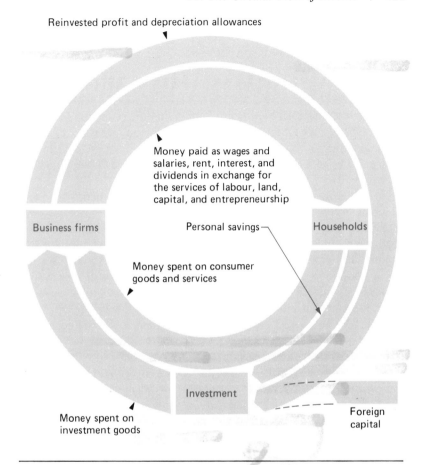

Figure 21:2 The Circular Flow, Showing the Relationship between Savings and Investment

working-capital needs will usually be loaned at interest to a bank. Consequently, the money saved is made available for investment by someone else.

Lastly, a portion of a business firm's profit may be paid to the owners, or shareholders, in the form of dividends. So long as these dividends are spent and not hoarded by their recipients, there will again be no reduction in the circular flow of income.

Of course, not all business firms make a profit. In many businesses, particularly new ones, expenditures exceed revenues. If a business firm makes a loss, how does this affect the circular flow? In order to pay out more than it takes in, a firm will either have to borrow money from someone else or reduce its assets. If it borrows from a bank, it is spending money that someone else has saved—so it is helping to maintain the circular flow.

What happens if households wish to save more than business firms wish to invest? The answer is that the level of income will fall. This decline in income will result from the fact that the reduction in spending by households is not being fully offset by the increase in investment spending by business firms. In other words, the leakage in the circular flow of income, caused by savings, exceeds the injection caused by investment.

Let us assume, first, that individuals, out of a total income of $100 billion, spend $80 billion on consumption goods and services (*C*), and save $20 billion (*S*). If business firms spend $20 billion on investment goods and services (*I*), the total spending (*C* + *I*) will still be $100 billion. This is because the savings leakage has been exactly offset by the investment injection. As a result, the circular flow of money and the level of national income remain unchanged in size.

But assume that business firms, because of an uncertain economic outlook, decide to reduce investment spending to $15 billion. This means that the savings leakage of $20 billion will now be greater than the investment injection of $15 billion. And this will cause the circular flow of income to contract. When this occurs we are said to be experiencing an *economic recession*. Conversely, if business firms decide to increase investment to $25 billion, (compared with household savings of $20 billion), the money flow and income level would increase. Then we are said to be experiencing an *economic boom*.

21.4: GOVERNMENTS AND THE CIRCULAR FLOW OF INCOME

Our next step in understanding Canada's basic economic structure is to consider how governments affect the circular flow of income. In Figures 21:1 and 21:2, our first simplified economic models, we deliberately left them out of account. Economic models enable us to simplify reality so that we can focus our attention on a particular problem or explain a particular relationship. But we must not forget our underlying assumptions. Now we abandon the assumption that there are no governments.

Many government-owned enterprises, such as Air Canada, operate almost exactly like private business firms. They make factor payments to households; and the households in turn spend money on the goods and services provided by these government-owned enterprises. Therefore, in understanding Canada's basic economic structure, we can logically include these government-owned enterprises with private business firms in the business firms sector of our circular-flow model.

The role played by the federal, provincial, and municipal governments themselves is somewhat more complex. Governments at all levels provide a wide variety of services to business firms and households. These services range from garbage collection to the maintenance of law and order. Government services also include a variety of payments such as regional-development grants to business firms and family allowances to households. These payments by governments are called, in economics, *transfer payments*. By taking money from business firms and individuals through taxes and giving it to other business firms and individuals through grants and subsidies, the government is in effect "transferring" income between different members of society. To a certain extent, of course, many of those who pay also receive. All these various government services and transfer payments are shown in Figure 21:3 as part of the circles linking governments to business firms and to households.

As well as providing services and making transfer payments, governments have another economic relationship with business firms and households. They purchase goods—for example, in ordering office supplies. They also purchase the services of various factors of production—for example, by payment of wages and salaries to government employees, rent on land, and interest on government bonds. This government expenditure (G) is also illustrated in Figure 21:3.

By levying various kind of taxes to help finance their expenditures (also shown in Figure 21:3), governments reduce the amount of money that individuals and business firms have to spend. Taxes (T), therefore, like savings, act as another leakage in the circular flow of money. However, governments do not usually hoard their tax revenues. They need the money, often very urgently, to meet all their expenditures. These government expenditures (G) represent an injection into the circular flow.

As far as the size of the circular flow of income is concerned, government taxation and spending must be considered in conjunction with the savings and investment of households and business firms. If the circular flow of income (defined so far as $C + I + G$) is to remain unchanged at, say $100 billion, then the total of leakages $(S + T)$ must be equal to the total of injections $(I + G)$. Thus, if consumption is $80 billion, both $(S + T)$ and $(I + G)$ must be $20 billion. However, S need not be equal to I, or I to G. In fact, a part of S (the amount by which it exceeds I) can go to finance a government deficit — the excess of G over T.

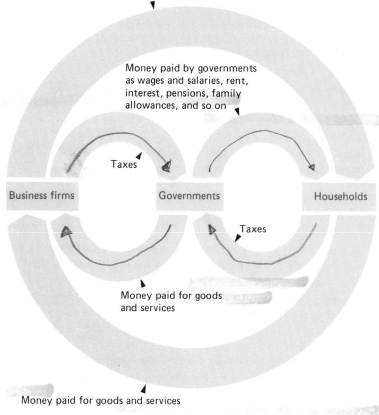

Money paid by business firms as wages and salaries, rent, interest, and dividends in exchange for the services of labour, land, capital, and entrepreneurship.

Money paid by governments as wages and salaries, rent, interest, pensions, family allowances, and so on

Taxes

Business firms

Governments

Households

Taxes

Money paid for goods and services

Money paid for goods and services

Figure 21:3   The Circular Flow, Showing the Position of Governments

21.5: OTHER COUNTRIES AND THE CIRCULAR FLOW OF INCOME

How do Canada's economic transactions with other countries affect the circular flow of money? First of all, Canadian households, business firms, and governments pay money to foreigners for goods and ser-

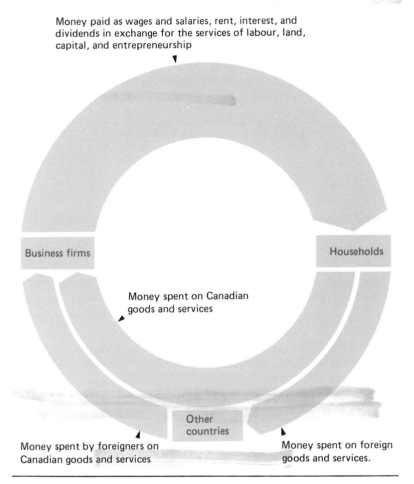

Money paid as wages and salaries, rent, interest, and
dividends in exchange for the services of labour, land,
capital, and entrepreneurship

Business firms

Households

Money spent on Canadian
goods and services

Other
countries

Money spent by foreigners on
Canadian goods and services

Money spent on foreign
goods and services.

Figure 21:4 The Circular Flow, Showing the Position of Other
Countries

vices provided by them, including the use of their capital and know-
how, and to finance Canadian foreign investment. These payments for
imports of goods and services and for money invested abroad (together
labelled *M*) represent a leakage in Canada's circular flow (see Figure
21:4). Second, business firms and governments receive money from
abroad in payment for Canadian exports and to finance foreign investment in Canada. These payments for exports, etc. (*X*) act as an injec-

tion in Canada's circular flow.

With regard to the size of the circular flow, we cannot view M and X in isolation from savings and investment, and from taxes and government expenditure. The circular flow will be in equilibrium (as we shall discuss in more detail in Chapter 24) only when the total of all the leakages is equal to the total of all the injections. In other words, equilibrium is attained only when $(S + T + M) = (I + G + X)$.

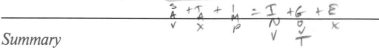

Summary

1. A circular-flow model is an economic model that demonstrates, by use of the expenditure-income relationship, how the various sectors of the economy—business firms, households, governments, and foreign trade and investment—operate in relation to each other.

2. The first version of the circular-flow model includes only business firms and households. Money paid as income to households in exchange for services of the factors of production is in turn spent by households on goods and services produced by business firms. Thus there is a circular flow of money from business firms to households and back again to business firms.

3. All the various inter-industry flows of goods and services can be summarized in the form of an input-output table that can be used for economic forecasting.

4. Saving is defined as the act of abstaining from consumption. These savings (S) constitute a leakage in the circular flow of money.

5. Investment is (a) the purchase of new machinery, equipment, and buildings and (b) increases in business inventories of goods and materials. This investment (I) acts as an injection in the circular flow of money.

6. If savings is the only leakage and investment the only injection, then savings and investment must remain equal if the size of the circular flow of the money is to remain unchanged. If savings exceed investment, the level of income will fall. If investment exceeds savings, the level of income will rise.

7. Government taxes (T) represent an additional leakage and government expenditure (G) an additional injection.

8. Imports and investment abroad (M) constitute another leakage and exports and investment from abroad (X) another injection.

9. The circular flow is in equilibrium when $(S + T + M) = (I + G + X)$.

Key Terms

Review Questions

1. What does a circular-flow model help to illustrate?
2. What is the basic relationship in our society between business firms and households?
3. Distinguish between money income and real income in terms of the circular flow.
4. What are the two basic types of payments made by business firms?
5. What is meant by "value added" in production?
6. Distinguish between saving and dis-saving. What is meant by business saving?
7. How do savings and investment affect the circular flow of money?
8. How do governments affect the circular flow of money?
9. How do transactions with other countries affect the circular flow of money?
10. What conditions must exist if the circular flow of money is to be in equilibrium?

Reference

1. Wassily Leontief, *The Structure of the American Economy, 1919-1939*, Oxford University Press, New York, 1951. Also by the same author, *Input-Output Economics*, Oxford University Press, New York, 1966.

*"Polly, it looks like the GNP is down
again this year. ."*

22. THE NATIONAL ACCOUNTS

CHAPTER OBJECTIVES

A. To explain the nature and purpose of the "national accounts"
B. To discuss the concept of the Gross National Product, or GNP
C. To indicate how the GNP can be calculated, by either the expenditure approach or the income approach
D. To explain the concepts of GNE, NNI, Potential GNP, NNP, GDP, PI, PDI, and PNS
E. To indicate how national accounts figures can be meaningfully compared from year to year despite the effects of inflation.
F. To explain how GNP figures can be used to show a country's standard of living and to make international economic comparisons

CHAPTER OUTLINE:

22.1: NATURE AND ORIGIN OF THE NATIONAL ACCOUNTS

Anyone who wants to keep his or her personal finances in order will make a careful record of personal income and expenditures. Similarly, every business firm maintains a set of "books" so that the owners and managers can know how the business is performing. What does a country do if it wishes to keep a record of its economic activities? Very simply, it keeps a set of "national accounts."

These *national accounts* summarize the economic transactions that have taken place in the economy during the past year and during each quarter of it. They reveal a country's national output and income, and the importance, relative to each other, of the various sectors of the economy—households, business firms, government, and foreign trade—that we referred to in the previous chapter.

The first estimates of Canada's national income were made as early as 1919 and Statistics Canada and its predecessors have kept national accounts for Canada for every year from 1926 on. However, national accounting in its present form is relatively new. Canada, Britain, and the United States together first established the main essentials of the present system in 1944.

22.2: PURPOSE OF THE NATIONAL ACCOUNTS

Most governments, including that of Canada, find it worthwhile to keep national accounts. This is because the information provided is very useful in the study of such important economic problems as the growth of the economy; structural changes in the economy; the causes and effects of business cycles; and the role of the private and public sectors in the economy. The national accounts reveal, for example, a country's level of output and income; the amount of foreign trade; the flow of capital investment to and from abroad; the various sources of saving; the relative importance of different types of industries in the economy; how government, by taxes and transfer payments, affects the distribution of income; and the geographical distribution of income in Canada. The information provided by the national accounts has also been extremely useful to business firms and governments in their economic forecasting and policy making. Thus, business firms base their sales forecasts to a large extent on the expected level of economic activity in the country. Governments use the information to help draw up their budgets and to plan and evaluate the effects of other economic policy measures. The information provided by the national accounts is also useful for making international economic comparisons.

22.3: GNP AND ITS MEASUREMENT

In the national accounts, current output, perhaps the most important item of information, is call the *Gross National Product*, or GNP.

Two Approaches

Statistics Canada uses two different methods to calculate Canada's Gross National Product—the expenditure approach and the income approach, both of which provide the same answer, as illustrated in Figure 22:1.

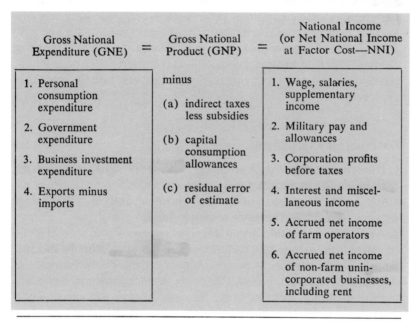

Gross National Expenditure (GNE)	=	Gross National Product (GNP)	=	National Income (or Net National Income at Factor Cost—NNI)
1. Personal consumption expenditure		minus		1. Wage, salaries, supplementary income
2. Government expenditure		(a) indirect taxes less subsidies		2. Military pay and allowances
3. Business investment expenditure		(b) capital consumption allowances		3. Corporation profits before taxes
4. Exports minus imports		(c) residual error of estimate		4. Interest and miscellaneous income
				5. Accrued net income of farm operators
				6. Accrued net income of non-farm unincorporated businesses, including rent

Figure 22:1 Two Methods of Measuring Gross National Product

22.4: GROSS NATIONAL EXPENDITURE

This is the total of all expenditures by the public, governments, business firms, and foreigners on final goods and services produced in Canada, and is equal to the Gross National Product. The GNE is broken down in the national accounts (See Table S.14) into spending on final goods and services by four major sectors: consumers, governments, business, and foreigners. It is summarized by the following formula:

$$GNE = C + G + I + (X - M)$$

where C = personal consumption expenditure; G = government expenditure; I = business investment expenditure; X = exports; and M = imports. The composition of each of these items is now briefly discussed.

Personal Consumption Expenditure

This is spending by the general public on such goods and services as food, clothing, shelter, and entertainment that will be consumed immediately or in a few years at the most. In the case of shelter, an estimated rent is included in personal expenditure if a house is occupied by the owner. Durable consumer goods such as cars, television sets, and kitchen appliances are also included in personal expenditure. The term *postponable consumer spending* is sometimes used to describe spending on these durable consumer goods. This is because, in time of economic recession, consumers postpone this type of expenditure for months or even years.

Government Expenditure

1. Government Current Expenditure. This is spending by the federal, provincial, and municipal governments on goods and services (for example, public employees, office space, printing, and cleaning) that are necessary for the performance of public duties.
2. Gross Fixed Capital Formation. This is government spending of a capital nature, such as expenditure on new highways, schools, and hospitals. Capital investment by government-owned enterprises such as Air Canada, Canadian National Railways, and the Canadian Broadcasting Corporation is included in the business category. No adjustment is made in the value of fixed capital formation for depreciation during the year of buildings and machinery. Hence the use of the term *gross*.
3. Value of Physical Change in Inventories. This is the amount by which government inventories of supplies and materials have changed over the year.

Business Investment Expenditure

1. Gross Fixed Capital Formation. This is business spending on (a) residential construction, (b) industrial and commercial construction, and (c) machinery and equipment.
2. Value of Physical Change in Inventories. This is the amount by which business inventories of materials and parts have increased or decreased over the course of the year. Many materials and parts pro-

Table S.14
Gross National Expenditure, in millions of dollars, 1950-1982

| Year | Personal expenditure on consumer goods and services | Government current expenditure on goods and services | Gross fixed capital formation | | | | Value of physical change in inventories | Exports of goods and services | Imports of goods and services | Residual error of estimate | Gross National expenditure at market prices |
			Total	Government	Business	Housing					
1950	12 482	1 928	3 862	521	2 388	953	549	4 158	-4 492	4	18 491
1955	18 388	4 036	6 422	948	3 689	1 785	285	5 749	-6 390	38	28 528
1960	25 479	5 281	8 473	1 560	5 119	1 794	409	7 004	-8 092	-195	38 359
1965	33 947	8 358	13 179	2 440	8 105	2 634	1 244	11 182	-12 341	-205	55 364
1966	36 890	9 748	15 361	2 841	9 915	2 605	1 225	13 045	-14 259	-182	61 828
1967	39 972	11 153	15 628	2 954	9 865	2 809	260	14 663	-15 234	-33	66 409
1968	43 704	12 684	15 754	2 983	9 518	3 253	745	16 719	-17 010	-10	72 586
1969	47 492	14 241	17 232	3 055	10 332	3 845	1 467	18 761	-19 821	443	79 815
1970	50 327	16 630	18 015	3 173	11 342	3 500	105	21 167	-20 214	-345	85 685
1971	55 616	18 368	20 800	3 754	12 230	4 816	392	22 181	-22 016	-891	94 450
1972	62 208	20 291	23 051	3 968	13 263	5 820	544	24 580	-25 250	-190	105 234
1973	71 278	23 037	27 848	4 305	16 156	7 387	1 588	30 718	-30 954	45	123 560
1974	83 388	27 816	34 260	5 462	20 022	8 776	3 451	38 992	-41 009	630	147 528
1975	96 995	33 380	40 044	6 323	24 489	9 232	-239	40 452	-45 589	300	165 343
1976	110 886	38 325	44 895	6 318	26 256	12 321	1 563	45 601	-49 973	-266	191 031
1977	122 530	43 374	48 193	6 790	28 597	12 806	374	52 548	-57 262	-889	208 868
1978	135 153	47 811	52 261	7 140	31 598	13 523	494	62 985	-67 970	-244	230 490
1979	150 521	52 301	60 654	7 397	39 113	14 144	-3 711	77 181	-82 807	15	261 576
1980	168 395	58 538	68 905	8 277	46 635	13 993	-1 754	90 944	-93 287	128	291 869
1981	191 025	66 749	80 802	9 524	55 131	16 147	653	99 468	-106 375	-984	331 338
1982	205 952	75 748	76 393	10 620	53 039	12 734	-8 692	100 395	-99 150	-1 721	348 925

Source: Statistics Canada, *National Income and Expenditure Accounts*

duced last year are used in production this year. So long as year-end inventories are the same, such materials and parts have been offset by an equal value of materials and parts produced this year. An increase in inventories means that more materials and parts have been produced than have been used and incorporated into this year's final goods. To get an accurate picture of this year's production, the net increase must be added to the value of the final goods and services produced. A decrease in inventories means that more materials and parts were used in production than were actually produced this year. This decrease must be subtracted from the total value of the final goods and services produced. Otherwise the GNE would be overstated by that amount.

The change in business inventories for which allowance must be made are actual physical changes. No adjustment is made for the fact that the replacement cost of the materials or parts may have increased or decreased.

The value of the physical change in business inventories is divided in the national accounts into two parts: (a) non-farm business inventories, and (b) farm inventories and grain in commercial channels.

Foreign Trade

1. Exports. This is spending by foreigners on goods and service produced in Canada. Although not purchased by Canadian residents, these goods and services nevertheless form part of the country's current output. Consequently, this amount must be included in the GNE.
2. Imports. This is spending by Canadian residents on goods and services produced by foreigners. It is, in fact, already included in the totals of Canadian consumer, government, and business spending. To determine the GNE, which is total spending by Canadians and foreigners on *Canadian* final goods and services, the value of imports must be subtracted from the total spending—for the obvious reason that such goods are produced outside Canada.

Double Counting

In calculating GNE, Statistics Canada tries to avoid double counting. This can arise if a good is the final product of one industry, but is also the raw or processed material, or part, sub-assembly or assembly of another. For example, a windshield is the final product of the firm that supplies it to a car manufacturer. The same windshield is also one of the many parts that the car manufacturer will assemble to produce the final product, the car. By including the final output of both the windshield manufacturer and the car manufacturer in the GNE, we would be double counting the windshield. That is why spending on all raw materials, processed materials, parts etc. is excluded.

However, any increase or decrease in business inventories of materials and parts at the end of the year is included in GNE. An increase, in this case, represents items produced but not incorporated into final goods during the year. A decrease represents the incorporation into final goods during the year of some of last year's materials and parts as well as those that were actually produced in the current year.

Some goods—fruit and vegetables grown and consumed on farms, for example—are included in the GNE by means of an estimated value. Others, notably the services of homemakers, are excluded.

Changes in Canada's GNE

How has Canada's GNE changed over the years? If we look at Table S.15, we can see that Canada's GNE (calculated in constant 1971 dollars) has greatly increased over the period 1950 to 1982, although the rate of increase has recently faltered.

What is the relative importance of the various types of expenditure? And how has it changed over the years? The answers to these questions are found in Table S.16. One of the most striking facts is that personal expenditure on consumer goods and services has declined in relative importance—even though it is still the major component. By contrast, government current spending has increased.

22.5: NATIONAL INCOME

The other method used to estimate Gross National Product is the income approach—which involves adding together all the incomes earned by the various factors of production.

Factor Incomes

The various incomes earned by "permanent residents" of Canada are grouped in the national accounts into six categories:

1. Wages, salaries and supplementary labour income before taxes. The supplementary labour income includes employer and employee contributions to social insurance and pension funds.

2. Military pay and allowances.

3. Corporation profits before taxes. This item includes only the profits of non-government business enterprises.

4. Interest and miscellaneous investment income. This item includes the profits (net of losses) of government business enterprises and other government investment income.

Table S.15
Gross National Expenditure, in millions of constant 1971 dollars, 1950-1982

| Years | Personal expenditure on consumer goods and services | Government current expenditure on goods and services | Gross fixed capital formation | | | | Value of physical change in inventories | Exports of goods and services | Imports of goods and services | Residual error of estimate | Gross National expenditure | Annual Rate of increase (%) |
			Total	Government	Business	Housing						
1950	20 394	5 367	7 042	884	4 385	1 773	789	5 956	-6 469	10	33 762	7.6
1955	26 456	8 736	9 678	1 308	5 594	2 776	410	7 442	-8 799	61	43 891	9.4
1960	33 392	9 218	11 790	2 142	7 017	2 631	523	8 717	-10 347	-271	53 231	2.9
1965	41 606	12 253	16 259	3 003	9 843	3 413	1 441	12 606	-14 140	-256	69 981	6.7
1970	51 526	17 650	18 904	3 329	11 857	3 718	84	21 223	-20 588	-341	88 390	2.5
1971	55 616	18 368	20 800	3 754	12 230	4 816	392	22 181	-22 016	-891	94 450	6.9
1972	59 841	18 930	21 955	3 772	12 751	5 432	515	23 655	-24 489	-159	100 248	6.1
1973	63 879	19 795	24 384	3 751	14 667	5 966	1 346	26 156	-27 824	76	107 812	7.5
1974	67 160	20 584	25 694	3 957	15 802	5 935	2 642	25 620	-30 538	516	111 678	3.6
1975	70 645	21 399	26 661	4 127	17 031	5 503	-252	23 993	-29 684	243	113 005	1.2
1976	75 251	21 689	27 397	3 860	16 973	6 564	988	26 225	-32 166	-135	119 249	5.5
1977	77 416	22 392	27 173	3 859	17 162	6 152	82	28 046	-32 844	-503	121 762	2.1
1978	79 539	22 797	27 166	3 769	17 355	6 042	244	30 958	-34 393	-120	126 191	3.6
1979	81 123	23 011	28 936	3 560	19 503	5 873	1 735	31 868	-36 857	34	129 850	2.9
1980	81 984	22 782	30 054	3 591	20 951	5 512	-775	32 447	-36 113	88	130 467	0.5
1981	83 535	22 988	31 777	3 670	22 286	5 821	687	32 979	-37 064	-362	134 540	3.1
1982	81 485	23 145	27 927	3 748	19 724	4 455	-3 170	32 493	-33 219	-604	128 057	-4.8

Source: Statistics Canada, *National Income and Expenditure Accounts*

Table S.16
Structural Changes in Demand, 1950-1982 (Percentage Distribution of Gross National Expenditure by Components)

Years	Personal expenditure on consumer goods and services	Government current expenditure on good and services	Gross fixed capital formation				Value of physical change in inventories	Exports of goods and services	Imports of goods and services	Residual error of estimate
			Total	Government	Business	Housing				
1950	67.5	10.4	20.9	2.8	12.9	5.2	3.0	22.5	-24.3	0.0
1955	64.5	14.1	22.5	3.3	12.9	6.3	1.0	20.2	-22.4	0.1
1960	66.4	13.8	22.1	4.1	13.3	4.7	1.1	18.3	-21.1	-0.5
1965	61.3	15.1	23.8	4.4	14.6	4.8	2.2	20.2	-22.3	-0.4
1970	58.7	19.4	21.0	3.7	13.2	4.1	0.1	24.7	-23.6	-0.4
1971	58.9	19.4	22.0	4.0	12.9	5.1	0.4	23.5	-23.3	-0.9
1972	59.1	19.3	21.9	3.8	12.6	5.5	0.5	23.4	-24.0	-0.2
1973	57.7	18.6	22.5	3.5	13.1	6.0	1.3	24.9	-25.1	0.0
1974	56.5	18.9	23.2	3.7	13.6	5.9	2.3	26.4	-27.8	0.4
1975	58.7	20.2	24.2	3.8	14.8	5.6	-0.1	24.5	-27.6	0.2
1976	58.0	20.1	23.5	3.3	13.7	6.4	0.8	23.9	-26.2	-0.1
1977	58.6	20.8	23.1	3.3	13.7	6.1	0.2	25.2	-27.4	-0.4
1978	58.7	20.7	22.7	3.1	13.7	5.9	0.2	27.3	-29.5	-0.1
1979	57.5	20.0	23.2	2.8	14.9	5.4	1.4	29.5	-31.7	0.0
1980	57.7	20.1	23.6	2.8	16.0	4.8	-0.6	31.2	-32.0	-0.0
1981	57.6	20.1	24.4	2.9	16.6	4.9	0.2	30.0	-32.1	-0.3
1982	59.0	21.7	21.9	3.0	15.2	3.7	-2.5	28.8	-28.4	-0.5

Source: Statistics Canada, National Income and Expenditure Accounts

5. Accrued net income of farm operators from farm production. This net income includes changes in the value of farm inventories.

6. Accrued net income of non-farm unincorporated business, including rent. This is a separate category because of the difficulty, in practice, of dividing the net income of sole proprietors and partners into salaries, rent, interest, and profit. It includes the net income of independent professional practitioners. It also includes all net rental income, regardless of who receives it.

These six categories are called *factor incomes*, for they represent income earned by the various factors of production—labour, land, and capital. They include, it should be noted, only payment made in exchange for production services. In other words, transfer payments such as family allowances and old-age pensions made for social security reasons are excluded. The sum of the incomes of permanent residents of Canada is called the *National Income*, or more precisely the *Net National Income at factor cost*, or *NNI*.

National Income is said to be at factor cost because it excludes indirect taxes but includes subsidies. Indirect taxes include excise taxes and duties, customs duties, sales taxes, property taxes, licences, and any other indirect tax that helps to raise the market price of a good above the level that it would otherwise be. Subsidies include payments to various type of farmers and are added to the market price to represent the true factor cost.

National Income is considered to be "net" because capital consumption allowances have been deducted in calculating business net income. Such allowances, we should remember, are included in the GNP. They represent an estimate of how much the country's capital stock has depreciated over the course of the year.

Gross National Product exceeds, therefore, Net National Income at factor cost by (a) the amount of indirect taxes less subsidies, (b) the amount of capital consumption allowances, and (c) the residual error of estimate.

The growth and composition of Canada's National Income over the years 1950 to 1982 are shown in Table S.17.

Structural Changes

Has there been any significant change in the distribution of Canada's National Income over the years? Is labour receiving more or less of the National Income than it was ten or twenty years ago? Are business corporations now taking a larger share of the National Income? What is the income position of farmers and small businesses in Canada? The answers to these questions are to be found in Table S.18, which shows

Table S.17
National Income and Gross National Product, in millions of dollars, 1950-1982

Year	Wages salaries and supplementary labour income (1)	Corporation profits before taxes	Dividends paid to non-residents	Interest and miscellaneous investment income	Accrued net income of farm operators from farm production	Net income of non-farm unincorporated business including rents	Inventory valuation adjustment	Net National Income at factor cost	Indirect taxes less subsidies	Capital consumption allowances and Miscellaneous valuation adjustments	Residual error of estimate	Gross National Product at market prices
1950	9 152	2 608	-412	396	1 301	1 882	-374	14 553	2 065	1 876	-3	18 491
1955	14 369	3 485	-396	764	1 120	2 748	-182	21 908	3 321	3 337	-38	28 528
1960	20 141	3 870	-495	1 129	1 026	3 192	-26	28 837	4 587	4 739	196	38 359
1965	28 878	6 318	-828	1 891	1 389	3 893	-322	41 219	7 284	6 655	206	55 364
1970	47 620	7 699	-952	3 428	1 211	5 424	-195	64 235	11 299	9 806	345	85 685
1971	52 436	8 681	-1 079	3 906	1 576	5 928	-665	70 783	12 276	10 500	891	94 450
1972	58 549	10 799	-1 031	4 577	1 662	6 170	-1 032	79 694	13 876	11 474	190	105 234
1973	67 849	15 417	-1 277	5 359	3 009	6 656	-2 362	94 651	15 598	13 355	-44	123 560
1974	81 289	20 062	-1 645	7 632	3 859	6 901	-4 244	113 854	18 257	16 046	-629	147 528
1975	94 625	19 663	-1 835	8 661	3 944	7 669	-2 938	129 789	17 584	18 270	-300	165 343
1976	109 375	19 985	-1 719	11 175	3 317	8 438	-2 064	148 507	21 520	20 738	266	191 031
1977	120 523	20 928	-2 094	13 147	2 831	9 113	-3 419	161 029	23 907	23 043	889	208 868
1978	131 380	25 668	-2 843	15 923	3 616	9 853	-4 653	178 944	25 563	25 739	244	230 490
1979	146 761	33 941	-3 064	19 101	3 909	10 685	-7 114	204 219	27 815	29 557	-15	261 576
1980	165 455	36 456	-3 117	22 164	4 005	11 669	-7 096	229 536	29 012	33 448	-127	291 869
1981	188 497	32 638	-3 740	26 951	4 473	13 290	-7 002	255 107	37 627	37 620	984	331 338
1982	201 736	21 777	-3 356	29 704	4 646	14 031	-3 784	264 754	40 588	41 862	1 721	348 925

Source: Statistics Canada, *National Income and Expenditure Accounts*

Note: (1) Includes military pay and allowances.

Table S.18
Structural Changes in Income, 1950-82 (Percentage Distribution of Gross National Product by Components)

Years	Wages salaries and supplementary labour income (1)	Corporation profits before taxes	Dividends paid to non-residents	Interest and miscellaneous investment income	Accrued net income of farm operators from farm production	Net income of non-farm unincorporated business including rents	Inventory valuation adjustment	Net national income at factor cost	Indirect taxes less subsidies	Capital consumption allowances and miscellaneous valuation adjustments	Residual error of estimate
1950	49.5	14.1	-2.2	2.1	7.0	10.2	-2.0	78.7	11.2	10.1	0.0
1955	50.4	12.2	-1.4	2.7	3.9	9.6	-0.6	76.8	11.6	11.7	-0.1
1960	52.5	10.1	-1.3	2.9	2.7	8.3	-0.1	75.2	12.0	12.4	0.5
1965	52.2	11.4	-1.5	3.4	2.5	7.0	-0.6	74.5	13.2	12.0	0.4
1970	55.6	9.0	-1.1	4.0	1.4	6.3	-0.2	75.0	13.2	11.4	0.4
1971	55.5	9.2	-1.1	4.1	1.7	6.3	-0.7	74.9	13.0	11.1	0.9
1972	55.6	10.3	-1.0	4.3	1.6	5.9	-1.0	75.7	13.2	10.9	0.2
1973	54.9	12.5	-1.0	4.3	2.4	5.4	-1.9	76.6	12.6	10.8	0.0
1974	55.1	13.6	-1.1	5.2	2.6	4.7	-2.9	77.2	12.4	10.9	-0.4
1975	57.2	11.9	-1.1	5.2	2.4	4.6	-1.8	78.5	10.6	11.0	-0.2
1976	57.3	10.5	-0.9	5.8	1.7	4.4	-1.1	77.7	11.3	10.9	0.1
1977	57.7	10.0	-1.0	6.3	1.4	4.4	-1.6	77.1	11.4	11.0	0.4
1978	57.0	11.1	-1.2	6.9	1.6	4.3	-2.0	77.6	11.1	11.2	0.1
1979	56.1	13.0	-1.2	7.3	1.5	4.1	-2.7	78.1	10.6	11.3	0.0
1980	56.7	12.5	-1.1	7.6	1.4	4.0	-2.4	78.0	9.9	11.5	0.0
1981	56.9	9.9	-1.1	8.1	1.4	4.0	-2.1	77.0	11.4	11.4	0.3
1982	57.8	6.2	-1.0	8.5	1.3	4.0	-1.1	75.9	11.6	12.0	0.5

Source: Statistics Canada, *National Income and Expenditure Accounts*
Note: (1) Includes military pay and allowances

the percentage distribution of the income components of Canada's GNP over the years 1950 to 1982.

22.6: ACTUAL VERSUS POTENTIAL GNP

Gross National Product, calculated in the two ways just described, attempts to measure the *actual* volume of goods and services produced in a country. However, it is also extremely useful for governments to have an estimate of the *potential* GNP—or, in other words, what *could be* produced if all the factors of production were reasonably fully employed. With this information, government economic policies can be designed to help ensure the fullest use of the country's productive resources with a minimum of inflationary pressure. The potential GNP also enables governments and other interested persons to have an estimate of what could have been produced in the past if government economic policies had been more suitable or effective.

22.7: NET NATIONAL PRODUCT

The term *gross* in Gross National Product indicates that the GNP includes, in addition to all consumer goods and services, all capital goods—buildings, machinery, and equipment—produced. No adjustment is made for the capital goods used to replace others that have worn out or become obsolete. This, clearly, is like estimating Canada's annual population growth by including births and immigration but omitting deaths and emigration. Theoretically, it would be more accurate to deduct, from the amount of capital goods produced, the amount of capital goods that wears out each year. A rough indication of this wear and tear is provided by the capital consumption allowances or depreciation that each business firm is permitted to add to expenses each year for income-tax purposes. Where these allowances are deducted from the GNP, the resultant amount is called the *Net National Product*, or *NNP*. In practice, it is extremely difficult to make any reasonable estimate of capital attrition. Consequently, most countries, including Canada, commonly use GNP as the measure of their economy's annual performance.

22.8: GROSS DOMESTIC PRODUCT

In addition to the GNP, it is useful to have a measurement of goods and services produced solely in Canada. This measurement is called the *Gross Domestic Product*, or GDP. In calculating the GDP, we include the output of foreign-owned factors of production located in this country. However, we exclude the output of factors of production located abroad, even though they are owned by permanent residents of Canada.

22.9: OTHER MEASUREMENTS OF INCOME AND THEIR USES

The NNI at factor cost, explained previously, can be used not only as a means of calculating the GNP, but also as a source of information about personal spending and saving.

Personal Income

Net National Income includes only the money received by the factors of production in exchange for their services. Governments, however, take money from the public and from business by taxes and compulsory contributions, then give some of it back in the form of family allowances, pensions, bond interest, and subsidies. These payments by the government, which are not in exchange for services rendered, are called *transfer payments* and represent a transfer of income from some people to others.

By adding to the Net National Income the various transfer payments mentioned and deducting from it corporate income taxes paid and undistributed corporation profits after tax, we obtain *Personal Income*, or *PI*. This is the amount of money that persons in Canada actually receive in a year.

The Personal Income section of the national accounts is studied by the government when it is considering changes in taxation. This is because the account shows the amount of income the public has, and the way in which it is distributed. It can help the government to decide what are the most effective ways of raising more money with the minimum adverse political repercussions.

Personal Disposable Income

Personal Income is a person's income before taxes; *Personal Disposable Income*, or *PDI*, is the amount that remains after direct taxes (mainly income tax) are deducted. Personal Disposable Income is an important indicator of the spending power of the public and therefore the public's potential demand for goods and services. Thus, if the PDI has risen over a period of time, it is likely that more money will be spent on consumer products and, as a result, on capital investment. Of course, the cost and availability of credit will also influence actual spending by the public. So also will the public's economic expectations.

The relationship between GNP, NNI, PI, and PDI, is illustrated in Table 22:1.

Table 22:1

Relationship of GNP, NNI, PI, and PDI

Gross National Product (GNP)			
Consumer goods and services	+ Government goods and services	+ Capital goods	+ Export minus imports

minus: Indirect taxes less subsidies
       Capital consumption allowances
       Residual error of estimate
equals: Net National Income (NNI)

Wages and salaries	+ Profits	+ Rent	+ Interest

minus: Undistributed corporation profits
       Corporation profit taxes
       Social insurance and government pension
       contributions
plus: Transfer payments (including interest on the
      public debt)
equals: Personal Income (PI)

Wages and salaries after deductions	+ Distributed profits	+ Rent + Interest +	Transfer payments

minus: Personal income taxes
equals: Personal Disposable Income (PDI)

Personal expenditure on consumer goods and services	+	Personal net saving	

Personal Net Savings

Usually the public will save some part of its disposable income, rather than spend it all. Only in a situation of runaway inflation would all disposable income be immediately spent. In normal times, the amount actually saved can be determined by subtracting the total amount spent on consumer goods and services from the total disposable income. The balance, called *Personal Net Savings*, or *PNS*, is an important item of information for the government in its measures to promote greater employment and prosperity in the country. One important reason for this is that any attempt by government to increase its own spending so as to increase the demand for goods and service may be offset by a reduction in the public's savings. In fact, in time of economic recession, the public usually increases its rate of savings which is just what the government does not want.

The ratio of Personal Savings to Personal Disposable Income as well as other information about personal income and expenditure in Canada in the period 1950 to 1982 is shown in Table S.19.

22.10: MEASURING OUTPUT OVER TIME

Real versus Money Terms

All the many different goods and services produced by a country constitute its *real* national output. However, we do not know how desirable these different products are to society, nor can we add, for example, kilograms of potatoes and tonnes of cement. The use of money, fortunately, solves both these problems. The market price of a product reflects what society thinks a unit of that product is worth. To obtain the total value of each type of good or service, we need only multiply this market price by the quantity produced. The use of the dollar as a common denominator enables us to add together the total values of all the different goods and services produced to obtain the national output.

Adjusting for Price Changes

The use of money does, however, cause one serious problem. If the dollar gradually loses its real worth, then an increase in the dollar value of national output may not signify a corresponding increase in the quantity of goods and services produced. For example, out of a total annual increase in the value of national output of 8 per cent, perhaps two-thirds can be attributed to real growth and one-third to an increase in the price level. To overcome this problem and facilitate comparisons between different years, Statistics Canada issues certain national accounts figures calculated in *constant dollars*. To do this, it uses a price index—the percentage relationship between prices in a chosen year and those in each successive year. Such a price index indicates how much prices have generally risen each year. Statistics Canada chooses a year as its base year, then "deflates" each year's current dollar amounts by the base year figure. The final result is that each year's output is expressed in *constant dollars*—that is to say, base-year dollars. Differences between dollar amounts in various years are then purely real ones. The price changes in dollars have, by the application of this technique, been eliminated.

Table S.19
Personal Income and Expenditure, 1950-1982

Years	Personal Income	Personal disposable income	Personal expenditure	Personal saving	Ratio of PS to PDI (%)	PDI per capita	PE per capita
		(Millions of dollars)				(Dollars)	
1950	14 262	13 285	12 482	738	5.6	969	910
1955	21 265	19 331	18 388	797	4.1	1 231	1 171
1960	29 595	26 567	25 479	867	3.3	1 487	1 426
1965	41 071	36 263	33 947	2 001	5.5	1 846	1 728
1970	66 633	54 009	50 327	2 872	5.3	2 536	2 363
1971	74 092	59 943	55 616	3 509	5.9	2 779	2 579
1972	83 767	68 100	62 208	5 015	7.4	3 124	2 853
1973	97 832	79 719	71 278	7 230	9.0	3 617	3 234
1974	116 867	94 545	83 388	9 406	9.9	4 228	3 729
1975	136 205	110 996	96 995	12 139	10.9	4 890	4 273
1976	155 343	125 510	110 886	12 560	10.0	5 459	4 823
1977	171 303	138 094	122 530	13 367	9.7	5 930	5 262
1978	190 403	154 975	135 153	17 172	11.1	6 585	5 743
1979	212 867	173 810	150 521	19 378	11.1	7 313	6 333
1980	239 891	195 338	168 395	21 889	11.2	8 120	7 000
1981	280 413	225 989	191 025	28 114	12.4	9 284	7 848
1982	307 750	247 074	205 952	33 850	13.7	10 042	8 371

Source: Statistics Canada, National Income and Expenditure Accounts

22.11: GNP AND ECONOMIC WELFARE

One important use of GNP statistics is as a measure of a country's economic welfare, or standard of living. However, an increase in Canada's GNP alone does not necessarily mean an increase in the economic welfare of Canadians. This is because population growth may have reduced each person's share of the GNP. Therefore, Canada's GNP is divided by the number of persons living in this country to arrive at *per capita GNP*, the average output per person. In this way, the effect of population growth on the standard of living in a country is taken into account. Also, we should remember that many goods and services sold or traded privately (the "underground economy") do not enter the GNP statistics; nor do such products as vegetables and livestock grown at home or fish caught non-commercially in lakes, rivers or seas.

22.12: INTERNATIONAL ECONOMIC COMPARISONS

In 1947, uniform international standards were proposed by the United Nations and adopted by most countries. In 1968, a major revision of the Canadian national accounts was undertaken in order to bring the definitions and structural presentation closer to the United Nations' System of National Accounts. Consequently, the information provided by Canada's national accounts is now more easily and accurately compared with that of other countries.

Summary

1. National accounts summarize the economic transactions that take place during a quarter or year among the various sectors (households, business firms, governments, and other countries) in an economy and reveal a country's national output and income. Such accounts have been kept in Canada since 1926.
2. The information provided by the national accounts serves a variety of useful purposes—for example, it helps guide government and business policy decisions.
3. The item that is used in the national accounts to measure current output is called the Gross National Product, or GNP.
4. GNP can be calculated by the expenditure approach or the income approach.
5. Gross National Expenditure, or GNE, is the total of all the expenditures by the public, government, business, and foreigners, on

final goods and services produced in Canada. It is equal to GNP.
GNE $= C + G + I + (X - M)$.

6. Net National Income at factor cost, or NNI, is the sum of the incomes of permanent residents of Canada.
7. Potential GNP is an estimate of what could be produced in a country if all the factors of production were fully employed. Actual GNP is what is actually produced.
8. Net National Product, or NNP, equals GNP minus capital consumption allowances.
9. Gross Domestic Product, or GDP, is the total value of the goods and services produced *within* the country—whether by Canadian or foreign-owned factors of production.
10. NNI plus transfer payments minus corporate income taxes and undistributed corporation profits equals Personal Income, or PI.
11. Personal Income minus direct taxes (mainly income tax) equals Personal Disposable Income, or PDI.
12. Personal Disposable Income minus personal expenditure equals Personal Net Saving, or PNS.
13. In order to show the real growth in national output, the national accounts are calculated in constant as well as current dollars.
14. Economic welfare, or the standard of living, is indicated by per capita GNP—obtained by dividing the GNP by the population.
15. Uniform national accounts standards now permit international comparisons.

Key Terms

Review Questions

1. What are the national accounts?
2. What is their purpose?
3. How did they originate?
4. What is meant by the Gross National Product?
5. What are the two basic methods of calculating GNP?
6. What is Gross National Expenditure? Explain the formula GNE = C + G + I + (X − M).
7. What is included under the heading "Gross Fixed Capital Formation"?
8. What is the significance for GNE of a decrease in year-end inventories of materials and parts?
9. How is GNE affected by exports and imports?
10. Why is spending on raw materials, processed materials, and parts excluded from the calculation of GNE?
11. Why do we include in the GNP any increase or decrease at the end of the year in business inventories of materials and parts?
12. Why are some goods given an imputed value for GNE purposes? Give examples.
13. What are the most significant changes in Canada's GNE in recent years?
14. The National Income includes six basic types of factor income. What are they?
15. Why is National Income said to be at factor cost? Why is it considered to be "net"?
16. How does GNP differ in amount from Net National Income?
17. What structural changes have taken place in Canada's National Income over the years?
18. What is potential GNP? What purpose does this concept serve?
19. Distinguish between actual and potential GNP.
20. What is the significance of the term "gross" in "Gross National Product"?
21. Distinguish between GNP and NNP.
22. Distinguish between GNP and GDP. Under what circumstances would they differ greatly in amount?
23. How is Personal Income calculated? What is the usefulness of this national accounting concept?
24. Distinguish between Personal Income and Personal Disposable Income.
25. What is Personal Net Saving? What is its economic significance?
26. Why is national output measured in monetary rather than real terms?

27. What serious problem is created by the measurement of national output in monetary terms? How is this problem overcome?
28. How is GNP used to measure economic welfare?
29. Examine the National Accounts, then answer the following questions:
    (a) How has Canada's GNE increased since 1960? How much of this is the result of inflation?
    (b) What percentage of total spending is by the public? How has this changed over the years?
    (c) How important is government in total spending? How do you account for any changes?
    (d) What has been the rate of growth in GNE? Why has the rate varied so much?
    (e) How important is business in total spending?
    (f) Why are exports added to GNE and imports subtracted?
    (g) Who gets the largest share of Canada's National Income?
    (h) What significant changes, if any, have taken place in the distribution of Canada's GNP over the last twenty years?
    (i) What has happened to business profits?
30. Why has the ratio of personal savings to personal disposable income increased? What significance, if any, does this have for government economic policy?
31. If Canada's GNP is $160 billion and its population 25 million, what is the average GNP per person?
32. If Canada's GNP in *constant dollars* is increasing by 4 per cent a year, and its population is increasing by 6 per cent a year, what would be happening to the average standard of living? Answer, with a numerical example.
33. Suppose the GNP in current dollars is increasing by 7 per cent a year and the general price level is rising by 10 per cent a year. What is happening to the country's output of goods and services?
34. In one year, a country's GNP rose by 7 per cent and its real GNP per capita increased by 5 per cent. In the following year, the GNP also rose by 7 per cent, but the real GNP per capita increased by only 1 per cent. The next year GNP increased by 5 per cent and real GNP per capita fell by 2 per cent. What happened?
35. How does Canada's GNP compare with that of other countries?
36. One way of calculating GNP is by adding together the values added in production plus the services of government. What contribution would the following hypothetical transaction make to GNP?
    (a) A farmer grows 40 m³ of wheat and sells them to a flour mill for $80.00/m³.

(b) The flour mill grinds the wheat and sells it to several bakeries for $45000.

(c) The bakers use the flour to make 100000 loaves which they sell to retailers for 55 cents each.

(d) The retailers sell the loaves to the public for 75 cents each.

(e) The government requires the retailers to collect a sales tax of 5 cents on each loaf.

23. UNEMPLOYMENT AND ITS CAUSES

CHAPTER OBJECTIVES

A. To explain how Statistics Canada defines the unemployed and the rate of unemployment in Canada
B. To review Canada's unemployment record and the age, sex, and geographical characteristics of Canada's unemployed
C. To examine the many different types of unemployment in Canada and their causes
D. To outline the government's various job creation programs
E. To examine government work-sharing initiatives

CHAPTER OUTLINE

One of the biggest economic headaches that afflicts modern industrial societies is the very high level of unemployment. It is now a seemingly impossible task to find jobs for all the persons who are able and willing to work. In fact, it is now considered a great achievement if the number of unemployed persons is no greater than 5 or even 10 per cent of the total civilian labour force. And the unemployment rate is much greater than this among young people, particularly males.

23.1: UNEMPLOYMENT DEFINED

The *unemployed* are defined by Statistics Canada as all persons fifteen years of age and over who: (a) were without work and seeking work or (b) were temporarily laid off for the full week during which StatsCan conducted its survey of 56 000 representative households across Canada.

The first category comprises persons who did no work during the survey week and were looking for work, or would have looked for work except that they were temporarily ill, were on indefinite or prolonged layoff, or believed no suitable work was available in the community. The second category comprises persons who were temporarily laid off for the full week—that is, were waiting to be called back to a job from which they had been laid off for less than thirty days.

The *unemployment rate* is the number of persons unemployed expressed as a percentage of the total labour force—that is, of the total of employed and unemployed persons.

Some persons are formally excluded from the StatsCan calculation of the unemployed. They are: member of the armed forces, persons in jail, residents of the Yukon and Northwest Territories, inmates of institutions, and Indians living on reserves.

The Hidden Unemployed

There are also many other persons who, although not unemployed according to the StatsCan definition, are in fact unemployed or underemployed. These "hidden unemployed" consist of persons who, for one reason or another, did not look for work in the week in which the StatsCan survey was made and persons who have managed to find part-time work but who really want full-time work. According to the StatsCan definition, a person is officially employed even if he or she worked only one hour per week. According to one estimate, the hidden unemployed in Canada total almost a million persons, meaning that the true unemployment rate might be 70% higher than that officially announced.

*"According to the newspaper, you're one
of the 'hidden unemployed'!"*

23.2: CANADA'S UNEMPLOYMENT RECORD

Since 1926, Canada's unemployment rate (see Table S.20) has varied from a high of 20.0 per cent in 1933 to a low of 1.6 per cent in 1945. In absolute terms, unemployment was as high as 851 000 persons in 1933 (a year of world-wide economic depression), as low as 70 000 persons in 1945 (the last year of World War II), and up to a new high of over one million persons in recent years. *Full employment* of labour has for many years been defined in Western industrial societies as a situation in which there is 3 per cent or less of the civilian labour force unemployed. Canada last achieved this situation in 1953. More recently, however, Canada's Finance and Employment Ministers have suggested that 7 to 8 per cent be considered the norm.

In term of age groups, the unemployment rate (see Table S.21) is well above average for persons 15 to 24 years of age. However, the unemployment rate is slightly lower for females, compared with males.

Geographically, the unemployment rate (see Table S.22) is highest in the Atlantic region of Canada and lowest in the Prairie region. Also, unemployment is higher in Quebec than in Ontario. Internationally, Canada's unemployment rate has been higher than that of many other industrialized countries. Among the non-communist countries, Japan, West Germany, and Norway have had the lowest rate of unemployment in recent years. Both Canada and the U.S. experienced high rates of unemployment in the early 1980s because of economic recession, with the rate being somewhat lower in the U.S.

The problem of finding enough jobs for everyone has been made more difficult in recent decades by a change in the female participation rate. The *participation rate* is the number of persons actively seeking work out of the eligible population, expressed as a percentage. Over the years, the participation rate for males has remained reasonably steady, at just below 80 per cent. However, for females, it has climbed dramatically from about 35 per cent in 1965 to over 50 per cent in recent years as economic pressures and career interests attract more women into the work force. It has been estimated that, if the labour force participation rate of the 1960s still prevailed in Canada, the current unemployment rate would be reduced to about half. This fact should not, of course, be interpreted to mean that women are to blame for Canada's unemployment woes. It can equally be argued that if more men stayed home, or joined the armed forces, the jobless rate would be lower.

Table S.20
Unemployment in Canada, thousands of persons, 1926-1982

Year	Employed	Unemployed	Rate (%)
1926	3 578	107	3.0
1927	3 684	106	2.9
1928	3 794	89	2.3
1929	3 909	93	2.4
1930	4 009	285	7.1
1931	4 110	532	12.9
1932	4 182	777	18.6
1933	4 246	851	20.0
1934	4 312	740	17.2
1935	4 372	736	16.8
1936	4 432	729	16.4
1937	4 490	627	14.0
1938	4 549	696	15.3
1939	4 592	680	14.8
1940	4 537	539	11.9
1941	4 423	156	3.5
1945	4 478	70	1.6
1946	4 829	163	3.4
1947	4 942	110	2.2
1948	4 988	114	2.3
1949	5 055	141	2.8
1950	5 163	186	3.6
1951	5 223	126	2.4
1952	5 324	155	2.9
1953	5 397	162	3.0
1954	5 493	250	4.6
1955	5 610	245	4.4
1956	5 782	197	3.4
1957	6 003	278	4.6
1958	6 127	432	7.1
1959	6 228	373	6.0
1960	6 403	448	7.0
1961	6 521	466	7.1
1962	6 615	390	5.9
1963	6 748	374	5.5
1964	6 933	324	4.7
1965	7 142	280	3.9
1966	7 242	251	3.4
1967	7 451	296	3.8
1968	7 593	358	4.4
1969	7 832	362	4.4
1970	7 919	476	5.7

Continued on page 456

Table S.20 Continued from page 455
Unemployment in Canada, thousands of persons, 1926-1982

Year	Employed	Unemployed	Rate %
1971	8 104	535	6.2
1972	8 345	553	6.2
1973	8 761	515	5.5
1974	9 125	514	5.3
1975	9 284	690	6.9
1976	9 479	727	7.1
1977	9 648	850	8.1
1978	9 972	911	8.4
1979	10 369	838	7.5
1980	10 655	867	7.5
1981	10 933	897	7.6
1982	11 864	1 305	11.0

Source: Statistics Canada, *The Labour Force*

Note: In January 1976, a revised Labour Force Survey replaced the previous one. Revised data have been estimated by Statistics Canada back to 1966.

Table S.21
Percentage Unemployment Rates, by Sex and Age Groups, 1966-1982

Years	Male Total	15-24	25 +	Female Total	15-24	25 +	Total
1966	3.3	6.3	2.6	3.4	4.8	2.7	3.4
1967	3.9	7.2	3.0	3.7	5.5	2.8	3.8
1968	4.6	8.7	3.5	4.4	6.5	3.7	4.4
1969	4.3	8.3	3.2	4.7	6.5	3.7	4.4
1970	5.6	11.2	4.1	5.8	8.5	4.4	5.7
1971	6.0	12.1	4.3	6.6	9.8	5.0	6.2
1972	5.8	11.9	4.1	7.0	9.5	5.7	6.2
1973	4.9	10.1	3.4	6.7	9.2	5.4	5.5
1974	4.8	9.7	3.3	6.4	8.9	5.1	5.3
1975	6.2	12.6	4.3	8.1	11.4	6.5	6.9
1976	6.4	13.3	4.2	8.4	12.1	6.6	7.1
1977	7.3	15.0	4.9	9.4	13.8	7.4	8.1
1978	7.6	15.2	5.2	9.6	13.9	7.7	8.4
1979	6.7	13.4	4.6	8.8	12.7	7.0	7.5
1980	6.9	13.8	4.8	8.4	12.7	6.5	7.5
1981	7.1	14.2	4.9	8.3	12.3	6.7	7.6
1982	11.1	21.1	8.1	10.8	16.1	8.8	11.0

Source: Statistics Canada, *The Labour Force* and *Historical Labour Force Statistics*

Table S.22
Unemployment, Canada and by Region, thousands of persons,
1966-1982

Years	Canada	Atlantic region	Quebec	Ontario	Prairie region	British Columbia
1966	251	33	86	72	30	33
1967	296	33	100	92	30	39
1968	358	38	124	107	43	47
1969	362	40	137	99	45	43
1970	476	40	160	139	70	67
1971	535	46	171	178	74	65
1972	553	54	178	171	78	73
1973	515	57	169	152	71	66
1974	514	65	169	164	53	64
1975	690	77	214	242	65	92
1976	727	88	233	240	71	96
1977	850	104	284	279	86	97
1978	911	108	307	300	96	98
1979	838	105	277	280	83	94
1980	867	103	292	300	86	87
1981	898	109	311	295	93	90
1982	1 305	135	407	441	158	163
		Unemployment Rate (%)				
1966	3.4	5.4	4.1	2.6	2.4	4.6
1967	3.8	5.3	4.6	3.2	2.3	5.1
1968	4.5	6.0	5.6	3.6	3.2	5.9
1969	4.4	6.2	6.1	3.2	3.3	5.1
1970	5.7	6.2	7.0	4.4	4.9	7.7
1971	6.2	7.0	7.3	5.4	5.2	7.2
1972	6.2	7.7	7.5	5.0	5.3	7.8
1973	5.5	7.8	6.8	4.3	4.7	6.7
1974	5.3	8.4	6.6	4.4	3.4	6.2
1975	6.9	9.8	8.1	6.3	3.9	8.5
1976	7.1	10.9	8.7	6.2	4.1	8.6
1977	8.1	12.6	10.3	7.0	4.9	8.5
1978	8.4	12.5	10.9	7.2	5.2	8.3
1979	7.5	11.8	9.6	6.5	4.3	7.7
1980	7.5	11.2	9.9	6.9	4.3	6.8
1981	7.6	11.7	10.4	6.6	4.5	6.7
1982	11.0	14.4	13.8	9.8	7.4	12.1

Source: Statistics Canada, *The Labour Force* and *Historical Labour Force Statistics*

More and more women are entering the labour force . . .

Female Participation Rate (%)

1966: 35.4
1970: 38.3
1975: 44.4
1980: 50.3
1982: 51.6

Participation Rates by Sex and Age Groups, 1966—1982

	Male			Female		
	Total	15-24	25 +	Total	15-24	25 +
1966	79.8	64.1	84.9	35.4	48.4	31.2
1967	79.3	64.1	84.5	36.5	49.1	32.3
1968	78.6	63.3	84.0	37.1	49.8	32.8
1969	78.3	62.7	83.8	38.0	50.2	33.8
1970	77.8	62.5	83.3	38.3	49.5	34.5
1971	77.3	62.7	82.7	39.4	50.8	35.4
1972	77.5	64.4	82.3	40.2	51.8	36.2
1973	78.2	66.8	82.3	41.9	54.2	37.6
1974	78.7	68.9	82.2	43.0	56.0	38.5
1975	78.4	68.8	81.9	44.4	56.8	40.0
1976	77.6	67.9	81.1	45.2	56.8	41.1
1977	77.6	68.8	80.9	46.0	57.5	42.1
1978	77.9	69.7	81.0	47.8	58.9	44.0
1979	78.4	71.4	80.9	48.9	61.0	44.9
1980	78.3	72.0	80.5	50.3	62.6	46.2
1981	78.3	72.5	80.3	51.6	63.2	47.9
1982	76.9	69.5	79.3	51.6	62.3	48.3

Source: Statistics Canada, *The Labour Force*

In order to understand why unemployment occurs, we can examine unemployment under the following headings: frictional, structural, technological, seasonal, cyclical, government-induced, labour-induced, and replacement.

23.3: FRICTIONAL UNEMPLOYMENT

In Canada, people have the freedom to leave their jobs and employers the right to dismiss or lay off employees. Therefore many persons are always to be found, at any point in time, in the process of moving from one job to another, and even from one part of the country to another, seeking to improve their lot. There are also many persons entering the labour force from high school, college, and university who cannot find a suitable job, or even any job, right away.

The first type of frictional unemployment—delays in movement between jobs—is reduced to some extent by government and private employment agencies trying to put persons seeking jobs quickly in touch with employers offering jobs. However, a certain amount of this frictional employment will always continue to exist in our type of society. Only if persons were forbidden to change jobs without government permission, or without another job to go to, could this type of unemployment be significantly reduced.

The second type of frictional unemployment—that among young people trying to find their first full-time job—is not only high, but has been increasing in recent years. The situation is particularly bad nowadays because of various factors: the rapid increase in the number of young job seekers (the products of the post-war "baby boom"), the relatively high average level of formal education and job expectations of these new entrants to the labour force, and the reduction in the rate of growth of new job opportunities. This type of unemployment can be reduced to some extent by better career counselling, by guiding school-leavers into areas which have the greatest number of job openings, by offering subsidies to employers, and perhaps by breaking down artificial barriers to certain trades and professions for which public need greatly exceeds the supply of trained personnel.

Other types of persons who could logically be included among the frictionally unemployed include those suffering from language disabilities and lack of skills, including literacy.

23.4: STRUCTURAL UNEMPLOYMENT

As time goes by, consumer demand patterns change, with the result that some industries grow while others decline and even disappear.

"Not everyone finds it easy to choose a career."

This inevitable process of economic change means that while new jobs are being created in some industries, employment is stagnant or falling in others. Unfortunately, from the employment point of view, most workers cannot easily move from one industry to another. Job retraining programs and relocation expenses provided by government are trying to help overcome this labour immobility. However, there is the important human factor that, once a person is established in his or her way of life and place of work, there is a natural reluctance to uproot self and family to seek a job elsewhere. This reluctance is strengthened financially because unemployment insurance benefits and welfare assistance now make it economically possible for an unemployed person to remain where he or she is.

Sometimes this type of structural unemployment affects industries that are vital to the economic well-being of a whole region. This has happened, for example, in the Atlantic provinces of Canada, where shipbuilding was once a dominant industry. Or, more recently, to car makers in Southern Ontario, and to mines throughout the country. In addition, because of different economic circumstances, including closeness to markets and availability of means of transportation, certain regions of a country develop economically, while others tend to stagnate. Favourable conditions encourage new industries to locate in certain areas, while other areas find it hard to attract new industries, even just to replace the ones that have shut down. As a result, some regions persistently suffer a much higher rate of unemployment than others. This is sometimes called *regional unemployment*. Such unemployment cannot, however, be considered entirely structural.

A new type of structural unemployment, now gradually appearing, is what has been called *environmental unemployment*. This is where the need to install expensive anti-pollution equipment has forced the closing of marginally profitable industrial plants.

Other persons who might be included in the ranks of the structurally unemployed are those who, rightly or wrongly, are considered too old for a particular job; those who are unwilling to accept a lower-paid job or a different type of job than that previously held; and those who are unwilling to work at all (the "unemployables") and who are included in the unemployment statistics because of their claim that no suitable work exists for them in their community.

23.5: TECHNOLOGICAL UNEMPLOYMENT

Unemployment can be caused by changes in technology as well as by changes in demand. Thus, it may become more profitable for a firm, because of the invention of new machinery to employ more capital-intensive methods of production. If the firm is growing, it may not need to dismiss anybody. However, it will most likely reduce the rate of hiring, which in turn aggravates local unemployment. If the firm is not growing, it may very well dismiss some of its present employees as well as cut the rate of recruitment. Even if wage rates remain the same, more advanced equipment or new materials may reduce employment.

One example of technological unemployment is the introduction of the microcomputer in the small business. Thus a law firm, medical or dental centre, or accounting firm may purchase a microcomputer and appropriate software instead of hiring an additional person or replacing someone who has left. Another example is the growing use of robots in manufacturing industry (for example, auto production) and eventually in non-manufacturing jobs. This "robotics revolution" is spurred by the fact that the cost of capital-intensive robotic techniques is steadily decreasing relative to prices in general, whereas the cost of traditional labour-intensive production methods is steadily increasing. Also, of course, robots do not go on strike or demand overtime pay. On the positive side, it has been suggested that the introduction of robots may well reduce unemployment in the long run, if the resultant increase in productivity can lower the relative prices of the goods produced and so extend the market for them. Thus the introduction of the assembly line and mass production into the automobile industry early in this century so reduced production costs that the price could eventually be reduced to permit almost everyone to own a car. As a result, the number of workers employed in the automobile industry grew rather than declined. However, other studies suggest that the new technology will not create enough new jobs to replace those that disappear. In fact, it has been estimated that Canada may well lose between one and two million jobs in the 1980s due to technological and structural changes. Unfortunately, some of the new technologies, such as microelectronics, use not only less labour but also less capital equipment which also means fewer jobs in the capital goods industries. Whereas three million new jobs were estimated to have been created in Canada in the nineteen seventies, it would seem difficult to emulate this feat in the nineteen-eighties. Consequently, despite private and government job-creation efforts, the unemployment rate is predicted to remain high. On the more positive side, the new technology will be introduced only gradually, giving time for adjustment. Also, some economists anticipate that the greater productivity will generate higher earnings that will be spent on other goods and services, causing additional jobs to be created in other areas.

"Well, what exactly DID the computer say, when it fired you?"

23.6: SEASONAL UNEMPLOYMENT

Canada also has unemployment caused by variations in the climate. Farming, lumbering, fishing, construction, and port operations are all examples of the victims of this seasonal unemployment. To reduce it, many municipalities have undertaken winter-works projects, usually with federal government financial support. Furthermore, industries that provide Winter employment have sometimes been given government financial assistance.

23.7: CYCLICAL UNEMPLOYMENT

The most serious type of unemployment in Canada, in terms of the sheer number of persons deprived of jobs,is that caused by cyclical variations in the general level of economic activity. The world economic depression of the 1930s was the most severe example of this type of unemployment, raising the unemployment rate in Canada in 1933 to as high as 20 per cent of the labour force. But other reductions in economic activity, both before and since the 1930s, have had the same origin. On the positive side, such unemployment is usually only temporary.

Although our federal and provincial governments have some ability, through spending and other economic measures, to stimulate business activity and so reduce cyclical unemployment, their hands have often been tied by the desire to restrain inflation. Even when they do take action, the difficulty of predicting the exact effects of their policies on income and employment, as well as the time lags involved before the measures make themselves felt, give such policies very much a "stop-and-go" character.

23.8: GOVERNMENT-INDUCED UNEMPLOYMENT

Government, as well as being able to play a key role in maintaining a high level of consumer demand in the economy, can also be guilty of creating unemployment by adopting restrictive economic policies. In winning one battle (inflation), the government may easily lose another (unemployment). Thus, if a government, through the country's central bank, restricts too much the country's money supply and raises interest rates very high in order to combat inflation, the level of consumer demand tends to fall, investment is reduced, and unemployment increases. This apparently inverse relationship between the rate of unemployment and the rate of inflation is discussed later in this chapter (Unit 23:11).

Another type of government-induced unemployment arises when a firm finds that it has become unprofitable for firms to employ as many workers as before, because of government-set minimum wage rates. The firm may either cease operations or use more capital-intensive methods of production. The workers still employed will receive higher wages, but those who have been dismissed must look for other jobs.

23.9: LABOUR-INDUCED UNEMPLOYMENT

As labour unions succeed in negotiating higher wages and fringe benefits for their members, it becomes more and more attractive for firms to use machines instead of labour, or even to close down plants altogether. Paradoxically, the more successful a labour union is in pressing its members' claims, the greater the likelihood of reduced employment in that industry. And this is occurring throughout the economy. Thus, it is more economical for municipalities to employ highly mechanized street-cleaning methods than human labour, even though many able-bodied persons may be unemployed and even on welfare. The question is, of course, whether it is better that everyone should have a job (even a menial one) at a relatively low wage, or that most people, but not all, have a job at a higher wage.

23.10: REPLACEMENT UNEMPLOYMENT

This term describes the unemployment caused in Canada and other Western industrial countries by the replacement of goods that traditionally have been produced locally, by lower-cost and often better-quality ones made in S.E. Asia and in other countries such as Brazil. This type of unemployment has gradually worsened in recent decades and is now a major cause of chronically high unemployment rates in Canada, the U.S., and Western Europe.

In Canada, more and more firms in such industries as clothing, footwear, home appliances, etc. have disappeared and others, notably in the auto industry, have had to cut back production as their market share has diminished. Even many finished goods, still assembled in Canada, contain many foreign-made components. Hence the claim by many Canadian workers that their jobs are being "exported abroad".

According to traditional international trade theory and the principles of the General Agreement on Tariffs and Trade, or GATT, to which Canada is a signatory, greater liberalization of international trade should be an unquestioned goal. However, many Western countries have now erected barriers of one sort or another to stem the flow of foreign imports, particularly of manufactured goods, in an effort to prevent local unemployment from growing any worse. Thus Canada has import quotas for footwear and clothing. For many years, particularly in Western Europe, the agricultural industry has also been protected from foreign competition.

Only if business firms in the Western countries can become more cost and quality conscious than such S.E. Asian suppliers as S. Korea, Hong Kong, Japan, Malaysia, and so on, can they and their employees' jobs be made secure under a situation of relatively free international trade. Another possibility is the development of high-technology, resource-based industries in Canada that can compete effectively with foreign-made goods both at home and abroad.

23.11: UNEMPLOYMENT AND INFLATION

Over the years, a trade-off relationship between the rate of unemployment and the rate of inflation has from time to time been observed: as unemployment is decreased, so inflation seems to increase; and as inflation is decreased, so unemployment seems to increase. In other words, it seems that more of one can be achieved only at the expense of less of the other. And vice versa.

The Phillips Curve

Many countries in the world, not only Canada and the United States, have witnessed this tradeoff relationship between inflation and unemployment. It has even been depicted graphically in the form of a Phillips curve (see Figure 23.1) named after its author, Professor Alban W. Phillips, of the London School of Economics and the Australian National University.

The Phillips curve, it should be noted, attempts to describe the *short-term* relationship between inflation and unemployment. In the long run, the relationship can change. Thus, if the public gradually adopts an inflationary psychology (because of constantly rising prices and wages) the Phillips curve will shift to the right. This will mean that the government, to reduce the rate of inflation, will have to restrict aggregate demand much more than would previously have been necessary. This in turn would mean a substantial increase in unemployment.

Stagflation

In practice, the trade-off relationship between inflation and unemployment is not as exact or permanent as the Phillips curve suggests. Thus, it was noted in both Canada and the United States in the 1950s and again in the 1970s, that even with considerable unemployment, prices

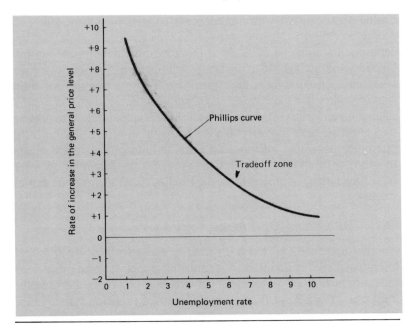

Figure 23:1 The Phillips Curve

continued to rise. The apparent reason is that inflation today has assumed an increasingly cost-push character. Labour contracts with built-in wage increases have lengthened in duration. Also large business firms and large labour unions have become much more independent of competitive market pressures. The laws of demand and supply do not affect large firms with regard to market price as effectively as they do smaller firms. Labour unions, despite unemployment of their own members, still insist on substantial wage increases for those still employed. In addition, despite unemployment in other industries, labour unions and professional associations carefully restrict entry of new workers into their own. This relative independence of large firms and labour unions from normal market pressures makes cost-push inflation increasingly serious, as well as difficult to control.

Economists in Western industrial countries have also been seriously disturbed by another apparent weakness of the Phillips curve. Although a tight-money policy is usually accompanied by increased unemployment, the converse does not always seem true. Thus, an easy-money policy (and consequently increased inflation) is often extremely slow in reducing unemployment. The cause seems to be that business executives, with confidence shattered by a period of economic recession or (particularly in Canada in recent years) by uncertainty and apprehension about the government's attitude towards business and by high wage demands, will postpone or even forgo new investment in equipment and inventory. Thus, a country can easily start to wallow in what is called *stagflation*—a combination of economic stagnation and inflation. Another disturbing feature is that government may push its easy-money policy so hard, in an effort to reduce the unemployment, that inflation can easily get out of hand. This means that the degree of inflation required to reduce unemployment seems to be getting larger. In other words, the Phillips curve seems to be getting steeper.

23.12: JOB CREATION PROGRAMS

Another approach that has been used by our governments to reduce unemployment, in addition to stimulating public spending, has been the introduction of a variety of job-creation programs. Perhaps the most well-known was LIP, the Local Initiatives Program, started in the Winter of 1971-72, which provided financial aid for local job-creation ideas until its termination in 1976-77. Another program, OFY, or Opportunites for Youth, lasted from 1972 to 1977 when it was replaced by Young Canada Works, the youth version of the Canada Works job scheme. Job creation programs now in existence at the federal level include the following:

1. CCDP, or Canada Community Development Projects. Here, money is given to each federal riding to be spent on community development projects.

2. CCSP, or Canada Community Service Projects. In this case, money is given to community service groups for job-creation projects.

3. Summer Canada. This is a youth employment program aimed at creating summer jobs.

4. LEAP, or Local Employment Assistance Program. This program begun in 1973, aims at helping chronically unemployed persons to upgrade their skills so as to improve their employment prospects.

5. LEDA, or Local Economic Development Assistance program. This program, started in 1980, provides investment money to corporations of local residents in various communities who can devise feasible ways of creating jobs.

6. NETP, or the New Technology Employment Program. This program, also begun in 1980, provides wage subsidies for up to one year for persons with high skills training who have recently entered the work force but are unemployed or underemployed. The employment that is subsidized usually involves research with small companies or research institutes.

7. Section 38. This job-creation program, begun in 1982, based on Section 38 of the Unemployment Insurance Act, involves the payment of a supplement to people otherwise drawing unemployment benefits who agree to work at temporary jobs, on average six months long, notably in development of the country's fisheries and forests.

8. NEED, or New Employment Expansion and Development program. This program, also started in 1982, is designed to help provide work for unemployed people who have used up all the unemployment insurance benefits to which they are entitled and who have had to turn to municipal welfare for financial assistance.

Conclusion

An analysis of the effectiveness of such government job-creation programs usually involves a comparison between the cost to the taxpayer and the amount of work created—in person-years, which could be one person working for a year, three people each working for four months or some other combination adding up to a year. However, two other factors to take into account are: the money saved in unemployment benefits and the social cost that unemployment would have meant to the persons assisted and their families. In conclusion, one might say that these job-creation programs, and similar ones by provincial governments, represent no more than a band-aid solution to Canada's unemployment problem. Cynics might say that their emergence is due as much to political as to economic or social reasons. And that better results for the dollar might have been obtained in some other way. Nevertheless, a small dent has been made in Canada's unemployment total (now about 1.4 million persons) and for the people helped, the programs have undoubtedly been beneficial. However, the main thrust by government should be (a) to maintain a high level of public demand for goods and services and (b) to encourage Canadian firms to be more competitive internationally (as discussed in Chapter 20).

23.13: WORK-SHARING

For some years, the federal Department of Employment and Immigration has sponsored a temporary work-sharing program. Under this program, which requires a prior agreement between the employer and the employees, the Department pays unemployment insurance benefits for one or two days a week for up to 26 weeks to employees who agree to work a shorter work week as part of a scheme to avoid a temporary reduction in an employer's work force. In 1983, a new expanded program offered such assistance for up to 50 weeks in situations where there would have been permanent layoffs. However, it also required a prior arrangement for retraining of workers during the 50-week period. What has made the program attractive for workers has been the fact that the combination of wages and unemployment insurance benefit for employees who give up one day of work a week amounts to as much as 95 per cent of after-tax income.

From the economic point of view, it can be argued that, with such a scheme, workers and employers in general, with their unemployment insurance contributions, are subsidizing a four-day week for certain employees. Some of the benefits may also be considered, of course, a refund of these employees' own past contributions. Some school boards have also experimented with job-sharing programs for teachers whereby a teacher accepts a reduction in regular pay for so many years and then takes a self-financed sabbatical year. Another type of work-sharing that is sometimes practised is the sharing of one job by two or more people each working on a part-time basis.

In 1983, the federal Employment Minister suggested that in the nineteen-eighties much more should be done in the way of job-sharing in Canada as one means of reducing the high unemployment rate. However, reaction from employers and organized labour was generally unfavourable—the main criticism being that this was a defeatist attitude by the federal minister towards Canada's serious unemployment problem.

Summary

1. One of the biggest economic headaches that afflicts modern industrial societies is the very high level of unemployment.
2. The unemployed are defined as persons fifteen years of age or over without work and seeking work or temporarily laid off for the full week in which Statistics Canada conducts its survey.
3. The unemployment rate is the number of persons unemployed expressed as a percentage of the total labour force, both employed and unemployed.
4. Unemployment in Canada since 1926 has varied from a high of 20.0 per cent of the civilian labour force in 1933 to a low of 1.6 per cent in 1945. In recent years, unemployment for Canada as a whole has gone as high as 12 per cent. Unemployment is highest among the young. Regionally, the Atlantic provinces have the highest unemployment rates. A higher female participation rate in

recent years has added to the demand for jobs.

5. Full employment of labour is usually defined in Western societies as a situation in which there is 3 per cent or less of the civilian labour force unemployed. Canada last achieved this situation in 1953. Nowadays, 7 or 8 per cent is being cited as the target.

6. There are many different types of unemployment which together cause a high unemployment rate.

7. *Frictional unemployment* results from delays in persons obtaining their first jobs or in moving to new jobs.

8. *Structural unemployment* results from the decline of industries that no longer satisfy consumer or other demand at competitive prices. Where this decline seriously affects a whole region, the term "regional unemployment" is also used. Structural unemployment can also be the result of changes in pollution-control requirements.

9. *Technological unemployment* results from the use of more capital-intensive methods of production. (e.g. computers and robots).

10. *Seasonal unemployment* results from variations in climate.

11. *Cyclical unemployment* results from cyclical changes in economic activity and is the most severe type of unemployment in numbers of persons put out of work. However, it is usually of temporary duration.

12. *Government-induced unemployment* results from the adoption of severe fiscal and monetary measures by the government to restrain inflation, or from the establishment and raising of minimum wage-rates.

13. *Labour-induced unemployment* results from higher union-negotiated wage-rates, which encourage employers to use more machines and fewer workers.

14. *Replacement unemployment* results from the replacement of relatively high-cost, goods produced in Canada by relatively low-cost, often higher-quality goods produced abroad, mainly in S.E. Asia.

15. It has been observed that in practice measures to reduce inflation can easily increase unemployment. The Phillips curve depicts the inverse relationship, often observed, between the rate of inflation and the rate of unemployment. The term *stagflation* describes a situation in which there is both economic stagnation and inflation.

16. To combat unemployment, the federal and provincial governments, as well as stimulating public spending, have also initiated a variety of job-creation and work-sharing programs.

Key Terms

Review Questions

1. When is a person officially considered "unemployed" in Canada? Who are the "hidden unemployed"?
2. How is the rate of unemployment determined? How has this rate varied in Canada?
3. What is meant by "full employment"? When has Canada been most successful in achieving this goal? And when least successful?
4. Why do Canada's young and old seem to have the most difficulty in finding jobs? Discuss.
5. Why is unemployment lower among females than among males? Discuss.
6. Why is unemployment greater in some parts of Canada than in others? Discuss.
7. What is frictional unemployment? Why is it considered to be unavoidable?
8. What is structural unemployment? Why has it affected certain areas of Canada more than others?
9. Explain and discuss some specific modern examples of technological unemployment.
10. What is seasonal unemployment? Give examples. What has been done to reduce it?
11. What is cyclical unemployment? What has been Canada's experience with it since World War II?
12. To what extent can government be held responsible for creating unemployment?
13. "Paradoxically, the more successful labour unions are in pressing their members' claims, the greater the likelihood of reduced em-

ployment in that industry." Explain and discuss.

14. What is meant by "replacement unemployment"? Give some examples of your own of jobs that have been lost in this way.

15. In your opinion, which types of unemployment now account for most of our high unemployment rate?

16. Explain and discuss how changes in the "participation rate" have worsened Canada's unemployment problem.

17. "Why can't our municipal governments be given unemployment and welfare funds to provide community improvement jobs for anyone who is temporarily ouut of work?" Discuss.

18. A person who is unemployed should be required to accept any job, not just one similar to that previously held. Discuss

19. Many large Canadian retailers now find it cheaper to have their goods manufactured abroad rather than in Canada. Discuss.

20. Country A has a labour force of 15.2 million, of which 2.1 million are currently unemployed; Country B, a labour force of 9.7 million, and 1.3 million unemployed. Which country is economically worse off?

21. What are the most effective measures that the federal government can use to increase employment in Canada? Discuss.

22. Explain and discuss the various federal job-creation programs.

23. What job-creation programs, if any, are being undertaken by your provincial government?

24. "Stagflation has made the Phillips curve obsolete". Discuss.

25. What are the various types of work-sharing practised in Canada?

26. "Job-sharing is both economically and socially desirable in Canada." Discuss.

24. EMPLOYMENT THEORY

CHAPTER OBJECTIVES

A. To explain the classical belief in long-run full employment
B. To describe how Keynes challenged the classical view and suggested that full employment was an unusual and unlikely state of affairs
C. To explain how, according to Keynes, national output, income, and employment are determined
D. To distinguish between inflationary and deflationary gaps
E. To explain the concept of the Keynesian multiplier
F. To explain what is meant by "supply-side economics"

CHAPTER OUTLINE

24.1: THE CLASSICAL BELIEF ABOUT UNEMPLOYMENT

Until the 1930s, most economists believed that labour and the other factors of production of a country would automatically be fully employed. Cyclical unemployment could occur, it was recognized, but only as a temporary and exceptional phenomenon. This classical belief in long-run full employment had its roots in Say's Law (an economic principle named after J.B. Say, a French economist, who lived from 1767 to 1832). According to this law, the production of any good or service automatically creates, through the flow of income to wage earners and others, enough additional purchasing power in the economy to enable the public to buy the additional goods and services produced. In other words, there can be no general overproduction in the economy.

Changes can, however, occur in the pattern of production. Thus, if production of one type of good tends to be excessive in relation to demand, its price will fall, output will decline, and some of the factors of production involved in its manufacture will become unemployed. And so long as wage rates and other factor payments are flexible, so long as competition exists, and so long as the factors of production are mobile and can move into industries for whose output demand is increasing, this unemployment will gradually disappear.

24.2: THE KEYNESIAN VIEW

This classical line of reasoning was repudiated in the 1930s by an English economist, John Maynard Keynes (later Lord Keynes). Keynes asserted that full employment was *not* the long-run equilibrium towards which the economy would gravitate. And that even if it were, in the long run we would all be dead! On the contrary, full employment, according to Keynes, was an exceptional state of affairs. Equilibrium was more likely a situation of less than full employment.

Since the publication in 1936 of Keynes' famous book *The General Theory of Employment, Interest and Money*, there has been a spate of articles and books, adding to, criticizing, and improving the concepts expounded by Keynes. The body of economic theory that has evolved is now often referred to as *Keynesian economics*.

24.3: DETERMINANTS OF NATIONAL OUTPUT, INCOME, AND EMPLOYMENT

According to Keynes, the most important determinant of a country's income and employment is the *aggregate demand* for its goods and services. This is the total amount of money spent in say, a year, on the final goods and services produced in a country. Aggregate demand *(AD)* for Canadian-produced goods and services comprises consumption expenditures by domestic households, investment expenditure by business firms, government expenditure, and the value of exports (spending by foreigners on Canadian goods) minus the value of imports. In algebraic terms, $AD = C + I + G + E$. In this definition, C, I and G are net of imports.

These are the factors, or "injections" that add to the circular flow of income discussed in Chapter 21. In addition, of course, there are "leakages": savings, imports, and taxes.

24.4: CONSUMPTION

The most important factor determining the level of consumption expenditure in a country is considered to be the level of national income. Thus the higher the level of national income, the higher will be the level of consumption expenditure. Conversely, the lower the level of national income, the lower the level of consumption expenditure. However, not all national income is available for spending by consumers. Part is set aside in undistributed corporation profits, part in corporation income taxes, and part in social insurance and pension contributions. What is left, plus any transfer payments from government such as family allowances, equals total *Personal Income*. After personal income tax is deducted, we have what is called total *Personal Disposable Income*, which is the amount that consumers are able to save or spend at their own discretion. And it is this amount that critically influences consumption expenditure.

Several other factors, as well as income, influence the level of consumption expenditure in a country. Individual wealth is one factor. Age is another: young people, for example, are usually willing to spend more than are the old. Advertising is another factor, for it persuades people to buy. Easy availability of credit also increases expenditure by making it possible for consumers to buy goods without first accumulating the necessary cash. As a result, people tend to buy more than they otherwise would. The degree of social security that the public enjoys is another factor that affects consumption spending. Old-age pensions, medical insurance, unemployment insurance, and other government and private benefits all reduce the need for a person to accumulate savings as protection against the uncertainties of the future. Another factor that may sometimes influence the level of consumption expenditure is people's expectations as to the future. During a period of severe inflation, for example, people may increase their consumption because savings held in the form of money rapidly lose their real worth as the value of money declines. In addition, if people expect their incomes to rise in the future, as in a period of economic boom, they may increase the proportion of their disposable income currently allotted to consumer expenditure. In times of economic recession, with people worrying about job security, the proportion of disposable income saved usually increases.

APC, MPC

The *average propensity to consume (APC)* is the ratio between total disposable income and total consumption expenditure or, in other words, consumption expenditure divided by disposable income. Thus, if $35 billion were spent on consumer goods and services out of a total disposable income of $40 billion, the APC would be 35/40, or ⅞. This ratio is usually expressed by the formula APC $= C/Yd$, where C stands for consumption and Yd for disposable income.

The *marginal propensity to consume (MPC)* is the relationship between changes in total disposable income and consequent changes in total consumption expenditure. If, for example, personal disposable income increased by $5 billion and spending on consumer goods and services increased by $4 billion from one year to the next, the marginal propensity to consume would be ⅘. The marginal propensity to consume is expressed by the formula

$$\text{MPC} = \frac{\triangle C}{\triangle Yd} \quad \text{where } \triangle \text{ stands for change}$$

At low levels of disposable income, people tend to spend more than they earn. As their income increases, they begin to save part of it. And as income rises even more, a larger percentage of each additional amount of income is saved. In other words, at low levels of income, the APC and MPC are very high. However, as income rises, both the APC and MPC tend to decline.

The Consumption Function

The relationship between the amount of personal disposable income and the amount of consumption expenditure is called the *propensity to consume*, or *consumption function*. This can be represented by a chart showing the amount of money that would be spent on consumer goods and services at different levels of disposable income (see Figure 24:1).

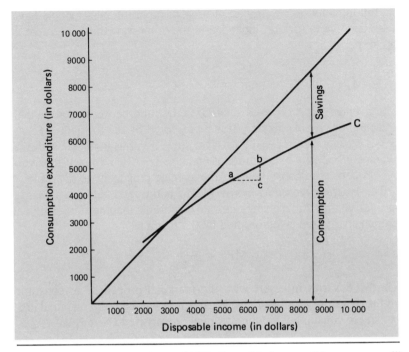

Note: The chart shows that at $8500 disposable income, this consumer will spend $6000 and save $2500. At $3000 disposable income our consumer would consume all the income. Below $3000, our consumer would consume more than the disposable income by drawing on past savings or by borrowing.

The marginal propensity to consume is also illustrated by the chart. Line ac represents an increase in disposable income of $1000; line bc, a consequent increase in consumption of $500. The MPC over this range is therefore 500/1000 or ½.

Figure 24:1 The Propensity To Consume Schedule

24.5: SAVINGS

That part of disposable income that is not consumed is saved. Consumption and savings therefore vary inversely. If, for example, 75 per cent of disposable income is consumed, then 25 per cent is saved.

Determinants of Savings

Like consumption, savings are determined mainly by the level of income. The less income a person has, the harder it is to save. The more income he or she has, the easier it is to save. The other determinants of consumption also affect savings, since savings is the converse of consumption. Thus, for example, in time of rapid inflation, people have less incentive to save or, looked at in the other way, more incentive to consume.

APS, MPS

The *average propensity to save (APS)* is the ratio between total savings and total disposable income. It is represented by the formula: APS = *S/Y*. The average propensity to save, since it varies inversely with the average propensity to consume, is equal to $1 - $ APC. Thus, if the average propensity to consume is ⅞, the average propensity to save is ⅛.

The *marginal propensity to save (MPS)* is the ratio between a change in total savings and a change in total disposable income. The marginal propensity to save is represented by the formula:

$$\text{MPS} = \frac{\triangle S}{\triangle Yd}$$

The MPS varies inversely with the marginal propensity to consume and is therefore equal to $1 - $ MPC. In other words, if the marginal propensity to consume is ⅘, the marginal propensity to save is ⅕.

The Savings Function

The relationship between total disposable income and total savings is called the *propensity to save*. Figure 24:2 illustrates, in chart form, the savings function in terms of the amount of savings that takes place at different levels of disposable income.

24.6: INVESTMENT

Investment, as we saw previously, means spending on new buildings, machinery, and equipment. It does not include the purchase of capital goods that are already in existence. Such purchases add nothing to the country's capital stock: they only cause a change in the ownership of such goods.

Determinants of Investment

One important determinant of the level of investment by business firms is management expectations about future consumer demand. If business executives are optimistic about future demand for their various products, perhaps because of a buoyant economy or a more positive government economic policy, they will increase investment spending. If

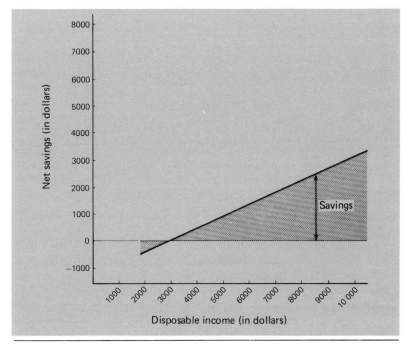

Figure 24:2   The Propensity To Save Schedule

they are pessimistic because of, for example, economic or political uncertainty, price controls, labour unrest, or rising foreign competition,
they will reduce it. Other determinants of investment spending include
expectations about future production costs. Thus, increased labour-
union demands or higher minimum wage rates would tend to discourage
investment. So also would higher income-tax rates and higher interest
charges on business borrowings.

Marginal Efficiency of Investment

This is the anticipated rate of return on an additional unit of investment. If, for example, a business firm invests $100000 in new equip-
ment and as a result expects the firm's annual net profit to increase by
$10000, the marginal efficiency of investment would be 10 per cent.

When a firm commences production, the marginal efficiency of investment is often very high because of the benefits of specialization, or
division of labour. However, as the firm grows larger, it eventually
goes beyond its optimum size. Production is no longer as efficient as

before and the market is already adequately supplied with the firm's products. Also, the prices of the materials and equipment used tend to rise as the firm expands and its demands increase. As a result, the return on any new investment tends to be smaller than before. In other words, beyond a certain amount of investment, a firm (unless it moves to a larger plant or enlarges its range of products) is usually faced with a declining marginal efficiency of investment.

New Investment Opportunities

One might at first expect that business firms would run out of attractive investment opportunities. This is not true for a variety of reasons. First, the growth of Canada's population and national income gives rise to an increasing demand for all existing types of goods as well as for the materials, parts and machinery with which to manufacture them. Added to this there is the export demand that offers almost unlimited possibilities for Canadian manufacturers and other types of producers. Second, there is always the possibility for a new product or service that will satisfy the consumer more completely than an existing product or service, or for a new type of machine to manufacture goods more efficiently than an old one. Third, there is always the possibility for a new product or service to satisfy a consumer demand not previously satisfied. Fourth, it may become profitable to use already known or newly discovered oil or other mineral deposits, hydro-electric sources, or other natural resources. Fifth, the running down of inventories of materials and finished goods and the deterioration of industrial machinery and equipment both provide the need for new investment. At the consumer level, the wearing out of semi-durable goods such as cars, appliances, and entertainment equipment helps increase consumer demand and indirectly helps create investment opportunities for industries producing these goods. Sixth, new technology may make it cheaper to produce goods—thereby shifting a firm's whole cost curve downwards and encouraging an expansion in its productive capacity to satisfy a larger market.

Rates of Interest

A business firm, in deciding whether to undertake new investment, must look not only at the expected rate of return, but also at the cost of the investment. This is the rate of interest on the money used. If the money comes from the firm's own sources (from reinvested profits, for example) a rate of interest must be imputed. This would be the *opportunity cost* or, in other words, what the firm could otherwise earn by lending this money to someone else. If part or all of the money is borrowed, the cost of the investment is the rate of interest to be paid.

For an investment to be worthwhile, the rate of return, or marginal efficiency of investment, must, in the long run, exceed the rate of interest. In the short run a firm may sometimes be willing to accept a loss on its investment to get established in a market, to dislodge a competitor, or to await better times.

The relationship between investment and the rate of interest can be illustrated by a *marginal efficiency of investment curve* (see Figure 24:3). In the diagram, investment projects are spread along the horizontal axis—the ones with the highest expected return being closest to the point of origin. At a high rate of interest (measured on the vertical axis), only the most profitable projects will be undertaken. However, as the rate of interest drops, more and more projects, offering lower expected rates of return, will be undertaken. Consequently, the MEI curve slopes downward from left to right, signifying that the lower the rate of interest, the greater the amount of investment.

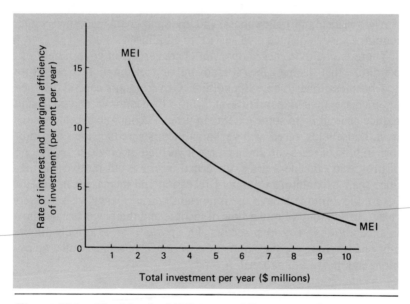

Figure 24:3   The Marginal Efficiency of Investment Curve

The MEI curve assumes, of course, that the expected rate of return on the various investment projects remains constant. In practice, a change in business outlook could make the *expected* rate of return for all projects higher or lower. This would mean a shift in the MEI curve. If entrepreneurs become more pessimistic because of, for example, a government tight-money, high-interest rate policy, then the curve might shift to the left—meaning that fewer investment projects would now be undertaken at any given rate of interest. On the other hand, if entrepreneurs become more optimistic about the future, the curve would shift to the right, signifying that more projects would be undertaken at any given rate of interest.

24.7: GOVERNMENT EXPENDITURE

The federal, provincial, and municipal governments in Canada together account for a large proportion of aggregate demand. This government spending has been increasing over the years, both in absolute size and as a percentage of the country's total expenditure. The increase has reflected the expansion by our governments of traditional community services, such as education, police and fire protection, and the construction of roads and bridges, and the assumption of new responsibilities such as regional development, job retraining, health care, pension plans, family allowances, and unemployment insurance, which require a vastly enlarged civil service to administer.

There is one extremely important characteristic of government expenditure that distinguishes it from public consumption expenditure and business investment expenditure. Governments can, if they see fit, increase their expenditure at a time of economic recession and reduce or limit it (to some extent) in time of economic boom. By contrast, households, faced with declining incomes, reduce their expenditure in time of recession and increase it, as their incomes go up, in time of prosperity. Business firms, governed by the profit motive, also reduce their expenditure in time of recession and increase it in time of boom. Governments have the important power, if they wish to exercise it, to add to the circular flow of income and thereby offset declines in expenditure in the other sectors. This power is an extremely important one when we consider how the economy is to achieve full employment and maximum national income.

24.8: GOVERNMENT TAXATION AND BORROWING

Our governments levy a variety of income, sales, property and other taxes. These taxes have the effect of reducing the circular flow of income in the economy. Additional taxes can be levied, if deemed necessary, to offset excessive spending in the private sector. Government borrowing also reduces the circular flow of income.

24.9: EXPORTS

The fourth type of expenditure that forms part of Canada's aggregate demand is spending by foreigners on Canadian goods and services. The actual level depends on several factors. First, there is the foreign need for Canadian goods and services. Second, there is the competitiveness of Canadian products in term of quality and price. Import duties in foreign countries, it should be noted, raise the price of our goods and reduce their competitiveness. Import quotas and other non-tariff barriers may prevent them competing at all. Third, there is the ability or not of foreigners to pay for Canadian goods and services, perhaps because of low per capita income or because of a shortage of U.S. dollars, the usual currency of payment for our exports.

Unlike the other types of expenditures, spending by foreigners on Canadian goods and services is partly beyond Canadian control. Thus, if there is an economic recession in the United States, Canada's most important export market, there will be a fall in demand for Canadian goods and services. The more important exports are, compared with the other main types of expenditure, the more severe will be the decline in aggregate demand in Canada.

24.10: IMPORTS

Not all expenditure by Canadian households, business firms, and governments is on Canadian goods and services. Part goes for goods and services produced by foreigners, including the payment of interest and dividends on foreign capital and payment of travel costs. The purchase of foreign goods and services reduces the demand for Canadian goods and services.

Determinants of the level of imports include the competitiveness of foreign versus Canadian goods, consumer tastes in Canada, government restrictions on imports, the level of income in Canada, the extent of government and business borrowing abroad, and the amount of travel, insurance, shipping, etc. required.

The relationship between total disposable income and total imports is called the *average propensity to import (APM)*.

The relationship between changes in total disposable income and change in total imports is called the *marginal propensity to import (MPM)*. It is formulated as follows:

$$\text{MPM} = \frac{\triangle M}{\triangle Yd},$$

where M = imports, Yd = disposable income, and $\triangle$ = change.

24.11: EQUILIBRIUM LEVEL OF NATIONAL OUTPUT, INCOME, AND EMPLOYMENT

An *equilibrium level of income* is considered to be a stable, self-perpetuating level of output, income, and employment. According to Keynes, this level would be achieved only if aggregate demand were equal to aggregate supply. (By aggregate supply [*AS*] we mean the value of all final goods and services produced—in other words, the Gross National Product.) If, for example, Canada's aggregate demand were $100 billion and aggregate supply $80 billion, falling inventories of finished products would encourage business investment. This, in turn, would cause aggregate supply to increase until it eventually equalled aggregate demand. Conversely, if Canada's aggregate demand were $80 billion and aggregate supply $100 billion, the unsold inventories would bring about a reduction in investment and production until AD = AS. This movement towards equilibrium is illustrated in Table 24:1 and in Figure 24:4.

Table 24:1
The Equilibrium Level of Income and Employment

Aggregate Demand (C + I + G + X) ($ billions)	Aggregate Supply GNP ($ billions)	Employment (millions)	Change in Income, Employment, and Production
65	50	7.5	
70	60	8.0	
75	70	8.5	↓
80	80	9.0	equilibrium
85	90	9.5	↑
90	100	F/E 10.0	
95	110	10.0	
100	120	10.0	

A comparison of aggregate demand and aggregate supply is one way of understanding how the equilibrium level of income is determined. Another way, already familiar from Chapter 21, is by comparing leakages in the circular flow of income with injections. The various leakages (*L*) are savings, taxes, and imports or *S* + *T* + *M*. The various injections (*J*) are investments, government expenditure, and exports,

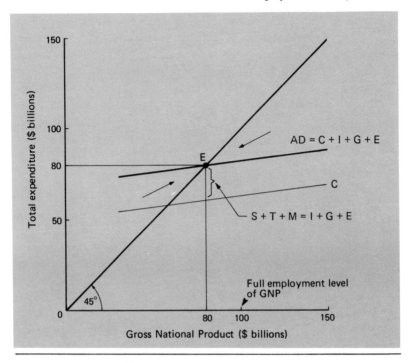

Note: Potential equilibrium exists at any point along the 45° line, for anywhere along this line total expenditure will equal total output.

Actual equilibrium is where the aggregate demand curve (AD) intersects the 45° line. At this point total expenditure of $80 billion equals total output of $80 billion.

To the left of this point aggregate demand (AD) exceeds aggregate supply (AS). To the right of this point, AS > AD.

Note that the equilibrium level of output ($80 billion) is lower than the full-employment level ($100 billion).

Figure 24:4   The Equilibrium Level of National Income

or $I + G + X$. If L exceeds J, the level of income will fall. Conversely, if J exceeds L, the level of income will rise. Only when $L = J$ will the level of income neither fall nor rise. And it will be at this point that aggregate demand equals aggregate supply. Unfortunately, there is little likelihood (without deliberate government intervention) that this equilibrium will be attained at the point at which a country's factors of production are fully employed. The various leakages and injections in the circular flow of income are shown in Figure 24:5.

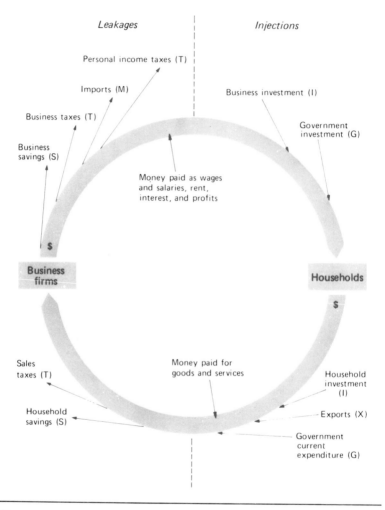

Figure 24:5   Leakages and Injections in the Circular Flow

24.12: PERIOD ANALYSIS

Keynes, in *The General Theory of Employment, Interest, and Money*, treated savings as the sole leakage and investment as the sole injection in the circular flow. And he declared that savings and investment are always equal. His reasoning was as follows: since national income can be either saved or spent, then national income must be equal to consumption plus saving. Therefore: Savings = Income minus Consumption. Since national income is also equivalent to national output (the other side of the coin), then national income must also be equal to the output of consumption goods plus the output of capital goods. In other words, national income consists of consumption plus investment. Therefore: Investment = Income minus Consumption. Finally, since savings and investment are each equal to income minus consumption, then: Savings = Investment.

In more recent analysis, as we saw earlier, the effects of governments and foreign trade are also taken into account. Both these sectors account for a sizeable portion of Canada's GNE. We now say, therefore, that:

$$(S + T + M) = (I + G + X) \text{ or: } L = J.$$

If, logically, *L* must equal *J*, why is it that we also talk about *L* exceeding *J*, and vice versa? The answer lies in the fact that different time periods are involved. There is a difference between *planned* or *intended* saving and investment (which are not necessarily equal) and *actual* or *realized* saving and investment (which must by definition be equal). This distinction is sometimes referred to as the *ex ante* and *ex post* equality of S and I. If intended savings and investment differ in period one, the level of income will change so that they will be equal in period two. Or, with our broader concept, whatever the differences between intended *L* and *J* in the present, changes in the level of income will tend to bring about equality in the future. Of course, if intentions continually change, the actual equality of *L* and *J* in the future may never, in fact, come about. The level of national income will, instead, continue to fluctuate. And this is, in fact, perhaps the most logical explanation yet advanced for the existence of the business cycle—the subject of the next chapter.

24.13: INFLATIONARY AND DEFLATIONARY GAPS

At any one time, there is a maximum possible output of goods and services in an economy. This is the output achieved when all the country's resources are fully employed—in other words, the *full employment level* of production. So long as the economy is operating below this level, an increase in aggregate demand (a money flow) will induce a higher level of employment and national output. However, once the full-employment level is reached, an increase in aggregate demand will only cause an increase in prices, for output cannot be further increased.

In practice, prices tend to rise even when the economy is operating below the full-employment level. This is because the economy does not operate as smoothly as is suggested by our economic models. And, in practice, even at the full-employment level, some increase in production is still possible by more intensive use of plant and equipment. Nevertheless, our major conclusion remains valid—once the full-employment level is reached, any further increase in aggregate demand will have a mainly inflationary effect, raising prices rather than output.

There is an optimum level of aggregate demand that will cause the economy to operate just at full employment. It is this level that governments aim for with their income-stabilization policies. Unfortunately, for reasons explained later in this chapter, it is rarely achieved. In practice, aggregate demand is often greater than that required for full employment. Thus, in Figure 24:6, AD (the actual aggregate demand curve) intersects the 45° line at an NNP of $120 billion rather than at the full-employment level of $100 billion. In other words, households, governments, and business firms are trying to spend more at current prices than there are goods and services being produced. The vertical difference between the AD curve and the full-employment point on

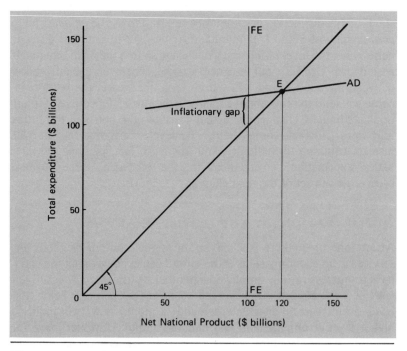

Figure 24:6 Inflationary Gap

the 45° line is called the *inflationary gap*. It indicates the extent to which total intended expenditure exceeds the amount required for a full-employment level of Net National Product. The result, unless government intervenes, is rapidly rising prices as money income exceeds real national product.

We have considered the situation where the equilibrium level of income, without government intervention, may settle at more than full employment. However, just the opposite may happen. The equilibrium level may be at less than full employment. Thus, in Figure 24:7, aggregate demand intersects the 45° line at an NNP of $80 billion rather than at the full-employment level of $100 billion. The vertical distance between the aggregate demand curve and the 45° line at the full-employment level of $100 billion is called the *deflationary gap*. It measures the shortfall between total intended expenditure and the amount required for a full-employment level of Net National Product.

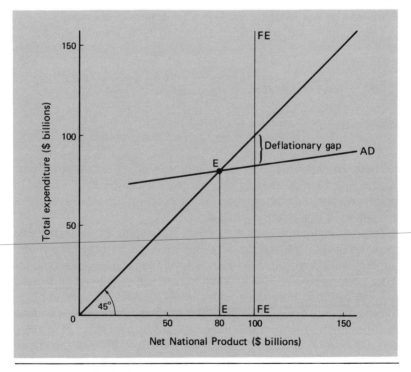

Figure 24:7   Deflationary Gap

24.14: THE MULTIPLIER

Any increase in spending on Canadian goods and services—by consumers, business, government, or foreigners— will cause Canada's national income to rise by several times the initial increase in spending. The ratio of this increase in income to the increase in spending is called the *multiplier*. If, for example, national income increased by $9 billion following an additional investment expenditure of $3 billion, the multiplier would be 3. If the increase in national income is $15 billion, the multiplier would be 5.

The level of national income will only remain higher, of course, if there is a permanent rather than "one shot" increase in spending.

We should emphasize that the multiplier effect takes place with any kind of additional spending—for consumption, business investment, government purposes, or by foreigners buying more Canadian goods and services. Also, of course, the multiplier can work in reverse. Thus, for example, an increase in taxes or a reduction in exports can cause a more than proportionate *decrease* in Canada's national income.

The multiplier can be calculated by using the following formula:

$$K = \frac{\Delta Y}{\Delta E}$$

where   Y is the change in national income
E is the change in expenditure that caused it, and
K is the multiplier

These various multipliers can reinforce or offset each other. Thus, for example, a reduction in national income caused by a decline in exports may in turn bring about a reduction in business investment that will itself cause national income to fall.

The reason for the multiplier effect on income of an increase in spending is that the recipients of this money (the original income-earners) will spend part of it. This part will then constitute income for those persons who receive it. They in turn will spend part of it. And this will continue until the amount involved in the last round of respending is only a minute fraction of the original increase in spending. If, for example, the marginal propensity to consume is ¼, an increase of $10 000 in investment spending will provide $10 000 of income to the first round of recipients, $7500 to the second round, $5625 to the third round, $4219 to the fourth round, and so on.

The actual change in income can be calculated by the application of the formula:

$$\frac{1}{1 - MPC} \times \text{ change in spending}$$

$$= \frac{1}{MPS} \times \text{ change in spending.}$$

In the previous example, the increase in income would therefore be $\frac{1}{\frac{1}{4}} \times \$10\,000$, or $\$40\,000$. The larger the marginal propensity to save (MPS), the greater the leakage of spending power in the form of savings. Also, the larger the MPS, the smaller the multiplier. We should note here that the MPC and MPS can only be used in this way if we exclude imports from consumption, since they constitute a leakage.

The multiplier has considerable practical significance. Suppose, for example, that entrepreneurs reduce investment expenditure. Then the corresponding reduction in national income would be much greater than the decrease in expenditure. Or if, for example, the government were to increase its spending in time of economic recession, the effect on national income would be much greater than the outlay.

24.15: INCOME-STABILIZATION POLICIES

At first sight, it may seem fairly obvious how a government could stabilize income at the full-employment level. In time of inflationary gap, it would merely have to reduce aggregate demand. In time of deflationary gap, it would have to increase it. Later on in this book, we shall see how the government can to some extent manipulate aggregate demand by using its three main economic weapons—fiscal policy, monetary policy, and exchange-rate policy.

What is the situation in practice? First of all, the inflationary situation caused by excessive demand—called *demand-pull inflation*—is only one type of inflation. More important in recent years has been what is called *cost-push inflation* where strong labour unions and big business push up wages and prices regardless of government tight-money policies. A reduction in aggregate demand may therefore do little to dampen inflation but much to increase unemployment.

A second weakness of income-stabilization policies is that, in times of deflationary gap, despite expansionary economic policies, governments often find it hard to restore consumer and business confidence, vital ingredients in economic expansion.

A third weakness of such policies is that our governments' understanding of the working of the economy is nowhere near as precise as our economic model suggests. What is the size of the multiplier? What is the exact effect of spending on imports? What actually determines the size of business investment in Canada? The answers to these questions are by no means clear-cut.

A fourth weakness of income-stabilization policies is the delay in obtaining statistical evidence as to what the economic situation actually is. Much statistical data is available only months or years after the event.

A fifth weakness is that government economic policies are by no means precise or immediate in their effects. Thus, despite our conceptual understanding of the multiplier, it is still not easy to predict the exact effects on the economy of, for example, a cut in personal income taxes or an increase in government spending. Also, there are considerable (and uncertain) *time lags* between the implementation of a policy and its effects on the economy.

As a result of these various uncertainties, government economic policy usually tends to go from one extreme to the other—driving furiously in one direction to get results that seem slow in coming, then braking hard (and even reversing) as the results of the first policy turn out to be greater than anticipated—hence the term *stop-go economic policy.*

24.16 SUPPLY-SIDE ECONOMICS

In the Keynesian theory that we have outlined in this chapter, an increase in aggregate demand should automatically cause economic activity, including employment, to increase. However, in practice, the economy sometimes remains relatively stagnant even though aggregate demand and prices (perhaps because of changes in fiscal and monetary policy) are increasing. This is the phenomenon of "stagflation", described in the previous chapter.

Some economists have consequently criticized Keynesian theory on the grounds that it presents aggregate demand as the active variable in a country's economic system, or model, and aggregate supply as an essentially passive one. Instead, they have argued (as a possible explanation of "stagflation") supply (for example, production costs) can also affect the level of income and employment. In other words, aggregate supply is just as much an active variable as aggregate demand. The term used to describe this approach in economic thinking is *supply-side economics.* Its advocates are termed "supply-side economists", or "supply-siders".

Factors Affecting Aggregate Supply

There are various factors that can affect production costs and thereby aggregate supply. Some are temporary in nature (such as inclement weather, earthquakes, and other natural phenomena; labour strikes; the sharp OPEC oil price increases; or an increase in inflationary expectations. Other factors are more permanent and structured. Of particular concern to the supply-side economists is the tremendous increase over the years in the size of the public sector of the economy.

According to the supply-siders, the growth in the public sector has had various effects on aggregate supply. First, the increase in sales, excise and other taxes as a percentage of national income has meant that prices have been pushed up as business firms seek to recover these taxes from consumers, rather than suffer a reduction in profits. Most taxes, according to their point of view, act as a "wedge" between the cost of the various resources, or factors of production, and the price paid by the public for the final product. Consequently, the larger the amount of taxes, the higher the price that must be charged, the less that will be bought, and the greater the degree of stagflation.

The second, and even more detrimental effect of the growth of the public sector, according to the supply-siders, has been the reduction in incentives to work, innovate, invest, and undertake entrepreneurial risk. Higher taxes, associated with progressively increasing marginal income tax rates, mean that an employee keeps less and less of each additional dollar earned. So people are less willing to work longer hours. Similarly, a businessperson is discouraged from taking entrepreneurial risks as the potential rewards are that much less. Also, people are less willing to save and invest because the after-tax returns are so poor. As a result, business managers tend to refrain from purchasing new machinery and equipment, and technologically tend to fall behind their foreign competitors.

At the same time, the other side of the coin, much of the money collected in taxes is paid out by the government in a variety of social-security programs which, although desirable in principle, have a negative effect on people's willingness to seek work, and to work in a disciplined way when employed. In other words, the tax-transfer social security system helps reduce labour productivity and so increases per unit production costs. This in turn makes such goods higher priced and less competitive with imports and so also contributes to stagflation.

A third effect of the growth of the public sector has been increased regulation of industrial activity. This regulation, which often takes the form of government-operated or regulated monopolies (airlines, railways, postal service, telephone service, liquor, agricultural marketing boards, etc.) usually means the reduction or elimination of competition in that particular industry and an increase in the cost of providing the goods or services. Pollution, safety, and other statutory requirements (however desirable they may be) also add to production costs in all industries.

Substantial Tax Cuts

There are various ways in which the costs of production can be reduced so as to encourage consumption and investment without inflation. One way is to encourage labour to moderate its pay demands, by pay restraints, moral suasion, and by example. Another is to deregulate some of the entrenched private and government monopolies and oligopolies in the economy so as to obtain, by means of competition, a better product at lower cost. But most important of all to "supply-siders", as an answer to stagflation, is a substantial reduction in taxes. Such a reduction would mean that the total cost of the product is less. This reduction in cost, when passed on in whole or part to the consumer, would cause more goods to be bought and therefore more employment created—and without inflation. As a result the Phillips curve would shift downward, to indicate that the economy has less inflation but with less unemployment (rather than more—the usual case).

Keynesian economists argue, on the other hand, that a substantial tax cut in time of recession can only create a large budget deficit. And this in turn can only cause a rapid increase in the rate of inflation. However, Arthur Laffer, a prominent U.S. supply-sider, has argued that tax cuts do not necessarily mean a reduction in tax revenue. Because of their stimulative effects on the economy, the tax cuts may in fact cause the opposite—an increase in tax revenues because of the increased economic activity and the additional sales and income tax revenue that it generates. According to Laffer, once tax rates climb too high, there is a decline in total tax revenue—because of reduced economic activity following a loss of motivation for employees, entrepreneurs, and investors. Conversely, if tax rates are dropped, total tax revenue may well increase. This relationship between the tax rate and total tax revenue is depicted in a Laffer Curve (Figure 24:8). This approach was made an integral part of President Ronald Reagan's economic policy in the U.S. in the early 1980s and earned the label "Reagonomics".

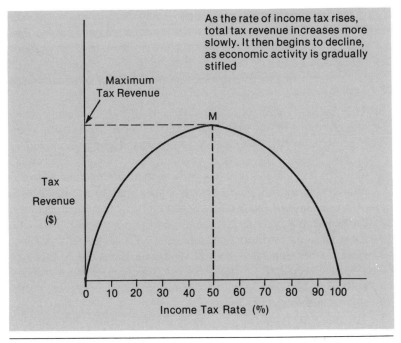

As the rate of income tax rises, total tax revenue increases more slowly. It then begins to decline, as economic activity is gradually stifled

Maximum Tax Revenue

M

Tax Revenue ($)

0 10 20 30 40 50 60 70 80 90 100

Income Tax Rate (%)

Figure 24:8 The Laffer Curve

Summary

1. Most economists used to believe that the factors of production of a society would automatically tend to be fully employed.

2. This belief was challenged in the 1930s by the English economist John Maynard Keynes. He asserted, instead, that equilibrium was more likely in a situation of less than full employment of the factors of production.

3. According to Keynes, the most important determinant of a country's income and employment is the aggregate demand (AD) for its goods and services. $AD = C + I + G + (X - M)$.

4. The amount of consumption expenditure in a society depends primarily on the level of national income. The propensity to consume is the relationship between the amount of personal disposable income and the amount of consumption expenditure.

5. The average propensity to consume (APC) is the ratio between *total* disposable income and *total* consumption expenditure. The marginal propensity to consume (MPC) is the relationship between *changes* in total disposable income and consequent *changes*

in total consumption expenditure.

6. That part of disposable income that is not consumed is saved. Two concepts are used: the average propensity to save and the marginal propensity to save.

7. Other determinants of consumption include total personal wealth, age, advertising, credit, social security, and expectations.

8. The marginal efficiency of investment (MEI) is the anticipated rate of return on an additional unit of investment. For an investment to be worth while, the MEI must, in the long run, exceed the rate of interest—the actual or imputed cost of investment funds.

9. Government expenditure has become increasingly large. Governments have the important power, if they wish to use it, to partly offset declines or increases in expenditure by the other sectors of the economy.

10. Exports, or expenditure by foreigners on Canadian goods and services, is an important part of aggregate demand. A recession abroad, particularly in the U.S., can greatly affect Canadian exports and therefore aggregate demand in Canada. Imports reduce aggregate demand in Canada.

11. The marginal propensity to import (MPM) is the relationship between changes in total disposable income and consequent changes in total imports.

12. An equilibrium level of income is a stable, self-perpetuating level of income and employment. This is achieved when aggregate demand equals aggregate supply, or, in terms of the circular flow of money, when total leakages equal total injections.

13. There is a difference between *planned* or *intended* leakages and injections, which are not necessarily equal, and *actual* or *realized* leakages and injections, which must be equal.

14. The extent to which total intended expenditure exceeds the amount required for a full-employment level of Net National Product is called the *inflationary gap*. The shortfall between total intended expenditure and the amount required for a full-employment level of NNP is called the *deflationary gap*.

15. The ratio of the increase in total income to the increase in investment (or other injection) that caused it, is called the *multiplier*.

16. Government income-stabilization policies suffer from various weaknesses—the prevalence of cost-push (rather than demand-pull) inflation; the difficulty of restoring consumer and business confidence once shattered; lack of understanding on the part of government of the working of the economy; delays in obtaining statistical data; and time-lags between the adoption of policy mea-

sures and their effects on the economy.

17. In practice, an economy can be quite stagnant despite a relatively high rate of inflation—hence the term "stagflation".

18. Some economists criticize Keynesian economics theory on the grounds that it treats aggregate demand as the key factor affecting a country's level of economic activity. Instead, they argue that aggregate supply is just as important. Such economists are called "supply-siders".

19. The supply-siders recommend substantial tax cuts as a means of reducing product costs and prices and thereby stimulating consumer and investor demand and consequently national income and employment. However, the Keynesians argue that this would only produce budget deficits and inflation.

20. Arthur Laffer, a supply-sider, counters this argument with the suggestion that a lower tax rate, because of its positive effect on economic activity, may in fact increase rather than reduce total tax revenue. The relationship between tax rates and tax revenue is illustrated by the Laffer Curve.

Key Terms

Review Questions

1. How did Keynes differ from the classical economists in his view of long-run full employment?
2. What, according to Keynes, is the most important determinant of a country's income and employment?
3. What are the other determinants of a country's national output, income, and employment?
4. How is consumption expenditure defined? What determines the level of consumption expenditure in a country?
5. Distinguish between the average propensity to consume and the marginal propensity to consume. What is the consumption function?
6. What is the relationship between consumption and savings? What determines the level of savings?
7. Distinguish between the average propensity to save and the marginal propensity to save.
8. How is investment defined in economics?
9. What determines the level of investment in a country?
10. What is meant by the marginal efficiency of investment?
11. What usually happens to the marginal efficiency of investment when a firm increases output?
12. What are the various type of new investment opportunities available to business?
13. How do changes in the rate of interest affect business investment decisions?
14. What factors can affect entrepreneurs' expectations as to the future rate of return on investments?
15. How does spending by foreigners affect employment and income in Canada? What effect do imports have on aggregate demand?
16. What characteristic of government expenditure distinguishes it from consumption expenditure and business investment expenditure?
17. How can taxation affect the level of output, income, and employment?
18. What, according to Keynes, is the equilibrium level of national income and employment? What is the modern view?
19. Distinguish between the *ex ante* and *ex post* equality of savings and investment.
20. What is meant by the term "inflationary gap"? What is its significance?
21. What is a deflationary gap? What are its implications for the economy?

22. What is the multiplier? Give a numerical example.
23. How can the government attempt to stabilize income at the full-employment level?
24. What are the weaknesses of income-stabilization policies?
25. Explain what is meant by "stagflation". Why is this considered to be an exception to Keynesian economic theory?
26. Who are "supply-siders"? Why have they earned this title?
27. Why do supply-siders advocate substantial tax cuts?
28. What is the "Laffer Curve"? What is its relevance to supply-side economics?

25. BUSINESS CYCLES

CHAPTER OBJECTIVES

A. To explain the meaning of the term "business cycle"
B. To distinguish between the various phases of the typical business cycle
C. To describe Canada's cyclical record
D. To point out U.S. economic influence on Canada
E. To indicate the possible causes of the business cycle
F. To explain how changes in national income can have an accelerated as well as a multiplier effect

CHAPTER OUTLINE

25.1 Business Cyle Defined
25.2 Phases of the Business Cycle
25.3 Canada's Cyclical Record
25.4 U.S. Economic Influence on Canada
25.5 Possible Causes of the Business Cycle
25.6 The Accelerator Theory

25.1: BUSINESS CYCLE DEFINED

In the previous chapter, we concluded that the level of a country's income has to vary in order to keep intended leakages in the circular flow equal to intended injections. During Canada's history there have, in fact, been marked fluctuations in the level of national income and output which have varied in length from many months to many years. Such fluctuations in national income, with a period of economic expansion followed by a period of economic contraction and so on alternately, have traditionally been called *business cycles*. More recently, however, the term *growth cycle* has been used by more and more economists. This new term recognizes that many changes in economic activity have been relatively slight deviations from long-term growth trends rather than severe and sustained fluctuations in business activity.

25.2: PHASES OF THE BUSINESS CYCLE

A business cycle usually passes through four phases: contraction (or downswing), trough, expansion (or upswing), and peak, as outlined in Figure 25:1.

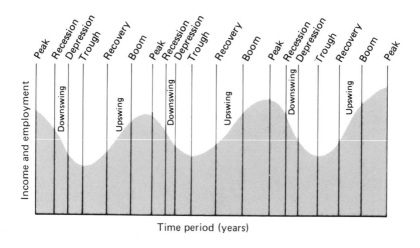

Figure 25:1 Phases of the Business Cycle

Contraction

The contraction phase of the business cycle may be subdivided into two parts, recession and depression.

Recession. In this part of the business cycle, the level of economic activity in a country quickly declines. This down-turn may be caused by a fall in demand for consumption goods, for raw and semi processed materials, or for plant and equipment. In economic contractions in Canada since World War II, personal expenditure on consumer goods and services has been remarkably stable. So also has been government expenditure. The largest reductions have been in inventories, in plant and equipment, and in exports, particularly of industrial raw materials.

At the start of a recession, business optimism gives way to pessimism. Various factors may trigger this change in outlook: a government tight-money policy, high interest rates, a fall in exports, a cutback in too rapidly accumulated inventories, or stock-market pessimism.

During the recession, business profits fall, mainly as a result of a decline in sales and partly as a result of price reductions to clear inventories. As profits decline and pessimism as to the business outlook grows, business executives refrain from investing in new plants and equipment and let inventories of raw materials and finished goods run down. As a result, demand for the output of industries producing these goods falls and many firms (for example, steel producers) have to reduce the number of hours worked or close their plants completely.

Employees working short-time or laid off altogether have less money to spend, so personal expenditure on consumer goods and services also falls. This in turn causes a reduction in the income and employment of firms producing such goods and services. They in turn cut investment expenditures. This action results in a reduction in new investment, which has a magnified or "accelerated" effect on industries producing building materials (for example lumber) and manufacturing machinery and equipment. Such industries, in time of economic recession, endure a much greater reduction in sales than do producers of consumer goods.

Depression. This term is used to describe that part of the economic contraction in which income and employment, although still falling, have become extremely low. In this stage, unemployment is high, many businesses are bankrupt, and a sense of economic helplessness prevails. The term "depression" is commonly associated with the severely depressed economic conditions of the 1930s which despite numerous predictions have never since been repeated.

Trough

Eventually, the fall in national income comes to a halt. This is called the *trough* of the business cycle.

Expansion

The expansion phase of the business cycle may be divided into two parts: recovery and boom.

Recovery. There comes a time when consumers and business firms start to replace goods that have worn out. Purchases such as clothing and appliances, for example, eventually must be made. Hopeful of an eventual revival in economic activity, business firms also begin to replace machinery and equipment. Government spending on public

"It wasn't really your fault that you went broke; you just got caught in the downphase of the business cycle."

works and various types of social relief also puts money into circulation and helps bolster consumer demand. Interest rates start to fall. The stock market perks up. Gradually the business outlook seems to improve. People begin to believe that the depression cannot last much longer. Business firms, in anticipation of an increase in demand, start to build up inventories of materials and finished goods and bring their plants up to maximum efficiency. This optimism spreads to others and before long national income and employment begin to rise. The country then enters a period of *recovery*.

Boom. After some time, the cautious optimism that characterizes the economic recovery phase gives way to unbridled consumer and business enthusiasm. Demand for all types of goods and services rises rapidly as income increases; unemployment drops to a relatively small percentage of the labour force; manufacturers can raise prices without reducing sales; profits show a healthy increase every year; and expectations for sales and profits become extremely high. This euphoric stage of the economic expansion is known as the *boom*.

As confidence about the future increases, business firms are willing to invest more and assume greater risks. Cash held in reserve during the depression is now spent relatively freely; a large proportion of profits is reinvested; and investors, with their own funds, help swell the volume of investment money available. Business spending (added to government spending and receipts from exports) provides the income with which the general public can purchase consumer goods and services. Of each dollar received, a large part is respent. Therefore, each initial dollar spent causes a multiple increase in income and expenditures. Demand for new plants and equipment (to provide enough goods and services to meet the anticipated increase in consumer demand) causes an unusually rapid increase in the demand for the output of industries producing industrial machinery and other capital goods.

During the boom, as unemployment diminishes, production costs tend to rise. Labour and other factors of production are more difficult to obtain, and firms, competing to get them, drive up their prices. As profits are high and management has no wish to halt production in a time of rapidly increasing sales, labour unions can successfully press claims for higher wages and better fringe benefits. Speculative buying of materials, land, and securities, encouraged by the general mood of optimism, also helps drive up prices.

Peak

The economic expansion phase, perhaps lasting several years, finally reaches a climax. This *peak* of the business cycle is then followed by a period of contraction—gradual or fast, depending on the forces at play e.g. in Canada's case a contraction in the U.S. market for Canadian goods or a high interest-rate policy to defend the foreign exchange rate of the Canadian dollar. In Canada, the economic expansion following the Depression of the 1930s continued with the help of World War II spending until 1944.

25.3: CANADA'S CYCLICAL RECORD

The dates and duration in months of the many business cycles that have taken place in Canada in the period 1873 to 1961 are shown in Table 25:1. Compared with earlier periods, the contractions since World War II have been shorter and the expansions longer. Annual statistics of GNP are available only from 1926 on. For the years previous to 1926, we must rely in the main on statistics of trade, employment, and output of various individual industries, and on written accounts of the economic history of those years. A summary of the rise and fall of economic activity in Canada over the last one hundred years, and of some of the factors commonly held to be fully or partly responsible for these fluctuations, is presented in the following paragraphs.

After Confederation in 1867, Canada entered a period of mild economic prosperity stimulated by the construction of the Intercolonial Railway, the large British and U.S. demand for such Canadian exports as lumber, and the economic recovery in the United States following the end of the Civil War. This prosperity lasted until 1873 when economic activity in Canada began to decline, partly as a result of a fall in the prices of Canada's principal exports.

The replacement of wooden sailing ships constructed in Canada by ships built of iron and powered by steam (constructed in the U.S.) and the general expansion of agricultural output in the United States contributed significantly to this economic decline. Over the next twenty years, in fact, Canada experienced hard times, relieved only occasionally, as in the early 1880s, by a period of accelerated business activity. During this time, tariff protection was provided for Canadian manufacturers.

Commencing in 1890, the country began a period of economic boom that continued, despite minor recessions, until 1920. At the start of this period, the settlement of Western Canada, the building of two transcontinental railroads, and the construction of storage and handling facilities for Prairie wheat were important contributing factors to Canada's high level of economic activity. The earnings from wheat exports

Table 25:1
Business Cycles in Canada, 1873-1961

Dates			Duration in Months		
					Complete
			Contraction	Expansion	Cycle
			(peak to	(trough to	(peak to
Trough		Peak	trough)	peak)	peak)
		November 1873	—	—	—
May	1879	July 1882	66	38	104
March	1885	February 1887	32	23	55
February	1888	July 1890	12	29	41
March	1891	February 1893	8	23	31
March	1894	August 1895	13	17	30
August	1896	April 1900	12	44	56
February	1901	December 1902	10	22	32
June	1904	December 1906	18	30	48
July	1908	March 1910	19	20	39
July	1911	November 1912	16	16	32
January	1915	January 1918	26	36	62
April	1919	June 1920	15	<u>14</u>	<u>29</u>
September	1921	June 1923	15	21	36
August	1924	April 1929	14	56	70
March	1933	July 1937	47	52	99
October	1938	n.a.	15	n.a.	n.a.
February	1946.	October 1948	n.a.	32	n.a.
September	1949	May 1953	11	44	<u>55</u>
June	1954	April 1957	13	<u>34</u>	<u>47</u>
April	1958	January 1960	12	21	33

Note: Underlined figures are the wartime expansions and the full cycles that include the wartime expansions.

Source: D. A. White, *Business Cycles in Canada*, Staff Study No. 17, Economic Council of Canada, p. 236. Reproduced by permission of the Minister of Supply and Services Canada.

to Britain and other countries enabled Canadian prairie farmers to purchase lumber from British Columbia and manufactured goods from Ontario and Quebec, and so spread the prosperity to all parts of the country. During this period new mines were established in Ontario, British Columbia, and the Yukon; factories were built in central Canada; hydro-electric power was made available in Ontario; rail and lake shipping was improved; and foreign capital, mainly British, flowed into Canada.

World War I, beginning in 1914, caused a large demand for such products as base metals, pulp and paper, woollens, ships, and particularly munitions. The demand for food also increased greatly; so farmers shared in the general prosperity. The economy continued to prosper for some time after the end of the War, as business firms produced machinery and equipment to replace that which had worn out and as the demand for food and clothing at home and abroad continued at a high level. At the end of 1920, demand fell and Canada experienced a short but severe economic recession.

During most of the remainder of the 1920s, however, the country continued to prosper: wheat and other grain crops were good and demand for them was high; the automobile industry was developing and new roads were constructed; and capital from the United States was invested in the mining and wood-pulp industries. The Maritime provinces did not, however, share in this general economic prosperity.

Unfortunately, towards the end of 1929, economic confidence disappeared in Canada and the United States; and the stock-market crashes of that year were followed by a rapidly falling level of investment and economic activity in general. North America and Europe then experienced the "Great Depression" with its bankruptcies, suicides, soup kitchens, and bread lines. Not until 1933 did the Canadian economy start to revive. This expansion continued, except for a slight recession in 1938, into the economic boom years of World War II.

In 1945, the economic depression that was expected to follow the war failed to materialize: Canada continued to prosper. The pent-up demand for consumer goods was released in a flood of spending. Foreign demand for this country's exports was high, and Canadian and U.S. investment in Canadian manufacturing, mining, and housing was large. Periods of accelerated economic activity were experienced in 1950 (due to large military expenditures for the Korean War) and in 1955-56 (due to heavy U.S. investment in Canadian resource development). Economic recessions in the United States in 1949, 1954, and 1957-58, on the other hand, caused a slight decline in economic activity in Canada in those years. After 1958, Canadian economic growth slowed down and the unemployment rate among the labour force was quite high. The economy picked up in 1962 and until 1969 Canada enjoyed a period of economic boom. Some of the factors responsible for this prosperity included: a steady expansion in manufacturing facilities; a substantial increase in the money supply; large wheat sales to the Soviet Union and China; increasing exports to the United States (where spending for the Vietnam War helped to raise the total level of expenditure); a high level of government spending in Canada on education, roads, bridges, and health; and the large Expo 67 construction program. In 1969 the economy began to suffer an economic recession brought about by a government tight-money policy designed to fight inflation. This policy lasted until 1971 when credit was loosened and the economy again began to pick up speed. Despite severe inflation, the economy continued to operate at less than full employment. However, by early 1978, the rate of inflation had been significantly lowered by the use of compulsory wage-and-price controls. Nevertheless, unemployment, particularly among young people had reached alarming levels. The economy continued to stagger along until the early 1980s, when a high interest-rate policy in the United States, Canada's major export market, was followed by a similar one in Canada. Canada's high interest-rate policy, designed to help defend the foreign exchange value of the Canadian dollar as well as to fight inflation, slowed investment spending and discouraged house-buying and other consumer expenditures and so helped bring about a fall in Canada's GNP. Also, the continuing low level of foreign and Canadian demand for raw materials and equipment caused many firms, in manufacturing, mining, and other resource-based industries such as lumber, to lay off workers, either permanently or temporarily. Furthermore, a more nationalistic economic policy, symbolized by the Foreign Investment Review Agency and the National Energy Program, scared away many foreign investors. The result of all this was a severe economic recession that lasted until 1983.

25.4: U.S. ECONOMIC INFLUENCE ON CANADA

Canada depends on other countries, particularly the United States, for the sale of many of its products. This heavy dependence on foreign demand makes the Canadian economy extremely susceptible to changes in the level of economic activity abroad. Thus, if the United States experiences an economic recession, this is quickly felt in Canada as exports fall.

Also Canada, because of its dependence on a large amount of foreign investment, is vulnerable in another way to changes abroad. If economic activity declines in the United States, American investment in Canada also declines, resulting in a fall in the general level of demand for goods and service in this country.

25.5: POSSIBLE CAUSES OF THE BUSINESS CYCLE

So far, there is no generally accepted theory as to the causes of business cycles. However, the income and employment theory discussed in the previous chapter provides at least a partial explanation. Also there is no doubt that government economic policies are often crucial in triggering an expansion or contraction of the economy. In Canada's case, the actions of the U.S. government can be just as important as those of our own government.

Changes in Investment

Until World War II, the main components of total expenditure were personal consumption, business investment, and exports. Since then, a fourth component, government expenditure, has become very important. Of these four components, business investment is by far the most unstable element, because it depends largely on business expectations of the future.

In Table 25:2, we can see that in the economic depression from 1929 to 1933, total final demand for goods and services fell by about 40 per cent. However, the fall in investment expenditure was much more pronounced. Spending on non-residential construction declined by 84 per cent and spending on machinery and equipment by 81 per cent. In the 1957-58 economic recession, as another example, investment in housing, in non-residential construction, and in machinery and equipment fell substantially, while personal expenditure and government expenditure both increased. A decline in Canadian exports contributed significantly to all but the most recent cyclical contractions. In the 1929-33 contraction, a substantial decline in government expenditure (28 per cent) was an important element in the overall reduction in final demand expenditures and so helped intensify the contraction. In all later periods of economic contraction, government spending has increased and has to some extent offset the reduction in spending by the other components.

25.6: THE ACCELERATOR THEORY

The level of investment in a country varies considerably over time. Economists have suggested, as an explanation, that investment depends more on the *rate of change* in national income than on its *absolute level*. This is because of the predominantly *induced* nature of business investment. Let us explain.

Business investment consists of two parts; first, replacement of plant and equipment that has worn out and, second, additions to the existing capital stock. In both cases the level of investment depends on what business firms consider to be the necessary amount of plant and equipment to produce the goods and services that the economy demands. If business firms anticipate that demand for their goods will remain at the

Table 25:2

Percentage Changes in Components of Canadian Final Demand
Expenditures (in Current Dollars) during Cyclical Contractions

	1929 to 1933	1937 to 1938	IVQ 1948 to IVQ 1949	IIIQ 1953 to IIIQ 1954	IIIQ 1957 to IIQ 1958	IIQ 1960 to IQ 1961
Personal expenditure	−35.4	0.3	5.8	3.5	5.4	3.0
Government expenditure	−27.8	7.6	16.9	2.3	8.5	4.8
Residential construction	−68.7	−9.7	7.7	0.7	29.0	−11.8
Non-residential construction	−84.1	−9.6	3.6	−1.7	−8.1	−4.1
Machinery and equipment	−80.7	−2.7	—	−5.0	−18.6	−8.6
Exports	−49.4	−14.8	−7.3	−7.5	2.6	0.4
Imports	−57.4	10.8	1.2	6.8	8.0	0.5
Total final demand (equals GNE excluding error and inventory change)	−39.8	−1.2	4.8	2.1	6.3	1.6

Note: The change in each component is expressed as a percentage of the peak level of GNE (excluding error). Each component shows, therefore, its percentage contribution to the total percentage change in GNE (excluding error).

Source: D. A. White, *Business Cycles in Canada*, p. 96. Reproduced by permission of the Minister of Supply and Services Canada.

same level, they need only replace plant and equipment that has worn out. For example, an individual industry with plant and equipment worth $30 million might replace 5 per cent of it each year to maintain sales at $10 million. This 5 per cent would mean an investment expenditure of $1.5 million. The assumed *capital output ratio* is 3:1.

Investment expenditure is not made, however, solely for replacement. There is also *induced investment*, which takes place in response to an increase in the demand for the industry's output. If, in our highly simplified example, the industry anticipated a 10 per cent increase in sales (and the existing production capacity could not be more fully utilized), it would need to purchase plant and equipment worth $4.5

million ($1.5 million of replacement investment and $3 million of induced investment).

The significance of the induced nature of most business investment is that a change in national income and therefore sales (see Table 25:3) can cause an *accelerated* change in business investment. Thus, if national income starts to rise after an economic recession, business investment may show a startling increase. Conversely, if national income starts to decline, business investment (reflecting business managers' pessimistic outlook as to expected sales) can fall even faster. And this fall may be in replacement investment as well as in induced investment. This relationship between the rate of change in national income and the level of business investment is explained by the *accelerator theory*, or *accelerator principle*. Using this principle, we can predict that when national income is rising, the level of business investment will be high. However, once the level of national income is relatively stable, business investment will decline. The ratio between the change in demand for business output and the change in investment, although difficult in practice to measure, is called the *acceleration factor*.

Table 25:3
An Example of the Accelerator Theory of Investment
(Hypothetical Data in $1000s)

Year	Annual Sales	Required Capital Stock (assuming a 3:1 capital-output ratio)	Required Change in Investment from previous year
1	180	540	—
2	200	600	+ 60
3	240	720	+120
4	300	900	+180
5	400	1200	+300
6	420	1260	+ 60
7	420	1260	—
8	400	1200	− 60
9	360	1080	−120
10	300	900	−180

Accelerator-Multiplier Interaction

A fall in business investment, once the rate of increase in national income falls off, can have disastrous effects on the economy. This is because the decline in investment will have a multiplier effect. If the multiplier (determined, as we saw in the previous chapter, by the marginal propensity to consume) is 4, then a decline in investment of $5 million would cause a fall in national income of $20 million. In addition, as national income falls, sales expectations drop. This results in less investment, which in turn reduces national income even further. This *cumulative* effect can also work in reverse. If a government pumps money into the hands of consumers during an economic depression, the increase in income and spending (if considered to be of relatively permanent duration) will tend to cause an increase in investment spending because of the accelerator effect. We say "tend" because in practice the effect of the government spending may be partly offset by a negative outlook among business managers. However, assuming that this is not the case, the business spending will in turn create new jobs and income and, through the multiplier process, raise national income by four times the amount of investment. And as national income rises, more investment spending will result in further income expansion. Optimism will replace pessimism and consumers and business firms, spending freely, will push national income to new heights—until the rate of growth slackens and (unless there is deliberate government expenditure to boost demand) causes investment to drop off, initiating a cumulative decline in national income.

From our discussion, we can see that the accelerator nature of induced business investment, combined with the multiplier effects of changes in business investment on national income, can cause national income and output to change significantly and cumulatively, either up or down. However, as we saw in the previous chapter, there is no guarantee that the economy will stabilize at a full-employment level. Rather, since we live in a dynamic world, the levels of output, income and employment will tend to be changing all the time.

Other Factors

The accelerator-multiplier effects of investment are not the only relationships that have been advanced to explain cyclical changes in economic activity. Other factors include changes in the rate of interest; the marginal efficiency of investment; changes in the money supply; and the cost of capital goods compared with the cost of other inputs. Cyclical behaviour is also considered to be influenced by "shocks" such as wars, technological developments, changes in the weather, natural disasters (for example, earthquakes), major strikes, major natural-resource discoveries, significant changes in government economic policy (e.g. wage and price controls), major increases or reductions in tariffs, changes in the availability of business credit, and crises in international liquidity. Human nature is also considered to be an important factor affecting business cycles. Thus, in a period of economic expansion, human over-optimism and lack of customary caution become increasingly evident and help to intensify the expansion. In a period of economic contraction, pessimism and excessive caution tend to heighten the economic depression and postpone the recovery.

Summary

1. Marked fluctuations in the level of national income and output over the course of many years are known as business cycles or, more optimistically, as growth cycles.
2. The contraction phase of the business cycle can be divided into two parts: recession and depression. Recession is a period of declining business activity. Depression is a situation where income and employment, although still falling, have become extremely low.
3. The trough of a business cycle is the lowest point of business activity.
4. The expansion phase of the business cycle can be divided into two parts: recovery and boom. Recovery is a situation of cautiously rising business activity, following a recession or depression. Boom is a situation of rapidly increasing business activity, characterized by optimism as to the future.
5. The peak of the business cycle is the highest point of business activity.
6. Contractions of business activity in Canada since the Second World War, compared with those of previous years,have been shorter and expansions longer.
7. Because of Canada's heavy reliance on export markets, particularly the United States, for the sale of many of its goods and services, economic contractions abroad are quickly felt at home.
8. So far, there is no generally accepted theory of business cycles. The most plausible explanation to date has been the Keynesian income and employment theory.
9. It has been suggested that fluctuations in the level of investment take place because investment depends on the rate of change in national income rather than on its absolute level. This is called the accelerator theory.
10. Accelerated changes in business investment combined with the

multiplier effect discussed in the previous chapter can cause tremendous changes, upward and downward, in national income.

11. Other factors, including human nature, have been pinpointed as possible contributory causes of the business cycle.

Key Terms

Business cycle   503
Growth cycle   503
Contraction   504
Recession   504
Depression   505
Trough   505
Expansion   505

Recovery   505
Boom   507
Peak   507
Accelerator theory   512
Induced investment   513
Accelerator-multiplier
   interaction   514

Review Questions

1. What is a business cycle? What are its various phases?
2. Distinguish between a recession and a depression.
3. Distinguish between the trough and the peak of a business cycle.
4. What are the characteristics of a business boom?
5. What has been Canada's recent cyclical experience?
6. How is Canada affected by cyclical changes in economic activity abroad, particularly in the United States?
7. What is induced investment?
8. What is the accelerator theory?
9. What is the accelerator-multiplier interaction?
10. What factors, other than changes in investment, can cause cyclical changes in economic activity?

26. ECONOMIC GROWTH AND REGIONAL INCOME DISPARITIES

CHAPTER OBJECTIVES

A. To discuss the relationship between economic growth and the standard of living of a country
B. To identify the requirements for economic growth
C. To explain the causes of economic growth
D. To describe government assistance for economic growth in Canada
E. To discuss the nature and causes of regional income disparities in Canada
F. To emphasize that, as economic growth takes place, many non-renewable natural resources are depleted

CHAPTER OUTLINE

26.1: ECONOMIC GROWTH DEFINED

Apart from political independence, nothing is more vital to a country's well-being than economic growth. For *economic growth*—the rate at which a country increases its output of goods and services—is the key to a higher standard of living. In fact, Canada's rate of economic growth, as measured by annual increases in real GNP, has varied considerably (see Table S.23)—ranging from 7 or 8 per cent in some years to almost nothing or even a slight decline in others.

In Canada, despite its relatively high average standard of living, the need for rapid economic growth is no less acute than in many other parts of the world. The elimination of poverty, the reduction of unemployment, the lessening of regional disparities in wealth and opportunity, and the provision of adequate medical, dental, and hospital care, are all examples of objectives requiring economic growth, as well as political resolve, for their achievement. However, we should not forget that economic growth also has disadvantages—notably, pollution of the environment and depletion of natural resources.

26.2: POPULATION GROWTH AND THE STANDARD OF LIVING

A high rate of economic growth does not automatically mean a rising standard of living because the increase in output may be more than offset by an increase in the population. For example, the present rate of economic growth in India is hardly sufficient to maintain the existing standard of living for its rapidly expanding population. And, in China, birth control is an integral part of the new economic program. With this in mind, many economists measure economic growth in terms of *per-capita output* or *per-capita national income*. This is the average output or average income per person—obtained by dividing the value of a country's GNP or its national income by the number of its population. Canada's experience since 1950 is shown in Table S.24.

A visitor from outer space would consider Canada to be a vast land with a tiny population. He or she would think that everyone would have more than enough food; and there would be no shortage of work. In fact, although Canada is by no means the paradise that our visitor might expect, it is a rich land compared with many others. Also, average per capita income is one of the highest in the world, even though it has slipped down the international scale over the last few decades from its once number four position to its present fourteenth.

Obviously, if a country's population is growing faster than its real national income, the average standard of living will decline. Indeed, a visitor from outer space might well wonder how people could multiply so rapidly, yet still be able to continue feeding themselves for so long with the surface of the earth fixed in size. The problem has also been foreseen and discussed by many people on earth. One of these was Thomas Robert Malthus, a young English clergyman, who wrote a

Table S.23
Canada's Gross National Product, 1950-1982

Year	Millions of Current Dollars	Millions of Constant (1971) Dollars	Percentage Increase in Real GNP
1950	18 491	33 762	7.6
1951	21 640	35 450	8.9
1952	24 588	38 617	5.1
1953	25 833	40 605	-1.2
1954	25 918	40 106	9.4
1955	28 528	43 891	9.4
1956	32 058	47 599	8.4
1957	33 513	48 718	2.4
1958	34 777	49 844	2.3
1959	36 846	51 737	3.8
1960	38 359	53 231	2.9
1961	39 646	54 741	2.8
1962	42 927	58 475	6.8
1963	45 978	61 487	5.2
1964	50 280	65 610	6.7
1965	55 364	69 981	6.7
1966	61 828	74 844	6.9
1967	66 409	77 344	3.3
1968	72 586	81 864	5.8
1969	79 815	86 225	5.3
1970	85 685	88 390	2.5
1971	94 450	94 450	6.9
1972	105 234	100 248	6.1
1973	123 560	107 812	7.5
1974	147 528	111 678	3.6
1975	165 343	113 005	1.2
1976	191 031	119 249	5.5
1977	208 868	121 762	2.1
1978	230 490	126 191	3.6
1979	261 576	129 850	2.9
1980	291 869	130 467	0.5
1981	331 338	134 540	3.1
1982	348 925	128 057	-4.8

Source: Statistics Canada, *National Income and Expenditure Accounts*

Table S.24
Canada's Per Capita Real GNP, 1950-1982

Year	GNP in Millions of Constant (1971) Dollars	Population as of June (thousands)	Per Capita Real GNP (1971) Dollars	Percentage Annual Increase
1950	33 762	13 712	2 462	5.5
1951	35 450	14 009	2 531	2.8
1952	38 617	14 459	2 671	5.5
1953	40 605	14 845	2 735	2.4
1954	40 106	15 287	2 624	-4.1
1955	43 891	15 698	2 796	6.6
1956	47 599	16 081	2 960	5.9
1957	48 718	16 610	2 933	-0.9
1958	49 844	17 080	2 918	-0.5
1959	51 737	17 483	2 959	1.4
1960	53 231	17 870	2 979	0.7
1961	54 741	18 238	3 001	0.7
1962	58 475	18 583	3 147	4.9
1963	61 487	18 931	3 248	3.2
1964	65 610	19 291	3 401	4.7
1965	69 981	19 644	3 562	4.7
1966	74 844	20 015	3 739	5.0
1967	77 344	20 378	3 795	1.5
1968	81 864	20 701	3 955	4.2
1969	86 225	21 001	4 106	3.8
1970	88 390	21 297	4 150	0.1
1971	94 450	21 568	4 379	5.5
1972	100 248	21 802	4 598	5.0
1973	107 812	22 043	4 891	6.4
1974	111 678	22 364	4 994	2.1
1975	113 005	22 697	4 979	-0.3
1976	119 249	22 993	5 186	4.2
1977	121 762	23 287	5 229	0.8
1978	126 191	23 534	5 362	2.5
1979	129 850	23 769	5 463	1.9
1980	130 467	24 058	5 423	-0.7
1981	134 540	24 342	5 527	1.9
1982	128 057	24 603	5 205	-5.8

Source: Statistics Canada, *National Income and Expenditure Accounts* and *Estimated Population of Canada*

book, *Essay on the Principle of Population* that was published in 1798 and has had considerable world influence ever since.

The principal point made by Malthus in his essay was that the world's population tends to double itself every twenty-five years or so—a much faster rate of growth than that of the world's food supply. This meant, according to Malthus, that the world's population, if left to grow unchecked, would eventually starve itself to death. However, Malthus argued, various checks operate to prevent this catastrophe. First of all, *positive checks*, such as famine, disease, and war, tend to increase the death rate. Second, *preventive checks*, such as later marriages, and more modest ambitions as to family size, tend to reduce the birth rate.

What has happened since Malthus helped make people uncomfortably aware of the fate that might one day overtake us? In 1880, world population was estimated to be about 919 million. By 1980, it had grown to 4381 million—an almost fivefold increase. During that period, the positive checks (including two world wars, influenza and other epidemics, famines, and earthquakes) have on the one hand helped to slow population growth. So also, in more recent years, have such preventive checks as new and improved birth-control devices. However, new medical discoveries, better sanitation, and improved nutrition have on the other hand helped to reduce the death rate among both young and old. The world population has certainly not doubled every twenty-five years. Nevertheless, its rate of growth has been enough to cause continued alarm. And by 1990, according to World Bank estimates, it should reach 5025 million.

Another point to remember when we talk about economic growth and the standard of living is the proportion of a country's wealth devoted to military purposes. If a country uses part of its materials, capital, and labour to staff and equip an army, air force, and navy, it is forgoing its ability to produce other goods and services. Such military expenditure may be well justified if it is to protect the independence of the country. Military security, just like law and order, may be considered part of a country's standard of living. Canada is fortunate, because of its proximity to the United States, not to have to devote as large a percentage of its resources to the maintenance of military security as do many other countries.

In the case of countries that depend on exports for a major part of their national income, a very important influence on the standard of living is the price received for these exports. Thus, although there may be economic growth in the sense of more production, there may be little increase in a country's real income. Third World countries, with

Despite its size and wealth, Canada has a relatively tiny population

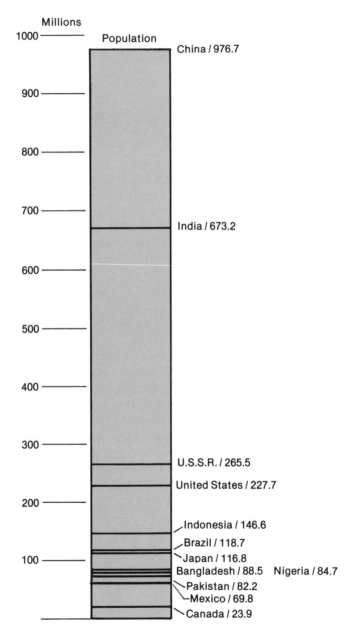

Source of data: World Bank, *World Development Report, 1982*

predominantly agricultural or mineral exports, have in fact found that world market prices for such products have not kept pace with the prices of the manufactured goods that they import. In other words, the *terms of trade* (which is the relationship between a country's export prices and import prices) have become less favourable. That is one of the reasons why the oil-exporting countries decided to raise their oil prices in 1973. And that is why many such countries have taken part in price-fixing cartels such as the Organization of Petroleum Exporting Countries (OPEC) and the Inter-Governmental Council of Copper Exporting Countries (CIPEC).

Finally, we should remember that per-capita national income is an average. If, as is often the case in many economically underdeveloped countries, the distribution of income greatly favours a small ruling class, the standard of living of the mass of the population will be lower than that suggested by the per-capita income statistics. On the other hand, many goods, such as home-grown farm produce and livestock, never enter the official statistics of these countries; nor do the people face large heating, transportation, and clothing costs. Thus the low per-capita income may not really be as bad as it may initially sound to a Canadian. Moreover, in all countries, national-income statistics ignore that many goods have greatly improved in quality without a proportionate increase in price—for example, the average car today is much better value than the average car of thirty years ago. National-income statistics also ignore that people can now buy goods and services that were not available before—such as air travel or printed words. They also ignore the amount of leisure time a population enjoys.

26.3: REQUIREMENTS FOR ECONOMIC GROWTH

If a country is to be able to produce more goods and services, it will obviously require a larger supply of the various factors of production, including technology.

Natural Resources

Without natural resources such as farmland, mineral deposits, and hydro-electric potential, a country is severely handicapped in its efforts to achieve economic growth. Labour, capital, and technology alone do not usually suffice. Most countries, however poor, usually have at least one or two valuable natural resources locally available. An island in the Pacific, for example, has one of the highest per-capita incomes in the world, based on only one natural resource—the phosphate of which the island is composed. Japan, one of the world's leading manufacturing nations, imports most of its raw materials and much of its fuel. Canada, by contrast, has a variety of valuable natural resources, ranging from forests and fisheries to mineral deposits and fresh water. Where raw materials and even fuel need to be imported, a country can be severely handicapped. Only Japan, with its highly productive labour force and advanced technology, has been able in recent years to overcome this handicap. Western Europe, by contrast, has fared less well—although discoveries of oil and natural gas in the North Sea have helped to improve the situation.

Unlike capital and labour, natural resources cannot be indefinitely increased. Some new resources, such as mineral deposits, are, it is true, periodically being found and new uses for others being devised. But we are fortunate if these new discoveries more than offset resources like iron ore that are being used up, or resources like fishing grounds that are being destroyed. That is why there is so much concern that Canada is exporting so many of its natural resources in a relatively unprocessed state rather than using them here in the production of manufactured goods that could be sold abroad, if the price and quality were reasonable enough.

Labour

Without people to develop and operate a country's factories, farms, and mines, there can be no investment and no production: a country's natural resources would lie practically unused—just as they did in Canada for so many centuries.

What is the labour-force situation in Canada? Since Confederation, heavy immigration and a high birth rate (until recent years) have provided the country with a steadily increasing labour force. (See Table S.2, in Chapter 1).

In the last decade, Canada's labour force has rapidly increased. There have been three basic reasons for this: first, the larger number of new workers entering the labour force because of the post-war baby boom; second, the larger percentage of women entering the labour force; third, increased immigration. Whether the quality of labour has increased in recent years as a result of massive spending on education is a debatable point as many employers argue that the "basics" are being neglected.

Also of importance to economic growth is the mobility of the labour force. Many Canadians have shown themselves willing to move to other part of the country in search of better jobs. Portable pension rights under the Canada Pension Plan have increased this labour mobility. However, unemployment-insurance benefits and welfare assistance, can have the opposite effect because they reduce the incentive to move elsewhere in search of work.

Capital

A country's capital is of two main kinds: *business capital*, such as manufacturing plants and transportation equipment; and *social capital*, such as roads, hospitals, houses, and schools. Canada is considered to have one of the highest average amounts of capital per worker in the world.

Statistical records of private and public investment in Canada show that utilities, manufacturing, and primary and construction industries account for well over half the total investment. Housing now absorbs about one-fifth of total investment funds. Over the years, capital investment in Canada has been rapidly increasing, except in periods of economic recession.

The relationship between a given amount of investment and the resultant output is called the *capital-output ratio*. Since capital is scarce, investment is often in projects with the highest capital-output ratio. However, where there is a high degree of actual or "hidden" unemployment, it would seem to make more sense to favour labour-intensive projects over capital-intensive ones. Employment tax credits and wage subsidies, whereby an employer is given a financial incentive to take on more employees, are a step in this direction.

Technology

Another important ingredient of economic growth is technology. This is the technical knowledge of how to produce goods and services. As we have said before, a country can have a good labour force and sufficient capital, but not have the technology to make the best use of its natural resources. Furthermore, it is improved technology that permits an increase in the capital-output ratio.

Research and Development (R & D)

Scientific and industrial research and development usually go hand in hand with economic growth. Thus, Britain became the "workshop of the world" in the nineteenth century partly because of the steam engine, the cotton spinning jenny, and other industrial inventions. Nowadays, improvements in communications and the licensing of foreign manufacturing rights mean that the benefits of new inventions can be quickly spread throughout the world. Indeed, Japan's rapid economic growth after World War II was initially based on the copying, improvement, and more efficient production of products already invented else-where. As one example, it produced relatively few cars until the 1960s, but once production started, it took only a relatively short time before Japanese firms became world-leading car manufacturers. The same story is true of motor-cycles, cameras, television sets, radios, calcula-tors, etc.

Canada, although not without its own inventions and discoveries (for example, the telephone, insulin, the snowmobile, and Telidon), has relied mainly on copying products researched and developed else-where. Because of the United States' advanced industrial technology, wealth of investment capital, and close geographical proximity, much of Canada's technology has been imported from that country. British, German, French, and other foreign firms have also established manu-facturing subsidiaries in Canada.

With a few notable exceptions, private industry in Canada has tended to neglect the important functions of research and develop-ment. One reason for this is that the U.S. parent companies of many firms in Canada prefer to carry out this function at their research labo-ratories in the United States. Thus, total private research spending in Canada compares unfavourably with that in West European countries and Japan. Moreover, the scientific knowledge acquired by private re-search in Canada has not always been readily available to the govern-ment or the country in general.

Unlike the private sector, government spending on scientific and industrial research compares very favourably with that of other coun-tries. Research is carried on by most federal government departments and agencies.

26.4: CAUSES OF ECONOMIC GROWTH

There is no one universally accepted theory of economic growth. De-pending on the time and circumstances, different forces have assumed a key role in propelling a country or region forward economically.

The Staple Theory

One long-advanced explanation of Canada's economic growth is the *staple theory*. This theory states in essence that a prime motivating force in the country's economic growth has been the production and export of various staple products. These products have changed over the years—the most notable being fur and codfish from the time of Con-federation until the early twentieth century; wheat from 1896 to 1914 and again in more recent times; and forest products and non-ferrous metals since World War II. The earnings from these exports have had a beneficial, ripple effect throughout the economy. When staple exports have declined, there have been periods of relative economic stagnation.

Certainly, there can be little doubt that, when Canada's domestic market was very small, the income and employment created by exports of one or more staple products was relatively great. However, as the Canadian economy has grown and diversified, the relative importance of individual export products has declined.

Social Capital

Another possible way in which a country's economic growth can be accelerated is by the provision of social capital—namely, roads, ports, railways, electric power, schools, housing, and hospitals. If these are lacking in an area (for example, Canada's North-West), it is difficult, if not impossible, for mining, processing, or manufacturing industries to be established. If a private firm must itself supply these basic requirements, the overall cost of establishing a plant is usually prohibitive. Since the benefits of roads and other public facilities are spread throughout the area, providing substantial "external economies" to all, it is usually considered to be the responsibility of government to provide them. In many countries, governments do in fact consider such public investment, together with other incentives such as tax holidays, to be the most effective way of stimulating economic growth.

Innovations

A U.S. economist, Alvin Hansen, after examining the great economic expansions of the past, attributed them to increases in investment caused by one of three factors: fast population growth; the opening up for settlement of vast new areas; and innovations. By "innovations," he meant new ways of doing things—such as travelling by rail—that would offer profitable investment opportunities. The role of innovations in economic growth was also stressed by another great economist, Joseph Schumpeter.[1] Today, four different types of innovation are recognized: (a) the discovery and use of new types of resources; (b) the development of new uses for existing resources; (c) the development of new products; and (d) the modification of existing products. Each type of innovation can spur economic growth, so long as it permits the production of new goods that will satisfy customer wants previously unfilled or permit the production of existing goods at lower cost. Closely associated with all these types of innovation is the develop-

"How can you expect Canada to grow, if you don't buy our cars?"

ment of new technologies—sometimes considered as a category of innovation in itself.

Today, governments recognize the importance of all these factors. But not many countries still have new territories to develop; Canada is one of the lucky few. Population growth is also slowing down in many countries of the world. There can be no doubt, however, that profitable investment opportunities still abound. The problem is, of course, being able to recognize them or to develop the necessary technology.

Innovations are considered most likely to occur if certain favourable conditions are present in society. These conditions have been categorized as: (a) *underlying conditions*, (b) *enabling conditions*, and (c) *incentives to innovate*.[2] Favourable *underlying conditions* exist where people are not heavily bound by tradition, but have an open, dynamic outlook. Favourable *enabling conditions* exist, where the institutional framework of society, including law and order, research and development facilities, financial institutions, and competition, encourages innovation. Favourable *incentives to innovate* exist where private property rights, capital cost and depletion allowances, rates of income taxation, and development grants help make innovation financially worthwhile. Canada rates fairly well by all these criteria.

26.5: GOVERNMENT ASSISTANCE

Something that is relatively new today is the much more active role of government in the economy. Instead of relying purely on private investment, governments are themselves investing vast sums in a wide variety of projects. They are also offering incentives of all kinds—such as "tax holidays" and "forgivable loans"—to stimulate private investment in designated areas. At the federal level, the Department of Regional and Industrial Expansion is very active in this field. So also is the Canada Development Corporation. To assist the growth of small Canadian businesses, there is the Federal Business Development Bank. All of these are examined below.

Department of Regional Economic Expansion

In April 1969, the federal government established a new department, called the Department of Regional Economic Expansion, or DREE. This department, the instrument of a major federal effort to reduce regional economic and social disparities through economic growth, was to offer financial and other assistance to "designated regions" and "special areas" of Canada. These regions and areas were those considered to be in need of special federal help because of high chronic unemployment, slow rates of economic growth, and low levels of income. The general philosophy of the department was to give priority to assisting growth centres, as well as to improving the economic infrastructure (roads, bridges, schools) of these regions. With this policy, the department hoped to avoid the error too frequently committed in the past of providing some measure of temporary relief but doing little to help make an area economically viable.

Prior to the establishment of this new government department, federal assistance for regional economic development had been scattered among a variety of departments, boards, and agencies. One of the purposes in establishing this new department was to centralize and coordinate many of these diverse activities.

DREE attempted to promote economic growth in the designated areas in various ways. One way was to offer regional industrial incentives. These incentives, of a once-and-for-all nature, were of two types: first, there was the *primary development incentive*, a grant made to a manufacturing or processing firm that expanded or modernized its existing plant; second, there was the *secondary development incentive*, an additional grant made to a firm that established new facilities or undertook new product expansion. For the special areas, the assistance provided by the department could take the form of a development incentive grant, a settling-in grant, a loan guarantee and/or a loan.

A second way that the department had of promoting economic growth in the designated regions was by *area programs* of financial assistance to build roads, bridges, electric-power plants, sewage systems, and other elements of the economicinfrastructure.

The third type of assistance, of a social nature, consisted of programs, such as NEWSTART vocational training, designed to help people in the special areas adjust to the new employment opportunities.

The Department of Regional Economic Expansion was organized for its development activities into three regions: Atlantic, Centre (Quebec and Ontario), and West. Field offices were located in all provincial capitals. There was also a regional office for the West in Regina.

Department of Regional and Industrial Expansion

In 1983, the Department of Regional Economic Expansion (DREE) was to be merged with the Department of Industry, Trade and Commerce (ITC) to form a new department, the Department of Regional and Industrial Expansion (DRIE). This Department, as we saw in Chapter 17, is to implement the federal government's new Industrial and Regional Development Program, or IRDP for short. Like the

DREE, the DRIE will rely mainly on financial grants to industry to achieve its economic growth objectives.

Canada Development Corporation

The Canada Development Corporation, or CDC, was established by the Federal Government in 1971 as a national development corporation for Canada. Its purpose was to act as a vehicle for raising substantial funds from the Canadian public and for investing these funds, in the form of equity capital, in Canadian business corporations. The money was to be used to help establish significant new enterprises and to assist in the expansion of existing companies. The size of the investment in a corporation was normally large enough, either alone or in combination with funds from other Canadian investors, to ensure Canadian control. The CDC was expected to play a leadership role, along the lines of a merchant bank, in organizing major, viable, Canadian business ventures such as natural-gas and oil pipelines and in arranging mergers of smaller Canadian companies, where significant administrative, financial, production, or marketing benefits would accrue. Since the date of its establishment, the CDC has also actively involved itself in increasing the amount of venture capital available to small and medium-sized businesses. It has done this by purchasing part ownership of existing venture capital firms and by co-operating with private institutional investors in setting up new ones. It has also purchased from the federal government a number of former crown corporations. Two wholly-owned subsidiaries are Polysar Limited, formerly a crown corporation, and Connaught Laboratories Limited, purchased in 1972 from the University of Toronto.

Funds at the disposal of the CDC are eventually to total about $2 billion, of which half will come from the sale of preferred shares and the other half from the sale of common shares. Under the terms of the CDC Act, the federal government share of ownership must not fall below 10 per cent. Furthermore, no provincial government or single investor may acquire more than a 3 per cent share of ownership. When shares are eventually offered to the general public, only Canadian residents will be allowed to purchase them.

Direction and management of the corporation is entrusted to a board of eighteen to twenty-one directors and a president, all of whom must be Canadian citizens. Although they were initially appointed by the federal government, mainly from the business community, the directors are intended to act as an independent body. However, in their investment policies, they are expected to take into account Canada's national interest as well as profitability.

Federal Business Development Bank

The FBDB, a crown corporation, was established in 1975 as a successor to the Industrial Development Bank.

Its main purpose is to encourage the establishment and development of business enterprises in Canada by providing them with financial and management services. It supplements such services available from others. And it pays particular attention to the needs of smaller enterprises.

FBDB financing is available by means of loans, loan guarantees, equity financing, or leasing, or by any combination of these methods, in whatever manner best suits the particular needs of the business. Loans are made at interest rates in line with those generally available to businesses.

Many of the bank's customers use FBDB funds to acquire land, buildings, or equipment. Others use them to strengthen the working capital of their business, to establish new businesses, and for other purposes.

FBDB financing ranges in size from a few thousand dollars upwards. The amount that can be borrowed for a specific purpose depends on the borrower's ability to satisfy the general requirements of the bank. Businesses may obtain FBDB assistance on more than one occasion if they meet its requirements.

FBDB loans are usually repaid by way of monthly instalments of principal and interest. However, where the particular needs of the business would make it appropriate, other arrangements may be considered. Most FBDB loans must be repaid within ten years.

FBDB can extend financial assistance to new or existing businesses of almost every type in Canada that do not have other sources of financing available to them on reasonable terms and conditions.

The qualifications for FBDB financing are:

(a) that the amount and character of investment in such a business by persons other than FBDB may reasonably be expected to ensure the continuing commitment of these persons to the business; and

(b) that the business may reasonably be expected to prove successful.

Transportation Subsidies

Another federal measure to help spur economic growth in the poorer parts of Canada has been the provision of subsidized railway freight rates. Thus the Maritime Freight Rates Act, passed in 1927, lowered freight rates by 20 per cent on goods being moved by rail within that part of Canada lying east of Lévis, Quebec, or being moved from that area to other parts of Canada. This transportation subsidy was designed to make it easier for Maritime producers to sell their goods in the growing market of the central provinces. In 1928, additional federal rail subsidies were introduced to reduce the cost of shipping coal from the Maritimes to the steel mills of Ontario and Quebec. And in 1957, the reduction in railway freight rates on all goods being shipped from the area east of Lévis, Quebec, to other parts of Canada was increased to 30 per cent. In 1965, with the sale of coal seriously affected by the growing use of oil, the federal government established some new subsidies. These subsidies were for the transportation to Canadian markets of coal mined in the Atlantic and Prairie provinces, and for the transportation of coal from Alberta and British Columbia to west-coast ports for shipment abroad.

Provincial Development Corporations

Not all regional economic development aid is federal. Provincial governments also encourage, with varying degrees of intensity, the development of the less prosperous parts of their provinces. Most provinces have, in fact, a development corporation. Thus, as one example, the Ontario Development Corporation was established by the government of Ontario in June 1966 with the purpose of promoting the industrial and economic development of the province. It has its own board of directors, comprising representatives from business, finance, and labour, and reports to the provincial legislature through the Minister of Industry and Trade. The corporation attempts to promote the province's development in various ways: by providing technical, financial, and managerial advice; by assisting in the introduction of new products or techniques; by assisting Ontario-based companies to obtain financing from the regular lending institutions, and by providing financial aid to companies unable to obtain such financing.

Government Efforts: A Mixed Reaction

Government efforts to promote regional economic growth have by no means received unanimous approval. It is alleged, first of all, that the government is being naïvely optimistic in trying to promote industrial growth in areas which do not have the necessary economic potential. This argument has also been made of government efforts in many under-developed economies. In many cases, however, the building of an area's *economic infrastructure* (or *social capital*) has made such growth quite feasible and self-sustaining. On the other hand, it would be foolhardy to ignore that many government-sponsored industrial schemes, such as Clairtone Sound Industries in Nova Scotia, the forest-products complex at the Pas, Manitoba, and Georgetown Seafoods Ltd. in Prince Edward Island, have in the past only succeeded in losing vast sums of the public's money. So much has in fact been lost that a book has even been written about it.[3]

If the sparsely settled regions of Canada, particularly the North, are to be developed, the federal and provincial governments must undoubtedly take the initiative. Much has already been done, particularly in the field of hydro-electric development and oil-and-mineral exploration. Now, with government blessing, a major pipeline is eventually to be constructed to bring natural gas from the Arctic fields to southern markets in Canada and the United States.

Much research has already been carried out by a private firm, Acres Research and Planning Limited, regarding the possibilities of a Mid-Canada Development Corridor. This concept, originally advanced by Toronto lawyer Richard Rohmer, envisages the settlement and development of an area stretching right across Canada immediately to the north of the present populated areas. This corridor would have the following characteristics: an acceptable climate for working and living; land that is accessible and suitable for development; abundant and well-distributed resources; existing settlements; potential urban growth centres; proximity to existing north-south transportation routes; and suitability for the provision of new east-west transportation routes. Let us hope that this is not just a pipe-dream.

26.6: REGIONAL INCOME DISPARITIES

One characteristic of Canada's economic growth is that it is taking place unevenly across the country. As a result, the income disparities among provinces (see Table S.25) show little sign of abating. As the saying goes, "The rich get richer, and the poor get poorer." Even per capita (see Table S.26), the situation is the same.

The wealthiest, as well as the most populous provinces are Ontario and Quebec, followed by British Columbia. In recent years, with its oil wealth, Alberta has improved its relative position.

Average per capita income is highest in B.C., Alberta, and Ontario and lowest in Newfoundland and P.E.I.

Table S.25
Percentage Distribution of Personal Income, by Province, 1960 to 1981

Years	Nfld.	P.E.I.	N.S.	N.B.	Que.	Ont.	Man.	Sask.	Alta.	B.C.	Y.T. & N.W.T.	Canada ($ millions)
1960	1.4	0.3	3.1	2.2	25.1	40.3	5.0	4.6	7.2	10.3	0.2	29 595
1961	1.5	0.3	3.1	2.2	25.1	40.3	4.8	3.6	7.3	10.3	0.2	30 104
1962	1.4	0.3	3.0	2.2	25.8	39.9	4.9	4.7	7.4	10.0	0.2	32 788
1963	1.4	0.3	3.0	2.2	25.6	40.1	4.7	4.8	7.3	10.1	0.2	34 829
1964	1.4	0.3	3.0	2.1	26.1	40.3	4.8	4.1	7.1	10.3	0.2	37 282
1965	1.5	0.3	2.9	2.1	26.0	40.3	4.6	4.4	7.2	10.4	0.2	41 071
1966	1.5	0.3	2.8	2.1	25.8	40.5	4.4	4.4	7.3	10.5	0.2	46 094
1967	1.5	0.3	2.9	2.1	26.0	40.6	4.5	3.8	7.2	10.6	0.2	50 579
1968	1.5	0.3	2.8	2.1	25.5	41.0	4.5	3.9	7.4	10.5	0.2	55 677
1969	1.5	0.3	2.9	2.1	25.2	41.5	4.4	3.7	7.4	10.8	0.2	61 804
1970	1.5	0.3	2.8	2.1	25.0	42.0	4.3	3.2	7.4	10.9	0.2	66 633
1971	1.6	0.3	2.8	2.1	24.8	41.8	4.3	3.4	7.5	11.0	0.2	74 092
1972	1.6	0.3	2.9	2.2	24.9	41.6	4.3	3.3	7.5	11.2	0.2	83 767
1973	1.6	0.4	2.9	2.2	24.6	40.8	4.3	3.8	7.6	11.6	0.2	97 832
1974	1.6	0.3	2.9	2.2	24.8	40.3	4.3	3.9	7.7	11.7	0.3	116 867
1975	1.7	0.4	2.9	2.3	24.8	39.6	4.3	4.2	8.1	11.6	0.3	136 205
1976	1.7	0.4	2.8	2.2	25.2	39.2	4.2	4.0	8.2	11.7	0.3	155 343
1977	1.7	0.3	2.9	2.2	25.1	39.2	4.1	3.7	8.5	11.9	0.3	171 303
1978	1.6	0.4	2.9	2.2	24.9	39.0	4.1	3.7	8.8	12.0	0.3	190 403
1979	1.6	0.4	2.9	2.2	24.7	38.7	4.0	3.7	9.4	12.1	0.3	212 867
1980	1.6	0.4	2.8	2.1	24.8	38.4	3.8	3.7	9.8	12.4	0.3	239 891
1981	1.5	0.3	2.7	2.1	24.5	38.1	4.0	4.0	10.2	12.3	0.3	280 413

Source: Statistics Canada, *National Income and Expenditure Accounts*

Table S.26
Personal Income Per Capita, Canada and by Province, 1960-1981

Province	Per cent of national average					Dollars
	1960	1965	1970	1975	1981	(1981)
Nfld.	55.5	59.2	63.4	68.6	65.4	7 528
P.E.I.	56.9	60.1	66.5	70.2	68.0	7 829
N.S.	76.4	74.7	77.5	79.1	78.5	9 041
N.B.	68.1	68.4	72.0	77.2	71.8	8 272
Que.	87.2	89.9	88.7	91.2	92.5	10 661
Ont.	117.8	116.5	118.4	109.9	107.5	12 386
Man.	99.4	93.8	92.9	96.4	93.8	10 806
Sask.	89.2	90.1	72.4	104.0	100.5	11 853
Alta.	99.8	97.0	99.3	103.0	110.9	12 779
B.C.	115.2	113.7	108.8	108.1	108.8	12 538
Y.T. & N.W.T.	105.7	80.5	94.6	91.5	102.4	11 797
Canada	100.0	100.0	100.0	100.0	100.0	11 520

Source: Statistics Canada, *Estimates of Population for Canada at June 1; National Income and Expenditure Accounts*

Note: Personal income per capita is obtained by dividing Personal Income by Population as of June

Economic Differences

The reasons for differences in regional economic growth rates and consequent income disparities are not hard to find. Different areas have different endowments of natural resources, labour, and social and private capital. Moreover, many regions are too isolated and small in themselves to provide a substantial local market and they are unable to sell effectively abroad or to other parts of Canada. If we think in terms of the factors that govern the location of a new industry, we can better appreciate why, for example, manufacturing (perhaps the most dynamic income producer) tends to favour one region of Canada rather than another. These factors are as follows:

1. Adequately sized markets. A large local market is the ideal. However, many industries, depending on the type of product, successfully sell to markets, both domestic and foreign, many hundreds and even thousands of miles away.

2. Available raw materials. Industry cannot exist without crude or processed raw materials, or manufactured parts, to use for its finished products. Many industries, such as sawmills, locate very close to their materials. Others successfully bring their materials from distant locations. Large local supplies of crude oil, natural gas, or metal ores can form the basis for a substantial refining and manufacturing complex.

3. Available land. A large supply of good farmland, with adequate water and sunshine, can help an area to become reasonably prosperous on the basis of agriculture alone. If the area is scenic and well located, tourism may also become a major source of income.

4. Suitable means of transportation. Finished products must be taken to the market. Materials must be brought in to the manufacturing or processing plant. Only if suitable transportation facilities exist can this be done cheaply enough. If the products or materials are bulky, heavy, and of relatively low value per unit of weight, then river- or ocean-shipping facilities are essential. For goods with greater value per ton, road and rail facilities may be sufficient. For high-value items, the presence of an airport may be enough. In Canada, government rail-transportation subsidies enable large-scale manufacturers in Central Canada to compete more effectively with smaller local firms in more distant provinces.

5. Adequate electric power. An adequate supply of relatively cheap electricity is vital to most modern industrial plants. It provides the power to drive the great variety of machines now used and the lighting by which to work. Electricity can be brought a considerable distance from its source of generation—hydroelectric, thermal, or nuclear power plant—to its place of use. However, the longer the distance, the greater the transmission loss and, therefore, the greater the cost.

6. Suitable labour supply. A modern industrial plant requires a large and varied staff. Some key personnel can be brought in from other locations; but usually, for reasons of cost and good-will the bulk of the labour force must be recruited locally. The local labour supply must in the long run therefore provide most of the managerial, skilled, and semi-skilled workers needed for the new plant. Sometimes, where only unskilled labour is available, crash training programs to upgrade the local workers can be successfully used.

7. Entrepreneurship. Without effective entrepreneurship—that is to say, human willingness and ability to establish new businesses—a region's resources can lie idle. With good business leadership, even currently unprofitable industries can sometimes be made profitable.

8. Investment capital. It often takes large sums of money to start a new business or re-equip an existing one. If this money is not available from private investors, government funds may have to fill the breach.

9. Others. Several other factors are often conducive to the economic prosperity of an area. These include the availability of a low-cost fuel such as coal, oil, or natural gas; the availability of a plentiful supply of water, sometimes of a certain mineral content; a positive community attitude, manifested in such things as subsidized industrial parks, cash incentives, or temporary "tax holidays"; good community facilities, such as housing, schools, churches, hospitals, parks, stores, and banks; and a suitable climate.

Provincial Comparisons. Ontario and Quebec, huge in size and well endowed with natural resources, now generate about two thirds of Canada's national income. Inevitably, their large population (62% of Canada's total) plus nearby U.S. markets and good transportation routes have greatly encouraged manufacturing and agricultural development. Next in importance in their share of national income, are B.C. and Alberta, with 21 per cent of Canada's population and a smaller share of natural resources.

In terms of standard of living, as measured by personal income per capita, Alberta and B.C. are now the leading provinces (see Table S:26), thanks in part to the increase in world oil and gas prices and related developments. Close behind is Ontario, followed by Manitoba and Quebec. Newfoundland and P.E.I., although relatively better off than before, still have the lowest standard of living. Nova Scotia and New Brunswick, with more industrial development, are closer to the national average. Hopefully, the development of offshore oil and gas resources will raise the standard of living in Canada's Atlantic provinces in the 1980s.

26.7: DEPLETION OF CANADA'S NATURAL RESOURCES

One important disadvantage of economic growth is the depletion of Canada's natural resources. In its worst form, this includes the erosion of the top soil, the disappearance of forests, and the decimation of the fish stock, as discussed in the next chapter. In addition, metal ores such as iron, copper, and nickel, which cannot be replaced, are exported with relatively little processing in Canada. Also, unless Arctic reserves can be drawn on, and East coast offshore deposits developed, the supply of Canadian crude petroleum is expected to peter out in the 1980s.

Some people argue that Canada cannot go on exploiting its natural resources at the rate it has done in the past. Also, that it is foolish not to make better use of them in terms of income and jobs rather than to export much of them, relatively unprocessed. They predict also that the already high cost of energy will force Canadians to accept a much lower rate of annual economic growth than in the past. This will mean, if the population continues to grow, that Canadians will have to become accustomed to a lower material standard of living. Some people argue that a *zero-growth economy* will become the pattern of the future. But this view gives little credit to human ingenuity, particularly in the field of scientific and technical innovation, in overcoming economic problems.

Summary

1. Canada's rate of economic growth, as measured by annual increases in real GNP, has varied considerably.
2. Economic growth is important because it is the key to a higher standard of living for everyone; however, economic growth also has disadvantages.
3. The effect of a high rate of economic growth on a country's standard of living may be offset by population increase. Therefore, many economists measure economic growth in terms of per-capita output or income.
4. Thomas Robert Malthus, a young English clergyman, published a theory of population growth in 1798. His thesis was that the world's population grows at a much faster rate than the world's food supply. Consequently, only various positive and preventive checks can head off catastrophe. Despite immense increases in world food production, the present rate of growth of world popula-

tion is cause for alarm. A reduction in the birth-rate, on a global scale, seems essential.

5. If a country is to be able to produce more goods and services, it must have a larger supply of the various factors of production, including improved technology.

6. Canada is well endowed with natural resources and is in an enviable position compared with most other countries of the world.

7. Although Canada's population has grown substantially, the rate of growth has declined in recent years.

8. Over the years, capital investment in Canada has been rapidly increasing.

9. Canada has had access to the latest technical knowledge of how to produce goods and services. However, most of this technology has been imported.

10. With a few notable exceptions, private industry in Canada has tended (for various reasons) to neglect the important function of research and development. On the other hand, government spending in this area has been relatively substantial.

11. The staple theory of Canadian economic growth states, in essence, that a prime motivating force in Canada's economic growth has been the production and export of various staple products.

12. Government investment in social capital is considered in many countries to be one of the most effective ways of promoting economic growth.

13. Innovations (or new ways of doing things) are also considered to be a prime stimulus to economic growth. Innovations are most likely to occur if certain favourable conditions are present in socieety.

14. Governments are now playing a much more active role in promoting economic growth than in the past.

15. The federal government's Department of Regional Industrial Expansion provides financial and other assistance to promote the economic growth of the poorer parts of Canada. The Federal Business Development Bank also helps promote industrial growth. The Canada Development Corporation has been established to help raise equity capital for Canadian business ventures.

16. Provincial governments also provide economic development assistance, often through their own development corporations.

17. The possibilities for developing Canada's North, including the Mid-Canada Development Corridor, are being researched. Some ventures are being undertaken.

18. Economic growth is taking place unevenly across Canada. Conse-

quently, regional income disparities show no signs of abating.

19. Regional differences in economic growth can be explained in terms of relative availability of markets, materials, and other industrial requirements.
20. One important disadvantage of economic growth is the depletion of Canada's natural resources.

Key Terms

Review Questions

1. What is economic growth? Why is it such a high-priority national goal?
2. What has been Canada's record of economic growth?
3. Explain the relationship between economic growth, population growth, and the standard of living.
4. What is Malthus' theory of population growth? What has actually happened?
5. Why do countries that depend on agricultural exports for a large part of their national income often fail to enjoy the benefits of increased output?
6. How realistically do per-capita national-income statistics reflect living standards in different parts of the world?
7. What are the basic requirements for economic growth? Comment on Canada's situation.
8. What are the most important recent trends in Canadian population growth? What is the future outlook?

9. What are the main characteristics of Canada's labour force?
10. Distinguish between business capital and social capital.
11. What is the capital-output ratio? What is its significance?
12. What is technology? Why is it considered so vital to economic growth?
13. Why has private industry in Canada tended, with a few notable exceptions, to neglect the important function of research and development?
14. What is the "staple theory" of economic growth?
15. Explain how the provision of social capital acts as a source of economic growth.
16. Explain what is meant by "innovations" as a source of economic growth. How can they be encouraged?
17. What is the Department of Regional and Industrial Expansion? How does it try to promote economic growth?
18. Explain the nature and purpose of the Canada Development Corporation.
19. What is the purpose of the FBDB? What are its methods?
20. Explain the nature, purpose, and effects of subsidized railway freight rates in Canada.
21. Government efforts to stimulate economic growth in Canada have met with mixed success. Comment.
22. What is the Mid-Canada Corridor? What is the purpose behind the concept?
23. What are the factors that help make one region of a country economically more prosperous than another region?
24. How does personal income vary in Canada from one province to another?
25. The depletion of a country's natural resources is an inevitable result of economic growth. Comment.
26. What are the implications of zero economic growth?

References

1. Joseph Schumpeter, *The Theory of Economic Development*, Harvard University Press, Cambridge, Mass., 1934
2. John M. Clark, *Competition as a Dynamic Process*, The Brookings Institution, Washington, D.C., 1961
3. Philip Mathias, *Forced Growth, Five Studies of Government Involvement in the Development of Canada*, James Lewis and Samuel, Toronto, 1971.

27. POLLUTION OF THE ENVIRONMENT

CHAPTER OBJECTIVES

A. To stress the environmental cost of economic and population growth
B. To explain the different kinds of environmental pollution
C. To examine the economics of pollution
D. To discuss pollution control legislation
E. To stress the resource allocation aspect of pollution

CHAPTER OUTLINE

27.1 Types of Pollution
27.2 Economics of Pollution
27.3 Pollution Control Legislation
27.4 Resource Allocation

27.1: TYPES OF POLLUTION

A serious disadvantage of economic growth and population expansion has been the pollution of our environment. The air, water, and land (to say nothing of the birds, fish and animals that inhabit them) are all suffering in varying degrees from (a) inefficient disposal of waste products (from cars, factories and homes); (b) great use of chemicals to fertilize crops, destroy pests, and even to wage wars; and (c) adornment of the landscape with ugly buildings, power lines, strip mines, and billboards. Although this problem has been recognized for many years, it has assumed a new urgency today. This is because of the relentless growth of world population; its increasing concentration in urban areas; its increasing per-capita consumption of fuel and energy; and its greater material possessions which, together with their packaging material, are often quickly discarded.

Air Pollution

The air that we breathe is constantly being contaminated by all kinds of foreign matter. This contamination has been going on for thousands of years, often caused by natural sources such as volcanoes. But the chief source of air contamination has been people: as they have multiplied, so has the contamination. When air contamination is sufficiently great that the population is harmed in some way, we call the situation *air pollution.*

Sources of Air Pollution. For many years, the main source of air pollution was the burning of coal for heat and energy. Today, however, the combustion of petroleum products by industry, homeowners, and car users has become a major source. Air pollution is also caused by vaporization, whereby the application of heat and pressure in certain chemical and other manufacturing operations causes some of the component materials to vaporize into the atmosphere. Another cause of air pollution is mechanical attrition—the crushing, grinding, and other industrial activities that produce dusts and mists.

The federal Department of Energy has estimated that, in Canada, industrial fuels cause 46 per cent of total air pollution, domestic fuels almost 20 per cent, motor gasoline over 19 per cent, commercial fuels (less gasoline) 11 per cent, and other industrial sources about 4 per cent. Coal provides a relatively small portion of the total amount.

One of the chief culprits of air pollution is the automobile. In addition to carbon dioxide and water vapour, automobile exhaust contains carbon monoxide, nitrogen oxides, unburned hydrocarbons, and lead. All of these gases are harmful to people if breathed in sufficient quantities. Fortunately, government legislation, by requiring the installation of emission control devices of all new cars, is helping to solve this problem. However, more could be done in Canada—for example, in reducing the lead level in Canadian gasoline to at least the U.S. standards.

Acid Rain. An extremely critical air pollution problem for Eastern Canada is the estimated 20 million tons of sulphur dioxide that each year spews out of hundreds of U.S. and Canadian coal-fired power plants, blows long distances, and falls as sulphuric acid rain. In fact, a million square miles of Canadian lakes and forests are already suffering from acid rain pollution. To reduce such pollution would require the installation of smoke-cleaning "scrubbers" in smokestacks, and the pre-cleaning of coal before it is burned or a switch to cleaner coal from Western Canada or the Western U.S. So far, the Canadian and U.S. authorities have not been able to agree on a joint plan to start tackling

"I think the biggest problem that faces Canada today, Steve, is pollution of the environment."

this environmental problem. The biggest obstacle is, of course, the cost. Another is the likelihood that thousands of eastern coal miners in Canada and the U.S. would be thrown out of work.

Water Pollution

The water in our streams, rivers, lakes, and oceans is constantly being polluted: in some places the level of pollution is now dangerously high. Thanks to the dumping of vast quantities of untreated human and industrial wastes into the nearest water, many of Canada's lakes, rivers, and ocean beaches are now unfit for bathing; and fresh water from many rivers and lakes is now drunk at great risk. Salmon and other fish, once to be found in abundance even far upstream, have in many places disappeared; too often, hundreds and thousands of dead fish, killed by pollution, are washed ashore. And even the live ones, because of high levels of mercury, etc., are often unfit to eat. The contrast with early Canada, when clear, sparkling rivers and lakes teemed with fish, is an unhappy one. Only in the more remote parts of Canada is unpolluted water still to be found and enjoyed.

Domestic and Commercial Wastes. One source of water pollution is domestic wastes. These include wastes discharged from our homes—from toilets, baths, showers, dishwashers, and laundry machines. Another source is wastes discharged from schools, restaurants, hospitals, and commercial establishments. Nowadays, sewage-treatment plants can effectively separate and remove most of these wastes from the water in which they are carried. However, many municipalities in Canada have not yet built sufficient facilities to handle the quantity of sewage discharged (see Table 27:1). Also, even where sewage-treatment facilities exist, they are often overloaded, run out of chlorine, or are deliberately by-passed by illegal sewer connections that put raw sewage straight into lakes and rivers. Furthermore, domestic waste, accidentally or deliberately discharged into storm sewers, normally bypasses any sewage-treatment facilities. To complicate matters, many families still reply on septic tank systems: in some cases, particularly cottages, on even more primitive sewage disposal methods.

Industrial and Agricultural Wastes. Manufacturing industries, such as pulp and paper, aluminum, steel, plastic, oil, and chemicals, discharge large quantities of waste products into the rivers and lakes. Canada is particularly affected by highly toxic chemicals flowing into the Great Lakes from U.S. industry and from old chemical dumps, especially along the Niagara River. Together these pose a serious threat to Lake Ontario drinking water. Many of these industrial wastes, includ-

Table 27:1

Sewage Treatment in Selected Urban Areas, 1969

Metropolitan Area	Waste-Water Flow (million litres per day)	Percentage of Waste-Water Flow Subject to:		
		No Treatment	Primary Treatment	Secondary Treatment
St. John's	57.9	100.0		
Halifax-Dartmouth	45.1	99.0	1.0	
Saint John	24.6	99.8		0.2
Quebec	191.5	100.0		
Montreal	1323.2	91.6	2.6	5.8
Ottawa	182.4		100.0	
Toronto	884.6			100.0
Hamilton	273.6		100.0	
Sudbury	50.1			100.0
London	127.8			100.0
Windsor	18.2	85.0		15.0
Winnipeg	211.4	4.0		96.0
Regina	54.7			100.0
Saskatoon	45.6	93.0		7.0
Edmonton	171.0		46.5	53.5
Calgary	177.0		100.0	
Vancouver	456.0	59.0	41.0	
Victoria	82.1	98.9		1.1

Note: Primary treatment removes 30–50 per cent of non-suspended solids; secondary treatment removes about 80–85 per cent of total solids and reduces the biological oxygen demand by about the same proportion.

Source: Economic Council of Canada, *Sixth Annual Review* (Ottawa: Queen's Printer, 1969), Tables 3–7, p. 44. Reproduced by permission of the Minister of Supply and Services Canada.

ing acids and other chemicals, oil, grease, and animal and vegetable matter, are left unaltered by normal methods of municipal sewage treatment. Therefore, special disposal plants for liquid industrial waste are urgently needed. On the farm, mishandling of animal wastes, improper soil fertilization and crop irrigation, and unwise use of pesticides and herbicides also cause contamination of ground and surface water. Meat packing plants have been identified as a major source of fecal coliform—a critical form of bacterial water pollution.

Oil Spills. The use of large tankers to carry oil from the source of production to the areas of consumption has meant that a shipwreck or collision can have disastrous effects on neighbouring shorelines. Canada had one bad experience of this type in 1970, with the sinking of the oil tanker *Arrow* off the coast of Nova Scotia. Other countries such as Britain, the United States, and Japan have had even worse experiences. Despite the development of new methods of combatting oil spills (notably the use of sponge-squeeze barges), oil pollution is still very much feared because of the possible damage to beaches, birds, and fish. That is why the residents of British Columbia so fiercely oppose the shipping of Arctic oil by ocean tanker from Alaska along their coast. Oil pollution of the ocean, and even of inland waterways, is not only the result of accidental spills. Deliberate discharge of oil and other waste by merchant ships also occurs even though government aerial surveillance and penalties have been increased. As Thor Heyerdahl, the noted sea traveller, has pointed out, significant parts of the ocean are already covered with all kinds of floating waste.

Effects of Water Pollution. Water pollution from sewage and other waste discharge is costly to our society. First of all, it endangers human health by supporting various bacteria, viruses, protozoans, and parasites that cause such diseases as typhoid. Second, nutrients (particularly phosphates) found in treated and untreated sewage have greatly stimulated the growth of aquatic vegetation, especially algae. As the algae decay, further plant growth is stimulated. This process, known as entrophication, gradually depletes the oxygen level and in some lakes, such as Lake Erie, has killed off much of the fish population.

Pollution also eliminates recreational facilities by making the water unsightly, smelly, unfit to bathe in, and devoid of game fish. Pollution also increases the cost of the treatment facilities needed to provide drinking water for the population. This demand for water is constantly increasing, not only with the growth in the population but also with the greater per capita water consumption which is now estimated at 680 L per person per week, compared with 13 to 23 L in pioneer days. Large amounts of water are also needed by new industrial plants: it has been estimated that it requires 318 200 L of water to make a ton of steel, nearly 909 200 L in some paper mills to make a ton of newsprint, and 2 227 000 L to produce a ton of aluminum.

Soil Pollution

The soil we use to grow crops for human and animal consumption is suffering from pollution in some areas of Canada. The chief reasons for this deteriorating situation are: (a) the large quantities of domestic and industrial waste dumped on the soil or carried into it by liquid discharge; (b) the intensive use in modern farming and forestry operations of chemical fertilizers, pesticides, and herbicides; and (c) the raising of poultry, pigs, and other livestock in high-density confinement housing. Just like the air and water, the soil can only handle a certain amount of waste materials before the soil itself begins to be damaged, causing lower crop yields, poorer-quality crops, and even danger to human and animal health. Pollution of the soil also contributes, indirectly, to air and water pollution.

What are the main problems? Although pesticides have been of great aid to the farmer and to society in general in reducing the numbers of unwanted insects such as grasshoppers and mosquitoes, they also constitute a pollution problem. However, the long-term effects on the environment of the use of the various chemical pesticides is still being investigated. Already, the use of the pesticide DDT, once so popular throughout the world, has been banned in many countries. Another problem is sanitary landfills. Although an inexpensive method of disposing of the waste of many urban communities, landfills frequently become ideal breeding grounds for rats, flies, and other disease-carrying pests, as well as sources of smoke and bad smells.

One of the most recent problems concerning soil pollution is the possible effects that oil spills may have on the permafrost in Canada's North.

Visual Pollution

A somewhat different type of pollution from those previously discussed is the pollution of the landscape. By this is meant the destruction of the natural beauty of the countryside by industrial and commercial activities and by waste-disposal habits. No one should oppose the construction of new factories, roads, and homes that will make life more pleasant for the population. But one can insist that these developments be planned with due regard for the environment. Too many urban and suburban areas have been built with little or no provision for parks and other recreational space. New expressways have cut towns and cities apart and deluged residential streets with commuters' cars. Power-transmission lines stretch across some of the most beautiful countryside; billboards, bottles, cans, paper, and other discarded objects litter much of the land. Mining operations, too, have contributed to this type of pollution. Open-strip mining has meant the removal of the topsoil and its covering trees and other vegetation, usually leaving an ugly scar in their place. And a wild variety of signs adorn every commercial block.

Of course, visual pollution is a much more debatable matter than air,

water, and soil pollution. An ugly building to one person may be a thing of beauty to another. Just listen to the variety of comment that may be heard about some of Canada's newest skyscrapers. In other cases, such as electric-power lines, many people would prefer underground wiring, but would be unwilling to pay the extra cost involved; just as many people prefer, given the choice, to have their own TV antenna, despite its ugliness, rather than pay for cable TV. And now dish receivers are beginning to sprout across the land. The cost of this type of pollution is impossible to measure, since it is a psychic one. Nevertheless, it is a very real cost, as more and more people are coming to realize.

Noise Pollution

Another type of environmental pollution is the growing amount of noise in certain places. This has become particularly acute in the neighbourhood of airports, expressways, and new industrial areas. Efforts are being made, for example, with regard to aircraft, to reduce noise emission and to restrict flying times and flight paths. In this category, we can include excessive commercial advertising on radio and television.

27.2: THE ECONOMICS OF POLLUTION

At one time, economists assumed that clean air and water were always available in unlimited supply. And since they were available free of charge, they were not "economic goods" that people, in the allocation of scarce resources, had consciously to choose to produce. Nowadays, however, the story is becoming quite different. If we want to breathe clean air in our cities, we may have to pay extra (in the price of a new car) for a special exhaust-control device. Or we may have to pay more for household electricity produced in a thermal-power plant using natural gas which is a cleaner but more expensive fuel than coal. Or we may have to pay more for sewage treatment and disposal to keep lakes and other recreational facilities fit for bathing. So, in other words, clean air and water are gradually becoming economic goods just like any other.

Why is it, we may ask, perhaps ingenuously, that individuals, households, and firms do not dispose of their waste products in a non-polluting way? Part of the answer is that technologically we still have not found efficient, low-cost methods of doing this. For example, we are still struggling to invent a car engine that does not pollute the atmosphere, but we do not want to give up the use of our present cars, even though they are a major source of pollution. The other part of the answer is that, even where it is possible to control pollution, we are often unwilling to do so (for example, using unleaded rather than regular gasoline) unless we are given some special incentive, such as lower prices, or refunds on returnable bottles, or forced to by the government, by laws, inspections, and fines.

But the main reason for pollution is that it is cheaper and more convenient for a person or firm to dump wastes than to dispose of them in a non-polluting way. And here we have a divergence between the interests of the individual and the interests of society. The householder or business manager, in making the decision to pollute, does not take into account the cost of this pollution to society as a whole. Only the *private costs* are considered—what it would cost to dispose of wastes in a non-polluting way versus the cost of dumping them. We do not consider the cost to society of smoked-filled lungs, dead fish, and polluted bathing areas. But these *social costs* of pollution cannot and should not be ignored. Indeed, the only effective way to control pollution would be to make these social costs part of private costs.

The Pollution Equation

The economic relationship between production and pollution has been analyzed in various books.[1] Basically, manufacturers, when they bother to think about it, compare two different sets of costs. They estimate on the one hand what it will cost to dispose of wastes in a non-polluting way by, for example, taking them to an industrial waste disposal plant or, if possible, by recycling them—that is, converting them into new products. They would then subtract from this cost, in the case of recycled products, any revenue that may be received from their sale. The final sum is the net cost of the non-polluting disposal of waste products. They will estimate on the other hand the cost of dumping untreated wastes into the air or into the nearest stream, river, or lake, plus any fines or other penalties that may be incurred.

The first of these costs can be summarized algebraically as $WC_w - W_tP_w$, where W equals the quantity of untreated waste products, C_w equals the per unit cost of recycling or treating waste products, W_t equals the quantity of recycled or treated waste products, and P_w equals the per unit revenue obtained, if any, from the sale of the recycled or treated waste products.

The second of these costs can be summarized algebraically as D_w, the disposal cost of untreated waste products, including fines and other penalties.

If a firm can recycle its waste products (for example, used envelopes into new ones) and sell them for more than the recycling and other costs involved, it will be financially motivated to reduce pollution even though the disposal cost of untreated wastes is nil. Algebraically, this situation would exist if WtPw > WCw, and Dw = 0. The same reasoning applies to a firm which can convert its waste products into other products (for example, sawdust into fire logs). Even if the cost of treatment exceeds the revenue from the treated waste, treatment may still be financially worthwhile if the cost of dumping the untreated waste products, including any possible fines, is greater. Algebraically, this would be if (WCw − WtPw) < Dw. Public-spiritedness is another factor that may tip the scale in favour of the recycling or treating of waste products. Thus, if the cost of treating the waste products exceeds the cost of dumping them untreated by $5000, a firm may choose the former alternative out of public-spiritedness in the same way that many householders insist on purchasing soft drinks etc. in returnable bottles despite the inconvenience.

Unfortunately, except for the very public-spirited, manufacturers do not usually take into account, in the waste-disposal decision, the cost to society of pollution. If they did, they would only be tempted to pollute if: (WCw − WtPw) > (Dw + Ew), where Ew equals the social costs of pollution. In many instances, manufacturers (as well as municipalities, householders, or individuals) will commit an act of pollution, although, if the social cost were included in the calculation, they would not do so. Clearly, then, as far as pollution is concerned, the private and public interest are frequently in conflict. This conflict can perhaps only be resolved by government intervention.

27.3: POLLUTION-CONTROL LEGISLATION

Clean air, water, and soil, as well as an unpolluted landscape, can be placed in the same category of economic goods as public education, medical and hospital care, law and order, and roads and bridges. All these goods are extremely desirable from society's point of view, but they are not usually provided by our private-enterprise system of production in the quantity and quality that society wants. That is why governments have over the years assumed more and more responsibility for providing them. But, whereas police protection has long been a service provided by the government, pollution control is relatively new.

In many countries of the world, pollution is still considered to be the necessary price of economic growth. If some pollution of the air and the neighbouring river is to be the price of a new manufacturing plant that will provide jobs and income for many families now living in poverty, there is no doubt what the choice will be. In North America, Europe, and other economically developed countries, however, the public is more able to accept pollution control—even though it may slow economic growth and raise the price of goods now being produced. In these countries, including Canada, there has been much more public support in recent years for anti-pollution measures. This support has been strengthened by various factors: first, people's awareness, through personal discomfort in smoggy cities, murky rivers, and dirty beaches, of the seriousness of the problem; second, the realization that clean air and water are no longer in inexhaustible supply; third, the knowledge that a great deal of pollution can be prevented; and, fourth, a growing unwillingness to sacrifice the quality of life on the altar of economic growth. Already, advances in fuel and combustion technology, as well as better waste-disposal habits induced by government controls and public pressure, have slowed the rate of pollution. But, certainly, much remains to be done.

Governments can, if they wish, pass laws regulating the disposal of waste. Until recently in Canada, legislation of this type was incomplete and the fines that could be imposed on offenders were relatively small. Today, anti-pollution laws are much more comprehensive, the fines and possible prison terms much stiffer, and the degree of inspection and enforcement much greater.

Organizationally, the federal government established, in 1971, a Department of the Environment, also known as Environment Canada. It brought together, in one department, all those agencies within the federal government already involved in work related to the environment and renewable resources. Also, in 1973, the federal government approved a review process to ensure that environmental matters are taken into account in government projects. In 1979, the Department of the Environment was split into two: a Department of Fisheries and Oceans and a new Department of the Environment. Parks Canada was added to the latter Department.

Jurisdictionally, the federal government has responsibility for environmental and resource matters clearly within its jurisdiction such as the territories, national parks, and oceans and for matters which the provinces cannot readily or cost-effectively undertake, such as weather services. The provinces have direct management responsibility for most environmental and resource matters within their borders.

Within the Department of the Environment, the Environmental Protection Service (EPS) develops national environmental guidelines,

requirements and regulations in consultation with the provinces and industry. Important concerns for Environment Canada in the 1980s are the control of toxic substances, the long-range transport of air pollutants, and hazardous waste management. Other important parts of Environment Canada are the Environmental Conservation Services, the Canadian Forestry Service, the Canadian Wildlife Service, the Inland Waters Directorate, the Lands Directorate, and the Atmospheric Environment Service.

27.4: RESOURCE ALLOCATION

Pollution control involves basically a question of resource allocation. If the people of a country are sufficiently concerned about damage to their physical environment, they can devote more of their resources to pollution control. These resources might at present be used for less important purposes or even be unemployed. Once a government senses that the electorate is willing to support anti-pollution measures, even though they require the outlay of public or private money, an increase in the price of a firm's product to the consumer, or the closure of marginally profitable plants (causing unemployment), it will take action.

In Canada, the United States, Western Europe, and elsewhere, concern about pollution has been rapidly mounting and governments have started to respond. These countries are fortunate in that they have sufficient resources to afford both a good average standard of living and a high degree of pollution control. In other, poorer countries, the choice is much harder. In real terms, the cost of a municipal sewage plant may be the equivalent of a small manufacturing or assembly plant that could generate more employment and income for the community. This is one area in which economic aid programs by the richer countries can make a very useful contribution.

Government action to protect the environment can, as we saw earlier, take various forms. Legislation to prohibit certain practices as well as to encourage others is one form. Equally important are the enforcement of the laws and the imposition of penalties that really act as deterrents. The provision of financial aid to both municipal governments and private firms for the installation of pollution-control equipment is another form. But most important of all is the eventual achievement, through technology, as well as legislation, of a system whereby waste products: (a) are reduced to a minimum; (b) can be easily and cheaply disposed of; and (c) are the responsibility of the person or firm producing them to dispose of them in a non-polluting way.

Summary

1. An economic and social problem of mounting concern in Canada and other countries of the world is pollution.
2. Air pollution exists when the degree of contamination becomes harmful. The main source of air pollution used to be the burning of coal. Today, it is the combustion of petroleum products, particularly in the car. Harmful effects include human and animal ill-health and death; the soiling of clothing and buildings; the corrosion of metal; the deterioration of stone and masonry; damage to trees and crops; and reduction in visibility that can, in turn, lead to traffic accidents.
3. Water pollution of streams, rivers, lakes, and oceans has resulted from wastes discharged from our homes, schools, restaurants, hospitals, commercial establishments, manufacturing industries, and farms, and from oil spills. Harmful effects include human ill-health, destruction of fish, elimination of recreational facilities, and increased cost of providing water for drinking and other purposes.
4. Soil pollution has been caused by: (a) the large quantities of domestic and industrial waste dumped on the land or carried into it by liquid discharge; (b) the intensive use in modern farming of chemical fertilizers, pesticides, and herbicides; and (c) the raising of poultry, pigs, and other livestock in high-density confinement housing. Key problems are the possible dangers from pesticides, sanitary landfills, and from oil spills.
5. Landscape pollution, a more controversial topic, refers to the disfigurement of the countryside and towns with billboards, signs, so-called tourist attractions, ugly buildings, electric power lines, and expressways.
6. Noise pollution has increased due to growing numbers of aircraft, cars, and factories. Excessive commercial advertising on radio and television may also be included in this category.
7. The main reason for pollution is that it is cheaper and more convenient for a person or firm to dump wastes rather than dispose of them in a non-polluting way; in other words, there is a divergence between the private costs and social costs of pollution.
8. The economic relationship between production and pollution can be expressed in the form of a pollution equation.
9. Clean air, water, and soil, as well as an unpolluted landscape, can be placed in the same category of economic goods as public education, medical and hospital care, law and order, and roads and

bridges. All these goods are very desirable from society's point of view, but are not usually provided (unless by the government) in the quality that society wants.

10. Various measures have been taken by the federal and provincial governments in recent years to reduce pollution. Also, more staff are now being provided to enforce anti-pollution legislation and stiffer fines are being imposed on polluters. Financial assistance is also being provided for the purchase of polution-control equipment.

11. The Department of the Environment co-ordinates federal pollution-control efforts. The provincial governments are also very active in this area.

12. The cost of pollution control is very great and must inevitably be borne by the consumer. Fortunately, Canada is better able to afford such control than many other countries. From the economic point of view, pollution control is basically a matter of resource allocation.

Key Terms

Air pollution   546
Acid rain   546
Water pollution   548
Oil spills   549
Entrophication   550
Soil pollution   550
Visual pollution   551

Noise pollution   553
Economic goods   553
Pollution equation   554
Pollution control
 legislation   555
Resource allocation   558

Review Questions

1. What are the various types of pollution of our environment?
2. How has economic growth caused pollution of the environment?
3. Should economic growth be restricted if it causes environmental pollution? Discuss.
4. What does "noise pollution" mean to you? Is it something to be concerned about?
5. Clean air and water have now become "economic goods" in many cities of Canada. Discuss.
6. Explain and discuss the phenomenon of "acid rain".
7. Explain and discuss the the phenomenon of "entrophication".

8. What is the "pollution equation"?
9. What laws help control pollution in your province?
10. Pollution control is nothing more than a question of resource allocation. Discuss.
11. Why has nothing substantial yet been done to resolve the problem of "acid rain"?
12. "Only in North America is pollution a problem". Discuss.
13. "The recycling of waste should be encouraged by government subsidy". Discuss.
14. "In the space-age society, economic growth will take place without pollution". Discuss.

Reference

1. See, for example, J.H. Dales, *Pollution, Property and Prices*, University of Toronto Press, Toronto 1968; and D.A.L. Auld, "An Economic Analysis of Environmental Pollution" in D.E. Eldrick, ed., *Environmental Change: Focus on Ontario*, Science Research Associates (Canada) Limited, Toronto, 1970.

The biggest item in the federal government's budget is social affairs, followed by interest on the public debt . . . .

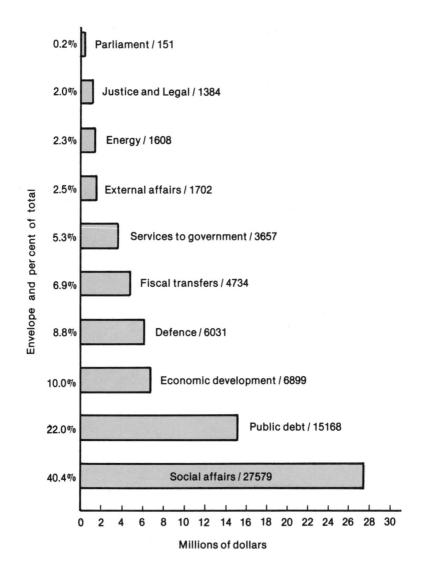

Envelope and per cent of total

0.2% | Parliament / 151

2.0% | Justice and Legal / 1384

2.3% | Energy / 1608

2.5% | External affairs / 1702

5.3% | Services to government / 3657

6.9% | Fiscal transfers / 4734

8.8% | Defence / 6031

10.0% | Economic development / 6899

22.0% | Public debt / 15168

40.4% | Social affairs / 27579

0 2 4 6 8 10 12 14 16 18 20 22 24 26 28 30

Millions of dollars

Part G:
THE PUBLIC FINANCES

In this part of the book, we consider how much our governments are spending and on what; where the money is coming from; and how taxation and borrowing by our governments affect the economy.

"Come, come, gentlemen. The deficit's still getting bigger; so the Minister says we've just got to tighten our belts, even if it does mean abandoning some of our pet projects."

28. GOVERNMENT EXPENDITURE

In recent years, our three levels of government—federal, provincial, and municipal—have together accounted for almost half of all spending in Canada (see Table S.27). In contrast, before World War II, government spending accounted for only about one-tenth of Canada's national expenditure. One of the most noticeable changes over the years in the way that governments in Canada have spent the taxpayers' money is the increase in *transfer payments*—as pensions, family allowances, and other social security benefits are called.

Instinctively, we tend to criticize this growth in government spending. One reason is that most of the money comes from us in the form of taxes. Another reason is that the enlargement of government activity is often seen as a threat to the Canadian way of life, with its tradi-

Table S.27
Total Government Expenditure as a Percentage of Canada's GNE,
1950-1982

Year	Total Government Expenditure ($ millions)	Gross National Expenditure ($ millions)	Total Government Expenditure (as a % of GNE)
1950	4 080	18 491	22.1
1951	5 227	21 640	24.1
1952	6 605	24 588	26.9
1953	6 812	25 833	26.4
1954	7 091	25 918	27.4
1955	7 498	28 528	26.3
1956	8 224	32 058	25.7
1957	8 906	33 513	26.6
1958	9 946	34 777	28.6
1959	10 647	36 846	28.9
1960	11 380	38 359	29.7
1961	12 200	39 646	30.8
1962	13 197	42 927	30.7
1963	13 932	45 978	30.3
1964	14 905	50 280	29.6
1965	16 554	55 364	29.9
1966	19 101	61 828	30.9
1967	21 828	66 409	32.9
1968	24 472	72 586	33.7
1969	27 226	79 815	34.1
1970	31 148	85 685	36.4
1971	35 205	94 450	37.3
1972	39 738	105 234	37.8
1973	45 045	123 560	36.5
1974	55 961	147 528	37.9
1975	68 288	165 343	41.3
1976	76 718	191 031	40.2
1977	86 315	208 868	41.3
1978	96 881	230 490	42.0
1979	106 475	261 576	40.7
1980	121 851	291 869	41.7
1981	141 410	331 338	42.7
1982	165 557	348 925	47.4

Source: Calculated from data in Statistics Canada, *National Income and Expenditure Accounts*

tional (though perhaps declining) emphasis on private initiative, thrift, and hard work. We cannot deny, however, that we are glad to have many government services: good roads, schools, hospitals, unemployment benefits, and old-age pensions—the list is almost endless. If governments do not provide these services, who would? Not everyone has the ability, foresight, opportunity, or even sheer good luck always to be able to take care of himself, herself, and perhaps dependents. The question is: where do we draw the line? This is to some extent a political question, outside the scope of this book. However, if we heed the arguments of the "supply-side" economists, discussed in Chapter 24 (Employment Theory), the growth of the public sector is also an economic question. This is because high marginal income tax rates reduce people's willingness to work hard and undertake entrepreneurial risks whilst unemployment benefits and other tax-transfer payments reduce the incentive to look for work or to hold on to a job.

28.1: DIVISION OF RESPONSIBILITIES

Unlike many countries with a high degree of political centralization, Canada has divided its economic and social responsibilities between a federal government on the one hand and a number of provincial governments on the other. According to the Constitution Act, 1867, which established the Canadian Confederation, the federal Parliament was given legislative jurisdiction over all matters of national concern, such as foreign policy and national defence. The provincial legislatures were given jurisdiction over all matters of local concern, such as education and roads. Each provincial legislature was also given the power to delegate part of its authority to municipal governments.

At the time of Confederation, the provincial and municipal governments were expected to account for the bulk of government spending. In practice, this did not turn out to be the case. A few years after Confederation, the federal government was found to be spending over half the total. However, as the provincial and municipal governments began to provide more services, the federal share of spending began to decline. This decline, although interrupted by World War I, continued until 1933. During World War II, for obvious reasons, federal spending as a percentage of the total shot up. Since that time, it has declined in importance compared with combined provincial and municipal expenditures.

28.2: FEDERAL EXPENDITURE

In accordance with the letter and the spirit of the Constitution Act, the federal government restricted its activities for many years to such matters of broad national interest as defence, foreign relations, trade and commerce, currency and banking, and the administration of justice. It also helped to finance the construction of canals and railways that would better link Canada together. Indeed, it was a condition of British Columbia's entry into Confederation in 1871 that the federal government construct the Canadian Pacific Railway within ten years. The federal government also established, in the form of government departments or crown corporations, a number of business enterprises, such as the Post Office and, later, Air Canada which would operate nation-wide.

More recently, the federal government has extended its activities into areas once considered to be of purely local or provincial interest. It has done this mainly by offering to help finance joint federal-provincial programs. The most common of these are *conditional-grant programs* such as hospital insurance, medicare, and the Canada Assistance Plan (the major source of welfare payments), under which the federal government undertook to pay half the cost of the program so long as certain minimum standards were met.

Federal government expenditures since 1950 are shown in Table S.28.

Pattern of Spending

Every spending program has certain objectives. The federal government's principal economic and social goals for Canada in recent years seem to have been the following: a reduction in the high level of unemployment; economic growth, however slight; a continued battle against inflation; more competition among business firms; less foreign ownership of Canadian industry; and a viable balance of international payments. Government expenditure is one important means of promoting these goals. Other means include changes in taxation or enactment of laws restricting certain activities (for example, the Act establishing the Foreign Investment Review Agency, or FIRA; or the Act establishing the National Energy Program, or NEP). Of course, it is extremely difficult, if not impossible, for a government to pursue all its goals at the same time. For example, in the early 1980s, greater price stability was achieved only at the cost of greater unemployment and slower economic growth. A choice, or *tradeoff*, is therefore usually necessary.

An examination of the recent pattern of federal government spending reveals that health and welfare is by far the largest area of expenditure, followed by economic development and support, interest on the public debt, defence, fiscal transfer (equalization) payments to the

Table S.28
Federal Government Expenditures, millions of dollars, 1950-1982

Years	Goods and services	National defence(1)	Transfers to persons	Interest on the public debt	Sub-sidies	Capital assist-ance(2)	Transfer payments to non-residents	Transfers to other levels of government	Gross capital formation	Total expenditures	Deficit (−) or surplus
1950	923	493	615	427	60	1	14	251	79	2 370	650
1955	2 364	1 760	1 229	487	75	3	36	450	162	4 806	202
1960	2 426	1 546	1 973	753	283	15	74	994	228	6 746	-229
1965	2 829	1 559	2 311	1 052	372	86	119	1 431	351	8 551	544
1970	4 551	1 868	4 057	1 862	589	97	244	3 397	465	15 262	266
1971	4 958	1 926	4 684	1 974	513	171	249	4 323	514	17 386	-145
1972	5 452	1 963	6 186	2 253	596	181	277	4 558	623	20 126	-566
1973	6 087	2 174	7 008	2 518	738	227	315	4 807	722	22 422	387
1974	7 408	2 548	8 705	2 961	2 060	193	403	6 165	974	28 869	1 109
1975	8 329	2 780	10 620	3 705	3 183	288	588	7 670	1 125	35 508	-3 805
1976	9 670	3 220	11 533	4 519	2 398	367	537	8 522	1 158	38 704	-3 391
1977	11 143	3 693	13 089	5 101	2 222	497	630	9 967	1 163	43 812	-7 303
1978	12 018	4 080	14 647	6 410	2 301	615	1 003	10 875	1 206	49 075	-10 685
1979	12 793	4 245	14 657	8 080	3 225	629	756	11 754	911	52 805	-9 264
1980	13 802	4 936	16 470	9 653	5 523	708	804	12 831	1 008	60 799	-10 153
1981	16 365	5 743	18 785	13 351	6 494	760	859	14 073	1 029	71 716	-7 979
1982	18 636	6 969	24 644	16 440	5 649	2 288	1 039	15 768	1 493	85 957	-21 083

Source: Statistics Canada, National Income and Expenditure Accounts
Note: (1) Includes national defence. (2) From 1961 on, this item is treated as government current expenditures; prior to 1961, it was treated as a capital transfer

provinces, and transportation and communications.

A major area of concern in the 1960s and 1970s was social security. By the end of the 1960s, the federal government was paying half the cost of provincial hospitalization, welfare assistance, and, in most cases, medical care programs. It was also providing pensions for the old, and family allowances for the young; it had a Canada Pension Plan to provide portable retirement pensions and an Unemployment Insurance Fund to provide financial benefits for persons out of work. Some politicians had argued in favour of a guaranteed minimum income for all, but this was rejected by the government on grounds of cost. Also, mainly for financial reasons, it was felt inappropriate to introduce a government-financed program of dental care.

In the early 1970s, the government reorganized some of the existing social-security schemes, increased some of the benefits, such as those for the unemployed, and, extremely important, reduced universal eligibility for many of the benefits. As one example of the latter, the government instead of increasing old-age pensions for all, introduced a guaranteed-income supplement for needy pensioners. As another example, it increased family-allowance payments, but made them subject to income tax. This meant, in effect, that families with a higher taxable income returned part of the money to the government.

In the late 1970s and early 1980s, the federal and provincial governments experienced increasingly large budgetary deficits. These were caused by two main factors: (a) less tax revenue than anticipated as a result of a poor national economic performance and (b) larger than anticipated expenditures in four main areas: federal contributions to the unemployment insurance fund; Canada Assistance Plan payments to the provinces for welfare; cash payments to the provinces for tax equalization; and service charges on the national debt because of high interest rates and increased government borrowing.

Equalization Payments

One major problem that the federal government, through its spending program, has tried to help resolve is that of regional disparities of income. While Ontario, Alberta, and British Columbia are relatively rich economically, many of the other provinces find it difficult to make ends meet. To help offset these differences, the federal government has for many years made "equalization" payments to the poorer provinces. Under the *Federal-Provincial Fiscal Arrangements and Established Programs Financing Act, 1977*, the federal government gives money to the governments of the poorer provinces in the form of fiscal-need grants and revenue-equalization grants. Fiscal-need grants are payments made to help provincial governments provide standards of health, education, welfare, and other public services comparable with those of the country as a whole without having to levy abnormally high taxes. The amount of money a province receives is determined according to a formula that takes into account both the expenditure needs of that province and its means of revenue. *Revenue-equalization grants* are payments made to provincial governments to cover the difference between the provincial average revenue per capita and the national average. Thus, a province that can raise only a limited average amount of revenue per person from taxes, fees, fines, permits, and so on, compared with other provinces, although the tax rates are approximately the same, would receive financial assistance from the federal government.[1]

In 1974, after the escalation of world oil prices, the equalization formula was changed so that only one-third of increases in oil-and-gas revenues of producing provinces above the 1973-74 levels would be taken into account. In 1977, the formula was again changed to include only half of provincial revenues from all non-renewable resources.

Shared-Cost Programs

The cost of many government programs in Canada, notably Hospital Insurance, Medicare, post-secondary education, have been shared by the federal and provincial governments. Many of these programs have been the result of federal government initiative and the provinces' natural reluctance to refuse the offer of federal funds. In most cases, the federal government has matched dollar for dollar the spending by provincial governments. However, from 1977 on, contributions from the federal government were no longer directly related to provincial expenditures, but instead were to increase in accordance with the growth of the economy. The only exception was the sharing of the cost of the Canada Assistance Plan—the basis for welfare payments. The provincial governments have agreed to maintain certain minimum standards for the shared-cost programs, including portability and degree of coverage. Also, since provincial spending is no longer matched dollar for dollar, the provincial governments now have an additional incentive to exercise economy in these programs and this is what has taken place in, for example, the area of post-secondary education. In the 1980s, the federal government has announced its intention to limit the amount of money that it transfers to the provinces for health and education.

Historical Origins

Federal financial assistance to the provinces is not a recent development. From the start of Confederation, well over a hundred years ago, the federal government has been granting subsidies to the poorer provinces. However, until relatively recently, such aid was *ad hoc*—money was made available to cover a specific, temporary need. Today, the principle that richer provinces in the Confederation should continue to help the poorer provinces has become one of the main planks of federal-government policy. The principle has also been accepted, though not without misgivings, by the governments of the provinces called upon to do the giving. It is sometimes pointed out that a standard of living cannot be measured solely in economic terms. A Maritimer, for example, would resent the allegation that he or she is "poorer" than someone in, say, Southern Ontario earning one-and-a-half times or even twice as much money.

Expenditure Estimates

The federal government's spending plans for the fiscal year beginning April 1 are submitted to Parliament in the preceding February by the President of the Treasury Board. The *Main Estimates*, as they are called, are then divided by subject matter and sent by the House of Commons to its appropriate standing committees for examination. These committees are required to report back to the House of Commons by May 31. Since the fiscal year begins April 1, Parliament, by voting *Interim Supply* at the end of March, authorizes the government to continue spending through the use of an Appropriation Act, usually until June 30 or such time as the Main Estimates are approved by Parliament. The committees, comprising Members of Parliament from all the main political parties, are able to supplement their examination and discussion of the expenditure estimates by questioning Ministers, department officials, and outside experts. The committees can recommend to the House of Commons the reduction or even elimination of particular items. However, without the government's agreement, such recommendations have little chance of being accepted.

Amendments to the federal government's spending plans, often for purposes of fiscal policy, are submitted to Parliament usually in November and March of each fiscal year. These amendments, called *Supplementary Estimates*, are presented in the form of a *supply bill* and after examination in the standing committees, are approved by Parliament as an Appropriation Act. In each year, there are normally four Appropriation Acts—one in March for *Interim Supply*, one in June for the

Main Estimates, one in December for the first set of *Supplementary Estimates*, and one in the following March for the final *Supplementary Estimates*. Sometimes additional amendments to the government's spending plans may become necessary, resulting in *Further Supplementary Estimates*.

28.3: PROVINCIAL EXPENDITURE

The Constitution Act, 1867, gave the provincial legislatures jurisdiction over all matters of local interest. This meant, in practice, such matters as health, education, welfare, fire prevention, police protection, and the construction and maintenance of roads. The provincial governments were also given the power to delegate part of their authority to local municipal governments.

The two largest areas of provincial expenditure are education and health.

28.4: MUNICIPAL EXPENDITURE

Canada has a great variety of municipal governments—in cities, towns, villages, counties, districts, regional municipalities, and metropolitan areas. The powers of these local governments vary considerably from one province to another and even within one province itself. Generally speaking, however, these local governments have been given power by their respective provincial governments to carry out functions best provided locally. Thus, local governments provide police and fire protection, run the schools, operate public libraries, and supply water and other utilities.

In some instances the provincial and the municipal governments divide between them a responsibility such as police protection. As times change, this allocation of powers is sometimes altered. Thus, special school districts may replace the local municipal school board; a number of local municipalities may be combined into a regional municipality; or, a number of urban municipalities may be joined into a metropolitan area to provide certain common services.

28.5: BUILT-IN STABILIZERS

Government expenditures play an extremely important role in helping to stabilize the level of income and employment in Canada. In times of economic pessimism, spending by our governments (unlike most business investments and, to some extent, consumer spending) rarely goes down. In fact, considering the large number of persons now employed directly or indirectly by government and the large amount of "transfer

payments" such as old-age pensions, unemployment-insurance benefits, and family allowances, it would probably be political suicide for
our federal, provincial, and municipal governments to undertake any
drastic reduction in their spending. In other words, the expenditures
are now built in to our economy; that is, even if business investment
declines because of a poor economic outlook, government spending
will form a prop for a sagging economy. We consider built-in stabilizers
in more detail in Chapter 31 (Canadian Fiscal Policy.)

Summary

1. Government now accounts for about one-half of all spending in
   Canada. This includes transfer payments.
2. Economic and social responsibilities are divided, under the terms
   of the Constitution Act, 1867, between the federal government
   and the provincial governments. The provincial governments in
   turn delegate certain of their powers to municipal governments.
3. In recent years, the federal government has extended its activities
   into areas that were once considered to be of purely local or provincial interest. Health and welfare are by far the largest areas of
   expenditure.
4. Equalization payments are made by the federal government to certain provinces to help reduce regional income disparities.
5. The two largest areas of provincial expenditure are education and
   health.
6. Municipal governments carry out functions best provided on a local basis, such as fire protection.
7. Government expenditures play an extremely important role in
   helping to stabilize the level of income and employment in
   Canada.

Key Terms

Transfer payments   565
Legislative jurisdiction   567
Federal expenditure   567
Conditional-grant
   programs   568
Social security   570
Budgetary deficit   570
Equalization   570

Fiscal-need grants   571
Revenue-equalization
   grants   571
Shared-cost programs   571
Expenditure estimates   572
Supplementary estimates   572
Provincial expenditure   573
Municipal expenditure   573

Review Questions

1. What percentage of Canada's national expenditure today is made by government, rather than by business firms or the public?
2. What are the major areas of federal and provincial government expenditure?
3. Why is government spending considered necessary? Why has it grown substantially in recent years?
4. How are public responsibilities divided among the federal, provincial, and municipal governments in Canada?
5. What is the percentage of expenditure made by each level of government in Canada?
6. What are the basic goals that now seem to guide federal-government spending?
7. What has been the pattern of federal-government spending in recent years?
8. Explain how the federal government, through fiscal means, attempts to reduce regional income disparities.
9. What are the most important areas of provincial- and municipal-government spending?

Reference

1. For a detailed discussion, see, for example: Douglas H. Clark, *Fiscal Need and Revenue Equalization Grants*, Canadian Tax Papers No. 49, Canadian Tax Foundation, Toronto, 1969.

*"Believe me, Mr. Shaw, we wouldn't ask
for the money if we didn't need it."*

29. GOVERNMENT REVENUE

CHAPTER OBJECTIVES

A. To indicate where our governments obtain their money from
B. To review the different type of taxes imposed
C. To outline the history of federal-provincial tax relations
D. To discuss briefly Canada's income tax system
E. To analyze the incidence of sales taxes

CHAPTER OUTLINE:

29.1: SOURCES OF REVENUE

In the modern Western industrial democracies, including Canada, governments have been elected on political platforms of social reform. These involve a variety of social security measures such as unemployment insurance, old age pensions, education, health, welfare assistance, etc. all of which require an army of public and semi-public employees for their administration. Consequently, the government demand for revenue to meet its expenditure needs has now become huge.

The money to finance the spending by our governments has to come mainly from the private sector of the economy—from individuals and business firms. The most important way that governments obtain this money is by taxation, notably by personal and corporate income taxes and by sales taxes. Other private sources include contributions by employers and employees to social-insurance and government-pension funds. Then there are public sources such as profits from government enterprises. The various sources of federal government revenue are shown in Table S.29. As we consider in the next chapter, our governments also raise money by borrowing, both at home and abroad, to permit them to spend more than they collect in taxes and investment income.

The largest source of revenue for the federal government (see Table S.30) is the personal income tax, followed by the corporation income tax and indirect taxes such as the sales tax and customs duties. Non-tax revenue—notably the return on investments in government business enterprises—is of less importance.

The provincial governments rely heavily on income and sales taxes for their revenue. The municipal governments have the property tax as their mainstay.

29.2: TYPES OF TAX

Throughout history, many different types of taxes have been imposed by governments to raise revenue.

Direct versus Indirect Taxes

One way of classifying the various taxes levied is into direct and indirect taxes. And this distinction was made in the Constitution Act, 1867, in the allocation of tax powers between the Federal Parliament and the provincial legislatures.

A *direct tax* is levied on the person intended to pay it. Thus, a person who has to pay personal income tax cannot transfer the tax to someone else. An *indirect tax*, conversely, is a tax that can be passed on to someone else. Thus, the manufacturer who pays excise taxes can add them to the selling price of the goods. In this way, the consumer, rather than the manufacturer, eventually pays the tax.

Progressive, Proportional, and Regressive Taxes

To stress the varied effect that taxes can have on different income levels of society, economists sometimes classify taxes as progressive,

Table S.29
Federal Government Revenues, millions of dollars, 1950-1982

Years	Direct taxes persons	Direct taxes corporations	Withholding taxes	Indirect taxes	Transfers from persons	Investment income	Capital consumption allowances	Total revenues
1950	806	847	54	1 115	7	133	58	3 020
1955	1 647	1 248	67	1 743	1	220	82	5 008
1960	2 503	1 308	79	2 177	3	336	111	6 517
1965	3 332	1 652	167	3 245	3	545	151	9 095
1966	3 634	1 774	204	3 570	3	632	167	9 984
1967	4 305	1 758	218	3 705	3	738	179	10 906
1968	5 125	2 107	209	3 761	4	821	191	12 218
1969	6 503	2 402	234	4 028	2	1 108	213	14 490
1970	7 436	2 276	269	4 034	2	1 279	232	15 528
1971	8 299	2 477	278	4 480	4	1 458	245	17 241
1972	9 285	2 901	287	5 121	5	1 684	277	19 560
1973	10 861	3 644	322	5 837	6	1 827	312	22 809
1974	13 538	5 012	430	8 495	8	2 116	379	29 978
1975	15 231	5 372	465	7 882	8	2 304	441	31 703
1976	18 042	5 046	504	8 601	11	2 608	501	35 313
1977	18 042	5 157	534	9 085	13	3 124	554	36 509
1978	17 708	5 813	582	9 750	15	3 879	643	38 390
1979	20 252	6 945	754	10 661	17	4 183	729	43 541
1980	23 456	8 425	995	12 131	17	4 816	806	50 646
1981	29 096	8 399	1 110	18 838	22	5 349	923	63 737
1982	32 254	6 745	1 178	17 324	24	6 294	1 055	64 874

Source: Statistics Canada, National Income and Expenditure Accounts

Table S.30
Federal Government Budgetary Revenue by Major Source, millions of dollars, 1982

Fiscal Year ended March 31	1982	Per cent of total
Tax revenue		
Income tax		
Personal	24 046	44.5
Corporation	8 118	15.0
Non-resident	1 018	1.9
Petroleum & gas revenue tax	864	1.6
Sub-total.	34 046	63.0
Excise taxes & duties		
Sales tax	6 185	11.4
Customs import duties.	3 439	6.4
Excise duties	1 175	2.2
Natural gas and gas liquids tax	998	1.8
Oil export charges	519	1.0
Special petroleum compensation charge	473	0.9
Special excise tax-gasoline	436	0.8
Other.	564	1.0
Sub-total.	13 789	25.5
Other tax revenue	120	0.2
Total tax revenue.	47 955	88.7
Non-tax revenue		
Return on investments		
Bank of Canada	1 853	3.4
Canada Mortgage & Housing Corp	873	1.6
Exchange Fund Account	763	1.4
Interest on bank deposits.	701	1.3
Farm Credit Corporation	285	0.5
Other return on investments	620	1.1
Sub-total.	5 095	9.4
Other non-tax revenue.	1 018	1.9
Total non-tax revenue	6 113	11.3
Total revenue	54 068	100.0

Source: Public Accounts of Canada

proportional, or regressive. A *progressive tax* is one that takes a larger percentage of a rich person's income than of a poor person's income. Examples of such taxes in Canada include the personal income tax and succession duties. A *proportional tax* is one that takes the same percentage of a rich person's income as of a poor person's income. A hypothetical example would be an equal-percentage levy on everyone's total income. A *regressive tax* is one that takes a larger percentage of a poor person's income than of a rich person's income — for example, the general sales tax and customs duties.

Point of Impact

Taxes may also be classified according to their point of impact. From this viewpoint, there are three basic forms of taxes in Canada: (a) income taxes, (b) sales taxes, and (c) wealth taxes. We now consider each of these.

29.3: INCOME TAXES

In each province, both the federal government and the provincial government levy a personal income tax and a corporation income tax.

Personal Income Tax

The personal income tax is *graduated*; that is to say, the larger a person's taxable income, the higher the rate of tax on any additional income. Because of the increasing tax rate, the personal income tax is said to be a *progressive* tax. The provincial personal income tax is collected by the federal government at the same time as it collects its own; the provincial tax is then remitted to each provincial government. Quebec, however, collects its own provincial personal income tax.

The logic behind graduated rates of personal income tax is that a person with a low income cannot afford to give the government very much money. This person needs it all for food, shelter, and other basic necessities. The person with a high income, on the other hand, can better afford a large tax payment. This person will not go hungry if the government takes a larger portion of his or her earnings. The graduated personal income tax is also an extremely effective tool for achieving income redistribution, because: (a) more is taken from the upper- and middle-income groups than from the lower-income ones and (b) part of what is taken from the upper- and middle-income groups is given to the lower-income groups in the form of family allowances, child credits, pension supplements, and other government transfer payments geared to a person's income.

Most people agree that low-income earners should pay proportionately less tax than high-income earners. However, there is considerable dispute as to how steeply graduated the tax rate should be. If the rates increase too sharply, it is argued, most people will lose the incentive to work harder. Furthermore, a sole proprietor or partner, for instance, who pays personal income tax on any business income, may be less inclined to take business risks. Also, there is considerable argument as to how high the top rate of income tax should be. For the government to take over 60 cents of each additional dollar earned, as is now the case, seems to many people, confiscatory.

A person's taxable income comprises any salary, wage, or commissions, plus any business, investment, or other income, minus various personal exemptions and other allowable deductions. Since 1972, one-half of certain capital gains, as well as various other types of income, have to be included when taxable income is calculated. Conversely, one half of any capital losses may be used to reduce other taxable income.

Corporation Income Tax

Every business corporation in Canada must pay federal and provincial corporation income taxes on its annual net income. At present, the combined rate of tax is about 40 per cent on income from manufacturing and processing, varying slightly according to the province. Other types of business income are taxed at a rate of 46 per cent. As a small-business incentive, Canadian-controlled private business corporations are taxed at a rate in most provinces of 25 per cent on their first $200000 of annual business income. This incentive applies only to firms with an accumulated taxable income, over the years, of less than $1000000. Investment income does not benefit from the reduced rate; nor does income received by various professional service firms such as medical doctors.

In all provinces except Ontario and Quebec, the federal and provincial corporation income taxes are collected together by the federal government.

The net income of a corporation after these income taxes have been deducted may be retained in the business or paid out as dividends. Dividends must be included by shareholders in their personal income tax returns.

Naturally enough, most business owners argue that the rate of corporation income tax in Canada is far too high. Of course, the higher the rate, the less incentive there is to establish and expand businesses. And without business expansion, there can be no increase in income and employment opportunities. In fact, without business expansion, there can be no economic growth. Business owners also argue that it is unfair to tax business income when it is earned, then tax it again when part is paid out as dividends.

There are, however, two sides to most arguments. Governments need money to pay for the services they provide. Many of these services—for example, education of the future labour force and maintenance of law and order—are of direct benefit to business. Other services, such as pollution control, are remedies for problems created partly by business corporations. A rate of corporation income tax should reflect both points of view. The actual rate is obviously a political decision. And governments reduce double taxation to some extent by allowing a person who receives dividends from Canadian-controlled corporations to subtract a dividend tax credit from the amount of personal income tax payable.

29.4: SALES TAXES

There are many different sales taxes in Canada. The federal government levies a general sales tax, an excise tax, a special excise tax, and customs duties. In addition, each provincial government, except Alberta, levies its own sales tax.

The *general sales tax*, which the federal government levies on a large number of goods in Canada, is based on the price of goods manufactured in Canada or on the duty-paid value of goods imported from abroad. It is payable by the manufacturer at the time of delivery to the purchaser, or by the importer at the time of importation. The present rate of tax is 9 per cent, except for some building materials (5 per cent). There are many exemptions from the general sales tax: for example, materials and equipment for manufacturing production; farm machinery; drugs; heating fuels; electricity; most products of farms, forests, fisheries, and mines; and books, magazines, and newspapers.

The *excise tax* is a federal sales tax levied on special classes of goods or services: for example, the net premiums of certain non-Canadian insurance companies; tobacco, cigarettes, and cigars; and alcoholic products. The tax may be a percentage of the value (*ad valorem*)—for example, 10 per cent of the value of net insurance premiums. Or it may be *specific*—for example, 9¢/L (42 cents per gallon) of beer or $2.69/L (12.25 per gallon) of Canadian brandy.

The *special excise tax* is a sales tax levied on the sale in Canada of items such as jewellery, clocks, and watches; toilet articles and cosmetics; playing cards; tobacco and smoker's accessories; and wines. As with the general excise tax, some of these special excise taxes are *ad valorem* and others are specific. In the case of tobacco products, there is both an excise tax and a special excise tax. There is also the general sales tax.

Why does the government levy excise taxes on various products? One reason is that it is useful to have a source of revenue additional to the general sales tax. However, in the case of products such as tobacco and liquor, the excise tax is imposed because the public accepts the fact that it is desirable to discourage the consumption of these products and is not therefore as outraged, as it might be, if such high taxes were levied on food, clothing, or other more necessary goods. Also, conveniently for the government, the demand for tobacco and liquor is relatively price-inelastic. This means that the high rate of tax and therefore the high price of the good, although discouraging consumption, does not discourage it enough to cause the government to forgo too much tax revenue. A third reason for excise taxes on luxury and semi-luxury goods is that people who can afford to buy them can also presumably afford to pay extra sales taxes. In the case of gasoline, the excise tax is justified on the grounds that the proceeds are, at least ostensibly, required to help pay for new roads. This is what is sometimes called a *pseudo-benefit tax.*

Customs duties, also called *tariffs* or *import duties*, are taxes on goods imported into the country. They are *ad valorem*, specific, or a combination of both. For example, the customs duty on a good may be 15 per cent of its import price, 10 cents per pound, or the greater of the two.

Customs duties have long been a source of government tax revenue because they have always been relatively easy to collect compared with other taxes. As well as providing tax revenue, they have the advantage of helping to protect domestic industry from foreign competition. However, by restricting imports, they cause prices in the domestic market to be higher for the consumer than they would otherwise be. Moreover, if the customs duties are prohibitive ones, they may restrict the consumer's choice by barring some foreign goods completely. Another possible disadvantage, depending on one's point of view, is that they reduce international specialization and trade.

Each provincial government, except that of Alberta, has its own provincial sales tax. The taxes are set as a percentage of the retail price or, in some provinces, of the "fair value" of the goods sold.

How satisfactory are these various types of federal and provincial sales taxes? Sales taxes are sometimes criticized because a low-income person pays the same amount of tax on a good as a high-income person. Because a dollar paid in tax means more to a poor person than to a rich one, the low-income person, it is argued, bears greater hardship. Money, like any other good, is subject to diminishing marginal utility.

According to this argument, the rich should pay more in order to suffer the same loss in satisfaction or utility. Because sales taxes take a larger bite of a poor person's income than of a rich person's income, they are said to be *regressive*. However, some goods, particularly necessities, are exempted from the general sales tax. Furthermore, some sales taxes, such as the excise tax, are levied only on goods purchased mainly by higher-income families. At the provincial level, the regressiveness of the sales tax is reduced in two ways: first, by exempting most necessities; second, by levying special taxes on semi-luxury goods or services such as tobacco or race-horse betting that, in theory at least, low-income persons cannot afford.

29.5: TAXES ON WEALTH

Taxes on wealth include the capital gains tax levied by the federal government, the gift tax and succession duties levied by the provincial governments, and the property tax levied by the municipal governments. The gift tax and succession duties, since they are levied on wealth being transferred from one person to another, are often called *transfer taxes*. The estate tax on inheritances, levied by the federal government until 1972, was also of this type. The *capital gains tax*, introduced in 1972, is not a separate tax but is part of the income-tax system. Generally, one-half of the gain or loss on the sale or disposal of most property is to be taken into account when computing a taxpayer's taxable income.

The *gift tax* is a tax levied on the transfer by an individual, during his or her life, of cash or any property with value to other persons, except as part of a normal business transaction. Such a tax was levied by the federal government until 1972. Most provinces have now introduced a gift tax partly to raise revenue and partly to prevent people from avoiding succession duties.

Succession duties are provincial taxes levied on the transfer of cash and other valuable property as a result of inheritance. Succession duties, apart from being a source of revenue for provincial governments, have the merit for some people of helping to give everyone an equal start in life. Because of this tax, millionaires cannot pass all their wealth on to their sons or daughters. Succession duties also have the merit in some people's opinion of being a relatively painless way of raising tax revenue, since, as the saying goes, "you can't take it with you." However, there is undoubtedly a lot of pain to those persons who stood to inherit the money paid in tax. Also, many people would argue that if a person has worked hard to accumulate some wealth, he or she should have the right to leave most, if not all, of it to whomsoever that person chooses. The same reasoning is also often applied to the gift tax.

The *property tax* is a tax levied on persons owning land and buildings. In Canada, this tax is levied by municipal governments on real property in their area. The only exception to the tax is government-owned property, for which grants are received by the municipality instead. Each property has an assessed value as determined by municipal assessors. (If the assessment is an old one, the assessed value may be much less than the market value of the property.) The municipal government, after having determined the amount of tax revenue it needs to obtain, divides this amount by the total assessment. This gives the tax rate. For example, to raise $3 million with a total taxable property assessment of $200 million, the municipal government has to strike a tax rate of 15 "mills" (or one-thousandths). The owner of a house assessed at $30 000 then has to pay $450 ($30 000 × 15/1000). There are, in practice, two mill rates—one for residential properties and another slightly higher one for commercial properties.

Municipal property taxes are often considered to be regressive because they are based not on the income and wealth of a person but on the assessed value of the residence. Usually, however, a high-income person lives in an expensive home and consequently pays more tax. If the person owns income-producing properties, tax must be paid on them too. Property-tax rates have risen considerably in recent years, owing mainly to higher costs of education.

In addition to the taxes previously described, provincial and municipal governments obtain revenue from individuals and business firms in various other ways. A few examples are motor vehicle licences and fees, hospital and medical care premiums, mining taxes, and "place of business" taxes.

29.6: FEDERAL-PROVINCIAL TAX RELATIONS

The Constitution Act, 1867, as well as dividing legislative power between the federal and provincial governments, specified the tax powers that each level of government was to have. The federal Parliament, on the one hand, was given the right to raise money "by any mode or system of taxation." The provincial legislatures, on the other, were given the right to "direct taxation within the province in order to the raising of a revenue for provincial purposes." This meant, in theory, that the federal government was given a free hand to impose direct or indirect taxes, whereas the provincial governments (and the municipal governments, which derive their powers from the provincial governments) were limited to direct taxes. In practice, the provincial governments were able to levy an indirect tax—the provincial sales tax—by treating retailers as legally-appointed collection agencies rather than as taxpayers.

At the time of Confederation, two indirect taxes—customs duties and excise taxes—were the major sources of government revenue. Customs duties are taxes on goods imported into Canada. Excise taxes are taxes levied on many goods sold in Canada, whether produced here or abroad. These two indirect taxes, it was hoped, would provide the federal government with sufficient funds to pay for its activities. The provincial and municipal governments, whose responsibilities were considered at that time to be quite modest, were left to make do with the politically unpopular right to impose direct taxes. It was agreed, however, that the federal government would provide some financial assistance to the provincial governments. This assistance took two forms: first, a per-capita subsidy to all provinces, which varied according to the needs of each; second, a "debt allowance" to those provinces that had less debt taken over by the federal government on Confederation than the average per capita amount for all the provinces.

By the beginning of the twentieth century, the provincial governments, faced with rising expenditures, had found it necessary to levy three direct taxes: a personal income tax, a corporate income tax, and succession duties. The municipal governments, also facing rising financial demands, relied mainly on the property tax plus even bigger grants from their respective provincial governments.

The next nail in the taxpayers' coffin, as many people see it, was World War I. To help finance the country's war effort, the federal government introduced its own personal and corporate income taxes. This meant that the government was now exercising its right to levy direct taxes as well as indirect taxes. Thus, individuals and business firms in Canada were now confronted with two income taxes—one provincial, the other federal. In addition, at the end of World War I, the federal government introduced a 1 per cent general sales tax at the manufacturer's level.

During the 1920s and 1930s the provincial governments found other new sources of revenue. One important source was the eatablishment of government liquor boards with monopoly power to sell liquor in the province. Others were the imposition of sales taxes on gasoline and other products, as well as the charging of fees for vehicle licences, driver licences and building permits.

World War II meant additional spending by the federal government and fresh demands for tax money. As a consequence, the federal government not only raised its rates of personal and corporate income tax considerably, but also introduced a special excise tax on many different goods and an estate tax on property left to others. This estate tax was similar to the succession duties already being collected by the provincial governments.

In 1941, the federal government and all the provincial governments signed a tax-rental agreement. This agreement, to last for the duration of the War and for one year after, stipulated that the provincial governments ceded the right to levy personal and corporate income taxes and succession duties in exchange for an annual cash grant from the federal government.

In 1947, a new tax-rental agreement was signed to cover the period 1947 to 1952. This time, the provincial governments of Ontario and Quebec refused to take part. Instead, they reintroduced their own corporate income tax and succession duties. But they did not at this time reintroduce the provincial personal income tax. Since these two provinces were levying their own corporate income tax, the federal government allowed an "abatement" or reduction in its own federal corporate income tax to business corporations in these two provinces. However, this abatement was only 5 per cent of taxable income, compared with a provincial income tax of 7 per cent. Consequently, business corporations in Ontario and Quebec ended up paying more tax than they would have if they had been located elsewhere. The federal government also allowed a 50 per cent abatement on its estate tax to take into account the succession duties levied by Ontario and Quebec.

In 1952 a new tax-rental agreement was signed between the federal and provincial governments. The major change from the previous agreement was that Ontario now agreed to take part. Specifically, Ontario agreed, in exchange for an annual cash grant, to abolish its own corporate income tax and not introduce a personal income tax. Both Ontario and Quebec continued, however, to levy their own succession duties. Quebec, furthermore, not only retained its corporate income tax, but also went a step further towards tax independence.

In 1954 the government of that province reintroduced its own personal income tax at a rate equivalent to about 10 per cent of the federal personal income tax. The federal government, to reduce double taxation, at first allowed taxpayers in Quebec an abatement of 5 per cent of the federal tax. Later in 1954, after considerable dispute, it raised the abatement to 10 per cent.

In 1957, another agreement, this time called a tax-sharing agreement, was signed by the federal and provincial governments. By this agreement, Ontario took back its right to collect its own corporate income tax but continued to agree, in exchange for an annual cash grant, not to impose a provincial personal income tax. Quebec maintained its go-it-alone tax policy. The cash grants to provincial governments that participated fully in the tax-sharing agreement were made up of three parts: first, a grant to make up for the tax revenue lost by a province because it does not levy its own personal income tax, corporate income tax, and inheritance tax; second, an equalization payment to help a province with a per-capita tax revenue below the national average; and third a stabilization payment to prevent the total payment to each province from varying too greatly from that received under the previous tax agreement.

In 1962, federal-provincial tax relations took a shift in the opposite direction. All the provinces reasserted their right to levy their own personal and corporate income taxes. However, most of them agreed to permit the federal governments to collect the money for them. Since the proceeds of the provincial personal and corporate income taxes, less a collection cost, were now to be remitted to the provincial government, equalization payments by the federal government were drastically reduced. This was one step towards greater provincial control of tax revenues.

Another and even more noteworthy step towards provincial fiscal autonomy was the federal government's agreement to gradually reduce the federal personal income tax. An abatement of 16 per cent to tax-payers was allowed in 1962 for provinces levying their own provincial income tax. It was agreed that this abatement was to be increased by 2 per cent a year until it reached 24 per cent in 1966. Thus, the federal government was reducing its share of the possible revenue from this type of direct tax in favour of the provinces. As a result of further federal-provincial tax conferences, the taxpayers' abatement was reduced even more than previously agreed: by 1972 it was 28 per cent. This abatement was then converted by the tax reform of 1972 into a provincial tax rate of 30.5 per cent of federal tax payable, from 1972 to 1976.

Under the Federal-Provincial Fiscal Arrangement and Established Programs Financing Act, 1977 (effective April 1, 1977), the federal government relinquished two more percentage points of its personal income tax to the provinces. This Act settled all outstanding tax issues, notably the Revenue Guarantee under which the federal government had agreed to reimburse any province that suffered a tax loss as a result of the new tax structure introduced in 1972.

29.7: CANADA'S INCOME TAX SYSTEM

A country's tax system usually has two basic aims: (a) to raise enough money to meet most or all of the cost of government spending programs and (b) to help a government achieve various political, economic and social goals.

Over the years, government spending (including transfer payments) in Canada has grown to almost one-half the country's Gross National Expenditure. And as spending programs continue to increase, so also does the need for more tax revenue. In the early 1980s, a period of economic recession, government revenue remains woefully insufficient to meet government expenditures—with the result that government borrowing continues unabated.

The second basic aim of a country's income tax system is to help achieve various political, and social goals. Politically, the government wishes to remain in power—therefore, it tries to please groups within society that account for most votes. The closer it is to election time, the greater the pressure on the government to undertake new spending programs and not to cut existing ones. Sometimes, of course, the government will, in the national interest, take politically unpopular steps.

Canada's economic and social goals, as we saw at the beginning of this book, are numerous and from time to time vary in priority. One of these goals is a more equitable distribution of income and, particularly, the reduction of poverty. Canada's tax system, by providing, for example, basic exemptions for everyone, larger exemptions to elderly taxpayers, deductions for child-care expenses incurred by working mothers, and for employment and moving expenses incurred by all employees, has meant a higher *tax threshold*—the level of income at which a person starts to pay tax. This means that many low-income persons no longer pay income tax, and many others pay much less. However, the combined federal and provincial tax rates are quite high. Thus, income is being shifted from the middle-income group to the lower-income one.

How does the upper-income group fare under Canada's income tax system? The rate of tax on taxable income beyond $78 420 is now fixed at 61.3 per cent (in Ontario) rather than increasing up to 82.4 per cent as it did some years ago. Thus, the upper-income taxpayer is taxed less on income beyond this amount. However, the capital-gains tax generates most revenue from the upper-income group, so that the net tax position of this group is probably not as good as it was before the capital gains tax was introduced in 1972. In other words, income is also shifted away from the upper-income group to the lower-income group. From the viewpoint of achieving a more equitable distribution of income, Canada's income-tax system appears to be successful.

Another important federal goal is economic growth. By lowering the top personal income-tax rate, the government has increased the motivation for employed and self-employed persons to work harder. The personal income tax, we should remember, is paid on business income from sole proprietorships and partnerships. In addition, by reducing the corporation income tax rate to 46 per cent and to 40 per cent for profits from manufacturing and processing, the government has provided more motivation to business corporations. Canadian-owned small-business corporations are also encouraged by a relatively low rate of about 25 per cent on the first $200000 of annual business income. The abolition of the federal estate tax and gift tax might at first seem to have provided more incentive for people to earn income and accumulate wealth. There would seem to be greater opportunity to pass on such wealth, often in the form of family farms and businesses, to sons and daughters. Previously, many people sold out, often to foreign investors, and spent their money during their lifetime rather than leave it for the tax collector later. Now, however, a capital gains tax is payable on sale of property or following the owner's death. Moreover, provincial governments now levy succession duties. So, on the whole, the incentive to accumulate wealth rather than spend it has not been increased. By substantially raising the maximum deductible contributions that a person may make to registered retirement savings plans, the government should increase the amount of savings available for investment. Furthermore, by requiring that no more than 10 per cent of the funds be invested in foreign assets, the government will ensure the most of these savings will be invested in Canada. On the whole, therefore, Canada's present tax system (compared with the old) stimulates rather than hinders Canadian economic growth.

A third important federal goal is reasonable price stability. In so far as the new tax system redistributes income from the middle- and upper-income groups to the lower-income groups, there is not only a reduction in poverty, but also an increase in consumer demand. This is because lower-income groups spend a larger percentage of additional income than higher-income groups. To use economic terminology, the marginal propensity to consume of lower-income groups is higher. This increase in aggregate demand, as a result of the tax system, may therefore encourage inflation. However, if consumer demand and the rate of inflation are too high, the government can reduce them by various means—for example, by high interest rates or by restricting its own spending. Also, with the cost-push nature of so much of today's inflation, any changes in consumer demand caused by the tax system should have only a limited effect on prices.

Canada's income-tax system was not made overnight. In fact, its origins go back to 1962 when a special commission, under the chairmanship of the late Kenneth Carter, was appointed by the federal government to review the federal tax system. The report of the Carter Commission, as it came to be known, was published in 1967 and contained many novel and, to many people, revolutionary proposals. In 1969 the newly elected Trudeau government published its own White Paper proposals for income-tax reform. These proposals, called "Benson's Iceberg" by some critics, because the bulk of the reforms seemed hidden beneath the surface, provoked heated debate throughout the country. They even led to the holding of mass rallies across Canada by a newly established citizens' group, the Canadian Council for Fair Taxation. After the proposals had been thoroughly debated by the public and mass media and special committees of the House of Commons and the Senate had reported on them, the federal government finally introduced its tax-reform bill in June 1971 for implementation in 1972. This bill contained many of the proposals of the original White Paper, but others had been modified or withdrawn—for example, the proposed capital gains tax on private homes. Since that time, a variety of minor changes have been made to Canada's income tax system, mainly to raise more tax revenue, or to stimulate certain types of activity, creating a bewildering mass of rules and regulations.

The most serious criticisms that can be made of Canada's income tax system are: (a) the increasingly large amount of income diverted from the private to the public purse and its dampening effect on human industry and initiative; (b) the complexity of the tax system; and (c) the allegedly preferential treatment accorded the federal revenue needs as compared with those of the provincial and municipal governments. The latter criticism is considered unfounded by the federal government, which argues that the provincial and municipal governments are receiving a larger share of total revenue. Another criticism, that the sales and property taxes should also have been overhauled, seems less valid, considering the problems encountered in revising one type of tax alone. However, the system of sales taxes may eventually be revised. One possible change is the adoption of a *value-added tax*, or VAT.

Value Added Tax

This is a tax levied on the value added by a firm to a good at each stage of the manufacturing and marketing process. Unlike our present provincial sales tax, which is levied when the goods are sold to the final customer, the VAT is levied in installments as the materials, parts, or goods proceed through the manufacturing and marketing process. Each business is taxed on its output, but can claim offsetting credits for the cumulative amounts of tax paid on its inputs of goods and services.

The tax payable is, in other words, the difference between the total tax shown on a firm's sales invoices minus the total tax shown on its purchase invoices. This type of tax is used by Britain and the other Common Market countries of Western Europe. One advantage of the value-added tax, from a government's point of view, is that the government obtains its tax revenue sooner. Another advantage, particularly important for an exporting country such as Canada, is that under international rules, a government may rebate the tax paid on goods subsequently exported. This can help keep export prices more competitive.

Summary

1. The most important way in which government finances its expenditure is by taxation.
2. The three basic forms of taxation in Canada are: (a) income taxes, (b) sales taxes, and (c) wealth taxes.
3. Persons and corporations pay different income taxes. The personal income tax is graduated. Candian-controlled incorporated small businesses have a special low rate of corporation income tax.
4. Sales taxes include the general sales tax, the excise tax, the special excise tax, tariffs, and provincial sales taxes. The incidence of sales taxes depends on the elasticities of demand and supply for the product. The same is also true of subsidies.
5. Taxes on wealth include the capital gains tax, the gift tax, the estate tax, succession duties, and the property tax.
6. The Constitution Act, 1867, authorized the federal government to impose any type of tax, whereas the provincial governments were restricted to direct taxes.
7. Canada's income tax system was overhauled in 1972. The new system appears to satisfy several of the requirements of a good tax system. However, there are also some major criticisms.

Key Terms

Government revenue   577
Direct taxes   578
Indirect taxes   578
Progressive tax   578
Proportional tax   581
Regressive tax   581

Personal income tax   581
Taxable income   582
Capital gains   582
Corporaton
  income tax   582
Sales tax   583

Review Questions

1. What are the various source of government revenue in Canada? Specify the three main forms of taxation.
2. Distinguish between direct and indirect taxes. Why is this distinction still important in Canada?
3. Distinguish between a progressive tax, a proportional tax, and a regressive tax. What is the purpose of such a classification?
4. Why do most countries have graduated rates of personal income tax? What is the top rate in Canada?
5. How are corporations taxed on their income? What tax incentives are provided to incorporated small businesses?
6. What is double taxation? How is its effect reduced in practice?
7. What is the general sales tax?
8. Distinguish between an *ad valorem* sales tax and a *specific* sales tax.
9. What are excise taxes? What is their purpose?
10. What happens when the sales tax is increased on a product for which the demand is (a) elastic, and (b) inelastic? (See Appendix 29-A).
11. Who receives the benefit of a government subsidy—the producer or the consumer? (See Appendix 29-A).
12. What is the capital gains tax? How is it calculated?
13. What is the municipal property tax? How is it calculated What is a mill rate?
14. How are tax powers shared by the various levels of government?
15. What are the basic aims of a tax system? How satisfactory is Canada's income tax system? Discuss.
16. Explain the pros and cons of a "value-added tax".

APPENDIX 29-A:
THE INCIDENCE OF SALES TAXES

Sales taxes are of many different kinds. They include the general sales tax, excise taxes, and customs duties levied by the federal government, and the sales taxes levied by each provincial government. All have one feature in common—they are taxes levied on the sale of goods or services. The result is that on a good costing, for example, $10 to produce and market, a total of perhaps $3 goes in various taxes to the federal and provincial governments.

What effect does the imposition of a sales tax have on the market for a product? To answer this question, we make use of a diagram. In Figure 29:1, we can see that, before the addition of a sales tax, the market demand curve DD intersects the industry supply curve S_1S_1 at point A—where the market price is OP_1 and the quantity sold OQ_1. After the imposition of a sales tax, an industry is willing to supply the same quantity as before, but only at a price equivalent to the previous price plus the sales tax. This means that the new supply curve S_2S_2 will be higher than the previous one by the amount of the tax. The demand curve remains unchanged. In our illustration, the supply curve S_2S_2 intersects the existing demand curve DD at point B. At this new equilibrium position, price is now P_2 and the quantity sold is Q_2. The effect of the sales tax has therefore been to raise the price of the good sold and reduce the quantity sold.

The extent to which price and volume sold are affected by a sales tax will depend on the nature of demand and supply. The more elastic the demand, the greater the reduction in the quantity sold and the less the increase in price after the imposition of a sales tax. That is why governments prefer to place sales taxes on goods such as tobacco products that have a very inelastic demand. With such products, consumers cannot "cheat" the government by substantially reducing their purchases. The more elastic the supply, the greater also the change in the quantity sold and the less the increase in price.

Another question regarding the sales tax that remains to be answered is: who bears the burden of the tax—the producer or consumer? In fact, the burden is normally shared, its actual distribution depending on the elasticities of demand and supply. In Figure 29:2, we show how a sales tax is distributed, if demand is very inelastic. Of the sale tax, equivalent to AC in our diagram, the producer pays only an amount AB (the amount by which the producer's after-tax price is

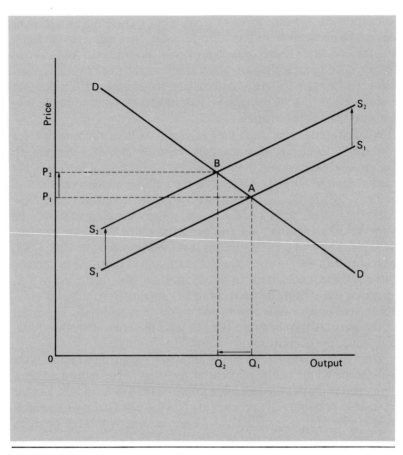

Note: The imposition of a sales tax causes the supply curve to shift upward from S_1S_1 to S_2S_2. The new market equilibrium is at point B instead of A. Price has risen from OP_1 to OP_2; the quantity sold has declined from OQ_1 to OQ_2.

Figure 29:1 Effects of an Imposition of a Sales Tax on the Market Price and Quantity Sold of a Product

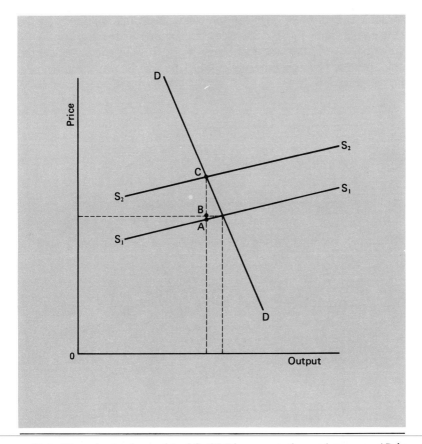

Note: The sales tax is equal to AC. Of this amount, the producer pays AB in the form of a lower price received than before. The consumer pays BC in the form of a higher price than before. The consumer, in this case, bears most of the burden of the sales tax.

Figure 29:2 How the Burden of a Sales Tax is Shared by Producer and Consumer when Demand is Very Inelastic

lower than before). The consumer, however, sees the price rise by the amount BC. Obviously, the consumer, because of the desire to have the product at all costs, has to bear the major part of the tax burden.

But what happens if supply rather than demand is very inelastic? If we look at Figure 29:3, we can see what effects this will have. At the new equilibrium, most of the sales tax is borne by the producer. Of a tax equal to AC, the producer bears, in the form of a lower price, the amount AB. The consumer bears only the part BC, in the form of a higher price.

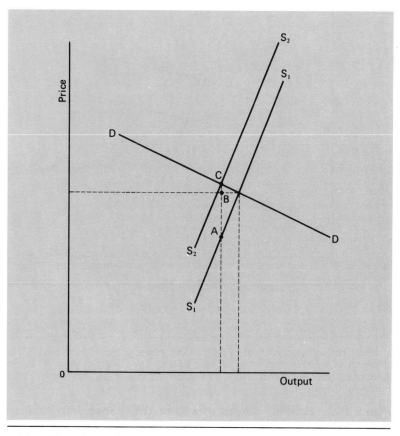

Note: The sales tax is equal to AC. Of this amount, the lion's share is borne by the producer. The price received per unit of sales has dropped by the amount AB. The consumer, however, faces a price increase equivalent to only BC.

Figure 29:3 How the Burden of a Sales Tax is Shared by Producer and Consumer when Supply is Very Inelastic

Subsidies

Sometimes a government grants a subsidy to farmers or other producers. In this case (instead of imposing a sales tax of $3 on each $10 product that is sold, for example) a government gives each producer a $3 bonus for each unit sold. This means that the industry can now afford to supply each previous quantity at a price $3 lower per unit than before. Instead of receiving $3 from the customer, the producer receives it from the government. The supply curve, instead of shifting

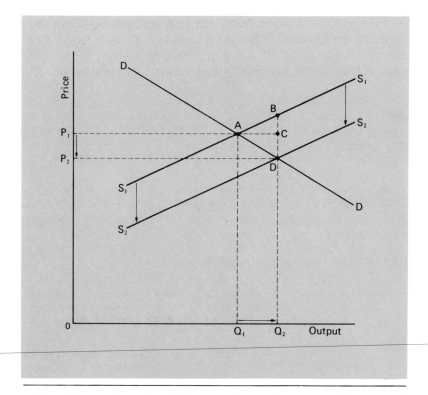

Note: The provision of a subsidy causes the supply curve to shift downward from S_1S_1 to S_2S_2. The new market equilibrium is now at point D—where price has fallen to OP_2, and quantity sold has increased to OQ_2. The producer now receives a total price of Q_2B, which is higher, by the amount BC, than the previous market price OP_1. The consumer now pays a price OP_2 that is lower than the previous market price OP_1 by the amount CD. Thus the producer and consumer have shared the benefit of the subsidy.

Figure 29:4 Effects of the Provision of a Subsidy on the Market Price and Quantity Sold of a Good

upwards as with a sales tax, now shifts downwards. This is shown in Figure 29:4, where the market equilibrium, after the introduction of the subsidy, is at point D instead of C. The effects of the subsidy have in fact been to reduce the market price (from OP_1 to OP_2) and to increase the quantity sold (from OQ_1 to OQ_2). Of course, not all the subsidy will in practice accrue to the producer. Depending on the elasticities of demand and supply, the benefit of the subsidy, just like the burden of the sale tax, will be shared between the producer and the consumer. In Figure 29:4, the introduction of the subsidy causes the price to drop not by the full amount of the subsidy, but only as far as OP_2. As a result, producers now receive a total price Q_2B, which is higher by the amount BC than the previous price they received. Consumers are also better off. They now have to pay only a price OP_2, which is lower by the amount CD than the previous market price, OP_1.

30. GOVERNMENT BORROWING AND THE PUBLIC DEBT

CHAPTER OBJECTIVES

A. To explain why governments need to borrow
B. To indicate the disadvantages of government borrowing
C. To explain how governments borrow by selling treasury bills and bonds
D. To indicate the size of Canada's public debt and the burden that it may be said to impose
E. To explain how the public debt is managed by the Bank of Canada

CHAPTER OUTLINE

30.1 Need for Borrowing
30.2 Disadvantages of Government Borrowing
30.3 Methods of Borrowing
30.4 The Burden of the Public Debt
30.5 Management of the Public Debt

In some countries, an excess of government expenditure over tax and other revenue is met simply by printing more money. This is one way for a government to divert a larger share of the national resources from the private to the public sector. As there is a larger money supply and the same physical amount of wealth, the real value of each dollar in the hands of the private sector declines.

To governments in some countries, printing extra money is politically more palatable than raising taxes. It is certainly much cheaper than borrowing money, for there is no interest to be paid. The price of this policy can, however, be a high one—galloping inflation. In many countries that have resorted to raising revenue in this way, increases in the general price level of 20 or even 50 per cent or more per annum have not been uncommon.

In Canada, the federal government finances any excess of expenditure over tax and other revenue by means of borrowing. Payment of interest is a relatively cheap price to pay, so it is considered, for greater price stability.

30.1: NEED FOR BORROWING

The greatest need for borrowing money occurs in time of war, when governments have to pay for large armed forces and considerable munitions production. Thus, the sale of Victory and other bonds by governments during World War II resulted in a vast increase in the public debt in many countries, including Canada. A *government bond*, it should be noted, is a written promise by a government to repay the money that it has borrowed and to pay interest at a specified rate and on specified dates on the amount borrowed.

In peacetime, the federal government in Canada has also frequently spent more than its revenue (see Table S.31). In some years this policy has been a deliberate one—adopted to stimulate activity at a time of economic contraction. In other years, it has reflected the ambitious efforts of government to undertake more programs involving public spending than can be financed by normal revenues. Borrowing, rather than raising taxes or reducing other expenditures, has been the easy way out.

The federal government also finds it necessary to borrow money to repay money that it has borrowed previously. When a government bond matures—that is, falls due for repayment—the government may repay all or part of it by a new bond issue. This is called *refunding*. The part not covered by the new issue is repaid out of tax revenue and thus the size of the country's outstanding public debt is reduced.

Not all government borrowing is long term. Irregularity in the government's cash flow during the course of the fiscal year also creates a considerable need for short-term financing. Thus expenditures in the early part of a year may be much greater than the cash inflow during these months, even though revenue and expenditure are expected to be in balance for the year as a whole. In these circumstances the government borrows money for three or more months.

Provincial and municipal governments are also substantial borrowers. Provincial governments need money to finance unusually large expenditures such as the building of highways and bridges and the con-

Table S.31
Federal Government Revenue, Expenditure, and Surplus or Deficit, in millions of dollars, 1950-1982

Year	Revenue	Expenditure	Surplus or Deficit
1950	3 020	2 370	650
1951	4 165	3 194	971
1952	4 687	4 492	195
1953	4 809	4 658	151
1954	4 608	4 654	-46
1955	5 008	4 806	202
1956	5 698	5 100	598
1957	5 672	5 422	250
1958	5 409	6 176	-767
1959	6 139	6 478	-339
1960	6 517	6 746	-229
1961	6 779	7 189	-410
1962	6 979	7 486	-507
1963	7 323	7 609	-286
1964	8 355	8 010	345
1965	9 095	8 551	544
1966	9 984	9 753	231
1967	10 906	10 990	-84
1968	12 218	12 229	-11
1969	14 490	13 469	1 021
1970	15 528	15 262	266
1971	17 241	17 386	-145
1972	19 560	20 126	-566
1973	22 809	22 422	387
1974	29 978	28 869	1 109
1975	31 703	35 508	-3 805
1976	35 313	38 704	-3 391
1977	36 509	43 812	-7 303
1978	38 390	49 075	-10 685
1979	43 541	52 805	-9 264
1980	50 646	60 799	-10 153
1981	63 737	71 716	-7 979
1982	64 874	85 957	-21 082

Source: Statistics Canada, *National Income and Expenditure Accounts*

struction of electric-power generating and transmission facilities. Municipal governments need money for such costly projects as new schools, waterworks, sewage systems, and road-widening schemes.

30.2: DISADVANTAGES OF GOVERNMENT BORROWING

Government borrowing brings with it a number of disadvantages for both the government and the economy. First, interest must be paid to the lender. Second, the money borrowed must eventually be repaid. If the lender is a foreign one, payment of interest and repayment of principal will require the purchase of the foreign currency. Consequently, pressure will be put on Canada's balance of international payments tending to depress the foreign-exchange rate of the Canadian dollar because of the increased demand for the foreign currency. Also, if the loan is denominated in a foreign currency that appreciates in value (like the U.S. dollar or Swiss franc), the cost of the loan will rise in terms of Canadian dollars.

A third disadvantage of heavy government borrowing is that it adds to the demand for loan funds at home and helps force up current rates of interest. Consequently, business firms and private individuals find it more costly and difficult to borrow. This in turn may discourage business investment and consumer spending at a time when they are needed to stimulate economic activity. Fourth, a government may borrow so much that the payment of interest and repayment of principal may become so onerous as to bankrupt it. Because of the taxing power that a government has, this is unlikely. However, many municipal government did suspend payments during the economic depression of the 1930s.

30.3: METHODS OF BORROWING

The federal government borrows money by selling marketable and non-marketable securities to financial institutions and the general public. *Marketable securities* consist of bonds of varying maturity. Once issued, they can be bought and sold in the bond market at any time and their current market price is determined by demand and supply. *Non-marketable securities* issued by the federal government consist of treasury bills, Canada Savings Bonds, Unemployment Insurance Commission bonds, and Canada Pension Fund bonds.

Money borrowed by the government for short periods of time (by the sale of treasury bills, for example) is known as *floating debt*. Money borrowed for longer periods of time, by the issue of bonds, is called *funded debt*.

Treasury Bills

These are promissory notes (also called bonds) that the federal government issues each week in exchange for short-term loans. They are issued in denominations of $1 000, $5 000, $25 000, $100 000, and $1 million. They usually mature ninety-one days from date of issue. Some treasury bills are issued, however, for six months and longer.

The bills are sold by competitive tender to the highest bidder by the Bank of Canada, Canada's central bank, acting on behalf of the federal government. Bidders include the chartered banks, money-market dealers, and the Bank of Canada. The Bank of Canada submits two bids: one for bills that it would like for itself; the other as a reserve bid for the entire issue. The reserve bid is to ensure that the entire issue is sold and that other bidders cannot collude to hold down the price. Other investors buy their treasury bills at second-hand—from chartered banks or money-market dealers.

Treasury bills are attractive to investors for three reasons: first, the investor's absolute certainty that the money loaned to the government will be repaid; second, the ease with which the bills can be sold if necessary; and third, the reasonable rate of return, or *yield*, to be obtained—determined by relating the nominal rate of interest to the purchase price.

The federal government also occasionally sells certificates of deposit, or CDs, to the chartered banks in exchange for short-term financing. The maturity is usually six months and the price is a negotiated one. These certificates are not marketable and are issued on the understanding that they will be held to maturity.

Bonds

Government bonds are written promises by a government to repay money that it has borrowed and to pay interest at a certain rate at specified intervals. They are similar to treasury bills except for their date of maturity. Bonds are issued for longer periods of time—many of them maturing only after ten or more years. In Canada, bonds are sold by all levels of government—federal, provincial, and municipal. They are sold mainly to chartered banks and other financial institutions. Many of them are sold outside Canada, in the United States and Europe.

Government of Canada Bonds: Bonds issued by the federal government can be divided into marketable and non-marketable bonds. The fact that the federal government, with its unlimited tax powers, is the borrower means that the security for repayment is practically impeccable. The only risk is that the government might suddenly decide to

repudiate its debt or that a foreign power might capture the country—
two events that are extremely unlikely. Marketable bonds can be
bought and sold by investors at any time. In total, they represent about
one-half of the federal government's outstanding debt.

The most important type of non-marketable bond is the Canada Savings Bond, or CSB. This is a successor to the Victory Bond sold to the
public during World War II to help finance the Canadian war effort.
CSBs differ from marketable federal government bonds in several
ways. First, CSBs can be surrendered at a chartered bank at any time
for full face value plus interest. Because of the government's willingness to redeem them in this way, CSBs do not fluctuate in value as do
marketable bonds that can be redeemed only on the agreed maturity
date. A second difference is that CSBs are not marketable—the holder
of such bonds cannot sell them to someone else. A third difference is
that CSBs, for the convenience of the small investor, are available in
small denominations as well as large—$50, $100, $500, $1000, and
$5000.

Once the federal government has decided to borrow money, how is
the bond issue made? The procedure is that the Bank of Canada invites
a select group of investment dealers and chartered banks to place
orders at a set price. This group—the *primary distributors*—then resell
the bonds, at a slightly higher price, to a variety of investors.

Provincial and Municipal Bonds: Provincial governments issue *debenture bonds* or *debentures* for short, to raise money for important
public works and even to finance full-employment budget deficits.
Many provincial governments also guarantee repayment of money borrowed by municipal governments and school boards. The term *debenture* means that the lender, or bondholder, has a general claim on the
assets of the borrower. With a mortgage bond, by contrast, a specific
asset such as a building is earmarked as security for repayment of the
loan. Provincial debenture bonds are issued in a wide variety of denominations ranging from $500 to over $100000.

Municipal governments across Canada also issue debentures to help
pay for local improvements such as road construction, water supply,
and sewage treatment. It is considered reasonable to spread the cost of
these projects over many years so that future local inhabitants who will
later enjoy these facilities can also help pay for them. Moreover, it
would be politically unwise to try to raise the money all at once, even if
a municipal government were so disposed. Most municipal debentures
are in *serial* form; that is, repayment of the money borrowed is stag-
gered over a number of consecutive years rather than being undertaken all in the same year. Thus, a $10 million debenture might be

repaid over ten years, $1 million each year, beginning so many years from date of issue. In this way, the repayment is less onerous.

Provincial and municipal governments issue their bonds in two ways. Very often they sell them directly to investors, employing a group, or *syndicate*, of investment dealers and banks as a "fiscal agent" to negotiate the price and other terms. Alternatively, the bonds may be sold by competitive tender, the investment dealers being invited to submit purchase offers. A considerable part of the money needed is often obtained by the sale of these government bonds in the United States and Western Europe. To avoid the risk of a decline in the foreign exchange value of the borrowing country's currency, lenders sometimes insist that the principal and interest payments be specified in terms of the lender's own currency. Thus many Canadian loans from abroad are denominated in U.S. dollars, German marks, etc.

30.4: THE BURDEN OF THE PUBLIC DEBT

Over the years Canada's public debt has steadily increased (see Table S. 32). This reflects partly the existence of inflation — the federal government needs to borrow more each year to purchase the same amount of goods and services as in the previous years. It also reflects the fact that governments constantly spend more than they collect in taxes. However, when the public debt is divided by the total population, the increase has not been as great. As a percentage of Canada's GNP, the public debt is now in the 25 to 30% range.

Many people believe that a large public debt imposes a great burden on Canada. Money borrowed by our federal, provincial, and municipal governments, they argue, must eventually be repaid. Consequently, a government's policy of living beyond its tax and other revenue means is ruthlessly placing a millstone of debt around the necks of later generations.

This view of the public debt arises because people often apply to the public finances the same principles that they apply to their own personal finances. If a person has borrowed money from someone else, that money must eventually be repaid. When it is, the borrower is financially worse off.

However, if a brother owes money to a sister, for instance, repayment of the loan does not make the family any poorer. All that occurs is a redistribution of wealth within the family. Similarly, when our governments pay interest on the public debt or repay part of the principal, the country is no worse off. However, this is the case only so long as the money is paid to Canadian residents who are, as it were, "members of the family."

Table S.32
The Public Debt, 1962-1982

As of March 31	Net Federal Government Debt		Net Public Debt Charges	
	$ millions	% of GNP	$ millions	% of GNP
1962	14 767	37.2	532	1.3
1963	15 522	36.2	606	1.4
1963	16 657	36.2	627	1.4
1965	16 986	33.8	629	1.3
1966	16 745	30.2	673	1.2
1967	17 013	27.5	671	1.1
1968	17 713	26.7	689	1.0
1969	18 117	25.0	785	1.1
1970	17 621	22.1	857	1.1
1971	18 030	21.0	920	1.1
1972	18 811	19.9	1 004	1.1
1973	19 810	18.8	1 036	1.0
1974	21 194	17.2	1 077	0.9
1975	22 927	15.5	1 408	1.0
1976	28 390	17.2	1 875	1.1
1977	34 600	18.1	2 309	1.2
1978	44 889	21.5	2 958	1.4
1979	57 115	24.8	3 902	1.7
1980	68 595	26.2	5 180	2.0
1981	81 263	27.8	6 557	2.2
1982	94 869	28.6	10 073	3.0

Source: Public Accounts of Canada

The very real burdens that exist as the result of a large public debt held within the same country are: first, the depressing effect on business investment of high interest rates caused by governments seeking to refinance or increase their debt; second, the depressing effect on economic growth of high levels of taxation that are required to help meet the government's interest payments; and, third, less flexibility in government fiscal policy because of the gradual reduction in the amount of discretionary spending.

If payments of principal and interest are made to persons in other countries, then the public debt imposes an even greater real burden on Canadians. This is because the money paid to foreign lenders can be used by them, or their fellow citizens, to buy Canadian goods and services that could otherwise be consumed within Canada or sold abroad to pay for imports.

Should a government borrow at all? The answer is usually yes — so long as the expected benefit versus the interest cost is worthwhile; the interest payments are within the person's means; and the money borrowed can eventually be repaid. Logically, therefore, we can complain of the burden of the public debt only if our governments have borrowed money irresponsibly. However, if a provincial government borrows money in the United States or Europe to finance an essential electric-power project that will benefit the inhabitants of that province, then it would seem reasonable that those persons should be prepared to help repay this money through future taxation.

Over the years, the public debt has greatly increased in Canada, particularly in time of war. However, Canada's population and its ability to produce goods and services have also been growing. If all the public debt were owed to foreigners (which it is not), how much would the interest payments deprive us of in terms of goods and services? The answer is: not very much. In relation to Canada's Gross National Product, net interest payments on the federal public debt amount to only about 3 per cent. We should also remember that, as inflation continues and the value of money falls, it becomes easier to repay sums borrowed in the past. To repay a thousand dollars borrowed many years ago requires much less sacrifice in terms of purchasing power today than it would have when the debt was contracted. Nevertheless, heavy interest payments on the public debt do impose a heavy burden on the public purse. And the scale of federal budget deficits in the 1970s and early 1980s has caused some people to conclude that the federal and some provincial governments have a chronic, or structural deficit problem.

30.5: MANAGEMENT OF THE PUBLIC DEBT

One of the functions performed by the Bank of Canada, Canada's central bank, is the management of the public debt. Like any prudent debt manager, it tries to obtain the funds required by the federal government at the lowest cost. However, it also takes into account the effect of its actions on the money market and the bond market in particular and on the economy in general. In order to neutralize the effects of its debt operations on the financial markets, the Bank tries to keep such operations—new issues and refunding—as regular and predictable as possible.

With regard to the economy, the Bank should ideally try to ensure that its debt operations support rather than oppose government economic policy. Thus, when the government is trying to dampen economic expansion, the Bank should try to "lengthen" the public debt—in other words, raise new funds by selling longer-term securities, refund maturing bonds with longer-term ones, and sell long-term bonds presently held in official accounts. The net effect of this policy would be to increase the supply of long-term securities, depress their market price, and thereby raise long-term interest rates in general. The opposite policy should be followed when the government's purpose is to promote economic expansion. In practice, the Bank of Canada has not manipulated the public debt in a counter-cyclical fashion. In fact, its policy after World War II and up to 1958 was considered to have had the opposite effect. However, debt management has been used quite effectively at times to help Canada's balance of international payments and to protect the foreign exchange rate of the Canadian dollar. Thus, when Canada's foreign exchange reserves have been low, or the dollar has been slipping in external value, debt management has been used to push up interest rates in Canada, thereby attracting an inflow of short-term capital funds and increasing the demand for Canadian dollars. It should be noted, however, that the use of debt management to reinforce government economic policy can mean that other goals, such as minimizing the cost of borrowing or exerting a neutral effect on the money market, may have to be thrown overboard. In the early 1980s, in fact, the Bank's actions to keep up interest rates to support the foreign exchange value of the Canadian dollar, helped deepen the economic recession in Canada.

Summary

1. Governments in Canada finance any excess of expenditure over tax and other revenue by means of borrowing.
2. The need for borrowing arises either because of ambitious government spending plans or from the desire of government to stimulate economic activity by spending more than tax and other receipts.
3. The federal government borrows money by selling marketable and non-marketable securities to financial institutions and the general public. Marketable securities consist of bonds of varying maturities. Non-marketable securities comprise treasury bills, Canada Savings Bonds, Unemployment Insurance Commission bonds, and Canada Pension Fund bonds.
4. Over the years, Canada's public debt has greatly increased, particularly in the 1970s and early 1980s. As a percentage of Canada's GNP, the public debt is now in the 25 to 30% range.
5. The very real burdens that exist as a result of a large public debt are (a) the effects on interest rates of government borrowing; (b) the depressing effect on economic growth of high tax levels caused partly by public debt servicing requirements; and (c) the reduction in flexibility of government fiscal policy.
6. The Bank of Canada manages the public debt. It tries to obtain funds as cheaply as possible, and to keep its debt operations — new issues and refunding — reasonably regular and predictable so as to have a neutral effect on the economy.

Key Terms

Government bond 602	CSB 606
Refunding 602	Debenture bond 606
Marketable securities 604	Mortgage bond 606
Non-marketable	Syndicate 607
securities 604	Fiscal agent 607
Floating debt 604	Public debt 607
Funded debt 604	Debt per capita 607
Treasury bills 605	Burden of debt 607
Bonds 605	Debt management 610

Review Questions

1. How does the federal government in Canada finance any excess of expenditure over tax and other revenue? What else could it do, and with what probable results?
2. At what times does a government usually need to increase its borrowing?
3. What is refunding? What is its purpose?
4. Distinguish between floating debt and funded debt.
5. Why do provincial governments need to borrow?
6. How does the federal government borrow money?
7. What are Treasury bills? How are they issued? Why are they attractive to investors?
8. What is a government bond? Distinguish between marketable and non-marketable bonds.
9. What is a debenture bond?
10. How do provincial and municipal governments issue their bonds?
11. How big is Canada's public debt?
12. What is meant by "management of the public debt"? Who performs this job and with what objectives?
13. What is the relationship between management of the public debt on the one hand and Canada's balance of international payments and the foreign exchange rate of the Canadian dollar on the other?

31. CANADIAN FISCAL POLICY

CHAPTER OBJECTIVES

A. To explain the nature and purpose of fiscal policy
B. To explain how governments are restricted in their ability to vary revenue and expenditures
C. To emphasize the role of fiscal policy in removing inflationary or deflationary gaps
D. To explain how certain automatic tax and revenue changes help stabilize the economy without conscious government effort
E. To review the different types of fiscal policy that have been practised in Canada
F. To discuss the limitations of fiscal policy

CHAPTER OUTLINE

31.1: FISCAL POLICY DEFINED

Fiscal policy is the use by a government of its powers of taxation, expenditure, and borrowing to alter the size of the circular flow of income in the economy so as to bring about greater consumer demand, more employment, inflationary restraint, or other economic goals. If spending by households and business firms is too small, government can increase aggregate demand by increasing its own spending or by encouraging private spending—for example, by tax cuts. In trying to stimulate economic activity, it can finance its additional expenditure by borrowing rather than by higher taxation. In other words, it can run a budget deficit, even though it increases the national debt. Conversely, when private spending is too great, so that the economy is threatened with excessive inflation, government can reduce aggregate demand. It can do this by restricting its own spending and by discouraging private spending—for example, by tax increases.

31.2: DISCRETIONARY FISCAL POLICY

Governments in Canada have certain, though limited, powers of discretion in deciding what their expenditures and revenues in any year will be. As a result, they can take steps to counteract an economic recession or to restrain an economic boom so as to move towards the ideal economic goal of non-inflationary full employment.

Changes in Spending

If a government wishes to stimulate the economy, it can increase spending in all areas of its normal budgetary program—health and welfare, economic development, education, roads, and so on. Every government department would welcome more money, and every recipient of the old-age or other pension, family allowance, unemployment benefits, or welfare assistance certainly would welcome more financial help. The government can also authorize special public works programs. These are projects, such as the extension of an expressway or the building of an airport that would not normally be undertaken, at least for some years to come. Unless they are well planned, however, their benefits can be very small compared with their costs. That is why a prudent government will have a number of public works projects up its sleeve, so to speak, to be carried out when more public spending is called for.

Governments do not, however, have a completely free hand in deciding what their expenditures and revenues will be. Many expenditures, such as municipal spending on police forces for example, are largely determined by community needs. And many expenditures, for example, pensions, could not be reduced without great public outcry. In fact, it is much easier to increase government spending than to reduce it. Furthermore, there is a time-lag of six months or more before increased or reduced government spending really exerts any great effect on the economy.

Changes in Taxation

To restrain or stimulate economic activity, the government can also change *tax rates*. One method of doing this is by raising or lowering personal and corporate income, sales, and excise taxes. A second method of changing tax rates is by altering *tax exemptions* in order to make more or less income, taxable. A third method is to provide special *tax incentives* for investment, such as larger capital cost allowances on new buildings and equipment. One problem in making major tax changes relates to the past practice of introducing such changes only in the annual budget usually announced between mid-March and mid-April, in time for the fiscal year beginning April 1. However, the greater use of supplementary or "baby" budgets at other times of the year appears to be making this type of federal fiscal policy more flexible in Canada. So far, Parliament has, for obvious reasons, been unwilling to give the government "stand-by authority" to make tax changes without prior parliamentary debate and consent.

31.3: REMOVING INFLATIONARY OR DEFLATIONARY GAPS

The modern view of discretionary fiscal policy is that the government should endeavour to remove any inflationary or deflationary gaps. An *inflationary gap*, as discussed in Chapter 24 (Employment Theory), is the extent to which aggregate demand exceeds full-employment output at current prices. In Figure 31:1(a), the inflationary gap is eliminated by reducing aggregate demand from AD_1 to AD_2. This can be achieved by raising taxes, reducing government spending, or both. A *deflationary gap* is the shortfall between actual total expenditure and that required to achieve non-inflationary full employment. To remove it, government needs to increase aggregate demand. In Figure 31:1(b), government deficit financing (that is, spending more than is received) raises aggregate demand and so ensures a full-employment level of employment and output. This elimination of the deflationary gap can be achieved by cutting taxes, increasing government spending, or by both combined.

31.4: THE BALANCED-BUDGET MULTIPLIER

We would think, at first glance, that an increase in taxes of, say, $100 million and an equal increase in government expenditure would have a neutral effect on a country's circular flow of income—for one would seem to cancel out the other. However, this would be true only if tax-

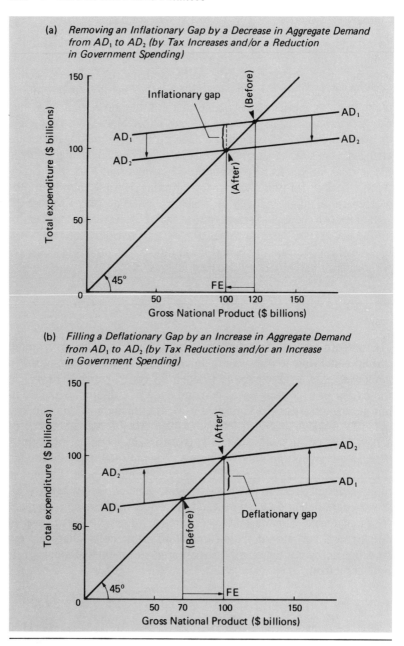

Figure 31:1 Using Fiscal Policy to Offset Inflationary and Deflationary Gaps

payers would otherwise have spent all the $100 million on domestic goods. In practice, part of this amount would have been saved and part spent on imported goods. Thus, an increase in taxes of $100 million might only reduce consumer demand by $75 million. Therefore, if the government increases its own expenditure on domestic goods and services by $100 million, the net effect on the economy is an increase in aggregate demand of $25 million. This situation arises because the government's marginal propensity to spend ($100 million out of an extra $100 million of extra tax revenue = 100%) is much greater than the general public's marginal propensity to spend on domestic goods (75%). We can see, therefore, that an increase in the *size* of a balanced budget can have an expansionary effect on the economy. Conversely, a decrease in the size of a balanced budget can have a contractionary effect. The actual extent to which the economy expands or contracts as a result of a change in the size of a balanced budget is known as the *balanced-budget multiplier*.

31.5: BUILT-IN STABILIZERS

Certain *built-in* or *automatic stabilizers* in our economy automatically tend to restrict any variations in economic activity. These come into play without any change in discretionary fiscal policy. When the economy is in recession, they tend to slow the decline in income and employment. Unfortunately, when the economy is recovering from a recession, they also slow the rate of recovery. In time of boom, their dampening effect is usually welcomed.

Automatic Changes in Tax Revenue

The amount of personal and corporate income taxes, capital gains taxes, and sales and excise taxes collected by governments in Canada varies with the level of national income. During an economic recession, incomes are lower. But government takes less from the taxpayer because of the progressive nature of the income tax. Conversely, in time of boom, government takes more as incomes rise. If government were to take a fixed amount (as it does in the case of the municipal property tax) whatever the level of income, there would, in an economic recession, be no tax check on the fall in personal disposable income. In a boom, when incomes rise, the government would not be helping to reduce demand and the rise in incomes.

The most important of these built-in stabilizers, then, is the personal income tax. As national income increases, the public has a larger total income to be taxed. But more important, as personal incomes rise, the progressive rates of personal income tax take more and more from each additional dollar of taxable income. Conversely, in time of economic recession, when personal incomes fall, the government take less and less from each dollar earned.

Corporation income tax revenues also vary considerably as the level of economic activity fluctuates. In time of economic recession, profits and tax receipts are low. In time of economic boom, the opposite is true.

Sales taxes and excise taxes are not progressive in nature. Nevertheless, their total amount increases in time of economic expansion because of increased expenditure and decreases in time of economic contraction. Consequently, they also help, though less significantly, in dampening fluctations in economic activity.

Automatic Changes in Social-Security Payments

The amount of welfare assistance, unemployment benefits, and other government social-security payments changes with the level of employment. In time of economic recession, when the number of unemployed persons begins to grow, the fall in earned income is partly offset by larger government expenditure on welfare assistance or unemployment benefits. In time of economic recovery, the number of unemployed drops, the total amount of welfare and unemployment payments is reduced, and contributions to the Unemployment Insurance Fund increase.

Price-Support Programs

Another built-in stabilizer is government price-support programs. When national income and the level of prices fall, the purchase by government of agricultural products at prices higher than those that would be set by the free play of market forces helps keep up farm income. Conversely, when national income and the general level of prices rise, the release of stored surpluses tends to keep down farm income.

Family and Corporate Savings

These savings constitute another stabilizer because most families save less when their income falls and more when it rises. This tends to dampen cyclical fluctuations in national income. Moreover, business corporations, despite fluctuations in their income, usually try to keep the level of dividends steady from bad times to good. Thus, they tend to retain a larger percentage of their profit in good times (not all of which may be invested) and a smaller percentage in bad times.

Imports

In times of economic prosperity, Canadian consumers tend to spend a higher percentage than usual of their disposable income on imported goods. This means that imports act as an automatic stabilizer, drawing off more Canadian income as national income rises. Conversely, in times of economic recession, Canadians spend more on Canadian-made goods and less on imported goods.

Fiscal Drag

This term is used, particularly in periods of slow economic recovery, to describe the slowing effect that automatic or built-in stabilizers can have on government-induced economic expansion. Together with discretionary fiscal policies and other appropriate economic measures such as changes in monetary policy, the built-in stabilizers can greatly reduce the degree of cyclical fluctuations in national output and income.

31.6: CANADIAN FISCAL POLICY IN PRACTICE

The Annually Balanced Budget

Until the 1930s, the primary aim of fiscal policy in Canada was to ensure that government expenditure each year did not exceed revenue—in other words, to *balance the annual budget*. Every citizen was indoctrinated in church, school, and home, with the view that to spend more than one's income was to invite economic and social disaster. It was only logical, therefore, that the country's politicians would apply, to the public finances, the same principles that governed their own personal affairs.

In the 1930s, J.M. Keynes and other economists severely criticized the logic behind the annually balanced budget. Such a policy, they argued, could only accentuate cyclical variations in the country's levels of income and employment. In time of economic recession, for example, the fall in business activity would mean a reduction in government tax revenue. To maintain a balanced budget, the government would therefore have to reduce its expenditure. This would cause an undesirable further reduction in national income and employment—the actual amount depending on the size of the multiplier. In time of economic boom, increasing business activity would provide the government with greater tax revenues. For the government to reduce taxes or to increase its own spending at this time would add to the general level of demand. If factors of production were already fully employed, the government's balanced budget would then only serve to drive up prices even more.

The Cyclically-Balanced Budget

According to early Keynesian economists, governments should use their fiscal policy to achieve a high, stable level of national income with neither unemployment nor inflation. If an economic recession were to begin, the government should start to spend more than it received. By such a policy of *deficit financing*, the government would increase the country's aggregate demand for goods and services and so brake or even counteract the falling levels of income and employment. If an economic boom were to occur, the government should take in more (by raising taxes or reducing expenditures) than it paid out. This policy of *surplus financing* would reduce the level of aggregate demand in the economy and so dampen any inflationary pressure. Instead of balancing revenue and expenditure over the course of a year, the government should aim, according to this view, at balancing the budget over the course of a business cycle. This would mean balancing the budget over a number of years rather than just one.

In 1945, in its White Paper on Employment and Income, the Canadian government declared its intention of pursuing a cyclically balanced budget rather than an annually balanced one.

> ... The Government will be prepared, in periods when unemployment threatens, to incur the deficits and increase in the national debt resulting from its employment and income policy, whether that policy in the circumstances is best applied through increased expenditures or reduced taxation. In periods of buoyant employment and income, budget plans will call for surpluses. The Government's policy will be to keep the national debt within manageable proportions, and maintain a proper balance in its budget over a period longer than a single year.[1]

The federal government, expecting an economic depression rather than a boom, concentrated on setting up machinery to boost employment. The most important part of this machinery was a program of public investments that could be quickly undertaken once unemployment started to become critical. It was at first hoped that this "public works shelf," as it came to be known, would include provincial and municipal, as well as federal, construction projects. However, at the 1945 Dominion-Provincial Conference, the federal government was unable to reach agreement with the provinces and municipalities and consequently decided to set up its own public works shelf, with a target of $150 million worth of projects. Unfortunately, the government's good intentions fell short of the mark, so that by mid-1947 there was still only $54 million worth of projects on the shelf, despite considerable inflation since the end of the war. This deficiency was attributed to shortages of technical and supervisory staff, to lack of co-operation among goverment departments, and to the tendency to start a project as soon as it had been placed on the shelf.

In December 1949, the public works shelf was officially abandoned. Since that time there has been very little advanced planning by the federal government of public works projects specifically for economic stabilization purposes. The decline of federal interest in this area was due in large part to the fact that the main economic problem of the immediate post-war era turned out to be inflation rather than unemployment.

Although the public works shelf was not a great success, the federal government did contribute to the stability of the Canadian economy in the two decades after World War II by its budgetary surpluses and deficits. Thus, the large surpluses in 1947 and 1948 helped reduce the strong inflationary pressures of those years. Generally speaking, however, fiscal policy was not as exact or as useful in offsetting cyclical changes in economic activity, particularly economic boom, as had been hoped. Politically, for example, it was not easy to persuade the public to accept tax increases when the budget was already in surplus, even though such a policy was desirable to curtail consumer demand. Moreover, in Canada the federal government could have any budgetary surpluses offset by the deficits of the provincial and municipal governments—a critical weakness in Canada's economic system and fiscal maneuverability.

After World War II, aggregate demand in Canada continued to be quite buoyant. As a result, until 1953 the country experienced a steady period of economic growth, interrupted only by a relatively minor recession in 1949. The maximum unemployment rate was just over 3 per cent. However, after 1953 unemployment rates began to creep upwards so that, by the early 1980s, 10 per cent or more seemed to have become the norm. Equally bad, the economy was usually operating below its potential. Governments in Canada during this period did, however, use fiscal policy in an effort to combat this trend. During the 1960s, governments at all levels in Canada, but particularly the federal government, consistently ran budget deficits in order to promote economic expansion. However, the fight against inflation and the already large deficits pevented greater government action. A study of Canadian fiscal policy between 1945 and 1963 has concluded that government action, although increasing the national debt, definitely helped stabilize the Canadian economy.[2] Despite the acknowledged time lags, and the stop-and-go character of much Canadian fiscal policy in subsequent years, fiscal policy has undoubtedly been a useful tool in restraining inflation on the one hand and promoting economic growth, employment, and income on the other.

The Full-Employment Budget

The latest thinking on fiscal policy is that governments should go beyond the cyclically balanced budget. It is now argued that they should try to achieve a non-inflationary, full-employment level of output. This policy, sometimes called *functional finance*, has had a mixed reception so far in government circles.

To judge the suitability of government fiscal policy, economists have developed the concepts of the *full-employment surplus* and *full-employment deficit*. The full-employment surplus is the excess of government revenue over expenditure that would be necessary to obtain the non-inflationary, full-employment level of GNP. The full-employment deficit is just the opposite—the excess of government expenditure over revenue that would be necessary to achieve this same level. With this concept as a measure, it is possible to estimate how a government's actual budgetary surplus or deficit compares with the country's actual needs.

31.7: LIMITATIONS OF FISCAL POLICY

In practice, several factors limit the usefulness of fiscal policy. First of all, there is the problem of *time lags*. Some fiscal measures, such as tax changes, and even new government spending programs are decided and implemented relatively quickly. Certainly, compared with the United States, Canada's federal political structure (with the government usually able to rely on a majority of votes in Parliament) means that the so-called *decision lag* is not too prolonged. However, fiscal policy is often very slow in making its effects felt. Thus, even after the decision has been taken to implement a public works program, for instance, it takes considerable time to get the projects under way: plans must be prepared, land purchased, tenders invited, and contracts drawn up.

A second important limitation of fiscal policy is that only a relatively small percentage of total government expenditure can be easily varied. Many items such as health and welfare, interest on the public debt, and salaries and pensions for government employees are relatively fixed.

The Full Employment Budget

To achieve full-employment, the government may need to have:

a. a budget surplus (T > G);
b. a balanced budget (T = G); or
c. a budget deficit (T < G).

(T = government revenue, or taxation; and G = government expenditure). Thus, in the diagram below, if Y1 is the full-employment level of income, the government should incur a budget surplus; if it is Y2, the government should balance its budget; and if it is Y3, the government should incur a budget deficit.

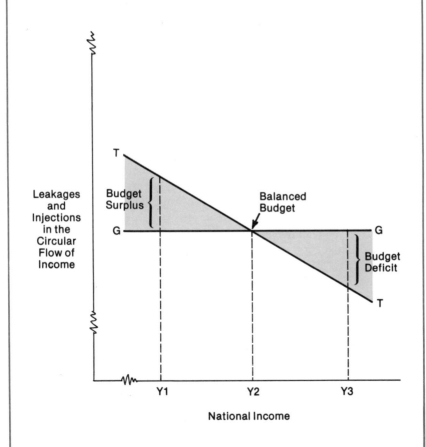

A third important limitation is that government expenditure in Canada is spread among three different levels of government. This means that spending by provincial and municipal governments could conceivably be expanded at a time when spending by the federal government is being restricted. Particularly important is that most public works such as roads, schools, hospitals, and sewage-treatment plants are the responsibility of the provincial or municipal governments. The federal government can encourage the provincial and municipal governments to spend more by means of grants and shared-cost programs. However, if a provincial government disagrees with federal policy (as occasionally happens), the federal policy can be partly thwarted. For example, a provincial government has the power, if it wishes to use it, to increase income taxes at the same time that the federal government is reducing them.

31.8: CANADA'S BUDGET DEFICITS

In Canada, both the federal and provincial governments have for some years incurred large annual budget deficits. This has not been the result of a deliberate government effort to expand consumer demand in time of economic recession. Rather, Canada and many other Western countries have become the victims of what has been called the *fiscal trap*.

On the one hand, because of slow economic growth and even at times economic standstill, government revenues have fallen. On the other hand, because the amount paid out in unemployment benefits and other financial assistance has increased, government expenditures have risen steeply. With government revenue down, and expenditure up, the fiscal deficit has increased—even though governments would have preferred it to decrease. Far from having the ability to achieve a balanced-budget, or even a cyclically-balanced budget, most of our governments, for political reasons, now drift helplessly along waiting for better economic times to automatically increase revenue and decrease expenditure. From 1945 to 1975, the federal deficit averaged zero. But since then the deficit has mushroomed so that financial analysts now talk of a "structural deficit" of $12 to $15 billion per annum.

Unfortunately, large federal and provincial government budget deficits, although they mean more money pumped into the economy, have several serious drawbacks. First, the government borrowing that is required to finance the deficit removes money from the capital market and makes it harder for private business firms to borrow money, at reasonable terms, for investment. Second, the deficits tend to counteract any monetary measures, such as restricting the growth of the money supply, designed to slow inflation. Third, they increase the size of the country's national debt which in turn, because of the larger interest payments, tends to make the budget deficit even greater. Today, in fact, Canada's federal government deficit is larger, as a percentage of GNP, than that of any other major industrial country.

Summary

1. Fiscal policy is the use by a government of its powers of taxation, expenditure, and borrowing to help achieve its various economic goals.
2. Discretionary fiscal policy includes changes in spending and in taxation.
3. The modern view of discretionary fiscal policy is that the government should aim to remove any inflationary or deflationary gaps.
4. Because the public does not spend all its income, an increase in the size of a balanced budget cannot be said to have a neutral effect on the circular flow of income in the economy.
5. There are certain built-in stabilizers in our economy that automatically tend to restrict any variations in economic activity. They include automatic changes in tax revenue, automatic changes in welfare payments, price-support programs, family and corporate savings, and imports.
6. Canadian fiscal policy has moved from the annually balanced budget to the cyclically balanced budget to the full-employment budget.
7. Fiscal policy has several limitations: time-lags; the relatively small amount of discretionary spending available to the government; and the division of spending among three levels of government.
8. Because of economic recession, Canada has been caught in a *fiscal trap*, with budget deficits increasingly out of control.

Key Terms

Review Questions

1. What is discretionary fiscal policy? What are its principal tools?
2. What are inflationary and deflationary gaps? Why should fiscal policy be directed towards their removal?
3. What is the balanced-budget multiplier?
4. What are built-in stabilizers? What are the most important types? What effect do they have?
5. What is an annually balanced budget? Why was it considered desirable for so many years?
6. What is a cyclically balanced budget? What are its advantages, if any, over an annually balanced budget?
7. Explain deficit financing and surplus financing.
8. What is meant by a "public works shelf"?
9. What is a full-employment budget?
10. Explain the meaning of "full-employment surplus" and "full-employment deficit."
11. What are the limitations of fiscal policy?
12. What is the "fiscal trap"? How inevitable is it? What are its implications?

References

1   *Employment and Income*, King's Printer, Ottawa 1945, p. 21. Reproduced by permission of The Minister of Supply and Services Canada.
2   R.M. Will, *Canadian Fiscal Policy, 1945-1963*, Study No. 17, Royal Commission on Taxation, Queen's Printer, Ottawa, 1966, Chapter 5.

Part H:
MONEY, BANKING, AND INVESTMENT

What is money? How large is Canada's money supply? What causes inflation? How do banks create money? What is the role of the Bank of Canada in the management of Canada's monetary affairs? What are stocks and bonds? And how are they issued and traded? These are some of the questions we seek to answer in this part of the book.

32. MONEY, PRICES, AND INFLATION

CHAPTER OBJECTIVES

A. To indicate the various kinds of money in Canada, the various functions that such money performs, and the characteristics that any item used as money must possess
B. To outline the growth that has taken place in Canada's money supply and level of prices over the years
C. To define "inflation" and to consider its effects
D. To outline the various theories that have been advanced to explain the existence of inflation
E. To point out the connection between the money supply and the level of national income and output

CHAPTER OUTLINE

32.1: KINDS OF MONEY

Three main kinds of money are used in Canada today: coins, bank notes, and chequable bank deposits.

Coins represent only a very small part of Canada's total money supply. They are issued in the following denominations: five cents, ten cents, twenty-five cents, and one dollar. Sometimes called *token* money (because the value of their metal is worth much less than their face value), coins are legal tender only up to certain amounts—bronze coins up to 25 cents, nickel coins up to $5, and silver coins up to $10. If a person wishes to give larger quantities (e.g., paying tuition fees with sacks of pennies), the intended receiver must first give his or her consent.

Bank notes (issued by the Bank of Canada in denominations of 1, 2, 5, 10, 20, 50, 100 and 1000 dollars) comprise about 10 per cent of Canada's money supply. At one time, the central banks of many countries were willing to give the bearer of a bank note, gold or silver in exchange. However, the Bank of Canada's promise to pay the bearer, on demand, the face value of a note has never meant anything more than that other paper money would be given in exchange. With the new bank notes, the pretence of gold or silver backing has been dropped; they state only that "This note is legal tender." Bank of Canada notes were first issued in 1935. Until that time there were two kinds of bank notes in circulation in Canada: Dominion notes issued by the federal Department of Finance and bank notes issued by the various privately-owned chartered banks.

Although coins and bank notes are the popular concept of money, a far more important type is chequable bank deposits. This is because most people pay their bills by cheque or by electronic transfer rather than by notes or coin. Chequable bank deposits comprise, in fact, the vast bulk of Canada's money supply. Cheques are a convenient way of making payment because they can be easily carried around or sent by mail; they can be cancelled if lost or stolen; and they can be used, in connection with a monthly bank statement, as a means of recording and evidencing payments.

Coins, notes, and chequable bank deposits are not the only possible kinds of money. All kinds of objects have in fact been used as money at different times and in different places. Precious and non-precious metals, shells, animal skins, and cattle are some examples. All the goods offered for trade by the Hudson's Bay Company were at one time given a "price" in beaver skins.

32.2: FUNCTIONS OF MONEY

Money, in its various forms, performs several useful functions in our society. It serves as a medium of exchange, a measure of value, a unit of account, and as a store of wealth.

Medium of Exchange

Without money, workers would have to find employers willing to accept their services or products in exchange for the things they needed. For example, a dairy worker would either have to agree to being paid with butter, milk, or cheese, or the employer would have to keep a stock of assorted items—food, clothing, and so on—with which to pay wages. Furthermore, since the dairy worker has to purchase a variety of goods and services, people willing to accept dairy products in exchange would have to be found. In other words, there would have to be what is called in economics a "double coincidence of wants." In practice, a dairy worker might have to go through a whole series of transactions to obtain the needed goods. Thus, to obtain a new television set, he or she might first have to swap cheese for furniture, swap the furniture for a sailboat, swap the sailboat for a motorcycle, then swap the motorcycle for a television set. Obviously, our whole economic system would break down. People would spend most of their time trying to barter or swap what they had for what they really wanted. From an employer's point of view, it is also much more convenient to pay money wages rather than goods to workers in order to avoid being a storekeeper as well as the owner of, say, a manufacturing business.

Measure of Value

In our money society, each good or service has a value, or price, expressed in dollars and cents—the common denominator. This price is usually determined by the interaction of demand and supply. Anyone wishing to obtain the good or service is required to give that much money in exchange. Since everyone uses money, this measure of value is meaningful to all. Moreover, because each item has a money price, comparisons between one item and another are easily made. With money as a measure of value, transactions are much simpler—there is only one basic price to be determined, in dollars and cents, whoever may be the buyer. Also, with a decimal system of currency, whereby each amount can be easily divided or multiplied by ten, the value of each transaction can be easily calculated, either mentally or electronically. This contrasts with the clumsiness of the old sterling system once used in Canada and until recently in Britain in which a pound was divided into twenty shillings and a shilling into twelve pence.

Unit of Account

Without money as a common denominator, it would be impossible to add in any meaningful way the values of, for example, a car, a house, and a piece of furniture. But with values expressed in dollars and cents, we can easily add, subtract, divide, and multiply the prices of various goods and services. In addition, when we purchase goods on credit or borrow money, the balance owing and any interest charges are computed in monetary terms. Some economists consider this a separate function of money—namely, as a *standard of deferred payment.*

Store of Wealth

As a store of wealth, money has the great advantage of being highly liquid; that is, it can be converted into other assets almost immediately. It does, however, have some drawbacks. Notes and coins can be easily stolen or lost. Cheques can be forged and bank deposits fraudulently withdrawn. The biggest disadvantage that money has, as a store of wealth, is its vulnerability to inflation. As the prices of various goods and services rise, each dollar buys less and less. This decline in the real value of money means that a thousand dollars in a year's time will buy fewer goods and services than a thousand dollars today. If we use money rather than real estate or other goods to store our wealth, the real value of our accumulated savings will gradually decline.

32.3: CHARACTERISTICS OF MONEY

What causes one object to be used as money rather than another? The answer is that an item must have certain characteristics that make it suitable for use as money. To be a satisfactory medium of exchange, money needs to be portable, durable, divisible, and, above all, acceptable. Money must be sufficiently light and compact that it can easily be carried around. Coins, notes, and cheques have this characteristic. Money must not easily wear out. That is why metal coins have been popular throughout the centuries. Our paper money certainly is not as durable as coin. However, with normal treatment, it has a reasonably long life. We must also be able to use money to purchase items of greatly different values. For example, we may need thousands of dollars to purchase a house or only a dollar (looking ahead) to purchase a cup of coffee. Although an item may have many of the required characteristics, it can never be successfully used as money if people lack confidence in it. In this respect, Canadian notes and coin are readily acceptable by the general public because they are issued by the Bank of Canada, Canada's government-owned central bank. Even more important, they can legally be used to settle debts of any amount. Chequable bank deposits are also money. But not all personal cheques are as readily acceptable as notes and coins. Sometimes, the intended recipient may insist that a cheque first be "certified"—a pledge by the bank upon which it is drawn that it will honour it when presented for payment.

As a measure of value, money need not be portable or durable. It must, however, be divisible. We must be able to measure the value of each good or service in terms of this scale. One item may be worth ten thousand dollars, another only ten cents. Money must also be acceptable as a measure of value in the sense that everyone recognizes this common measure and is familiar with it.

As a unit of account, money must be easy to add, subtract, divide, and multiply. We are fortunate in Canada to have a decimal system of currency, in which a dollar divides into a hundred cents. Nothing can be simpler as a unit of account. By contrast, the old British system, with 240 pence in a pound, was a bookkeeper's nightmare.

As a store of wealth, money should retain its value in terms of other assets. However, with constantly rising prices, a thousand dollars will not buy as many goods and services today as it would have a year ago or whenever the money was saved. In fact, with, say, a 10 per cent rate of inflation, it would buy only nine-tenths. As a store of wealth, our present money is consequently not very satisfactory. That is why many people (who can afford it) keep antiques, real estate, paintings, and even racehorses instead.

32.4: THE MONEY SUPPLY

We have said that money consists of coins, notes, and chequable bank deposits. However, to calculate Canada's money supply, we need to be more precise. The Bank of Canada now defines the money supply in the following ways:

M1 is the sum of Canadian currency (notes and coin) in circulation plus Canadian-dollar demand deposits at chartered banks (excluding federal-government deposits). This is the money supply most narrowly defined.

M1B consists of currency and all chequable deposits—that is, M1 plus Canadian-dollar chequable notice deposits at the chartered banks. This is the closest equivalent to the American definition of M-1.

M2 comprises currency and all chequable notice and personal term deposits—that is, M1B plus other notice and personal term deposits at the chartered banks. This is similar to the American definition of M-2.

M3 consists of M2 plus Canadian-dollar non-personal, fixed-term deposits at chartered banks plus foreign currency deposits of residents at chartered banks in Canada. This definition differs greatly from the American M-3 definition, which excludes highly interest-sensitive commercial deposits.

Some economists argue that chequable and other deposits held in financial institutions, such as credit unions and trust companies, should also be included in the definition and calculation of Canada's money supply.

As well as currency and deposits, the public holds various types of government bonds (such as Treasury bills and Canada Savings Bonds). These bonds are called *near-money*, for they can be quickly exchanged for cash. In determining monetary policy or examining the state of the economy, economists and others keep these other relatively liquid assets, or "near-money," in mind.

How has Canada's money supply changed over the years? If we look at Table S.33, we can see that currency and chartered-bank deposits held by the public have increased in every year except 1959. Sometimes the rate of increase has been extremely high—for example, over 18 per cent in 1973. This constant increase in the money supply has undoubtedly been a prime culprit in Canada's inflation. The chief reason for the increase in the money supply has been the rapid rise in government expenditures, particularly on social-security programs. Although socially desirable, such programs (for example, family allowances) have had the economic effect of reducing the savings of the middle- and upper-income classes and increasing the spending of the lower-income ones. Changes in income taxation in Canada in recent years have had a similar effect, by leaving more money in the hands of the lower-income groups. Also, it has been suggested that democratic societies such as Canada are inflation-prone in the sense that political parties, in order to be elected or re-elected, are constantly advocating new, costly programs. Furthermore, it can be argued that the governments of many countries, including Canada, now suffer from "Keynesian overreaction"—to avoid economic recession they are constantly tending to overspend, justifying their deficit spending with Keynesian economic theory.

Table S.33
Canada's Money Supply, 1970-1982

Years (average of Wednesdays)	Currency and demand deposits (M1)	Currency and all chequable deposits (M1B)	Currency and all chequable, notice and term deposits (M2)	Currency plus total privately held chartered bank deposits (M3)
		(Millions of dollars)		
1970	9 023	14 716	25 580	32 175
1971	10 170	16 074	28 755	35 495
1972	11 622	18 098	31 785	40 462
1973	13 312	20 256	36 291	46 510
1974	14 551	21 405	43 554	58 014
1975	16 557	23 465	50 118	66 610
1976	17 883	24 922	56 414	78 860
1977	19 377	26 700	64 343	91 344
1978	21 318	29 039	71 194	103 821
1979	22 813	30 471	82 395	123 898
1980	24 228	31 781	97 263	141 586
1981	25 255	32 800	111 377	158 931
1982	25 760	33 676	127 718	182 550
		(Per cent change)		
1970	2.4	-4.1	6.8	—
1971	12.7	9.2	12.4	10.3
1972	14.3	12.6	10.5	14.0
1973	14.5	11.9	14.2	14.9
1974	9.3	5.7	20.0	24.7
1975	13.8	9.6	15.1	14.8
1976	8.0	6.2	12.6	18.4
1977	8.4	7.2	14.1	15.8
1978	10.0	8.8	10.7	13.7
1979	7.0	4.9	15.7	19.3
1980	6.2	4.3	18.0	14.3
1981	4.2	3.2	14.5	12.3
1982	2.0	2.7	14.7	14.8

Source: Bank of Canada, *Review,* monthly

32.5: PRICES

An important consideration for every Canadian is the current level of prices. For if prices go up and a person's income remains fixed, that person's standard of living will decline. More usually, incomes also rise—but often not as fast as prices. That is why a government wage-restraint policy that sets a target rate of increase in wages well below the rate of inflation is received with so much dismay.

The Consumer Price Index

Every month, Statistics Canada issues the latest figures for the *Consumer Price Index*. This index (see Table S.34) represents the combined retail prices of some three hundred different consumer goods and services from the general categories of food, housing, clothing, transportation, health and personal care, recreation and reading, tobacco and alcohol. The choice of items (the "shopping basket") and the weighting given to each are based on expenditures in the chosen base-year of a representative cross-section of middle-sized urban families with medium incomes.

The overall, or composite, consumer index is based on individual index numbers for each category of good or service. The individual index numbers (for example, for food) are obtained by dividing the present prices by the prices in the starting, or base, year and multiplying by one hundred. In other words, the present prices are calculated as a percentage of the base-year prices. The base year is consequently expressed as equal to 100. Because prices have risen since the base year, the price index is greater than 100 in every category. The Consumer Price Index, we should remember, applies to the average of the total urban population. Specific segments of the population, such as country dwellers, senior citizens, students, and others, can be affected differently by an overall increase in prices.

The Consumer Price Index, or CPI, is the official measurement of changes in Canada's price level. Therefore many groups rely on it—for example, labour unions whose contracts with employers often contain "cost-of-living clauses" that provide for additional wage increases based on changes in the general price level.

Statistics Canada also calculates indexes of manufacturers' prices, primary producers' prices, wholesale prices, farm prices, and stock prices.

Table S.34
Consumer Price Indexes: Standard Classifications, 1961-1982 (1971 = 100)

Year	All Items	Food	Housing	Clothing	Transport- ation	Health and Personal Care	Recre- ation and Reading	Tobacco and Alcohol	Annual Increase %
1961	74.9	76.1	73.1	77.7	77.0	70.2	73.7	77.8	0.9
1962	75.8	77.5	73.9	78.4	76.9	71.6	74.4	78.7	1.2
1963	77.2	80.0	74.8	80.4	76.9	73.4	75.4	78.9	1.8
1964	78.6	81.3	76.0	82.4	77.7	75.9	76.6	80.4	1.8
1965	80.5	83.4	77.3	83.8	80.7	79.4	77.9	81.7	2.4
1966	83.5	88.7	79.4	87.0	82.6	81.8	80.1	83.7	3.7
1967	86.5	89.9	82.9	91.3	86.1	86.0	84.2	85.8	3.6
1968	90.0	92.8	86.7	94.1	88.3	89.5	88.3	93.6	4.0
1969	94.1	96.7	91.2	96.7	92.4	93.8	93.6	97.2	4.6
1970	97.2	98.9	95.7	98.5	96.1	98.0	96.8	98.4	3.3
1971	100.0	100.0	100.0	100.0	100.0	100.0	100.0	100.0	2.9
1972	104.8	107.6	104.7	102.6	102.6	104.8	102.8	102.7	4.8
1973	112.8	123.3	111.4	107.7	105.3	109.4	107.1	106.0	7.6
1974	125.0	143.4	121.1	118.0	115.8	119.4	116.5	111.8	10.9
1975	138.5	161.9	133.2	125.1	129.4	133.0	128.5	125.3	10.8
1976	148.9	166.2	148.0	132.0	143.3	144.3	136.2	134.3	7.5
1977	160.8	180.1	161.9	141.0	153.3	155.0	142.7	143.8	8.0
1978	175.1	208.0	174.1	146.4	162.2	166.2	148.2	155.5	8.9
1979	191.2	235.3	186.2	159.9	178.0	181.2	158.4	166.7	9.1
1980	210.6	260.6	201.4	178.7	200.7	199.3	173.5	185.2	10.2
1981	236.9	290.4	226.4	191.4	237.6	221.0	191.0	209.2	12.5
1982	262.5	311.4	254.7	202.0	271.1	244.4	207.5	241.6	10.8

Source: Statistics Canada, *The Consumer Price Index*, Cat.62-001

32.6: INFLATION DEFINED

The term *inflation* describes a situation in which the general price level in a country is increasing. Where this increase is relatively small, say, 1, 2, 3 or even 5 per cent per annum, the term *mild inflation*, or *creeping inflation*, is often used. Some economists argue that mild inflation is a normal and even healthy state of affairs. The gradual increase in prices, according to this view, tends to increase business profits and investment opportunities and so encourages full employment and economic growth. However, others argue that mild inflation, if continuous, can still bring about great hardship to fixed-income receivers. Furthermore, it can gradually encourage an "inflationary psychology" among the public, which can in turn help spark more severe inflation. *Price stability*, according to the Economic Council of Canada, is an increase in the general level of prices of less than 2 per cent per annum. Where the increase in prices in a country is very fast (for example, the 60 to 90 per cent rates seen in Mexico in recent years) the terms *hyperinflation*, *galloping inflation*, or *runaway inflation* are often used.

The term *deflation* is used to describe the much less common state of affairs in which the general level of prices of a country is falling. Such a situation, because of its effect on profits, usually causes a decline in business activity and a consequent fall in national income and employment. Sometimes, however, deflation can be an effect rather than a cause. Thus, if an economic recession occurs, the increase in unemployment and fall in income may tend to force prices down.

32.7: INFLATION IN CANADA

Over the long run, prices in Canada have climbed steadily (as shown in Table S.34). As a result, the real value of money has constantly been declining. Thus, the goods and services that could have been bought with $100 not so long ago now cost much more. Particularly alarming for Canadians is the fact that the rate of inflation has increased in recent years. Instead of mild inflation (in the order of one to five per cent a year), Canadians have been faced with inflation rates in the 6 to 12 per cent range.

32.8: GOVERNMENT ANTI-INFLATION POLICY

One approach to the problem of inflation is for the government to adopt, as part of its overall monetary and fiscal program, an *incomes policy*. This is the setting by the government of a maximum desirable annual rate of increase in profits, wages, and other forms of income in the economy. Such a policy is considered appropriate by many economists because of the cost-push nature of much recent inflation. Such a policy can take the form of "guideposts" or government suggestions as to a desirable maximum percentage wage or price increase. It can also take the form of more definite wage-and-price controls.

Wage-and-Price Controls

With such a policy, any changes in wages, salaries, rent, interest, and other forms of income, as well as changes in prices of materials, parts, finished products, and services, would have to conform with guidelines laid down by the government. Wage rates could continue to be negotiated by management and labour, but the resultant agreement would have to conform to the guidelines. One guideline in Canada in the past has been a maximum of 8 per cent per annum for any wage or price increase. An alternative could be that any wage increase be limited to the average increase in real output per person in the particular firm, industry, or country as a whole. Business firms could also continue to set the prices for their products and services so long as any increases did not exceed the official guideline. Some advocates of wage-and-price controls also suggest that corporation profits be limited to a certain percentage return on invested capital or sales, based on the long-term experience of the firm or industry.

Wage and price controls may be either *voluntary* or *mandatory*. Voluntary controls are obviously limited in their effectiveness because the only pressures to observe them are public opinion, government exhortation, newspaper and television criticism, and the public-spiritedness of labour and business. Mandatory controls occur when the wage and price guidelines are enforced by the courts and/or by a government agency such as the Anti-Inflation Board (AIB) that the federal government set up in 1975. Although mandatory controls can be much more effective than purely voluntary ones, they require a complex system of government officials to police and enforce them. They also represent a large step towards complete government control of the economy— something that is unwelcome to the vast bulk of the public in Canada and the United States. Furthermore, any control on profits might severely discourage capital investment and thus aggravate unemployment.

Wage and price controls may also be either *partial* or *complete*. With partial controls, only certain industries or sectors of the economy are subject to wage and price regulation. Such industries may be "pattern setting" ones, such as the steel or car industries, ones that operate like Bell Canada under conditions of monopoly or near-monopoly, or ones such as construction, where labour unions are extremely aggressive in seeking wage increases. Such partial controls would invite the accusation of unfairness, since they are discriminatory in application. Complete controls would be comprehensive in scope, embracing all sectors of the economy, and, because of this, more costly and difficult to enforce. In Canada, only key groups within society have been subject to compulsory price-and-income restraint.

Canada's Experience

During World War II, the federal government imposed mandatory price controls on a wide variety of products, and established a Wartime Prices and Trade Board to supervise them. Although fairly successful in restraining inflation, these controls, despite the patriotism of wartime, were extremely difficult to enforce, in part because of excess demand in the economy and rationing of scarce products amongst consumers. In 1969, the federal government as part of its program to halt inflation, established a Prices and Incomes Commission. In 1970, the government, through the Commission, launched a program of voluntary wage and price restraint, setting, as a guideline, a 6 per cent annual maximum wage and price increase. However, due in large measure to the opposition of organized labour, the program was only able to achieve a temporary slow-down in the rate of inflation.

Finally, in October 1975, the federal government instituted a short-term policy of price and income restraint with the following main characteristics:

1. Maximum emphasis on voluntary compliance with price and income guidelines.

2. Fullest possible consultation with provincial governments, business, labour and others.

3. Statutory enforcement of the guidelines in the case of key groups within society.

4. Minimum "red tape" and bureaucracy.

Despite strong opposition from organized labour, the new policy was energetically enforced with the help of an Anti-Inflation Board, and was given credit for substantially lowering the rate of inflation in Canada. With high oil prices, heavy government deficit spending, and a growing money supply continuing to fuel inflation, the federal government in 1982 imposed wage controls (6 per cent for the first year, and 5 per cent for the next year) on public sector employees and for business firms within its jurisdiction such as Crown corporations and firms requiring federal government assistance. It also restricted price increases wherever possible—for example, by Crown Corporations. Some provinces also restricted pay increases for their own public sector employees (e.g. British Columbia and Ontario). In 1981 and 1982, the Bank of Canada also imposed extremely high interest rates that deterred private borrowing. However, underlying government causes of inflation—heavy government deficit spending and an increase in the money supply—continued relatively unchecked.

In 1983, with the annual inflation rate in Canada down to 5 per cent, the possibility of any reintroduction of full wage and price controls by the federal government as part of its economic policy seems out of the question. However, the federal and provincial governments, with their large budget deficits, may well be tempted to continue with public sector pay restraint programs. Such programs would also perhaps serve as an example for the private sector—a complete reversal of the situation in the mid-1960s, when large public sector pay increases (as, for example, with the St. Lawrence Seaway workers) helped trigger the inflation of the nineteen-seventies.

32.9: EFFECTS OF INFLATION

The upward trend in the general level of prices in Canada has benefited some groups and penalized others.

Fixed-Money-Income Groups

Many persons in Canada rely wholly or partly on a fixed-money income to cover their living expenses. The various types of fixed-money income include veteran, old-age, and retirement pensions, annuity payments (bought, for example, by a widow with the proceeds of her husband's life-insurance policies) and interest on government and corporation bonds. When prices rise, persons receiving fixed-money incomes are adversely affected. They receive the same monetary income but must pay more for the same amount of food, clothing, and shelter. In other words, as prices rise, the real income of such persons falls. As one result, older workers become more reluctant to retire early despite high unemployment among younger persons.

Creditors and Debtors

Persons or firms who have lent money (or given goods in exchange for a promise of payment at a later date) to other persons are called *creditors*. The persons who have borrowed the money (or received the credit) are called *debtors*. When the general level of prices rises, creditors are worse off because the money they have loaned is worth less in real terms when it is paid back. Conversely, debtors are better off if prices rise. They repay their creditors with money that is now worth less (and consequently easier to obtain). Today, in Canada, the eroding effect of inflation is encouraging many large lenders such as insurance and trust companies to insist on a combination of mortgage loans plus a share of ownership in the ventures for which their mortgage money is being used. In the case of "conventional" house mortgage loans, the term for repayment (or renewal at a new, possibly higher, rate of interest) has been reduced to 5 years or less.

Wage Earners

When prices rise, wage-earners find that their take-home pay is buying fewer goods and services. As a result, they begin to demand an increase in wages to maintain or, even better, to increase their real standard of living. Their success in doing so will depend on their numbers, the ability of the industry to pay higher wages, the organization and militancy of the workers, and the public importance of their industry. Severe inflation can cause workers in one industry to compete vigorously with workers in other industries, as well as with management, to retain or enlarge their share of the country's real national income. Strikes, lockouts, and physical violence all slow down the country's production; finally, if the inflation becomes severe enough, a flight from money ensues.

Most people, having lost confidence in money as a store of wealth, try to exchange their wages and other income, as quickly as they receive it, for other assets such as food, clothing, and furniture. They also try to withdraw their savings from the banks and convert the money into other assets. This unwillingness to hold money causes the price level to rise even more rapidly. Under such circumstances, normal business activity ceases and the seeds of social and political disorder are sown. Germany, in the period 1918-1923, is the classic example of this desperate situation. There, workers used barrows and suitcases to carry their paper-money wages from their places of employment to the nearest stores willing to accept paper money in exchange for goods. Whereas the price of a loaf of bread was a quarter of a mark in 1918, it had reached 240 marks by the end of 1922, 5000 marks by Summer 1923, and a horrifying 260 billion marks by Fall 1923. Argentina is a more recent example of runaway inflation. In 1983, it had to replace its currency with a new one because, as their Economy Minister said "the computers in the central bank and other government institutions just couldn't handle any more zeros." With the old currency, one U.S. dollar was worth 80000 pesos; with the new currency, created by dropping four zeros from the old, its worth became eight.

Business Firms

For various reasons, a general rise in prices tends to increase business profits. First, materials and parts are bought at yesterday's prices, while the finished goods are sold at today's prices. Secondly, wage and rent increases tend to lag behind the increase in the prices of the finished products. Thirdly, the general increase in incomes, as wages, profits, rent, and so on rise, causes the demand for goods and services to increase also and so enables even the moderately efficient business firm to sell its products at a profit.

Governments

When prices rise, government revenue from corporation income taxes and sales taxes also rises. The increase in revenue may not be sufficient, however, to meet sharply rising costs, such as higher wages for government employees. Furthermore, many federal-government payments are now linked by law to the Consumer Price Index. As the price level rises, so does the amount of these payments. Payments now indexed in this way include the old-age security pension, the guaranteed income supplement, the Canada Pension Plan, veterans' allowances, and welfare assistance. Also, on the revenue side, the personal income-tax system is now indexed so that, with inflation, personal exemptions automatically rise and tax revenue does not increase as much as it otherwise would. However, such indexing is now being reduced in scope because of government revenue needs.

32.10: CAUSES OF INFLATION

Several theories have been advanced to explain why changes take place in a country's general level of prices. The traditional explanation, which we shall consider first, is the *Quantity Theory* that links the price level directly to the supply of money. Other theories include the *Demand-Pull Theory*, the *Cost-Push Theory*, and the *Imported Inflation Theory*.

The Quantity Theory of Money

This theory, in its simplest form, states that a change in the quantity of money in circulation will cause a proportionate change in the level of prices and therefore an inverse change in the value of money. Thus, if the amount of money in circulation is doubled, the general level of prices will also be doubled and the real value of money will be halved. The quantity theory of money offers a simple cause-effect relationship between the quantity of money and the general price level. In practice, it was found that other factors besides the quantity of money affected prices, particularly in the short run. The "crude" quantity theory, as it is now called, was therefore set aside as a useful but incomplete explanation of price changes, except, perhaps, in the very long run.

However, before we consider the various "refinements" that have been made to the quantity theory, let us emphasize that this traditional approach has enjoyed a comeback among economists in recent years. It has been argued by these economists, collectively known as the "monetarist school" and led by Professor Milton Friedman of the United States, that this approach is fundamental to our understanding of the economic problems that beset us today. Many of these problems can be attributed, they say, to the rapid increase over the years in the money supply of most Western countries.

The Transactions-Velocity Approach (or Fisher Equation)

A basic weakness of the crude quantity theory was its assumptions that the amount of business transacted in the economy and the number of times that a unit of money was used would remain relatively stable. Only on the basis of these assumptions could a change in the quantity of money cause a directly proportionate change in the general price level. Early in this century, Professor Irving Fisher, a U.S. economist, re-examined these assumptions and formulated what is now known as the *Fisher Equation*:

$$MV = PT$$

In the equation, M stands for the *money supply*—that is, the total amount of coin, paper money, and bank deposits in the economy; V represents the *velocity of circulation* or, in other words, the average number of times that each unit of money is used to make a purchase during a given time period; P is the *average price* of each business transaction; and T represents the *number of transactions* in the economy during that time period. Thus, the left-hand side of the equation, MV, is equivalent to the total value of all monetary payments in the economy during the time period considered. The right-hand side of the equation, PT, represents the total value of business transactions in the economy during the chosen time period. MV and PT are equal because they represent nothing more than two aspects of the same thing—one the monetary and the other the physical. For example, when a car is sold for $10000, the *MV* or monetary aspect is that $10000 has changed hands once; from the *PT* or physical aspect, a car worth $10000 has been sold.

The significance of the Fisher Equation is that it brings into the open the role of the two factors—the velocity of circulation of money and the number of transactions—assumed to be stable in the crude quantity theory. Let us consider each of these.

The velocity of circulation is the average number of times that a unit of money is used during, say, a year to purchase goods and services. Why should this vary? The most important reason is loss of confidence by the public in the value of money. In a time of runaway inflation, for example, people are unwilling to hold money because, as prices continue to rise, this money declines in value. People will try to spend money as fast as possible; the shopkeepers or other recipients will in turn quickly respend it on new goods for resale or for personal requirements, so this circle of rapid spending continues. As a result, in a time of severe inflation, the velocity of circulation of money increases sharply. Thus, even if the amount of money in circulation were to remain unchanged, the total value of monetary payments in the economy might increase severalfold. For, as we know, the size of *MV* can be enlarged by an increase in *M*, an increase in *V*, or by an increase in both.

The number of transactions in the economy also does not remain stationary for very long. Gross National Product is usually increasing or decreasing. Consequently, an increase in *MV* may not cause an increase in the price level if the number of transactions is rapidly increasing. An increase in the supply of money, for example, may be offset by this increase in transactions; for, although *PT* must increase if *MV* increases, this increase may be in *T* rather than in *P*.

The Fisher Equation can be reshaped to indicate more clearly the effects on the price level of changes in the supply of money, in the velocity of circulation, or in the number of transactions.

The new equation is as follows:

$$P = \frac{MV}{T}$$

Thus, if *M*, the supply of money, is $3 billion; if *V*, the velocity of circulation, is 100; and if *T*, the number of transactions during the year is 60 billion; then *P*, the average price paid during the period in question, would be:

$$\$5.00 = \frac{\$3 \text{ billion} \times 100}{60 \text{ billion}}$$

The Cash-Balance (or Liquidity-Preference) Approach

Another approach developed to explain changes in the price level is the *cash-balance approach*. This was developed concurrently with the transactions-velocity approach and stresses the psychological forces involved in people's behaviour towards money. This approach is also summarized in the form of an equation:

$$P = \frac{M}{kY}$$

In this equation, known as the *cash-balances equation*, or *Cambridge Equation, P* is the price level; *M* is the country's money supply; *Y* is the level of national income; and *k* is the *cash balance*, or fraction of the national income, for a certain period, that the public wishes to hold in the form of money.

The desire of the public to hold money is called its *liquidity preference*. This preference is based on three factors: (a) the transactions motive, (b) the precautionary motive, and (c) the speculative motive. The *transactions motive* is the need for money that individuals, business firms, and governments have in order to carry on their daily business. The most important factor that causes a change in the amount of money required for transactions purposes is a change in national income and employment. The *precautionary motive* is people's desire to hold money to provide for emergencies. The need to carry cash, however, tends to be reduced as more and more people use credit cards. Moreover, the need to hold emergency bank balances declines as life, income, and medical insurance become more widespread. Nevertheless, the precautionary motive remains an important part of the total demand for money by the public. The *speculative motive* is a person's preference for holding money rather than other assets because of the hope of financial gain, or, more often, the hope of avoiding financial loss. Thus, if a person fears that the market value of bonds, stocks, or real estate is likely to fall—as in time of economic recession—the person may find it financially advantageous to sell these assets and hold the money until the fall in prices has reached its lowest point. The rate of interest that the public can obtain on savings deposits is also an important factor influencing the decision to hold money rather than other assets.

As an explanation of changes in the price level, the cash-balance approach stresses the importance of the desire to hold money. This desire can vary over time because of any one of the three motives outlined. If the public's desire to hold money increases and the supply of money remains unchanged, then prices will tend to fall. Conversely, if the public's desire to hold money declines and the supply of money is the same, prices will tend to rise. Thus, if M, the supply of money, is $80 billion; if Y, the level of national income, is $40 billion, and if k, the fraction of the national income that people want to hold in money, is $\frac{1}{4}$; then P will be equal to:

$$\frac{\$80 \text{ billion}}{1/4 \times \$40 \text{ billion}} \text{ or } \$8.00.$$

If the public's *liquidity preference* increases to $\frac{1}{3}$ (instead of remaining at $\frac{1}{4}$), the average price will decline to $6.00, so long as other factors remain unchanged.

We should note that the cash-balance approach and the transactions-velocity approach to explaining changes in the general price level are very similar. Thus, an increase in the velocity of circulation of money (V in the Fisher Equation) is the same as a reduction in the public's liquidity preference (k of the Cash-Balance Equation).

32.11: DEMAND-PULL INFLATION

According to the *demand-pull theory*, inflation can be explained in terms of the relationship between a country's aggregate demand for goods and services and the degree of use of its factor resources. Thus, once a country's resources are fully employed, an increase in aggregate demand can only cause a rise in prices. If, for example, total spending is increased by 15 per cent over the level necessary for full employment, then the general level of prices will also tend to rise by 15 per cent. Business firms, competing to expand output, will also tend to raise wage rates. Eventually, prices, wages, and profits will all have increased by approximately 15 per cent. This assumes that labour and management continue to receive the same relative rewards. In real terms, despite higher monetary rewards, no one will be better off. The increase in aggregate demand has succeeded in pulling up the prices of outputs and of factor inputs—hence the name "demand-pull" inflation. The extent to which the level of Gross National Expenditure exceeds that required for full employment of the country's resources is called the *inflationary gap*.

To combat demand-pull inflation successfully, government must ensure that aggregate demand is at or below the full-employment level. Thus, if investment by business firms rises substantially so that total injections (G + I + X) start to exceed total leakages (S + T + M), as defined in Chapter 21 (The Circular Flow of Income), the government can hold down the increase in the flow of income by decreasing its own expenditure or by increasing taxes. However, because of the time lags involved as well as changes in other circumstances, such action can easily be too little, too much, or too late.

32.12: COST-PUSH INFLATION

In the late 1950s, economists noticed that, while output and employment in North America were declining as a result of an economic recession, the general price level was rising. Since this was obviously inconsistent with the traditional demand-pull theory of inflation, a new explanation was sought. This explanation, known as the *cost-push theory of inflation*, holds that a rise in the general price level is possible even with less than full employment, because of the bargaining strength of labour unions. These unions push up wage rates; and the increased operating costs in turn encourage business firms, justifiably or not, to raise the selling prices of their products.

However, it has been observed that business firms often raise prices to increase profits, rather than just to offset additional expenses. Consequently, the cost-push theory of inflation has more recently been broadened to include price increases caused by increases in non-labour costs as well as in labour costs. The name for this new, broader concept is *sellers' inflation*: sellers of factor services and sellers of goods and services are all trying to obtain more total revenue than the current value of national output. This forces market prices upwards as each seller scrambles to obtain a larger slice of the national or global pie. The most notable example of this inflationary factor in recent years has been the policy of the major oil-exporting countries in raising drastically the price of their oil.

In time of full employment, both demand-pull and cost-push, or sellers' inflation, can exist at the same time. Consequently, a government, if it is to be successful in restraining inflation, must be careful to understand just what type of inflation it is dealing with. If it is predominantly cost-push inflation, then the government might have to adopt extremely tough monetary and fiscal restraints, including even wage-and-price controls, before the inflation is slowed. At the same time, these restraints may bring about a major slow-down in the country's economic growth and a considerable rise in unemployment.

32.13: IMPORTED-INFLATION THEORY

If a country imports raw materials, food, fuel, equipment, and other goods, any increase in their prices intensifies inflation in that country. Thus, for example, world-wide increases in commodity prices and in oil prices have helped inflation reach double figures annually in many countries. Canada, as a prime supplier of food and raw materials, was not hit as hard as other countries. Nevertheless, the increases in foreign oil prices did severely affect Canada, for most of the oil consumed in Quebec and the Maritime provinces has for many years been imported from abroad. Furthermore, the Prairie provinces, notably Alberta, were successful in obtaining a substantial increase in the price of their oil sold in Canada. Also, the high prices to be obtained abroad for various commodities—for example, animal feedstuffs—inevitably helped to raise their price at home; hence, at least one political party called for a two-price system for Canada's principal exports, namely an export price and a lower home-market price. The producer would receive the same price whatever the market, but the foreign buyer would have to pay a price that includes a Canadian export tax as well.

32.14: MONEY SUPPLY AND THE NATIONAL INCOME

In classical economic theory, the money supply played a central role in determining national income. But this view was discredited in the 1930s by Keynes and other prominent economists.

Nowadays people are becoming more and more critical of excessive government spending. This spending is often justified as being necessary to stimulate the economy or, in Keynesian terms, to increase aggregate demand. Often, in practice, however, such spending seems only to increase the rate of inflation rather than lower the rate of unemployment. As a result there has been a revival of interest in monetary policy—or more specifically the alteration of the money supply—as a more efficient means of raising or lowering aggregate demand and thereby determining the level of national income and employment without the abuses of runaway government spending.

The "monetarists," led by Professor Milton Friedman of the United States, argue that there is a normal relationship between the level of national income and the quantity of money that persons and firms wish to hold. If the money supply is increased beyond this amount, the excess money will be spent, thereby raising national income. Conversely, if the money supply is reduced, spending will drop and national income will fall until the normal relationship is re-established.

Fiscal policy, so it is argued, is only a special case of monetary policy—thus, a tax increase, for example, affects aggregate demand through a reduction in the money supply—and would be more effective if recognized as such. Also, rather than let politicians have a free hand with spending, with consequent inflationary effects, Professor Friedman recommends that the annual increase in a country's money supply be the same as that forecast for growth in the country's real GNP.

Summary

1. There are three main kinds of money used in Canada today—coins, bank notes, and chequable bank deposits. Chequable bank deposits are by far the most important kind. All kinds of objects have been used as money at different times and in different places.
2. Money, in its various forms, serves as a medium of exchange, a measure of value, a unit of account, and as a store of wealth.
3. To be a satisfactory medium of exchange, money needs to be portable, durable, divisible, and, above all, acceptable. As a measure of value, it must be divisible and commonly recognized. As a unit of account, it must be easy to add, subtract, divide and multiply. And as a store of wealth, it should retain its value in terms of other assets.
4. Canada's money supply is commonly defined as: notes and coin held by the public plus all chartered bank deposits held by the public. A distinction is sometimes made between the money supply narrowly defined (called M1) which includes only chequable bank deposits, and the money supply broadly defined (or M2), which includes chequable and non-chequable deposits.
5. Statistics Canada calculates indexes of consumer and other prices in Canada to reveal changes that have taken place.
6. The term "inflation" describes a situation in which the general price level in a country is increasing. This inflation can be mild or galloping. Deflation is a situation of generally falling prices.
7. Over the long run, prices have marched steadily upward in Canada.
8. The federal government has, from time to time, tried to combat inflation with wage and price controls and high interest rates.
9. Various groups are affected differently by inflation—fixed-money—income groups, creditors and debtors, wage-earners, business firms, and governments.
10. Several theories have been advanced as a full or partial explanation of inflation. These include: the quantity theory of money and its two refinements, the transactions-velocity approach (or Fisher Equation) and the cash-balance, or liquidity, approach; the demand-pull theory; the cost-push theory; and the imported-inflation theory.
11. The "monetarist school" argues that deliberate changes in the money supply are a more efficient way of raising or lower aggregate demand than changes in government spending.

Key Terms

Money 630
Coins 630
Token money 630
Legal tender 630
Bank notes 630
Chequable bank deposits 630
Medium of exchange 631
Measure of value 631
Unit of account 632
Store of wealth 632
Portability 632
Durability 632
Divisibility 633
Acceptability 633
Certified cheque 633
Money supply 633
M1 633
M1B 633
M2 634
M3 634
Near money 634
Consumer price index 636

Inflation 638
Mild inflation 638
Hyperinflation 638
Deflation 638
Incomes policy 638
Fixed money income 641
Creditors 641
Debtors 641
Quantity theory 643
Fisher equation 644
Velocity of circulation 644
Liquidity preference 646
Cambridge equation 646
Transactions motive 646
Precautionary motive 646
Speculative motive 646
Demand-pull theory 647
Cost-push theory 648
Sellers' inflation 648
Imported inflation 648
Monetarist school 649

Review Questions

1. What are the three main kinds of money in use in Canada? What is their relative importance?
2. Coins are sometimes called "token money." Explain.
3. Why are bank deposits considered to be money?
4. "Money is used as a medium of exchange." Explain.
5. What are the other main functions of money?
6. What are the advantages and disadvantages of money as a store of wealth?
7. What characteristics does an object need to be a satisfactory medium of exchange?
8. What characteristics should money have to serve as (a) a measure of value, and (b) a unit of account?
9. How efficient has the Canadian dollar been as a store of wealth? Compare it with other currencies.

10. What constitutes Canada's money supply? How has it grown in recent years?
11. What is near-money? Why do some economists believe that it should be included in the calculation of a country's money supply?
12. What is the Consumer Price Index? How is it calculated? What purpose does it serve?
13. Distinguish between inflation and deflation.
14. How have prices changed in Canada since the 1930s?
15. What effects does inflation have on pensioners and other fixed-money income receivers?
16. What effects does inflation have on creditors and debtors?
17. What is the quantity theory of money?
18. What is the Fisher Equation? What is its significance?
19. What is meant by the "velocity of circulation" of money? What causes it to change?
20. What is the cash-balance, or liquidity, approach to explaining price changes? What does it emphasize?
21. What are the various motives that the public has for holding money?
22. Distinguish between the demand-pull and cost-push theories of inflation.
23. Explain the "imported-inflation" theory. Does it apply to Canada?
24. What is the "monetarist school"? What is their main thesis? How plausible does it seem?

33. THE CHARTERED BANKS AND MONEY CREATION

CHAPTER OBJECTIVES

A. To describe Canada's system of banks
B. To indicate the various functions that a bank performs
C. To compare Canada's system of branch banking with the U.S. system of unit banking
D. To examine the assets and liabilities of Canada's chartered banks
E. To explain how banks can create money, but are restricted in doing so by cash-reserve requirements

CHAPTER OUTLINE

33.1: CANADA'S CHARTERED BANKS

Canada now has 69 privately-owned chartered banks, divided into two classes: Schedule A and Schedule B. Schedule A banks (11 out of the 69), are ones in which no shareholder or group of associated shareholders owns more than 10 per cent of the bank's voting shares. Schedule B banks are ones that are permitted to be closely held upon incorporation—that is, one or just a few shareholders own more than

10 per cent of the voting shares. Under the Bank Act, Schedule B banks automatically include the subsidiaries of foreign banks. Both classes of banks, A and B, have the same general powers, restrictions, and obligations under the Bank Act.

The eleven Schedule A banks include the Big Five (the Royal Bank of Canada, the Canadian Imperial Bank of Commerce, the Bank of Montreal, the Bank of Nova Scotia, and the Toronto-Dominion Bank) which together account for the vast bulk of total bank assets (see Table S.35). Each of these banks has a network of branches spread across the country. The other Schedule A banks, which operate mainly regionally, are in order of amount of assets: the National Bank of Canada, the Mercantile Bank of Canada, the Continental Bank of Canada, the Bank of British Columbia, the Canadian Commercial Bank, and the Northland Bank.

At one time (1875) Canada had as many as fifty-one chartered banks, but over the years many failed, merged with others, or had their charter repealed so that by the 1970s there were less than a dozen left. Now, in the 1980s, the number of chartered banks in Canada has again increased dramatically as the result of a new Bank Act, passed in December 1980, which has allowed foreign banks to set up branch operations in Canada in return for Canadian banking privileges abroad. However, the activities of the foreign bank subsidiaries are restricted at the present time, compared to their Canadian counterparts, by a ceiling on the value of their assets in Canada of 8 per cent of the total for the banking industry as a whole.

33.2: ESTABLISHMENT OF A BANK

No new bank may be established in Canada without the approval of the federal Parliament because, at the time of Confederation, Parliament was given authority over money and banking in Canada. Applications to establish a new bank are closely examined by the Treasury Board (the federal cabinet, meeting under the chairmanship of the Minister of Finance) and by the Senate Banking Committee.

Bank charters are granted under the Bank Act. This Act, which sets out the conditions under which the banks must operate, is revised and renewed by Parliament every ten years. The present Bank Act came into force on December 1, 1980. Chartered banks, like other privately-owned business firms, have as their main obligation the earning of profits for their shareholders. However, the Bank Act helps to reduce the conflict between the interests of the public and those of the banks by requiring minimum cash reserves, audits by public accountants, and a system of inspection by the federal Department of Finance.

Table S.35
Chartered Banks of Canada — Statement of Assets, in million of dollars, Aug. 31. 1983

BANKS	Cash Resources			Securities			Investment dealers and brokers	Loans		Mortgages	Acceptances fixed and other assets	TOTAL ASSETS
	Cash at and deposits with Bank of Canada	Deposits with other banks	Cheques and other items in transit	Canada	Other government securities	Other		Banks	Other			
Royal Bank of Canada	1 667.8	12 062.7	177.0	3 126.0	71.3	4 304.0	289.6	1 588.9	46 881.9	8 204.3	6 819.8	85 193.2
Cdn. Imp. Bank of Commerce	1 501.5	5 378.9	933.3	3 474.9	23.6	2 608.1	539.6	1 563.0	40 003.8	7 894.9	4 677.6	68 419.2
Bank of Montreal	1 206.0	7 366.5	0.0	5 300.6	244.6	3 277.0	572.1	2 037.1	33,563.9	5 141.6	5 437.4	64 146.8
Bank of Nova Scotia	1 208.4	1 131.1	0.0	1 364.4	136.1	2 025.2	342.3	1 847.7	29 321.3	3 765.8	3 464.7	54 787.0
Toronto-Dominion Bank	886.2	3 452.0	0.0	2 258.0	31.4	2 044.8	463.3	2 013.5	23 766.0	4 699.4	3 279.8	42 894.4
National Bank of Canada	308.3	1 105.4	169.4	867.6	118.3	650.0	386.5	994.2	9 656.5	2 711.1	1 087.0	18 045.3
Continental Bank of Canada	23.8	164.4	31.3	147.4	0.0	344.4	9.9	95.2	3 244.6	380.7	177.4	4 601.1
Mercantile Bank of Canada	15.1	86.7	33.1	185.5	0.0	119.2	219.0	75.4	3 070.8	88./	387.0	4 279.9
Bank of British Columbia	59.1	196.8	25.2	117.9	6.0	124.0	6.0	57.4	2 104.2	219.9	152.1	3 068.4
Canadian Commercial Bank	11.5	42.3	35.3	47.8	0.0	93.8	6.0	0.0	1 799.8	26.0	104.7	2 167.1
Northland Bank	11.2	0.6	0.0	24.3	1.4	50.4	0.0	18.7	550.8	0.0	32.2	689.6
Western and Pacific Bank	0.0	15.6	0.0	1.9	0.0	1.5	0.0	0.0	0.8	1.7	1.6	23.0
TOTAL Schedule A Banks	6 898.9	41 164.9	1 404.7	16 916.3	632.6	15 642.4	2 654.2	10 291.1	193 964.2	33 133.6	25 612.4	348 315.3
TOTAL Schedule B Banks	12.8	5 049.4	26.7	544.0	41.8	460.8	403.6	197.1	11 611.4	1 219.3	1 691.4	21 258.3
TOTAL as of August 83	6 911.6	46 214.3	1 431.4	17 460.3	674.4	16 103.2	3 057.8	10 488.2	205 575.6	34 352.9	27 303.9	369 573.6

Source: The Canadian Bankers' Association

Note: Figures may not add due to rounding

33.3: FUNCTIONS OF A BANK

The most important functions performed by the chartered banks are: (a) the receiving of deposits (repayable on demand or short notice and usually transferable by cheque) from households, business firms, and governments, (b) the paying of interest on deposits; (c) the lending and investing of these funds; and (d) the charging of interest on loans. Other functions performed by the chartered banks include foreign exchange transactions; buying and selling of domestic or foreign bills of exchange (or drafts); collecting of monies owing on bills of exchange; making remittances; clearing cheques; issuing letters of credit; giving financial guarantees; providing financial information and counselling; safekeeping securities or other valuables; handling security transactions; financial leasing; factoring (i.e. buying a firm's accounts receivable); the provision of venture capital; data processing services; and renting of safety deposit boxes. All these activities, it should be noted, are also carried out in varying degree by other financial institutions in Canada. Because loans to business or "commerce" are such a fundamental part of a bank's lending activities, the chartered banks, and their equivalent in other countries, are known as *commercial banks.*

Over the last thirty years, owing to a widening of the banks' powers under successive Bank Acts, the chartered banks have greatly enlarged their range of financial services. As well as making short and medium-term loans to business, the banks are now predominant among financial institutions in the consumer-loan field. They also make long-term mortgage loans for house purchases. And they have sponsored a far-reaching credit-card system (Visa) which together with Mastercard, has, for many people, drastically reduced the need for carrying cash, as well as provided computerized bookkeeping for the individual household. In addition, new financial services are still being introduced to take advantage of the banks' widespread network of branches. The banks have also been successful in attracting the bulk of the public's savings.

33.4: BRANCH BANKING

The Canadian commercial-banking system is known as *branch banking* because the five largest banks have branches spread across the country. This system is similar to the British one.

In the United States, by contrast, Federal law prohibits commercial banks from operating in more than one state; and in some states, state law prohibits commercial banks from having any branches at all. As a result, there are many thousands of banks in the United States, most of them quite small. The name for this kind of banking is *unit banking.*

"What d'you mean, 'that's the new manager'?"

What are the advantages, if any, of the Canadian system of having a relatively small number of large banks, with many branches? First, because of their size, large banks are financially much more stable than small local banks. In fact, there has not been a bank failure in Canada since 1923. Second, because of the wide geographical dispersion of the branch banks, sudden withdrawals in one locality can be covered by funds from other branches. For a small local bank, a regional economic upset or major embezzlement can be financially disastrous. Third, because of its wide geographical coverage, a large bank can put savings from one area to work in another. And, fourth, because of its size, a large bank can have a better system of staff training, providing its managers and future managers with a wider variety of experience, than can a small bank.

33.5: BANK ASSETS AND LIABILITIES

The chartered banks use the funds at their disposal to provide loans and make investments. The earnings from these various loans and investments enable the banks to cover their expenses and earn a profit for their shareholders. The actual choice of assets represents a compromise between two different goals: (a) maintaining a high degree of liquidity, and (b) obtaining as high a rate of return as possible. In most cases, the less liquid the asset, the higher the rate of return; and vice-versa. The degree of liquidity is not, of course, left to the banks' discretion. Under the Bank Act, the banks must keep minimum *cash reserves* (Bank of Canada deposits and notes) equal to a certain percentage of demand deposits and of notice deposits. These percentages relate to deposits in Canadian currency. The most liquid assets, other than cash, are day-to-day loans and Government of Canada treasury bills. These constitute the chartered banks' *secondary reserves*, which must also, by law, be kept at a certain minimum level—one that is varied from time to time depending on the federal government's monetary policy.

If we examine the consolidated balance sheet of Canada's chartered banks (see Table S.36), we can see that the largest portion of the banks' assets comprises general loans—money owed to the banks by households, business, and government borrowers. The next largest item is foreign currency assets. The vast bulk of the bank's liabilities consists of short-term debt—namely, the banks' obligations to their depositors—and foreign currency liabilities.

Bank deposits are traditionally divided into two main groups: demand deposits and notice deposits. *Demand deposits* (notably business and government current accounts and personal chequing accounts) are deposits that can be withdrawn on demand—that is, without prior no-

Table S.36
Chartered Banks' Assets and Liabilities, end of 1982

Assets	$ millions	%
Bank of Canada deposits and notes	7067	1.9
Day-to-day loans	85	0.0
Treasury bills	9 883	2.7
Govt. of Canada direct and guaranteed bonds	1 667	0.5
Call and short loans	2 363	0.6
Loans in Canadian dollars:		
Provinces and municipal	2 685	0.7
Canada Savings Bonds	908	0.2
General loans	119 362	32.3
Residential and other mortgages	31 599	8.6
Leasing receivables	2 549	0.7
Canadian securities:		
Provincial and municipal	523	0.1
Corporate shares	4 841	1.3
Other corporate, etc.	4 619	1.3
Canadian dollar deposits with other banks	4 776	1.3
Canadian dollar items in transit (net)	856	0.2
Customers' liability under acceptances	12 647	3.4
All other assets	6 143	1.7
Total Canadian dollar assets	212 572	57.6
Total foreign currency assets	156 490	42.4
Total Assets	369 062	100.0

Liabilities and Shareholders' Equity		
Canadian dollar deposits		
Personal savings deposits	100 037	27.1
Non-personal term and notice deposits	48 541	13.2
Personal chequing and other demand deposits	19 114	5.2
Government of Canada	6 906	1.9
Advances from Bank of Canada	143	0.0
Bankers' acceptances	12 647	3.4
Liabilities of subsidiaries other than deposits	1 520	0.4
Other liabilities, etc.	4 723	1.3
Bank debentures issued and outstanding	2 552	0.7
Appropriations for contingencies	1 002	0.3
Capital stock	3 905	1.1
Contributed surplus and general reserve	1 422	0.4
Retained earnings	7 146	1.9
Total foreign currency liabilities	209 658	56.8
Total liabilities	159 404	43.2
	369 062	100.00

Source: Bank of Canada, Review, monthly

tice. As well as being highly liquid assets for the banks, they are used as the chief medium of payment in Canada. *Notice deposits* are deposits for which the banks reserve the right to demand prior notice of withdrawal. Such a requirement would only be enforced if there were a sudden rash of withdrawals through loss of public confidence in a bank—a highly unusual event in Canada.

33.6: HOW BANKS CREATE MONEY

We have seen so far that the chartered banks perform two main functions: on the one hand, they collect the savings of individuals, business firms and governments; on the other hand, they lend this money to business firms, individuals, and governments who wish to use it for investment or consumption. But what is distinctive about our chartered banks, as compared with other financial institutions, is their ability to create or destroy money. No one bank, as a bank manager may argue, can create money. But chartered banks, as a whole, do have this seemingly magical power. To explain, it is helpful to go back in time to the beginning of modern banking.

Origins of Deposit-Money

In the early days of banking history, many wealthy people would leave their gold and silver coins and other valuables with the local goldsmith, paying a fee for the safekeeping services provided. The owners could always collect their valuables by bringing along the receipt. Gradually, instead of drawing out gold and silver coins every time they needed cash to settle a debt, the depositors would use the goldsmith's receipts to make payment. In other words, the receipts came to serve as money.

The goldsmiths, as well as accepting gold and silver for safekeeping, also engaged in lending. At first these early banks would lend out only their own money. As a result, their balance sheets might have looked like that shown in Table 33:1. On the left-hand or asset side, there is $100000 in gold and silver coin belonging to depositors. This is offset, on the right-hand side, by $100000 of deposit liabilities. Also on the left-hand side, there is $10000 of loans and investments—in other words, I.O.U.s of borrowers and securities purchased by the goldsmith. This, in turn, is offset on the right-hand side by the $10000 of capital that was invested in the bank by its goldsmith owners. In this case, the bank is holding a 100 per cent cash reserve. For every dollar owed to its depositors, it has one dollar in gold or silver coin in its vaults. The only money loaned out is what the goldsmiths themselves have invested as ownership capital in the business.

Table 33:1
Balance Sheet of Early Bank

Assets		Liabilities and owners' equity	
Gold and silver	$100 000	Liability to depositors	$100 000
Loans and investments	10 000	Owners' equity	10 000
	$110 000		$110 000

The money that people deposited with the goldsmith was always payable on demand. In other words, the depositors could collect their gold and silver coin and other valuables at any time, without giving prior notice. The goldsmiths soon came to realize, however, that most people were content to leave their valuables in the vaults. If they needed to make a payment, they would use the goldsmith's receipts in lieu of coin. The coin that was occasionally withdrawn from the goldsmith's vaults by depositors was normally offset by new deposits of coin. Of course, the public's willingness to leave their valuables with the goldsmiths depended on the depositors' confidence in the honesty and financial stability of the goldsmiths. If this confidence were destroyed, there would be a rush by depositors to withdraw their wealth.

It did not take long for the goldsmiths to start lending and investing their depositors' money as well as their own. Not only was this more profitable, it also entailed little risk so long as a large enough reserve was kept to satisfy those few depositors who wished to withdraw their funds. The cash reserves held by these goldsmith banks to satisfy their deposit liabilities soon became far less than 100 per cent. The goldsmiths' enthusiasm for reducing cash reserves was not for their benefit alone; they could also now afford to pay depositors for the privilege of looking after their money and charge borrowers less for their loans. As a result, everyone was happy.

Over the years, more and more depositors acquired the habit of writing *cheques* on their deposit accounts. A cheque was a written instruction authorizing the bank to pay money from the depositor's account to the person named on the cheque. This meant, in theory, that the bank would need to have the cash ready to pay such a person. In practice, however, very little of this cash was ever required. Most of the persons who were given cheques (the *payees*) did not bother to go to the bank of the cheque-writer (or *payor*) and draw out the cash. Instead, the payees deposited the cheques at their own banks—in effect authorizing

"These aren't the 'old days', Mr. Smith. We know exactly how much you owe and to whom."

their own banks to collect on their behalf. At the end of each day, most of the money to be collected by, for example, bank A from banks B, C, and D (the *clearing drain*, as it is now called) was offset by the amounts to be paid by Bank A to these other banks.

Consequently, only a relatively small amount of cash was required to be paid by one bank to another to settle the outstanding balance. Nowadays, any such balance is settled by one bank writing a cheque, in favour of another bank, on its deposit account with Canada's central bank, the Bank of Canada. So, in fact, no cash actually changes hands.

How Banks Increase Deposit-Money

With the growing, widespread use of deposit-money (often more convenient than gold or silver coin or even paper money) to finance transactions, the banks discovered another important fact. If they wished to lend money, they did not need to pay out cash. All they had to do was to increase the balance in the borrower's account by the amount of the loan. The borrower would then write cheques on the account that would later be offset by cheques written on accounts in other banks. In other words, without having more cash on hand, a bank had actually created money. This money was, of course, deposit-money. But, as we have seen previously, this type of money is even more useful than notes or coin in settling debts and paying for goods and services. The banks had, in economic terminology, *monetized private debt.*

As well as lending money at interest, the banks also invested in various types of securities—notably government and business bonds. Here again, the banks found that they did not need to use cash. They could pay for their investments by means of cheques drawn on themselves. The sellers of the securities would then deposit the bankers' cheques in their own bank deposit accounts. At the end of the day, most payments by, for example, bank A to depositors in Banks C, D, and E would be offset by payments by these other banks to depositors in bank A.

How Cash Reserves Control Deposit-Money

If the banks can create money merely by increasing the balance in a depositor's account, what is to prevent the money supply from being increased indefinitely? The answer is the *cash-reserve requirement.* Not all cheques will be deposited with other banks. A certain amount of cash will always be drawn out. Consequently, the banks will always need to keep a cash reserve. However, this need only be a fraction of the banks' total deposits—hence the term *fractional reserves.*

The size of the cash reserve that the banks must maintain in relation to their deposit liabilities is in fact set by law. It is not left up to the banks' own discretion, for they might be tempted, in their pursuit of profit, to keep the reserve dangerously low. As the Canadian Bankers' Association has said:

It is of course technically true that the Canadian banking system can expand its assets (in the form of loans and investments) and its liabilities (in the form of deposits) but only within limits fixed by the amount of cash reserves the Bank of Canada allows them. However, the banks themselves cannot determine these limits. It is entirely up to the national monetary authorities to decide what level of bank deposits is appropriate.[1]

Until June 30, 1967, the legal requirement in Canada was that the chartered banks keep a cash reserve equal to 8 per cent of all demand and notice deposits in Canadian dollars. By the terms of the Bank Act of 1967, the cash reserve ratio was gradually changed, so that, since February 1968, the required ratios have been 12 per cent for demand deposits and 4 per cent for notice deposits. However, as a result of the 1980 Bank Act, the ratios are being gradually lowered once more to: (a) 10% of Canadian currency demand deposits; (b) 3% of Canadian currency notice deposits used to finance domestic transactions (with 2% on the first $500 million); and (c) 3% of foreign currency deposit liabilities used to finance domestic transactions. About one-third of the cash reserves is kept in the form of bank notes and about two-thirds in the form of deposits with the Bank of Canada. Just how large, as a percentage of deposits, the reserves should be in normal times is a matter of opinion. Some bankers have asserted that, so long as public confidence in the banking system remains high, a 5 per cent over-all average reserve is more than enough.

To ensure a high degree of liquidity, chartered banks voluntarily maintained secondary reserves comprising excess cash reserves, day-to-day loans, and treasury bills. However, since 1968, the Bank of Canada has stipulated the amount of secondary reserves the chartered banks should hold as a percentage of total Canadian dollar deposit liabilities. The Bank of Canada can set the secondary reserve ratio, depending on the monetary situation, anywhere between 6 and 12 per cent.

One important purpose of the reserve requirements is to ensure that a significant portion of the banks' assets are available as cash or in securities that can be quickly converted into cash. However, the legal reserve requirements also provide the means (as explained in the next chapter) whereby the federal government, through the Bank of Canada, can control the country's money supply. And without such control, the government would be relatively helpless in fighting inflation.

33.7: THE MONEY MULTIPLIER

As we have just seen, the chartered banks have the power to create demand deposit-money by a multiple of any additional cash reserves. This figure, called the *money multiplier*, is the reciprocal of the reserve ratio. The lower the reserve requirement, the greater the multiplier. Thus, with a 6 per cent cash reserve (see Table 33:2), the money supply can be increased 16.7 times any additional cash reserve. Conversely, the higher the reserve requirement, the lower the multiplier and the multiple expansion. The money multiplier is also smaller if the public hoards cash or the banks hold excess cash reserves.

Table 33:2

Process of Multiple Expansion of Bank Deposits Following an Initial Deposit of $1000, with a 6 Per Cent Cash Reserve

Circular Flow	New Deposits	Additional Cash Reserves	New Loans and Investments
First round	$ 1 000.00	$ 60.00	$ 940.00
Second round	940.00	56.40	883.60
Third round	883.60	53.02	830.58
Fourth round	830.58	49.83	780.75
Fifth round	780.75	46.85	733.90
Sixth round	733.90	44.03	689.87
Seventh round	689.87	41.39	648.48
Eighth round	648.48	38.91	609.57
Ninth round	609.57	36.57	573.00
Tenth round	573.00	34.38	538.62
	7 689.75	461.38	7 228.37
Subsequent rounds	8 976.91	538.62	8 438.29
Total for all banks	$16 666.66	$1000.00	$15 666.66

We should also note that this whole process of money creation can work in reverse. If the banks lose $1000 of their cash reserves, then, if they are to maintain a 6 per cent cash reserve ratio, they must reduce bank deposits by 16.7 times. Finally, we should remember that the process of money creation depends entirely on the public's willingness to make most of their payments by cheque. If they were not willing to do so, the banks would have to keep much higher cash reserves. If these reserves were 100 per cent of deposit liabilities, there could be no multiple expansion or contraction of deposit money. And no money

---

Summary

1. Canada has sixty-nine privately-owned chartered banks. Of these, five account for the vast bulk of total assets.
2. A federal Bank Act, revised and renewed by parliament every ten years, regulates the establishment and operation of Canada's chartered banks.
3. The most important functions of the chartered banks are receiving deposits and making loans. However, the banks have greatly increased their range of other financial services over the last twenty years.
4. The five largest banks have branches right across Canada, hence the description of Canada's commercial banking system as *branch banking*. This contrasts with the U.S. system of *unit banking*.
5. In providing loans and making investments, the banks try to balance two different goals: maintaining a high degree of liquidity and obtaining a satisfactory profit. With regard to liquidity, the Bank Act prescribes minimum cash reserves and secondary reserves that all chartered banks must hold.
6. Bank assets include Bank of Canada deposits and notes, Canadian day-to-day loans, treasury bills, Government of Canada bonds, net foreign currency, call and short loans, short-term loans in Canadian currency, mortgage loans, provincial, municipal, and corporate bonds, Canadian dollar items in transit, and customers' liability under acceptances, guarantees, and letters.
7. Bank liabilities include Canadian dollar deposits, advances from the Bank of Canada, acceptances, guarantees, letters of credit, debentures, and accumulated appropriations for losses. Deposits comprise demand deposits and notice deposits, the former withdrawable without notice.
8. The chartered banks are the primary source of short-term business working capital. They usually establish, formally or informally, a line of credit for each important customer, and provide financing

in the form of demand loans, secured or unsecured.

9. In recent years, the chartered banks have aggressively promoted consumer loans, usually secured by a chattel mortgage on a car or other asset. The banks have also greatly increased their residential mortgage lending activities.

10. Banks had their origin as depositories for the coin and other valuables of the wealthy. Gradually, however, depositors acquired the habit of writing cheques on their deposit accounts, authorizing the transfer of funds to other people. Persons receiving cheques usually did not require the cash but were content to deposit the funds in their own banks. Since claims on one bank were largely offset by claims on the others, there was little actual cash transfer between banks. Also there was little or no withdrawal of cash by the public from the banking system as a whole.

11. Since the banks required, in practice, only a small cash reserve (compared with their deposit liabilities), they were able to earn a profit by making loans and investments. By increasing a borrower's bank balance, instead of giving him or her cash, the banks were in fact creating money, or *monetizing private debt*. All the banks as a whole had to do was to maintain a cash reserve equal to a fraction of the new money created.

12. To prevent the banks expanding the money supply excessively, and thereby keeping their cash reserves dangerously low, governments now impose minimum cash reserve requirements. In Canada, the required cash reserve ratios are 10% of demand deposits, 3% of notice deposits (with 2% on the first $500 million), and 3% of foreign currency deposit liabilities. The chartered banks are also required to keep a secondary reserve, comprising excess cash reserves, day-to-day loans, and treasury bills.

13. When additional cash is deposited with the banks, the money supply can be gradually increased (with an average cash reserve ratio of 6 per cent) by about seventeen times the additional cash reserve. This number is called the *money multiplier* and is the reciprocal of the reserve ratio.

Key Terms

Review Questions

1. Distinguish between Schedule A and Schedule B banks.
2. What is the procedure for establishing a chartered bank in Canada? What functions do the chartered banks perform?
3. What is meant by "branch banking"? What are the advantages of this system compared with other systems?
4. What assets do the chartered banks hold? What aims govern the banks' choice of assets?
5. What are the banks' principal liabilities? Distinguish between demand and notice deposits.
6. How did deposit-money originate?
7. How are the banks as a whole able to increase the money supply?
8. How does the size of the cash reserves held by the banks control the size of the money supply?
9. What are the minimum cash reserves that the banks must maintain by law?
10. What are secondary reserves? What is their purpose?
11. What is the money multiplier?

Reference

1 *Submission to the Royal Commission on Banking and Finance*, p. 5. Reproduced by permission of the Minister of Supply and Services Canada.

34. THE BANK OF CANADA AND CANADIAN MONETARY POLICY

CHAPTER OBJECTIVES

A. To explain how the Bank of Canada is owned and managed
B. To describe the functions that the Bank of Canada performs
C. To explain the nature and purpose of Canadian monetary policy
D. To indicate the relationship between monetary policy, fiscal policy, and exchange rate policy

CHAPTER OUTLINE

34.1 Management of the Bank of Canada
34.2 Functions of the Bank of Canada
34.3 Monetary Policy
34.4 Tools of Monetary Policy
34.5 Monetary, Fiscal, and Exchange Rate Policies
34.6 Canada's Recent Monetary Policy

One of the results of the economic depression of the 1930s was a demand for better monetary management in Canada. This led to the establishment by the federal government in 1934 of the Bank of Canada as Canada's central bank. Prior to 1934 the federal Department of Finance had exercised many of the powers of a central bank. For example, it had issued paper money called Dominion Notes and administered a series of Finance Acts. Britain, by way of contrast, had established its central bank, the Bank of England, in 1694, and the United States, its Federal Reserve System, in 1913.

To keep the Bank of Canada's policies immune from political pressures, ownership was at first placed in private hands. However, in 1936, a new federal government, wishing to have a stronger say in the Bank's policies, acquired 51 per cent of the ownership. Finally, in 1938, the government purchased the remainder of the capital stock. However, as we shall see later, the Bank of Canada, through its governor, has continued to exercise a strong mind of its own.

34.1: MANAGEMENT OF THE BANK OF CANADA

This is the responsibility of a board of directors, consisting of a governor, a deputy governor, and twelve directors. The directors are appointed for three-year terms by the federal Minister of Finance, with the approval of the federal cabinet. The directors in turn appoint the governor and deputy governor for seven-year terms, again with approval of the federal cabinet.

The directors, from diverse occupations, are usually appointed from the various regions of Canada and may not include a person who is a director, partner, officer, or employee of a firm or organization, such as a chartered bank or investment dealer, with whom the Bank has direct dealings. Each director, including the governor and deputy governor, has one vote at board meetings. The Deputy Minister of Finance is also a board member, but has no vote. Normally there are eight meetings of the board every year. Between meetings, an executive committee (comprising the governor, deputy governor, two directors chosen by the board, and the Deputy Minister of Finance, again without a vote) meets every week and acts on behalf of the board. The presence of the Deputy Minister of Finance on the board and on the executive committee provides a formal channel of communication between the Department of Finance and the Bank of Canada. There are also many other more informal contacts. The governor, who is chairman of the board and chief executive officer of the Bank, has a power of veto over any decisions of the board or executive committee, that can in turn be upheld or disallowed by the federal government.

Within two months of the end of the financial year, the Bank must provide the Minister of Finance with a statement of its accounts and an annual report by the governor. The Bank is also required to publish a statement of its assets and liabilities as at each Wednesday and each month end. In addition, the bank issues, each Thursday, *Weekly Financial Statistics*, a summary of the more liquid assets of the chartered banks as of the day before, and of all their major asset and liability items as of eight days before. The Bank also publishes each month a *Bank of Canada Review*, containing key financial and other economic data. It also publishes staff studies on various economic topics.

Usually, the Bank of Canada shows a substantial profit on its activities. This is mainly because Canada's private sector banks are required to hold minimum reserves at the Bank of Canada on which no interest is paid. The Bank of Canada uses this money, now well over $6 billion, to earn interest for itself.

34.2: FUNCTIONS OF THE BANK OF CANADA

The Bank of Canada performs several important functions. They include: issuing bank notes; acting as the federal government's fiscal agent; and acting as a "bankers' bank." It also performs the extremely important function of implementing, and helping to formulate, the government's monetary policy.

Sole Issuer of Bank Notes

Prior to 1934, paper money was issued in Canada by the federal Department of Finance and by the privately owned chartered banks. As one of its functions, the Bank of Canada took over the issuing of paper money from the government. Eventually, in 1945, the note-issuing privileges of the chartered banks were withdrawn. As a result, the Bank of Canada is now the sole issuer of bank notes for circulation in Canada.

The Bank of Canada may not just give paper money away. Each note that it issues is a liability. The Bank must, consequently, acquire some asset in exchange. The bulk of these assets, as we can see in the Bank's balance sheet (Table S.37), are government securities. These are written promises by the federal government to repay money borrowed, as well as to pay interest. By exchanging Bank of Canada notes for these government securities, the central bank is said to be *monetizing public debt*. In other words, the Bank of Canada finances part of the government's debt by creating money. The larger the proportion of the federal budget deficit that is financed by printing money, the smaller the amount that the federal government has to borrow in the private capital market and the less the upward pressure on interest rates. However, because the printing of money gave such a boost to inflation in the 1970s, the Bank, as part of its anti-inflation policy, decided in 1975 to keep the printing of new money only within certain target limits—limits that were abandoned only in 1982 in favour of a more flexible approach to changes in the money supply.

The Currency, Mint and Exchange Fund Act provides that Bank of Canada notes are legal tender and, except for gold coin, and subsidiary

Table S.37
Bank of Canada—Assets and Liabilities, December 31, 1982

Assets	$ millions	%
Government of Canada direct and guaranteed securities:		
Treasury bills	2 426.5	12.5
Other maturities	12 944.7	66.6
Advances to chartered and savings banks	143.0	0.7
Other investments	1 240.9	6.4
Foreign currency deposits	263.9	1.4
Cheques on other banks	1 635.4	8.4
Net amount of Govt. of Canada items in process of settlement	283.8	1.5
Accrued interest on investments	387.6	2.0
All other accounts	97.2	0.5
	19 422.9	100.0

Liabilities		
Notes in circulation:		
Held by chartered banks	2 228.1	11.5
Held by others	10 490.7	54.0
Canadian dollar deposits		
Government of Canada	81.0	0.4
Chartered banks	4 838.4	24.9
Government of Canada enterprises	0.6	0.0
Foreign central banks and official institutions	122.5	0.6
Other	39.5	0.2
Foreign currency liabilities	80.8	0.4
All other liabilities		
Bank of Canada cheques outstanding	1 506.2	7.8
All other accounts	35.1	0.2
	19 422.9	100.0

Source: Bank of Canada, *Review*

coins in very small amounts, the only form of legal tender in Canada. The biggest asset in the Bank of Canada's balance sheet is government securities — particularly long-term ones.

The biggest liability in the Bank of Canada's balance sheet is the amount of notes in circulation. Deposit accounts by the chartered banks comprise the next most important liability.

Fiscal Agent

Another function of the Bank of Canada is to act as the federal government's fiscal agent. Although the government is responsible for management of the national debt, the Bank of Canada provides advice and implements any changes. Thus, on behalf of the federal government, the Bank arranges the sale of new government securities, handles the withdrawal of existing ones, pays interest to security holders, and keeps all the necessary records. As fiscal agent, the Bank also operates the deposit account which the federal government keeps with the Bank and through which practically all government revenues and expenditures flow; undertakes foreign exchange transactions for the government; manages a foreign exchange fund account (designed to help stabilize the foreign exchange value of the Canadian dollar) on instructions from the federal Minister of Finance; and acts as a financial advisor to the federal government.

Bankers' Bank

A third function of the Bank of Canada is to act as a "bankers' bank." In this role, it keeps deposit accounts for the chartered banks, for various savings banks, for foreign central banks, and for various international financial institutions. It does not, it should be noted, accept deposits from the general public. The deposits that the chartered banks maintain with Canada's central bank comprise a substantial portion of their legally required cash reserves. When one chartered bank has an outstanding claim on another—for example, at the end of the cheque-clearing process—the second bank will write a cheque on its deposit account at the Bank of Canada to settle the obligation.

In its role as a bankers' bank, the Bank of Canada also has the power to make short-term loans to the chartered banks and to banks operating under the Quebec Savings Act. It can also make loans to the federal government. The minimum rate of interest that it charges is known as the *bank rate*. This rate must be made public at all times. The Bank of Canada also has the power to provide money to a chartered bank faced with unusually heavy withdrawals. Thus, if a "run" develops on a bank, the Bank of Canada can step in as a lender of last resort. The Bank also enters into purchase and resale agreements with money-market dealers. The *money-market rate* is the rate of interest at which the Bank is prepared to enter into such agreements. The minimum rate charged is slightly less than the bank rate.

Before World War II, the Bank of Canada also used to hold the country's gold reserves. It was required by law to hold, as backing for the country's money supply, gold equivalent in value to 25 per cent of its combined note and deposit liabilities. However, this requirement was abolished early in the War when it became obvious that Canada's money supply would have to be greatly increased and that gold, instead of lying in the Bank of Canada's vaults, could be more usefully employed elsewhere. Since that time, Canada has had no gold backing for its currency. The backing for the Canadian dollar is in fact the country's real output, or GNP. The larger this is in relation to the money supply, the more valuable the dollar becomes. Conversely, the larger the money supply (the total number of dollars) relative to real output, the less each dollar is actually worth in terms of purchasing power.

34.3: MONETARY POLICY

Another extremely important function of the Bank of Canada, is the establishment, in consultation with the federal government, of Canada's monetary policy and the implementation of that policy.

Monetary policy is the alteration of a country's level of interest rates and money supply so as to help achieve various economic goals, such as reducing inflation, or encouraging economic growth. There are two extremes of monetary policy—"tight" money and "easy" money, as explained below. There are also various intermediate stages of monetary policy. Usually, because of time lags, changes in monetary policy make their effects felt in the economy relatively slowly.

Tight-Money Policy

This is a policy of raising interest rates and reducing the country's money supply, or at least slowing the rate of its growth, so as to bring about a reduction in aggregate demand.

One effect of a tight-money policy is to reduce consumption. This occurs because individuals find it harder and more expensive under such a policy to borrow money or obtain credit. Furthermore, since increased unemployment and reduced job security usually accompany a tight-money policy, consumers are less willing to spend.

Another effect of a tight-money policy is to reduce business investment. On the one hand, loans for investment purposes are more difficult to obtain and, because of higher interest rates, more expensive even when obtained. On the other hand, declining consumption expenditures mean reduced sales and lower profits, and therefore less incentive to invest. This decline in investment, together with cutbacks in production, results in lower incomes and fewer jobs. As a result, consumption expenditures decline even further. And so it can continue in a steadily widening circle.

The reduced demand for goods and services that results from the decline in consumption and investment spending means, of course, a fall in the country's aggregate demand, $C + I + G + (X - M)$. This can in theory have two possible results: first, it can reduce inflationary pressure; second, it can reduce real national output and income. In practice, a tight-money policy designed to fight inflation often ends up reducing national output rather than inflation because of the highly cost-push character of inflation today.

Easy-Money Policy

This is a policy of lowering interest rates and deliberately expanding the money supply to stimulate investment and consumption and thereby increase aggregate demand. The increased money supply makes it easier and cheaper (through lower interest rates) for the public to borrow money or obtain credit. Consequently, the public is able to buy more goods and services, and consumption spending goes up. Business firms also find it easier and cheaper to borrow money and, since consumption spending is on the increase, the sales outlook for their products looks much more promising than it did before. With the improved economic climate that accompanies an easy-money policy, business people regain confidence and begin to find that investment opportunities are once more attractive. As a result, investment spending increases and the flow of income that it generates provides the means for further consumption and investment spending. In practice, governments often find that an easy-money policy has to be supplemented by other measures such as fast writeoffs on capital investments and reductions in corporate income tax rates, to say nothing of increased government spending. Restoring economic confidence is, in fact, a slow and difficult process. At the worst, a country may wallow, for some time, in a situation of *stagflation*—a combination of stagnant economic activity and inflation.

Who Decides Monetary Policy?

The Bank of Canada appeared to have been given the responsibility, when it was established in 1934, of formulating and applying Canada's monetary policy. According to the preamble of the Bank of Canada Act, Canada's central bank was to

> ... regulate credit and currency in the best interests of the economic life of the nation, to control and protect the external value of the national monetary unit and to mitigate by its influence fluctuations in the general level of production, trade, prices and employment, so far as may be possible within the scope of monetary action, and generally to promote the economic and financial welfare of the Dominion.

This statement led many people to believe that the Bank alone was responsible for determining as well as implementing a monetary policy for Canada. Others believed that the Bank was responsible for managing interest rates and the country's money supply, but in such a way as to promote the government's monetary policy. This difference of opinion came to a climax in 1960. At that time the Bank was pursuing a tight-money policy while the government was trying to stimulate the economy by budget-deficit spending. Despite Prime Minister John Diefenbaker's requests, the governor of the Bank of Canada, James Coyne, refused to alter its monetary policy, and only agreed to resign after the government had introduced legislation in Parliament declaring his job vacant.

Following the report of a Royal Commission on Banking and Finance, the Bank of Canada Act was amended in 1967, and the responsibilities of the Bank and of the government were more clearly defined. As a result, it is now laid down that the Bank is to formulate and execute Canada's monetary policy. However, the government is to have full and continuous responsibility for the policy and in the event of disagreement can issue a written and binding directive to the Bank as to the monetary policy to be followed.

In 1971, Finance Minister Edgar Benson stated that he accepted responsibility for monetary policy in Canada: "I can instruct the Bank of Canada what I want done." He said, furthermore, that the governor of the central bank does not "run off with monetary policy," without discussing it with the Minister of Finance. At the same time, however, the Finance Minister does not make significant fiscal changes without talking to the governor.[1]

"There's no need to sulk, just because I said you're setting the Bank Rate too high."

Although the federal government clearly has ultimate responsibility for monetary policy in Canada, we should note that the central bank in Canada, as well as those in other countries, has traditionally enjoyed a high degree of autonomy. The most important reason for this is that, without a relatively independent central bank, charged with the task of issuing currency, a government might finance its spending requirements merely by printing more money. This could cause a drastic increase in the money supply and in price levels. As a result, each unit of money would be worth less in real terms, and resources would have been diverted from the private to the public sector. Moreover, if the inflation were severe enough, the country's economic life could be disrupted. With a relatively autonomous central bank in sole control of the power to issue bank notes, there is a check on any increase in the money supply. The central bank, in other words, has a special role as watchdog over a country's price stability. Unfortunately, price stability and unemployment often seem to bear an inverse relationship to each other. Consequently, in trying to maintain price stability, a central bank may be thwarting a government's attempts to increase employment. This is, in fact, what happened in Canada in 1960. Consequently, as is now agreed in Canada, the central bank must, in the final analysis, accede to the government's wishes. Price stability cannot be considered to have priority over all other economic, social, and political goals, although in recent years it has certainly been given high priority in North America.

A second important reason for at least some central bank autonomy is that it encourages the central bank to give its expert advice on economic policy in general, free from political pressure; and to give a warning to the public if there seems to be a threat that government policies are endangering the stability of the currency.

A third reason for a relatively autonomous central bank is that it helps give confidence to foreign and domestic investors that financial markets in a country will remain relatively stable—that a government will not, for political purposes, interfere capriciously to upset the market value of various investments.

34.4: TOOLS OF MONETARY POLICY

There are different ways in which the Bank of Canada can implement monetary policy. First, it can alter the cash reserves of the chartered banks, so that they will have to alter, in multiple fashion, the amount of bank deposit money. Second, it can alter the secondary reserve ratio so that the same amount of secondary reserves will permit a smaller or larger amount of bank deposit-money. Third, it can alter the bank rate to encourage or discourage borrowing. And, fourth, it can use "moral suasion" to persuade the banks to reduce or expand the volume of loans.

Altering Cash Reserves

The most important way in which the Bank of Canada can alter the chartered banks' cash reserves is by selling or buying assets—notably government securities, but also gold and foreign exchange. These transactions are known as *open-market operations.*

If the Bank of Canada wishes to reduce the money supply, as part of its tight-money policy, it will sell government securities. If the securities are sold to the chartered banks (see Table 34:1), they will pay for them with cheques drawn on their deposit accounts with the central bank. Since the balances in these deposit accounts form part of the chartered banks' cash reserves, their reduction will therefore mean a fall in the banks' reserves. If some of the securities are sold to the general public, the payment for them will be made by cheques drawn on the public's deposit accounts with the banks. To settle these cheques, the banks will have to pay the Bank of Canada a similar

---

Table 34:1

Effects of the Sale of Securities by the Central Bank to the Chartered Banks

Bank of Canada's balance sheet

Assets		*Liabilities*	
Foreign Exchange		Bank of Canada notes	
Securities	−$1000	Deposits:	
Other assets		Federal government	
		Chartered banks −$1000	
		Other deposits ———	−$1000
		Other liabilities	
	−$1000		−$1000

Chartered Banks' combined balance sheet

Assets		*Liabilities*	
Cash[1]	−$1000	Deposits	
Loans and investments	+$1000	Other Liabilities	
Other assets			

---

[1]Includes deposits with the Bank of Canada.

amount from their own deposits at the central bank. This also means a fall in the chartered banks' cash reserves. If the chartered banks have excess reserves, the Bank of Canada can also "mop up" this amount by selling securities. In this way, it will effectively prevent any monetary expansion from taking place. If there are no excess reserves (or, in other words, the banks are "fully loaned up"), open-market operations will cause a reduction in cash reserves and thereby force a contraction in the money supply.

What happens if the Bank of Canada wishes to relax a tight-money policy or pursue an easy-money policy? The Bank in this case has to buy securities from the chartered banks or the general public. Where the banks are the sellers, they receive cheques drawn by the Bank of Canada on itself. When deposited, these cheques increase the balance of the chartered banks' deposits with the central bank. Thus the banks' cash reserves rise (see Table 34:2). When the Bank of Canada buys securities from the general public, it also pays for them with its own cheques. These cheques are then deposited by the public in their bank accounts. The chartered banks then present them to the Bank of Canada for payment, with the result that once again the chartered banks'

Table 34:2

Effects of the Purchase of Securities by the Central Bank from the Chartered Banks

Bank of Canada's Balance Sheet

Assets		Liabilities	
Foreign Exchange		Bank of Canada notes	
Securities	+$1000	Deposits:	
Other assets		Federal government	
		Chartered banks +$1000	
		Other deposits ———	
			+$1000
		Other liabilities	
	+$1000		+$1000

Chartered Banks' Combined Balance Sheet

Assets		Liabilities	
Cash	+$1000	Deposits	
Loans and investments	−$1000	Other liabilities	
Other assets			

deposit balances with the central bank increase. This means that cash reserves have gone up. This *may* cause an increase in the money supply, depending on the enthusiasm with which the banks promote personal and business loans. However, some of the cash may be held as excess reserves. This is where Bank of Canada persuasion becomes important.

The change in the chartered banks' cash reserves as a result of the central banks' open market operations will, as we saw in the previous chapter, cause the amount of bank deposit-money to expand or contract. With, for example, a 6 per cent cash reserve ratio, demand deposits *could* increase up to 16.7 times for every extra dollar of reserves. Conversely, demand deposits *will* decline up to 16.7 times for every dollar withdrawn from reserves. The Bank of Canada, by issuing, for example, an extra one million dollars in exchange for government bonds, can cause an expansion in Canada's supply of demand deposit money by $16.7 million. Conversely, if the Bank of Canada were to withdraw $1 million cash by selling bonds to the public, the chartered banks would lose this amount of cash and consequently would have to reduce their demand-deposit liabilities by $16.7 million. The actual expansion or contraction will depend on various factors—for example, the ability of the banks to increase or decrease deposits, the relative changes in demand deposits versus notice deposits, the willingness of the public to hold the same amount of cash as before, and the amount of any excess reserves held by the banks.

Switching Government Funds

In addition to open-market operations, the Bank of Canada can alter the chartered banks' cash reserves by switching federal government deposits from the chartered banks to the central bank, or vice versa. Such a step requires the consent of the federal Minister of Finance.

Let us assume that government funds are switched from the chartered banks to the central bank. The Bank of Canada would, on the one hand, increase the balance in the deposit account that it holds for the federal government by the amount of these funds. On the other hand, it would decrease the balances in the deposit accounts that it operates for the chartered banks. Since these deposit accounts form part of the chartered banks' cash reserves, the banks' cash reserves would therefore have been decreased. This would lead in turn, for reasons explained previously, to a multiple reduction in the amount of deposit money.

Conversely, if the Bank of Canada switches government funds from itself to the chartered banks, it reduces the balance of the federal government's account at the central bank and increases the balances of the chartered banks' accounts. This means that the banks' cash reserves have risen, permitting a multiple expansion in bank deposit-money. By switching government deposits from itself to the chartered banks, or vice versa, the Bank of Canada can alter the cash reserves of the chartered banks and the amount of bank deposit-money more quickly than by open-market operations. The Bank of Canada uses this tool of monetary policy quite frequently.

Altering the Secondary-Reserve Ratio

Until 1967, the Bank of Canada had the power to alter the chartered banks' cash reserve ratio. The 1954 Bank Act gave the Bank of Canada the power to alter the minimum legal reserve ratio to between 8 and 12 per cent of the chartered banks' deposit liabilities in Canadian dollars. In practice, however, Canada's central bank left the minimum reserve ratio at 8 per cent, on the informal understanding that the chartered banks would carry secondary reserves equivalent to 7 per cent of their deposit liabilities. These secondary, or "liquid", reserves comprised excess cash reserves, day-to-day loans to money-market dealers, and Treasury bills. Altogether, therefore, the chartered banks held a combined ratio of cash reserves and highly liquid secondary reserves equal to 15 per cent of deposit liabilities.

In 1967, when the new Bank Act was passed, certain fundamental changes were made. Instead of one legal minimum cash reserve ratio, two ratios were established—one for demand deposits (12 per cent) and another for notice deposits (4 per cent). In addition, the central bank's power to vary the cash reserve ratio was abolished. However, the chartered banks' secondary reserves were now legally recognized and the Bank of Canada authorized to set the minimum ratio for these reserves. By requiring larger secondary reserves, the Bank could force the chartered banks to switch other assets into secondary reserves and thereby restrict funds available for loans.

In 1980, as the result of a new Bank Act, the reserve ratios were changed once more. Instead of two ratios, there are now three: 10% on demand deposits, 3% on notice deposits (with 2% on the first $500 million), and 3% on foreign currency deposit liabilities. The two last ratios apply only to deposits used to finance domestic transactions.

Altering the Bank Rate

The bank rate, as stated earlier, is the minimum rate of interest that the Bank of Canada charges for loans to the chartered banks. The role of the bank rate in monetary policy is to supplement the Bank's open-market operations by signalling and enforcing desired changes in credit conditions. Thus, an increase in the bank rate generally indicates the Bank's intention to restrict credit in the economy; a reduction in the bank rate, its intention to make credit more easily available. Since the chartered banks' own interest rates to their customers vary in accordance with changes in the bank rate, the Bank of Canada in effect therefore controls the level of interest rates in Canada.

Usually the bank rate is set slightly above the rate that the chartered bank can earn on short-term investments. This means that if the banks' cash reserves are reduced by the Bank's open-market operations, the banks would find it unprofitable to borrow from the Bank of Canada, even though they wished to maintain existing credit conditions.

Not all changes in the bank rate are indications of the central bank's intentions to make money tighter or easier. Some changes are technical adjustments. The need for these arises because of the central bank's desire not to let the bank rate remain too far above the rates which the banks charge for their day-to-day loans. By keeping the gap reasonably narrow, the Bank of Canada can ensure that if the banks run extremely short of cash they will turn to the central bank for help rather than call in all their day-to-day loans and so disrupt the money market. When such a technical adjustment takes place, the governor of the Bank of Canada usually takes great pains to explain that it is only a technical adjustment and not a signal of a change in monetary policy.

Moral Suasion

Moral suasion (or "jawboning") is the practice, undertaken mainly by the central bank, of trying to persuade the chartered banks to adjust their investment and lending policies to suit current national needs. Thus, when the central bank wishes to tighten money and credit, it will ask the banks to restrict their lending. Obviously, in heeding the central bank's call, the chartered banks may have to forgo the possible profit on the loans that could have been made. They are in fact being asked to place the national interest before their own. That is why the term "moral" is used in describing this monetary tool. The governor of the Bank of Canada usually plays a leading role in the use of moral suasion. However, the Prime Minister of Canada, the federal Minister of Finance, and senior treasury officials, can also by personal contacts or public statements exert considerable influence on the banks.

Moral suasion, as a tool of monetary policy, has the advantage of being selective in its application. And the relatively small number of large chartered banks in Canada—the Big Five—makes personal persuasion, as a tool of monetary policy, quite feasible. Nevertheless, moral suasion is by no means a perfect tool. First of all, it interferes with the free operation of the capital markets. Second, the chartered banks naturally resent being told what to do. And third, the banks are often slow to act on the advice.

34.5: MONETARY, FISCAL, AND EXCHANGE-RATE POLICIES

For many years, monetary policy (changes in interest rates and the money supply) was overshadowed by fiscal policy (changes in government revenue and expenditure) in any serious discussion of income stabilization. However, for some years, a growing body of economists, led by Professor Milton Friedman, has claimed that monetary policy determines not only the level of prices, but, more important, the level of a country's Gross National Product. This monetarist school, as it is called, argues that because cash is really held only for day-to-day transactions, the velocity of circulation of money is relatively constant. Therefore, any change in the money supply will automatically cause a corresponding change in a country's aggregate demand. Consequently, if aggregate demand is less than that required for a high level of employment and economic growth, all the government need do is to increase the money supply—by, for example, open-market operations. Conversely, if there is too much inflation, all the government need do is to reduce the money supply. Monetary policy by itself, it is argued, can stabilize national income at a desirable level; fiscal policy, therefore, is unnecessary.

The other school of thought is the Keynesian one. Its adherents argue that changes in the money supply are less important than changes in credit conditions generally, and that both are less important than fiscal policy in determining the level of a country's national income, output, and employment. According to Keynesian theory, an increase in the money supply (unless offset by a fall in the velocity of circulation) causes the amount of money held by the public for speculative purposes to increase. As more money is spent on financial assets (stocks and bonds), the prices charged for them will tend to increase and interest rates will tend to fall. This decline in interest rates will help stimulate spending by consumers, business firms, and governments, and thereby help raise the level of GNP. However, the cost of borrowing is only one consideration in consumer and business spending. More important, as regards the consumer, is the expectation that he or she will continue to hold a job and earn an income. In the case of business firms, a more important consideration is the expectation that future sales will justify any new investment. Only housing is considered to be very sensitive to interest-rate reductions. Even governments are often relatively insensitive to the cost of borrowing when they believe that some public work should be undertaken. They may postpone the investment for some months, but most likely they will shop around, often abroad, to get the cheapest money at prevailing rates. In conclusion, therefore, Keynesians believe that a change in the money supply is, at best, only a slow and imprecise means of determining a country's GNP.

Canada's recent monetary experience seems to confirm the Keynesian point of view. Despite large increases in the money supply in the 1970s, long-term interest rates, rather than falling, actually climbed. The reason advanced for this apparent monetary paradox is that an increase in the money supply creates inflationary expectations; lenders, therefore, add an inflation premium to their interest rates to offset the expected rise in prices. Another explanation that has been advanced is that a lot of the extra money has been in the form of chartered bank non-personal term and notice deposits. Since these earn a substantial rate of interest and are relatively risk-free, there is no incentive to use the money to buy stocks and bonds and thereby bid up their prices. Only if the Bank of Canada were able to require a reserve ratio against these deposits higher than the present statutory 3 per cent would the banks be forced to reduce the interest paid and so encourage this money to act in the manner traditionally conceived. Also, Canada's exchange-rate policy affects the level of interest rates. In order to attract short-term capital to Canada, the Bank of Canada may need to set the bank rate at a level higher than that in the U.S. Whatever the reasons, it would seem that changes in the money supply are not as powerful in stimulating an increase in national income and GNP as the monetarists suggest. There can be little doubt, however, that high interest rates and a reduction in the rate of growth of the money supply can eventually curtail economic growth (as with the 1980-83 recession) and that an increase in the money supply is a necessary condition for continuing economic growth. Nevertheless, fiscal policy—that is, changes in government revenue and expenditure, with its direct multiplier effect on income and employment—does seem to be a much more effective and efficient tool for helping to stabilize a country's GNP at a desirable level than does monetary policy.

A critical problem in Canada today is that the large government budget deficit (fiscal policy) creates a government demand for funds in the capital market which at the same time is trying to meet a rising demand for funds from the private sector. And this puts government fiscal policy on a collision course with monetary policy. This is because the Bank of Canada can only ease the pressure on the capital market by satisfying a larger proportion of the government's need for cash by printing more money—and thereby adding to inflation.

Exchange Rate Policy

No discussion of monetary and fiscal policies can legitimately ignore a country's exchange rate policy. Unless there is harmony of purpose among these three types of economic policy, the effects of one may cancel the effects of another. Thus, if the federal government adopts an expansionary monetary policy, yet at the same time restricts government spending, there may be little increase in employment. Or if the government encourages employment by an easy-money policy, it may, on the other hand, reduce exports and employment in Canada by holding the foreign exchange value of the Canadian dollar at too high a level. This would mean that Canadian goods are priced out of foreign markets, and imports into Canada are encouraged, often at the expense of domestically produced goods. In recent years, a partially floating exchange rate for the Canadian dollar has reduced this danger. Nevertheless, high interest rates in Canada in recent years (compared with rates in Western Europe) have caused the Canadian dollar to appreciate compared with the European and other foreign currencies. Because Canada's interest rate levels are similar to the U.S. ones, there has been very little appreciation of the Canadian dollar against the U.S. one.

34.6: CANADA'S RECENT MONETARY POLICY

In the mid-1970s, Canada, like other Western industrial democracies, began to suffer from "stagflation"—a combination of both relatively stagnant economic activity and inflation. Whereas real GNP grew by an average of 5 per cent per annum during the period 1966-1973, it increased by an average of only 2.8 per cent per annum in the period 1974-1981. And unemployment, which had averaged 5.0 per cent during 1966-1973, rose to 7.3 per cent during the 1974-1981 period. Inflation, which had averaged 5.0 per cent per annum during the period 1966-1973 (as measured by the Consumer Price Index), instead of slowing down, as the economy puttered along, rose sharply to 10.9 per cent in 1974.

To combat this sharp increase in the inflation rate the federal government announced a new economic policy in October 1975. This involved strict control over the growth of Canada's money supply, with a gradual reduction in the rate of growth, and a temporary three-year program of wage and price controls. Other non-monetary aspects of this policy were restraint in government spending and measures to improve competition in the market-place.

In accordance with this policy, the Bank of Canada set specific target rates of growth for Canada's money supply, gradually lowering the rate of increase from between 10 and 15 per cent a year in 1975 to between 4 and 8 per cent of M1 in 1981, with the aim of lowering aggregate demand. The Bank of Canada also used higher interest rates as part of its anti-inflation policy but was forced to raise the Bank rate to record levels in the early 1980s in step with those set by the U.S. Federal Reserve Board (the chief monetary authority in the United States).

Despite the Bank of Canada's reduction in the rate of increase in the money supply, the rate of inflation continued at a high level during the second half of the 1970s. This was due partly to the size of the federal deficit but also to structural reasons: wage and price expectations (cost-push inflation); productivity performance; prices of imported manufactured goods; and world price movements, particularly for crude oil and food.

In November, 1982, Gerald Bouey, the Governor of the Bank of Canada, announced that the Bank's seven-year experiment in monetary targeting had been abandoned. Although unstated, the implication was that the Bank would, instead, react as required to each new set of economic circumstances. Disillusionment with monetary targeting seems to have stemmed from the fact that there were always too many extraneous factors at work to permit a policy of gradualism in the increase of Canada's money supply. Thus, for example, the impact of the introduction of Canada's National Energy Program in 1980 with the resultant outflow of capital from Canada and pressure on the Canadian dollar forced the Bank to switch its emphasis at that time to exchange rate policy.

There seems little doubt in the early 1980s that the Bank of Canada, headed by its Governor, Gerald Bouey, will continue to give priority to the fight against inflation. And one important tool will be control of the growth in Canada's money supply. According to Bouey: "... We continue to believe that monetary policy must move toward a trend of monetary expansion that will permit economic growth without inflation. With careful interpretation, the aggregates that are available provide a basis for judging the trend"[2] In the past, the Bank focused its attention on M1 (currency in circulation plus demand deposits) in setting its monetary growth targets. However, because of the existence of other types of money, it may turn to another aggregate, M1A, which adds "non-personal notice deposits" to the M1 figure. The Bank Governor has also stressed the need for a stable exchange rate, but not necessarily at its present level.

Canadian monetary policy, we should recognize, cannot differ greatly from that followed in the U.S. This is because over 70 per cent, by value, of Canada's international trade is with that country. Consequently, if the inflation rate in Canada exceeds that in the U.S., Canadian exports will become less competitive. And if the Bank of Canada lets the foreign exchange rate for the Canadian dollar drop even further to keep export prices down, Canadian imports would then cost more in Canadian dollars. So also would the servicing and repayment cost of the heavy Canadian borrowing abroad that has occurred in the past and which is denominated, both interest and principal, in U.S. dollars or other hard currencies.

Canadian monetary policy is not only tied to that of the U.S. in the area of monetary growth (and thereby the rate of inflation) but also in the area of interest rates. There is an enormous amount of private capital (from corporations, banks and individuals) that is on short-term deposit in Canada to pay for daily commercial transactions; capital that can easily be transferred out of the country if interest rates become lower than in the U.S. This outflow of funds would severely impact Canada's international balance of payments and force down the foreign exchange rate for the Canadian dollar—something that the federal government and the Bank of Canada would seem reluctant to see occur for both political and economic reasons, particularly below 80 cents U.S.

It was no coincidence therefore that the abandonment of monetary targeting in Canada in 1982 occurred about the same time that Paul Volcker, the Chairman of the Federal Reserve Board, announced a similar change in the U.S. Nor was it a coincidence that the Bank of Canada's interest rate (on which all other Canadian ones are based) marched steeply upward, in line with the Federal Reserve Board rate, as Mr. Volcker set out, in September 1979 to break the inflationary spiral in the U.S. with a policy of strict monetarism that lasted until Fall 1982. Nor was it a coincidence that interest rates in Canada came down in 1983 in line with the U.S. ones.

Future U.S. monetary policy is expected to be more flexible than it was in the years 1979 to 1982—when monetary targets decided how the Federal Reserve Board would set interest rates and carry out its money market operations. Now that the U.S. inflation rate has dropped to a range of 4 to 5 per cent, the emphasis is on economic recovery. Although also facing, as in Canada, huge government budget deficits, the Federal Reserve Board believes that it can afford to place less stress on strict monetary targets. Instead it will take into account the whole performance of the U.S. economy in deciding when and for how long it will permit extra large increases in the money supply. Also two broader definitions of the money supply, M-2 and M-3, which include interest-bearing deposits, will be used instead of M-1 to provide guidance.

Summary

1. The Bank of Canada was established by the federal government in 1934 to serve as Canada's central bank. All of its capital stock is now owned by the federal government.
2. Management of the Bank is entrusted to a government-appointed board of directors. The federal Deputy Minister of Finance is a non-voting board member.
3. The Bank's functions include: issuing bank notes; acting as a "bankers' bank"; and helping to formulate, and actually implementing, the government's monetary policy.
4. The Bank issues its notes to the government in exchange for government securities; in other words, it monetizes public debt.
5. As fiscal agent, the Bank manages the national debt, operates the government's deposit account, undertakes foreign exchange transactions for the government, manages a foreign exchange fund account, and provides financial advice to the government.
6. As a bankers' bank, the Bank of Canada keeps deposit accounts for the chartered banks, for various savings banks, for foreign central banks, and for various international financial institutions. It can also make short-term loans to the federal government, to the chartered banks, and to banks operating under the Quebec Savings Act. It can also enter into purchase and resale agreements with money-market dealers.
7. The Bank of Canada helps to establish the country's monetary policy and is responsible for its implementation.
8. Monetary policy is the process of altering a country's money supply so as to help achieve various economic goals. There are two extremes of monetary policy — "tight" money and "easy" money, with various intermediate stages.
9. A tight-money policy is a policy of raising interest rates and reducing the rate of growth of the country's money supply so as to bring about a reduction in aggregate demand. Usually a tight-money policy succeeds more in reducing national output and income than in reducing inflationary pressures. This is because of the predominantly cost-push nature of inflation today.
10. An easy-money policy is a policy of lowering interest rates and

increasing the rate of growth of the country's money supply so as to bring about an increase in aggregate demand. By itself, this policy is not usually very effective or quick in raising aggregate demand. This is because business firms need more than easily available funds to persuade them to invest, and business investment is a prime component of aggregate demand.

11. The federal government is responsible for monetary policy in Canada, and, if necessary, can issue direct instructions to the Bank of Canda. Monetary policy and fiscal policy are usually co-ordinated.

12. There are various good reasons why a country's central bank should posses a high degree of autonomy. The most important is to ensure that a government does not indulge in a money-printing and spending orgy that would debase the value of the currency.

13. The Bank of Canada can implement its monetary policy by altering the chartered banks' cash reserves, by altering the bank rate, and by using "moral suasion".

14. The Bank of Canada can alter the chartered banks' cash reserves by open-market operations (by buying or selling of government securities) and by switching government funds from itself to the chartered banks, or vice versa.

15. The 1967 Bank Act abolished the Bank of Canada's power to vary the cash reserve ratio. However, it gave the Bank the power to set the minimum secondary reserve ratio.

16. *Bank rate* is the minimum rate of interest that the Bank of Canada charges for loans to the chartered banks. This rate, on which the chartered banks' own lending rates are based, acts as a signal of desired credit conditions, and can be altered by the Bank.

17. The Governor of the Bank of Canada uses personal persuasion (called "moral suasion" or "jawboning") to encourage the chartered banks and other financial institutions to support the government's monetary policy by their own borrowing and lending activities.

18. Monetary policy should not be viewed in isolation. Equally important in Canada are the government's fiscal and exchange rate policies. For maximum results, the three types of economic policy should be part of a concerted government economic program.

19. Top priorities in Canada's future monetary policy are continued monetary restraint and exchange rate stability. However, Canada's monetary policy must be kept in line with the U.S. one, because of trade and capital ties.

Key Terms

Central bank   671
Bank notes   673
Monetizing public
   debt   673
Fiscal agent   675
Bankers' bank   675
Cheque-clearing
   process   675
Bank rate   675
Money-market rate   676
Monetary policy   676
Tight money   676

Easy money   677
Cash reserves   681
Open-market operations   681
Moral suasion
   (jawboning)   685
Switching government
   funds   683
Secondary-reserve
   ratio   684
Fiscal policy   686
Exchange rate policy   688
Monetary targets   689

Review Questions

1. When and why was the Bank of Canada established?
2. How is the Bank of Canada owned and managed?
3. How does the Bank of Canada exercise its note-issuing function?
4. What is involved in the Bank of Canada's role as fiscal agent for the federal government?
5. "The Bank of Canada acts as a 'bankers' bank'." Explain.
6. What is the "backing" for the Canadian dollar?
7. What is monetary policy? Distinguish between tight money and easy money.
8. How can a tight-money policy reduce aggregate demand? How effective can a tight-money policy be in fighting inflation?
9. What shortcomings does an easy-money policy have in overcoming an economic recession?
10. Who decides monetary policy in Canada?
11. Why should a central bank enjoy a high degree of autonomy?
12. "The Bank of Canada can increase or reduce the chartered banks' cash reserves by open-market operations and by switching government funds." Explain.
13. Why is it that a change in the chartered banks' cash reserves does not always mean an automatic change in the size of the country's money supply?
14. What is meant by the secondary-reserve ratio? How can the Bank of Canada affect the country's money supply by altering the size of this ratio?

15. What is bank rate? How is it used as a tool of monetary policy?
16. What is "moral suasion"? What are its advantages and disadvantages as a tool of monetary policy?
17. "Monetary policy cannot be viewed in isolation from other economic policies." Explain and discuss.
18. Can Canada pursue a monetary policy independent of the U.S. one? If so, at what cost?
19. Explain and discuss the role of monetary policy in the world economic recession of 1980-83.

References

1   Finance Minister's press conference, report in *The Globe and Mail*, Toronto, June 19, 1971.
2   *Annual Report*, Bank of Canada, Ottawa, 1983.

35. INTEREST RATES

CHAPTER OBJECTIVES

A. To emphasize the fact that high interest rates can depress a country's economic activity
B. To explain why there are many different interest rates
C. To examine the demand for loans in Canada by the public, governments, and business firms
D. To examine the supply of loans from different sources
E. To indicate how the interaction of demand for and supply of funds influences the level of interest rates

CHAPTER OUTLINE

35.1 Effect of High Interest Rates
35.2 Different Rates of Interest
35.3 Demand for Funds
35.4 Supply of Funds
35.5 Demand, Supply, and the Rate of Interest

35.1: EFFECT OF HIGH INTEREST RATES

In the early 1980s, interest rates in Canada reached record highs. As a result, an unusually large number of business firms slid into bankruptcy as borrowing costs became a major expense. Even industrial giants looked as if they might go under and in some cases (for example, Dome Petroleum) had to be bailed out by the federal government. In the consumer area, thousands of private individuals and their families were forced to abandon their homes as mortgage renewal time arrived and others already living in rental accommodation were forced to abandon their dreams of home ownership. Other individuals, considering the purchase of cars, furniture, appliances and other consumer durables on credit, were stopped in their tracks. Conversely, when interest rates are low, business firms are much more willing to borrow and invest. Consumers also are more confident in signing for mortgage and other consumer loans and buying on credit.

35.2: DIFFERENT RATES OF INTEREST

Interest is the money paid by a borrower to a lender for the use of the lender's money. The percentage rate of interest is the amount of interest divided by the sum borrowed (the *principal*) multiplied by 100. The rate of interest may be considered to be the "price" that a borrower pays for the use of someone else's money. There are in fact many different interest rates in Canada, depending on the type of loan, its purpose, size, the risk involved, the time period involved, the credit rating of the borrower, and a number of other factors. The underlying market forces that help to determine the rates of interest are the demand for, and supply of, loanable funds.

The rate of interest that the Bank of Canada charges (see Table S.38) on loans to the chartered banks is called the "Bank rate". The rate that the chartered banks charge their best customers is called the *prime rate*. Other business customers are charged a rate that is one or two percentage points above the prime rate, according to their credit standing and availability of *collateral*—assets that can be pledged to the bank by the borrower as security for repayment of the loan. The general public is charged even more for "consumer loans" for the purchase of cars, boats, etc. and other "consumer durables". And some credit card interest rates exceed 20 per cent per annum.

Until 1967, the federal government, by means of the Bank Act, set a maximum rate of interest that the banks could charge. Now the banks set their own rates, usually in line with those of each other, in accordance with the Bank of Canada's rate of interest. The large chartered banks, we should remember, are relatively few in number and have every incentive to minimize price competition amongst themselves and to keep the "spread" between their own borrowing rates and their lending rates as wide as possible. Instead, they concentrate on non-price competition such as advertising, conveniently located banking facilities, financial advice, pleasant, courteous staff, and, at one time, quick service. Trust companies and other financial institutions, specializing in long-term loans, also stress non-price competition, including the establishment of their own real-estate sales offices as a means of obtaining a dependable outlet for their mortgage funds.

Table S.38
Interest Rates in Canada, 1970-1982

Years	Bank rate	3-month Treasury Bills	Government of Canada bonds: over 10 years	Prime corporate paper: 90 days	Bank prime lending rate	5-year conventional mortgage rate
		(Annual average, in per cent)				
1970	7.13	5.99	7.91	7.34	8.17	10.45
1971	5.19	3.56	6.95	4.51	6.48	9.43
1972	4.75	3.56	7.23	5.10	6.00	9.21
1973	6.13	5.47	7.56	7.45	7.65	9.59
1974	8.50	7.82	8.90	10.51	10.75	11.24
1975	8.50	7.39	9.03	7.94	9.42	11.43
1976	9.29	8.87	9.18	9.17	10.04	11.78
1977	7.71	7.33	8.70	7.47	8.50	10.36
1978	8.98	8.68	9.27	8.83	9.69	10.59
1979	12.10	11.69	10.21	12.07	12.90	11.98
1980	12.89	12.79	12.48	13.15	14.25	14.32
1981	17.93	17.72	15.22	18.33	19.29	18.15
1982	13.96	13.66	14.26	14.15	15.81	17.90

Source: Bank of Canada, *Review*, monthly

35.3: DEMAND FOR LOANS

The demand for loans within a country comes from three main sources: individuals, governments, and business firms. There is also a certain amount of overseas demand. Let us consider each source in turn.

Public Demand

There are many goods that we, as individuals, would like to have but do not usually have enough money to pay for. We can, if we are patient, put aside part of our income each week or month. However, for large purchases such as a car or house, this process of saving could take many years. By the time that we have saved enough money to buy a house, any children that we might have could have grown up and left home and one of the main reasons for owning a house would have disappeared. It is not surprising, therefore, that many individuals are willing to pay more to have an item now than to wait until the distant future when the need may no longer exist. They can do this by borrowing money and paying interest on the amount borrowed, or *principal* of the loan.

This desire to have something now rather than wait until later is called, in economics, the consumer's *time preference*. This time preference will, of course, vary from person to person. Some people will pay practically any price to have an item now, while others will patiently save and bide their time. Certainly, in times of inflation, it makes sense to borrow now to buy a house rather than wait until the future when it may cost a lot more. Also, of course, as inflation reduces the purchasing power of the dollar, the repayments become less onerous as the years go by. However, to offset the effects of inflation, lenders are now charging much higher rates of interest than they used to do.

Another consideration is the vast amount of advertising pressure put on the average family to buy more goods and services. This makes it extremely difficult for people to save enough to finance any major purchase. Borrowing money and having to repay the principal involved gradually, is in effect a kind of forced saving that many people find quite necessary. The fact that so much of the spending of the average Canadian family is for costly *consumer durables*, such as a house, a car, household appliances, television, and furniture, also helps make borrowing a normal part of our way of life.

Borrowing by the public takes two basic forms. A sum of money may be borrowed from a bank, finance company, or other lender and the money used to pay for the good desired. Alternatively, the seller of the good may do the lending. The individual, instead of borrowing the money from someone else to pay the purchase price, obtains the good from the seller with little or no immediate payment. What the seller is really doing is lending the purchaser the money to buy the seller's own goods. Each month the purchaser is required to pay to the seller, interest on the amount of credit received together with some repayment of the principal. Often the financing is arranged on behalf of the seller by a finance company or bank. In many cases, the buyer has been pre-screened for his or her credit-worthiness, and given a *credit rating* (or assessment of credit-worthiness). He or she may also have been provided with a *credit card*, authorizing credit purchases up to a certain amount, or more with telephone authorization up to an agreed credit limit. Nowadays, the use of credit cards has become extremely widespread. In the future, it is predicted that most, if not all of our purchases will be made in this way. Whatever form the individual's borrowing takes—either bank loan or store credit—it comprises part of the total demand by individuals for loans and so helps to determine the level of interest rates that are charged.

The demand for loans by individuals reflects, to a considerable extent, the public's confidence in the future. If the economy is booming and jobs are easy to find, people are more willing to assume a large burden of debt. In time of economic stagnation, uncertainty about future income makes people more cautious about assuming new debt obligations. Whatever the state of demand, consumers tend to borrow more when the interest rate falls. In other words, the individual's demand curve for loans is downward-sloping from left to right.

Government Demand

Another important component of the total demand for loans is borrowing by federal, provincial, and municipal governments, and by their various agencies. The money is used, in the case of governments, to help make up any difference between total expenditure on the one hand and total tax and other revenue on the other. Part of the expenditure, such as that on income-security programs, may be considered as consumption. The other part—for example, the construction of highways and the payment of public employee salaries—may be considered as production. This means, therefore, that only part of the money borrowed is being used as capital in the sense of a factor of production.

Because of political and social pressures, government spending needs in Canada are constantly expanding. However, because of the already high level of taxation, it is not easy for the government to increase its tax and other revenues without further discouragement of private investment. With very few exceptions, government spending plans are constantly outrunning revenues, with the result that governments are competing more and more with business firms and individuals for a share of the existing supply of loanable funds. This competition would be even more intense if foreign capital markets were not also available to satisfy some of our governments' borrowing needs. Because governments are now such an important component in the demand for loanable funds, they are one of the main determinants of the level of interest rates. Unlike individuals, the government does not necessarily increase its demand for funds when interest rates fall. In other words, the government demand curve is much more inelastic than the consumer one.

Business Demand

The largest source of demand for loans is business firms. This money is normally used in conjunction with the ownership or *equity* capital, to provide working capital and fixed capital for the various types of businesses.

Working capital is money used to buy stocks of materials and merchandise and to pay for employee services and other manufacturing or marketing expenses. The finished product is then sold either for cash or on credit and finally cash flows back into the firm. The funds invested in working capital can therefore be imagined as a pool which is constantly being drained on the one hand by expenses and replenished on the other by revenue received. The borrowed money, not used for working capital, is used to pay for fixed assets. This *fixed capital* of a business consists of land, buildings, machinery, tools, furniture, trucks, and cars. Of course, not all the fixed capital is owned by the business. Nowadays, most firms, to improve their working capital position, lease a large part of their fixed assets—ranging from cars to computers—from leasing firms.

For a business firm, the decision to borrow money is based on considerations quite different from those of individuals or governments. A business firm looks on borrowed money as a factor of production. The money capital enables it to cover operating expenses and pay for fixed assets. Consequently, the business firm, in deciding to borrow, will compare the expected return from this extra money with the rate of interest—the cost of borrowing it. The same comparison is made when considering the reinvestment of profit or the raising of additional outside equity capital; the only difference is that the rate of interest is an imputed one, reflecting the "opportunity cost" (or what such funds could have earned if invested elsewhere). The expected return (called in economics the *marginal revenue product*) can, for convenience, be expressed as a percentage of the cost of the additional machine or other capital good purchased with the borrowed money. Thus, if a machine costing $1000 results in additional, annual net income of $200, the marginal revenue product of the machine is 20 per cent per annum. If the loan costs 16 per cent per annum, then it is profitable for a firm to borrow the money and purchase the machine.

The business demand for loans (Figure 35:1) varies directly with the rate of interest at which the money can be borrowed. If the rate is reduced, investment opportunities not profitable before will now look attractive. The demand curve for loans (called the *marginal efficiency of capital*, or *MEC curve*) is, in other words, relatively elastic—that is, considerably more money will be demanded at a lower price than at a higher price. Thus, in Figure 35:1 only $1.4 million of investment will be undertaken when the cost of borrowing is 25 per cent per year, but there will be $6 million of investment at an interest rate of 5 per cent.

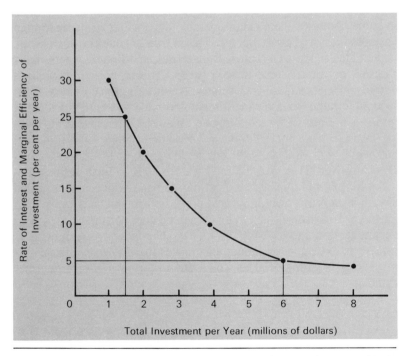

Note: Investment projects are spread along the horizontal axis, those with the highest expected rate of return being closest to the point of origin.

Figure 35:1   The Marginal Efficiency of Investment

The actual level of demand will also depend very much on the general economic climate and business expectations as to the future. If the country is prospering, business executives will tend to take an optimistic view of the future. And since it is the *expected* rate of return that counts because it takes time for an investment to be completed and start yielding a return, demand for loans will be high. The exact opposite will be the case in time of economic contraction.

In Canada, the business demand for funds in recent years has also included another and unusual element. This has been the borrowing to help pay for "take-overs" of firms previously owned by foreigners.

We have seen that both business (the major borrower) and the public have a relatively elastic demand for loans. Only government demand is relatively interest-insensitive. The demand for loans as a whole tends therefore to be relatively interest-elastic. As a result, the total demand curve for loans is downward-sloping from left to right.

Investment Abroad

In some countries there is considerable demand for loans by foreign business firms and governments. This is true of countries such as the United States, West Germany, Switzerland, and Britain, where many overseas borrowers come to seek funds. Canada, as an industralized but nevertheless still underdeveloped country, is capital hungry. Consequently, rather than having foreign firms and governments looking for loans in Canada, we see our governments and business firms seeking loans in New York, Bonn, and elsewhere. Some large Canadian business firms, particularly the chartered banks, do invest funds overseas, however. This investment therefore adds to total business demand for loans in Canada. Much of this demand is, of course, satisfied directly by a firm's own reinvested profit (a form of equity capital). In other words, a firm wishing to invest abroad does not always need to go outside its doors to look for the money. The federal government, as part of its foreign-aid program, also makes loans to economically underdeveloped countries. This, too, adds to the total government demand.

35.4: SUPPLY OF LOANS

We have briefly considered the nature of the demand for loans. Let us now consider the sources of supply.

The Public

Whereas many people borrow money to enable them to spend more than their current disposable income, others save and invest part of their income. Some individuals are also borrowing and saving at the same time. For most households, there is a common pattern of borrowing and saving. When a family is young, the demand for money is exceptionally heavy. Feeding, clothing, and otherwise caring for young children; buying, furnishing, and equipping a house; paying for medical, educational, transportation, and vacation needs are all expenses that tend to be large initially but decline as the family grows older. Also, income often increases as a mother re-enters the labour force. Indeed, when the house is paid for and the children have left home, the average married couple are often at their earnings peak. The higher this disposable income becomes, the easier it is to save. Changes in the rate of interest as an inducement to save are by contrast relatively insignificant.

Saving money from one's disposable income is, of course, one thing. Lending it is another. As we said at the beginning of this chapter, a person, by lending money, is giving up its use. Some people, in fact, prefer to keep their savings hidden around the house—but these people are the exception rather than the rule. However, the public in general will not want to lend all the cash it has. The amount that the public wishes to hold, called its *liquidity preference*, depends on three factors: the transactions motive, the precautionary motive, and the speculative motive.

The *transactions motive* is the need of individuals (and also of business firms and governments) to have enough cash to carry on their daily business. The *precautionary motive* is a person's desire to hold cash for emergencies. The *speculative motive* is a person's desire to hold cash rather than stocks, bonds, and other assets in order to be able quickly to take advantage of some unforeseen investment opportunity.

Although the public's willingness to save is not considered to be greatly influenced by the rate of interest, the same cannot be said of the public's willingness to lend its money. If the rate of interest is very low, people tend to hold more of their savings in the form of cash, including non-interest-bearing bank deposits. Conversely, if the rate of interest is high, people tend to reduce their cash balances and lend more money.

Governments

We must remember that not all the money obtained from individuals and business firms in the form of taxes, unemployment insurance, and pension-plan contributions is used by government to pay for current operating expenses. As well as paying salaries and wages to the civil service and meeting the cost of supplies, governments also use a part of their revenue to finance investment expenditures. Many of these are undertaken by government agencies which borrow money from the government. Also, money borrowed from the goverment by such agencies as the Federal Business Development Bank is used to make loans to the business sector. These loans constitute part of a country's total supply of loans.

Business firms

As an original source of long-term loans, other than for reinvestment, business firms are relatively unimportant. We exclude, of course, from this general statement firms such as trust companies, life-insurance companies, mutual funds, and mortgage corporations that act as financial intermediaries. Such firms are really "go-betweens", channelling savings from private individuals, trusts, pension funds, etc. on the one hand to individuals, government, and business borrowers on the other.

The most important form of lending that the average business firm undertakes is to invest any temporary surplus of working capital in short-term interest-bearing money-market instruments such as bank certificates of deposit. These temporary surpluses are usually caused by seasonal variations in business activity. At peak periods of the year, a firm may be extremely busy and require a great deal of working capital. At other times, it may have more than it needs. The surplus is therefore available for short-term lending.

Banks

To some degree, the chartered banks act as financial intermediaries, receiving the savings of individuals, business firms, and even governments on the one hand and lending it out to other individuals and business firms on the other. But the banks also have the power to expand the money supply so long as they maintain the required cash reserve ratios. This expansion of the money supply is implemented by the banks by means of the purchase of more investments or an increase in loans. As a result, the banks must be considered important original suppliers of short-term loans.

Foreign Lenders

Canada, ever since its inception, has looked abroad for a major part of its capital needs. Most of the major investment projects such as oil, mining, and hydro-electric power development, have depended upon foreign lenders or investors for a considerable part of their financing.

This means that the supply of loans is much larger than that available within the country alone.

There is also a vast amount of short-term capital switched from one country to another according to relative international levels of interest rates. Thus, if the rates are higher in Canada than in the United States, short-term funds flow into this country adding to the existing domestic supply. Conversely, when Canadian rates are relatively low, short-term funds flow out, reducing the local supply.

35.5: DEMAND, SUPPLY, AND THE RATE OF INTEREST

We have now looked at the demand for and supply of loans. Within a country, the public, governments, and business firms all exert varying influences on total demand and total supply. However, the most important determinant of the level of interest rates in Canada is undoubtedly the federal government. This importance is based partly on the effects that government demands for borrowed funds have on the total capital market. In wartime this demand is overwhelming. But, even in peacetime, with a large public debt to be periodically refunded, and persistently huge budget deficits to be financed, it is quite substantial. In fact, one of the major criticisms of Canada's present fiscal policy, with its consistently large deficits, is its disruptive influence on the capital market—making it harder and more expensive for the private sector to obtain investment funds.

On the supply side, the Bank of Canada, as part of the Government's monetary policy, can increase or decrease chartered bank reserves and so make bank loans easier or harder to obtain. It can also use its powers of "moral suasion" (or "jawboning") to persuade banks and other financial institutions to make credit easier or harder to obtain. And, extremely important, it can set the *bank rate*—the rate of interest that the Bank charges on money loaned to the chartered banks and which, indirectly, determines the rates of interest that the banks and other lenders charge to their customers. That is why we talk about the government's *interest rate policy*—the level of interest rates that the government decides is suitable for the country as part of its overall economic policy. The action of the Bank of Canada, in setting the Bank rate, is similar in effect on the Canadian capital market to the government setting prices (e.g. wage rates, or rental rates) in any other market. Thus a high bank rate will increase the supply of funds and decrease the demand for them. And a low rate, the opposite.

A complicating factor, in Canada's case, is the balance of international payments. If it is in a critical condition, relatively high interest rates may be necessary in Canada to attract and keep short-term investment funds from abroad, thereby increasing the surplus on the capital account in Canada's balance of international payments. This factor seemed the predominant one behind the high interest-rate policy of the early 1980s when it was felt necessary to match the high interest rates prevalent in the U.S.

Also of great importance, the availability of loanable funds in foreign capital markets helps relieve the pressure on the domestic market. For the foreseeable future, it appears that Canadians will continue to seek money abroad to supplement local supplies of loan capital rather than that foreigners will come to seek money in capital-hungry Canada.

Summary

1. The cost of borrowing money is called the *rate of interest*. If rates of interest become very high, the economy can slowly grind to a halt. If they are low, business investment and consumer borrowing and credit buying are encouraged.
2. In practice, there are many different rate of interest because of the type of loan, its purpose, size, the risk involved, the time period, and the credit standing of the borrower.
3. The "Bank rate" is the rate of interest charged by the Bank of Canada to the chartered banks. The "prime rate" is the rate of interest charged by the chartered banks to their best customers.
4. The demand for loans comes from the public, governments, business firms, and foreigners.
5. Individuals borrow according to their *time preference*; that is, the desire to have something now rather than wait until the future, when enough money might have been accumulated. Borrowing may take the form of actual cash borrowed or the purchase of goods on credit. The demand for loans by the public reflects, to a considerable extent, the public's confidence in the country's economic future.
6. Governments borrow to cover any excess of expenditure over revenue, or to refinance existing government debt.
7. Business firms constitute the largest source of demand for loans. The money is used, in conjunction with ownership capital, to provide (a) *working capital*—the money used to buy stocks of materials and merchandise and to pay for employee services and other manufacturing or marketing expenses; and (b) *fixed capital*—such fixed assets as land, buildings, machinery, tools, furniture, trucks, and cars.

8. In deciding whether to borrow, the business firm compares the expected return on this capital (the *marginal efficiency of capital*) with the rate of interest (the cost of borrowing it). The actual level of business demand for loans will depend very much on the general economic climate and businesspeople's expectations as to the future. Canada, a capital-hungry country, does not experience a large foreign demand for loans.

9. The main sources of supply of loans are the public, governments, business firms, and foreign lenders.

10. The amount of money that the public wishes to hold is called its *liquidity preference* which is, in turn, determined by three factors: (a) the *transactions motive*—the need for enough cash to carry on daily business; (b) the *precautionary motive*—the desire by individuals to hold cash for emergencies; and (c) the *speculative motive*—the desire to hold cash rather than stocks, bonds, or other assets for fear of loss. Interest rate levels greatly influence the public's willingness to lend money.

11. Governments use part of their revenue to make loans to various government agencies. Business firms, other than financial intermediaries, are a relatively unimportant original source of long-term loans. However, they do make a considerable amount of short-term loans. The banks are very important short-term lenders. Foreign lenders supply large amounts of short and long-term loans to Canadian borrowers.

12. Various sectors of the economy participate in the demand for and supply of loans. However, the federal government, with its large budget deficits, is making it harder for private business firms to obtain investment funds at reasonable cost.

Key Terms

Interest 696
Rate of interest 696
Principal 696
Bank rate 696
Prime rate 696
Collateral 696
Consumer loans 696
Consumer durables 696
Demand for loans 698
Time preference 698

Borrowing 698
Credit rating 699
Credit card 699
Working capital 700
Fixed capital 700
Opportunity cost 700
Marginal revenue
  product 701
Marginal efficiency
  of capital 701

Review Questions

1. What is the rate of interest? What significance does it have for business investment?
2. Why are there many different rate of interest, not just one? What is the pure rate of interest?
3. How do individuals borrow? Why do they borrow? What factors can cause the amount of borrowing by individuals to vary considerably?
4. What types of borrowing do governments in Canada undertake? For what purposes do governments borrow?
5. Distinguish between the working capital and the fixed capital of a business.
6. Why do business firms borrow?
7. What is the marginal efficiency of investment? What is its significance for business borrowing?
8. To what extent do foreigners constitute a part of the total demand for loans in Canada?
9. How do individuals contribute to the supply of loans in Canada?
10. What is liquidity preference? How is it determined? And what is its significance?
11. What is the relationship between the rate of interest and the amount of savings by individuals?
12. How do governments in Canada contribute to the supply of loans?
13. What is the most usual type of short-term lending by business firms? Explain the special role of financial intermediaries.
14. To what extent do foreign lenders contribute to the supply of loans in Canada? Explain the special position of short-term funds.
15. The most important determinant of the level of interest rates in Canada is the government. Discuss.
16. How have interest rates varied in Canada in recent years?
17. Explain the role of the "Bank rate" in Canada's capital market.

36. STOCKS, BONDS, AND THE CANADIAN CAPITAL MARKET

CHAPTER OBJECTIVES

A. To explain the need for a capital, or securities, market in a modern industrial society

B. To examine the three main parts of the Canadian capital market: the money market, the stock market, and the bond market

C. To explain the functions of each part of the Canadian capital market and the financial instruments used

D. To discuss the role of the investment dealer

E. To examine the various financial intermediaries that gather funds and invest them in the capital market

CHAPTER OUTLINE

36.1: NEED FOR A BORROWING AND LENDING MECHANISM

Throughout history, whatever the society, there have been people who wish to borrow and others who wish to lend. In a modern industrial society, governments seek to borrow large amounts of short- and long-term funds to finance budget deficits and to bridge temporary differences between revenue and expenditure flows. Business corporations seek both borrowed capital and equity capital to enable them to start new ventures and enlarge existing production facilities. There are, on the other hand, many institutions such as banks, trust companies, insurance companies, mutual funds and pension funds, as well as private individuals, with money to invest.

36.2: CAPITAL MARKET AND OTHER TERMS DEFINED

If the government is to be able to function properly, and if business corporations are to be able to grow, there must be a mechanism for moving funds from would-be lenders to would-be borrowers. In fact, there is in Canada and most other economically developed countries, an intricate network of institutions and individuals, called the *capital* or *securities market*, specializing in just this task. Their work includes the transferring of funds, the changing of ownership of the financial claims involved, and the provision of financial advice. The process of transferring funds is known as *financial intermediation*; and the participants, the chartered banks for example, are known as *financial intermediaries*. The process of handling changes in ownership of financial claims is known as *financial brokerage*; and its participants are known as *stockbrokers* and *investment dealers*. The financial claims handled included both primary securities and indirect securities. *Primary securities* are bills, notes, stocks, and bonds issued by the ultimate borrower such as a government or a business corporation. *Indirect securities* are claims such as bank deposits or mutual fund shares that are issued by financial intermediaries as part of the process of raising funds from the public. The money obtained is subsequently invested in primary securities or even in indirect securities of other financial institutions. The provision of financial advice is known as *financial* or *investment counselling*.

In practice, financial intermediation, financial brokerage, and financial or investment counselling are often performed by the same institution. For example, a trust company, as well as being an important supplier of investment funds (obtained from the public), often handles changes in ownership of industrial shares as stock transfer agent for the corporation concerned. It also gives investment advice.

The Canadian capital market can be divided, for analysis, into three parts: (a) the money market; (b) the stock market; and (c) the bond market. The *money market* is the short-term part of the over-all capital market. It is concerned with short-term borrowing by governments and business corporations. The *stock market* is the equity part of the long-term capital market —that is, the part that is concerned with the sale of shares of ownership in business corporations. The *bond market* is the other part of the long-term capital market—the part that is concerned with obtaining borrowed capital by the sale of medium- and long-term government and corporation bonds. Many financial institutions, private as well as public, participate in both the short-term and long-term parts of the capital market. In addition, their activity may not be confined to one role alone.

36.3: THE MONEY MARKET

The term *money market* refers to the activities of various government and private financial institutions that specialize in the issue, purchase, and trading of highly liquid, short-term *debt instruments* (or, in other words, written acknowledgements of money borrowed). The financial institutions involved include the Bank of Canada, the chartered banks, money-market dealers, investment dealers, sales finance companies, and large, non-financial business corporations. The debt instruments are many and varied, ranging from Treasury Bills to *corporate paper* (the name given to notes issued by large business corporations in which they promise to repay money borrowed plus interest at a certain date in the future). Most of the debts mature within one year, but some are for as long as three years. Canada today enjoys a large, well-organized money market—in marked contrast to the situation in 1934 when the first Treasury bills were issued.

Unlike a stock exchange, the money market does not operate within a single building. It is scattered throughout each main financial centre, notably Toronto, Montreal, and Vancouver, with each participating institution linked to the others mainly by telephone.

Functions

A large and active money market performs several useful functions. First of all, it provides an orderly and effective means for governments and business firms to borrow funds at short term, and for financial intermediaries such as banks and large, non-financial business corporations to lend funds. Second, it provides liquidity to these short-term instruments. Thus, a firm is easily able, should the need arise, to sell any such short-term assets that it may possess without a substantial loss on their original purchase price. A third important function of the money market is to facilitate the central bank's implementation of the federal government's monetary policy. Thus, if the government wishes to restrict the supply of credit, the Bank of Canada can quickly make this policy felt by its actions in the money market.

Instruments

The most important debt instruments bought and sold in the money market include: Treasury bills, short-term government bonds, day-to-day loans, certificates of deposit, bankers' acceptances, repurchase agreements, finance company paper, and corporate paper. Let us examine each of these in turn.

Treasury Bills. Every week the Bank of Canada, acting on behalf of the federal government, issues Treasury bills, in units, or denominations of $1000, $5000, $25 000, $100 000 and $1 million. These bills are sold, on the basis of a competitive tender, to the chartered banks and money-market dealers. The Bank of Canada also places a bid to make sure that the whole issue is taken up. Although anyone can submit a bid, financial institutions (other than the banks) and non-financial business corporations usually purchase their requirements at second-hand—either from the banks or from the money-market dealers.

About 80 per cent, by value, of the bills issued are for three months, and most of the remainder for six months. Sometimes, however, bills for more than six months but less than a year are issued. By issuing a Treasury bill, the federal government is, in effect, borrowing money for ninety-one days or more. The Treasury bill is the written acknowledgement of the federal government's indebtedness. For an investor with funds available to lend for a relatively short period of time, Treasury bills provide not only an interest-bearing investment, but an asset that is highly liquid. This liquidity arises from two facts: the standing of the Canadian government as a borrower and the existence of a well-developed money market to handle any resale.

Short-Term Government Bonds. Short-term marketable bonds issued by the federal government form a substantial part of the total value of securities handled by the money market. These bonds differ from Treasury bills in that they have a much longer life, ranging from two to seven years from date of issue. However, the security—the backing of the federal government—is the same.

Day-to-Day Loans. These are loans, usually for over $100 000 each, made on a day-to-day basis by the chartered banks to a group of investment dealers. These loans, which require Treasury bills, short-term government bonds, or bankers' acceptances from other banks as collateral (or security for repayment), can be called in any day so long as notice is given before noon. As a protection against being financially embarrassed, the investment dealers can, if necessary, obtain financing (at a higher rate of interest) from the Bank of Canada.

Certificates of Deposit. Since 1964, the chartered banks have issued negotiable certificates of deposit, commonly called CDs, to investors who deposit money with them for a minimum period of time. These certificates of deposits were established to compete with other short-term debt instruments that business firms were purchasing to obtain a higher rate of return on temporary surpluses of funds.

Bankers' Acceptances. When one business firm sells goods to another on credit, the purchaser is often required to make written acknowledgement of its debt by signing a document called a *time draft*. In this document, the purchaser states that he will pay the vendor the sum owing plus interest at the end of the stipulated period of credit—sixty or ninety days, for example. The vendor of the goods, instead of waiting for his money, usually discounts the draft at his bank—that is to say, sells it to the bank for slightly less than its face value. Since 1962, the banks, instead of holding to maturity drafts of over $100 000, have in turn sold them to money-market investors. Before doing so, the bank concerned has endorsed or "accepted" the draft—thereby pledging the bank's guarantee of repayment in case the purchaser of the goods defaults. The banks have also accepted promissory notes issued by corporations for the express purpose of obtaining short-term funds even when fully "loaned-up" at the bank. These drafts or notes, called bankers' acceptances, may, if necessary, be rediscounted by the Bank of Canada. This means, therefore, that their liquidity is very high. So far, however, bankers' acceptances form a relatively small part of the total value of debt instruments traded in the money market.

Repurchase Agreements. Sometimes a business corporation or financial institution with funds to invest for a certain number of months will find that there is no short-term government bond that fits the required time period. Consequently, the investor, rather than lending his money to a bank or trust company, may enter into a repurchase, or "buy-back", agreement with a money market dealer. This agreement permits the investor to purchase a short-term government bond, even though it matures after the date on which the investor wishes to have its money back. It does this by giving the investor the undertaking of the dealer to repurchase the bond at a specified date. Thus, the investor is able to invest its funds at a good rate for the exact time period that it wants; and the dealer is able to make a profit by selling the bond at one price and repurchasing it at a slightly lower price.

Finance Company Paper. Sales finance companies are important borrowers of short-term funds, which they use, indirectly, to extend credit to consumers. They provide this credit by purchasing conditional sales contracts from car dealers, furniture stores, and other retailers who sell their goods on credit. These sales contracts—in which the consumer agrees to pay for the good in instalments, with interest—are "packaged" by the sales finance companies usually according to maturity. They are then used by the sales finance companies as backing for the promissory notes or certificates that they sell in the money market in exchange for the funds that they need.

Corporate Paper. Corporate paper began to become important in the Canadian money market in the late 1950s. Large business corporations with a good financial reputation often find it cheaper to obtain short-term funds by selling their own promissory notes at a discount than by borrowing from a bank. Simpsons, National Cash Register, and Robin Hood Multifoods would be examples of such firms. These notes, usually maturing in from thirty to ninety days, are purchased and resold by investment dealers.

36.4: THE STOCK MARKET

As already discussed in some detail in Chapter 19 (Business Organization), the ownership, or *equity*, of a business corporation is represented by its capital stock. The issue of this stock is authorized by the articles of incorporation, letters patent, or memorandum of association, that brought the corporation into being. When the shares of capital stock (called *common shares*) are sold, the money received is used to provide working capital and to purchase various fixed assets.

Common and Preferred Shares

Every corporation issues *common shares*, which confer voting rights on the holder as well as the right to receive a share of the profits, called *dividends*. Many corporations also issue *preferred* (or *preference*) *shares*, which confer on the owner a prior claim to a fixed share of the profits (usually expressed as a percentage of the face value of the share), but no voting rights. These preferred shares are either cumulative or non-cumulative. With *cumulative* preferred shares, the corporation, if unable to pay the fixed dividend in the current year, must pay it in later years along with the fixed dividend of those subsequent years. Until this is done, no dividends may be paid on the common shares. Preferred shares, as an investment, appeal to persons desiring a high degree of security as well as a good return. Common shares appeal to persons wishing a possibly very high rate of return as well as the right to vote at shareholders' meetings. The owner of capital stock, whether common or preferred shares, is known as a *shareholder* or *stockholder*.

The specific value indicated on the stock certificate when a share is issued is called the *par value*. However, the issue price may be above or below this par value, depending on the public's demand for the shares. Since the actual value of a share is its market value (or what it will fetch in the stock market), which can vary from day to day, most corporations now issue their common shares *without par value*. Preferred shares, however, are still issued with a par value, since their fixed dividend is usually set as a percentage of this amount.

Once having invested money in common or preferred shares, a shareholder can only regain his or her cash by selling the shares to someone else. The shareholder cannot get it back from the corporation, unless, perhaps, its existence is voluntarily terminated and its assets sold. At any one time there are many individuals and financial institutions wishing to sell shares. There are also investors wishing to buy shares, both new and old. The firms that specialize in the trading of shares are known as *stockbrokers*. They receive a commission for acting as selling or buying agent. The whole network of stockbrokers, investors, and trading facilities is known as the *stock market*. For convenience, it can be divided into two main parts: the stock exchanges and the over-the-counter market.

Stock Exchanges

The *stock exchanges* are buildings that contain a trading floor on which *floor traders* employed by member stockbrokers meet to buy or sell shares on behalf of their employer's clients. They also contain elaborate computer and communications equipment to record transactions and to keep stockbrokers and investors informed of the latest bid and ask prices. Canada now has five stock exchanges: one each in Toronto, Montreal, Vancouver, Winnipeg, and Calgary. Toronto accounts for the vast bulk of shares traded. However, with the rapid development of communications equipment, the need for centralized trading floors may eventually disappear.

Operation. The operation of each stock exchange and the conduct of its members are governed by provincial statute; by its bylaws (which are made effective through a majority vote of the members); and by the rulings of its Board of Governors, which meets regularly each week. A president, assisted by a small staff, is in charge of day-to-day operations.

Purpose. The basic purpose of the stock exchange is to provide a place and the necessary facilities, particularly communications equipment, for the efficient buying and selling of listed stocks by its members. In a broader sense, it satisfies an investor's need to be able to sell stocks quickly if the need for cash arises. Because of this ease of liquidity, the existence of a stock exchange encourages persons and institutions to invest money in stocks and thereby help provide long-term funds for business expansion.

Income. As a non-profit organization, the stock exchange meets its costs of operation by an annual levy on its members; by attorney fees; clerk fees; telephone booth fees; and transaction charges. The two largest sources of revenue are, first, the fees charged to corporations for having the stock exchange list their stocks and, second, the transaction charges imposed on member brokers for transactions made on the floor of the exchange.

Stocks Traded. The facilities of the stock exchange are available to members only for the trading of listed stocks—not bonds or unlisted stocks. A *listed stock* is one that has been registered with the provincial securities commission and approved for trading by the stock exchange.

Approval for listing on the exchange is normally granted to corporations that meet minimum financial standards set by the stock exchange and can provide the exchange with satisfactory evidence of management performance. Canada's stock exchanges vary in their listing requirements.

Trading Facilities. The trading floor of the exchange has a number of booths, known as *trading posts*, for the more actively traded stocks. Each of these trading posts specializes in a particular type of stock (oils, mines, and so on). The buying and selling of stocks in each category takes place around the respective posts. Each offer to buy or sell is shouted out for all traders to hear. At each trading post are quote boards, which record the latest bid and ask prices for the listed stocks. Around the floor of the exchange are telephone booths in which each member has a telephone clerk to receive orders and relay them to the member's floor traders.

Stock Quotations. The transactions which take place in the stock exchange are published daily in the newspapers.

The information usually given is the abbreviated name of the stock; the dividend paid in the current year; the highest price per share paid that day; the lowest price per share paid that day; the last (or closing) price paid that day; the net change or difference between yesterday's and today's closing price; and the total number of shares traded on that day. The prices quoted are in dollars and fractions of dollars ranging from ⅛ to ⅞. Some daily summaries also include the highest and lowest prices paid during the current year.

Weekly summaries of trading (as for example, in the *Financial Post*) usually include such additional information as the indicated dividend rate, earnings per share for the last two years, and the latest price/earnings ratio.

Stock Values

The market price of a stock is a classic example of the interaction of the economic forces of demand and supply. However, because the emotions of buyers and sellers are very much involved, the market can be quite volatile. As good rumours about a company spread, the price of the stock may quickly shoot up as people rush to buy. Conversely, as some bad news about a company begins to circulate, the price of the stock may just as rapidly fall, as people rush to sell. Good or bad news, accurate or not, can affect a complete industry or even all industries together. Thus a belief that the auto industry is in serious trouble from imports can cause auto stocks to fall. Or an anticipated rise in interest rates may cause stock prices in general to decline. Such rises or falls in stock prices are accelerated by the "herd instinct"—whereby people rush to imitate each other, often stampeding in the wrong direction.

Normally, when no state of panic exists, investors try to be rational in their purchases of stocks. In deciding what they would be willing to pay for a stock, they consider various factors, notably their expectations as to the state of the economy, their expectations as to the prosperity of the industry, and their expectations as to the profitability and solvency of the company whose stock they are considering buying. To find out about the economy, the industry, and the company, they may, at various times, consult the newspapers, magazines, investment letters, statistics, stock services, company reports, etc. and seek advice from stockbrokers, friends, neighbours, investment clubs, fortune tellers, and so on. Although they are looking to the future, they can also seek clues from the past—for example, past trends in stock prices and company earnings over recent years. They can also try to determine whether a stock is currently overvalued or undervalued when compared with its recent earnings (or net profit) record. If it seems to be overvalued, then it is not a "good buy", unless there are some other stronger factors that more than offset this negative one. If it seems to be undervalued, then it may be a "good buy". This relationship between the market price of a stock and the recent earnings of the company is called the *price-earnings ratio*. It is the current market price of the stock divided by the earnings per share. (The *earnings per share* is calculated by dividing total company earnings for the most recent

"Last month, he put all his money into a new gold mining stock."

year by the number of shares outstanding.) Thus, if the current price of a company's stock is $20.00, and the company earned $4.00 per share last year, the price-earnings ratio is 5. These ratios can be compared, year by year, for the same company, and for each year between companies in the same industry.

We stated previously that investors are influenced in their buying and selling decisions by "expectations". So, although a company's current price-earnings ratio is high, its stock may still not be a good buy if the sales outlook for the company, for whatever reason, is bleak. More important, therefore, for the investor is the *projected* price-earnings ratio. Although the relationship is by no means clear-cut, the most important factor affecting the market price of a stock is its expected future earnings. If earnings do increase as expected, the investor stands to benefit from possibly higher dividends (the share of the profits paid out to the shareholders) and, usually much more important, from an increase in the market price of the stock. Then, by selling the stock at the higher price, the investor will make a *capital gain*. The great difficulty for the investor is, of course, trying to make an accurate prediction of a company's future earnings when other factors such as unexpected competition, or a change in government policy, may drastically alter the company's fortunes.

For those investors primarily concerned with dividends paid, an important consideration is the *yield* on the stock. This is the current rate of dividends (for example, $1.00 per year) divided by the market value of the share (for example, $20.00) — a yield of 5%.

Stock Indexes

To indicate how the prices of stocks are changing from day-to-day, month-to-month, and year-to-year, various types of stock indexes are calculated. First of all, various stocks are selected to represent (depending on the type of stock index) stocks in general or certain types of stocks (oil, mining, etc.) in particular. The average price of these selected stocks on a certain day in a year (called the *base year*) is then calculated. And the resultant average price is considered to be equal to 100. The average price of the same stocks is then calculated on subsequent dates and compared with the base-year average price and the index figure thereby determined. Thus if the base-year average price was $10.00 and the average price two years later was $15.00, the index would have increased from 100 to 150.

Stock indexes are maintained on a daily basis by the various stock exchanges—e.g. the Toronto Stock Exchange index of 300 prices, known as the TSE 300 Composite. Another prominent stock index is the Dow Jones Index—an average of 30 representative industrial stocks listed on the New York Stock Exchange. Stock indexes are also kept for specialized stocks: minerals, golds, oil and gas, forest products, etc.

The stock exchanges also keep a daily record of the total number of shares traded and indicate the most active stocks.

Stock-Trading Process

A person may buy or sell stocks personally. Usually, however, the services of a stockbroker are used. A person can establish an account with a stockbroker by providing personal identification and a satisfactory bank reference. The customer will normally deal with an employee of the firm known as an *account executive*. The account executive will, if requested, provide advice about stocks to buy, taking into consideration the customer's financial circumstances and wishes. He or she may also, once the customer's credit standing has been satisfactorily established, arrange for stock purchases to be partly financed by the stockbroker. When a customer uses such credit, he or she is said to be *buying on margin*. Usually the maximum credit permissible is 50 per cent of the market price of the stock. The stock itself is held by the stockbroker firm as security for repayment of the loan.

Once the customer has given a firm order (either in person or by telephone, mail, telex, or cable), the account executive records the details on a stock ticket. He or she then arranges for the order to be sent by direct private telephone to the firm's order clerk, located in the firm's booth on the edge of the trading floor of the exchange. The clerk will then call over one of the firm's floor traders, who will take the order to the appropriate trading post and shout it out. The order may be to buy or sell a stock at a definite price or *at market*, that is, at the best price obtainable.

Once the floor trader has found another floor trader willing to do business at an agreeable price, the transaction is made and recorded on a floor ticket, which is sent immediately to the ticker room of the exchange. The details contained in the floor ticket, which provides a permanent record of the transaction, are then sent out by the exchange to all parts of the country over the ticker tape. On the floor itself, the trader informs the firm's order clerk that the transaction has been completed; the clerk relays this information back to the stockholder's office; and the account executive then telephones the customer that the stock has been bought or sold. An official confirmation is mailed the same day. Payment, in the case of a purchase, must be made within three days of the transaction. The rate of commission charged by the stockbroker varies with the value of the order. The stock certificate, issued by the transfer agent (usually a trust company) of the corporation whose shares have been bought, may take one or two weeks to reach the new shareholder.

Stockbroker's Office

A typical stockbroker firm is likely to comprise many partners, including possibly a senior partner, a managing partner, and partners in charge of each of the different business departments. These departments usually include a managed accounts department; an unlisted department and wire room; an underwriting department; and a research department. Some firms also have a money department, a bond department, and a commodities department. In addition to the partners, there are account executives, bond traders, research staff, accountants, floor traders, and clerical and secretarial staff.

To supplement the activities of the account executive in his or her dealings with clients, the research department will often provide weekly or monthly reports on market trends and on the record and prospects of individual stocks.

There is also a variety of communications equipment in the stockbroker's office to bring market news immediately to staff and customers. This equipment includes a long, narrow screen, on to which is projected the moving ticker tape. The *ticker tape* is a running report, in partly codified form, of the transactions which have just taken place on the floor of the stock exchange and of the latest bid and ask quotations.

Sometimes, when the volume of trading on the Exchange floor is extremely heavy—for example, because a rumoured mining "strike"—the information may be minutes behind the time when the transaction actually took place. This is called *late tape*.

Another communications device in the stockbroker's office is the tele-register board, which automatically shows price changes for a selection of the most popular stocks. The details given usually include: the stock symbol; the previous day's closing price; the current day's opening price; the highest price; lowest price; latest price; and volume of trading. Sometimes, to save space, only the stock symbol and latest price are shown.

An account executive can also use *Candat*, a communications system which provides instant access by remote terminal (in, for example, a stockbroker's office) to the stock exchange data computer. Enquiries about stock prices, trading volumes, and a wide range of other stock market data are immediately answered.

Unlisted Shares

Not all stocks are "listed"—that is to say, have been approved for trading in a particular stock exchange. Some firms have no particular wish to have their shares listed since no public trading is desired. Others would not meet the listing requirements such as a specified minimum amount of capital and a proven dividend record. And others are waiting to have their shares listed. Unlisted stocks are nevertheless bought and sold. This trading, conducted by stockbrokers, now mainly over the telephone, forms part of what is known as the *over-the-counter market*. The other important part of the over-the-counter market, the trading of bonds, is discussed in the next Unit of this chapter.

The advantages of listing a stock are that it (a) helps the shares to become well-known, (b) enables investors to buy and sell them easily, and (c) consequently helps to raise their market value.

36.5: THE BOND MARKET

Business corporations finance a large part of their long-term capital needs by selling equity shares and reinvesting their profits. The purchasers of common and preferred shares, in exchange for their money, became part-owners of the business firms involved. However, business corporations also finance another large part of their long-term capital needs by borrowing money from investors. This money, unlike the equity capital, requires the payment of interest to the lender, and the sum borrowed, the *principal*, must eventually be repaid.

Business corporations are by no means the only ones who need to borrow money for long periods of time. As we have already seen, governments—federal, provincial, and municipal—are also heavy borrowers. This is because their tax revenues often fall short of their spending needs. As well as providing for operating expenses, governments require funds to finance capital expenditures for roads, bridges, power dams, and other public works that are necessary in a developing economy. Government borrowing is in fact much more important, in total value, than business borrowing.

Bonds and Debentures

A *bond* is the written acknowledgement that a government or a business corporation makes of its indebtedness. Strictly speaking, the written contract that sets out in detail the terms of the loan is a *bond trust deed*, or *debenture indenture*. This document specifies such matters as the principal, or sum borrowed; the rate of interest; the maturity date—that is to say, when the loan has to be repaid; the collateral, if any, pledged as security for repayment of the loan; and the names of the *bond trustees*—the persons appointed to look after the interests of the bondholders, or lenders. It is on the basis of this indenture, or contract, that a business corporation or government issues individual bond certificates, or "bonds". Each of these bonds contains a summary of the main features of the bond indenture and is normally for a minimum denomination of $1000. These bonds are negotiable.

Some bonds have specific assets such as land and buildings pledged in the bond indenture as security for repayment of the principal. Such bonds are known as *mortgage bonds*, because of the legal claim that the bondholders have on the borrower's assets. According to the priority of this claim to the assets, compared with the claims of other lenders, a bond may be a first-mortgage bond or a second-mortgage bond. If no specific asset is pledged as security for repayment of principal, the term *debenture*, or *debenture bond*, is often used. In such a case, the bondholders have what is called a "floating charge" on the assets and earning ability of the borrower. All federal government bonds and most provincial and municipal bonds are of this type. In practice, the term "bond" is frequently used to describe both mortgage bonds and debentures.

The *bond market* is the name used to describe collectively the persons, firms, and institutions involved in the issue and trading of bonds. Sometimes the term is used to refer to persons involved only in the *secondary trading* of bonds—that is to say, the buying and selling that takes place once the bonds have been issued.

The Investment Dealer

This is a firm that advises upon and underwrites new issues of government and corporate bonds, and corporate stocks. By *underwriting*, we mean buying part or all of a new issue in the hope of being able to resell it later at a slightly higher price to various long-term investors. Frequently, to share the risk of a particular issue, several investment dealers will conbine to form an *underwriting syndicate*. Some stockbroker firms also do underwriting.

Business corporations that wish to borrow long-term funds usually rely heavily on the advice of the investment dealer as to the size and type of bond they should issue and the date it should be offered for sale. This advice will take into account the financial position and other characteristics of the firm, the nature of the industry of which the firm is a part, and the state of the capital market. The bond, once its nature and size have been determined, may then be placed privately, or offered for sale to the public. In the case of a "private placement", the investment dealer acts as agent for the business corporation in negotiating the sale of the bonds to large personal or institutional investors. For this service, the investment dealer receives a commission. Business corporations do not always use the services of an investment dealer to raise long-term funds. Some large, well-known firms sell their own new stocks and bonds directly to investors.

Prospectus

When bonds are to be sold to the investing public, the corporation, or the investment dealer in consultation with the issuing corporation, will first prepare a *prospectus*. This is a document that must be approved by the provincial securities commission before the bonds may be sold. Such a prospectus must contain the following information:

1. the details of the issue, such as price, commissions, and delivery date;

2. a description of the corporation, covering its history, financial position, operations, and purpose of the loan;

3. audited financial statements;

4. statutory information—that is to say, answers to a number of questions set out in the Provincial Securities Act or, if applicable, in the Federal Corporations Act; and

5. signatures of auditors, directors, and others.

Other documents required before the sale of the bonds may proceed include: the trust deed, or trust indenture, setting out the terms of the bond; the underwriting agreement or agency contract specifying the relationship between the issuing corporation and the investment dealer; the banking group agreement, whereby various other investment dealers agree to participate in the underwriting; the selling-group agreement, whereby other investment dealers (often all the members of the Investment Dealers' Association of Canada and all the members of the leading Canadian stock exchanges) are given the chance to buy bonds for resale to their customers; and the banking-group advertisement by means of which the new issue is announced to the public.

Bond Trading

The trading of bonds, once the primary distribution is completed, is carried out by investment dealers, bond houses, and the bond departments of stockbroker firms. These firms buy and sell the bonds both on their own account and as agents for banks, trust companies, pension funds, life insurance companies, mutual funds, and other financial institutions that invest in bonds. Although bonds can, technically speaking, be traded on a stock exchange, practically all bonds are traded by dealers operating from their own offices, using the telephone to communicate with each other. Unlike the floor trader in a stock exchange, the trader in the bond market must constantly telephone around to inform other traders of his or her requirements and availabilities. This manner of trading is the same as that for unlisted stocks. Traditionally referred to as the over-the-counter market, it dates back to the times when traders had to call upon each other in person to conduct business. Most of the buying and selling now takes place over the telephone. Unlike the stock market, there is no central clearing house. The *over-the-counter* market (or, more aptly, the *over-the-telephone* market) is used instead.

The Bond Trading Process. The trading department of an investment dealer contains a number of *trading desks* or *turrets*. Each trader has a telephone and a number of *key boxes*, so that by merely pulling a key above a certain label, he or she can get into touch immediately with the trading desk of another firm.

A typical trade would be as follows:

Trader A: "How are you on Imperial Oil 12 to 93?"

Trader B: "99 to 101."

Trader A: "Sold you 5 and I've got 10 to go."

Trader B: "I'll take the other 10 and I'm still bidding."

In this transaction, trader A has asked trader B for his or her buying and selling prices for a 12 per cent bond issued by Imperial Oil and due for repayment in 1993.

Trader B has indicated that her or she is willing to buy these bonds at $99 per $100 face value, or sell them at $101 per $100 face value. (This bid, or offer, applies to a minimum of five bonds of $1000 each—known as a *board lot*.)

Trader A, accepting Trader B's offer to buy at $99, has sold him or her $15 000 par value for $14 850. Each of the two traders would note the details on a transaction slip, which would then be sent to their respective accounting departments.

In this example, because of the attractive interest rate, the bonds are being traded close to their face value. If they are sold for more than their face value (for example, at the $101 price quoted by the buyer), they are said to be trading *at a premium*. Normally, however, most bonds sell *at a discount*.

Bond Prices. The latest prices at which bonds are bought and sold are published in the newspapers. So also are bond indexes—Government of Canada, provincial and guaranteed, municipal, corporates, and convertibles.

36.6: SECURITIES LEGISLATION

Each province has a Securities Act, as well as a number of other laws affecting in various ways the raising of funds for business purposes from the general public. Most of the Securities Acts closely resemble each other and provide for a Securities Commission to regulate the securities industry in various ways: by the approval and registration of practically every person in any way connected with security issuing or trading; by the investigation of individuals; or companies' books and affairs generally; by the right to give or deny consent to the operation of a stock exchange; by the right to accept or reject prospectuses (setting out the company's background, capital, provisional directors, purposes, and so on), which must be approved before funds may be solicited from the public; and by requiring that a corporation make "full, true and plain disclosure" of all relevant facts before the distribution of its shares to the public.

As a further safeguard of the public interest, certain rules are enforced by the various stock exchanges, by the Investment Dealers' Association in Canada, and by the local Broker-Dealers Association, to ensure an ethical standard of conduct by their members.

Despite all these precautions, however, it is still possible for the public to be hoodwinked by a fraudulent stock or bond promoter.

36.7: BUYING STOCKS AND BONDS

A person buying securities normally has one or more of the following motives: the desire to preserve his or her savings; the desire to obtain a high return on the investment; and the desire to have the investment in as liquid a form possible—that is, easily convertible into cash, without taking a substantial loss on the principal sum. Common shares, preferred shares, bonds, and all their variations—for example, convertible preferred—offer the investor different attractions.

Safety of Principal

If an investor's foremost concern is the desire to preserve savings, then he or she should first consider bonds. On the maturity date, say 20 years hence, he or she will get from the firm or government that has issued the bond the exact amount of principal stated on the bond certificate. The investor will also receive each year a reasonably high, fixed rate of interest on the investment. This is the reasoning behind government legislation that encourages insurance companies and trust companies to invest a large proportion of their funds in this type of security.

What I said was: "If I'd switched from common shares to fixed-income convertibles at the optimum price relationship, then I could've reversed the switch or sold short when the relationship changed."

Unfortunately, because of inflation, $1000 in the future will buy less than $1000 today. To preserve savings, therefore, an investor must receive back more than his or her present $1000. One way to do this is to buy common shares, since their prices tend to keep pace with most other prices. Buying common shares involves a much greater risk, however, of losing one's investment if the company fails. The answer then, for many people, is investment in selected *blue chip* stocks (shares of financially strong and stable companies with proven records of steady earnings and dividends) or in a diversified selection of common stocks—for example, by purchasing shares of a mutual fund. A less certain answer, known as *averaging*, is to invest a fixed sum of money in one stock, irrespective of price movements, at fixed intervals over a long period of time. The weakness of this method is that the price of the stock may be gradually declining.

High Rate of Return

The desire to obtain a high rate of return is another motive for investing. In recent years, bonds have offered a rate of interest usually higher than the yield (the dividend paid as a percentage of the price of the stock) of common and preferred stocks. However, one important advantage of a common stock is that its market price may rise considerably, even over a short period of time. In other words, an investor may buy at one price and soon be able to re-sell at a higher price. Thus, in addition to his or her dividends, the common stock investor may also make a capital gain. And only half of this gain is subject to personal income tax. The possibility of a capital gain makes common stocks a particularly attractive investment for the person whose main concern is a good return on his or her money, as well as protection from the effects of inflation.

The reasons for the rapid price changes in common stocks lie in the nature of the demand for and supply of these securities. The people who own stocks and the people who wish to buy stocks can be greatly influenced by such factors as political events, economic recessions, and rumours. People often wish to buy or sell stocks, not because of any rise or fall in the earnings and assets of the companies concerned, but because of what they believe will happen to the price of these stocks. Obviously, in trying to forecast the future, there is ample room for error and difference of opinion. Also, when a wave of buying or selling begins, many people, however irrationally, will join in. When stock prices are increasing, the market is termed a *bull market*. When they are decreasing, it is termed a *bear market*.

Some people—professional and amateur speculators—attempt to make money by concentrating their attention on short-term changes in stock prices. One method of speculation is to buy stock when prices are low (perhaps after a change in government) and sell soon afterwards if and when they are higher. Another method, called *selling short*, is to make an arrangement to sell particular stocks to someone at an agreed price at a certain future date. Implicit in this transaction is the speculator's belief that he or she can buy these shares later, before the delivery date, at a price lower than the previously agreed sale price. If the market price of the stock rises rather than falls, the speculator will have to buy the shares for more than he or she has previously arranged to sell them for and will thus suffer a loss. Legally, to sell short, the speculator must possess the stocks which he or she is agreeing to sell at a future date. What the speculator does is borrow them, for a fee, from a stock broker and return them when he or she buys the same stock later to meet the previously agreed delivery date.

Liquidity of Investment

The third motive that an investor may have in buying stocks or bonds is a desire for liquidity. Fortunately, the existence of the stock exchanges and the over-the-counter market makes it relatively easy for a person to sell stocks and bonds at short notice. However, when the investment is in stocks, selling at short notice may mean a substantial loss in the principal sum, depending on the level of prices at the time. With bonds there is less risk of a loss in principal, though many bond investors have in fact seen the market value of their investments substantially decline in the past decade as inflation and other factors have caused interest rates to rise.

36.8: CONCLUSION

The Canadian stock and bond markets, concentrated in the major financial centres of Toronto and Montreal and, to a lesser extent, in Vancouver, Calgary, Winnipeg, and other key provincial cities are now considered to be highly developed. As a result, more and more stock and bond issues of varying sizes are successfully being made in Canada, particularly in time of general economic expansion. Nevertheless, the Canadian long-term capital market does have its limitations. Government and corporate borrowers requiring very large sums often cannot hope to raise sufficient amounts in Canada and must look to New York, London, Bonn, and other foreign centres for the money. This does not mean that there are insufficient funds saved in Canada. In practice, many of Canada's leading financial institutions find it more attractive to invest long-term funds at their disposal in investment opportunities abroad, particularly in the United States, rather than in Canada. One factor behind this preference is that, in recent years, the chances for stock price appreciation have been greater in the United States than in Canada. Another factor is that it is much easier to dispose of large amounts of stock in the United States, without depressing the market price, than it is in Canada. However, the deductions permitted under Canada's Income Tax Act for contributions to registered retirement savings plans and the requirements concerning their investment in Canada has helped to increase the supply of funds in this country. The difficulty of disposing of large amounts of stock will only disappear as the Canadian stock market becomes larger.

Summary

1. The intricate network of institutions and individuals specializing in the task of moving funds from would-be lenders to would-be borrowers is known as the *capital* or *securities market*.
2. The process of transferring funds is called *financial intermediation* and the participants are called *financial intermediaries*.
3. The Canadian capital market can be divided, for analysis, into three parts: (a) the money market, (b) the stock market, and (c) the bond market.
4. The term *money market* refers to the activities of various government and private financial institutions that specialize in the issue, purchase, and trading of highly liquid, short-term debt instruments.
5. The most important short-term debt instruments bought and sold in the money market include: treasury bills, short-term government bonds, day-to-day loans, certificates of deposit, banker's acceptances, repurchase agreements, finance company paper, and corporate paper.
6. The *stock market* consists of two separate parts: (a) the *stock exchanges*—well-known, formal meeting-places where member stockbrokers, using floor traders, can buy and sell shares; and (b) the *over-the-counter market*—the network of brokers and dealers who trade unlisted stocks mainly by telephone.
7. A *bond* is the written acknowledgement that a government or a business corporation makes of its indebtedness. If no specific asset is pledged as security for repayment of the sum borrowed, the term *debenture* or *debenture bond* is often used.

8. The term *bond market* is used to describe the persons, firms, and institutions involved in the issue and trading of bonds.
9. An *investment dealer* is a firm that advises upon and underwrites new issues of government and corporate bonds, and corporate stocks.
10. The trading of bonds, once the primary distribution is completed, is carried out (mainly over the telephone) by investment dealers, bond houses, and the bond departments of stockbroker firms.
11. Most of the funds used to purchase corporation and government securities, as well as to make mortgage and other loans, come from a variety of financial institutions rather than directly from the public.

Key Terms

Review Questions

1. What is the capital market? What are its three major components?
2. Distinguish between financial intermediation and financial brokerage.
3. Distinguish between primary securities and indirect securities.
4. Why do many Canadian financial institutions invest a large percentage of their funds abroad?
5. What is the money market? Where is it located?
6. How does the money market operate?
7. What are Certificates of Deposit? Why are they popular in the business community?
8. What is a banker's acceptance?
9. What are repurchase agreements? What purpose do they serve?
10. Distinguish between finance company paper and corporate paper.
11. What is capital stock? What is a shareholder?
12. Explain the nature and purpose of a stock exchange.
13. What is a stockbroker? What function does he or she perform?
14. Explain how a stock is sold through a stock exchange.
15. Distinguish between the stock exchanges and the over-the-counter market.
16. How is the market value of a stock determined?
17. Explain how the price-earnings ratio of a stock is calculated. What is the significance of this ratio?
18. Explain the nature and purpose of a stock index. What are the different types?
19. What is a bond? Distinguish between a mortgage bond and a debenture.
20. What is the bond market? What functions does it perform?
21. What is an investment dealer? What is the underwriting function that such a firm often performs?
22. What is the typical procedure for issuing corporate bonds?
23. Explain the nature and purpose of a company prospectus.
24. How is the secondary trading of government and corporate bonds carried out?
25. What motives can govern a person's decision to buy stocks or bonds? What types of securities do you recommend to make money quickly, regardless of risk?

APPENDIX 36-A:
FINANCIAL INTERMEDIARIES

Most of the funds that are used to purchase corporation stocks and government and corporation bonds, as well as to make mortgage and other loans, do not come directly from the individuals or business firms that provide the savings for investment. They come, instead, from a variety of financial institutions, that collect the savings and then invest them in the capital market or lend them to the public. These institutions are the *financial intermediaries* mentioned at the beginning of this chapter. There are also a number of government financial institutions, such as the Federal Business Development Bank, the Canada Mortgage and Housing Corporation, and the various provincial Development Corporations, that lend public funds to business and the public.

Like any other business firms, private financial intermediaries undertake their activities for profit. On the one hand, they obtain funds from the public and other sources in the form of interest-bearing savings deposits, and funds entrusted for investment, and through the sale of debentures. On the other hand, they invest this money in loans, stocks, and bonds, in the hope of a return high enough not only to cover the interest that may have to be paid and the administrative costs involved, but also to provide a profit.

The investment policy of each institution depends upon the emphasis that it places on security as well as profitability. At one extreme, the banks are very cautious investors; at the other, the so-called "go-go" mutual funds are willing to buy high-risk junior industrial stocks in the hope of a fast capital gain.

Government financial intermediaries such as the Canada Mortgage and Housing Corporation have as their main purpose the achievement of a particular government aim—in the CMHC's case, an increase in the supply of low-cost housing. Although profitability is not usually the principal goal of government financial intermediaries, security is very important since such agencies have no wish to lose the taxpayers' funds.

Chartered Banks

The privately-owned chartered banks are far and away the most important financial institutions in Canada in terms of total assets and liabilities. They were the object of our attention in Chapter 33.

Quebec Savings Banks

These banks play an important role in the Province of Quebec in collecting the public's savings and investing it, predominantly in mortgage loans and provincial government securities.

Life Insurance Companies

These companies in Canada have gradually accumulated large sums of money from insurance policy premiums and from the reinvestment of profits. As a result, they now rank next to the banks in terms of total assets. Depending on the type of insurance policy, the premiums paid by individuals and business firms may be partly a payment for protection against financial loss when a person dies and partly savings that may later be reimbursed with interest. Whatever the case, this money must be invested in assets that will not only provide money for paying claims and for meeting operating expenses, but that will also provide a reasonable rate of return on policyholders' savings. A large part of the money is used for making long-term mortgage loans and for purchasing corporate and government bonds. Relatively little, because of safety precautions imposed by law, is used for purchasing stocks. However, life insurance companies do nowadays also sell shares in mutual funds to persons willing to take greater risks with their savings. Life insurance companies also operate annuity and insured pension plans. Under an *annuity contract*, a person pays a lump sum or a series of smaller amounts to an insurance company. In exchange, he or she receives from the company, after a certain date, fixed regular payments for a fixed number of years or for the remainder of his or her life. Obviously, in providing this service, an insurance company handles large sums of money that must be carefully invested. The same applies to pension funds where the company assumes the responsibility of looking after the funds that have been accumulated by the prospective pensioners.

Life insurance companies are now permitted to invest up to 25 per cent of their assets in common shares that meet certain minimum earnings requirements.

Pension Funds

Many employees contribute to a private pension fund so that they will have a pension on retirement additional to that provided under the federal government's Canada Pension Plan. In the case of an insured private plan, the money that is contributed is administered by a life insurance company. In the case of an uninsured plan, the money is administered by a trust company, by a pension fund society, or by independent trustees. Whatever the case, a vast sum of the public's money is being invested in pension funds each year. Because of the need for safety of principal, the major part of this money is invested in government and corporate bonds. Every employee also contributes to the Canada Pension Plan (or, in Quebec, to the provincial pension plan), and the money that remains after payment of benefits and operating costs is invested in provincial bonds.

Finance Companies

Sales finance companies are firms that specialize in financing the purchase of cars and other durable consumer goods. When a car dealer or furniture retailer sells his product on credit, the customer signs a *conditional sales contract* that specifies, among other things, how the balance of the purchase price and the interest charges are to be paid.

These conditional sales contracts are then purchased at a discount by the sales finance companies who assume the responsibility for collecting the money. As well as providing retail credit of this kind, some sales finance companies engage in wholesale financing. For example, sales finance companies owned by Ford and General Motors provide financing to car dealers to enable them to carry their inventory. Nowadays, many sales finance companies also provide a variety of business loans. The money to finance all this lending was originally provided by the finance company owners' equity capital and reinvested profit, supplemented by bank loans. Today, however, sales finance companies also raise funds from other financial institutions and business corporations by the sale of promissory notes and debentures.

Consumer Loan Companies

These are firms that specialize in providing loans directly to consumers. A person borrowing money is required to sign a promissory note agreeing to repay the principal together with interest, usually in monthly instalments. The rates of interest charged are regulated by the federal Small Loans Act. Usually they are higher than that charged by a bank. Consequently, borrowers are usually persons who cannot, for various reasons, avail themselves of bank financing. The money that the consumer loan companies lend comes, in the case of the larger companies, from parent or associated companies. Smaller companies obtain most of their money from the sale of capital stock and by borrowing from the chartered banks.

Trust Companies

Trust companies are firms that originally specialized in the management and investment of funds entrusted to them as executors of wills or trustees of estates. Nowadays their sources of funds are more widespread, including the acceptance of demand and term deposits from the public, the sale of guaranteed investment certificates, and the administration of agency trust funds such as company pension plans.

The Trust Companies Act in each province imposes certain restrictions on the types of investments that a trust company may make. In most provinces, money may be loaned to business or the public only with the security of a first mortgage on real estate. Other permissible investments are federal, provincial, and municipal bonds, and school and hospital bonds. However, anyone entrusting money to the safekeeping of a trust company may, in the trust deed, authorize investment in stocks and bonds as well. A trust company may also be given wide discretionary investment powers by the depositor with regard to investments. Nowadays, funds from employee pension plans, profit-sharing plans, retirement savings plans, investment plans, and other private trusts, as well as being used to make mortgage loans and purchase government bonds, are being used to acquire common and preferred shares and corporate bonds. Recently, trust companies have started to make short-term personal loans, and have established their own real estate offices to ensure, amongst other reasons, a secure outlet for their mortgage funds.

Credit Unions

These are organizations formed on a voluntary basis usually by the employees of a particular firm or by the inhabitants of a particular area. Their main financial purpose is to collect together the savings of their members by selling shares and accepting interest-bearing deposits, and to make this money available to members in the form of relatively low-cost consumer loans secured by a promissory note. They also provide chequing and other financial services, including mortgage loans.

Caisses Populaires

These financial institutions originated in Quebec at the beginning of this century and are now to be found not only in that province, but also among French-speaking communities elsewhere in Canada. Usually organized around a Roman Catholic parish, they obtain most of their funds from members' deposits. Emphasizing thrift, they make only 50 per cent of their funds available in loans to members (compared with the credit union's 80 per cent). In most cases, they require as security a first mortgage on the borrower's residence. The remainder of their funds is usually invested in local municipal and school bonds.

Mortgage Loan Companies

These companies raise money by selling their own debentures (usually with maturities of five years or less) and, to a limited extent, by accepting deposits from the public. The larger companies also obtain short-term funds by selling their promissory notes in the money market and by borrowing from the chartered banks. These companies also obtain long-term funds by the sale of bonds and mortgages.

The money that is borrowed in these different ways is invested predominantly in what are termed "conventional" residential mortgage loans. By law, these loans may be for up to 75 per cent of the appraised value of the house, but can have a term of no more than five years (to prevent a borrower from being locked in with a high interest rate even though the current market rate may have declined). Mortgage loan companies are permitted by law to make personal and business loans so long as they are fully secured. They are also permitted to invest up to 25 per cent of their assets in common shares on which dividends have been paid for five consecutive years. However, collateral loans and common stocks have not proven very attractive.

Fire and Casualty Insurance Companies

These companies provide insurance against loss from a variety of hazards, including fire, hail, ill-health and injury, automobile collision, and public liability. The premiums collected from policyholders, together with income from previous investments, less any claims paid out, provide a substantial flow of new investment funds. This money is used to buy mainly federal and provincial government bonds.

Investment Companies

These are firms that sell their own stocks and bonds to the public and use the proceeds for investment in a variety of other bonds and stocks. *Closed-end investment companies* are those that have a fixed number of shares of ownership. First established in Canada in the 1920s, these companies became popular for three main reasons. First, the owners could supplement their equity capital by selling debentures to the public. Second, they could use the funds acquired to purchase a controlling interest in other non-investment companies. And, third, by the use of a large percentage of borrowed capital, the owners could obtain maximum financial leverage. Thus any increase in the value of the shares purchased would go, after debenture interest had been paid, to the investment company's equity shareholders. Closed-end investment companies, reflecting their basic purpose, invest their funds predominantly in stocks of junior industrial companies which have promising potential growth.

Open-end investment companies, more commonly known as *mutual funds,* also use their funds to purchase the stocks and bonds of other companies. However, in contrast to the closed-end investment companies, the mutual funds have no limit on the number of shareholders. Although first established in Canada in the late 1930s, mutual funds started to proliferate only in the late 1950s, as more and more individuals had surplus funds to invest. The mutual funds are able to attract savings because of several factors. First, mutual fund shares, sold through stockbrokers and the funds' own energetic sales forces, offer the public an easy way to invest. Second, the diversification of a mutual fund's own investments into a large number of different stocks gives the small investor a safety that he or she could not otherwise obtain. Third, the professional money management, although for a fee, enables the small investor to participate in the stock market with a minimum of personal attention. Fourth, the availability of mutual funds specializing in growth, income, security, oils, overseas stocks and so on, enables the investor to choose his preferred type of investment—"balanced" funds, for example, contain bonds as well as common and preferred shares in their investment portfolio; and "fully managed" funds vary their investment portfolio in the light of market changes. Lastly, the investor can always obtain cash, if the need should arise, by selling his or her shares back to the mutual fund at the going price, which is based on the current value of each share's portion of the fund's assets. However, the acquisition fee (or "front-end loading") that an investor pays when he or she purchases shares of a mutual fund cannot be regained.

Review Questions

1. What is a financial intermediary? What are the most important ones in Canada in terms of total assets?
2. How do life insurance companies obtain and invest their funds?
3. Why are pension funds becoming increasingly important in Canada? How do they invest their funds?

4. What is a conditional sales contract? What purposes does it serve?
5. Explain the functions of a trust company. How are its funds raised and invested?
6. What are credit unions? Why are they growing in importance?
7. Distinguish between closed-end investment companies and mutual funds. What functions do they perform for the investing public?

37. FOREIGN OWNERSHIP OF CANADIAN INDUSTRY

CHAPTER OBJECTIVES

A. To explain the difference between portfolio and direct investment
B. To describe the growth of foreign direct investment in Canada
C. To pinpoint the reasons for such growth
D. To point out the advantages for Canada of foreign direct investment
E. To point out the disadvantages of such investment
F. To outline government policy in Canada toward foreign direct investment

CHAPTER OUTLINE

37.1: HIGH DEGREE OF FOREIGN OWNERSHIP IN CANADA

One of the chief characteristics of the Canadian economy is that a substantial part of its industry is foreign owned and controlled. In fact, Canada has the reputation of being the industrial country with the highest degree of foreign ownership and control in the world. In the manufacturing sector, this foreign ownership and control has tended to concentrate in high-teçhnology industries—industries that possess the best growth prospects in the modern age. Because foreign ownership does not always imply foreign control, the amount of foreign ownership in Canada is slightly higher than the amount of foreign control. Hence, two different sets of figures are compiled by Statistics Canada.

In some industries, such as banking, finance and trust companies, and broadcasting and communications, government legislation has restricted the field to Canadian-controlled firms. In others, public ownership, such as provincial electricity monopolies, has ensured Canadian control; and in others which have limited growth prospects, there has been little foreign interest. However, in many other industries, such as oil, mining, and manufacturing, foreign ownership and control have reached alarming proportions.

37.2: PORTFOLIO VERSUS DIRECT INVESTMENT

By no means all foreign investment in Canada signifies foreign ownership and control. Thus, a distinction is made between portfolio investment and direct investment. *Portfolio investment* is the purchase of government and corporation bonds and scattered minority holdings of corporation shares. Such investment comprises either loans, with consequently no ownership rights, or shareholdings of capital stock so small as to make impossible any degree of control over the business corporation concerned. Most of the money supplied through portfolio investment must eventually be repaid, and the investors are concerned primarily with the rate of interest earned and the security of their investment. *Direct investment* is the purchase of a large enough amount of the capital stock (or equity) of business firms to provide the purchasers with control over them. Since loans do not confer ownership, direct investment comprises the purchase of corporation shares rather than bonds.

37.3: GROWTH OF FOREIGN DIRECT INVESTMENT IN CANADA

Canada, as a relatively new country with vast resources to develop, has had to rely mainly on foreign sources of capital since its earliest days for the funds needed to finance new mines, factories, etc. During the nineteenth century, much of this capital came from the sale of bonds in England; since these bonds signified portfolio investment, they did not require in return the surrender of any ownership rights. The money borrowed was used to help build railways, roads, power plants, and other public utilities; to exploit mineral resources; to help establish certain manufacturing industries; and to supplement government tax revenues. Direct investment, though not as great as portfolio investment, was used for manufacturing and resource development, particularly lumber. This investment increased considerably in the last quarter of the nineteenth century when high tariffs were imposed on imported manufactured goods in order to protect young domestic industries. Also, in the case of lumber, an export duty on logs in 1886 soon brought about the establishment of many U.S.-owned sawmills in Canada. Foreign direct investment in Canadian manufacturing can therefore be said to have begun in earnest in the last quarter of the nineteenth century. Whereas there was only one "branch plant" in 1870, there were 70 in 1900.

Total foreign investment gradually increased in Canada during the first half of the twentieth century. However, the rate of investment rose sharply in the 1950s and has stayed high ever since. Only very recently, with the restrictions (discussed later) placed by the Canadian government on such investments, has the pace slowed. More significant, as regards foreign ownership and control of Canadian industry, is that direct investment has gradually replaced portfolio investment as the main type of foreign investment in Canada.

During the nineteenth and early twentieth centuries, Britain was Canada's main source of foreign capital, most of which was of the portfolio type. However, World War I brought a halt to this traditional flow of funds. For many years, the United States, with vast natural and human resources, had been applying new technologies, including the techniques of mass production, in its industry. After World War I, consequently, the United States rather than Britain was the world's major economic power. During World War I, Canadian government and corporate borrowers had been forced to turn from the London capital market to the New York one; and this new borrowing relationship continued after the War.

With regard to direct investment, U.S. business firms had been setting up or taking over manufacturing and mining plants in Canada well before World War I. This tendency for U.S. direct investment in Canada steadily increased during the 1920s, 1930s, and 1940s. Later, starting in the 1950s, the flow became a veritable flood. Since World War I, the United States has been far and away Canada's largest supplier of direct and portfolio capital. By contrast, the flow of capital from Britain, both portfolio and direct, as a proportion of total foreign investment in Canada, dropped throughout this period. Since 1955, however, investment by other foreign countries has rapidly increased. Only in recent years has such investment in Canada been checked by the activities of Canada's Foreign Investment Review Agency (FIRA). This agency,

Table S.39
Contributors to Change in Book Value of Foreign Direct Investment
in Canada, in millions of dollars, 1946-1978

Year	Net capital inflow for foreign direct investment	Net increase in un-distributed earnings	Other factors	Net increase in book value	Book value
1946	40	120	-47	113	2 826
1950	225	150	14	389	3 975
1955	445	335	184	964	7 728
1960	670	280	16	966	12 872
1961	560	240	65	865	13 737
1962	505	325	93	923	14 660
1963	280	435	127	842	15 502
1964	270	480	-291	459	15 961
1965	535	735	125	1 395	17 356
1966	790	640	226	1 656	19 012
1967	691	845	162	1 698	20 710
1968	590	810	442	1 842	22 552
1969	720	1 045	143	1 908	24 460
1970	905	830	228	1 963	26 423
1971	925	1 335	-680	1 580	28 003
1972	620	1 545	-518	1 647	29 650
1973	830	2 165	228	3 223	32 873
1974	845	2 730	-63	3 512	36 385
1975	725	2 553	-2 274	1 004	37 389
1976	-300	2 744	478	2 922	40 311
1977	475	2 971	-74	3 372	43 683
1978	85	3 911	549	4 545	48 228

Source: Statistics Canada, Canada's International Investment Position

established by the Canadian government in 1973, tries to ensure, through a screening process, that such investment results in "significant benefit" for Canada. Originally, it screened and then approved or refused foreign takeovers of Canadian companies. Now it also screens and then approves or rejects new foreign investment in Canada, not just takeovers.

37.4: REASONS FOR GROWTH OF FOREIGN DIRECT INVESTMENT

Let us now consider the reasons why foreign direct investment in Canada, and consequently the increase in foreign ownership and control, has been so great.

Natural Resources

Canada possesses vast mineral and other natural resources. Industries in other countries have been eager to secure partial or full control of these in order to have a secure and, if possible, relatively cheap source of raw materials. This "vertical integration," in which a firm owns both manufacturing plant and raw-material sources, was evident as early as the nineteenth century when U.S. firms were buying up Canadian timber rights. And it became more evident in the twentieth century when foreign control in mining, petroleum, and natural gas rose substantially. As the U.S. shortage of raw materials and energy resources increases, the pressure to secure new supplies will grow even more acute.

Government Policy

Canadian government policy over the years has generally encouraged foreign investment, both direct and portfolio. Tariff policy, by making it more expensive to import manufactured goods, encouraged U.S. firms to set up production facilities in this country. Canada's membership in the British Commonwealth was also another incentive to foreign investment. Goods produced in Canada could be exported to Britain and other Commonwealth countries and, under Imperial Preference, pay only low rates of import duty.

Government economic development policy has also encouraged the establishment and expansion of foreign-controlled firms. Many federal and provincial schemes to encourage industrial development, particularly in slow-growth areas, have, until recently, made no distinction between Canadian or foreign-controlled firms. Perhaps most important of all in encouraging foreign investment has been the generally friendly attitude of the federal and provincial governments. Unlike many other countries, Canada has imposed relatively few laws to prohibit or restrict the activities of foreign firms. Thus, foreign firms do not, for example, have profit remittances limited to a certain percentage of their capital as they are elsewhere. Nor are they required to have a substantial or majority Canadian participation in their voting capital stock and, until recently, they faced little danger of government expropriation. In return for this "open-door" policy, the Canadian government was usually able, until the 1970s, to obtain special treatment from the U.S. government with regard to any U.S.restrictive measures, such as import quotas, that might harm the Canadian economy. Only in the last decade has the Canadian government tried seriously to regulate foreign investment.

Location

The fact that Canada is part of the North American continent (and that Toronto, for example, is closer to New York than are many U.S. cities) is an important stimulus to U.S. investment in this country. Compared with overseas subsidiaries, the Canadian subsidiary is much closer and therefore easier to control. Also, the transportation and communication links are much more efficient.

Culture

Many Americans believe that Canada has much the same culture as the United States. Certainly, there is great similarity of language, institutions, and even outlook which, through the impact of the mass media, grows greater every day. This similarity of culture, particularly language, helps make Canada the first choice when considering the establishment of manufacturing facilities outside the United States.

Security

One of the great attractions of Canada to most foreign investors is the safety it accords to their capital. Government expropriation of industry is highly unusual in Canada. Moreover, although Canada does not have large armed forces, its geographical position with oceans on both sides,and the closeness of U.S. military power, makes it almost as safe as the United States itself for investment. Also, there is good internal law and order.

Ease of Acquisition

It is quite difficult for Canadians to borrow funds to expand their businesses. It is also difficult to obtain a good price for businesses from Canadian buyers should they wish, for ill-health, retirement, or other reasons, to dispose of it. Consequently, American buyers, located just across the border, speaking the same language, financially well-endowed, and still largely unhampered by restrictions on foreigners, find it relatively easy to acquire a going Canadian business concern. Thus, the increase in foreign ownership and control in Canada has been as much by "takeover" as by the establishment of new enterprises.

Multinational Corporations

A new breed of business corporations, known as multinational corporations, has spread rapidly throughout the world since the 1950s. These firms, with head offices mainly in the United States, transact business on a worldwide scale. Unlike more traditional investors who lend their money at interest, these firms are interested only in direct investment. They desire complete or majority control of any new firm established or purchased abroad, so that the activities of each subsidiary may be part of a regional or worldwide production and marketing plan. With vast financial resources at their command, these multinational corporations, mainly U.S. owned, undertake new investment where the return is highest and the risk lowest. For the many reasons that we have already considered, they have found Canada to be one of the most favourable countries for such investment. Only Western Europe, since the formation of the EEC, has proved as attractive. Consequently, the growth of the multinational corporation, with its organization and expertise for foreign direct investment, has also meant the growth of foreign ownership and control in Canada. It could only have been prevented by deliberate Canadian government action and at the risk of a much slower rate of economic growth. Canada also, we should not neglect to mention, has, during this period, seen the growth of its own multinational corporations engaged in ownership and control abroad. In fact, in recent years, vast sums of Canadian money have been invested in the U.S.

37.5: ADVANTAGES OF FOREIGN DIRECT INVESTMENT

The main argument in favour of foreign direct investment in Canada is that it helps to raise the rate of growth of the Canadian economy; and by helping to provide more income and jobs, it helps to raise the average standard of living. However, it has been argued that Canada's economic growth performance and employment record have not in fact been better than those of many other countries which have relied much less on foreign direct investment. Consequently, we must try to understand just how foreign direct investment affects the Canadian economy.

Foreign direct investment can be broken down into various aspects, each of which makes its own individual contribution to economic growth. These are: *capital, entrepreneurship,* and *technology*. In every direct investment project, each of these elements is usually involved. However, their relative contribution may vary greatly.

Capital

At one time, the capital (or flow of funds) from abroad was a very important aspect of foreign direct investment. It meant that Canadian did not have to forgo current consumption in order to provide capital goods such as machinery and plant. The funds provided from abroad could be used to purchase such goods, often from overseas sellers.

However, as the total amount of foreign-owned assets in Canada gradually built up, reinvested profits, or *retained earnings*, became an increasingly important source of finance for foreign-controlled enterprises in Canada. Even more important was the capital-cost allowance, the item included among the expenses of a business to take into account that a firm's capital assets, such as plant and equipment, are gradually wearing out. Since such cash does not flow out of the business, as it does with operating expenses, the money is available for reinvestment, either in new capital items, inventory, accounts receivable, or cash in hand. In effect, therefore, capital cost allowance is similar to reinvested profit. If it did not exist, a firm's profit would be correspondingly higher, for total expenses would be less. Exactly the same in effect, although less important, is the depletion allowance that mining, oil, and natural-gas companies include among expenses in recognition of the gradual depletion of their mineral assets.

There are also sources of finance outside the business. Foreign-controlled firms are able to obtain money in the form of loans from banks and other financial institutions in Canada and abroad. They are also able to raise ownership capital from the sale of shares to Canadians, but without at the same time losing voting control of the enterprise.

When all the various sources of finance available to foreign-controlled firms are considered, the rather surprising conclusion emerges that in the years since World War II less than a quarter of the total financing of foreign-controlled enterprises in Canada has come from abroad. The most important sources of finance were internal: capital-consumption allowances and retained earnings. Thus, what is usually cited as an advantage of foreign direct investment—the flow of investment funds from abroad—does not now seem, in Canada's case, to be very great.

Another point to consider when discussing the role of foreign direct investment as a source of scarce capital is the amount of Canadian foreign investment. Logically, if capital funds are scarce in Canada, few or no funds will be available for investment abroad. In fact, Canadian total foreign investment, direct and portfolio, amounts to several billion dollars each year. Although retained earnings and capital cost allowances by Canadian subsidiaries abroad account for a large part of Canadian direct investment in foreign countries there is also a significant outflow of new funds from Canada and this has increased enormously in recent years. One reason for this is that Canadian financial institutions such as trust companies and mutual funds find securities in the United States usually more attractive in terms of earnings, safety, and liquidity than securities in Canada. However, Canada's Income Tax Act, which now restricts investment abroad by registered retirement savings plans (an important source of Canadian funds) to a certain percentage of total assets, should help to make more of these funds available in Canada. Another, and perhaps more important reason in the early 1980s was a rather hostile Canadian government attitude towards business firms in Canada generally. Whatever the case, scarcity of capital does not seem to be a reason for encouraging more foreign direct investment in Canada, unless, of course, it is for a project of such great magnitude as a Mackenzie River pipeline or development of the Athabaska tar sands. We should nevertheless readily concede that it is much easier for a foreign multinational corporation to obtain money both within and outside Canada for any particular investment project than it usually is for a Canadian firm. Thus, unlike the situation with a Canadian enterprise, shortage of funds is less likely to be a factor holding up new investment by a foreign multinational.

Entrepreneurship

This term is used to describe the creative, risk-taking ability that many business people exercise in pursuit of profit. This ability is used in introducing new products and services, and producing and marketing more efficiently those that already exist.

One of the advantages claimed for foreign direct investment is that it brings this entrepreneurial ability with it, in the form of managers from the parent corporation. Certainly, there are many examples of U.S.

firms establishing new enterprises in Canada that would otherwise not exist, or at least not have been established so soon. However, whether there is a dearth of entrepreneurship among Canadians is a debatable point. Some would argue that large financial resources or a guaranteed market in the United States often make the difference between the success of a U.S.-sponsored venture and a Canadian one. Others would argue that many of Canada's most creative business people are recruited by U.S.-controlled corporations and help to expand these firms' activities in Canada. In fact, many U.S. multinational corporations proudly claim that their operations in Canada are run almost exclusively by Canadian personnel. Others would argue that many of Canada's most talented business people emigrate to the United States in search of greater opportunity. However, with the emphasis being given to business training in colleges and universities throughout Canada, there should be a continuing flow of new talent available. Undoubtedly, many opportunities are present in Canada for both small and large businesses.

Today, the benefits of foreign entrepreneurship can be obtained by means of joint ventures in which Canadians have an equal stake in the enterprise. Certainly, there is concern that Canada's own entrepreneurial talent may be stifled if foreign ownership and control continue to spread so rapidly.

Technology

The third important ingredient of foreign direct investment is technology—the technical know-how needed to produce and market goods at a profit. If Canada is to achieve a satisfactory rate of economic growth and a higher standard of living for its people, it must continue to raise the productivity of its various resources—land, labour, capital, and entrepreneurship—by the application of new technology. To date, Canada has always relied heavily on foreign technology—for example, the vast majority of patents issued in Canada are registered to foreign owners, mainly U.S. residents. Of course, some notable discoveries and inventions, such as insulin, snowmobiles, and telidon, have been made in Canada.

So long as Canada can have access to new technology at reasonable cost, it can succeed in raising productivity. As Japan's example shows, a country can achieve rapid economic growth even though it has, at least initially, no great technological output of its own. Foreign direct investment has been one important way in which Canada has obtained access to new technology without having to invest vast sums in its own research and development (R & D). Of course, R & D tends to have been neglected in Canada, particularly in private industry, just because it has been more cheaply available from abroad. Naturally, this relative neglect has hastened the exodus of competent Canadian scientists and researchers to the United States. But the question arises: does Canada (a) need and (b) wish to pay for the R & D now carried out in the United States, a country with a population almost ten times as large?

If Canada is to continue to rely on mainly U.S. technology, is foreign direct investment so advantageous as a means of obtaining it? Can new technology be obtained only as part of a package deal that also includes foreign ownership and control of the firm in Canada that is to be the recipient? Two other ways of obtaining new technology—arm's-length licensing agreements and joint ventures—may be more beneficial for Canada. In the former case, a Canadian firm pays a fairly negotiated annual fee to a foreign firm for permission to use its "know-how". In the latter case, the Canadian and foreign firm jointly own the firm in Canada that uses the "know-how".

Other Advantages

We have seen that foreign direct investment can help provide a country with capital, entrepreneurship, and technology. But some other reasons also explain why the existence of U.S. or other foreign-owned multinational corporations in Canada can be advantageous. First, such corporations, by competing with Canadian-owned firms, can help keep industry as efficient as possible. Second, the fact that a multinational corporation owns manufacturing and assembly plants in a number of different countries enables it to achieve significant cost reductions (the economies of scale) from inter-plant specialization. This specialization has occurred, for example, in the auto industry in Canada and the U.S. following the auto pact. So long as Canada can capture some of the benefits of this specialization, this is all to the good. In fact, in recent years, more and more U.S. multinationals have given their Canadian subsidiaries a *world product mandate* for a particular product or product line—that is the sole responsibility for manufacturing and exporting the item (e.g. computer keyboards) to all the company's markets around the world, not just Canada. Third, the existence of a large, well-organized international sales force enables a multinational corporation, if it wishes, to promote the sale abroad of new products manufactured in Canada—thereby making a world product mandate for the Canadian subsidiary quite feasible. And, fourth, the ability of the multinational corporations to afford large research and development organizations, even though located in the United States, means that U.S. multinational corporations will continue to spearhead technological innovation and ensure its practical application in Canada as well as in the United States.

37.6: DISADVANTAGES OF FOREIGN DIRECT INVESTMENT

So far, in our discussion of foreign direct investment in Canada, we have suggested that the benefits of foreign capital, entrepreneurship, and technology may not be as great as supposed and could, furthermore, be obtained in other ways. Let us consider now what specific disadvantages arise from such a high degree of foreign ownership and control of Canadian industry.

Truncated Enterprises

First of all, direct investment has led to the establishment in Canada of what have been called *truncated enterprises*—that is, firms for which one or more important functions are performed abroad. Research and development is perhaps the best known type of activity that is performed in the country of the parent corporation, usually the United States. However, many other activities, such as production planning, marketing strategy, financial planning, and advertising, are to a varying extent directed from or performed abroad. As a result, not all decisions may be made in Canada's best interests. Thus, the head office of a multinational corporation may decide, for example, to produce only certain products in its Canadian subsidiary as part of a global production plan. This can mean that the Canadian subsidiary must refrain from producing other goods, even though they could be made and sold profitably at home or abroad. This can have disadvantages for Canada's balance of payments as well as for national income and employment.

The establishment of truncated enterprises, as a result of the growth of multinational corporations, also has another disadvantage. The performance of activities such as R & D in the country of the parent company means fewer job opportunities in Canada. And the resultant exodus of scientific personnel to the United States can only intensify Canada's reliance on foreign technology. But, as we suggested previously, this situation may be quite satisfactory. If the priority is a high rate of economic growth, it may be wiser to purchase foreign technology than to try to create it ourselves. However, lack of its own applied industrial research may well hamper a country such as Canada in creating new products and expending export markets. That is why such research is being encouraged by governments in Canada, particularly in high-technology ''growth'' industries—for example, by the establishment in Ontario of publicly-financed research centres.

Transfer Pricing

This is another example of a decision that may be detrimental to Canada.

The *transfer price* is the price that one branch of a multinational charges another branch for materials, parts, or finished goods supplied. Thus, the multinational corporation's head office in, say, the United States may set the prices for Canadian raw materials and parts sold to its plants in other countries too low. This could be designed to increase profits earned in the parent company and reduce them in the subsidiary company, which can mean a smaller total tax bill because of lower tax rates at home. Furthermore, the lower profit earned in Canada because of this practice can help prevent accusations of exploitation which otherwise might lead to higher taxes, withdrawal of concessions, or even expropriation.

Degree of Processing

This involves another decision that may be against Canada's best interests. The parent company in the United States, or even Japan, usually wishes to process the raw materials at its own home-country plants, whereas it would be in Canada's interests to encourage processing here because of the extra income and jobs for Canadians.

Takeover of Canadian Firms

Another disadvantage of so much foreign ownership and control in Canada relates to the much stronger competitive ability of the giant multinational corporations of which the Canadian subsidiary is only one part. This superior competitive ability (involving new production and marketing techniques, well-established markets in the U.S. and elsewhere, almost unlimited funds, and top-notch managers with wide international experience) can often mean the rapid disappearance of locally-owned competitors. Once a Canadian firm starts to lose sales as competition increases, it soon becomes amenable to a foreign takeover bid. And, if a Canadian firm is operating at a loss, the highest bidder is likely to be a U.S. multinational corporation. In West Germany, Japan, Britain, and elsewhere, governments have in fact encouraged the merger, or "rationalization", of large local firms. This is designed to increase their efficiency and thus better enable them to withstand the competition of the U.S.-based multinationals. In Canada, by contrast, there are relatively few large firms. Such business giants as Canadian Pacific, George Weston, Hudson's Bay Co., Bell Canada, Noranda Mines, and MacMillan Bloedel are the exception rather than the rule.

By permitting firms to engage in mergers designed to improve productive efficiency, the Canadian government is now beginning to follow the "rationalization" path.

Flow of Dividends Abroad

A third disadvantage of a high level of foreign direct investment relates to the flow of dividends abroad. As the amount of foreign capital grows (mainly from funds generated within the Canadian subsidiary rather than from funds brought from abroad), the greater becomes the amount of profit earned. Since the parent company is usually located in the United States, dividends will be remitted in ever larger amounts from Canada to that country. The same is also true of patent royalties, licence fees, management fees, and the subsidiary's share of head office expenditure, including research and development. This can impose an increasingly severe strain on Canada's balance of payments. In fact, Canada's substantial surplus on merchandise trade is more than offset by its deficit in the non-merchandise account (in which dividend and interest remittances abroad are the main culprit). And should the Canadian government attempt to restrict profit remittances in some way (for example, to a certain percentage of capital invested) this would invite retaliatory action with regard to Canada's exports to the United States which are now about a highly vulnerable 70 per cent of the total value of Canada's exports. In the case of foreign portfolio investment in Canada, the loans can eventually be repaid and the flow of interest abroad stemmed. With foreign direct investment, by contrast, the flow of dividends, royalty payments, management fees, and so on will continue *ad infinitum*.

Political Conflict

A fourth disadvantage of foreign direct investment is as much a political as an economic one. There may be a conflict of interests between the country in which the multinational corporation has its head office and the country in which the subsidiary is located. Thus, for example, U.S. government policy concerning trade with Cuba and China differed for many years from that of the Canadian government. Since the subsidiary tended to follow the orders of its U.S. head office, which in turn was obeying U.S. government policy and U.S. laws, this brought it into opposition with the Canadian government's policy. A similar complaint occurred some years ago when the U.S. government of President Johnson ordered U.S. multinational corporations to bring more of their funds home. More recently, U.S. subsidiaries in Western Europe wishing to supply gas pipe-line equipment to the Soviet Union have been caught between conflicting government policies. Fortunately, situations of this type have been relatively few, except perhaps in Third World countries. However, so long as a substantial part of a country's industry is foreign controlled, it makes it much more difficult for that country to pursue an independent political and economic policy both at home and abroad. The larger this foreign interest, the greater is the incentive for foreigners (mainly U.S. nationals) to intervene in a country's political affairs to ensure that their financial interests remain protected. Only the similarity of political outlook of the two peoples has so far prevented Canada's high degree of foreign ownership and control from being such an explosive problem as it has been elsewhere—for example, in Latin America. However, despite this similarity of outlook, the continued growth of foreign ownership and control at the pace seen in the last twenty-five years will inevitably make more and more Canadians wonder whether the benefits of rapid economic growth outweigh the loss of economic and perhaps political sovereignty.

Possibly Inefficient Use of Natural Resources

The United States faces an increasingly large deficit of energy resources and raw materials for its industries. This means that in the future it will inevitably have to increase, at an accelerating rate, its imports of crude oil, natural gas, iron ore, copper, nickel, lead, zinc, manganese, chromite, potash, uranium, pulpwood, timber, and electricity. And what more convenient place to look than Canada? From Canada's point of view, selling its raw materials has serious disadvantages. The processing of Canada's raw materials in Canada rather than in the U.S. offers the greatest income and employment prospects for Canadians, because resource industries are much more capital-intensive than labour-intensive. However, just to leave the resources untouched, as some people suggest, until Canadian manufacturing industry is ready for them, would be equally undesirable. Perhaps the answer is a good export price, combined with more processing in Canada.

37.7: GOVERNMENT POLICY TOWARD FOREIGN DIRECT INVESTMENT

We have already seen that, from the nineteenth century, Canadian tariff policy has encouraged foreign direct investment in Canada. In subsequent years, Canadian governments have held the view that stimulating industrial growth, and thereby income and employment opportunities for Canadians, has greater priority than limiting foreign ownership and control. Nevertheless, foreign direct investment has by no means had a free hand. And, in the early 1980s, economic national-ism seemed to have gained the upper hand for some time over employ-ment and income as the Canadian government's top priority.

Public Ownership

The existence of such federally-owned enterprises as Canadian Na-tional Railways, Air Canada, and the Canadian Broadcasting Cor-poration has tended to limit the degree of foreign penetration of the transportation and communications industries in Canada. Provincially and municipally-owned electricity boards, provincially-owned liquor boards, and, in some provinces, provincially-owned telephone compa-nies have also reduced the scope for foreign ownership and control.

Government Restrictions

Since the late 1950s, furthermore, foreign investment has been re-stricted and even prohibited in other key sectors of Canadian industry by means of government legislation.

1. Life insurance. In 1957, following the acquisition of six Canadian life-insurance companies by foreign firms, several amendments to the Canadian and British Insurance Companies Act were passed to pro-mote Canadian ownership. One amendment stipulated that a majority of the board of directors must be Canadian citizens ordinarily resident in Canada; another gave the directors the power to veto a transfer of shares from a resident to a non-resident; and another established a procedure whereby a firm could convert itself into a mutual company so that its Canadian policyholders could also become its owners. How-ever, as more takeovers of Canadian life-insurance companies subse-quently occurred, other amendments were passed in 1964-65. One of these limited the proportion of life-insurance company shares that could be transferred to non-residents to 25 per cent of the capital stock, or to the present proportion owned by non-residents if already higher than 25 per cent. Another forbade the transfer of such shares to any one non-resident if this would raise that person's proportion of a com-pany's capital stock to more than 10 per cent. These measures, al-though helping to prevent the takeover of Canadian-controlled firms, did not, however, prevent foreigners from starting new life-insurance companies in Canada. Only since the establishment of FIRA in 1973 has such prevention been possible.

2. Banking. In 1967, a new Bank Act placed the same limitations on the transfer of bank shares to non-residents as those that were imposed in 1964-65 on life insurance company shares. These limitations included a maximum total non-resident ownership of 25 per cent of the capital stock. A further limitation was, however, a 10 per cent maximum on the proportion of shares that could be owned by any one person, regardless of residence. Another limitation was that at least three-quarters of the board of directors of each bank should consist of Canadian citizens, ordinarily resident in Canada. On this point, the legislation is more severe than the life-insurance company legislation. However, this policy has now been relaxed so that foreign banks can undertake limited operations in Canada.

3. Loan and trust companies. Under other legislation, federally incorporated loan companies and trust companies are also required to meet the same 75 per cent Canadian requirement for their boards of directors as the banks. Governments of such provinces as Ontario, Manitoba, and Alberta have also passed similar legislation with regard to provincially incorporated loan and trust companies. Unlike the situation with banks, foreigners are free to start new companies in this financial sector, subject to FIRA approval.

4. Broadcasting. Legislation was passed in 1958 that restricted foreign ownership of any broadcasting undertaking other than cable television to 25 per cent. Foreign ownership of cable television was similarly restricted in 1964. In 1968, a new Broadcasting Act established the Canadian Radio-Television Commission with authority over conventional broadcasting and cable television. (It now has authority over telecommunications as well.) The main purpose of the Act was to ensure that the Canadian broadcasting system was effectively owned and controlled by Canadians in order to "safeguard, enrich and strengthen the cultural, political, social and economic fabric of Canada." Under the Act, broadcasting licences were restricted to Canadian citizens and eligible Canadian corporations. Foreigners presently owning Canadian broadcasting firms were required under the Act to reduce their holdings to a new legal maximum of 20 per cent. An eligible Canadian corporation was defined as a federally or provincially incorporated firm in which (a) the chairman and all the directors are Canadian citizens, and (b) at least 80 per cent of the voting shares and at least 80 per cent of the total paid-up share capital are beneficially owned by Canadian citizens or Canadian corporations. Measures were also taken to increase the amount of Canadian content in broadcast programs.

5. Newspapers, magazines, and periodicals. In 1965 the Income Tax Act was amended so that expenses incurred by business firms in advertising primarily for the Canadian market, in non-Canadian newspapers or periodicals, were no longer tax deductible. However, foreign newspapers or magazines, such as *Time* or *Reader's Digest*, that were already operating in Canada were made exempt. The Customs Tariff Act was also amended in that year so that foreign periodicals containing advertisements aimed primarily at the Canadian market were prohibited from entry. These measures meant that it would no longer be profitable for foreigners to establish new newspapers or periodicals in Canada or to take over existing Canadian ones. Since then, the exemption for *Time, Reader's Digest*, and other American-owned publications has been ended.

6. Satellite telecommunications. To prevent foreign control of satellite telecommunications in Canada, the federal government has established Telesat Canada, a semi-public enterprise with ownership divided between the federal government and its agents, approved telecommunications common carriers, and other Canadian citizens. Not more than 20 per cent of the shares owned by the last group may be held by non-residents, and all directors of Telesat Canada must be Canadian citizens normally resident in Canada.

7. Minerals. In this sector, the federal government attempted in 1960 to restrict foreign ownership and control by introducing what are known as Canadian Participation Provisions, or CPP. Under the CPP, oil and gas leases in the Yukon, the Northwest Territories and offshore are granted only to persons who are Canadian citizens over twenty-one years of age and to Canadian corporations which have satisfied the Minister responsible that:

> (a) at least 50 per cent of the issued shares are beneficially owned by persons who are Canadian citizens; or
>
> (b) the shares are listed on a recognized Canadian stock exchange and that Canadians will have an opportunity of participating in the financing and ownership of the corporation; or
>
> (c) the shares are wholly owned by a corporation that meets the qualifications outlined in (a) and (b) above.

However these requirements have not in fact done much to increase Canadian ownership and control of oil, gas, and mining in the areas concerned.

Measures have also been adopted by the federal government with regard to Canada as a whole to prevent foreign control of Canadian uranium deposits. Foreign ownership of any uranium property is now limited to one-third, and no single foreign investor or associated group of investors may own more than 10 per cent of the capital stock. However, firms which already had greater foreign ownership were permitted to continue as before, but the excess shares may not be sold to other foreigners.

Tax Incentives

To promote Canadian ownership of industry, the federal government has provided a number of tax incentives. First of all, Canadian residents can now deduct from their income tax an amount equal to 33 per cent of the net dividends they receive from taxable Canadian corporations. Since no tax credit is available for dividends from foreign-owned corporations, investors find it more profitable, at least in this respect, to hold Canadian stocks. Second, the withholding tax on dividends paid to non-residents was kept 5 per cent lower for corporations with some degree of Canadian ownership than for those completely foreign owned. Third, Canadian corporations are permitted to deduct as an expense the interest paid on money borrowed to finance the purchase of shares in other firms. Fourth, a special low rate of income tax is offered to Canadian-controlled private business corporations. The difference between this rate and that paid by other business corporations will have to be repaid only if control of the firm passes into foreign hands. Fifth, pension funds must pay a special tax of 1 per cent per month on that portion of their investments abroad that exceeds 10 per cent of their total assets. And, sixth federal estate taxes have been abolished, thereby reducing the need to sell a business (often to foreigners) on the death of the proprietor to raise funds. Of course, funds will be needed to pay capital-gains taxes, any provincial succession duties, and other expenses, but it should be easier to meet these payments out of life insurance proceeds, cash in the business, and other sources than it would have been if estate taxes had continued.

Canada Development Corporation

In 1971, the federal government established a development corporation for Canada. Along with its other goals, the corporation appears willing, at least occasionally, to buy all or part of major foreign-owned resource firms in Canada—as, for example, the Canadian operations of Texas Gulf Sulphur, subsequently renamed Kidd Creek Mines. Furthermore, when shares of this national development corporation are sold to the general public, only Canadian residents will be allowed to buy them.

Foreign Investment Review Agency

In December 1973, the federal parliament passed the Foreign Investment Review Act that authorized the federal government:

(a) to establish a screening agency to review proposed foreign takeovers of Canadian firms with assets of more than $250 000 or annual gross revenues of $3 million or more;
(b) to screen all new foreign investments in Canada; and
(c) to examine the expansion into unrelated lines of business of foreign-owned firms already in Canada.

The criterion to be used in judging such foreign investments is whether they offer "significant benefit" to Canada in terms of new jobs, increased exports, more processing of resources and raw materials in Canada, improved productivity, or of technological development. The agency began operations on April 9, 1974.

Since its inception, FIRA has aroused considerable opposition in the U.S. and other countries on the grounds that it unreasonably discriminates against foreign investment in Canada. Although most of the applications received have been approved, the applicants claim that they have been faced with unreasonable delays and have been forced to make costly concessions.

In the early 1980s, the Canadian government promised to relax somewhat FIRA's review procedure. And new regulations that came into force in July 1983 made many more foreign firms eligible for shorter review procedures.

The Key Sector Approach

As we saw earlier, the federal and provincial governments have restricted foreign ownership in key sectors of the Canadian economy. However, such a policy has been limited mainly to banking, transportation, and communications. It has been suggested that this policy should be broadened as in many other countries (for example, Mexico) to embrace manufacturing and resource industries as well. A Government of Ontario Task Force has suggested a clear division of the country's economic sectors into those in which:

(a) foreign ownership is prohibited;
(b) foreign ownership is allowed up to 25 per cent of equity;
(c) foreign ownership is allowed up to 49 per cent of equity; and
(d) foreign ownership is allowed without limitation.

The difficult question remains: which industries should be placed in which categories?

National Energy Program

The National Energy Program (described in Chapter 17) that the federal government introduced in 1980 had as one of its aims a substantial Canadianization of the petroleum industry—this meant doubling Canadian ownership from approximately 25 per cent in 1980 to about 50 per cent by 1990. This was to be achieved by making government off-shore exploration grants to the oil companies vary according to the degree of their Canadian ownership. Thus to receive the maximum grant, which would cover 80% of direct exploration spending, a company would need to have 75% Canadian ownership. Also, a more controversial feature, the federal government, through its Crown Corporation, Petrocan, was permitted to "back in" on existing oil exploration—that is, acquire a share of the development at minimum cost. Petrocan, the spearhead of the federal government's Canadianization program, was also provided with substantial government funds not only to participate in oil and gas exploration but to also acquire refinery and distribution facilities throughout Canada—for example, the assets of Petrofina in 1981 and the refining and marketing assets of BP Canada in 1982.

Transfer of Technology

Many present licensing agreements, involving the acquisition by Canadian firms of foreign production technology, restrict the Canadian firms from selling the product in other markets. This stipulation is considered by the federal government to be detrimental to Canada's interests. For example, the Northrop Corporation of Los Angeles launched a $17.5 million damages suit against the federal government of Canada in December 1973 for selling to Venezuela CF-5 fighter planes produced in Montreal by Canadair Limited under a licensing agreement between Northrop and the government. Also, because of such agreements, the incentive for domestic research and development is reduced. In future, the government proposes to subject all such licensing agreements to the "significant benefit" test. However, others argue that such agreements are the most economical and effective way for Canadian industry to obtain advanced technological know-how.

Provincial-Government Action

So far in this chapter, we have spoken mainly of federal-government policy toward foreign ownership and control, because the federal government, using the powers conferred on it by Section 91 of the Constitution Act, 1867, has played the predominant role in promoting

Canadian ownership of industry. These powers include the right to legislate with respect to the public debt and property; the regulation of trade and commerce; the raising of money by any mode or system of taxation, patents, and copyrights; aliens; and generally for the peace, order, and good government of Canada.

However, under Section 92, the provincial governments are empowered to levy direct taxes, manage and sell public lands, legislate with regard to local works and undertakings (except interprovincial transportation and communication lines and works declared by the federal government to be for the general advantage of Canada), incorporate companies with provincial purposes, legislate with regard to property and civil rights, and legislate with regard to matters of a purely local or private nature. Also, under Section 109, they are given power over natural resources within their provinces.

These powers have so far been used to regulate the ownership of provincial loan and trust companies, to establish provincial hydroelectric and liquor monopolies (which consequently prevent foreign ownership and control), to impose Canadian director requirements on provincially incorporated firms (for example, since 1972, a majority of the directors of Ontario-incorporated companies must be Canadian citizens ordinarily resident in Canada), to permit deduction of interest costs on money borrowed to purchase shares of other companies, to regulate sales of public land to non-Canadians, and to require advance notice of planned plant closures. Most provincial governments, except perhaps that of British Columbia, appear reluctant to impose further restrictions on foreign ownership and control, because they believe more restrictions would scare off new investment and consequently aggravate the serious unemployment situation in their respective provinces. However, the question remains, as the Government of Ontario Task Force so aptly put it, "Whether we do not delude ourselves by believing that we can retain one of the highest standards of living in the world by relying on imported technology, imported entrepreneurship, imported economic initiatives, imported trade marks, and imported patents and licenses. Will we be able to compete in manufactured products without bringing genuinely Canadian products and processes into the world market, under Canadian patents and trade marks?"

Summary

1. One of the chief characteristics of the Canadian economy is that a substantial part of its industry is foreign-owned and controlled.

2. A distinction is made between foreign portfolio investment and foreign direct investment in Canada. It is the latter that confers ownership and control.

3. Canada is a relatively new country with vast resources to develop. Consequently, it has had to rely, since its earliest days, mainly on foreign sources of capital. During the nineteenth and early twentieth centuries, Britain was Canada's main source of foreign capital, and investment was mostly of the portfolio type. As from World War I, the United States became Canada's principal source of foreign capital, and direct investment soon became more important than portfolio investment. Since the 1950s, U.S. direct investment in Canada has reached flood proportions.

4. The reasons for the growth of foreign, mainly U.S. direct investment in Canada include: the desire by foreign manufacturers to obtain a secure and relatively cheap source of supply of raw materials and energy; encouragement, until recent times, of foreign investment in Canada by the Canadian federal and provincial governments by such measures as tax concessions; Canada's geographical location next door to the United States; the similarity of culture, especially language, between Canada and the United States; the protection afforded to U.S. investment in Canada by a close U.S. military presence; the relative ease of acquisition of Canadian businesses; and the growth of mainly U.S. multinational corporations.

5. The main argument in favour of foreign direct investment in Canada is that it helps to raise the rate of growth of the Canadian economy. However, the validity of this argument has been questioned. Thus, it is argued that Canada has enough indigenous capital to finance its own economic growth; that its own entrepreneurs are sufficiently skilled and energetic to establish, operate, and expand Canada's business sector; and that, even if its own scientists cannot equal the results of the United States and other countries, Canada (following Japan's example) can still secure the benefits of foreign-produced technology—by licensing, joint ventures, and other means—without forfeiting ownership and control of its industries.

6. Specific disadvantages of a large degree of foreign ownership and control include: the establishment in Canada of "truncated" enterprises—ones that have activities such as research and development carried out at head office in the U.S.; the takeover of existing Canadian firms; the heavy flow of dividends abroad; the possibility of political conflict between Canada and the U.S. over the actions

of U.S. subsidiaries in Canada; and the inefficient use, from Canada's viewpoint, of Canada's natural resources—specifically, the export of raw materials with a minimum of processing, and therefore loss of jobs and income, in Canada.

7. Government policy toward foreign direct investment has included public ownership in certain key sectors such as airways, and restrictions on foreign ownership and control in other sectors such as banking and broadcasting.

8. To promote Canadian ownership of industry, the federal government has provided a number of tax incentives.

9. In 1971, the federal government established the Canada Development Corporation to increase the amount of venture capital available to Canadian business enterprises.

10. In 1973, the federal government established a Foreign Investment Review Agency to screen foreign investment to ensure "significant benefit" for Canada.

11. It has been suggested that Canada broaden its "Key Sector" approach to include manufacturing and resource industries.

12. The National Energy Program introduced by the federal government in 1980 is designed to increase Canadian ownership of the petroleum industry.

13. Restrictive licensing agreements, involving the use by Canadian firms of foreign technology, are also coming under federal government scrutiny.

14. Provincial governments have also taken steps to restrict foreign ownership and control—for example, minimum Canadian director requirements for provincially incorporated companies.

Key Terms

Review Questions

1. To what extent is Canadian industry foreign owned and controlled? In which industries is foreign penetration least? In which industries is it greatest?
2. Distinguish between portfolio investment and direct investment. Why is this distinction so important?
3. Why has Canada relied so heavily on foreign capital throughout its history? What have been the sources of this capital?
4. How has the nature of foreign investment in Canada changed over the years?
5. Why have Canada's natural resources been a source of attraction for foreign capital?
6. How has Canadian government policy encouraged foreign investment in Canada? To what extent has this policy now changed?
7. What significance does Canada's geographical location possess from the viewpoint of foreign investment?
8. Similarity of culture has been an important factor encouraging U.S. investment in Canada. Comment.
9. How secure are foreign investments in Canada from the military point of view?
10. Why have Americans found it relatively easy to acquire Canadian businesses?
11. What is a multinational corporation? What is its significance as regards foreign ownership and control in Canada?
12. "Foreign direct investment is no longer a major source of capital for Canada." Comment.
13. What is entrepreneurship? To what extent does foreign direct investment fill a need for entrepreneurship in Canada?
14. What is technology? Why is it so vital in industrial growth?
15. How essential is foreign direct investment as a means of obtaining the latest technology? How might Canada better obtain the fruits of modern technology?
16. "The competition offered by the Canadian subsidiaries of foreign firms to Canadian enterprises is beneficial to the Canadian economy." Comment.
17. "The auto pact shows how Canada can benefit from the inter-plant specialization offered by U.S. multinational corporations." Comment.
18. "The existence of a large, well-organized international sales force enables a multinational corporation to promote the sale abroad of Canadian-made products." Comment, with reference to "world product mandates".

19. What are "truncated" enterprises? What possible disadvantages can arise from their existence in Canada?
20. What is "transfer pricing"? How can it work to Canada's disadvantage?
21. "The Canadian subsidiaries of foreign firms should be required to process more of their materials in Canada before exporting them abroad." Comment.
22. How does the existence of truncated enterprises affect job opportunities for Canadian scientists?
23. "The fragmentation of Canadian industries appears to be very pronounced when compared with other industrially advanced nations." What is the meaning and significance of this statement?
24. To what extent is the flow of dividends abroad, as a result of foreign direct investment in Canada, a disadvantage for this country? Under what circumstances is it particularly so?
25. How can the activities of the Canadian subsidiaries of U.S. firms lead to political conflict between Canada and the United States? Give examples.
26. In what way can the increase of foreign direct investment in Canada lead to inefficient use of Canada's natural resources?
27. How have governments in Canada tried to restrict foreign ownership and control of Canadian industry in Canada?
28. What, in your opinion, are the most important of the guidelines put forward by the federal government in 1966 for the behaviour of the Canadian subsidiaries of foreign firms?
29. What tax incentives does the federal government now offer to promote Canadian ownership of industry?
30. Explain the nature and purpose of the Canadian Development Corporation.
31. What new foreign-ownership policy is now being implemented by the Canadian federal government?
32. What measures have provincial governments taken to restrict foreign ownership and control of Canadian industry?
33. Explain and discuss the pros and cons of Canada's National Energy Program.

Part I:
INTERNATIONAL TRADE
AND FINANCE

In this part of the book, we consider how Canadians try to improve their standard of living by engaging in international trade and finance. Thanks to a net inflow of foreign capital, both equity and borrowed capital, Canadians are able to continue running a deficit on current account—that is, making more payments abroad (for goods and services, including interest and dividend remittances), than foreigners make to us.

38. CANADA'S BALANCE OF INTERNATIONAL PAYMENTS

CHAPTER OBJECTIVES

A. To explain what is meant by Canada's balance of international payments
B. To examine the current account
C. To discuss some of the factors that have been affecting Canadian exports and imports
D. To examine the capital account
E. To explain the nature and purpose of official monetary movements
F. To explain the concept of a basic surplus or a basic deficit in a country's balance of international payments

CHAPTER OUTLINE

38.1 Balance of Payments Defined
38.2 The Current Account
38.3 The Capital Account
38.4 Official Monetary Movements
38.5 Basic Surplus or Deficit

38.1: BALANCE OF PAYMENTS DEFINED

Canada does not live in economic isolation. It engages in a variety of transactions with other countries of the world, predominantly with its huge neighbour to the south. Goods are exported and imported; Canadians travel abroad and foreigners visit Canada; immigrants send money home; interest and dividends are paid to foreigners for use of their capital and expertise, and income is received by Canadians on their investments abroad; the federal, provincial, and municipal governments float new bond issues in foreign capital markets; foreigners buy shares in Canadian companies and vice versa; and the Canadian government provides foreign aid.

All these and many other economic transactions with foreign countries are summarized (see Table S.40) in the form of a *balance of international payments*, or "balance of payments", for short. This balance shows, on the one hand, all the money received by Canada from foreign countries; on the other, all the money paid out. For simplification, the balance of international payments is divided into three main parts: the "current account", the "capital account", and "official monetary movements".

38.2: THE CURRENT ACCOUNT

This is a summary of all revenues from the export of goods and services and all expenditures on imports. The current account is itself divided into two sub-accounts: the "merchandise account" and the "non-merchandise account".

Merchandise Account. In this account are summarized the payments received from foreigners for goods exported, and payments made to foreigners for goods imported. Because this account is concerned only with goods or "merchandise", it is also known as the "visible trade account".

Non-Merchandise Account. This account includes all current transactions not included in the merchandise account. Because it relates mainly to services, this account is sometimes called the "invisible trade account". The principal service items in this account are travel, interest and dividends, and freight and shipping. For example, when Canadians visit the United States their spending on food, accommodation, and so on, constitutes an expenditure in Canada's non-merchandise account. Conversely, the money spent by U.S. tourists in this country represents a revenue in this account. Transfer receipts and payments, such as pensions remitted abroad, make up the remainder of this account.

Canada's Experience

For many years now, Canada has had a surplus in its merchandise account. Exports of goods have almost always been greater than imports. However, this favourable balance of "visible trade" has usually been more than offset by a deficit in the non-merchandise account. Since

Table S.40
Canada's Balance of International Payments, in millions of dollars, 1960-1982

Years	Merchandise trade exports	imports	balance	Service receipts	Service payments	Balance on goods and services	Net transfers	Balance on current account	Net capital movements Long-term	Short-term (1)	Special Drawing Rights allocations	Net official movements
1960	5 392	5 540	-148	1 590	2 549	-1 107	-126	-1 233	929	265	-	-39
1965	8 745	8 627	118	2 437	3 714	-1 159	29	-1 130	833	455	-	158
1966	10 326	10 102	224	2 719	4 157	-1 214	52	-1 162	1 228	-425	-	-359
1967	11 338	10 772	566	3 325	4 462	-571	72	-499	1 415	-896	-	20
1968	13 720	12 249	1 471	3 070	4 822	-281	184	-97	1 669	-1 223	-	349
1969	15 035	14 071	964	3 695	5 719	-1 060	143	-917	2 337	-1 355	-	65
1970	16 921	13 869	3 052	4 246	6 345	953	153	1 106	1 007	-583	133	1 663
1971	17 877	15 314	2 563	4 304	6 702	168	266	431	664	-318	119	896
1972	20 129	18 272	1 857	4 451	6 978	-670	284	-386	1 588	-983	117	336
1973	25 461	22 726	2 735	5 257	8 228	-236	344	108	628	-1 203	-	-467
1974	32 591	30 902	1 689	6 401	10 104	-2 017	557	-1 460	1 041	443	-	24
1975	33 511	33 962	-451	6 941	11 627	-5 137	380	-4 757	3 935	417	-	-405
1976	37 995	36 607	1 388	7 606	13 366	-4 372	530	-3 842	8 007	-3 643	-	522
1977	44 253	41 523	2 730	8 295	15 739	-4 714	413	-4 301	4 217	-1 337	-	-1421
1978	53 054	49 047	4 007	9 931	18 923	-4 985	50	-4 935	3 111	-1 475	-	3 299
1979	65 275	61 157	4 118	11 906	21 652	-5 626	664	-4 962	1 905	4 746	219	1 908
1980	76 772	68 284	8 488	14 172	25 003	-2 343	1 247	-1 096	1 907	-1 308	217	-1 280
1981	84 221	76 870	7 351	15 247	29 505	-6 907	1 560	-5 346	1 558	6 004	210	1 426
1982	84 486	66 740	17 746	15 909	32 410	1 245	1 424	2 669	8 561	-11 925	-	-695

Source: Statistics Canada, *Quarterly Estimates of the Canadian Balance of International Payments*, Cat. 67-001

Note: (1) Includes net errors and omissions

1974, Canadian expenditure on foreign services has exceeded, by a wide margin, foreign expenditures on Canadian services. The main reason for Canada's deficit in "invisible trade" is interest and dividends and Canadian travel abroad. Canada's payments of interest and dividends to foreigners (the result of considerable foreign investment in Canada) have always greatly exceeded interest and dividends received by Canadians from abroad. The other main factor, a relatively new one, is a large deficit in travel expenditure. Overall, Canada has for many years had a deficit on its current account. In other words, total Canadian expenditures on foreign goods and services have for many years exceeded total foreign spending on Canadian goods and services. A breakdown of Canada's merchandise trade and services accounts is shown in Tables S.41 and S.42.

Exports

Apart from motor vehicle exports, which have greatly benefited from the Canada-U.S. Automotive Products Agreement of 1965, and a few other key manufactured goods, such as telecommunications equipment, much of Canada's exports consists of goods that have undergone relatively little processing in Canada and in which the labour content in terms of value added in production is consequently relatively low. The key export items (see Table S.43) are, in descending order of importance, metal and mineral products, auto and related products, other fabricated materials, pulp, paper and board, machinery and equipment, wheat and wheat flour, other agricultural products, natural gas, other manufacturing goods, lumber and plywood, and crude petroleum.

Dependence on the U.S. Market

The biggest market for Canada's export goods, with about 70 per cent of the total value, is the United States. The second largest customer is Japan, followed by the United Kingdom. The full list of Canada's foreign customers is shown in Table S.44.

Most of Canada's manufactured goods go to the United States, which makes Canadian manufacturing income and employment particularly vulnerable to U.S. economic policy measures. Unfortunately, with Canadian manufacturing costs so high relative to those of many Asian and European producers, it is difficult for Canada to diversify its export market for manufactured goods, however economically and politically desirable this objective may be.

Table S.41
Canada's Merchandise Trade Balances, in billions of dollars, 1976-1982

	1976	1977	1978	1979	1980	1981	1982
Food and related products......	1.4	1.3	1.5	2.1	3.5	4.2	5.3
Crude material and related products.................	3.2	3.5	2.9	4.6	3.4	3.0	6.1
Fabricated materials...........	6.0	7.9	10.4	12.4	16.6	16.0	16.1
Autos and related products......	-1.2	-1.2	-0.8	-3.3	-2.7	-2.9	1.5
Other end products............	-8.9	-9.9	-11.6	-13.9	-15.1	-17.9	-14.1
Re-exports and special transactions..............	0.5	0.5	0.6	0.9	1.2	2.2	1.9
Total	1.0	2.2	3.1	2.8	6.9	4.5	16.8

Source: Statistics Canada, *Summary of External Trade,* Cat. 65-001
Note: Details may not add due to rounding

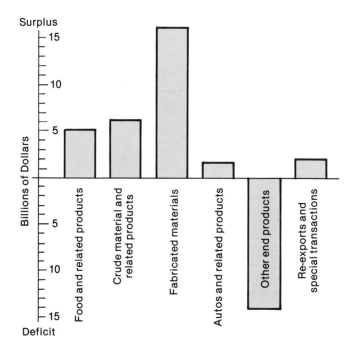

Source: Table S.41 (1982 data)

Table S.42
Canada's Services Account Balances, in billions of dollars, 1976-1982

	1976	1977	1978	1979	1980	1981	1982
Freight and shipping..........	-0.1	0.0	0.1	0.3	0.5	0.5	0.9
Travel......................	-1.2	-1.6	-1.7	-1.1	-1.2	-1.1	-1.3
Interest....................	-1.6	-2.5	-3.2	-3.7	-3.9	-4.5	-7.4
Dividends..................	-0.9	-1.2	-1.5	-1.6	-1.4	-1.9	-1.9
Other Services..............	-1.4	-1.6	-2.1	-3.0	-3.8	-6.0	-5.6
Miscellaneous Income.....	-0.3	-0.4	-0.7	-1.3	-1.6	-3.8	-3.2
Government business and other.............	-1.1	-1.2	-1.5	-1.7	-2.2	-2.2	-2.5
Withholding tax..............	-0.5	-0.5	-0.6	-0.8	-1.0	-1.1	-1.2
Total......................	-5.8	-7.4	-9.0	-9.7	-10.8	-14.3	-16.5

Source: Statistics Canada, *Quarterly Estimates of the Canadian Balance of International Payments,* Cat. 67-001

Note: Details may not add due to rounding

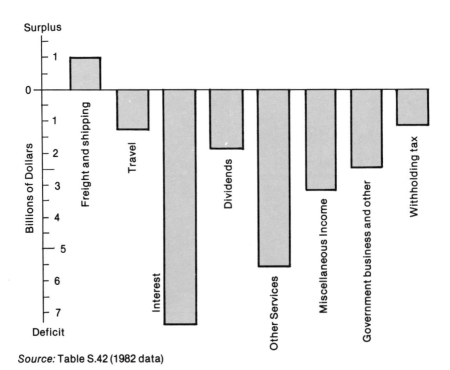

Source: Table S.42 (1982 data)

Table S.43
Canada's Principal Exports, 1982

Item	$ millions	Per cent
Wheat	4 286	5.1
Animals and other edible products	5 937	7.0
Ores and concentrates	3 187	3.8
Crude petroleum and natural gas	7 483	8.9
Other crude materials	4 105	4.9
Lumber	2 911	3.4
Woodpulp	3 234	3.8
Newsprint	4 080	4.8
Fabricated metals	6 781	8.0
Other fabricated materials	10 893	12.9
Motor vehicles and parts	16 382	19.4
Other machinery and equipment	9 956	11.8
Consumer goods and miscellaneous	2 478	2.9
Re-exports	2 690	3.2
Total	84 403	100.0

Source: Statistics Canada, *Summary of External Trade,* Cat. 65-001

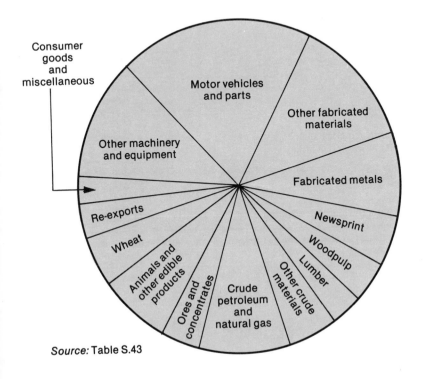

Source: Table S.43

Table S.44
Canada's Merchandise Exports, by Major Countries and Areas, 1982

	$ millions	Per cent
Countries		
United States	57 678.5	68.2
Japan	4 594.4	5.4
United Kingdom	2 725.5	3.2
U.S.S.R	2 073.7	2.5
West Germany	1 284.0	1.5
People's Republic of China	1 233.0	1.5
Netherlands	1 058.1	1.3
Belgium and Luxembourg	790.6	0.9
France	753.9	0.9
Italy	702.0	0.8
Australia	699.8	0.8
Venezuela	686.2	0.8
Mexico	456.3	0.5
India	295.6	0.3
Norway	256.3	0.3
Republic of South Africa	233.0	0.3
Others	9 013.7	10.7
Total	84.534.6	100.0
Areas		
Western Europe	8 761.4	10.4
Eastern Europe	2 590.2	3.1
Middle East	1 875.2	2.2
Other Africa	1 189.7	1.4
Other Asia	8 171.9	9.7
Oceania	85.3	0.1
Other: South America	206.8	0.2
Central America and Antilles	1 514.2	1.8
	24 394.7	28.9
United States	57 678.5	68.2
Others	2 461.4	2.9
Total Exports (including re-exports)	84 534.6	100.0

Source: Statistics Canada, *Summary of External Trade*, Cat. 65-001

The proximity of the United States gives Canadian manufacturers a competitive advantage, as regards transportation costs and after-sales service, over many foreign manufacturers. But once Canadian manufacturers have to ship overseas to reach their markets this advantage is lost. Nevertheless, exports of Canadian manufactured goods, as well as of more traditional resource-based products, to markets other than the United States have been gradually increasing.

Can excessive dependence on the U.S. market ever be avoided? It seems unlikely. First of all, the United States, with its population of some 250 million and one of the highest average per-capita incomes in the world, has enormous buying power. Second, this market is easily accessible to many Canadian manufacturers, particularly to those located in southern Ontario's manufacturing belt. Only if Canada could expand its own population to, say, 100 million in the next decade or two (a physically impossible feat without mass immigration), and provide them with employment and income, could Canadian reliance on export markets as a whole for income and jobs be greatly reduced. For those who wonder why we need to export at all, the answer lies in the gains to be obtained from international trade. Exports provide more income and jobs for Canadians than there would otherwise be. In fact, export-related jobs are estimated to account for a quarter of all jobs in Canada. Moreover, export earnings provide the means to pay for goods and services that Canadians wish to buy from abroad. Furthermore, many of the goods that Canadians sell to foreigners just could not find a sufficient market in Canada.

Britain's Entry into the European Economic Community

Canadian exports have suffered as a result of the United Kingdom's entry into the European Economic Community on January 1, 1973. Some Canadian products, such as plywood and veneers, have not yet been adversely affected, for the EEC affords them very favourable tariff treatment. But other goods, particularly the highly manufactured ones, as well as resource products such as lumber, pulp and newsprint and farm products such as wheat, have to face the EEC common external tariff that can be quite high on many products. No longer do Canadian goods enjoy the preferential tariff treatment they previously received from Britain because of Canadian membership in the British Commonwealth.

Freer Trade with the United States?

Some people have suggested that Canada should stop trying to fight the inevitable and work towards much freer trade with the United States. But such a path of action raises the question whether many Canadian manufacturing industries could survive the full effect of U.S. competition. This is because Canada's manufacturing industries are often characterized by small-scale—and more important, by rather unspecialized—production, and by high unit costs, despite advantages in supplies of basic materials and labour, and access to first-rate technology.

Certainly, in the case of the motor-vehicle industry, freer trade has meant much more income and employment in Canada. But minimum production requirements for Canada were stipulated in the Automotive Products Agreement (see Chapter 43—International Trade Cooperation). And these must claim a large part of the credit for increased Canadian production. It is possible that Canada might negotiate more trade agreements of this type, but the United States might require significant concessions in exchange—for example, a guaranteed share of Canadian water and energy resources. Not so many years ago, it was possible to conceive that Canada (one of the few industrial countries in the world without duty-free access to a large market for all of its manufactured products) might join some larger free-trade area such as an Atlantic Community, involving Britain and the United States. But today, this possibility seems remote. Nevertheless, the possibility of more free trade with the U.S., perhaps in certain types of products, keeps being raised in Canada.

Agricultural Products

Although tariffs have been reduced over the years on Canadian exports to many countries, this reduction has applied mainly to industrial goods. Most countries, for political as well as economic reasons, severely limit imports of agricultural products. As a result, Canada continues to face considerable problems in exporting its grains, beef, and other agricultural products. However, China and the Soviet Union have been major purchasers of Canadian wheat in recent years.

Ocean Freight Rates

A problem for Canadian exporters since the oil price increases beginning in 1973 has been the severe rise in ocean freight rates. The further the goods have to be shipped, the higher the freight charge and, consequently, the less competitive the price. By comparison, shipping to the U.S. market, by truck and rail, is far cheaper. Hence, the difficulty of reducing economic dependence on the U.S., despite all the federal government's aspirations, over the last decade, in this regard.

The Dollar Exchange Rate

Another problem that confronted all Canadian exports for many years was the high rate of foreign exchange for the Canadian dollar. If the Canadian dollar appreciates in external value, Canadian goods become more expensive to foreigners. If it depreciates, they become cheaper.

In the case of some products, particularly resource-based ones, the U.S. importer may still buy the Canadian product, particularly if the same product is not cheaper elsewhere. But, in the case of manufactured goods for which Canada may have only a slight cost advantage (usually the result of cheaper material), the U.S. customer will turn to lower-cost U.S. or other foreign sources of supply. Thus, the higher the foreign-exchange rate of the Canadian dollar, the more difficult it becomes to sell Canadian manufactured goods abroad. However, these manufactured goods are the ones that have the highest labour content. An increase in exports of resource-based products unfortunately does not create the same number of jobs and the same amount of labour income in Canada as does an increase in exports of manufactured goods.

Since the Canadian dollar was floated in 1970, it has moved both up and down in relation to the U.S. dollar—the major international trading currency. For some years, the movement has been downward. Thus, with a weak Canadian dollar, Canadian exports have been helped rather than hindered in their price competitiveness in the U.S. market. Elsewhere abroad it has been a different story—in terms of many European and Latin American currencies, for example, the Canadian dollar has appreciated—thus hindering our exports.

Imports

Canada's principal imports (see Table S.45) are, in descending order of importance: machinery and equipment, industrial materials, auto and related parts, crude petroleum, other consumer goods, food, and construction materials. Imports of machinery and equipment are almost three times the value of the exports; imports of auto and related parts are sometimes greater and sometimes less than the exports; and imports of crude petroleum are three times the exports.

With most of our imports from the United States (see Table S.46) and most of our exports sold to that country, Canada's major trade partner by far is the United States. Second in importance is Japan. Third is Britain.

Table S.45
Canada's Principal Imports, 1982

Item	$ millions	Per cent
Animals and edible products	4 940	7.3
Crude petroleum	4 973	7.4
Other crude materials	3 723	5.5
Fabricated materials	11 794	17.4
Motor vehicles and parts	14 898	22.0
Other machinery and equipment	19 391	28.7
Other end products and misc.	7 911	11.7
Total	67 629	100.0

Source: Statistics Canada, *Summary of External Trade,* Cat. 65-001

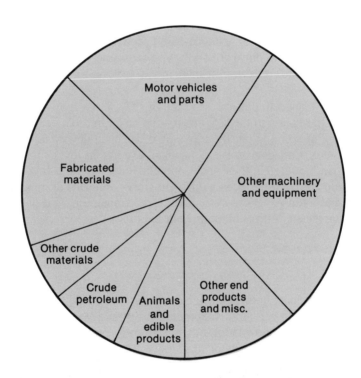

Source: Table S.45

Table S.46
Canada's Merchandise Imports, by Major Countries and Areas, 1982

	$ millions	Per cent
Countries		
United States	47 916.8	70.5
Japan	3 536.1	5.2
United Kingdom	1 903.7	2.8
Venezuela	1 810.5	2.7
West Germany	1 384.0	2.0
France	877.0	1.3
Saudi Arabia	731.3	1.1
Italy	724.9	1.1
Brazil	482.6	0.7
Australia	446.1	0.7
Netherlands	267.3	0.4
Belgium and Luxemburg	263.6	0.4
Jamaica	125.2	0.2
Iran	117.2	0.2
India	90.7	0.1
Others	7 374.3	10.9
Total	67 926.1	100.0
Areas		
Western Europe	7 026.1	10.3
Eastern Europe	241.3	0.4
Middle East	966.6	1.4
Other Africa	658.3	1.0
Other Asia	6 190.9	9.1
Oceania	594.6	0.9
Other South America	275.0	0.4
Central America and Antilles	128.0	0.2
	16 080.8	23.7
United States	47 916.8	70.5
Others	3 928.5	5.8
Total	67 926.1	100.0

Source: Statistics Canada, *Summary of External Trade,* Cat. 65-001

38.3: THE CAPITAL ACCOUNT

The second main part of Canada's balance of payments (see Table S.40) is the capital account. It includes two main items: (a) long-term capital movements, and (b) short-term capital investments.

Long-term Capital Movements.

These flows of long-term capital between Canada and foreign countries are grouped under three headings:

(1) *Direct Investment:* Funds used to provide additional working capital for a business or to purchase physical assets such as land, buildings and equipment and to obtain control of Canadian companies through the purchase of sufficient common shares.

(2) *Securities (or Portfolio Investment):* Funds used for the purchase of securities: new and existing government bonds and corporation bonds and common and preferred stocks. However, if the purchase of shares in a corporation provides a controlling interest, the capital investment would be classified as a direct investment.

(3) *Miscellaneous Long-term Capital Movements:* Funds used by the Government of Canada to make loans to foreign governments, to make capital subscriptions to international monetary agencies, and funds used for other purposes.

Short-term Capital Movements

These are funds that are transferred temporarily from one country to another because of differences in interest rates, political instability, or an anticipated change in the foreign exchange value of a currency. Such short-term capital movements from Canada to foreign countries are reflected in increases in Canadian resident holdings of foreign bank balances and other short-term investments. Short-term capital inflows take the form of increased holdings by foreigners of such investments in Canada as bank balances, commercial and finance-company paper, and Government of Canada Treasury bills.

Canada's Experience

As the statistics show, Canada usually enjoys a substantial surplus in its capital account—that is, more capital flows into the country each year than flows out. However, most of this surplus is due to long-term capital (foreign investment in Canada and borrowing by our governments and business corporations). Short-term capital flows are less certain, often registering a deficit rather than a surplus in that part of the capital account.

38.4: OFFICIAL MONETARY MOVEMENTS

The third main part of Canada's balance of payments is net official monetary movements. These movements act as a balancing item in Canada's balance of international payments. Any difference between the total of current and capital inflows and the total of current and capital outflows is covered by them.

Official monetary movements result in an increase or decrease in Canada's official *international monetary reserves*. These reserves consist of (a) gold and convertible currencies held by the Bank of Canada on behalf of the government and (b) Canada's net reserve position with the International Monetary Fund.

Gold has always been a readily acceptable international means of exchange: most countries are willing to accept it in return for their goods, services, and currency. *Convertible currencies* include the U.S. dollar and other major international trading currencies such as the Swiss franc, the German mark, and the Japanese yen that can be freely converted into other currencies. The reserve position with the International Monetary Fund represents the limit up to which Canada may purchase foreign currences from that international agency, using Canadian dollars.

38.5: BASIC SURPLUS OR DEFICIT

A *basic surplus* exists in a country's balance of international payments if the total receipts on current account and capital account exceed the total payments. A *basic deficit* exists if the opposite occurs. To make up the difference, official monetary movements are required—causing an increase or a decrease in the country's international monetary resources.

To counteract a basic surplus, a country would need to revalue its currency upwards and otherwise discourage exports and encourage imports. To counteract a basic deficit, it should devalue its currency and otherwise promote exports and restrict imports.

38.6: CANADA'S OVERALL BALANCE OF PAYMENTS SITUATION

Looking at Canada's overall balance of international payments (Table S.40), we can see that deficits on current account and even in net short-term capital movements have usually been more than offset by persistent surpluses in net long-term capital movements. In other words, Canada usually enjoys a basic surplus—with a resultant increase in its official international monetary reserves.

Without the long-term capital inflow, Canada would have had to reduce its imports to match its exports, or increase its exports to match its imports. Today, however, it would not be easy for Canada to reduce its deficit on current account because of the large remittance from Canada of interest and dividends to foreign investors. In other words, Canada is obliged to borrow considerable foreign capital, not only to help develop its economy, but also to remit dividend and interest payments to foreign owners and lenders. Recent substantial deficits in the travel and other services accounts have made a bad situation worse.

38.7: MONETARY POLICY AND THE BALANCE OF PAYMENTS

In recent years, economists have been perturbed by the strong effect that monetary policy has had on the U.S. balance of payments. Because of much higher interest rates in the U.S., compared with those in the rest of the world, together with greater political and economic stability, there has been a tremendous inflow of both long and short-term capital into the U.S. This in turn has caused the foreign exchange rate of the U.S. dollar to appreciate—so that U.S. exports have become more expensive to foreigners and U.S. imports cheaper. As a result, the U.S. current account has been adversely affected. This has led to the conclusion that monetary policy can cause a country to have a balance-of-payments situation in which the "capital account drives the current account, rather than vice-versa."

Summary

1. Canada's balance of international payments shows, on the one hand, all the money received by Canada from foreign countries and, on the other, all the money paid out. It is divided into three main parts: the current account, the capital account, and official monetary movements

2. The current account is a summary of all revenues from the export of goods and services and all expenditures on imports. The current account is itself divided into a merchandise account and a non-merchandise account.

4. The capital account includes two main items: long-term capital movements between Canada and foreign countries; and short-term capital movements.

5. The two main types of long-term capital movements are direct investment and portfolio investment.

6. Higher short-term rates of interest in one country compared with

another are a major reason for short-term international capital movements.

7. Net official monetary movements act as a balancing item in Canada's balance of international payments. These movements result in an increase or decrease in Canada's international monetary reserves.

8. If a country's total international receipts on current and capital accounts persistently exceed payments, it is considered to have a basic surplus. Conversely, if payments persistently exceed receipts, it has a basic deficit.

9. A country's monetary policy can influence the capital account of its balance of international payments and, through changes in the foreign exchange rate of its currency, indirectly influence the current account.

Key Terms

Balance of payments 769	Imports 779
Current account 770	Capital account 782
Merchandise account 770	Direct investment 782
Visible trade 770	Portfolio investment 782
Non-merchandise account 770	Official monetary
Invisible trade 770	movements 783
Exports 772	International monetary
U.S. market 772	reserves 783
EEC 777	Convertible currencies 783
Free trade 777	Basic surplus 783
Dollar exchange rate 779	Basic deficit 783

Review Questions

1. What is a country's "balance of international payments"?
2. What is the "current account" in a country's balance of international payments?
3. Distinguish between visible trade and invisible trade.
4. What is an unfavourable balance of trade? What has been Canada's experience in recent years?
5. What are Canada's principal exports?
6. Which countries are Canada's principal export markets?
7. Is Canada's dependence on the U.S. export market: (a) inevitable? (b) desirable?

8. How did Britain's entry into the European Economic Community affect Canada and other British Commonwealth countries?
9. Should Canada work towards free trade with the U.S.? Discuss the pros and cons.
10. Agricultural products are usually traded differently in international trade than manufactured goods. Discuss.
11. What effect have higher ocean freight rates had on Canadian exporters?
12. "A strong Canadian dollar means greater economic prosperity for Canada." Discuss.
13. What are Canada's principal imports?
14. From which countries does Canada import most? Why?
15. What does the pattern of trade reveal about Canada's economy?
16. What is the "capital account" in a country's balance of international payments? What are its two main components?
17. "There are two main types of long-term capital movements: direct investment and portfolio investment." Explain.
18. What has been Canada's experience in recent years with long-term capital movements?
19. What are the reasons for short-term international capital movements? How are these funds invested?
20. What is the form of Canada's international monetary reserves?
21. "Net official monetary movements act as a balancing item in Canada's balance of international payments." Explain. What has been Canada's experience in recent years?
22. What is meant by a basic surplus or basic deficit in a country's balance of international payments? What will happen if such a situation persists?
23. Explain the relationship, in a country's balance of international payments, between the current account and the capital account.
24. Does it make economic sense for a province to try, at the same time, to promote exports and attract foreign investment? Discuss.

39. FOREIGN EXCHANGE RATES

39.1: FOREIGN CURRENCY DEMAND AND SUPPLY

Canadian business firms, when they sell goods and services to foreigners, want eventually to be paid in Canadian dollars. Conversely, foreign business firms selling to Canada want eventually to be paid in their own money—for example, the U.S. dollar, the Japanese yen, or the Italian lira. Furthermore, when Canadians wish to invest abroad (or foreigners wish to invest in Canada), they need to obtain the currency of the country to which the funds are to be transferred. The same thing applies when dividends and interest have to be paid. At any one time, therefore, there are many foreigners wishing to exchange their own currencies for Canadian dollars. At the same time, there are also many Canadians wishing to exchange Canadian dollars for foreign currencies. For each currency, including the Canadian dollar, there is, consequently both a demand and a supply.

39.2: FOREIGN EXCHANGE RATE DEFINED

The "price" at which each foreign currency is bought and sold is known as its *exchange rate*. The Canadian exchange rates for a wide variety of foreign currencies are shown in Table S.47. Each rate indicates how many Canadian dollars and decimal fractions of a dollar are required to purchase one unit of the foreign currency. The foreign-exchange rate of a particular foreign currency can also be expressed in another way. Instead of saying how much a unit of foreign currency is worth in terms of Canadian dollars and/or cents, we can say how much a Canadian dollar is worth in terms of the foreign currency. Thus, if a U.S. dollar is worth $1.20 Canadian, then a Canadian dollar is worth $0.83 U.S. One ratio is the inverse of the other.

As practically every country quotes an exchange rate for the U.S. dollar, each country is easily able to compare the foreign-exchange worth of its own currency with those of other countries. In other words, the U.S. dollar, as well as being a major international currency for international trade purposes, is used as an international measure of value.

39.3: FLOATING EXCHANGE RATES

In many countries, the foreign exchange rates of the national currency are set by the government. These rates are known as *fixed exchange rates*. In other countries, the government allows the exchange rates to be determined in the foreign-exchange market. Where these rates are permitted to fluctuate each day according to the relative strengths of demand and supply, a country is said to have a *floating* or *flexible exchange rate*. When a country's central bank intervenes in the foreign exchange market (by buying or selling currencies) to make any changes more gradual or to provide some measure of support for its own currency, the term "dirty float" is sometimes used. This has been the situation with Canada ever since its currency was allowed to float in 1970.

In the absence of substantial government intervention, the foreign exchange rate of a currency will be determined by the interaction of

Table S.47
Foreign Exchange Rates, 1954-1982 (Canadian Dollars and/or Cents
Per Unit of Foreign Currency)

Years	French franc	German mark	Japanese yen	Swiss franc	Pound Sterling	U.S. dollar
			(Average of daily rates)			
1954	0.278	0.232	0.00270	0.227	2.734	0.973
1955	0.282	0.234	0.00274	0.230	2.754	0.986
1956	0.281	0.234	0.00273	0.230	2.752	0.984
1957	0.256	0.228	0.00266	0.224	2.679	0.959
1958	0.231	0.232	0.00270	0.226	2.728	0.971
1959	0.196	0.230	0.00267	0.222	2.694	0.959
1960	0.198	0.233	0.00270	0.225	2.723	0.970
1961	0.207	0.252	0.00281	0.235	2.839	1.013
1962	0.218	0.267	0.00297	0.247	3.001	1.069
1963	0.220	0.271	0.00300	0.250	3.020	1.079
1964	0.220	0.271	0.00300	0.250	3.012	1.079
1965	0.220	0.270	0.00300	0.249	3.014	1.078
1966	0.219	0.269	0.00298	0.249	3.009	1.077
1967	0.219	0.271	0.00298	0.249	2.962	1.079
1968	0.218	0.270	0.00299	0.250	2.579	1.077
1969	0.208	0.275	0.00301	0.250	2.574	1.077
1970	0.189	0.286	0.00292	0.242	2.502	1.044
1971	0.183	0.291	0.00291	0.246	2.469	1.010
1972	0.196	0.311	0.00327	0.259	2.479	0.991
1973	0.226	0.378	0.00370	0.317	2.452	1.000
1974	0.204	0.379	0.00336	0.330	2.288	0.978
1975	0.238	0.414	0.00343	0.393	2.258	1.017
1976	0.207	0.393	0.00333	0.395	1.781	0.986
1977	0.217	0.459	0.00398	0.445	1.857	1.063
1978	0.254	0.569	0.00548	0.644	2.191	1.141
1979	0.276	0.639	0.00537	0.705	2.486	1.171
1980	0.277	0.644	0.00519	0.698	2.721	1.169
1981	0.222	0.532	0.00545	0.613	2.430	1.199
1982	0.189	0.508	0.00497	0.609	2.158	1.234

Source: Bank of Canada, *Review*, monthly

demand and supply. Let us consider the Canadian exchange rate for U.S. dollars, the currency of our major trade partner, and the one that is used most in international trade.

The Canadian demand for U.S. dollars, on the one hand, results from those items in Canada's international balance of payments that cause an outflow of funds from Canada to the United States. The main items are Canadian purchases of U.S. goods and services, including tourist expenditures in the United States, plus interest and dividend remittances on U.S. investment in Canada. The supply of U.S. dollars, on the other hand, is the result of those items in Canada's international balance of payments that cause an inflow of funds from the United States. The major items in this respect are U.S. purchases of Canadian goods and services and U.S. investments in Canada. Americans wishing to buy Canadian currency to make payments for these items offer U.S. dollars in exchange.

The demand for, and supply of, U.S. dollars at different "prices", or rates of exchange, can be illustrated graphically by means of a demand curve and a supply curve (see Figure 39:1). The actual rate of exchange

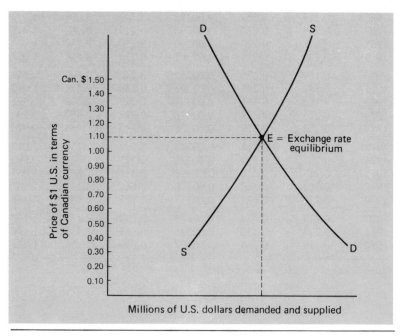

Figure 39:1   Demand and Supply Determine How Much Canadians Have to Pay for the U.S. Dollar

is where the Canadian demand for U.S. dollars is equal to the supply. This is at the point E in our graph where the demand curve DD intersects the supply curve SS. At this point, the exchange rate for the U.S. dollar is $1.10 Canadian. In other words, to buy a U.S. dollar, a Canadian will have to give one dollar and ten cents of Canadian currency in exchange.

Effect of an Increase in Canadian Demand for U.S. Dollars

What would happen to the U.S. dollar exchange rate, if Canadians began to import more U.S. goods, travel more in the United States, borrow more from that country, or increasingly engage in other transactions that caused an outflow of funds from Canada to the United States? There would obviously be an increase in Canadian demand for U.S. currency. In terms of the graph in Figure 39:2, this would mean a shift of the demand curve to the right. At each price (exchange rate) of the U.S. dollar, Canadians would want to buy a larger quantity of U.S. dollars than before. The consequence is that the new demand curve D_1D_1 would intersect the old supply curve SS (assuming that it has

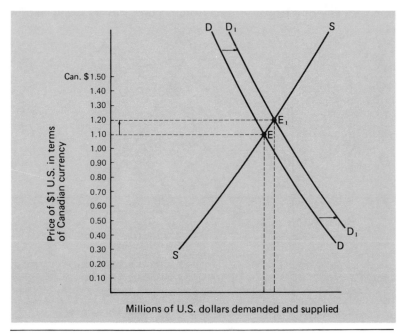

Figure 39:2 How an Increase in Demand for U.S. Dollars Raises the Exchange Rate

remained unchanged) at a new equilibrium point E_1. Because of the increase in demand, the exchange rate of the U.S. dollar will rise from $1.10 Canadian to $1.20 Canadian. This rise in the price of the U.S. dollar is called an *appreciation*.

Effect of an Increase in the Supply of U.S. Dollars

Conversely, we may ask: what would happen if Canadians were able to export more goods to the United States or attract more U.S. travellers or investment here? Clearly, the supply of U.S. dollars would increase. Americans would pay more to Canadian exporters and U.S. tourists and investors would buy more Canadian dollars to spend in this country. Even if they spent their U.S. dollars here, this money would soon be deposited by its recipient at a Canadian bank, adding to the supply of U.S. dollars available for exchange. The increase in the supply of U.S. dollars is shown in the graph in Figure 39:3 by a new supply curve S_1S_1. This new curve is to the right of the previous one, illustrating the fact that at every price, or exchange rate, more U.S. dollars are offered than before. The demand curve DD intersects the new supply curve S_1S_1 at a new equilibrium point E_1. As a result of this increase in supply, the

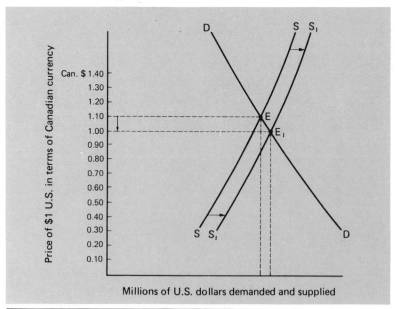

Figure 39:3   How an Increase in Supply of U.S. Dollars Reduces the Exchange Rate

exchange rate for the U.S. dollar would fall from $1.10 Canadian to $1.00 Canadian. This fall in the price of the U.S. dollar in terms of Canadian currency is called a *depreciation*.

Floating Exchange Rates: Good or Bad?

Canada has the distinction, enviable or not, of being one of the first countries in the world to have made use of a flexible exchange rate in the years since World War II. Specifically, the Canadian dollar floated freely in the foreign-exchange market during the period September 1950 to April 1962 and again during the period June 1970 to the present. Many other countries have followed suit, including the U.S.

Automatic Adjustments. One advantage of a freely floating exchange rate is that there can never be any imbalance between the Canadian demand for, and the foreign supply of, any foreign currency. Fluctuations in the exchange rate in response to these market forces will automatically equate demand with supply. Therefore, a persistent loss of international monetary reserves, with consequent implications for domestic economic policy, cannot occur. This is not true, however, of a "dirty float" in which the Bank of Canada intervenes to prop up the Canadian dollar by buying foreign currencies.

Insulation from Inflation Abroad. Another advantage of a freely floating exchange rate is that it helps to insulate a country from inflation abroad. As the foreign price level rises above that at home, the exchange rate will tend to alter in favour of the home country's currency. This is because foreign demand for the relatively cheaper home country's goods increases and home demand for the foreign country's relatively more expensive goods declines. As a result, foreign demand for the home country's currency also increases and home demand for the foreign currency decreases. As the foreign currency becomes cheaper in terms of the home currency, the cost of the imported good rises less than it would have done with a fixed rate of exchange.

Price Competitiveness. A flexible exchange rate also offers an advantage to a country whose price level rises above those of other countries. The automatic decline in the foreign-exchange rate of its currency will help prevent its goods being priced out of foreign markets. However, this can eventually turn into a disadvantage. As foreign demand for Canadian exports grows, the price of the Canadian dollar rises—because the supply of foreign currency (compared with demand) is increasing. As a result, Canadian goods can become higher priced for foreigners and demand for them be reduced. Canadian exporters, consequently, may get the impression that they are fighting a losing battle in trying to enlarge foreign sales. In summary, a weakening currency

will encourage exports; a strengthening currency will discourage them.
Effect of Capital Movements. These can be just as important as trade
payments in determining the exchange rate for a country's currency.
And such movements may cause the flexible exchange rate to increase
to the detriment of the country's economic interests. For example, in a
time of monetary restraint, high interest rates in Canada relative to the
United States and Europe may induce a heavy inflow of short-term
foreign capital. The increased supply of foreign currency, compared
with demand, will then cause an appreciation in the foreign exchange
value of the Canadian dollar. This, in turn, means that Canadian exports become more expensive to foreigners. The Canadian dollar price
has remained unchanged, but foreigners now have to pay more of their
own currency for each Canadian dollar. As a result, Canadian exports
decline, Canadian incomes fall, and unemployment increases.

But this is not the only consequence. At the same time as the Canadian dollar is becoming more expensive to foreigners, foreign currencies are becoming cheaper to Canadians, because, as we saw
previously, one exchange rate is the inverse of the other. Cheaper foreign currencies mean the Canadian importers now have to pay less for
foreign goods. (For example, an import priced at $10 U.S. per unit
now costs the Canadian importer $11 Canadian instead of $12, if the
rate has declined from $1.20 Canadian to $1.10 Canadian per U.S. dollar). More imports at lower prices mean more competition for the Canadian consumer's dollar. Instead of buying a Canadian-made product,
the consumer may now buy a foreign one. Insofar as the consumers
have paid less than before, they are better off. However, if the Canadian production of similar goods is reduced, plant and office workers
will be laid off or dismissed and incomes reduced. And the net effect
may be harmful to the country as a whole.
Uncertainty. Another disadvantage of a flexible exchange rate is its
uncertainty. Foreign importers like to know, naturally enough, what
they will have to pay for Canadian goods when they are delivered some
time in the future. Or what they will have to pay even later if the goods
are purchased on credit. An adverse change in the exchange rate in the
meantime could eliminate part, if not all, of the importer's profit margin. To avoid this uncertainty, the foreign importer will either have to
buy "future" dollars from the bank (i.e., dollars for delivery at a specified time in the future) at a premium, or require the Canadian exporter
to quote the export price in terms of the local currency (e.g., U.S.
dollars or Mexican pesos). This second alternative shifts the risk of an
exchange loss from the foreign importers' shoulders on to those of the
Canadian exporter. For example, assume that the Canadian exporter

has quoted an export price of $100 U.S. per tonne of product X when the exchange rate is $1.00 U.S. = $1.20 Canadian. This means that the Canadian exporter expects to receive $120 Canadian per tonne. However, if the exchange rate changes to $1.00 U.S. = $0.90 Canadian, the Canadian exporter will receive only $90 Canadian per tonne. The difference of $30 Canadian per tonne could well be the exporter's anticipated gross profit. Therefore, to eliminate the risk of an "exchange loss", the Canadian exporter would have to arrange to sell the foreign currency to its bank right away, with delivery in the future.

To keep the floating exchange rate from fluctuating wildly, the Bank of Canada intervenes in the foreign-exchange market. However, it does not buy or sell Canadian dollars as heavily as it would if it had to maintain a fixed official rate of exchange. Nevertheless, as mentioned before, it intervenes sufficiently for Canada's type of floating exchange rate to have merited the description of a "dirty float" — signifying that it is not a rate determined purely by normal market forces. And this intervention does cause some decrease or increase in Canada's international monetary reserves.

39.4: FIXED EXCHANGE RATES

A *fixed exchange rate* is a foreign exchange rate set, not by the interaction of demand and supply, but by government decree. For purposes of exchange stability, most currencies of the world do have rates of exchange that are fixed, or "pegged," by government. During the period 1962 to 1970, Canada had a fixed rate of exchange of just over $1.08 Canadian per U.S. dollar.

Maintaining a Fixed Exchange Rate

When Canada had a fixed foreign exchange rate, any tendency for the exchange market to set a rate beyond the permissible extremes had to be offset by government action. This was accomplished by the Bank of Canada's using its special Exchange Fund Account to buy or sell foreign currencies. If excessive demand for, say, U.S. dollars was pushing the rate above the permissible level, the Bank would sell U.S. currency. If an excessive supply of U.S. dollars was pushing the rate down, the Bank would buy U.S. currency.

To illustrate why the Bank of Canada would need to intervene in the foreign exchange market to maintain a fixed rate of exchange for the U.S. dollar, we can use a graph. Figure 39:4 shows the Canadian demand for and the American supply of U.S. currency at a particular time. The horizontal unbroken line indicates the fixed exchange rate, $1.10 Canadian per U.S. dollar. At that rate, Canadians wish to

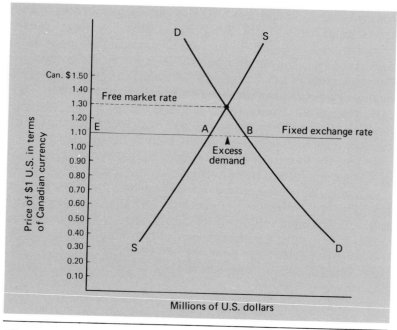

Figure 39:4   Why the Bank of Canada Needs to Sell Foreign Currency to Maintain a Fixed Exchange Rate

purchase EB millions of U.S. dollars. However, at this same rate, Americans are only willing to offer EA millions of U.S. dollars. Consequently, demand exceeds supply by AB millions of U.S. dollars. Therefore, to maintain the fixed rate, the Bank of Canada must make up this deficiency of supply by selling AB millions of U.S. dollars. If it did not, the free-market rate would settle at $1.30 Canadian per U.S. dollar, where normal demand and supply are equal—the point at which the demand and supply curves in our graph intersect.

We can also illustrate the opposite situation—where the Bank is required to buy U.S. currency to maintain the fixed exchange rate. Thus, in Figure 39:5, Canadian want to buy only EA millions of U.S. dollars at the official rate of exchange of $1.10 Canadian per U.S. dollar. However, at this rate, Americans want to sell EB millions of U.S. dollars. Without the Bank's intervention, the rate would drop to $0.90 Canadian per U.S. dollar—the rate at which demand would equal supply. To keep the exchange rate up to $1.10 Canadian per U.S. dollar, the Bank will have to buy AB millions of U.S. dollars. This will have the effect of

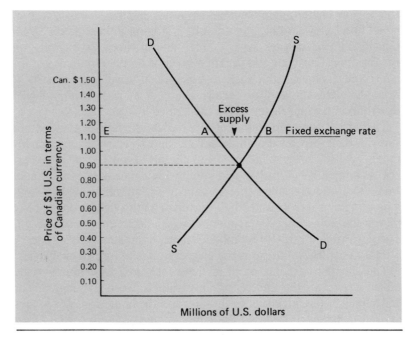

Figure 39:5   Why the Bank of Canada Needs to Buy Foreign
Currency to Maintain a Fixed Exchange Rate

increasing total demand to EB millions of U.S. dollars—so that demand
and supply are now equal at the official rate of exchange.

Persistent Shortage or Surplus of Foreign Currencies

But what if the demand for foreign currency at the fixed rate of
exchange persistently exceeds supply? In this case, the Bank must continue to sell foreign exchange to make up the shortage in supply. Eventually, Canada could lose all its international monetary reserves. To
prevent this calamity, the Bank of Canada and the federal government
would have to take other steps.

To reduce the demand for foreign currency the government can first
of all restrict imports. This can be done, in theory, by raising tariffs and
imposing import quotas. In practice, Canada's international obligations
make this course of action improbable, unless the economy were in
extremely critical shape. A more likely step is to use monetary and
fiscal policy to reduce the general level of demand in the country. Unfortunately, this step can have other undesirable effects for the coun-

try, notably higher unemployment. Another possible step is to restrict travel abroad by limiting the amount of foreign exchange that each Canadian tourist can purchase. Along the same lines, restrictions can be placed on Canadian investment abroad or on the remittance of interest and dividends. But such restrictions on travel and investment would be highly unusual for Canada, although practised quite widely in the world in recent years, even in the United States.

To increase the supply of foreign currency, the federal government and the Bank of Canada can do several things. They can, by a tight-money policy, combat inflation and thereby keep Canadian export prices competitive abroad. In addition, by high interest rates associated with a tight-money policy, they can encourage an inflow of short- and long-term capital from abroad. Unfortunately, this tight-money policy may at the same time slow economic growth and reduce employment. The government can also promote Canada to foreign tourists. Indeed, in many countries, tourism is the biggest source of foreign exchange.

The adoption of some or all of these measures may, however, be unable to correct the underlying imbalance between the demand for and supply of foreign currency. In this case, the home currency is considered to be *overvalued* and the government can do only one thing: reduce the official foreign exchange rate of its currency. This is known as *devaluation*. A Canadian dollar would then be worth less in terms of U.S. dollars. Faced with a severe imbalance of this sort, Britain devalued the pound sterling after World War II in 1948, in 1967, and in 1970, then followed Canada's example of a floating exchange rate in 1972.

Occasionally, a country will be faced with a situation in which the supply of foreign currency persistently exceeds demand. Instead of losing its international monetary reserves, a country may find them increasing at an embarrassingly high rate. This happened to West Germany some years ago. To relieve the pressure, a country can encourage imports, encourage its citizens to travel abroad, and promote official and private foreign investment and aid. However, if the country does nothing, of if the various measures fail to correct the problem, the country's currency would be considered *undervalued*. The country concerned may be forced as a last resort to *revalue* its currency upward. As a consequence, imports (because they are now cheaper) would be encouraged and exports (being more expensive for foreigners) discouraged.

Pros and Cons of Fixed Exchange Rates

It is not by chance that many countries of the world employ fixed rates of exchange. There is good reason why such governments "peg" the foreign exchange value of their currencies in terms of the U.S. dollar.

The great advantage of a fixed rate of exchange is the relative certainty that it affords to international monetary transactions. Foreign importers can predict with reasonable confidence how much of their own currency they will need to pay for imports from Canada. Canadian importers can know, ahead of payment time, how much each unit of imports will cost in Canadian dollars. Furthermore, Canadian exporters can know with reasonable certainty how many Canadian dollars their exports will earn. Foreigners investing here or Canadians investing abroad can be reasonably sure that the rate of return on their money and the value of their investment will not be reduced by adverse changes in the exchange rate of the currency. Exchange-rate stability removes one of the biggest headaches from international monetary transactions. It makes these transactions the same as transactions within a country—where, for example, an Edmonton purchaser of Toronto business machines knows that the $50 000 to be paid in 60 days will still be $50 000 when settlement day comes along. Exchange-rate stability encourages international trade and investment, which is generally considered to be much more beneficial to all than a policy of national economic self-sufficiency. For a major international trading currency such as the U.S. dollar, exchange-rate stability is imperative. However, it is less essential for the Canadian dollar.

The great disadvantage of a fixed exchange rate is that, in order to maintain it at its official level, a country may be forced to adopt undesirable internal economic policies. These policies, such as monetary restraint, may help maintain the fixed exchange rate, but at the expense of other economic goals such as economic growth and full employment. That is why some Canadian economists argue that the Canadian dollar should be allowed to drop until it finds its own level rather than make the country endure high-interest rate policies, etc. just to prop it up. However, a decline in the external value of the Canadian dollar means that imports and foreign debt servicing become that much more expensive in terms of Canadian dollars.

Foreign Exchange Speculation

When a country alters the official foreign exchange rate of its currency either downwards or upwards, some people stand to lose and others to gain. For example, assume that you had imported £1000 worth of goods from Britain, before it switched to a floating rate of exchange, with payment to be made in ninety days. In the meantime, the pound sterling is devalued from, say, $2.00 Canadian to $1.50 Canadian. This means that you will now have to pay $1500 instead of $2000, a saving of $500. On the other hand, if you had agreed to export some goods to Britain at a price of £1 per unit, you would now receive only $1.50 Canadian per unit instead of $2.00 Canadian.

If the revaluation (upward adjustment) of a currency seems likely, professional and amateur speculators will buy or sell the currency concerned. Thus, if a devaluation of the British pound seems imminent, persons holding pounds will exchange them for dollars or some other "hard" currency. Or, if a revaluation of the Swiss franc seems likely, persons will buy francs. This speculation worsens the foreign-exchange imbalance and actually hastens the change in the official rate. Sometimes a change in the official exchange rate is avoided: then foreign exchange speculators have lost their bet, since they cannot resell their holdings of the foreign currency at the expected higher price.

After a time, a country's official exchange rate may well lose touch with the underlying market forces of currency demand and supply. Thus, the currency may become overvalued or undervalued. This can lead, as we have seen, to speculation about a change in the official exchange rate. This speculation can last for months or even years. As a result, an air of uncertainty can overhang a country's currency, in effect destroying the principal advantage of the fixed exchange rate.

39.5 FLOATING VERSUS FIXED EXCHANGE RATES

We have completed our discussion of the nature and merits of floating and fixed exchange rates. Let us now, therefore, briefly contrast the advantages and disadvantages of each (see Table 39:1) from Canada's viewpoint.

A floating exchange rate has the great advantage of permitting a country to adopt fiscal and monetary policies designed to stimulate economic growth and a high level of employment without fear that its balance of payments will get out of line. This is a tremendous advantage for Canada, which needs expansionary monetary and fiscal policies to produce a high rate of economic growth and of new job opportunities. The disadvantage of a floating rate is the uncertainty that it creates in international transactions as to the future rate of exchange. However, this disadvantage for Canada is reduced in practice by forward selling of foreign exchange by Canadian exporters (when export prices are quoted in foreign currency) and by limited Bank of Canada intervention in the foreign-exchange market to smooth out fluctuations in the price of the Canadian dollar. Since the Canadian dollar is not a major trading or reserve currency like that of the United States, Canada

Table 39:1
Flexible versus Fixed Exchange Rates

Flexible Exchange Rate	Fixed Exchange Rate
Advantage	*Advantage*
1. Monetary independence — loss of international monetary reserves, with consequent implications for domestic monetary policy, does not occur.	1. Relative certainty that it affords to international monetary transactions — essential if a country's currency is a major trading currency; e.g., the U.S. dollar and British pound.
Disadvantages	*Disadvantage*
1. An increase in the price of the Canadian dollar (through increased foreign demand for Canadian goods or increased capital inflows) makes Canadian exports more expensive.	1. To maintain the official rate, a country may be forced to adopt undesirable domestic economic policies to increase exports, reduce imports, and alter capital flows.
2. Uncertainty as to the future rate of exchange complicates international trade and finance.	

does not have an international responsibility to maintain a fixed rate.

A fixed exchange rate affords some measure of stability in international transactions. However, as Britain's experience indicates, it can be a heavy burden to tie around a country's neck if it means economic stagnation at home. Only if a country is very strong economically or if international trade is of relatively small economic importance can it pursue expansionary policies at home and not worry unduly about the balance of payments and the exchange rate. In Britain's case, balance-of-payments difficulties have often led to restrictive monetary and fiscal policies at home. And even so, the official rate of exchange for the pound sterling has had to be devalued every few years and a floating rate adopted in June 1972. In the early 1980s, Canada also faced this situation and, in classical style, adopted a restrictive high-interest rate monetary policy at home to bolster the exchange rate and replenish its declining stock of international monetary reserves.

For Canada, it is now generally agreed among economists that a floating foreign exchange rate is preferable to a fixed one.

39.6: CANADA'S FOREIGN EXCHANGE RATE POLICY

In a major government policy decision, Canada moved in 1970 from a fixed exchange rate for the Canadian dollar to a floating one—albeit one that "floats" under the influence of a certain amount of Bank of Canada intervention in the foreign exchange market, to smooth out and even at times arrest changes in the exchange rate.

At first, the exchange rate remained close to par with the U.S. dollar and Canadian exporters claimed that a strong Canadian currency was making it difficult for them to makes sales abroad. However, over the last decade, the Canadian dollar has weakened considerably compared with the U.S. dollar (to about $1.30 Canadian for $1.00 U.S., or, the other way around, to about $0.77 U.S. for $1.00 Canadian). In terms of other foreign currencies, however, the Canadian dollar has recently been strengthening, making it more difficult to sell Canadian goods in Western Europe and other non-U.S. markets.

In recent years, some economists and politicians in Canada have argued that the Bank of Canada should let the Canadian dollar drop even further, perhaps to a 75-cent dollar. This would encourage exports and discourage Canadian purchases of foreign goods and services. It would also give the Bank of Canada the freedom to lower interest rates even more and thereby give a greater boost to business investment and consumer spending in Canada. Now, to help maintain the present exchange rate, the Bank of Canada must keep interest rates relatively high to attract short-term capital. However, according to the Bank of Canada, a lower Canadian dollar would merely push up the Canadian price of imported goods and services and so add to inflation in Canada which in turn would push up our export prices. And this would more than outweigh any advantages of further depreciation in the external value of the Canadian dollar.

39.7: U.S. EXCHANGE RATE POLICY

At the end of World War II and for many years thereafter, the U.S. dollar reigned supreme in the world. It was the "hard currency" or "convertible currency" *par excellence*, heavily in demand because of the strength of the U.S. economy, including its balance of international payments, the size of its gold and other international monetary reserves, and the consequent ease with which the U.S. dollar could be converted into other, softer currencies. Only the Swiss franc rivalled it in public esteem. Gradually, however, heavy U.S. spending abroad (including military and foreign aid commitments in Western Europe, Korea, and Vietnam), direct investment by U.S. multinational corporations, and a large volume of imports unmatched by an increase in exports undermined the international strength of the U.S. dollar. The Canadian dollar, also once strong, also weakened, even when compared with the U.S. dollar.

In the meantime, West Germany and Japan were busily rebuilding their war-torn economies and becoming extremely successful exporters of manufactured goods. In due course, the persistent surplus of their exports over their imports enabled these countries to amass large international monetary reserves and to permit the foreign exchange rates of their currencies, the mark and the yen, to steadily rise. These currencies, together with the already strong Swiss franc, became the new hard currencies.

In addition to Japan, S.E. Asian countries such as Taiwan, Hong Kong, South Korea, and Malaysia also became important exporters of manufactured goods to North America. The U.S. balance of payments situation was weakened even further when, in 1973, the world export price of crude oil, one of the United States' major import items, was substantially raised. Thus the nineteen-sixties and seventies witnessed the international weakening of the U.S. dollar (and of the Canadian one, too) mainly because of poor balance of payments' performance. Other countries, such as Britain, with its repeated devaluations of the official exchange rate for the pound sterling since World War II, had been the possessors of a "soft currency" all along. Such *devaluations* (or reduction in the fixed official exchange rate) saw the pound drop from about five U.S. dollars before World War II to less than two U.S. dollars today. Since 1971, the U.S. has also had a floating foreign exchange rate for its currency.

39.8: PROPOSAL FOR A MANAGED EXCHANGE RATE SYSTEM

In the early 1980s, France and other European countries called for a new Bretton-Woods style conference that would replace the existing floating rate system used by the Western industrial countries by a *managed exchange-rate system*. Such a system would link together the U.S. dollar, the Japanese yen, and the currencies of the European Monetary System (which vary, within fixed limits, with each other) within a narrow trading band.

One reason for European dissatisfaction with the floating rate for the U.S. dollar (the key trading currency) is that fluctuations in the exchange rate with other currencies have been extremely volatile, causing an air of monetary instability and having an unsettling effect on international trade flows. Another reason is that the U.S. high-interest-rate policy, as part of its anti-inflation program, has caused the foreign exchange value of the U.S. dollar to increase. This has meant that many European imports have gone up in price, particularly oil, which is priced in U.S. dollars per barrel. Also, to prevent their currencies weakening further (and this has also been true of Canada), the European countries have had to adopt high-interest rate policies that have discouraged economic growth. And France has been forced to devalue its currency three times in two years. A system of managed exchange rates, by contrast, would permit the exchange rate for the U.S. dollar to be adjusted downward—by means of the U.S. Federal Reserve Board buying foreign currencies in the exchange market—and relieve the pressure on the other countries.

So far, the U.S. government has not been very receptive to the French proposal. However, it may well move from its present policy of "benign neglect" to one of limited intervention—to eliminate the peaks and troughs in the fluctuations of the U.S. dollar exchange rate. However, if exchange rates are to be "managed", other countries will still be forced into devaluation if they let domestic inflation get out of control.

39.9: THE FOREIGN EXCHANGE MARKET

The term *foreign exchange* is used to describe foreign coins, bank notes, bank deposits, and other highly liquid foreign monetary claims that can be used, for example, to make investments in other countries, pay for imports, and buy foreign services. The most important type of foreign exchange consists of demand deposits in foreign banks and in the overseas branches and agencies of Canadian banks.

Making Payments Abroad

If a Canadian wishes to make a payment abroad, this can be done in various ways:

1. Cable transfer. This is a cable sent by a Canadian bank to its overseas branch, agency, or foreign correspondent bank telling it to pay funds to a particular person.

2. Mail transfer. This is the same as a cable transfer except that the order is sent by mail.

3. Bank draft. This is a written order from the Canadian bank instructing its overseas branch, agency, or correspondent to pay a certain sum in the specified foreign currency to the person named on the draft. The Canadian who purchases the draft from the Canadian bank sends it to the person abroad who then cashes it at the local bank.

4. Personal cheque. A person may send a personal cheque to make a payment in the U.S. and various other countries abroad and the recipient can arrange for the local bank to make collection, for a small fee.

Bills of Exchange

When Canadian importers purchase goods from abroad, they may make payment by one of the methods previously indicated. However, this presupposes that the foreign exporters trust them and are willing to send the goods or provide services such as shipping or insurance without receiving prior or simultaneous payment. In many cases, this is not so. Instead, foreign exporters usually send to Canadian importers a written document called a *bill of exchange*, in which the Canadian importer promises to pay to the exporter (or the person named by the exporter) the agreed sum of money immediately or on a specified future date. In the former case, the document is known as a *sight bill* or *sight draft*—and the importer is expected to pay when he or she signs the bill and receives in exchange the original copy of the bill of lading from the foreign exporter's representative. The *bill of lading*, which is an itemized list of the goods being shipped that is issued by the shipping company or other carrier, conveys ownership of the goods to its possessor. With it, the Canadian importer can claim the goods from the shipping company in the Canadian port. Sometimes, the importer will be given, say, 60 or 90 days in which to pay for the goods. In such a case, the bill of exchange that the Canadian importer signs is known as a *time draft*. Such a bill may then be "discounted" with the foreign exporter's own bank, thereby enabling the exporter to get its money (the "face value" minus the discount) for the goods sooner. If the foreign exporter is at all dubious about the trustworthiness of a Canadian importer, he or she may insist, before shipping goods to Canada, that the Canadian importer's bank agree to pay the sum owing, should the importer fail to do so. Such a written undertaking by a bank is called a *letter of credit*, and is normally *irrevocable*—that is, once issued, the importer may not change his or her mind and cancel it. The letter of credit sets out the terms under which the export shipment is to be made and the various documents (bill of lading, consular invoice, insurance certificate, etc.) to be provided. Once these terms have been complied with exactly, the Canadian bank's branch in the foreign country, or its foreign correspondent bank, will release the money to the foreign exporter.

Foreign Exchange Transactions

Unlike listed stock trading, foreign-exchange transactions are not confined to a particular building. Most transactions within Canada are arranged over the telephone by foreign exchange dealers (or brokers) employed by the Canadian Bankers' Association. These brokers act as intermediaries between the head-office trading departments of the chartered banks in Toronto and Montreal. The banks are the main buyers and sellers of foreign exchange in Canada. As well as using the Canadian interbank market, a bank may buy foreign exchange directly from banks and brokers in other countries and likewise sell directly to them.

Exchange Arbitrage

Because each financial centre is a foreign-exchange market of its own, there is the possibility that foreign-exchange rates for the same currency may differ. Thus, for example, the Canadian dollar might be worth 0.2136 French francs in Toronto, but only 0.2025 French francs in Paris. However, any substantial divergence between the rates is prevented by the practice of *exchange arbitrage*. This is the purchase by foreign exchange dealers of foreign exchange in one financial centre and its simultaneous sale in another. This practice increases demand for the currency in one market and increases the supply of it in the other. Consequently, the price of the currency tends to rise in the former and decline in the latter, until any difference between the exchange rates in the two markets is removed. Arbitrage also helps ensure that *cross-rates* keep in line. Thus if £1 costs $2 Canadian and 1 Venezuelan bolivar costs 25¢ Canadian, then £1 should equal 8 Venezuelan bolivars. But suppose £1 equals only 7 bolivars. Then it would be profitable for an exchange arbitrager in Canada to buy bolivars, sell them for British pounds, then use the pounds to buy Canadian dollars. This process will have the effect (a) of increasing the Canadian demand for bolivars (and thereby raising the dollar cost of the bolivar), and (b) of increasing the Venezuelan demand for British pounds (and so raising the bolivar cost of the pound). Eventually, the cross-rates will be in line and no profit can be made by further arbitrage.

Summary

1. International trade and investment cause foreigners to purchase Canadian dollars, and Canadians to purchase foreign currencies.

"What do you mean, 'there's none left'?!"

2. The price of the Canadian dollar, in terms of foreign currencies is known as its foreign exchange rate. Countries have either fixed or flexible foreign exchange rates. Canada has had both.

3. With a flexible exchange rate, the foreign exchange value of the Canadian dollar is determined by the interaction of demand and supply in the foreign currency market. A flexible exchange rate has the virtue of insulating a country to some extent from inflation and other unfavourable economic developments abroad. It can also have several disadvantages: adverse movements in the exchange rate, business uncertainty, and undesirable effects of capital movements.

4. With a fixed exchange rate, the foreign exchange value of the Canadian dollar is set by the government. If the official rate is above the market rate (the one that would be set by market demand and supply), the result will be a decline in Canada's international monetary reserves. If the official rate is below the market rate, the reserves will increase. A reduction in the fixed official foreign exchange rate is known as a *devaluation*. The great advantage of a fixed exchange rate is the relative certainty that it affords to international monetary transactions. The great disadvantages is that, to maintain the fixed rate, a country may be forced to adopt undesirable internal economic policies. People hold currencies as a speculative investment, in anticipation of a change in the foreign exchange rate in their favour.

5. In 1970, Canada moved from a fixed to a floating foreign exchange rate for its dollar.

6. For many years after World War II, the U.S. dollar reigned supreme. However, it was gradually replaced in status as a hard currency in the 1960s and 1970s by the W. German mark and the Japanese yen. Only in the 1980s has it become stronger again. The Swiss franc has always been hard. The U.K. pound sterling has been a good example of a soft currency. The Canadian dollar has weakened against the U.S. dollar in recent years and is rarely used as an international trading currency.

7. The Bank of Canada, which intervenes in the foreign exchange market to prevent drastic changes in the floating exchange rate for the Canadian dollar, has been criticized at times for not letting the rate drop further.

8. The European countries, after complaining for some years about a weak U.S. dollar, are now complaining that it is too strong.

9. Purchases and sales of foreign currencies are made through the foreign exchange market by foreign exchange dealers employed by

the banks.

10. An individual can transfer money abroad by cable or mail transfer, by bank draft, or even by personal Canadian dollar cheque.

11. A Canadian importer may be required to sign a bill of exchange (or "draft") to acknowledge that it owes money to the foreign exporter before possession of the goods can be obtained. The foreign exporter can then discount the bill at its bank and receive most of the money before the due date. (The reverse for the Canadian exporter).

12. The foreign exporter may require that the Canadian importer arrange for its bank to open a letter of credit in favour of the exporter before any goods are shipped to Canada. The bank agrees in its letter to pay the sum involved once all the conditions such as date of shipment, necessary documents etc. are met. (The reverse for the Canadian exporter.)

13. Arbitrage prevents cross-rates in the foreign exchange market from diverging significantly.

Key Terms

Foreign exchange rates 787
Foreign currency 787
Fixed exchange rate 788
Floating (or flexible)
   exchange rate 788
Dirty float 788
Undervalued currency 798
Exchange rate
   stability 799
Foreign exchange
   speculation 799
Hard (convertible)
   currency 802
Soft currency 803
Devaluation 803

Foreign exchange 804
Cable transfer 804
Bank draft 804
Bill of exchange 805
Time draft 805
Bill of lading 805
Discounting 805
Letter of credit 805
Foreign exchange
   transactions 806
Foreign exchange
   dealers 806
Exchange arbitrage 806
Cross-rates 806

Review Questions

1. What is a foreign exchange rate? What are the two different ways in which it can be expressed?

2. Distinguish between floating and fixed foreign exchange rates.

3. Show graphically how the foreign-exchange rate for the Canadian dollar would be determined in the absence of government intervention.

4. What would happen to Canada's exchange rate for U.S. dollars if Canadian demand for U.S. dollars increased? What might cause such an increase?

5. What would happen to Canada's exchange rate for U.S. dollars if the supply of U.S. dollars substantially increased? What might bring about such an increase?

6. Distinguish between the appreciation and depreciation of a currency. Distinguish between depreciation and devaluation; and between appreciation and revaluation. What has happened to the Canadian dollar in recent years?

7. What are the advantages of a floating foreign-exchange rate? Relate these advantages to Canada's situation.

8. What are the disadvantages of a floating foreign-exchange rate? How have these disadvantages affected Canada?

9. To what extent does the Bank of Canada intervene in the foreign-exchange market, despite the existence of a floating Canadian dollar?

10. What is a fixed foreign-exchange rate? How flexible is a fixed rate?

11. When Canada had a fixed exchange rate, how was this rate maintained?

12. What can happen if a country has a persistent shortage of foreign currencies?

13. When is a currency said to be undervalued? Overvalued? Give examples.

14. What are the advantages of fixed exchange rates? What are the disadvantages?

15. What is foreign-exchange speculation? Why does it exist?

16. What is Canada's present foreign exchange rate policy? What would be the effects of (a) a higher exchange rate and (b) a lower exchange rate for the Canadian dollar?

17. Explain the distinction between hard and soft currencies. Is Canada's currency getting harder or softer?

18. Why has France criticized U.S. foreign exchange rate policy? How justified is the criticism?

19. How can a person located in Canada make payment to someone located abroad?

20. Distinguish between a sight bill and a time bill of exchange. What purpose do they serve?

21. Explain the nature and purpose of a letter of credit.
22. Who deals in foreign exchange in Canada?
23. Explain the nature and purpose of exchange arbitrage.

"Wow! Will we ever get a good rating from the IMF. ."

40. THE INTERNATIONAL MONETARY SYSTEM

CHAPTER OBJECTIVES

A. To explain how the Gold Standard used to operate
B. To discuss the nature and purpose of the International Monetary Fund and related institutions
C. To indicate what constitutes a country's international monetary reserves
D. To describe the Eurodollar market
E. To indicate how OPEC tries to set the world price of crude oil
F. To explain how UNCTAD serves as a channel for the views on international trade and finance of the Third World countries

CHAPTER OUTLINE

40.1 The Gold Standard
40.2 The International Monetary Fund
40.3 Canada's International Monetary Reserves
40.4 The Eurodollar Market
40.5 The OPEC Oil Cartel
40.6 UNCTAD

40.1: THE GOLD STANDARD

This was a system of fixed foreign-exchange rates based on gold that was used by almost every major country in the world during the second half of the nineteenth century and up to the outbreak of World War I. It was used again, but in modified form, during the 1920s. It was finally abandoned, because of its disadvantages, in 1931.

To be *on the gold standard* meant, first of all, that each country's currency had a fixed value in terms of gold. Thus, the Canadian dollar was valued at 23.22 grains of gold. It meant, second, that the banks of a country would always be willing to buy and sell gold in any amount at this fixed rate. It meant, third, that people would be allowed to import and export gold freely. Finally, it meant that a country would vary its money supply in proportion to its reserves of gold. If a country obtained more gold, it would have to expand its money supply; if it lost gold, it would have to reduce it.

So long as all the major countries set a fixed value on their currencies in terms of gold, foreign-exchange rates were bound to remain stable. An example will help us to understand why. Assume, for simplicity, that the pound sterling was valued at 100 grains of gold; and the Canadian dollar at 25 grains. The exchange rate would therefore be £1 = $4.00. If the rate for the pound started to rise above this level, Canadian importers could always purchase gold in Canada and ship it to Britain to make payment. If the rate tended to drop below this level, British importers, conversely, could always purchase gold in Britain and ship it to Canada to meet their obligations. In other words, so long as each currency had a fixed gold value, at the rates indicated, a dollar would always be worth a quarter of a pound sterling.

Of course, account had to be taken of the various costs involved in shipping gold from one country to the other. These costs, which included freight, insurance, and packaging costs, as well as loss of interest during shipment, amounted to about two cents per hundred grains of gold. This meant that gold would only be shipped from Canada to Britain if the exchange rate for the pound exceeded $4.02. This was called the *gold export point*. Conversely, gold would only be shipped from Britain to Canada if the exchange rate for the pound fell below $3.98—the *gold import point*. Obviously, the currencies could get out of line with each other only by a negligible amount.

The big difference between the gold standard and a modern system of fixed exchange rates (in which each currency is given a fixed value in terms of, say, U.S. dollars) is in the way in which each system copes with a persistent excess of demand for foreign currencies over supply at the current fixed rate. Under a modern system of fixed exchange rates, a country that has a persistently greater demand for foreign currencies than supply of them must do one of two things. It must either successfully restrict imports and other foreign currency spending and promote exports, or it must devalue its currency. Under the gold standard, the imbalance of demand and supply was automatically corrected, without a change in the fixed exchange rate.

This automatic correction took place in the following way. Suppose Canada, for example, persistently had a greater demand for, than supply of, British currency. Then Canadian importers, rather than pay more than the standard rate for the British pound, would send gold to

Britain. This loss of gold would reduce Canada's monetary reserves and cause a contraction in Canada's money supply. Tight money at home would reduce the general level of demand and also reduce imports. Also, lower prices would make Canadian exports more attractive abroad and so increase the supply of foreign currency. Consequently, the demand for foreign currency would be reduced.

Britain, on the other hand, would experience an increase in its gold reserves. This would cause an expansion of its money supply and a rise in the general level of demand. An increased demand for imports would mean a larger demand for foreign currency, including the Canadian dollar. From Canada's point of view, there would therefore be an increase in the supply of British pounds. Also, higher prices in Britain would make British exports less attractive to Canadians with a consequent reduction in the demand for British pounds to pay for them.

Because of the movement of gold from Canada to Britain, the money supply in Canada has contracted and that in Britain has expanded. As a result, Canadian demand for British and other foreign goods has fallen and British demand for Canadian and other foreign goods has risen. The Canadian demand for British pounds has also fallen and the supply of British pounds risen. In other words, because of the gold movement, the imbalance in the demand for and supply of British pounds has been corrected, without devaluation of the Canadian dollar.

Despite the self-correcting mechanism just explained, most countries, including Canada, left the gold standard in 1914. The main reason was that they wished to increase their money supply far beyond the multiple expansion permitted by their gold reserves. This was essential if their governments were to mount a major war effort. Those countries, such as Britain, that were actively engaged in the war, also wished to use their gold to help pay for war supplies. Only slowly, after the war, did countries return to the gold standard: Canada in 1926, following Britain's example of the previous year. However, in 1929, Canada was forced to restrict the export of gold, so that, in effect, it once again unpegged its currency from gold. In 1931, Britain, wracked by economic depression, left the gold standard forever.

Why did the gold standard become so unpopular? It had the great advantage of providing an automatic means of correcting a fundamental disequilibrium in a country's balance of payments without changes in exchange rates. However, it meant that a country losing gold would be forced into a period of monetary contraction. This monetary contraction meant falling prices, less demand for goods and services, fewer jobs, less income, and so on, in a vicious circle. Adherence to the gold standard was often an extremely painful economic and social process. In Britain, in 1926, for example, it helped bring about a general strike. Later, in the 1930s, the advent of the Great Depression swept away any lingering willingness on the part of politicians to chain their country's domestic economic fortunes to the foreign-exchange rate of its currency and the gold standard was abandoned for good. In recent years, however, as the money supply in many countries has grown out of control, some people have started to talk nostalgically about the monetary discipline that a gold-backed currency can impose.

40.2: THE INTERNATIONAL MONETARY FUND

In 1944, with the end of World War II well in sight, economic experts from the United States, Britain, and other Allied and friendly nations, met at Bretton Woods, in the United States, to discuss economic plans for the future.

The Troubled Past

Looking back over the years, the experts could see how the gold standard, restored in many countries after World War I, had often acted as a straitjacket on economic growth. By abandoning the gold standard in the 1930s, each country had regained the freedom to decide its own internal monetary policies. However, most of these countries used their newly recovered economic freedom to engage in a policy of *economic nationalism*. By means of higher tariffs, smaller import quotas, and tighter exchange controls, the governments of these countries made every effort to protect domestic industries and jobs. Some countries, notably Germany under the guidance of its economic wizard, Dr. Hjalmar Schacht, drew considerable initial benefit from their protectionist schemes. But the benefits of these "beggar-my-neighbour" trade policies, which included competitive depreciation of currencies and bilateral clearing agreements, lasted for a relatively short period of time. Once other countries raised their own trade barriers in retaliation, every country began to suffer. As international trade drastically declined, export industries were forced to reduce their output and even shut down. High-cost local industries began to produce goods that had formerly been imported. And the benefits of international specialization and trade, in the form of lower prices for the consumer, soon began to disappear.

It was during this period that Britain, Canada, and other Commonwealth countries, at a conference in Ottawa in 1935, established a system of reciprocal tariff preferences for imports and talked of British

Commonwealth self-sufficiency. The United States, on the other hand, began in 1935 to negotiate a series of bilateral trade agreements with other countries, providing for a mutual reduction in tariffs. This movement towards freer, although bilateral rather than multilateral, trade was interrupted by the outbreak in 1939 of World War II.

These memories of the abandonment of the gold standard, the rise of economic nationalism, the resort to bilateralism in trade, and the outbreak of war haunted the minds of the delegates of the 44 countries represented at the Bretton Woods Conference. How could they reconcile exchange-rate stability (so necessary for an expanding volume of international trade) with the legitimate desire of governments to control their own monetary affairs? This was the problem which they had to resolve. For only with greater international specialization and trade, so it was believed, could countries raise the standard of living of their peoples. Only with greater international economic as well as political co-operation could the likelihood of future wars be reduced. The answer that the delegates produced was the International Monetary Fund, or IMF for short.

The *International Monetary Fund*, conceived at Bretton Woods in 1944, became a reality in 1945. Its objectives, formally stated in its charter, were:

1. to promote international co-operation by providing a mechanism for international consultation and collaboration on monetary, payment, and exchange problems;

2. to facilitate the balanced growth of international trade, thus contributing to high levels of employment and real income, and the development of production capacity;

3. to promote orderly exchange arrangements and avoid currency depreciation;

4. to foster a multilateral system of payments and transfers for current transactions and to seek the elimination of exchange restrictions that hinder the growth of world trade;

5. to make financial resources available to members on a temporary basis, with adequate safeguards to permit them to correct payment imbalances without resorting to measures destructive of national and international prosperity; and

6. to seek the reduction of both the duration and magnitude of payments imbalances

Official Exchange Rates

In a nutshell, the IMF hoped to obtain all the advantages of the gold standard, but without the disadvantages. To this end, each member country agreed to maintain the foreign-exchange value of its currency within a margin of 1 per cent on either side of an *official rate*—the one mutually agreed on by the member country and the IMF. If the member country found that its demand for a particular foreign currency within that range exceeded the supply and that its gold and foreign exchange reserves were being unduly depleted, it could borrow supplies of the scarce foreign exchange from the IMF. This assistance, even though temporary, meant that a country in foreign-exchange difficulties was not automatically forced to devalue its currency or impose additional import restrictions. In recent years, however, many countries (including Canada) have abandoned these fixed exchange rates and have floated their currencies instead.

Drawing Rights

A country borrows from the IMF by making use of what are called its *drawing rights*. These are the rights accorded to member countries to purchase foreign exchange from the IMF's reserves using the purchasing country's own currency. Thus, France, if faced with a shortage of German marks, can buy marks from the Fund, paying francs in exchange. Of course, these drawing rights are limited—a country may only purchase in any one year an amount equivalent to 25 per cent of its quota. Furthermore, a country's total indebtedness to the IMF must not be more than twice its quota. Otherwise, the IMF might find itself short of "hard" currencies (the freely convertible ones such as the German mark) and overstocked with "soft" currencies (the less easily convertible ones).

The assistance that the IMF gives to its member countries by means of the drawing rights is intended to be only temporary in nature. It provides a "breathing-spell," during which the member country can take steps to decrease the demand for the scarce foreign currency or increase the supply. Once the exchange crisis has passed, the country must buy back with gold or hard currencies the amounts of its own currency that it has previously sold to the IMF.

Basically, the IMF serves as a lender of last resort to financially troubled countries unable to obtain private loans. And any IMF loans are accompanied by strict conditions as to the domestic economic policy of the borrowing country—something that is often resented. In 1962, Canada drew an equivalent of $300 million U.S. from the Fund when the Canadian dollar was pegged at 95 cents U.S. It borrowed another $426 million U.S. in 1968 when the Canadian dollar was again under pressure following devaluation of the British pound and the introduction of a U.S. balance of payments program that reduced Canada's capital inflow.

Fundamental Disequilibrium

What happens if a country's shortage of foreign currency seems to be permanent? In other words, total payments on current and capital account (excluding net official monetary movements) persistently exceed total receipts—a situation of *basic deficit*. In this case, the country's balance of payments is considered to be in "fundamental disequilibrium." Consequently, the directors of the IMF, after consultation with the government of the member country concerned, will suggest what should be done. These suggestions would not include an extremely tight or deflationary monetary policy; otherwise, the country would in effect be back to the gold-standard days. They do include, however, recommendations for monetary and fiscal policy changes that for some countries have seemed in the past quite onerous and which are occasionally rejected by the country concerned.

Sometimes changes in a country's economic policies may fail to remedy the underlying balance-of-payments disequilibrium, and the basic deficit continues. In such a case, the directors of the Fund may authorize a further devaluation or revaluation of the member country's currency. Unlike pre-war days, all these changes are to be carried out in an orderly fashion, with the minimum possible disruption to foreign exchange markets.

Financial Resources

The IMF, with its head office in Washington, D.C., began its operations in 1946 with a capital of $6.8 billion U.S., of which $2.8 billion came from the U.S. Membership was mainly of the non-Communist countries. However, Poland was a member. And in the early 1980s, Hungary joined the IMF. Today, the IMF has 146 member countries. Each member country paid into the Fund gold or U.S. dollars equivalent to 25 per cent of its established quota. The remainder of its quota was to be paid in local currency as and when required. These financial resources soon proved insufficient in the face of rapidly increasing world trade. More and more reserves were required to cope with larger temporary imbalances in payments between different countries. The "dollar gap" that plagued most countries of the world in the post-war years imposed an exceptional strain. Many countries, particularly those of Western Europe, were importing far more goods and services from the United States than they were exporting to it. And the flow of investment capital from the United States was insufficient to offset the deficit in these countries' current accounts. Special U.S. economic- and military-aid programs did significantly increase the supply of dollars. But there was what seemed at the time to be a permanent shortage abroad of U.S. dollars.

To provide the additional international monetary reserves that were required to cope with rapidly growing world trade, member countries' quotas to the IMF were constantly enlarged.

Another remedy was a new set of rules for gold transactions among central banks. As from 1968, these were to be made at officially fixed prices regardless of prices prevailing in the private gold market. Another answer to the problem was for groups of countries to agree on additional credit arrangements among themselves to help a country in foreign exchange difficulties.

Debt Crisis

In the early 1980s, pressure mounted on the IMF once more to increase member countries' quotas. The main reason was the large amount of foreign debt that the developing countries had incurred due in part to their large import bill for oil, higher interest rates on their borrowings, and a slowing of their exports due to the world economic recession. However, the United States, the country with the largest quota, was reluctant to commit more U.S. funds to the agency unless strict financial conditions were attached to any new aid—for example, with regard to government spending, money supply increases, and balance of payments' deficits. The debt situation had been made worse by the fact that several oil-exporting countries such as Mexico, counting on rising oil export revenues, had borrowed heavily from private U.S., Canadian and W. European banks to finance rapid industrialization. When the world oil price dropped, these countries were immediately thrown into a balance of payments crisis, with a real possibility of their defaulting on their foreign debts. It was eventually agreed by the world's five largest industrialized democracies (the U.S., West Germany, Japan, France, and Britain) to increase the lending resources of the IMF by about $35 billion U.S. (of which only about half is in hard currencies), from $65 billion to $100 billion U.S.—to prevent loan defaults by Third World countries. The five lending countries together account for 42 per cent of the IMF's lending pool, with the U.S. being the largest single contributor at about 21 per cent—which gives it just enough veto power, if necessary, over IMF policy decisions. Amongst the borrowing countries, Mexico, Argentina, and Brazil stand out, with a combined total foreign debt of about $200 billion at present.

Special Drawing Rights

The biggest step towards increasing international liquidity was the establishment in 1970 of a system of Special Drawing Rights, or SDRs, operated by the International Monetary Fund. The SDR is, in effect, a new international currency, with each SDR initially equivalent in value to one U.S. dollar. Now, the rate is determined by the IMF each month according to a special valuation procedure. Each member country of the IMF is allocated a certain number of SDRs. This amount represents about 5 per cent of total international monetary reserves. A country possessing SDRs can use them in three different ways. It can exchange them, as the need arises, for certain convertible currencies, from countries specified by the IMF; it can use them to repurchase, by mutual agreement, amounts of its own currency held by other member countries; and it can use them to repay drawings that it has previously made from the regular IMF credit pool or to pay for its share of normal IMF operational charges.

Oil Program

The IMF also created a special $10 billion oil financing program. The IMF borrowed money from seven industrial countries and seven oil-producing nations and in turn lent it to countries that were encountering balance-of-payments problems as a result of large oil debts.

U.S. Influence

The IMF has been criticized from time to time, but particularly in the 1980s, as being a U.S. political tool. There is no denying that the U.S., as the largest financial contributor, has the most say. The IMF has also been criticized as representing "the interests of the bankers of the world"—presumably a response to the stringent conditions attached to IMF loans.

40.3: CANADA'S INTERNATIONAL MONETARY RESERVES

A country's total international monetary reserves consist of four items: foreign currencies, gold, Special Drawing Rights (SDRs) with the IMF, and its reserve position in the IMF. The Bank of Canada manages the Canadian government's funds of foreign exchange, gold, and credits with the IMF and intervenes in the foreign exchange market, as necessary, to stabilize the foreign exchange rate for the Canadian dollar. In recent years, Canada's reserves have been reasonably stable around the 4 billion dollar mark, as shown in Table S.48. Other countries' reserves are shown in Table S.49.

Table S.48
Canada's Official International Reserves, in millions of U.S. dollars, 1961-1982

End of year	Foreign currencies (1)		Gold	Special Drawing Rights	Reserve position in IMF	Total
	U.S. dollars	Other				
1961	1 123.0	10.7	946.2	-	212.1	2 292.0
1962	1 842.8	9.2	708.5	-		2 560.5
1963	1 786.6	9.5	817.2	-	-	2 613.3
1964	1 654.5	11.8	1 025.7	-	197.5	2 889.5
1965	1 519.9	12.8	1 150.8	-	353.4	3 036.9
1966	1 195.4	12.4	1 045.6	-	448.5	2 701.9
1967	1 255.2	13.4	1 014.9	-	433.4	2 716.9
1968	1 964.9	11.6	863.1	-	206.2	3 045.8
1969	1 743.6	12.3	872.3	-	478.1	3 106.3
1970	3 022.1	14.5	790.7	182.1	669.6	4 679.0
1971	4 060.0	13.6	791.8	371.9	332.6	5 570.4
1972	4 355.0	12.6	834.1	505.2	342.9	6 049.9
1973	3 927.2	12.2	926.9	563.7	338.2	5 768.2
1974	3 767.7	12.9	940.7	574.3	529.7	5 825.3
1975	3 207.1	15.7	899.4	555.4	648.0	5 325.6
1976	3 446.3	15.8	879.0	557.8	944.5	5 843.4
1977	2 298.7	15.8	935.6	505.3	852.1	4 607.5
1978	2 459.5	18.4	1 009.1	522.4	556.8	4 566.2
1979	1 863.9	23.9	1 022.6	585.9	390.6	3 886.9
1980	2 037.6	23.1	936.6	453.2	579.0	4 029.6
1981	2 865.3	95.8	833.7	174.0	402.4	4 371.1
1982	2 454.9	120.1	782.3	70.8	365.0	3 793.2

Source: Bank of Canada and Department of Finance

Note: (1) Convertible foreign currency of the Exchange Fund Account, the Receiver General for Canada and the Bank of Canada

Table S.49
Countries with Largest International Monetary Reserves, in millions
of SDRs, end of 1982

1.	Germany	43 909	23.	Israel	3 518
2.	United States	29 918	24.	Malaysia	3 497
3.	Saudi Arabia	26 948	25.	*Canada*	3 428
4.	Japan	22 001	26.	Sweden	3 397
5.	France	17 850	27.	Indonesia	2 959
6.	Switzerland	16 930	28.	Trinidad & Tobago	2 795
7.	Italy	15 108	29.	Lebanon	2 686
8.	United Kingdom	11 904	30.	Korea	2 556
9.	China	10 724	31.	Argentina	2 425
10.	Netherlands	10 723	32.	Algeria	2 391
11.	Singapore	7 687	33.	Ireland	2 390
12.	Spain	7 450	34.	Denmark	2 111
13.	Libya	6 525	35.	Chile	1 705
14.	Venezuela	6 365	36.	Philippines	1 624
15.	Norway	6 273	37.	Thailand	1 481
16.	Australia	6 053	38.	Finland	1 420
17.	Austria	5 544	39.	Bahrain	1 397
18.	Kuwait	5 449	40.	Oman	1 283
19.	Belgium	4 757	41.	Peru	1 271
20.	India	4 213	42.	Portugal	1 179
21.	Colombia	3 634	43.	Hungary	1 068
22.	Brazil	3 566			

Source: International Monetary Fund, *International Financial Statistics, 1983 Yearbook*

Note: International reserves consist of holdings of gold, Special Drawing Rights (SDRs), Reserve Positions in the IMF and foreign exchange. Gold is valued at SDR 35 per ounce. The conversion rate for each country's currency was based on a basket of five key currencies. Total international reserves at the end of 1982 amounted to 371 013 SDRs.

40.4: THE EURODOLLAR MARKET

An extremely important international source of financing that came into being in the 1960s is the Eurodollar market. A Eurodollar account is a bank deposit denominated in dollars and held by a person other than a resident of the United States. A Eurodollar is the name used to describe each dollar in such an account. Because this financial market developed in Western Europe, including Britain, the prefix "Euro" is used. Physically, the Eurodollar market is concentrated in London, England, where the head offices or branches of most participating banks are located.

The Eurodollar market originated because many persons receiving dollars (notably European exporters) did not want to convert them into their local currency. Instead, a European exporter would deposit dollar cheques with the local bank and have the amount credited to an account denominated in dollars. The European bank would then present the dollar cheques to the U.S. bank on which it was drawn, receiving in return a credit in the European bank's dollar account with the U.S. bank. Thus, as a result, the U.S. bank would owe the European bank so many dollars and the European bank would owe the European exporter the same amount, also denominated in dollars, or, as they came to be called, Eurodollars. Other important sources of Eurodollar deposits are the many U.S.-owned multinational corporations operating in Europe who wish to keep funds on hand and, particularly in recent years, the Arab oil-exporting countries which, for many years, earned U.S. dollars faster than they could spend them.

In order to attract deposits, the banks had to pay interest on the money placed in these Eurodollar accounts. This meant that the banks, in order to make a profit, had to lend the money out at higher rates of interest. This they were able to do—to multinational corporations needing short-term funds to meet cash flow requirements and to governments needing short-term funds to finance current-account deficits. Because at any one time a large amount of Eurodollars was always left on deposit, the banks were able to lend an amount several times larger than that placed on deposit. This was the usual process of bank money-creation, described in Chapter 33, except that no reserves other than the banks' sense of financial prudence were required. Because the U.S. dollar was freely acceptable in the various countries, the Eurodollar became in effect a new international currency.

To meet the needs of firms or governments wishing to borrow dollars for longer periods of time, the banks sold Eurobonds to themselves, other financial institutions and to corporate investors—the bond being the borrower's certificate of indebtedness, setting out the terms and conditions of the loan, including interest charged and repayment dates.

40.5: THE OPEC OIL CARTEL

In 1973, the Arab and several other oil-producing countries established a cartel, the Organization of Petroleum Exporting Countries (or OPEC). Beginning in late 1973, the steep increase in the price of crude petroleum imposed by the OPEC countries greatly strengthened the foreign exchange position of the member oil-producing countries such as Saudi Arabia and Venezuela. It also helped stave off economic disaster in other non-OPEC countries such as Britain. However, for most countries, the large increase in the price of oil has meant a much larger import bill, a consequent decline in international monetary reserves, and a weakening of the foreign-exchange rate of their currencies. Canada and the United States, despite reduced oil consumption, continue to pay vast sums for foreign oil. However, Canada still hopes to achieve oil self-sufficiency within this decade. The Soviet Union, by contrast, is already self-sufficient. Countries that have been hit particularly badly are the developing ones who lack the foreign exchange to pay for essential oil imports. Fortunately for the oil-consuming countries, the cutbacks in consumption, as consumers reacted to the much higher prices with oil-substitution programs, more economical use, etc. forced the OPEC countries to reduce the world price of oil in 1983 — and this despite greatly restricted output by Saudi Arabia, the largest producer. In fact, OPEC production was reduced from about 31 million bbl. per day in 1979 to about 14 million in 1983. Hastening this decline in the world oil price, after its devastating rise in the 1970s, was price-cutting by both OPEC and non-OPEC countries. Because of the depressed world oil market, OPEC was forced in 1983 to reduce its official benchmark price from oil for $34 U.S. per barrel to $29 U.S.

In the early 1980s, the OPEC managed to prevent the world price for oil slipping any further, not only by restricting output, but also by persuading non-OPEC countries that are net exporters of oil to keep their prices up. OPEC first successfully established links with Mexico, Britain, and Norway. It then went on to establish regular contacts with the Soviet Union, China, Egypt, Oman, Malaysia, and Brunei.

OPEC has also attempted to negotiate with the major oil-consuming countries a stable world oil price but has met with very little positive response. To advise them on the world oil situation, the major industrial oil-consuming countries have their own organization, the International Energy Agency, or IEA. In the past, the IEA has admonished the industrial countries about overconsuming oil and, in Canada's case, not letting the domestic price reach world levels. Just recently, it has been forecasting an excess of supply over demand.

40.6: UNCTAD

From time to time, the member countries of the United Nations meet together at what is called the United Nations Conference on Trade and Development. Because of the voting structure of the United Nations, with each member entitled to one vote, the resolutions approved are usually quite radical in nature, representing predominantly the interests of the numerous developing countries of the world. Most recently, the UNCTAD has called upon the IMF to issue additional special drawing rights (or SDRs), to double the quotas of IMF members, and to attach less stringent conditions to IMF loans—so as to improve international liquidity and ease the balance-of-payments situation of the developing countries. UNCTAD has also called for a minimum price for about 15 commodities traded internationally, to be maintained by using buffer stocks to restrict supplies and export quotas on producing countries, and to be financed by a special fund paid for mainly by the industrial countries and the IMF. UNCTAD has also called for an end to discriminatory tariffs by the industrial countries against exports of processed goods (e.g. steel bars) from the developing countries.

Summary

1. The gold standard was a system of fixed exchange rates based on gold that contained an automatic mechanism for correcting balance-of-payments disequilibria between participating countries. It was abandoned because it imposed monetary contraction, with consequent unemployment, on countries losing gold as a result of balance-of-payments difficulties.
2. An international organization, the International Monetary Fund, or IMF, was established in 1945 to promote foreign exchange stability, the elimination of foreign exchange restrictions, the establishment of a multilateral system of current payments, and the expansion and balanced growth of world trade.
3. Member countries, encountering balance of payments difficulties, can borrow scarce foreign exchange from the IMF. This provides time for domestic economic policies to correct the difficulties without resort to immediate and severe monetary contraction. Special drawing rights were later created as extra means of interna-

tional payment.

4. A country's international monetary reserves usually consist of monetary gold, SDRs, reserve positions in the IMF, and holdings of foreign exchange.
5. The Eurodollar market, centred in London, England, is an additional source of international currency.
6. The establishment in 1973 of the OPEC oil cartel, and the subsequent drastic increase in the world price of crude oil, helped weaken the U.S. dollar and other currencies. In the 1980s the world price of oil began to fall as supply exceeded demand.
7. The United Nations Conference on Trade and Development, or UNCTAD, serves as a channel for the views of the Third World countries about international monetary developments.

Key Terms

Gold standard   813
Gold point   814
Beggar-my-neighbour
   trade policies   816
Bilateral trade agreement   816
IMF   817
Official exchange rate   817
Drawing rights   818
Fundamental disequilibrium   819
IMF quota   819

Dollar gap   819
Special drawing rights   821
International monetary
   reserves   821
Eurodollar   824
Eurodollar account   824
Eurodollar market   824
OPEC   825
Cartel   825
UNCTAD   826

Review Questions

1. What was the gold standard?
2. How would a shortage of foreign currency be corrected under the gold standard?
3. Why did the gold standard become so unpopular?
4. What was the "troubled past" to which the economic experts at Bretton Woods could look back?
5. What is economic nationalism? What are "beggar-my-neighbour" economic policies?
6. What are the aims of the International Monetary Fund?
7. How does the IMF try to ensure exchange rate stability?
8. What are "drawing rights"? What is their purpose? What are their limitations?

9. What is meant by a "fundamental disequilibrium" in a country's balance of payments? What action can be taken under IMF rules to remedy such a situation?
10. How is the IMF financed? What is Canada's contribution?
11. How was the IMF able to cope in the 1960s with a growing shortage of international monetary reserves? What have countries been able to do, outside the IMF, to ease their exchange problems?
12. What are Special Drawing Rights? What is their purpose? How can they be used?
13. What constitutes a country's international monetary reserves? How large are Canada's? Why are they necessary?
14. What is the Eurodollar market? What purpose does it serve? How did it come about?
15. What is OPEC? How have its actions affected the international monetary situation?
16. Why has the world price of oil dropped in recent years? What have been the results for (a) Canada and (b) Mexico?
17. What is UNCTAD? What purpose does it serve?

41. BENEFITS OF INTERNATIONAL TRADE

CHAPTER OBJECTIVES

A. To explain why countries engage in international trade
B. To discuss the concept of absolute advantage
C. To explain why countries that can produce the same goods find it beneficial to specialize in production and to exchange part of the goods produced
D. To discuss some practical qualifications to the pure theory of international trade

CHAPTER OUTLINE

41.1 Absolute Advantage
41.2 Comparative Advantage
41.3 Practical Qualifications

Why is it that Canadians spend a large part of their income on goods imported from abroad? Japanese cars, Hong Kong toys, U.S. fruit and vegetables, Italian shoes, Spanish wine, and so on. Conversely, why is it that foreigners purchase many of our goods—motor vehicles, aircraft, farm machinery, telecommunications equipment, newsprint, wheat, lumber, coal, iron ore, fish and so on?

41.1: ABSOLUTE ADVANTAGE

We can easily appreciate the benefits of international trade in the case of products or services that are otherwise unobtainable. If Canada did not import orange juice from the U.S. or Brazil, for example, Canadians would not be able to enjoy this breakfast staple. Conversely, if Brazil did not buy Scotch whiskey from Britain, the Brazilians would have to do without. By engaging in trade, the inhabitants of both these countries are obviously better off, for they cannot produce the imported good in their own countries.

However, there are also benefits to be obtained from international trade even though two countries are able to produce the same goods and services. For example, let us assume, hypothetically, that Canada and the United States can both produce apples and oranges (or, for that matter, microcomputers and movies). Let us also suppose that (a) Canada can produce them in the ratio of one tonne of oranges to ten tonnes of apples, and (b) the United States can produce them in the ratio of one tonne of oranges to every 0.2 tonne of apples. Canada therefore has an *absolute advantage* in the production of apples; the United States, an *absolute advantage* in the production of oranges. This is illustrated in Figure 41:1. The opportunity cost of one tonne of apples and one tonne of oranges in the two countries is set out in Table 41:1.

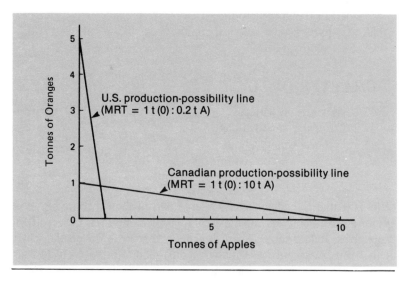

Note: (a) Canada has an opportunity cost or *marginal rate of transformation* (MRT) of one tonne of oranges for every ten tonnes of apples;

     (b) The United States has an opportunity cost (or MRT) of one tonne of oranges for every two-tenths of a tonne of apples.

Possible terms of trade: between 1 t.0 : 0.2 t A and 1 t.0 : 10 t A

Figure 41:1 The Case of Absolute Advantage

Table 41:1
Absolute Advantage—the Opportunity Cost of One Tonne of Apples and One Tonne of Oranges in Canada and the United States

	One Tonne of Apples	One Tonne of Oranges
Canada	0.1 t oranges	10.0 t apples
United States	5.0 t oranges	0.2 t apples

What are the benefits that these countries can obtain from international trade? The answer is that by each country specializing in the production of the good in which it has an absolute advantage, the two countries can greatly increase their total combined output. As Table 41.2 shows, if Canada produces one more tonne of apples (the product in which it has an absolute advantage in production) and the United States one more tonne of oranges, there is a net increase in total production of 0.8t of apples and 0.9t of oranges. International specialization, we should note, also takes place in the provision of services. Switzerland, for example, finds customers all over the world for its numbered bank accounts; and France, for its cuisine and fashions. Of course, there is a limit to international specialization—otherwise, Canada would end up, in our hypothetical example, producing only apples and the United States only oranges. The main reason for the limit on specialization, as we shall see later, is increasing costs. This would mean, in Figure 41.1, curving production-possibility lines rather than straight ones.

Table 41:2
Change in Total Output if Canada Produces One More Tonne of Apples and the United States One More Tonne of Oranges, with the Opportunity Costs Shown in Table 41:1

	Tonnes of Apples	Tonnes of Oranges
Canada	+1.0	−0.1
United States	−0.2	+1.0
Total	+0.8	+0.9

41.2: COMPARATIVE ADVANTAGE

We can easily understand how a country is better off by specializing in the production of goods and services in which it has an absolute advantage over other countries. By exporting some of these goods and services, and using the money to import goods and services that other countries can produce more cheaply, a country's real income can be larger than it would otherwise be.

But what if a country could produce everything more efficiently than other countries? Would there still be any benefit from international trade? This question was posed early in the nineteenth century by the British economist David Ricardo. His answer was the famous *theory of comparative advantage* (or *theory of comparative cost*). According to this theory, two countries can benefit from international trade even though one country can produce everything more cheaply than the other. The only requirement is that each country specialize in the production of those goods in which it has a *comparative advantage*—in other words, those goods that it can produce relatively more cheaply than other goods.

Assume that the United States can produce both apples and oranges more cheaply than Canada. Thus, with the same amount of resources, it might produce either ten tonnes of apples or five tonnes of oranges, as compared with Canada's eight tonnes of apples or one tonne of oranges. This situation is illustrated in Figure 41:2 with Canada's production-possibility line entirely inside that of the United States. Specialization and trade would be advantageous for both countries as long as the rate of exchange (called the *terms of trade*) of apples for oranges falls somewhere between one tonne of oranges for two tonnes of apples and one tonne of oranges for eight tonnes of apples.

Suppose, for example, the terms of trade are one tonne of oranges for three tonnes of apples. Then Canada, by specializing in the production of apples and exchanging some of them for U.S. oranges, can obtain twice as many oranges as it could by using its own resources. This can be shown as follows:

Canada: 100 R (units of resources)

(a) equal allocation of resources

$$50 \text{ R} = 400 \text{ tonnes of apples}$$
$$\underline{50 \text{ R} = 50 \text{ tonnes of oranges}}$$
$$100 \text{ R}$$

(b) specialization in apples

$$100 \text{ R} = 800 \text{ tonnes of apples}$$

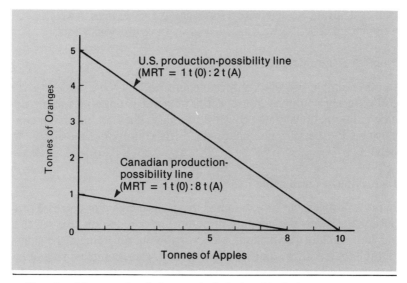

Note: Possible terms of trade: between 1 t.0 : 2t.A and 1 t.0 : 8t.A.

Figure 41:2 The Case of Comparative Advantage

(c) specialization and trade
$$100 \text{ R} = 500 \text{ tonnes of apples}$$
$$100 \text{ tonnes of oranges (imported in exchange for}$$
$$300 \text{ tonnes of apples)}$$

41.3: PRACTICAL QUALIFICATIONS

In order to explain how countries can benefit from international trade, we have used a highly simplified hypothetical example. Our simplification does not, however, mean that our conclusions are false. For reassurance, all we need do is to consider how our example differs from reality, and to consider what effect, if any, this difference makes.

Number of Products Involved

It makes no difference that countries trade many thousands of products, not just two. A glance at any country's list of principal exports quickly reveals which products that country can produce most efficiently. Thus five of Canada's leading exports (apart from motor vehicles and parts to the U.S. under the auto-pact) are newsprint, wheat, wood pulp, lumber, and iron-ore. A country will tend to specialize in the production of all those goods and services in which it has a significant cost advantage and import those goods and services in which it has a significant cost disadvantage, just as we have previously said.

Number of Countries Involved

In our example, we used only two countries. But there are now over 160 different countries in the world, all participating to a varying degree in international trade. However, this also does not impair our conclusions. By specialization and trade, every country has the chance to benefit.

Increasing or Decreasing Costs

In our examples, we have assumed that costs increase or decrease proportionately with the quantity of output. In other words, we say that per unit costs of production, whatever the output, remain the same. But, of course, this is not usually true. If it were, complete specialization would eventually occur. And, in our hypothetical example, only Canada would produce apples and only the United States would produce oranges (or one country produce both but the other country only one).

In practice, many industries find that the larger their output, the lower are their per unit costs of production. These "economies of scale" (or "economies of mass production") arise because of several factors. For example, manufacturing operations and materials handling can be more highly mechanized; head-office and plant overhead costs can be more widely spread; large volume buying of materials and parts permits quantity price discounts; a large sales volume helps finance a more effective marketing organization; and every advertising dollar goes much further. Decreasing costs means that the gains from international specialization of production are even greater than we have so far indicated. In fact, many regions of the world, such as Western Europe and Latin America, have formed free-trade areas in order to obtain these economies of scale—for only with a large market, can a firm sell enough of such goods as cars, trucks, stoves, and refrigerators to justify mass production. This is in fact the basis for Canada's automotive agreement with the United States. However, beyond a certain volume of output, a country runs into increasing costs (or "diseconomies of scale"). Certain types of labour become scarce and labour unions demand higher wages and greater fringe benefits. Capital funds become scarcer and more expensive. Raw materials and parts, because of greater demand in relation to supply, also rise in price. And the organization becomes unwieldy.

Transportation and Other Costs

Goods have to be transported from one country to another. Shipping companies and freight forwarders have to be paid. Insurance has to be taken out to cover the goods during their journey. Import duties and perhaps other taxes are incurred as well as customs brokerage fees, when the goods arrive. All these costs must be taken into account. Thus, if a good costs $10.00/t in Canada, it may, because of these additional expenses, cost $12.00/t for the foreign importer. This means that it will be worthwhile to import such goods only if they cannot be obtained in that country for less than $12.00/t. Clearly, the larger these transportation and other costs are, the less the scope for international trade. Conversely, as transportation and other costs fall—because of, for example, more efficient means of transportation—the goods of one country can compete more effectively in terms of price in the markets of another. International specialization and trade are still worthwhile, then, so long as the additional costs do not entirely offset the difference in production costs between one country and another. Thus, it might be cheaper to obtain nickel on the moon, but be too expensive to transport it to earth.

Use of Money

In practice, a country does not usually directly exchange or barter its goods and services for those of other countries—although "counter-trade", as it is called, has been growing in recent years, as Third World countries find themselves short of foreign exchange. Instead, a country usually sells its goods for a certain price and uses the money plus any other funds (for example, from foreign lenders) to pay for imports and for its own investments abroad. This movement of money into and out of a country therefore reflects the flow of goods and services that is taking place. And this international flow of goods and services is the result of the specialization that we have discussed.

The use of money, we should note, makes it possible for countries to engage in *multilateral* instead of just bilateral trade. In other words, a country need not buy its goods only from the country to which it sells its own. It can, if it sees fit, use its export earnings to pay for goods from any other country. Thus Canada may sell wheat to China to pay for cameras from Japan or suits from South Korea.

Without money, countries would not be able to specialize in production as much as they do. In exchange for imports, country A would have to produce and offer the goods and services that country B

wanted—not what, perhaps, countries C and D might like to have.

One complication in the use of money is that each country has its own currency. Consequently, a Canadian importer must purchase, for example, Japanese yen to pay for goods imported from Japan. And a foreign importer must purchase Canadian dollars to pay for imports from Canada. However, as we saw in Chapter 39, the mechanism for handling this problem exists and differences in currencies usually provide no impediment to the flow of international trade.

Another complication in the use of money, rather than direct barter, is that the prices of some goods increase more rapidly than others. In fact, the developing countries have long complained that the prices they receive for their exports of primary products have not increased as fast as the prices they must pay for their imports of manufactured goods. In other words, the *terms of trade* (i.e., the relationship between export prices and import prices) have been turning against them.

Summary

1. International trade permits the inhabitants of a country to enjoy goods and services that they themselves, for climatic and other reasons, are unable to produce.
2. Even when two countries can produce the same goods and services, specialization in production, combined with international trade, can enable both countries to produce and obtain more.
3. Countries can benefit from international trade by specializing in the production of the goods in which each has an *absolute advantage*. However, even though country A can produce *all* goods more efficiently than country B, both countries can benefit from international trade if country A specializes in the production of goods in which it has a *comparative advantage*.
4. The amount of goods that a country gives in exchange for those of its trading partner is called the *terms of trade*.
5. There are several practical qualifications to basic international trade theory, which do not, however, impair its validity. These include the number of products and countries involved, increasing or decreasing costs, transportation and other costs, and the use of money.

Key Terms

Absolute advantage   829   Specialization   831

Review Questions

1 Why does international trade take place?
2. What benefits, if any, does international specialization in production confer?
3. How can international trade affect consumers and producers in exporting and importing countries?
4. What is meant when we say that a country has an *absolute advantage* over another in the production of certain goods? Give an example of the benefits of international trade in such a case.
5. What is meant by "comparative advantage"? How can international trade be mutually beneficial in such a situation?
6. Who was David Ricardo? What is the theory of comparative advantage?
7. What is meant by the "terms of trade"? What are the limits beyond which mutually beneficial trade can no longer occur?
8. How does the fact that there are many products and many countries involved in international trade affect our conclusion about the benefits to be derived from it?
9. How do increasing or decreasing costs of production affect the gains to be derived from international trade?
10. How do transportation and other costs affect the extent of international trade?
11. How does the use of money affect the pattern of international trade?
12. Why have some countries turned to "countertrade"?

42. BARRIERS TO INTERNATIONAL TRADE

CHAPTER OBJECTIVES

A. To explain the various types of tariffs and how they act as barriers to international trade
B. To explain import quotas
C. To examine exchange controls as another means of restricting imports
D. To explain the various other types of non-tariff international trade barriers
E. To examine the purpose of import restrictions
F. To discuss the issue of free trade versus protectionism

CHAPTER OUTLINE

We have seen that, according to conventional international trade theory, every country can benefit substantially from international trade. It can do this by concentrating on the production of goods and services that it can produce relatively cheaply. It can then sell some or all of these abroad to pay for imports of goods and services that it can produce only at a relatively high cost, or not at all. In this way, it can have a larger and more varied quantity of goods and services than if it tries to produce everything itself. That is why most governments support the principle that international trade, like parenthood, is beneficial for the human race.

The governments of most countries actively encourage exports, particularly manufactured goods which, through a high value-added content, provide substantial income and employment for the exporting country. At the same time, however, they find it expedient to erect barriers of one kind or another to imports from other countries, particularly goods that can be produced within the importing country. These barriers, although not usually prohibitive, nevertheless impede the flow of international trade and help the country that erects them to have both the benefit of exports and the benefit of some protection for its industries in the home market. Thus, although paying lip-service to the principle of free international trade, few countries are willing to expose their own industries, agriculture as well as manufacturing, to the full blast of international competition. The most popular of the trade barriers is the tariff. Other barriers (often called ''non-tariff barriers'') include import quotas, exchange controls, and a variety of other devices. We examine tariff barriers first. Then we look at import quotas, exchange controls, and other ''non-tariff barriers''.

42.1: TARIFFS

A *tariff* is a tax that a government levies on an imported good. It is also called a *customs duty*, or *import duty*.

Types of Tariff

A tariff can be one of three different types: ad valorem, specific, or compound. An *ad valorem* duty is one that is calculated as a percentage of the value of the imported good. The duty may be set at, for ex-ample, 10, 30, or 45 per cent. This type of tariff is the one most com-monly used by Canada. A *specific* duty is a tax of so many dollars or cents per unit of the imported good—for example, 30¢/kg, 5¢/m, or 20¢/dozen. A *compound* duty is a combination of an ad valorem duty and a specific duty. Thus an import may have a compound duty of 10 per cent of value, plus 25¢/kg. Some goods, such as antiques, pay no duty at all. This non-dutiable merchandise is simply classified as ''free.''

Most tariffs are in force all year round. Sometimes, however, a tariff may be imposed only at certain times of the year. An example of such "seasonal" duties is the one that Canada levies on imports of U.S. fruit and vegetables at the time of year when Canadian farmers start to market their crops.

In addition to its regular tariffs, Canada sometimes imposes special *anti-dumping duties*. These additional customs duties are levied on goods (for example, canned tomatoes) that are being "dumped" in Canada—that is, being sold in Canada at a price lower than that being charged for them in their country of origin.

Also, some countries occasionally impose *countervailing duties*— these are additional import duties designed to offset any export subsidy paid to the foreign exporter by the government of the exporting country. Such duties may be imposed if a Canadian manufacturer can show sales have been lost to imports that have been made cheaper in this way.

Size of Tariff

The size of a tariff varies, first of all, according to the country from which the goods are imported. Canada has four levels of tariffs: British preferential, or BP; most-favoured-nation, or MFN; general, or Gen; and general preferential, or GP.

The lowest level of tariffs, the BP rate, applies to goods imported from all countries that are members of the British Commonwealth, except Hong Kong, plus the non-Commonwealth countries of Eire, South Africa and Pakistan.[1]

The second level of tariffs applies to goods imported from countries that are not members of the British Commonwealth but have signed special trade agreements with Canada. The rates of duty levied on these goods are called "most-favoured-nation" rates. This is because most bilateral and multilateral trade agreements contain a clause whereby each signatory country agrees to extend to the other the benefit of any trade concessions that each may later grant to other countries. For Canada, the most important of such agreements is the General Agreement on Tariffs and Trade (or GATT), explained and discussed in the next Chapter.

The third level of tariff is called "general." It applies to imports from countries that do not qualify either for British-preferential or most-favoured-nation-rates.

The fourth level, called "general preferential", and set lower than the general, applies to goods from developing Third World countries.

Most of Canada's imports fall under the first two categories: British preferential and most-favoured-nation.

As well as the four tariff rates outlined above, Canada offers special tariff privileges to certain goods from Australia, New Zealand, the West Indies, and the Republic of South Africa, with whom it has special trade agreements.

The size of a tariff also varies according to the nature of the goods imported. Thus goods imported under any one of the four categories may incur one of two rates. The lower rate applies if such goods are not made in Canada; the higher rate applies if they are.

42.2: IMPORT QUOTAS

The government of a country may not be satisfied with tariffs alone as a barrier to imports. It may also establish *import quotas* for certain types of goods. An import quota is a fixed quantity, or "quota," of a foreign good that importers may bring into the country during a twelve-month period at the prevailing tariff. Importers are required to obtain import licences from the government for the amount they wish to import. Once the quota has been filled, one of two things can occur. The government may stipulate that no more goods of this type may be imported until the next period. Or, the government may allow imports beyond the quota, but at a much higher tariff rate.

Import quotas sometimes specify the country in which the goods are produced. A *global* import quota specifies merely the total amount of a good that may be imported, whatever the country of origin. An *allocated* import quota specifies how much of a good may be imported from each foreign country. Canada now has import quotas on such items as clothing and footwear in order to help protect Canadian manufacturers of such goods.

42.3: EXCHANGE CONTROLS

Imports, we should remember, are responsible for only part of the demand for foreign currencies. Another part of this demand arises from the need to pay interest and dividends on foreign capital invested in Canada and to pay for services bought from foreigners, such as shipping, insurance, banking, and management, as well as for food, accommodation, and so on for Canadian tourists travelling abroad. All these items form part of the current account in a country's international balance of payments. There is also quite a large demand, in Canada's case, for foreign currencies to pay for items in the capital account—mainly short- and long-term investments abroad.

If a country is encountering balance-of-payments problems(that is, payments to foreigners for the various reasons indicated above exceed payments by foreigners to us) it can do two things. It can try to increase the supply of foreign currencies in various ways—for example, by promoting exports, by encouraging visits by foreign tourists, or by attracting foreign capital. It can also try to reduce the demand for foreign currencies. If tariffs and import quotas, cannot do this, a country may also institute a system of exchange controls.

With complete exchange control, anyone wishing to obtain foreign exchange must secure permission from the government. Such a system permits the government to restrict the demand for scarce foreign exchange and to ration it out among different needs. This rationing of foreign exchange also applies to importers: they must obtain a foreign exchange permit before they can import any goods. Exchange controls are therefore another and very effective way of restricting imports as well as other types of foreign exchange spending.

42.4: OTHER NON-TARIFF BARRIERS

We have just looked at two important kinds of non-tariff barriers that restrict the flow of international trade. Other non-tariff barriers include: customs delays; customs valuation procedures; government purchasing policies; technical barriers; voluntary restraints; and even boycotts.

Customs Delays

Exporters sometimes find that their goods are held up at foreign ports because of inexplicable delays by customs officials. These may be the result of deliberate government policy to restrict imports. The customs authorities may argue that the documentation or marking of the goods is not exactly as required. Canada used this technique for a short while in Vancouver to slow down the importation of Japanese cars. In other cases, delays may arise because the customs officials have not received a suitable "gift" from the importers. As another example, France restricted the import of Japanese video recorders by requiring each of them to be cleared through a tiny ten-man custom house in landlocked Poitiers.

Customs Valuation Procedures

Not all countries use the same method of valuing goods for purposes of assessing import duties. By using one method rather than another, an importing country can set a higher value on the merchandise and therefore levy a larger ad valorem duty. Canada is one of the importing countries that has been guilty of this practice. Its present customs code allows it to impose duty levels not directly related to the price paid for

"The government says we should spend our winters in Canada."

the good but to what is termed "fair market value". This has been branded by other countries, particularly the United States, as a non-tariff barrier and unfair protective device. It has been defended by Canada as a necessary measure to prevent predatory export pricing by foreign firms and the setting of artificially low transfer prices on goods sold to Canadian subsidiaries by foreign multinational parent corporations. However, at the Tokyo round of GATT trade negotiations that ended in 1979, Canada agreed to adopt in 1984 the standardized GATT customs valuation procedure. This will involve a switch from "fair market value" to "international transaction price" as the basis for assessment of import duties. At present, Canada Customs often sets values higher than the transaction price, giving Canadian firms an added degree of protection against imports.

Government Purchasing Policies

In some countries, government departments and agencies are required, officially or unofficially, to buy locally-made goods rather than imports. Japan, for example, has been accused of this practice. Here in Canada, governments encourage, by advertising, a "Buy Canadian" attitude among the Canadian public. In the United States, "Buy American" legislation requires that all or most goods bought by government departments and agencies be produced in that country.

In the latest GATT agreement, signatory countries are to drop this practice for contracts over $200000, except for certain specified types of goods—such as telecommunications and electrical generating equipment.

At this point, we should recall that the Soviet Union and most other communist countries are not members of GATT. In these countries, all purchasing of foreign goods is done by state agencies—which usually purchase foreign goods only if locally-made goods are not available.

Technical Barriers

These are phony technical standards set for imported goods designed to exclude them from the domestic market. One example might be the requirement that the product should be packed in special-size containers when it would clearly be uneconomic for the exporter to do so because of the small size of the market. Or unnecessary health regulations may be used to exclude foreign food products. Many foreign countries argue that Canada's product labelling requirements fall into this category.

Voluntary Restraints

Sometimes, when one of its domestic industries is being badly hurt by foreign imports, a government will undertake to persuade the exporting countries to "voluntarily" restrict their exports. The government usually obtains co-operation for such a program of voluntary restraint by making explicit or implicit their intention to impose import quotas or increase tariffs. As far as foreign exporters are concerned, voluntary restraint is the less disagreeable alternative. Canada, the United States, and the EEC have used this policy to slow the growth of imports of Japanese goods, particularly cars and steel. In 1981, the Canadian and Japanese governments reached an agreement to restrict exports of Japanese cars to Canada and a new six-month agreement was reached in 1982 after the Canadian government held up Japanese cars in the Port of Vancouver.

Boycotts

A country may refuse to buy goods from another country or from a firm that displeases it in one way or another. The most obvious current example is the Arab boycott of firms trading with Israel. As a result, for example, Arabs drink Pepsi, because Israelis drink Coke. When Canada planned to move its embassy in Israel to Jerusalem, the Arab countries threatened to boycott all Canadian exports. As another example, the U.S. refuses to trade with Cuba.

42.5: PURPOSES OF IMPORT RESTRICTIONS

In imposing tariffs, import quotas, and exchange controls, governments have one or more basic purposes: to obtain revenue; to improve the country's balance of payments; to protect local industry; to provide greater freedom in domestic economic policy; or to support political goals. Let us briefly examine each of these.

Source of Revenue

Many years ago, customs duties were an extremely important source of revenue for countries that carried on a considerable volume of international trade. They were also relatively easy to collect, despite the smuggling that always went on. Ports were relatively few and the goods could be counted as the ships were unloaded. In Canada, the introduction of the income tax during World War I and the extension of the sales tax to many more products, caused customs duties to decline in relative importance as a source of revenue. Even today, however, their contribution to the national treasury cannot be disregarded. Customs duties levied on goods imported into Canada nowadays provide about 6 per cent of total federal-government budgetary revenue.

Improvement in the Balance of Payments

By imposing tariffs, a government makes imported goods more expensive to local consumers. As a result, people tend to buy fewer imported goods and turn instead to the local product. Whatever happens, they will usually purchase a smaller total value of the imported good, so importers will in turn pay less to foreign exporters. The imposition of import duties therefore has the effect of reducing the demand for foreign currencies. If a country's demand for foreign currencies has been outstripping its supply so that its international reserves are becoming depleted, this reduction in demand would mean an improvement in the balance of payments.

The imposition of import quotas is a much more effective way of reducing imports. However, it does not usually produce revenue at the same time.

Exchange controls can be used to control all types of demand for foreign currency, not just payments for imports. For instance, exchange controls can restrict interest and dividend payments, tourist spending abroad, and the outflow of capital from a country.

Protection of Local Industry

If Canadian importers have to pay duty on imported goods, they will have to recover this additional expense by charging the public more for them. Otherwise, they will have to suffer a reduction in profit, which may already be quite small. However, by charging, say, $1.25 instead of $1.00 per item, they are not as competitive as before. Local Canadian producers who may be able to sell the same good for $1.15 can now outsell the imported product; previously they could not. In other words, an import duty helps protect the domestic producer from foreign competition. The larger the duty, the greater the protection. This is why many Canadian industries are continually lobbying the federal government and Members of Parliament for higher tariffs on imported goods. Import quotas, by restricting imports to a specified amount, can provide even greater protection to local industry.

If the government imposes a tariff greater than the cost difference between a domestic and imported product, it will no longer be profitable to import the foreign goods at all. Such a tariff is called a *prohibitive tariff*. Domestic industries will in such a case be the sole suppliers of the domestic market. Consumers will consequently be deprived of any of the benefits of international specialization and trade—in other words, they will have to pay more for the goods they buy and perhaps not be able to obtain certain goods at all.

Greater Freedom in Domestic Economic Policy

In the absence of exchange controls, government deficit spending and/ or an "easy-money" policy may cause a decline in the foreign exchange value of the country's currency. This will mean higher prices for imports and a higher cost of servicing foreign debt. A country's economic policy may also be partly thwarted by a flight of capital abroad. By imposing exchange controls, a government can, to some extent, have a free hand domestically in, for example, stimulating employment by a less restrictive monetary or fiscal policy.

Political Reasons

In time of war, hot or cold, a government may restrict or freeze capital movements and other financial transfers between itself and another country. This occurred in recent years between the U.S. and Iran, between Britain and Argentina, and between Poland and the West.

The Communist countries have always used exchange controls to help enforce political conformity at home (e.g., restrictions on trade and travel by nationals and foreigners) and to further their political interests abroad (e.g., the Soviet Union and Cuba).

42.6: FREE TRADE VERSUS PROTECTIONISM

Is a country better off with free trade or with some kind of tariff or other import protection? Most economists and governments believe that free trade is generally beneficial. However, this is not true of the Third World countries who generally restrict imports, particularly of manufactured "non-essential" goods. And in the case of the Soviet bloc, there is no free trade with the West. Even between the Communist countries themselves, most of the trade is conducted on a bilateral basis, governed by trade agreements. Let us now consider the nature and validity of some of the arguments in favour of trade protectionism.

Revenue

Undoubtedly, import duties can provide governments with a useful sum of money. However, the question is: who pays the import duty? If the general public pays, in the form of higher prices for the imported goods, then the government could obtain the money by other means, such as a higher sales tax. Since such a tax would apply to all goods, whether made at home or abroad, it would have the advantage of not interfering with the international division of labour. However, abolishing import duties would mean a break from tradition. Moreover, a higher sales tax might be politically more unpalatable. And in practice, political considerations often overrule economic ones.

It is possible, however, that the foreign exporters may bear part of the import duty, depending on the conditions of supply of the product. If foreign supply is relatively inelastic—in other words, a reduction in the price received will not cause very much reduction in the quantity supplied—the foreign exporters may accept a lower price for their goods, yet supply almost the same amount as before. For example, if the government imposes a 25¢ specific duty on a good formerly imported for $1.00 per unit, the foreign exporters may now accept $0.90 per unit. This will permit the good to be sold in the export market at $1.15 ($0.90 plus $0.25) instead of at $1.25 per unit and so remain competitive. By its import duty, the government has in effect caused a shift, in favour of its own country, of the *terms of trade*—the relationship between a country's export prices and its import prices.

Balance of Payments

Do countries need to restrict imports by tariffs, quotas, and exchange controls to improve their international balance of payments?

Certainly, so long as a country has a fixed exchange rate, an imbalance can develop between a country's demand for and its supply of foreign currencies. This imbalance can cause a rapid depletion in a country's reserves of gold and foreign exchange. By restricting imports, a government can effectively reduce this pressure. Many countries, when confronted with a foreign exchange crisis, do in fact impose additional import restrictions.

Import restrictions can undoubtedly be justified as a short-term measure. They afford a government "breathing space" for other measures to take effect. These other measures include "export drives" and changes in monetary and fiscal policy—all of which have a pronounced time lag. Import restrictions can also be used as a bargaining counter to induce trade concessions (such as a currency revaluation) from other countries.

If the underlying disequilibrium in the balance of payments cannot be corrected by any other measures, the only long-term solution is to devalue the foreign exchange rate of the currency. In other words, import restrictions are not a long-term answer. Nowadays many countries, including Canada, have a "floating" rather than a fixed rate of

"Either we learn to export more, or we have to start doing without some of those French wines, Italian shoes, and Japanese stereos."

exchange. Consequently, exchange-rate adjustments are made more gradually.

Local Industry

According to the "infant industry" argument, tariffs and other import restrictions are necessary if new industries are to be established in a country and are to be able to flourish. Only by shielding these new industries from foreign competition, can the country expect them to survive their first tender years. Such industries must be allowed to grow to the point where they will be large enough to benefit, in terms of lower per unit costs of production, from the economies of scale. Without protection, according to this viewpoint, they would never have a chance to reach a profitable size. In addition, to prevent such industries from getting established, foreign producers might even, in the short run, deliberately reduce the prices and profits on their own goods.

This argument is used by most of the developing countries as justification for their import barriers on foreign manufactured goods. However, it is difficult, to say the least, to determine which infant industries could eventually be as efficient as large foreign producers. Moreover, since tariffs are rarely removed once they have been imposed, it might be better, from the consumers' point of view, to assist infant industries by direct subsidies such as low-interest loans, outright grants, or income tax exemptions, all of which could be of relatively short duration. However, local industries do also provide local income and employment. So the calculation of net benefit is by no means straightforward.

Infant industries are not the only ones that clamour for protection. Sometimes even old, established industries lobby for increased tariffs and other import restrictions when lower-priced imports start to push their products out of the domestic market. This has happened in Canada with, for example, textiles, toys, television sets, and radios. Obviously, increased protection helps domestic industries. By making imports higher priced, it enables local producers to sell their goods and thus continue to provide income and jobs for their employees and taxes for the government. This argument is a perfectly valid one for the industries concerned. They are better off with more protection. Indirectly, the country as a whole will derive benefit from income and employment in these industries.

However, on the harmful side, increased protection for domestic industries prevents members of the public from buying lower-priced foreign goods. As they have to pay more for locally produced goods, their real income is lower than it might otherwise be. The fruits of international specialization and trade are taken from the population as a whole in order to protect the welfare of certain members of that population. Furthermore, if other countries restrict their imports from Canada in retaliation, Canadian exports will decline and thereby reduce income and employment. Of course, each Canadian industry threatened by competition from imports can be expected to fight in whatever way possible for its life. Often, therefore, the interests of the population as a whole (to be safeguarded by the government) are overlooked. It is often difficult to determine just what the net effect of increased protection would be for Canada as a whole. Theoretically, it is conceivable that a country's whole manufacturing sector could be wiped out if foreign manufacturers can produce and supply the goods more cheaply.

Sometimes protection for a particular industry is justified on military grounds. For example, to produce armaments it is essential to have steel-manufacturing capacity. Thus, the establishment of a steel mill, although domestic steel production may be less efficient than foreign production, may be encouraged by tariffs and import quotas. Again, the public as a whole is having to pay a higher price for domestically manufactured products. If international trade were permitted to flow unhindered, the public could buy the cheaper (but same quality) foreign products. However, in the event of war, the country can supply all or part of the steel required for tanks, munitions, and other military hardware.

Summary

1. Many countries restrict imports by means of tariffs, import quotas, exchange controls, and "voluntary" restraints on foreign exporters.
2. A tariff (also called a customs duty or import duty) is a tax that a government levies on an imported good. Tariffs can be *ad valorem*, specific, or compound.
3. Canada has four tariff levels: British preferential, most favoured nation, general, and general preferential.
4. An import quota is the fixed quantity of a foreign good that importers may bring into the country during a twelve-month period at the prevailing tariff. Import quotas may be global or allocated.
5. Exchange control, in its most rigorous form, means that anyone wishing to obtain foreign exchange must secure permission from the government. Such a system permits the government to restrict

the demand for scarce foreign exchange and to ration it among different needs.
6. Sometimes the government of an importing country will persuade the government or exporters of another country to impose "voluntary" restraints on their exports.
7. Import restrictions have one or more of three basic purposes: to obtain revenue, to improve a country's balance of payments, and to protect local industry.
8. In a discussion of the issue of free trade versus protectionism, the gains from specialization and international trade (which include the terms of trade) must be weighed against the reasons for imposing trade barriers.

Key Terms

Tariff   840
Ad valorem duty   840
Specific duty   840
Compound duty   840
Seasonal duty   841
Anti-dumping duty   841
Countervailing duty   841
British preferential
   rate   841
Most-favoured-nation
   rate   841
General rate   841
Non-tariff barrier   842
Import quota   842

Global import quota   842
Allocated import quota   842
Exchange control   842
Customs valuation   843
Fair market value   845
Purchasing policy   845
Technical barriers   845
Voluntary restraint   846
Boycott   846
Free trade   848
Protectionism   848
Non-essential goods   848
Infant industry   851

Review Questions

1. What are the main kinds of barriers to international trade?
2. What are the various types of tariffs?
3. Distinguish, with examples, between an anti-dumping and a countervailing duty.
4. "Canada has four levels of tariffs." What are they?
5. What is an import quota? Explain the different types.
6. Explain the nature and purpose of exchange controls.
7. What are the various types of "non-tariff barriers" other than import quotas and exchange controls?

8. What are the main purposes of import restrictions?
9. What are the merits of import duties as a source of government revenue? Why have they been used as such for so many years?
10. How can import restrictions improve a country's balance of payments? Which type is the most effective?
11. What is the "infant industry" argument for tariff protection? What are its merits?
12. Why is it that old, established industries often ask for tariff protection? Answer, with reference to a Canadian industry.
13. Summarize the arguments in favour of free trade.
14. Summarize the arguments in favour of protectionism.

Reference

1 The British Commonwealth is a voluntary association of forty-two sovereign independent countries. The member countries are: Britain, Canada, Australia, New Zealand, the Bahamas, Bangladesh, Barbados, Botswana, Cyprus, Dominica, Fiji, Gambia, Ghana, Grenada, Guyana, India, Jamaica, Kenya, Kiribati, Lesotho, Malawi, Malaysia, Malta, Mauritius, Nauru, Nigeria, Seychelles, Sierra Leone, Singapore, Solomon Islands, Sri Lanka, St. Lucia, St. Vincent, Swaziland, Tanzania, Trinidad and Tobago, Tuvalu, Uganda, Zambia, Tonga, Western Samoa, and Papua New Guinea.

43. INTERNATIONAL TRADE CO-OPERATION

CHAPTER OBJECTIVES

A. To explain the nature and purpose of the General Agreement on Tariffs and Trade, or GATT
B. To describe the steps that have been taken in Western Europe to establish regional free trade
C. To explain the nature, purpose, and results of Canada's auto-pact with the U.S.
D. To emphasize that many other countries have moved towards regional free trade
E. To discuss Canada's international trade policy

CHAPTER OUTLINE

43.1 The General Agreement on Tariffs and Trade (GATT)
43.2 West European Economic Co-operation
43.3 The Canada-U.S. Automotive Products Agreement
43.4 Trading Blocs
43.5 Canada's International Trade Policy

If international trade, with all its benefits, was to expand after World War II, there had to be some agreement among the various countries of the world to reduce tariffs and other trade barriers. The International Monetary Fund was designed to restore exchange rate stability; the World Bank (discussed in the next chapter) to promote post-war recovery and economic development; but the third prerequisite for greater international trade, an agreement on tariffs, was still lacking.

Consequently, in 1946, the Economic and Social Council of the United Nations decided to establish an international agency that would co-ordinate efforts to reduce trade barriers, establish rules of international trade practice, and settle international trade disputes. At a conference in Havana, Cuba, in 1947, the representatives of fifty-three countries approved, after some modification, a draft charter for such an agency. This agency, to be named the International Trade Organization (ITO), was to come into being when a majority of the governments represented at the conference had ratified the charter. However, the U.S. Congress refused to do so. Rightly or wrongly, members of Congress were unwilling to relinquish controls over U.S. tariffs and other trade practices to an international body. This meant that one of the most important trading nations would not take part. As a result, the agency was never established.

43.1: THE GENERAL AGREEMENT ON TARIFFS AND TRADE (GATT)

This setback, serious though it was, did not terminate United Nations' efforts to bring about an international agreement to reduce trade barriers. In that same year of 1947, the United Nations arranged a new conference in Geneva, Switzerland. Instead of trying to establish an international trade authority, the United Nations aimed, more modestly, at securing a voluntary agreement to reduce tariffs. Each country represented at the conference bargained bilaterally with every other country about the tariff reductions that it would make. This was on the understanding, as initially agreed, that the concessions made would automatically be extended to any other countries participating in the agreement. In other words, each country would extend to every other member country the lowest rate of duty that it had agreed to with any single country during the tariff negotiations. This rate of import duty was called the "most-favoured-nation" rate. After some hard bargaining, the delegates of twenty-three countries, including Canada, the United States, and Britain, signed an agreement that listed all the reductions in tariffs to which the various countries had agreed. This agreement, known as the General Agreement on Tariffs and Trade, or GATT, was to last three years. Since then, new agreements have been negotiated, embodying further tariff reductions and enlarging the number of participating countries. The last full-scale GATT talks took place in Geneva in November 1982.

The Soviet Union has never been a member of GATT but has recently been considering the possibility of "observer status"—something that Bulgaria has enjoyed since 1973. Amongst the communist countries (who are also members of Comecon, the Soviet trade bloc), Czechoslovakia was one of the original signatories of GATT; Poland joined in 1968; Romania in 1972; and Hungary in 1973.

*"In negotiating tariff reductions, Chris,
you've got to be prepared for some give
and take."*

Each country negotiated its own terms of access—for example, Poland agreed to a compound increase in the value of its imports from the other GATT members of 7 per cent a year. Hungary agreed to tariff and other concessions. However, the EEC countries, although GATT members, have kept their restrictions on imports from Poland, etc. because of claims of unfair export pricing policies. In October 1982, the United States withdrew most-favoured-nation status for Poland ostensibly on the grounds that Poland had not honoured its 7 per cent import growth commitment.

In the early 1980s, the members of GATT began to pay attention to the need for reducing widespread non-tariff trade barriers such as import quotas, exchange controls, etc.

Another area of concern has been the GATT mechanism for resolving disputes between member countries (e.g. U.S.-Canadian differences over Canada's Foreign Investment Review Agency). At present, a GATT panel is being formed to examine each particular problem and decide who is at fault. But there is no provision for follow-up to ensure that the situation is corrected.

Another item for discussion is the safeguards that countries can invoke when an imported good is causing harm to domestic producers. Thus, for example, Canada has used safeguard measures under GATT to limit the amount of footwear imported into this country. Canada, the U.S., and Japan favour "consensual selectivity" in applying restrictions to exports from other countries. This is another name for the "voluntary restraints" that Canada has already negotiated with Japan with regard to car exports to Canada. And it involves consultation with the exporting country and even provides for some measure of compensation. By contrast, the EEC prefers the right to unilateral action. The developing countries would like to stick with the GATT's present Most Favoured Nation clause that stipulates that countries must treat each other equally and not discriminate against any individual exporting country. Another item to attract the attention of GATT in the early 1980s is trade concessions between developed and developing countries.

An item of particular concern to Canada and to several developing countries is the treatment accorded to resource exports. So far, the GATT has applied to trade in manufactured goods rather than resource goods such as iron ore exported in raw or semi-manufactured form.

Of interest to the U.S. is the possibility of including the exports of services such as banking, investment, and shipping within the GATT framework. Along with Canada, Australia and other large agricultural producers, the U.S. is also interested in opening up the West European and other markets to its farm products. France and other EEC members are, however, highly protective of their domestic agriculture and subsidize both EEC farm output and agricultural exports—something that the U.S. and Canada feel constitutes an unfair trade practice. The U.S. claims that the EEC farm subsidy policy has enabled the EEC to become a leading exporter in several commodity markets—for example, from being the world's largest importer of poultry 20 years ago, it has now become the world's largest exporter; it has also become the second largest exporter of beef and veal; and it is challenging Australia as the third largest wheat exporter. Whereas GATT prohibits direct subsidies for exports of industrial goods, the EEC managed to negotiate an exemption for agricultural products during the Tokyo round of multilateral trade negotiations some years ago. The only restriction was that subsidies may not be used to gain an unfair share of the world markets—something that the U.S. claims is taking place. If the U.S. retaliates with export subsidies of its own, Canada may well see its farm exports drop as it cannot afford to subsidize their sale abroad.

43.2: WEST EUROPEAN ECONOMIC CO-OPERATION

For political as well as economic reasons, many countries of Western Europe were willing, after World War II, to extend their economic co-operation beyond the bounds envisaged in the international trade and exchange agreements previously discussed. These countries were willing, in fact, to abandon part of their economic, and even political, sovereignty in order to reap the economic benefit of a market comparable in size to that of the United States. They also hoped, by building greater economic interdependence, to reduce the possibility of future war in an area that had given origin to two previous world conflagrations.

Organization for European Economic Co-operation (OEEC)

The United States, in its foreign policy towards Western Europe, strongly urged that the member countries co-operate economically, both to raise the standard of living of their people and to promote future international peace. In extending economic assistance under the Marshall Plan, the United States had consequently insisted on the establishment of a special agency, representing the various European countries, to determine economic needs and to promote trade and other economic co-operation. This agency, set up in 1947 by sixteen different European countries, was the Organization for European Economic Co-operation (OEEC).

As well as determining aid priorities, the OEEC worked to reduce import quotas among member countries, so that, by 1956, most of these quotas had been abolished. The OEEC also worked hard to persuade member countries to reduce or eliminate duties on imports from each other. The OEEC endeavoured, furthermore, to promote a multilateral payments system among member countries so that, for example, French francs earned by British exporters could be used, if desired, to pay for British imports from other member countries. This aim was achieved with the establishment of the European Payments Union. The OEEC also promoted the idea of permitting workers in countries with large pockets of unemployment, such as Italy, to go to other countries, such as West Germany, that suffered at the time from a labour shortage.

Organization for Economic Co-operation and Development (OECD).

In 1961, the member countries of the OEEC, together with Canada and the United States, set up a new organization—the Organization for Economic Co-operation and Development (OECD). This new organization, which replaced the OEEC, was much broader in both scope and membership. Its objectives were threefold: to help promote the highest sustainable rate of economic growth and employment of member countries consistent with financial stability; to contribute to sound economic expansion in member as well as non-member countries in the process of economic development; and to contribute to the expansion of world trade on a multilateral, non-discriminatory basis in accordance with international obligations. The members of the OECD are: Australia, Belgium, Canada, Denmark, Finland, France, West Germany, Greece, Iceland, Ireland, Italy, Japan, Luxembourg, the Netherlands, New Zealand, Norway, Portugal, Spain, Sweden, Switzerland, Turkey, the United Kingdom, and the United States.

Benelux

The movement towards European economic integration received an early impetus when, in 1948, three West European countries—Belgium, the Netherlands, and Luxembourg (or Benelux, for short)—formed a customs union. This customs union provided for completely free trade between the three member countries and for a common tariff on goods from outside. Customs unions, by the way, were not new in Europe. In the nineteenth century, the various politically independent German states had operated their own Zollverein.

European Coal and Steel Community

At the individual industry level, another milestone on the road to European economic integration was erected in 1951 with the establishment of the European Coal and Steel Community. This was a supranational authority that was given jurisdiction over coal and steel production in the member countries: Belgium, France, Italy, Luxembourg, the Netherlands, and West Germany. Instead of each country, however efficiently, producing its own coal and steel and severely restricting imports from the others, the member countries would now concentrate production in their most efficient areas. They would, at the same time, remove barriers to trade in these products. Such a plan, which enabled all countries to derive economic benefit, had the additional advantage of reducing the possibility that a member country could unilaterally use its coal and steel capacity to produce munitions for war.

European Economic Community (EEC)

In March 1957, the six countries that were member of the European Coal and Steel Community took another and more important step towards economic integration. They signed a treaty providing for the establishment of a European Economic Community, known for short as the EEC. This was also to become known as the Common Market.

Under the Treaty of Rome, which came into force at the beginning of 1959, Belgium, France, Italy, Luxembourg, the Netherlands and West Germany agreed to the gradual removal of all trade barriers between themselves on almost all non-agricultural products manufactured within the region. They also agreed to the erection of a common tariff barrier on goods from outside. The removal of tariffs and import quotas between member countries was to take place over a period of twelve to fifteen years.

The combined population of the six member countries, when the Common Market was established in 1959, was over 160 million. (It now has 270 million with its enlarged membership). This compared favourably in size with the populations of the United States and the Soviet Union. Such a large market would obviously permit much greater specialization of production than had been previously possible. For example, a refrigerator manufacturer in Italy, instead of producing only 10000 refrigerators a year, could, with its product able to enter the other five countries duty-free, produce and sell 40000. With larger production, the Italian firm could now afford to use more highly mechanized means of production and materials handling. It could also spread the fixed costs of production and marketing over more units of output. These economies of large-scale production could then be shared in the form of higher profits and wages in the Italian plant and in the form of lower refrigerator prices, spurred by competition, in all the Common Market countries.

However, with the Treaty of Rome, the six countries sought more than just a customs union. They included in the Treaty various other provisions that would help bring about closer economic and political ties among themselves. Thus they provided in the treaty for the free movement of people, services, and capital from one country to another; and for the establishment of common hours of work, holidays, unemployment benefits, pensions, and other conditions of employment; for a common transport policy to ease the movement of people and goods; and for the support of agriculture through a common agricultural policy. They also arranged for the establishment of a European Investment Bank to make development loans to economically backward areas of the market. Under a separate treaty, the six countries also agreed to undertake a common program of atomic research and development. This was to be known as the European Atomic Community, or Euratom. To mitigate the social problems that would arise in adjusting each country's economy to increased competition, the six countries also provided for the establishment of a Social Fund. The money contributed by the member countries to this Fund would be used, wherever necessary, to help business firms convert their factories to new types of production and to help displaced workers train for and find new jobs.

In the years since the Treaty of Rome came into force, the member countries of the European Common Market, despite occasional difficulties and disagreements, have steadily pushed ahead with the unification of their economies. Trade barriers have been reduced more rapidly than was originally intended, and, partly as a result, the rate of economic growth of member countries, until the recent world economic recession, has been very high. Monetary co-operation has also been considerable and, eventually, member countries hope to have a common currency.

Proposal for an Industrial Free Trade Area.

Only six countries of Western Europe were willing in 1957 to contemplate the considerable sacrifice of national economic and political sovereignty that the Common market would eventually entail. At that time, the other eligible countries, notably Britain, felt that they would have more to lose than to gain by participation.

Britain, for example, had a long tradition of political independence. It also had a pattern of trade geared substantially to the British Commonwealth. Thus Britain had for many years imported a large percentage of its food and raw materials from Commonwealth countries. Britain's membership in the Common Market would mean that she would have to levy the common tariff rates on these outside goods but let in free those from the Common Market countries. This would certainly mean higher food prices for the British consumer. It would also mean an indignant outcry from Commonwealth countries, such as Australia, Canada, and New Zealand that would lose part or all of the British market for certain key products such as lamb, cheese, and butter.

However, a disquieting trend had long been evident in Britain's Commonwealth trade: Australia, Canada, New Zealand, and other Commonwealth countries were now developing their own manufacturing industries. As a result, British exporters of manufactured goods were finding it increasingly hard to compete with local industries. They were also finding it harder to compete in these Commonwealth markets, in many cases on the other side of the world, with more efficient Japanese and other S.E. Asian manufacturers.

It was also clear that the countries of Western Europe, close at hand, formed a market that was becoming more and more valuable to Britain, particularly to its high-technology industries such as electronics and chemicals. This meant that Britain could not afford to ignore the Common market and its implications for British exports. In fact, despite the common external tariff, the Common Market countries were Britain's principal customers.

Britain, in her best traditional form, proposed a compromise: an Industrial Free Trade Area that would include Britain, the Common Market, and any other European countries that cared to join. Within this area, there would be completely free trade in industrial goods. The Common Market countries would still be able to have their common tariff on goods from other countries. And Britain would be able to restrict food and raw material imports from Europe in favour of imports from the Commonwealth. However, France, with a large farming sector, strenuously opposed this plan. In exchange for permitting other countries' manufactured goods to enter freely, France, reasonably enough, wanted the right to export its agricultural products to other countries, including Britain. As a consequence, the Common Market countries rejected the British plan.

European Free Trade Association (EFTA)

Unwilling to enter the Common Market on the terms laid down, and thwarted in its attempt to establish an Industrial Free Trade Area with the Common Market countries, Britain joined with six other West European countries in November 1959, to form the European Free Trade Association. This was a new free trade area consisting of Austria, Denmark, Britain, Norway, Portugal, Sweden, and Switzerland—a group of countries later called the "Outer Seven". Members of this group agreed to remove tariffs and quotas on all imports of industrial and agricultural products from each other over the ten years beginning 1960. Unlike the Common Market, there was no intention of eventual political integration of member countries; no intention of close economic integration; and no restriction on a member country's rights to set its own tariff rate on imports from other countries. This meant that Britain could still give Commonwealth countries, including Canada, preferential treatment in the British market. It also meant, as a consequence, that Britain could still continue to enjoy preferential treatment for her manufactured goods in Commonwealth markets—a right that would have been lost if Commonwealth preference were abandoned because of Britain's entry into the Common Market.

Britain and the EEC

It did not take long for Britain and other EFTA countries to realize that their free trade area was a poor substitute for membership in the Common Market. For Britain, this conviction grew stronger as the economies of the Common Market countries boomed and Britain's industrial exports to these countries, despite the tariff barrier, grew larger. Europe was, in fact, becoming more important as a market for British goods than the Commonwealth. So, in 1961, Britain applied for membership despite protests from Canada and other Commonwealth countries. After lengthy negotiations as to the terms of Britain's entry, the Common Market countries, at French instigation, turned down the application. The main reason for this rejection, at least ostensibly, was that Britain was not sufficiently European in outlook. The member countries feared that once inside the Common Market, Britain might act as a brake on their basic goal of political and economic unification. Would Britain be willing, France argued, to put Europe before the British Commonwealth and the United States?

In 1966, with the retirement of France's president, General de Gaulle, French opposition to British entry into the Common Market quickly waned. As a result, Britain once more began negotiations with the Common Market countries. Finally, on January 1, 1973, it became a member, along with Denmark and Ireland. Norway, which also negotiated terms of entry, withdrew its application after a referendum in Norway produced a narrow majority against EEC membership.

Britain's membership in the EEC was perhaps inevitable, given its geographical and economic circumstances. However, entry into the Common Market has not been an unquestioned blessing,when costs are compared with economic benefits. The difficulty centres mainly around the CAP, or Common Agricultural Policy, which now eats up over 60 per cent of the EEC's budget. Under the CAP, agricultural prices are set at a high level and surplus production is purchased from farmers. If food is imported from outside the EEC, the importing country is required to pay any difference between the EEC price and the import price into the EEC budget. This means that food-producing countries such as France, Denmark, and Ireland, benefit greatly from the CAP, while food-importing countries, such as Britain and West Germany, lose. Britain in fact is a double loser. This is because it has the smallest per capita number of farmers in the EEC and therefore receives less agricultural subsidies than the other members. And because it imports more food from outside the EEC than the others—for which it must pay the differential into the EEC budget. British indignation at this situation has been mollified somewhat by a negotiated rebate of part of Britain's budgetary contribution.

Now that Britain is a member of the EEC, it no longer gives preferential rates of import duty to goods imported from Canada and other British Commonwealth countries.

The EEC in Review

Although the EEC has had its problems, particularly the dispute over the Common Agricultural Policy, and the overruling in May, 1982, of Britain's supposed veto on new farm prices, it has nevertheless achieved a great deal. For example, all tariff and quota barriers to trade between member countries have been abolished and trade with new-member Greece will be liberalized over a five-year transition period. The EEC also has a wide variety of trade agreements with other non-EEC countries. For example, there is now almost free trade in industrial goods with members of the European Free Trade Association (Norway, Sweden, Finland, Portugal, Austria, Switzerland, and Iceland). However, there are still some technical barriers that favour the EEC producers in the EEC market. Politically, there is very close contact amongst member countries, although the idea of the emergence of a single country is still a long way off. Progress has also been slow in the area of monetary union, although since March 1978, eight of the member countries have participated in a European Monetary System, or EMS, by which currency fluctuations are smoothed out and facilities for swapping credit, as and when necessary, are provided.

Other Western European countries had been barred from membership in the EEC because of their political regimes. Only those with a commitment to democracy were welcomed. However, the disappearance of political dictatorship in Greece, Spain, and Portugal paved the way for their entry. Greece had already negotiated associate status with the EEC before the establishment of a military dictatorship in 1967. And, with the restoration of democracy in 1980, Greece became the EEC's tenth member on January 1, 1981.

Portugal turned to democracy in 1974 and Spain, after the death of General Franco, followed suit in 1975. Although both countries applied soon afterwards for EEC membership, negotiations dragged on for many years. This was because of disillusionment by the six original members with the previous enlargement of the EEC in 1973. Also because of the fact that the entry of Spain and Portugal would provide unwelcome competition for farmers in France, Italy, and Greece and aggravate the existing farm surplus problem—for example, Spanish membership would raise EEC olive oil production by 60 per cent when the EEC is already 95 per cent self-sufficient in this product. However, the political advantages of an enlarged EEC membership are expected to overcome the economic snags.

43.3: THE CANADA-U.S. AUTOMOTIVE PRODUCTS AGREEMENT

Although the Canadian automobile industry has a long and creditable history, it has suffered along with many other Canadian secondary manufacturing industries from the limited size of the domestic market. Compared with the U.S. automobile industry, this has meant shorter production runs, higher per-unit production costs, and higher selling prices. Also, the workers employed are members of the same U.S.-based labour union, the United Automobile Workers of America, whose Canadian members insist on receiving the same rates of pay as their fellow union members south of the border, regardless of any differences in productivity.

Because of higher per unit production costs, the Canadian auto industry had always found it difficult to compete with foreign car and truck manufacturers, particularly in markets outside Canada. As a consequence, Canadian trade with the United States in automotive products in the early 1960s was showing a widening imbalance. Canada was importing far more than it was exporting.

In October 1963, to stimulate exports of automotive products and thereby the growth of the Canadian automotive industry, the Canadian government prepared to introduce a "duty-remission plan" whereby Canadian manufacturers would receive a rebate on their exports of automotive products to offset foreign import duties. However, since the U.S. government would automatically have imposed countervailing duties to neutralize these grants, there was the possibility of a serious deterioration in trade relations between Canada and the United States. To prevent such an occurrence, which could only have been harmful to both countries, the two governments, after discussions with the automobile industry, negotiated the Canada-United States Automotive Products Agreement. This agreement (known as the "autopact") was signed by Prime Minister Pearson and President Johnson on January 16, 1965.

Objectives of the Agreement

In Article 1 of the agreement, Canada and the United States agree to seek "the early achievement of the following objectives":

(a) the creation of a broader market for automotive products within which the full benefits of specialization and large-scale production can be achieved;

(b) the liberalization of Canadian and United States automotive trade in respect of tariff barriers and other factors tending to impede it, with a view to enabling the industries of both countries to participate on a fair and equitable basis in the expanding total market of the two countries; and

(c) the development of conditions in which market forces may operate effectively to attain the most economic pattern of investment, production and trade.

The two countries also agreed in Article I that "it shall be the policy of each Government to avoid actions which would frustrate the achievement of these objectives."

The Safeguards

Although both countries could obviously benefit from the lower production and marketing costs that would accompany increased specialization and longer production runs, it was likely that, without any special safeguards, production would gradually tend to concentrate in the United States. Consequently, although Canada agreed in Article II of the agreement to immediate duty-free entry of new cars, buses, and certain trucks, as well as of parts destined for them (but not replacement parts and tires), it also made certain restrictions set out in Annex A of the agreement and in separate "letters of undertaking." The first safeguard was that duty-free imports of automotive products would be permitted only to automobile manufacturers who met certain minimum Canadian production requirements for each type of vehicle—cars, trucks, and buses. To qualify, a firm has to produce at least 75 per cent of the vehicles it sells in this country, or failing this, the percentage reached in the 1964 model year in Canada (August 1, 1963-July 31, 1964).

The second safeguard was that the Canadian value added (the "Canadian Content") for each type of vehicle produced in Canada had to at least equal the dollar amount achieved in the 1964 model year.

The third safeguard, contained in separate letters of undertaking, provided for the future rate of growth of total value added in Canada. It was agreed that (a) the value added in Canada in each model year should be increased by an amount equal to 60 per cent of the growth in the value of cars sold in Canada (50 per cent for commercial vehicles) and (b) in addition to the value-added floor and the potential value-added growth already provided for, value added in Canada should be increased by the end of the 1968 model year by $260 million Canadian. However, the two commitments for value-added growth could be met either by more Canadian-produced vehicles or by more Canadian production of original parts for export, whichever was more efficient.

In the agreement, the removal of these safeguards was not provided for. However, it appears to have been the understanding of the U.S. government that the safeguards would be "transitional."

The effect of the agreement, with regard to Canada, was to stimulate the growth of the car and truck industry, vastly increase the two-way flow of vehicles, engines, and parts across the Canadian-U.S. border, and in the first few years (see Table S.50) gradually reduce Canada's foreign trade deficit in motor vehicles and parts. For the United States, the agreement meant, first of all, the avoidance of the protective trade measures previously envisaged by the Canadian government. It meant, second, lower production costs through greater specialization, which in turn would help North American sales in general. It also meant, though the reduction of a trade surplus with Canada in automotive products that Americans had come to regard as traditional. Thus, it helped aggravate a worsening overall U.S. balance-of-payments situation. Canadians claim that in recent years the U.S. has received more benefit from the pact than Canada.

Table S.50
Canada's Foreign Trade in Motor Vehicles and Parts, in millions of dollars, 1963-1982

Year	Exports	Imports	Balance
1963	88	669	-581
1964	177	818	-641
1965	356	1 125	-769
1966	1 012	1 581	-569
1967	1 739	2 168	-429
1968	2 672	3 001	-329
1969	3 514	3 546	-32
1970	3 499	3 252	+ 247
1971	4 171	4 110	+ 61
1972	4 718	4 934	-216
1973	5 415	6 081	-666
1974	5 717	7 124	-1 407
1975	6 432	8 236	-1 804
1976	8 225	9 440	-1 215
1977	10 424	11 576	-1 152
1978	12 540	13 386	-846
1979	11 900	15 161	-3 261
1980	10 924	13 609	-2 685
1981	13 084	15 996	-2 912
1982	16 382	14 898	-1 484

Source: Statistics Canada, *Summary of External Trade,* Cat. 65-001

Note: Imports are from Japan etc., as well as from the U.S.A.

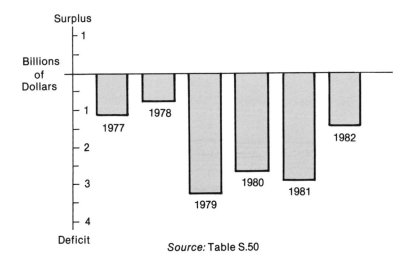

Source: Table S.50

Disagreement

From its very beginning, the agreement encountered criticism in the United States, particularly in Congress. And as the U.S. balance-of-payments situation deteriorated and the automotive trade balance with Canada worsened, this criticism became more outspoken. Finally, the removal of these safeguards became an important object in U.S. trade negotiations with Canada. In addition, the United States unilaterally adopted a domestic international sales corporation (DISC) program that, by means of large tax concessions, encouraged U.S. firms to pro--duce at home and to export, rather than produce in subsidiary manufacturing plants located in foreign markets. This program raised fears in Canada that U.S. automobile manufacturers would no longer expand plants in Canada but produce more in the United States. In practice, this is what seems to have occurred.

In Canada, Article I(b) of the agreement has been interpreted by many people to mean that Canada, to "participate on a fair and equitable basis in the expanding total market of the two countries," should have the same percentage share of total North American production as it does of total vehicle sales.

However, it must be remembered that the agreement can be terminated at any time by twelve months' written notice on the part of either government. In other words, if the agreement is not mutually beneficial, it can be quickly brought to an end.

How would the removal of the safeguards affect Canada? One point of view is that Canadian automobiles and parts production would continue to prosper. The U.S. automotive manufacturers, it is argued, have already completed major investments in Canada and will not close such plants in favour of those in the United States. A bigger danger, according to this view, is competition from Japan. The other point of view is that the Canadian automotive industry could be badly harmed, particularly in the long run, if the safeguards are dropped, for production will inevitably switch, albeit gradually, to U.S. plants.

43.4: TRADING BLOCS

The benefits of freer international trade, particularly at the regional level, have encouraged countries in different parts of the world to establish free trade areas. To many observers, the economic strength of the United States has been due in large measure to the large free trade area that it comprises. And in Western Europe, the faster rate of economic growth since the formation of the Common Market has provided confirmation of the benefits of regional free trade. Since the

Second World War, the Soviet Union has also welded itself and its satellite countries into one large trading bloc, the Comecon. However, this has been as much for political reasons as economic ones. But elsewhere in the world—in South America, Central America, South-east Asia, and Africa—countries have joined together in regional trading blocs.

43.5: CANADA'S INTERNATIONAL TRADE POLICY

Although steps are continuously being taken through GATT to reduce trade barriers on a world-wide basis, the various regional trading blocs will obviously maintain tariff and other trade barriers to imports from non-members. The question then arises as to Canada's future in world trade. Geographically, it is a natural member of a North American free trade area. But, politically, it fears economic and political domination by the United States. It seeks, instead, to diversify its trade so as not to be dependent on any one country. However, over 70 per cent of its imports and exports continue to be with the U.S. And the chances seem slim that it can successfully diversify in the face of increasing geographical compartmentalization of international trade.

As we mentioned earlier, there should perhaps be a limit to international specialization despite the theory of comparative advantage. Suppose for example, that the countries of S.E. Asia can produce manufactured goods more efficiently than Canada, should our government therefore stand idly by and let many of our existing manufacturing industries disappear when the rate of unemployment among young Canadians is already so high? Can Canada pin its hopes for greater employment on the so-called high technology industries (such as communications), particularly when other countries seem equally adept, if not more so, at industrial innovation and seem to have a stronger, more coherent industrial strategy? This, of course, is an argument for industrial protectionism.

Conversely, free traders would argue that Canada's market of just 25 million is too small to support an inward-looking manufacturing sector. They could cite examples of Canadian manufacturing firms that have been successful in developing their export markets. And they could cite examples of the Canadian subsidiaries of U.S. multinational corporations that have been given a *world product mandate* by their parent companies to manufacture a particular item in Canada for distribution and sale throughout the world.

Perhaps the answer lies in Canadian participation in a North American free trade area, with bilateral trade agreements with other countries. But this would of course mean a departure from Canada's present multilateral trade policy—as signified by Canada's membership in GATT. For the U.S., any move towards protectionism, however economically desirable it might be, has political implications (for example, Japanese antagonism) that, as a superpower, it probably could not afford. For Canada also, any move towards protectionism would counter its apparent policy towards the Third World countries of "trade as well as aid".

In discussing the issue of the health of Canada's manufacturing sector, in the face of foreign imports, we should keep in mind the following factors: (a) over 70 per cent of Canada's present international trade is with the United States; (b) the U.K., formerly Canada's second best trading partner, is now a member of the EEC, a large regional trading bloc, with its own protectionist devices, including a common external tariff, against goods from outside; (c) Japan, now Canada's second best trading partner, buys mainly food, minerals, lumber, and coal from Canada and sells in return a variety of manufactured goods; (d) more and more manufacturing jobs are disappearing every year in Canada and not just in the so-called traditional industries of textiles and footwear that are supposed to have had their day; (e) traditional international trade theory originated at a time when Britain had an effective monopoly on industrial technology, lots of cheap labour, no labour unions, and no welfare laws; and (e) the Canadian employee wants to be paid more rather than less for his or her work but does not usually seem to be as productive and dedicated as his S.E. Asian counterpart.

In the early 1980s, Canada's international trade policy was being seriously reviewed in Ottawa and the provincial capitals. This was in the aftermath of a serious world economic recession and growing economic protectionism that had contributed to an extraordinarily high unemployment rate in Canada. One argument heard in this review is that Canada is too small to take on trading giants such as the U.S. and the EEC in any bilateral negotiations and that it must rely on multilateral arrangements, notably the GATT, to protect its trading interests.

A serious concern has been the fact that industrial power has been shifting away from the U.S. in favour of other countries such as Western Europe, Japan, and the newly industrializing countries in South America, S.E. Asia, and the Middle East. Canada, instead of venturing into those expanding world export markets, has continued to depend on the U.S. market, with the result that Canada's share of world trade has declined from 5 per cent in 1970 to about 3.6 per cent today—just as the U.S. share has declined from about 25 per cent after World War II to about 10 per cent today.

Another concern has been whether Canadian exports are as competitive as before—since Canada has been losing its former share of numerous key markets, including Japan, Western Europe, and South America. In this regard, Canadian exporters have long complained that foreign exporters receive better income tax treatment and better government export financing than do Canadian firms. One suggestion in the review has been that Canada establish a series of free trade arrangements, similar to the Auto Pact with the U.S., for other products such as textiles and chemicals.

Efforts already made by the federal government in the early 1980s to improve Canada's international trade position include the establishment of a separate international trade cabinet portfolio; the reorganization of the Department of External Affairs, with a deputy minister responsible for trade; the transfer to External Affairs of the trade commissioner service previously under the Department of Industry, Trade and Commerce; the launching of a series of "special relationships" with a few countries such as Japan, Australia, and Mexico; and trade promotion visits to S.E. Asian and other countries by Canada's Prime Minister and International Trade Minister.

Summary

1. In 1946, the United Nations attempted to establish an international agency, the International Trade Organization, to co-ordinate efforts to reduce trade barriers, to establish rules of international trade practice, and to settle international trade disputes.
2. Although failing to establish the ITO, the United Nations succeeded in 1947 in bringing about a voluntary agreement to reduce tariffs—the General Agreement on Tariffs and Trade, or GATT. This agreement was to last three years, but has been renewed periodically following new international tariff negotiations.
3. Western Europe has been the scene of considerable international economic co-operation since the Second World War. Organizations that have been established include the Organization for European Economic Co-operation (or OEEC), which was broadened and renamed the Organization for Economic Co-operation and Development (or OECD) in 1961; and, even more important, the European Economic Community, or EEC, popularly known as the Common Market.
4. The Automotive Products Agreement provides for limited free trade between Canada and the United States in auto vehicles and parts.

"They say that if we want to sell them more wheat, we've got to start learning Chinese!"

5. The economic and, in some instances, political advantages of regional trading blocs have led to the establishment of free trade areas in many other parts of the world, including Latin America, Asia, Africa and Eastern Europe.
6. Canada's international trade policy seems to be at a cross-roads — whether to continue multilateral trade solely within the GATT framework, or to move towards greater economic protectionism with, perhaps, special bilateral trade arrangements, along the lines of the auto pact, with the U.S.

Key Terms

ITO 856	EFTA 864
GATT 856	CAP 865
Voluntary restraint 858	EMS 866
Export subsidies 859	Automotive Products
OEEC 859	Agreement 866
OECD 860	DISC 870
Benelux 860	Trading bloc 870
EEC 861	World product
Common market 861	mandate 871
Treaty of Rome 862	

Review Questions

1. What was the International Trade Organization? What was its purpose? Why was it never established?
2. Explain the nature and purpose of the General Agreement on Tariffs and Trade. How successful has it been?
3. Explain the nature and purpose of the OEEC.
4. What is the OECD? Why was it established? Why is Canada a member?
5. What is Benelux?
6. What is the European Coal and Steel Community?
7. What was agreed under the Treaty of Rome by the six initial members of the European Economic Community?
8. Explain the nature and purpose of the EEC's Social Fund.
9. What was Britain's original attitude towards the Common Market? What was its proposal for an Industrial Free Trade Area?
10. What was the European Free Trade Association?
11. Why did Britain eventually decide to apply for membership in the European Common Market?

12. What is the Canadian-U.S. Automotive Products Agreement? What are the benefits for Canada? What are the safeguards?
13. What has been the result of the Automotive Agreement on Canada's balance of international payments?
14. Distinguish between bilateral and multilateral trade.
15. Summarize from Canada's point of view, the arguments for freer international trade.
16. Summarize, from Canada's point of view, the arguments for more trade protectionism.
17. Should Canada join the U.S., if possible, in a North American free trade area? Explain and discuss the pros and cons.
18. Why is Brazil, a member of GATT, allowed to protect its manufacturing sector by tariffs, quotas, and exchange controls, when Canada, also an economically developing country, is not?
19. What has been done in other parts of the world to promote regional free trade? Why?

44. INTERNATIONAL ECONOMIC DEVELOPMENT AID

CHAPTER OBJECTIVES

A. To explain how Western Europe was aided in its economic recovery after World War II by UNRRA and the U.S. Marshall Plan

B. To show how the United Nations has provided technical and financial aid to the developing countries

C. To explain the role of the World Bank in helping the developing countries

D. To describe the Colombo Plan

E. To outline Canada's various economic aid programs, including the role of CIDA

F. To outline other countries' economic development aid programs

CHAPTER OUTLINE

44.1 Post-war Recovery
44.2 The United Nations
44.3 IBRD, or the World Bank
44.4 Inter-American Development Bank
44.5 Asian Development Bank
44.6 The Colombo Plan
44.7 Canadian Economic Development Aid
44.8 Other Countries' Economic Development Aid

In this last chapter, we look first of all at the steps that were taken after World War II to promote the economic recovery of Western Europe and other war-ravaged areas; and then at past and present international efforts, including our own Canadian ones, to promote the economic development of the economically poorer countries of the world.

44.1: POST-WAR RECOVERY

Most wars have left behind a trail of destruction. In some instance, whole civilizations, such as those of Carthage, early Mexico, and Peru, have been wiped off the face of the earth. In most cases, the possessions and often the lives of the conquered have been taken as the penalty for defeat. In many cases, as with modern Germany, countries have been left politically divided and parts or all of other countries have been absorbed into the conqueror's territory or sphere of political and economic influence—as with the present Soviet empire.

At the end of World War I, in line with classical practice, the Allies demanded heavy reparations (i.e. compensation for war damage and other losses) from Germany and other Axis powers. The financial burden of these reparations helped to depress the German economy during the 1920s, frustrate the Germans, and bring about the rise of Hitler.

UNRRA

At the end of World War II, therefore, the United States took a different approach. Instead of leaving the defeated, and those who had previously been subjugated by them, to look after themselves, the United States made great efforts to feed, clothe, and, where necessary, resettle them. The agency established as early as 1943 for this purpose was the United Nations Relief and Rehabilitation Administration (UNRRA). This agency was in existence until 1947. Over half its budget of $4 billion was provided by the United States; the rest was provided by other United Nations members. The target for revenue was 1 per cent of each country's national income in 1943. Canada's contribution, made on this basis, was $78 million. The Soviet Union, because of its own wartime suffering and destruction, was unwilling to join in this effort.

A large part of UNRRA's budget was allocated to Western Europe—to combat starvation and disease among the local populations; to feed, clothe, and temporarily house the millions of "displaced" persons; and, in many cases, to help them on their way to a new life in North America. The provision of food, clothing, medical supplies, and medical treatment was the chief priority in the use of UNRRA's limited funds. This meant that the rebuilding of agriculture, industry, and transportation, greatly devastated by the war, was left mainly up to the Europeans themselves. The problem in East Germany, incidentally, was aggravated by the fact that any machinery and equipment that still survived the hostilities had been quickly dismantled and shipped to the Soviet Union.

The Marshall Plan

To help the Western European countries rebuild their economies and thereby help check the spread of communism, the United States undertook, in the three years from 1948 to 1951, one of the largest foreign-aid programs the world has ever seen—the Marshall Plan, under which the U.S. government gave over $12 billion of economic aid to the countries of Western Europe. Of this amount, $10 billion was distributed as outright grants and $2 billion as low-interest loans.

The plan was named after the U.S. Secretary of State, George C. Marshall, who, in a speech at Harvard University on June 5, 1947, first announced the willingness of the U.S. government to provide large-scale economic assistance to Western Europe. In his speech, Mr. Marshall called on the West European countries to establish a committee to decide exactly what assistance was required from the United States to bring their productive capacities back to pre-war levels.

Although the Marshall Plan terminated a year earlier than intended, it is judged to have been a great success. By 1951, agricultural output in the OEEC countries was estimated to be at almost the pre-war level, while industrial output was judged to be far greater. Industrial output, in fact, was estimated to have gone from 87 per cent of the pre-war total in 1947, at the start of the Marshall Plan, to 134 per cent in 1951 when it was terminated. From the Western point of view, the most satisfying achievement, in light of the Cold War then well under way, was that the countries of Western Europe had remained politically non-communist—due in large part to their now rising economic prosperity.

The U.S. government also gave post-war recovery aid to countries on the opposite side of the globe—to Japan after 1945, and to South Korea after 1952. Canada, in addition to its contribution to UNRRA, gave direct financial aid to Britain in 1945 to help its economic recovery.

The OEEC

In direct response to this call, sixteen countries of Western Europe set up the Organization for European Economic Cooperation, or OEEC, with headquarters in Paris. The U.S. Congress then passed the Economic Co-operation Act, which authorized the provision of the necessary funds. The member countries of the OEEC then placed their requests for assistance with the European Co-operation Administration (ECA). This agency was set up by the government of the United States to procure the goods and services necessary for the reconstruction of the European economies.

NATO

The outbreak of the Korean War in 1950 led to the formation later in that same year of the North Atlantic Treaty Organization (NATO). This organization, comprising Canada, the United States, and most West European countries, was established to meet the desire for greater military security, although Canada's delegation pressed for economic co-operation as well. The United States' foreign aid to Western Europe now became predominantly military in character; and the European Co-operation Administration was replaced in 1951 by the Mutual Security Agency.

44.2: THE UNITED NATIONS

After World War II, many former colonies of the Western European countries such as Britain, France, Holland, and Belgium became politically independent. These and other new countries pointed out quite vociferously in the United Nations and elswhere that the richer countries of the world had a moral responsibility to help the poorer ones. At the same time, the emergence of the Cold War between the United States and the Soviet Union led to a keen rivalry to secure and retain the friendship of the various "neutral" countries of the world. This rivalry was intensified later on with the emergence of a communist regime in China—a major power, with a foreign policy of its own. Thus, a combination of moral virtue and political expediency resulted in a vast flow of technical and financial aid from the economically rich Western industrialized countries to the economically poor mainly African, Asian, and Latin American countries to promote their development.

Technical Assistance

The United Nations, although primarily concerned with the maintenance of international peace, has played a major role in channelling this technical and financial aid from its richer member countries to its poorer ones. Technical aid began in fact in 1946, when expert technical advice was provided free of charge to various member countries by the United Nations' specialized agencies such as the Food and Agriculture Organization (FAO), the World Health Organization (WHO), the United Nations Educational, Scientific, and Cultural Organization (UNESCO), and the International Labour Organization (ILO). It was not until 1949, however, that a large-scale program of U.N. technical assistance got under way, a direct result of the support for such a program advocated by President Truman of the United States in his Inaugural Address in January of that year.

This support, backed by U.S. government financial resources, led in 1949 to the establishment by the United Nations of an Expanded Program of Technical Assistance. Money for this program was to be contributed voluntarily by member countries. However, most of the funds were provided by the United States.

This program, administered by a new agency, the U.S. Technical Assistance Administration, provides three types of assistance. First, highly qualified experts employed by the United Nations go out, free of charge, to the less developed country (or LDC) requesting assistance. There they study local problems and advise the government on how to solve them. They also train personnel, whenever appropriate. The second type of assistance is the provision of fellowships and scholarships to enable the nationals of the LDC to obtain practical experience and academic training in the more developed countries. The third type of assistance is the establishment of regional study centres and local training centres. The regional centres, such as the U.N. Economic Commission for Latin America in Santiago, Chile, provide a place where experts from countries in that particular region can meet to study and discuss local problems. The training centres are well equipped and staffed and provide decentralized vocational training facilities throughout the world.

SUNFED

Although technical assistance is of great value, the economically less developed countries stressed that it was not sufficient in itself. They also needed help in building the infrastructure of their economies. Without outside financial help, they could not build enough power plants, roads, railways, airports, schools and hospitals, water and sewage systems, and other social capital to permit rapid economic growth. Such projects, they argued, yielded no direct revenue and therefore could not easily be financed by private investors. What was needed was outright grants or low-interest, long-term loans. Accordingly, in 1959, the United Nations established a special fund for this purpose, called the Special United Nations Fund for Economic Development (SUNFED). However, the funds contributed voluntarily by member countries were much less than expected. Consequently, SUNFED's activities have been limited so far to such projects as establishing major research institutes and undertaking large-scale engineering surveys to determine, among other things, hydro-electric power potential and mineral resources.

"On his last mission, they made him an honorary chief."

44.3: IBRD, or World Bank

At the Bretton Woods Economic Conference in 1944, the United States, Britain, and other allied and friendly countries decided to set up an International Bank for Reconstruction and Development. This World Bank, as it came to be known, based in Washington, D.C., was to channel long-term investment funds from the rich Western countries to the poorer countries of the world to help to build a better world for all, once World War II was over.

Sources of Funds

Funds were obtained from four different sources. First, the Bank sold capital stock to the governments of the richer countries according to predetermined quotas. Canada's quota was about 5 per cent of the total; the United States' quota, about 30 per cent. The Soviet Union, for various reasons, did not take part. Today, there are about 70 governments that are active lenders to the bank. When the Bank began operations in 1946, it had a subscribed capital of $9.2 billion. This amount has been increased since then by new issues of shares. Second, the Bank borrowed money from private investors and financial institutions in the United States, Canada, Switzerland, and elsewhere. It did this by selling its own International Bank bonds in the capital markets of these countries. These bonds offered investors a reasonable rate of interest plus a high degree of safety. The latter (an extremely attractive feature) was based on the fact that repayment of the money borrowed was guaranteed by the Bank's member countries up to the limit of their quotas. For a small charge, the Bank would also insure lenders against possible loss from non-repayment. This government backing, plus a careful lending policy, enabled the Bank to borrow large amounts of private capital. The third source of funds was the profits that the Bank made on its borrowing and lending operations. These profits were reinvested in new loans. A fourth source of funds was the resale to private investors of loans that the Bank had originally made. This meant that private investors took over the Bank's previous long-term financing and released the Bank's funds for new loans.

In recent years, many of the donor countries such as the U.S. are starting to reduce their multilateral aid commitments (such as to the World Bank) in favour of bilateral programs, especially "tied-aid" programs that require the money given in aid to be spent on goods and services from the country providing the aid. This means that the financial outlook for the Bank is not promising. Naturally, the less developed countries, the recipients of the aid, oppose this trend. The fact that the U.S. is moving in favour of bilateral aid is particularly significant because of the fact that, under the World Bank's weighted voting system, commensurate with each country's capital position with the Bank, the U.S. casts 20 per cent of the votes and its political allies many more.

Lending Activities

Between 1946 and 1948, the World Bank concentrated its lending activities on war-torn Western Europe. But, with the advent of the Marshall Plan, the Bank turned its attention away from Europe and started lending money to economically less developed countries in other parts of the world, with per capita income at less than a stated level. Loans are tied to specific projects and are usually made to the government of the country concerned; however, loans may also be made to private firms if the government of the country guarantees repayment. But such private loans have been very few. World Bank loans are provided only when private funds are not available at reasonable terms. The loans are repayable over periods as long as twenty years and bear interest at current market rates. Before a loan is made, the Bank sends out its experts to conduct a thorough appraisal of the proposed investment. These experts try to make sure that the project is economically sound, that it will strengthen the economy of the borrowing country, and that the loan is likely to be repaid. Often the Bank has been accused by the less developed countries of being overly cautious in its lending policy. It has also been accused at times of attaching too many conditions to its loans. The Bank's conservative lending policy has been reflected in the sizeable profit on its operations. Without such a policy, the Bank has argued, private investors would be unlikely to entrust their funds to the Bank.

The types of projects financed with World Bank loans have been as follows: about one-third for improvement in transportation facilities (roads, railways, airports, and ports); about one-third for electric-power generating facilities, including dams; and the remainder for a variety of projects such as the construction of water and sewer works, irrigation facilities, and steel mills.

Third World Debt

In the 1980s, a major concern of the World Bank, with its membership of 143 countries, is the large and rapidly growing amount of debt incurred by the less developed, or Third World countries. This increase in debt was partly the result of extra borrowing to help pay for much more expensive oil imports. And in the case of Mexico, an important oil exporter, by heavy borrowing to finance rapid industrialization. The principal and interest payments required on this debt is placing a heavy burden on the balance of international payments of these countries. In fact, by the early 1980s, low-income oil-importing countries were using on average, about 20 per cent of their export earnings for debt servicing.

International Finance Corporation (IFC)

This organization was established by the World Bank in 1956 to make loans to private business firms in less developed countries. As we saw previously, the World Bank required for its own loans that the government of the less developed country receiving the loan, guaranteed repayment. This condition meant in practice that very few loans were made to private firms in these countries. The International Finance Corporation, owned, supported, and managed by the World Bank, was designed to fill this gap. A considerable part of the Bank's profit from its own borrowing and lending activities has in fact been reinvested in the IFC. The money loaned by the IFC is usually channelled through development banks set up by the governments of the economically less developed countries. The IFC also helps to recruit competent management personnel for the projects if they are not locally available.

International Development Association (IDA)

In 1960, recognizing a further financing need in the economic development field, the World Bank established another subsidiary, the International Development Association. The purpose of the IDA was to help underdeveloped countries that needed more outside capital than they could afford to service conventionally—hence the description of the IDA as the World Bank's "soft-loan window". Many of these countries were in fact finding it difficult to obtain enough foreign exchange to pay for essential imports, let alone interest on foreign loans. To help overcome this problem, the IDA, with the financial assistance of 33 governments, has been making fifty-year interest-free loans with a 10-year grace period. The funds for the IDA's lending activities have come from the World Bank and a variety of Western nations. In recent years, "foreign-aid weariness" in the U.S. Congress has created funding problems for the World Bank and other multilateral aid agencies as the U.S. has been the largest individual donor.

44.4: INTER-AMERICAN DEVELOPMENT BANK

This international bank, with its headquarters in Washington, D.C., was established in 1959 to help finance economic and social development in Latin America. Originally, only the United States and nineteen Latin American countries were members. However, Canada joined in 1972 and Japan, Israel and many European countries joined in 1976 and 1977, bringing total membership up to 41 countries and enlarging the Bank's financial resources.

The Bank has offices in all of its Latin American member countries. These offices serve as a liaison with local authorities and borrowers, co-ordinate Bank activities, and supervise the implementation of Bank-supported projects. As well as agricultural and industrial development projects, including technical assistance, the IADB finances social development projects such as water supply and public health, urban development, and vocational, technical and higher education.

44.5: ASIAN DEVELOPMENT BANK

The ADB was formed in 1968, at the time of the Vietnam war, to help combat communism by lending funds to developing Asian countries. Today the Bank is an important lender in that region of the world. The bank's two largest shareholders are the U.S. and Japan, each with 13.6 per cent of the votes. Next comes India, with 6.5 per cent. Most of the Bank's funds have come from these three countries.

44.6: THE COLOMBO PLAN

Another major effort to promote the economic development of the poorer countries of the world is carried on under the auspices of the British Commonwealth of Nations. This development effort, called the Colombo Plan for Co-operative Economic Development in South and Southeast Asia, was conceived at a meeting of Commonwealth Foreign Ministers in Colombo, Ceylon, in January 1950. The original aim of the Colombo Plan was for the more advanced countries of the British Commonwealth to help the less advanced ones located in South and Southeast Asia. However, other countries were later invited to participate. As a result, the United States and Japan joined as donors, while other countries joined as recipients. Membership now includes Australia, Bhutan, Britain, Brunei, Burma, Cambodia, Canada, Ceylon, India, Indonesia, Japan, Korea, Laos, Malaysia, Maldive Islands, Nepal, New Zealand, Pakistan, the Philippines, Thailand, Vietnam, and the United States. A consultative committee, comprising ministers of the member countries, meets annually to discuss policy and review projects. The actual program of technical assistance is determined by a Council for Technical Co-operation that meets regularly in Ceylon. The plan was originally intended to last only until 1957. However, its life has been extended for five-year periods ever since. The Colombo Plan office was set up in 1950 within Canada's Department of Trade and Commerce, as it was then called.

Under the Colombo Plan, donor countries provide four basic types of assistance. First, they send experts free of charge to the underdeveloped countries to provide technical advice and training. Second, they pay for nationals of these countries to study in the more developed countries. Third, they provide equipment, financed either by outright grant or by low-interest, long-term loan, for development projects. And, fourth, they make gifts of raw materials and foodstuffs that can be resold locally to provide funds for development.

Since 1950, Canada has made grants for capital and technical assistance projects to Colombo Plan countries. Most of this money has gone to Ceylon, India, Malaysia, and Pakistan. It has been used for such diverse projects as multi-purpose irrigation and hydroelectric-power generation, the development of fisheries, and the construction and equipping of hospitals and schools. Gifts of raw materials and foodstuffs, used to raise funds to meet local costs of development projects, have also been made. Several thousands of persons from Colombo Plan countries have come to Canada for training in such fields as public administration and finance, agriculture, co-operatives, engineering, mining and geology, statistics, health education, and social welfare. In addition, several hundred Canadian experts have been sent to these countries to provide service in such fields as fisheries, agriculture, engineering, mining and prospecting, co-operatives, public administration, education and vocational training, and public health. They have also conducted aerial surveys of resources and helped to install and operate capital equipment.

44.7: CANADIAN ECONOMIC DEVELOPMENT AID

Canada, as we have just seen, makes a substantial contribution to the economic development of poorer countries by its participation in the United Nations and Colombo Plan programs of technical and other aid. It makes an additional contribution through various other programs that we briefly describe below. Until 1960, Canada's external aid, through all these bilateral and multilateral programs, was administered by the Department of Industry, Trade and Commerce. It now comes under the Department of External Affairs. Canada's agreed goal is to spend 0.5 per cent of the country's GNP on official development assistance, or ODA as it is called.

Canadian International Development Agency (CIDA)

In November 1960, Canada's external-aid programs were put under the charge of a special External Aid Office. In 1968, the name of this body was changed to the Canadian International Development Agency (CIDA). Its president reports to Parliament through the Secretary of State for External Affairs. And it is now responsible for the vast bulk of Canada's Official Development Assistance, or ODA, with a budget of over $1 billion.

The external financial aid administered by CIDA consists of bilateral assistance and contributions to multilateral agencies such as the United Nations. The bilateral aid (about 80 per cent of the total) is used mainly to provide Canadian goods and services to less developed countries. Originally, the minimum Canadian content of such goods had to be 80 per cent. Now it need be only 66.67 per cent, thereby permitting aid funds to be used for a much wider range of Canadian goods. Most of Canada's foreign aid has gone in recent years to Bangladesh, India, Pakistan, Kenya, Sri Lanka, and Tanzania. As well as financial aid, CIDA brings foreign students to Canada for training and sends Canadian experts abroad.

The CIDA program has been criticized in recent years as being wasteful and over-centralized. Also that too high a percentage of the total is "tied-aid"—that is, money that can only be used to purchase Canadian goods and services. A final criticism is that the total amount of aid is too small a percentage of Canada's GNP.

Commonwealth Caribbean Assistance

When Britain's colonies in the West Indies were being formed into a politically independent Federation of the West Indies in 1958, Canada undertook to provide a five-year $10 million program of economic and technical assistance. When the federation broke up four years later, Canada agreed to continue its assistance to each individual country. The assistance has taken the familiar pattern of experts being sent out from Canada, nationals coming to Canada for training, and Canada providing capital equipment. The types of development projects undertaken include the provision of passenger-cargo ships, construction of a deep-water wharf, the provision of port-handling equipment, construction of a prefabricated fish-packing plant, improvement of dairy herds, and construction of bridges.

"I just don't understand why they need all this foreign aid.."

Special Commonwealth African Assistance Plan

This is a British Commonwealth plan similar to the Colombo Plan, set up to provide technical and capital assistance to Commonwealth countries and territories in Africa. The chief donor countries are Britain, Canada, Australia, New Zealand, and, to a very limited extent, India and Pakistan. Canada began to contribute in 1961.

The Commonwealth Scholarship and Fellowship Plan

In 1958, a Commonwealth Trade and Economic Conference meeting in Montreal recommended a plan whereby 100 university scholarships would be offered to outstanding Commonwealth students. Britain agreed to provide half the number of scholarships; Canada, a quarter. The plan came into force in 1960 and was enlarged in 1965 to include a small number of research and visiting fellowships.

Assistance to French-Speaking Countries of Africa

Beginning in 1961, Canada has offered educational assistance to the French-speaking countries of Africa. Canadian teachers have been supplied, African students have studied in Canada, and educational equipment has been provided.

Latin American Program

In 1964, Canada made an agreement with the Inter-American Development Bank to provide funds for high-priority economic, technical, and educational projects in Latin America. Projects are processed by the Bank and submitted to the Canadian government for approval. Projects financed have included the expansion and improvement of port facilities in El Salvador and a resources survey in Ecuador. As mentioned previously, Canada has been a full member of the IADB since 1972 with a consequent increase in financial assistance.

International Development Research Centre (IDRC)

In May 1970, Parliament authorized the establishment of the International Development Research Centre of Canada. With federal financing, this centre provides research facilities and resources for experts from Canada and other countries. Research is conducted into the means for applying scientific and technical knowledge to the advancement of the developing countries. Also, in its role as a co-ordinator of international development research, it tries to assist developing countries to build up their own research capabilities to help solve their own problems. Projects are channelled through four program divisions: agriculture, food and nutrition sciences; health sciences; information sciences; and social sciences.

44.8: OTHER COUNTRIES' ECONOMIC DEVELOPMENT AID

The United States has played the major role in providing funds for the United Nations' technical-assistance program and even for the Colombo Plan, a British Commonwealth venture. It has also provided considerable direct assistance of its own.

Britain, France, and other former colonial powers, as well as contributing to the United Nations, have provided technical and economic aid to their former colonies.

The Soviet Union has been reluctant to contribute funds to the United Nations' programs of technical assistance, partly because it believes that they are predominantly U.S. run and controlled. It has also abstained from participation in the World Bank. Instead, it has provided economic aid directly, in the form of equipment and technical advice, provided through long-term, low-interest loans, rather than through outright gifts. The Aswan Dam in Egypt is one notable example of Soviet aid.

Japan has provided a great deal of technical assistance and financial aid in Southeast Asia. China, too, has helped its surrounding countries as well as others further afield, such as Albania and Tanzania.

The OPEC countries also provide aid to Third World countries through the OPEC Fund for International Development.

Summary

1   Abandoning the classical practice of war victors, the United States at the end of World War II made great efforts to feed, clothe, and where necessary, resettle the inhabitants of the defeated countries. The agency established for this purpose was the United Nations Relief and Rehabilitation Administration or UNRRA.

2. To help the West European countries rebuild their economies, and thereby to help check the spread of Soviet communism, the United States undertook, between 1948 and 1951, one of the largest foreign aid programs ever—the legendary Marshall Plan.

3. In addition to its political activities, the United Nations has played a major role in providing technical and financial assistance to the economically less developed countries, through both the Expanded Program of Technical Assistance and the Special United

Nations Fund for Economic Development.

4. In 1944, the United States, Britain, and other Allied and friendly countries decided to establish the International Bank for Reconstruction and Development, or IBRD. The World Bank, as it came to be known, channels long-term investment funds from the relatively rich Western industrialized countries to the economically poorer countries of the world. Loans are usually made to the governments of the countries concerned.

5. In 1956, the World Bank established a subsidiary, the International Finance Corporation, to make loans to private business firms in the less developed countries. In 1960, the World Bank established another subsidiary, the International Development Association, to make loans available on more generous terms than usual to countries unable to service conventional loans.

6. The Inter-American Development Bank, in which Canada is a member, helps to finance economic and social development projects in Latin America.

7. The British Commonwealth has a major economic assistance program of its own called the Colombo Plan.

8. Canada participates in the U.N. and Colombo Plan programs of technical and other aid. It also has various other aid programs of its own, which are administered by the Canadian International Development Agency, or CIDA.

9. Various other countries have extensive economic aid programs of their own.

Key Terms

Economic aid   877
Reparations   878
UNRRA   878
Marshall Plan   879
OEEC   879
NATO   879
United Nations   880
Technical assistance   880
LDC   881

SUNFED   881
IBRD   883
IFC   885
IDA   885
IADB   886
ADB   886
Colombo Plan   886
CIDA   888
IDRC   890

Review Questions

1. What was UNRRA? What was its purpose?

2. What was the Marshall Plan? What did it achieve?
3. What has been the role of the United Nations in providing technical assistance to economically less developed countries? What has been the major source of funds?
4. What types of assistance are provided under the U.N. Expanded Program of Technical Assistance?
5. What is SUNFED? What is its purpose? What has it achieved?
6. What is the IBRD? What is its purpose? How does it obtain its funds?
7. What types of loans are made by the IBRD? What is the usual loan procedure?
8. What is the International Finance Corporation? Why was it established? What is the International Development Association?
9. Explain the nature and purpose of the Inter-American Development Bank. Who are its members? What types of projects does it finance?
10. Explain the nature and purpose of the Asian Development Bank.
11. What is the Colombo Plan? What types of assistance does it provide?
12. What is CIDA? What criticisms have been made about it?
13. What are Canada's various foreign-aid programs?
14. What countries, in addition to Canada, have provided economic aid to the developing countries of the world? In what forms?

Index